SEAMANSHIP
IN THE AGE OF SAIL

P.⊖

Corvette vue par le travers en Pane mettant un Canot à la Mer.

P.⊖.

Corvette vue par le travers allant au mouillage et saluant la bande à babord

SEAMANSHIP
IN THE AGE OF SAIL

AN ACCOUNT OF THE SHIPHANDLING OF THE SAILING MAN-OF-WAR 1600–1860, BASED ON CONTEMPORARY SOURCES

JOHN HARLAND

ILLUSTRATED BY
MARK MYERS
RSMA, F/ASMA

NAVAL INSTITUTE PRESS

CASANOVA BOOKS
1601 W. GREENFIELD AVE.
MILWAUKEE, WIS. 53204
PHONE: (414) 672-3040

FRONTISPIECE
Two eighteenth century engravings by Pierre Ozanne,
showing a French corvette hove to and hoisting in a boat
(top), and a brig-of-war (bottom) running into an
anchorage with the lower shrouds manned and the crew
cheering to port. Ozanne's careful observation and fine
detail make his work a valuable source of information on
period seamanship. (Courtesy of The Mariner's
Museum, Newport News, Virginia)
ENDPAPERS
The French corvette *Galatee* under sail in Brest Roads.
(Osborne Studios)

© John Harland 1984

First published in 1984 by Conway Maritime Press Ltd,
24 Bride Lane, Fleet Street, London EC4Y 8DR

Published and distributed in the United States of
America and Canada by the Naval Institute Press,
Annapolis, Maryland 21402

Library of Congress Catalog Card No 83–43277

ISBN 0-87021-955-3

Manufactured in the United Kingdom

CONTENTS

ACKNOWLEDGEMENTS 7

INTRODUCTION 9

CHAPTER 1 **SOME WORDS AND PHRASES
USED IN SHIPHANDLING UNDER SAIL** 10

CHAPTER 2 **MASTS, RIGGING AND SAILS** 19
Masts 19
Yards 20
Standing Rigging 22
Running Rigging 25
Sails and their Gear 29

CHAPTER 3 **DEVELOPMENT OF THE
SAIL PLAN 1580–1900** 36

CHAPTER 4 **SOME THEORETICAL PRINCIPLES
UNDERLYING SHIPHANDLING** 40
Mathematical Principles 40
Some Theoretical Centres and Axes, and
their Relationships 41
Form of the Hull and Stability 43
Action of Wind on the Sails 49
Trimming the Sails 61
Geometric Problems with the Rigging 66
Working of the Rudder 69

CHAPTER 5 **SAILS CONSIDERED
INDIVIDUALLY** 72
The Courses 72

CHAPTER 6 **ORGANISATION OF CREW
FOR HANDLING THE SHIP** 91
Duties Allotted to the Different Parts of Ship 92
Sail Drill and Working Ship 93

CHAPTER 7 **BENDING, LOOSING AND
FURLING SAIL** 96
Bending Square Sail 96
Unbending Square Sail 101
Bending Fore and Aft Canvas 102

Loosing Sails to Dry 103
Furling Square Sail 104
Loosing Fore and Aft Sail 110
Furling Fore and Aft Sail 110
Shifting Sails 111
Sending Light Yards Up and Down 111
Shifting Topsail Yards 118
Striking and Shifting Topmasts 119
Striking Lower Yards 122
Squaring, Cockbilling and Manning Yards 122

CHAPTER 8 **MAKING AND SHORTENING
SAIL AT SEA** 124
Order of Making and Shortening Sail 124
Shortening Sail in Bad Weather 125
Handling the Individual Sails 131
Disposition of Crew for Making and
Shortening Sail 135
The Commands 135

CHAPTER 9 **REEFING** 137
Methods of Reefing 1600–1900 137
Other Gear Used in Reefing 143
Technique of Reefing 145

CHAPTER 10 **STUDDINGSAILS** 155
Evolution 155
Wind and Weather 156
Studdingsails on Different Points of Sail 157
The Sails 158
Other Gear Used with Studdingsails 161
Terminology, English and Otherwise 162
Setting Studdingsails 163
The Commands 171
Disposition of Crew for Handling Studdingsails 172

CHAPTER 11 **STEERING** 173

CHAPTER 12 **TACKING, WEARING
AND BOXHAULING** 181
Tacking 181
Sequence of Commands 182

Boxhauling 189
Wearing or Veering a Ship 191
Organisation of the Crew for Working Ship 193
To Tack Ship 194
Clubhauling 195

CHAPTER 13 **WORKING SHIP IN A TIDEWAY** 199

CHAPTER 14 **TOWING AND WARPING** 203

CHAPTER 15 **STORM** 209
Preparations 209
Scudding 213
Lying To 215

CHAPTER 16 **SQUALLS** 221

CHAPTER 17 **HEAVING TO** 225

CHAPTER 18 **THE SHIP AT ANCHOR** 231
General Preparations for Entering Harbour
and Anchoring 241
The Mechanics of Casting Anchor 242
Various Methods of Coming To Anchor 244
Management of the Ship at Single Anchor 247
Mooring 254

General Preparations for Going to Sea 258
Weighing Anchor 260
Catting, Fishing and Stowing the Anchor 267
Heaving In 269
Getting Under Way from Single Anchor 271
Laying Out an Anchor 277

CHAPTER 19 **SHIFTING HEAVY WEIGHTS** 280

CHAPTER 20 **LOWERING AND
HOISTING IN BOATS** 282

CHAPTER 21 **MAN OVERBOARD** 289

CHAPTER 22 **ACCIDENTS** 294
Accidents to Running Rigging 294
Accidents to Standing Rigging 298
Accidents to the Masts and Spars 299
Accidents to Wheel and Rudder 301
Leaks 303
Running Aground 305
Fire 310

BIBLIOGRAPHY 313

INDEX 316

AUTHOR'S
ACKNOWLEDGEMENTS

This book is founded on material collected over more than twenty years, together with conversations and correspondence with individuals for about the same period. Some of these communications were made so long ago that the people concerned may have long forgotten being quizzed on some obscure point. Photocopies of many of the rarer items in the bibliography were secured primarily from the Mariners' Museum, Newport News, Sjöhistoriska Museet, Stockholm and Marinens Biblioteket, Copenhagen, thanks to the unsparing help and expertise of John Lochhead, Anders Sandström and Capt Jørgen Teisen RDaN. Without their aid and patience the project would never have got off the stocks. The passage of time also accounts for the fact that many of the people who helped are, sad to say, no longer with us, notably: Dr R C Anderson, William A Baker, Howard Chapelle, Dexter L Dennis, Gershom Bradford, Archie Horka, Dr John Lyman, Alan Villiers and Arthur L Tucker.

Special thanks are due to Ruth Baker who, along with husband Bill, fielded many queries; Cdr Jaap F Brongers RNeN, who so freely shared his encyclopedic knowledge of Dutch sea-words; Ole Lisberg Jensen, Hans Jeppesen with whom I explored the attics of the Marinmuseet, Karlskrona, and the Orlogsmuseet, Copenhagen; Jac Muskens the modelmaker of the Prins Hendrik Museum, Rotterdam; J Bas Kist, who drew my attention to the collection of capstan models in the Rijks Museum, Amsterdam; Sten Johansson for many kindnesses; Dr Bertil Sandahl, for patiently answering many etymological questions, over many years; Commodore (E) Gunnar Schoerner RSwN, who took me aboard *Vasa*, and helped in many other ways besides; Korv Kapt Dr Heinrich Walle FGN, whose background in history and square-rig sailoring made his opinion on many technical points doubly valuable; Lt Cdr Peter Whitlock RN, who took the time to guide my wife and myself round *Victory*, and answered many queries.

The assistance of the following institutions is recognised: National Maritime Museum, Greenwich; Science Museum, South Kensington; City Museum, Liverpool; British Library; Sjøkrigsskolen, Bergen; Norsk Sjøfartsmuseet, Bygdøy; Norsk Forsvarets-museet, Oslo; Marinemuseet, Horten; Sjøfartsmuseet, Bergen; Orlogsmuseet, Copenhagen; Marinens Biblioteket, Copenhagen; Handels- og Søfartsmuseet på Kronborg; Historical Bureau of the Royal Dutch Navy; Maritiem Museum Prins Hendrik, Rotterdam; Rijks Museum, Amsterdam Nederlandse Scheepvaart Museum, Amsterdam; Sjöhistoriska Museet & Vasa Varvet, Stockholm; Sjöfartsmuseet, Gothenburg; Marinemuseet, Karlskrona; Deutsches Museum, Munich; Deutsches Schiffahrtsmuseum, Bremerhafen; Schiffahrtsmuseum, Kiel; Altonaer Museum, Altona; Marineschule, Mürwik; Marine Ehrenmal, Laboe; Museum of Hamburg's History; National Scheepvaart Museum, Antwerp; Musée de la Marine, Paris; French National Archives, Paris; Mariners Museum, Newport News; San Francisco Maritime Museum; Library of the US Coast Guard Academy, New London, Connecticut; Hart Nautical Museum, Cambridge, Massachusetts; Museum of the US Naval Academy, Annapolis, Maryland; Vancouver Maritime Museum; Victoria Maritime Museum; Maritime Museum of the Atlantic, Halifax; Ontario Maritime Museum, Toronto; British Columbia Medical Library; Kelowna Branch of the Okanagan Regional Library; the Commanding Officers of HMS *Victory*, USS *Constitution*, US Coast Guard Barque *Eagle*, and the Committee for the Restoration of *Constellation*, in Baltimore.

I must acknowledge the help of the following individuals: In France, Jean Boudriot, J Chantriot, Philippe Henrat, Cdt Marc Paillé, Henri Picard and Marcel Redouté. In Germany, Kapt z S Siegfried Bär FGN, Wolfgang Bohlayer, Willi Fraider, Franz Hahn, Dr Klaus Grimm, Kapt z S Dr Paul Heinsius FGN, Peter Mackens, Dr Jürgen Meyer, Dr Hans Thieme. In addition, my friend of many years, Arvid Göttlicher, and that larger than life personage Rolf Böttcher of Kiel. In Italy, Dr Giovanni Santi-Mazzini. In Norway, Lauritz Pettersen, Kapt Stein Moen RNoN and Capt Christopher Fasting. In Denmark, Dr Henning Henningsen, Ole Crumlin-Pedersen and Admiral Frits Hammer Kjølsen. In Finland, Lars Grönstrand. In Belgium, J van Beylen. In the Netherlands, L M Akveld, J Hazenberg, H Hazelhoff-Roelfzema and Herman Ketting. In Sweden, Gustav Alexandersson, Peter von Busch, Bo Johansson, Lars Åke Kvarning, Björn Landström, Ylva Lindström, Marie-Louise Lundin, Capt Stig Notini RSwN, and Eva-Marie Stolt. In the United Kingdom, Richard Cookson, Peter DuCane, Robert Gardiner, Peter A Hodges, Rick Hogben, Norman G Hurst, James Lees, Cdr W E May RN, David MacGregor, Caroline Mordaunt, Vice Admiral Brian B Schofield, Michael K Stammers, J D Storer, Arthur H Waite and Michael S Robinson. In the United States, Robert H Burgess, Joseph Bruzek, Harry Dring, Eugene S Ferguson, Karl Kortum, Philip K Lunderberg, Merrit A Edson, Andrew Nesdall, Leon and Shirley Polland, Erik A Ronnberg Jr, Norman Rubin, Henry Rusk and Giles M S Tod. In Canada, my good friend Dr Harold Bergman, Dr Arthur Chapman, André Christoffersen, Dan Gibson-Harris, John Holland, Niels Jannasch, Cdr L B Jenson RCN, Rear Admiral Desmond Piers RCN and Admiral Hugh F Pullen RCN, are among the many people who helped in one way or another. Finally my thanks to Lynne Smith, who typed the manuscript, and to my wife Janet, who prepared the Index, and constantly supported and encouraged the project at all stages.

John H Harland
Kelowna, B C
July, 1983

ILLUSTRATOR'S
ACKNOWLEDGEMENTS

The work of illustrating this remarkable text has been done with the advice and assistance of many people, but it is really due to the encouragement and kind persistence of one individual – the author, John Harland – that these line drawings appear at all. It was he who envisioned the work and introduced me to the project a dozen or more years ago, then shared with me the fruits of his considerable research into period seamanship. Throughout this long collaboration, John has steered me towards a wealth of new and unfamiliar source material, advised me on the style and substance of the drawings, and accepted patiently the delays brought about by my need to halt work on the book and get back to painting for a living.

Another great help has been the practical knowledge of sailing ship seamanship imparted to me by the masters and men of the ships in which I served some years ago. I feel particularly indebted to the late Capt Alan Villiers, Capt Adrian Small and Capt John A Linderman, and to Nigel Glassborow and George E Byrd for this rare and valuable experience.

For supplying the photographic illustrations for this book and for granting us permission to reproduce them, the author and illustrator would like to thank the following individuals and institutions: in Great Britain, Francis Greenacre and the Bristol Museum and Art Gallery, Nigel V Glassborow, Richard Green, Arthur G Credland and the Town Docks Museum, Hull, Alex A Hurst, James S Lucas and the Imperial War Museum, London, N R Omell, Osborne Studios and G Warrener; in the Netherlands, the Prins Hendrik Maritime Museum, Rotterdam, Rijks Museum, Amsterdam, and Nederlandse Scheepvaart Museum, Amsterdam; in Norway, the Norske Marinemuseet, Horten; in Sweden, the Marinmuseet, Karlskrona, Sjöhistoriska Museum, Stockholm, and *Vasa* Varvet, Stockholm; in Germany, the Schiffahrtsmuseum, Kiel; and in the USA, the Mariners Museum, Newport News, Virginia, Andrew J Nesdall and Giles M S Tod.

Special thanks are due to my father-in-law Michael Bouquet, for his knowledgeable advice and his generosity in passing into my care the long run of *Illustrated London News* issues from which many illustrations, both drawings and photographs, have come; and to Robert Gardiner of Conway Maritime Press for help in seeing this work through to publication.

Finally, I must acknowledge the cheerful support given throughout this project by my wife Peternella and daughters Mary and Katharine, who have endured great demands on their time and patience with wonderful forbearance.

Mark R Myers
Woolley, Cornwall
February, 1984

INTRODUCTION

The popularity of the sea romances by C S Forester, Dudley Pope, Alexander Kent, Patrick O'Brian and so on, indicates that many people are fascinated by the story of the 'wooden walls' and the men who sailed them. Reading these tales may prompt one to wonder about the exact manner in which things were managed aboard the old sailing man-of-war. How exactly was the anchor weighed, how was sail trimmed to best advantage, how did one heave to, and so on? A good deal of information about this sort of thing is to be found in the textbooks used by the young gentlemen who attended the naval schools in the 1800s, the most systematic and comprehensive accounts being in languages other than English. Seamanship was, and is, for the most part a practical subject, learnt primarily by doing rather than reading, and there was no overwhelming need to commit everything to paper. These accounts were written to complement rather than supplant practical instruction, and some technical points which are skated over because they were self-evident at the time, are often quite obscure to the modern reader. There are, moreover, formidable problems with some technical terms, since not all are to be found in the modern standard dictionaries. Initially, struggling with the blurred Gothic characters of a page of archaic Swedish, was like trying to decipher a passage in Minoan Linear B. Gradually, however, I was able to get things pretty well sorted out and reading through this material became relatively straightforward.

These books are hard to come by nowadays, since they formed part of the young sea-officer's working library, were taken to sea, and thumbed through until they disintegrated, still the fate, incidentally, of many a copy of Crenshaw's *Naval Shiphandling*. I do not know if Crenshaw is as widely used in Britain as in the United States, but it was for many years the only modern English language monograph on this topic. In any event, it seemed to me, there might be a place for a book on ship manoeuvring, based on the old written sources, a sort of 'Crenshaw' for the Hornblower *aficionado*, the naval historian,

or the armchair sailor and for readers who might be interested in shiphandling, as it applied to the old sailing warship.

I am only too acutely aware that, by virtue of personal experience in sail, there are many better qualified than myself to undertake this task. What follows is far from being the account of an old shellback, still wringing the sea-water out of his socks. My own practical experience is minimal, being limited to half a dozen trips moving motor fishing vessels (naval MFVs) from Cape Town to Durban, thirty years ago. I suppose this marginally qualifies as service in naval vessels under sail, but hardly suffices to confer expert status. This experience did, however, trigger a lifelong interest in how things were managed in centuries past in 'real' sailing ships. I live, to say the least, in one of the remoter backwaters, so far as nautical research is concerned. The vineyards of the Okanagan Valley lie three hundred miles from the Pacific Ocean, but with time, and through the good offices of others more strategically placed, I managed to accumulate a fairly comprehensive library of photocopies of the available material, and it became just a matter of extracting the meat from these old volumes. What follows, therefore, rather than representing my own opinions, is an attempt to put together an account of how things were done, based almost totally on contemporary authorities. While anxious to avoid an over-abundance of scholarly footnotes, I have tried to back up any points of possible contention with an appropriate citation (the authority and page number of the book where necessary are given in brackets; the reader is referred to the Bibliography for the titles of the works quoted). The old texts are full of obscurities and contradictions. Sometimes, after puzzling over a particularly knotty point for days, resolution would come out of the blue, perhaps while skiing along an abandoned logging trail on a winter's day. In other cases, the answers are still elusive, and I have by no means cleared up all the difficulties to my own satisfaction.

I hope our story will not be without interest to those with sea-time in 'modern'

square-rigged sailing vessels. They will find that the old methods differed quite a bit from practice on board *Pamir* and her sisters. The wooden masts and yards, and hemp rigging of the sailing man-of-war were nothing like as robust from an engineering point of view, as the steel spars and wire rope gear of the latter day 'windjammer'. In the latter, the available deck force barely sufficed to handle the vessel, whereas two men chased every job in the large man-of-war. (Brady mentions fifty men tailing on to the lower studdingsail halliards!).

This book is intended to complement James Lees' *Masting and Rigging of the English Ship of War 1625–1860*, one volume dealing with the anatomy or structure, as it were, and the other concerned with the physiology or function, of these old vessels. We start with a brief consideration of the masts, sails and rigging, emphasising the whys and wherefores of some of the gear and following the example of Captain Crenshaw, we concern ourselves not only with the 'how' but also with the 'why'. Although not intended as a theoretical treatise on the theory of sailing, ship stability, and so on, I have tried to give an overview of some of the abstract considerations which underlie the practice of shiphandling. Following a brief look at the evolution of the sailing ship over the relevant period, the body of the work concerns itself with the actual management of the ship under various conditions. While not strictly germane to the discussion, my fascination with foreign sea terms has resulted in some etymological digressions, which I hope will not bore the reader unduly.

Mark Myers' drawings make things come alive in a fashion quite beyond the ability of the written word. Some years ago, we collaborated in a study of the early history of the steering wheel, and happily he was agreeable to illustrating the present account. The artist has spent a good deal of time in small square-rigged wooden vessels, and his practical experience to some extent compensates for my lack of it.

CHAPTER 1
SOME WORDS AND PHRASES USED IN SHIPHANDLING UNDER SAIL

Sea language old and new. I start with the assumption that anyone interested enough to read this book has some acquaintance with the language of the sea, and access to a marine dictionary. Our period of interest spans roughly three centuries and it is not surprising to find that professional language evolved in parallel with technological change, during this period. For that matter, there has been further change since 1900, the modern sailor using words and expressions unknown to his predecessors, and sometimes employing the old terms in a slightly different fashion from that used originally. For example, a term like 'jack-line reef' representing as it did an innovation of the mid-1800s would not have been understood by Francis Drake. On the other hand, he might have spoken of a 'loom gale' (Boteler, 161), an expression which subsequently dropped completely out of favour, and would have been quite unintelligible to the Victorian seaman, who would have called it a 'whole topsail breeze'. We are attempting to focus on things more from the point of view of the seaman of the first half of the 1800s during the apotheosis of the sailing warship. When we refer to a word as 'archaic', we mean that it would have seemed so, viewed through 1850 spectacles. When in doubt, we accept Admiral William Smyth's posthumous *Sailor's Word-Book* of 1867 as the paramount authority. It is the more remarkable how many words held their original meaning throughout the whole period, reflecting perhaps the innate conservatism of the seaman.

Degrees and Points. During the heyday of the sailing man-of-war, angular change was reckoned in 'points' of eleven and a quarter degrees, the thirty-second part of the circle being about the smallest unit useful in manoeuvring the vessel. Instead of the 360° compass card familiar today, the helmsman was given the course in points, or if necessary, quarter points: 'Steer North by East, a quarter East!', and so on. It is appropriate, therefore, that we use points rather than degrees, in the ensuing discussion.

Words indicating relative position or bearing from the ship.
An object may be identified as lying 'ahead', 'astern', or 'abeam', corresponding to the cardinal points of the compass; 'on the bow' or 'on the quarter', corresponding to the half-cardinals; or 'fine on the bow', 'fine on the quarter', 'two points abaft the beam', and so on, answering to the 'three-letter' points. Everything to the right of the centreline, as one looks forward, is to 'starboard', and everything to the left, to 'port', or in older terminology 'larboard'. In sailing ships it was preferable much of the time to relate things to the wind, rather than using port and starboard. Everything on the side towards the wind was 'to windward' or 'a-weather', everything on the other side, 'to leeward' or 'a-lee'. Thus an object could be 'on the port quarter', 'on the weather bow', and so on.

I do not know if 'a-loof' ever meant exactly the same as 'a-weather'. Since we have for comparison German *Luvseite*, 'weather-side' and *luvwarts*, 'a-weather', this seems possible. In the late 1600s, it seems to have meant

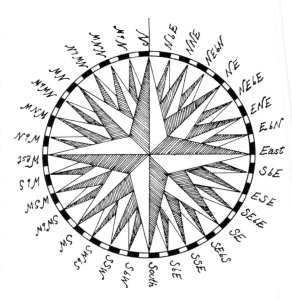

The mariner's compass of 32 points (after a design by Williams, 1724). The North point was often decorated, frequently with a fleur-de-lys, and up to the present century some card-makers also embellished the East point, which pointed towards the Holy Land.

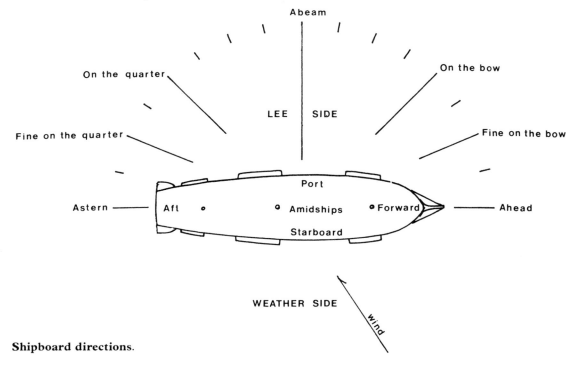

Shipboard directions.

Points of sailing
A Ship in the eye of the wind, sails aback; B ship all in the wind, sails shivering; C ship on the wind, close-hauled on the starboard tack, sails full; D ship off the wind, sailing free; E ship sailing large with a quartering wind, weather clew of mainsail hauled up; F ship running before the wind mainsail hauled up.

a point somewhere between abeam and on the bow, and the corresponding part of the ship was also called the 'loof'. By Smyth's time, this usage was quite obsolete, and people using the word 'aloof' today are usually quite unaware of its nautical origin. Nonetheless, the closely related verb 'to luff', to 'turn up into the wind' remains in use to this day.

Words indicating relative position within the ship. 'Amidships' is the centre of the vessel, whether considered in a fore and aft, or an athwartships direction, and an item may be 'forward of', 'abreast of', or 'abaft' this point. It may also lie to port or starboard, to weather or to lee. Thus we have the 'weather brace', the 'starboard lift', and so on.

Words indicating relationship to the wind. If the wind was dead ahead, the ship was said to be 'in the eye of the wind' or have 'the wind dead on end' (Uggla, 238) and of course she could not make immediate progress in this direction. The square sail instead of being 'full' curving forward, under the pressure of the wind would instead be 'aback', thrown aft against the masts and rigging. Sailing as close to the wind as possible, the ship was 'close-hauled', 'by the wind', 'on a bowline', 'on the wind', 'keeping the wind', 'touching the wind', 'lying dead upon the wind', and so on. A square-rigger could lie about six points from the wind, that is to say, if the wind were from the North, the ship could lie as close as East-North-East, or

West-North-West, but no nearer. In the first case, the wind coming from the port side, the ship was said to be 'on the port tack', the port 'tack', or rope securing the weather lower corner of the course, was 'boarded' or 'got down'. Heading West-North-West, she was said to be on the starboard tack.

If the ship were gradually 'jammed' as close to the wind as she would lie, the weather leeches of the square sails would initially flutter or 'lift' and then start to shake violently, at which point she was said to be 'all in the wind'. If pinching continued beyond that point, the sails would fly aback. If, however, the ship ceased to hug the wind and was kept away a little, until the sails were filled and drawing well, she was said to be 'a good full', 'clean full', 'rap full', or steering 'full and by'.

By appropriate 'trimming', or adjusting of sheets, tacks and yards, the sails can be got to draw on any point of sail between close-hauled and having the wind dead astern. As the wind drew aft of the point where the ship would be close-hauled, she was said to be so many points 'off the wind' or 'free', and the ship was said to be 'going free'. Thus a vessel with the wind abeam would be two points *off* the wind, or 'free' but eight points *from* the wind. If the wind was on the quarter, 'quartering', the ship was said to be 'running free' or in more remote times, 'lasking', 'going large', or 'going room'. These are all quite old-fashioned expressions, as is the phrase 'betwixt two sheets', to describe a

vessel sailing 'with the wind', 'before the wind', or having a 'following wind', all of which imply that the wind is more or less dead astern. In parentheses, one can see from the above, how the everyday expression 'by and large' arose; its nautical origin is not generally appreciated. To 'scud' was to run before the wind, under shortened canvas, as in a storm.

Favourable and contrary winds. If the wind were in the twenty point sector, which allowed the ship to head directly for her objective, she was said to be able to 'lay, or steer, her course'. If it was 'contrary' or 'foul', lying within the unfavourable twelve point sector, and thus preventing her from 'lying her course', she was obliged to 'work', 'beat', 'ply', or 'turn to windward'. This was also sometimes called 'laveering', following Dutch *laveeren* and French *louvoyer*, with the same meaning.

If the wind were such that the vessel could just manage to steer her course, it was said to be 'bare' or 'scant'. Should the wind draw round to become more favourable, the ship was said to be 'coming up', but if the wind were hauling in the opposite direction, she was said to be 'breaking off' (Nicholls, 254; Smyth). The technical meaning of 'scant' refers to the direction, rather than the force of the wind. Smyth defines a 'fair wind' as one coming from abeam, or anywhere abaft that.

Relative wind direction
A Following wind; **B** fair wind; **C** leading wind; **D** large wind; **E** soldier's wind; **F** scant wind; **G** foul wind; **H** dead muzzler; if into an anchorage, a traverse wind; **I** wind veers aft, and veers by compass; **J** wind hauls forward, and backs by compass.

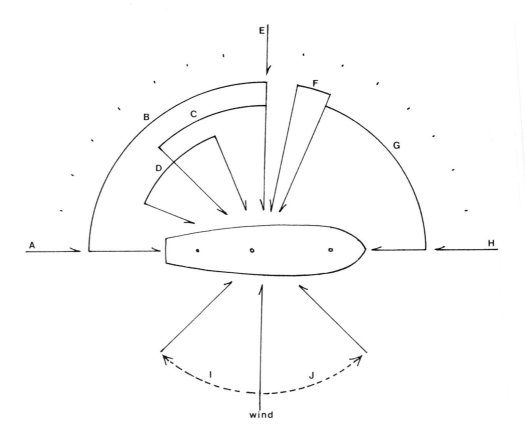

The term 'large wind' was less comprehensive, since it meant a wind more or less on the quarter, neither so far ahead as abeam, nor so far aft as dead astern. A 'leading wind' was a free wind from abeam to the quarter, giving ideal sailing conditions and the opposite of a scant wind. A beam wind was sometimes called a 'soldier's wind', since this was traditionally thought to demand the least nautical skill, the ship being able to travel in either direction with the same facility. A wind blowing directly into an anchorage, holding the vessels at anchor there 'wind-bound' or 'wind-fast', was sometimes called a 'traverse wind'. A strong, directly contrary, wind was sometimes called a 'muzzler' or 'dead muzzler' in the early 1900s. The expression 'in the teeth of the gale' came on the scene rather late in the day, and originally may not have been a strictly nautical expression.

Veering, hauling and backing of the wind. When the wind shifts around, so as to come from further aft, the modern convention is to say it has 'veered'. An older alternative was to say the wind 'larges'. If the wind draws forward, 'scants' as the old-timers put it, it is said to 'haul'. Thus the wind 'hauls forward', but 'veers aft'. I do not know how ancient this rule is, but I have seen it as far back as 1878 (Uggla). To find the principle violated, the wind 'hauling aft' is not unusual in the old accounts, some preferring 'draw aft', and 'haul forward'. Along the same lines, convention has it that the wind 'veers' when it shifts to the right or clockwise, as one looks at the horizon, or with the sun. Counter-clockwise movement is called 'backing'. This is another area where some confusion exists, some authorities considering 'haul' as synonymous with 'veer' in this particular context. Furthermore the idea underlying 'backing' is that the wind is moving contrary to the usual pattern of wind shifts, which in the Northern Hemisphere is clockwise. The exact opposite, however, is true in southern latitudes (Kemp; de Kerchove). A wind which kept changing direction was said to 'chop about', and Uggla says that a wind which had shifted about was said to have 'checked around'. In Danish, there were different words for a sudden marked change, *vinden springer*, 'the wind jumps', and a gradual change, *vinden skager sig*, 'the wind checks [itself]'. The

Elizabethan expression 'spring a-loof', meaning to turn abruptly to windward is using 'spring' in this sense. *Skage* literally means 'shake', but is closely connected with 'check' in its sea-sense.

Working to windward. If the ship could not steer her course, because she was being headed by the wind, she reached her goal by beating to windward, making a series of zigzags or 'boards', first on one tack, then on the other. At the end of each board, she was 'tacked' or 'stayed', going about head to wind onto the other tack. Another old term was to 'wind' (rhymes with 'bind') or 'wend' the ship. 'Stay' seems to have been commoner than 'tack' through the 1800s, although rarely heard today. If the distance between tacks was small, she was said to 'make short boards'. Running up into the wind, as if about to tack, but then falling off again on the same tack, was a 'half-board' or 'pilot's luff', and a succession of these was referred to as 'board and half-board'. If, in working to windward, along a coast, the ship were alternately to draw away from land and approach it, she was said to 'stand off and on'. A ship going astern was said to 'make a stern-board'. If the ship, instead of going about head to wind got on the other tack by turning stern to wind, she was said to 'wear' or 'veer'.

Underway. A vessel not at anchor, moored or aground but free to move in the water is 'underway'. If moving ahead, she is 'making headway'; if going astern, 'making sternway';

drifting to leeward, 'making leeway'; slowing down, 'losing way'. Incidentally, the ship 'gets underway', by 'weighing the anchor'. Although pronounced alike, the words, by convention, are spelt differently. It is by no means rare to see this rule breached, or reversed, in the old texts.

Tacking. In our period of interest, 'tacking' meant the operation of going about. The modern yachtsman tends to think of it as implying also the resulting progress, the 'beating to windward', but this appears to be a relatively recent extension of the original meaning. In the same vein, the old sailor would have been mystified by the modern terms 'broad reach' and 'beam reach', which he would have referred to as 'going large' and 'sailing with the wind abeam'. 'Reaching', when used, meant to sail by the wind, or with the wind somewhat forward of the beam, and sometimes implied 'standing off and on'. When a vessel luffs and turns up into the wind, as in tacking, she loses speed rapidly. However, her forward momentum carries her for some distance, and this is called 'forereaching'. A vessel lying to in bad weather, under shortened sail, with the wind forward of the beam, is sometimes said to be 'headreaching' (Nicholls, 254). In fact, the distinction between the two expressions is rather blurred.

Alteration of course. If a ship had the wind free, and the course was altered to sail by the wind, she was said to 'haul her wind', to 'come to', or sometimes 'come up' (Young). To 'luff', or 'spring a-luff', was to turn a close-hauled vessel towards the wind, so as to lift or shake the sails. To 'luff and lie' implies coming up as close as possible and holding there, while 'Luff and touch her!' was an order to luff but then fall off a fraction once more. To 'fall off' was to go off the wind. As the ship's head fell off the wind, after tacking successfully, she was said to 'pay off' on the new tack.

Pull and haul words. As regards handling ropes, 'veer' means to 'slacken off', 'pay out', the opposite of 'haul'. A rope may likewise be 'let go', 'let run', 'let fly', or 'come up' by 'casting it off' from the belaying pin, to which it is 'made fast', 'secured' or 'belayed'. If the rope under strain, instead of being thrown off, is 'eased' off a little and then belayed again, it is said to have been 'started' or 'checked'. By keeping a turn on the pin, it can be eased off in small increments, or 'snubbed'. 'Tending' is the operation of allowing a rope to pay out, without letting go of it entirely, as for example, tending the weather brace as a topsail is hoisted. A rope was 'manned' by putting an adequate number of men on it in preparation for hauling, as in 'Man the topsail halliards!'

When the fall, or rope rove through the blocks of a tackle, has been hauled to the point where its blocks have been drawn totally together, the purchase is said to be 'chock-a-block' or 'two-blocks'. It will be of no further use until the blocks are pulled apart, 'fleeting', 'overhauling' or 'coming up', the tackle fall. Taking down the slack of a tackle hanging vertically, the opposite of 'fleeting' it was called 'rounding up'. Anything hauled as taut as possible is referred to as 'chock'. When a topsail is all the way up, the halliards are 'chock up'. Nonetheless, the clews are 'sheeted home'.

There are some rather specific uses of some of these words. 'Light out to windward!' and 'Light over the head sheets!' are using the verb 'light' in an archaic sense of 'lift or pull', exactly following German *Anker lichten*, 'to weigh anchor'. 'Flow the head sheets!' uses 'flow' in the sense of 'hang loosely' as in 'her hair flowed over her shoulders'. I suppose a somewhat garbled understanding of the word accounts for Allan Cunningham's poetic reference to:

A wet sheet and a flowing sea
And a wind that follows fast.

Many colloquial variants which disappeared from use ashore, were retained afloat; for example 'lay' as an intransitive verb, instead of received English 'lie', 'now only illiterate', says the *OED*. Whatever the state of affairs in Britain, it is still widely used, even today, in Canada. In any case, it remained in regular use at sea as in 'Lay aloft!', 'Lay out!', 'Lay in!'. 'Rise' remained a common variant of 'raise' in the order 'Rise tacks and sheets!'

'Check', in the sense mentioned above, seems originally to have applied only to bowlines, but one finds some authors applying it to other pieces of gear, even halliards. This is a very old sea term, with cognates in other languages, in the sense of 'ease off', French *choquer*, Swedish *skaka* and *skräcka*, and so on. Unfortunately, its significance is the exact opposite of its everyday connotation, and for this reason it has completely dropped out of use (*Mariner's Mirror*, 61, 1975, 293). 'Steady out the bowlines!' was a specialised use of the word 'steady', applying only to bowlines. Hauling downwards was 'bousing', for instance to get lifts taut, whereas braces were 'rounded in', primarily a horizontal movement. Halliards were 'let go', or 'let fly', to strike a topsail in a hurry, but 'settled' to allow the yard to come down in a relatively controlled fashion. As to the manner in which an item was raised or lowered, 'handsomely' meant 'carefully'. 'Roundly' or 'cheerly' were expressions used when things were to be done briskly, with a will. To 'walk away', or 'run away', with the falls, in hoisting a boat, for example, indicated the speed with which the operation was to be done. Tacks were 'got down' or 'got on board' while the sheets were 'hauled aft'. Topgallant masts and light yards were 'swayed up' after being 'struck down'. 'Launch-ho!' was a special order to slacken

Working to windward
A Ship under way, making headway on the port tack; B ship in irons, making a sternboard all aback; C ship making a half-board, or pilot's luff; D ship tacking, or coming about; E ship sailing close-hauled on the starboard tack; F ship sailing close-hauled on the port tack; G ship wearing, or veering.

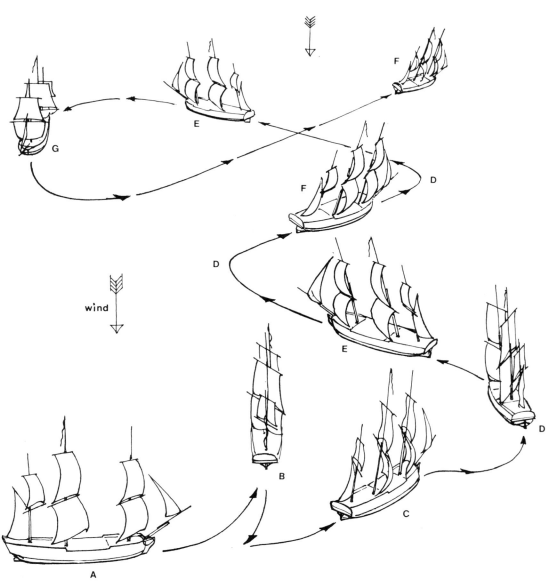

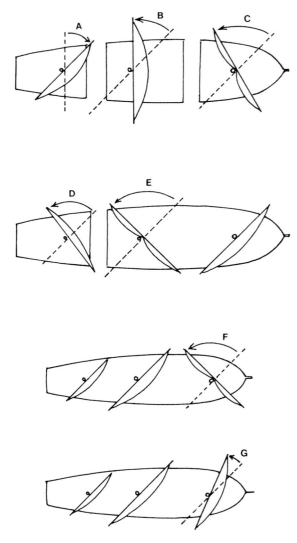

Trimming the yards
A Yard braced *up*; **B** yard braced *in*, or squared; **C** yard braced *aback*, or backed; **D** yard braced *about*, or braced round; **E** mainyard braced *by*, or counterbraced; **F** foreyard braced *abox*; **G** foreyard braced *to*.

the top-rope after a topmast had been hoisted, and the fid inserted to secure it (Smyth).

Upon coming to anchor, the cable was 'paid out' or 'veered'. To 'check' the cable was to stop momentarily the veering process, and thus was used in the ordinary landsman's sense, rather than the specialised meaning referred to earlier. As the barrel of the capstan rotated when weighing the anchor, the turns of cable around it continually rode downwards as the cable came in, and periodically had to be pried upward, or 'fleeted', on the barrel. To 'come up' the capstan, was to allow the cable to slacken. To keep the turns tightly around the capstan barrel, it was necessary to maintain tension on the inboard end, and this was called 'holding off'. To 'walk back' the capstan was to carefully ease the strain on the bars, so that the tension was

transferred from the bars to a cable stopper, or whatever. When a rope or fall had been hauled to the desired point, the order was given 'Well there, belay!'. 'Avast' as in the order 'Avast heaving!' meant to 'stop'. Smyth suggests that it derives from the Italian *basta!*, 'That's enough'.

Trimming of yards. When close-hauled, the lower yards made as acute an angle as possible with the keel-line. They were then said to be 'braced up' or 'braced sharp up'. As the wind drew aft, the yards were gradually 'braced in' or got more square, until they were right athwartships. It is important to realise that 'in' and 'up' are used here in a very specific way. That is to say, a yard would never be 'braced up square'. To 'check', or 'check in', a yard was to brace it in a little. Hourigan and Luce refer to laying the yard, so that the sail is 'alive', that is 'shivering'. This exactly parallels the Danish use of *levende* in the same technical sense (Bardenfleth, I, 165); the literal meaning is 'alive', 'living'. 'Canting', or 'bracing forward', is sometimes used synonymously with 'bracing up', from the 'in' position, although of course it is only the weather yardarm which moves forward. To 'brace about', or 'brace round', the yards was to swing them around for the opposite tack. To 'brace by', meant to 'counter-brace' the fore and main yards, swinging them in opposite directions, so that the vessel made no headway, and was 'hove to', or 'brought to', with the sails on one mast aback, and the other full. To 'brace aback', was to lay the yards so the sails were thrown back against the rigging. To 'brace full', implied swinging the yards so the sails filled once more. To 'brace a-box', was to brace the foreyard flat aback, swinging it well round, so that it would work to throw the bow off the wind. 'Bracing to', was a temporary easing or 'checking' of the lee fore brace, and a rounding in of the weather brace, in the early stages of tacking. Bringing the yards 'in' slightly from the sharp position was also called 'checking the yards' (*Mariner's Mirror* 61, 1975, 293).

Naming of sails. Kluge, Jal, and especially Sandahl, have a lot of interesting material about why sails have particular names. The English term 'course', for the lower sails, is based on the idea that this is the 'body' of the sail, to which additions are made, in the form of bonnet, and drabbler; Shakespeare's spelling 'corse', for 'corpse', would fit very well in this context. The word 'leech', for the edge of the sail, arises in a rather similar way from another old word for a dead body, surviving in the term 'lych-gate' of a church. Similar terms occur in the other northern European

languages, Dutch *lijk*, and so on, with the technical meaning 'boltrope', that is the rope outlining the 'body' of the sail.

One finds, upon looking through multi-lingual dictionaries, like Röding and Reehorst, that a similar word is sometimes used in different languages, with a definite shift of meaning. The most surprising example, of course, is the discrepancy between French *mât de misaine*, which means 'foremast', and English 'mizzen mast', Dutch *besaansmast*, Italian *albero di mezzana*, etc, which all mean 'mizzen mast'. However, we also have French *foc*, Italian *fiocco*, Spanish *fogue*, meaning 'jib', in parallel with Dutch *fok*, and similar words in Swedish, etc, which mean 'fore course'. The latter sail is *misaine* in French, but *trinchetta*, *trinquete*, in Italian and Spanish.

Dutch *kluiver*, 'jib', has the meaning 'cleaver', 'splitter', an understandable name for this sail, while the 'flying jib' is the *jager*, 'hunter', or 'chaser'. In French, this sail is the *clin-foc*, which arises from *Klein Fok*, literally 'little jib'. It is also called the *petit trinquette*, with similar diminutives in Spanish and Italian and Spanish, *trinchettina*, *trinquetilla*. The Dutch called the main staysail the 'deck-swabber', while the French word was *pouilleuse*. Exactly why, I do not know, but the meaning of *pouilleux* is 'miserable', 'abjectly poor'. *Aap*, the Dutch word for the mizzen staysail means 'monkey' or 'ape', and the term is adopted in several other languages, Swedish *apa*, and so on. The Italian name for the mizzen staysail was *carbonero*, 'collier', or something along those lines. In Portuguese, it was *rabeca*, 'fiddle', while it was *vela del humo*, 'smoke sail', in Spanish.

English 'topsail' is related to 'top' in the same way that French *hunier* is derived from *hune*. The latter has a common ancestry with the 'hounds' of the mast. Dutch *marszeil* derives from *mars*, 'top', and we have similar relationships in Italian, which has two words for 'top', *coffa* and *gabbia*. The second of these is the origin of the French word *gabier*, which means 'topman'. 'Topgallant', and the Dutch equivalent *bram*, both embrace the idea of 'showing off'. All the northern European languages name most of the top-sails and topgallants in a similar fashion *Vorbramzeil*, 'fore topgallant', *grootmarszeil*, 'main topsail', and so on. The mizzen topsail however, is called the *kruiszeil*, *kruismarszeil*, in Dutch, that is, 'cross-sail', 'cross-topsail'.

In Dutch, the 'royals' are the *boven-bramzeilen*, 'over topgallants'. In the 1800s, there developed a tendency to adopt English 'royal' instead, a change accelerated by the innovation of split topgallants, the upper-

Naming of sails
A Flying jib; **B** jib; **C** fore topmast staysail; **D** spritsail topsail; **E** spritsail; **F** fore royal; **G** fore topgallant sail; **H** fore topsail; **I** fore course or fore sail; **J** main topgallant staysail; **K** middle staysail; **L** main topmast staysail; **M** main staysail; **N** main royal; **O** main topgallant sail; **P** main topsail; **Q** main course or mainsail; **R** mizzen topgallant staysail; **S** mizzen topmast staysail; **T** mizzen staysail; **U** mizzen topgallant sail; **V** mizzen topsail; **W** mizzen sail.

most of which was naturally referred to as the *bovenbram*, necessitating some other word for the royal. The mizzen topgallant was called the *grietje*, or more formally *Grietje van dijk*, *Gretchen vom Deich*, in German. The underlying idea was that the mizzen topgallant was the last sail visible to Margriet, standing on the Dike, as she watched her sweetheart sail off, over the horizon.

In French, the main topsail was the *grand hunier*, and the fore topsail was the *petit hunier*. The fore and main topgallants were respectively the *petit* and *grand perroquet*. The mizzen topsail, being smaller than the others, was called the *perroquet de fougue*, that is to say, it had a name similar to the topgallants, rather than to the other topsails. The Spaniards called the mizzen topsail the *gata*, 'cat', while the Italians called it the *contramezzana*, 'counter mizzen', perhaps because it was square, in contradistinction to the regular mizzen. The Spanish word for the main topsail was *vela de gabia*, similarly in

---

SOME COMMON TERMS AND THEIR FOREIGN EQUIVALENTS

English	Dutch	German	Swedish	Danish	French	Italian	Spanish
Foremast	Fokkemast	Fockmast	Fockemast	Fokkemast	Mât de mizaine	Albero di trinchetto	Palo del trinquete
Mainmast	Grootmast	Grossmast	Stormast	Stormast	Grand mât	Albero maestro	Palo mayor
Mizzenmast	Bezaansmast	Besahnmast	Besansmast	Mesansmast	Mât d'artimon	Albero di mezzana	Palo de mezana
Topmast	Steng	Stenge	Stäng	Staeng	Mât de hune	Albero di gabbia	Mastelero
Topgallantmast	Bramsteng	Bramstenge	Bramstäng	Bramstaeng	Mât de perroquet	Albero di pappafico	Mastelero de juanete
Bowsprit	Boegspriet	Bugspriet	Bogspröt	Bovspryt	Beaupré	Copresso, Buonpresso	Baupres
Jibboom	Kluiverboom	Klüverboom	Klyvarebom	Klyverbom	Bâton de foc	Bastone di fiocco	Botalon del baupres
Foresail	Fokkezeil	Focksegel	Focksegel	Fok	Voile de mizaine	Vela del trinchetto	Vela de trinquete
Fore topsail	Voormarszeil	Vormarssegel	Förmärssegel	Formaersseil	Petit hunier	Vela di parrochetto	Vela de velacho
Fore topgallantsail	Voorbramzeil	Vorbramsegel	Förbramsegel	Forbramseil	Petit perroquet	Vela di pappafico di Parrachetto	Vela de juanete
Mizzentopsail	Kruiszeil	Kreuzsegel	Kryssegel				de proa
Mizzen topgallantsail	Kruisbramzeil (Grietje van Dijk)	Kreuzbramsegel (Gretchen vom Deich)	Krysbramsegel	Krydsseil	Perroquet de fougue	Vela di contramezzana	La Gata
				Krydsbramseil	Perruche	Belvedere	Periquito
Spritsail	Blinde	Blinde	Blinda	Blinde	Civadière	Civada	Cebedera
Shrouds	Wandt	Want	Vant	Vant	Haubans	Sarchie	Jarcia
Stay	Stag	Stag	Stag	Stag	Étai	Straggio	Estay
Braces	Brassen	Brassen	Brassar	Brasar	Bras	Braccj	Brazos
Lifts	Toppenants	Toppenants	Topläntor	Toplenter	Balancines	Amantigli	Amantillos
Tye	Draaireep	Drehreep	Drairep	Drajreeb	Itague	Ostaga	Ostaga
Halliards	Val	Fall	Fall	Fald	Drisse	Drizza	Driza
Buntlines	Buik-Gordingen	Bauch-Gordingen	Buk-Gårdingar	Bug-Gaardinger	Cargue-fonds	Mese	Brioles
Leechlines	Nok-Gordingen	Nok-Gordingen	Nock-Gårdingar	Nok-Gaardinger	Cargue-boulines	Serrapennoni	Apagapenoles
Studdingsail	Lijzeil	Lijsegel	Läsegel	Laeseil	Bonnette	Scopamare & Coltelazzi	Rastrera & Ala

HMS *Revenge* running for Portsmouth harbour. This painting by Thomas Luny may help to describe the terms which relate a ship to her surroundings. A sailor on board the *Revenge* would say that his ship was sailing large, or sailing off the wind, which blows on the starboard quarter. The two vessels ahead are sailing on the wind, close-hauled on the larboard (port) tack. The ship on the right he would describe as being on the weather (or starboard) beam, and appears to be in stays while passing through the eye of the wind. The small boat in the foreground bears a few points abaft the larboard beam, to leeward of the *Revenge*. (Courtesy Richard Green Galleries, London)

HM Brig *Sealark* is lying hove to in this photograph, making neither headway nor sternway, with her foresails full and aftersails aback. The yards on the foremast have been braced up on the starboard tack; those on the main have been braced in, or squared. The spanker has been sheeted in while the sheets of the jib and flying jib have been slacked well off, or flown, to take away their pulling power. (Imperial War Museum, London)

Foreign nicknames
A Mizzen topgallant – 'Grietje on the Dike' (Dutch and German); **B** mizzen staysail – 'Collier' (Italian), 'Smoke sail' (Spanish), 'Fiddle' (Portuguese), and 'Ape' (Dutch and German); **C** spritsail – 'Nosebag' (French and Spanish); **D** lubber's hole – 'Soldier's hole' (German), 'Cat hole' (French), 'Bear's hole' (Swedish), 'Wolf's throat' (Spanish).

Italian, while, in Spanish the fore topsail was *velacho* and in Italian *parrochetto*. The Italian word for the topgallant was *pappafico*, the Spanish equivalent *juanete*, a fore topgallant yardman, being a *juanetero*. The fore topgallant was *pappafico del parrochetto*, *juanete de proa*, respectively. *Perruche*, was the French word for the mizzen topgallant. This, like *perroquet* and *parrochetto*, means 'parrakeet'. Ornithologists will note that the *pappafico*, the warbler or blackcap, is of a different species.

Bagien-ra, *begijn-ra*, the word used for the crossjack yard, it related to the *Béguin* order of nuns, founded by Lambert le Bègue. Winschooten (17) engages in some speculation why this *vergue sèche*, 'barren yard', was named after the Sisters.

Making and shortening sail. The order 'Make Sail!' was given when more canvas was to be set, after it had been 'shortened' by reefing or furling. It was 'loosed' by casting off the gaskets, and then 'let fall'. When a square sail was taken in, the buntlines,

clewlines and leechlines were run up, and the sail was said to 'hang in the brails', or later, 'hang in its gear'. It was then formally 'furled', or 'handed'. The old definition of an able-bodied seaman was one who could 'hand, reef and steer'. To 'douse' something was to lower it suddenly. It was applied to taking in fore and aft sail as in 'Douse the jib!'. Reefs were 'taken', or 'turned in', and subsequently 'shaken out'. The convention in the United States Navy was that fore and aft sail was 'cleared away' and 'stowed', square sails were 'loosed' and 'furled', spanker and trysail 'cleared away' and 'furled', while studdingsails were 'got ready' and 'made up' (Hourigan, 21).

Modern sailing ship language. In any ship, on a protracted commission, there would have developed an idiolect, a language to some extent peculiar to that ship. The ship's company would have invented their own words for some new thing, and faced with several possible ways of saying the same thing, they would have tended to settle upon

one. In this way new terms were constantly coined, while others slipped into oblivion.

While preparing this book, I found Regan & Johnson's *Eagle Seamanship*, the manual used by the cadets of the United States Coast Guard Academy, extremely helpful. In terms of human activity, *Eagle* is the closest equivalent, still afloat in the English speaking world, to the old sailing warship, or, perhaps really more akin to the vessels of the Training Squadron, which were constantly dealing with a new intake of green hands. In this sort of context, the unwisdom of using language so salty as to be unintelligible, and the necessity of having exact agreement by all, on the meaning of the terms employed, is obvious. In the case of the Coast Guard, this is ensured by using *Eagle Seamanship* as the standard authority. As might be predicted, usage in *Eagle* shows some variation from that of the past. All sails are 'doused' rather than 'taken in', including those, like the courses, which actually are hauled up. The yachtsman's term 'luffing' for the shaking of a weather leech, is used instead of the old term 'lifting', which in turn, is used to describe the shivering of the whole sail when it is all in the wind. This choice may have been influenced by the Danish word *levende*, which is applied to a sail which is a-shiver, the literal meaning being 'alive'. Between 1942 and 1945, the cadets trained in *Danmark* with Danish officers, and it is possible that this has had an effect upon the sea terms preferred by the Coast Guard; at least I think it is still possible to detect traces of this influence on the sea-language of the Academy, even after thirty years. For instance, *brase op* and *brase ind*, have exactly the opposite technical meaning to 'brace up' and 'brace in' and this might explain a disinclination to use these time-honoured terms. Secondly, peculiar to the Academy is 'deadman: an improperly furled section of a sail, which looks as if a dead man could be furled inside it'. The standard, or at least older, meaning as given by Smyth, is 'dead-men: reef or gasket ends carelessly left dangling under the yard when the sail is furled, instead of being tucked in.' The idea underlying the term as used in *Eagle*, however, exactly parallels the old Danish sea expression *en kalv i revet*, 'a calf in the reef'. I know of no other English equivalent. However all that may be, I have no doubt that sea language will not remain static, in *Eagle*, or elsewhere, but will continue to evolve, while retaining many of the ancient terms.

Missionaries and anthropologists. There are two approaches to studying nautical language. The first is that of the missionary, who attempts to persuade the natives to act in a proper fashion. The second is that of the anthropologist, who observes and records the activities of the aborigines without making any moral judgement on them. As it concerns us, the interest lies in determining how a word actually was used, as distinct from how it should have been used. In the first case, it is most useful to find the term used in a narrative, rather than depending on a sterilised dictionary entry. There is honour among lexicographers, and the error of one is very likely to be transcribed unquestioningly by another. For instance, is 'fake' more correct than 'flake' in the sense of 'a single turn in a coil of rope', and the verb deriving from this? Almost every dictionary suggests that the answer is in the affirmative. However, F H Burgess, the compiler of the *Penguin Dictionary of Sailing*, told me that although he listed 'fake', he had never heard it during thirty years' service in the Royal Navy, coming across it, 'only in books'. In the *Admiralty Manual of Seamanship* (Volume II, 1951, 255) boat falls are 'flaked down'. Revision of the same passage, in Volume I (1964, 266), cleans it up, substituting 'fake'. For some reason 'fake' is considered correct, and 'flake' an illiterate variant, yet 'flake' has been in steady use, at least colloquially, since 1600, despite the efforts of the missionaries to cast it out! (Boteler, 169).

Oral tradition. Some words enjoy dual existence because of different written and spoken forms. 'Breaker', in the sense of a small barrel, is found side by side with 'barrico', 'bareka', etc, all presumably deriving from Spanish *baréca* with the same meaning. 'Timmynocky' with many variants, is a word used for a surprising variety of things, because it is a nautical equivalent to 'whatziz', 'thingamajig' (Nance, 160). Blanckley used it in the *Naval Expositor*, in 1750, as 'tyminoguy'. This was, mistakenly I am sure, assumed to be derived from a presumptive French form *timon au gui*, a term not found in any French nautical dictionary, but which would seem to mean 'a guyed tiller'. As a result it achieved respectability as 'timenoguy', now pronounced 'time-men-o-guy'.

Why the pronunciation of some words is so far removed from their spelling is a mystery. 'T'gant' for 'topgallant', 'stuns'l' for 'studdingsail' are so completely sanctioned by centuries of use, that they represent the 'proper' pronunciation. Sometimes we get a glimmering of how a pronunciation arose. It is usually suggested that 'forecastle' is traditionally pronounced 'fo'c'sl', because the illiterate sailor found this easier to say than 'fore-cast-el'. However, in the early 1400s, the 'fore sail' was known as the 'fokesail', and indeed remains *Fock-Segel* to this day in German (Sandahl, II, 39). As 'foresail' became the accepted English term, the old term was discarded, but almost certainly survived to influence the pronunciation of 'forecastle'.

It may be, however, that nowadays oral tradition is diminishing in importance. It is a little startling to hear American sailors pronouncing 'boatswain' exactly as spelled, but I am sure this alternative to 'bo'sun' reflects the fact that new entries into the United States Navy are totally literate before entering the service. In Nelson's day, the situation was quite otherwise, and terms were pronounced, not phonetically, but according to tradition.

CHAPTER 2
MASTS, RIGGING AND SAILS

In this section, we are concerned with function more than form. We wish to emphasise how things worked, rather than to deal with the topic in great structural detail. Contemporary writers on rigging and seamanship did not always fully explain matters which, although self-evident to the original readership, are quite obscure today, and we will try to clarify a few such points of difficulty. Excellent formal accounts of the rigging of the sailing man-of-war include those by Lees, Anderson, Longridge and, more remotely, those of Martelli, Biddlecombe, Lever and Steel. In addition texts by Boom, Pilaar, Mossel, Frick, Costé, and Bréart were helpful in getting an overview of this topic. The accompanying illustrations attempt to summarise what one needs to know about the anatomy of the spars and rigging, in order to grasp how things were managed in the sailing man-of-war. The table in the previous chapter shows the equivalent technical terms in other languages.

MASTS

The three masts differed in size, the main being the largest, and the mizzen the smallest. However, the proportions of the component spars on each mast remained constant. That is to say, if the fore topgallant mast is half the length of the fore topmast, the main topgallant likewise will be half the length of the main topmast. The bowsprit

Masts and yards
A Side view of the mainmast of a 36-gun ship (Steel's dimensions, 1794); **B** front view of mainmast of a 36-gun ship (Steel's dimensions, 1794); **C** detail of the main top and doubling; **D** detail of the main topmast crosstrees and doubling; **E** detail of the topgallant masthead; **F** detail of the main truck.
    a step; **b** partners; **c** top; **d** lowermast cap; **e** topmast trestletrees; **f** topmast cap; **g** topgallantmast head; **h** truck; **i** hounds; **j** bibbs; **k** trestletrees; **l** crosstrees; **m** heel; **n** lower yard; **o** topsail yard; **p** topgallant yard; **q** royal yard.
    a-d lower mast; **c-d** lower mast head; **c-f** topmast; **e-f** topmast head; **e-g** topgallant mast; **g-h** royal mast.
G Fidded royal mast; **H** royal mast fidded abaft topgallant mast; **I** funnel for topgallant rigging (late nineteenth century). **J** funnel and jack crosstree (late nineteenth century). **G, H, I** and **J** overleaf.

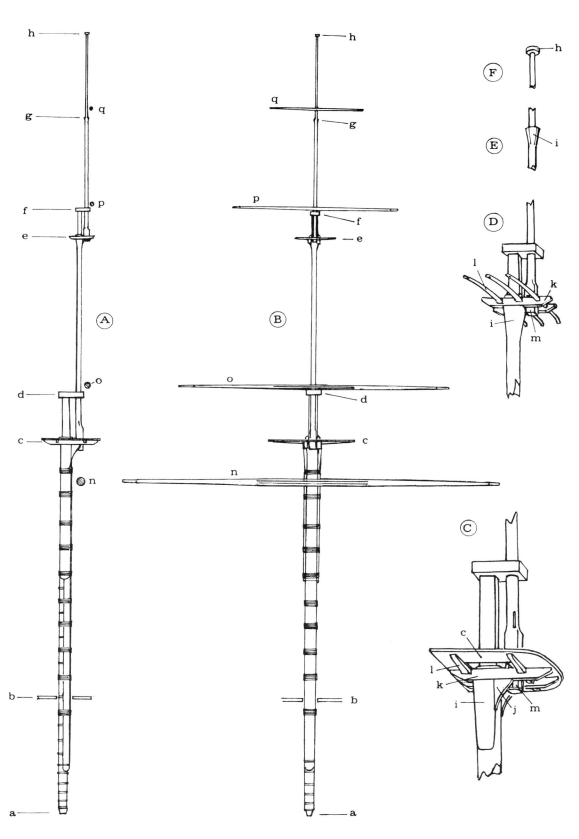

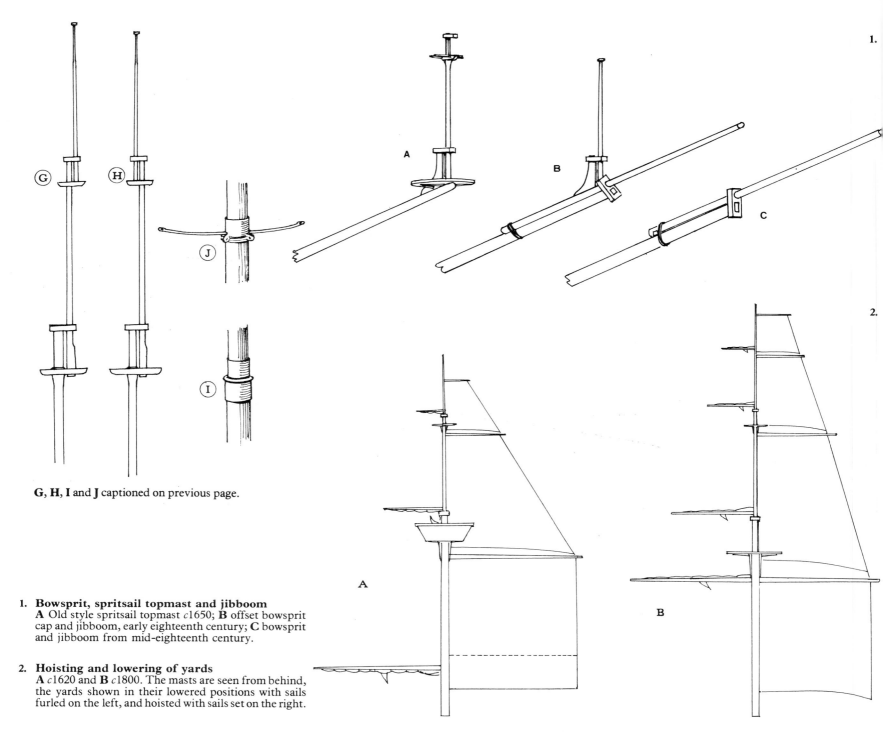

G, H, I and J captioned on previous page.

1. **Bowsprit, spritsail topmast and jibboom**
   A Old style spritsail topmast *c*1650; **B** offset bowsprit cap and jibboom, early eighteenth century; **C** bowsprit and jibboom from mid-eighteenth century.

2. **Hoisting and lowering of yards**
   A *c*1620 and **B** *c*1800. The masts are seen from behind, the yards shown in their lowered positions with sails furled on the left, and hoisted with sails set on the right.

corresponds to a fourth mast and was terminated by a cap, through which passed the jibboom, which thus was analogous to a topmast.

The topgallant mast overlapped the topmast, which in turn, overlapped the lower mast at the doublings. When first introduced, the royal mast was fitted in a similar fashion. Later on, topgallant and royal mast were fashioned from a single tree, a shoulder indicating the transition point. In the late 1800s, a funnel and jack-crosstree were fitted to the topgallant masthead, and the royal mast slipped into the funnel, but continued to be sent up and down together with the top-

gallant. The heads of the lower mast and topmast were surmounted by a cap which projected forward of the mast, and was pierced by a hole through which the mast above slid. In bad weather, the topgallant mast could be housed, partially lowered or struck, to reduce top weight, but was usually sent down completely.

Spritsail topmast. From about 1600 to 1715 a small vertical spritsail topmast perched at the end of the bowsprit. During the period when the jibboom and spritsail topmast coexisted, the bowsprit cap was slewed over to one side, to accommodate the knee of the topmast. After 1715, the cap was

placed vertically in English ships. The slewed bowsprit cap remained a feature of French rigging practice for many years after.

YARDS

Hoisting and striking yards. Corresponding to each element of the mast were the lower, topsail, topgallant and royal yards. The upper yards rested on the cap when they were struck or lowered for reefing, furling, or in harbour. 'Ties', or 'tyes', and halliards were used to hoist the upper yards, and the masts were slushed, or greased, rather than being painted, to facilitate the up and down movement. The lower yard was regularly

1.

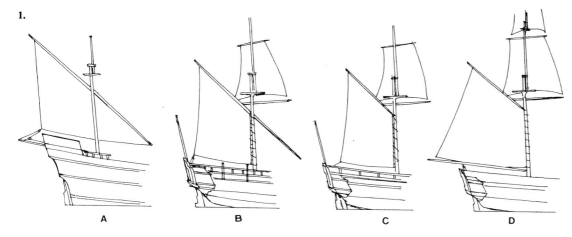

A   B   C   D

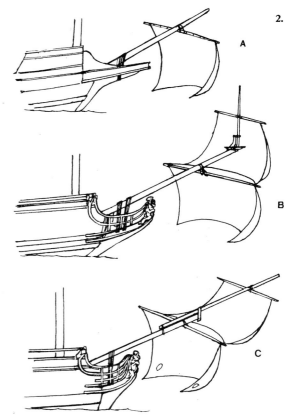

2.

A

B

C

hoisted and struck in Elizabethan times, but later, it became the practice to keep the yard aloft, more or less all the time, hung by a chain-sling. It was then struck only in exceptional circumstances, for example to ease mast and rigging, when riding hard in a stormy anchorage. The old term for this was 'riding a-portlast' (Boteler, 98).

Naming of yards. The yards were named for their respective masts, foreyard, mainyard, main topgallant yard, and so on, except that the yards for the topsails were always referred to as 'topsail yards' rather than 'topyards'. On the other hand, the studdingsails abreast the topsails, were called 'topmast studdingsails', as compared with 'topgallant studdingsails'.

The mizzen yard was unique in setting a fore and aft or lateen sail, the mizzen course. Originally, this was the only sail carried on the mizzen mast, but by about 1600, it was augmented by the square mizzen topsail, to be followed even later, by mizzen topgallant and royal. The yard, spreading the foot of the mizzen topsail, was called the crossjack (pronounced 'cro'jick') yard. Although it was analagous to the fore- and mainyards, the name 'mizzen yard' was already 'taken', so to

speak, and some other term was necessary. The mizzen course was subsequently replaced by a trapezoidal sail, whose forward leech was secured to the mizzen mast. The mizzen yard disappeared, or rather atrophied, being replaced by a gaff, which now supported the head of the smaller sail, which was still, however, called the mizzen. No square sail was set on the crossjack yard until very late in the 1800s.

Spritsail and spritsail topsail yards. The spritsail yard was slung under the bowsprit, about one third its length from the end, and like the lower yard, was fixed in this position. Between about 1600 and 1715, a spritsail topsail could be set on the spritsail topmast; between 1715 and 1800, retaining the old name, a spritsail topsail was run out on the jibboom, as a sort of 'under jib'. When furled, its yard rested on the bowsprit cap.

Yards and yardarms. Properly speaking, only the extreme ends of the yards were the 'yardarms'. These projected beyond the point where brace, lift and head-earing were secured and were about one twentieth the length of the yard, except in the case of the topsail yards, where they amounted to one-tenth. The centre of the yard was occasionally

1.
Changes to the mizzen yard
A lateen mizzen *c*1600; **B** smaller sail bent to whole mizzen yard *c*1760; **C** mizzen gaff *c*1790; **D** longer gaff and spanker boom, *c*1800.

2.
Spritsail and spritsail topsail
A *c*1600; **B** *c*1650; **C** *c*1780.

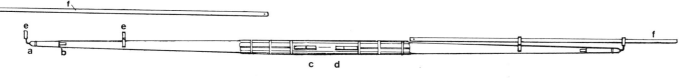

Yards and studdingsail booms
a-b yardarm; **b-c** quarters of yard; **c-d** slings of yard; **e** studdingsail boom irons; **f** studdingsail booms (shown fitted through boom irons on right).

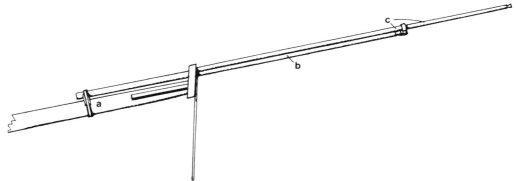

Bowsprit, jibboom and flying jibboom
a bowsprit; **b** jibboom; **c** flying jibboom.

called the 'bunt', but more usually the 'slings', the part of the yard between slings and a point half way out, being known as the 'quarters'.

Studdingsail booms. These were about half the length of their respective yards, and were found on fore and main topsail and lower yards. They were run out to spread the foot of the studdingsails, which set outside the principal sails. We will describe their fittings in greater detail later.

Flying jibboom. This was about the same length as the jibboom, and was run out through a ring very similar to a studdingsail boom iron, at the end of the jibboom. Its introduction in the 1790s brought about the adoption of a sort of jumper-strut, the dolphin-striker, to give it downward support, counteracting the upward pull of the flying jib. The martingale stay, running from flying jibboom end to the foot of the dolphin-striker, made it impossible to set the spritsail topsail, which accordingly vanished from the scene (*Mariner's Mirror* 63, 1977, 8). Incidentally, the term 'flying jibboom' had, somewhat earlier, been employed to describe what was later always referred to simply as the 'jibboom'.

STANDING RIGGING

The standing rigging supported the masts. Once set up, it was subject only to minor adjustments, rather than being extensively altered in the working of the ship. This does not strictly speaking apply to shifting backstays, but it is perhaps convenient to consider them at this point also.

Stays. The stays support the masts from forward and are named for the masthead they support. Usually, they run downwards and forwards from the mast at a fairly steep angle, but in the 1700s some of the upper stays are almost horizontal and contemporary paintings offer scattered examples of stays running slightly upwards and forwards. The 'staysails' were bent to the stays, and named for the stay on which they moved. The 'middle staysail', the 'flyer' or *vlieger* as the Dutch called it, is an exception to this: it set on a special stay running from halfway up the fore topmast to the main topmast head. In larger vessels, there were preventer stays parallel to the stay itself, and in men-of-war, they were 'snaked' to the stay itself prior to battle, in case one was shot away. The jib and flying jib stays were similar to the others except that their lower ends were secured to travellers, or rings, which ran out on the boom on which they were set. Storm staysails of very heavy canvas were set on the stays to the lower

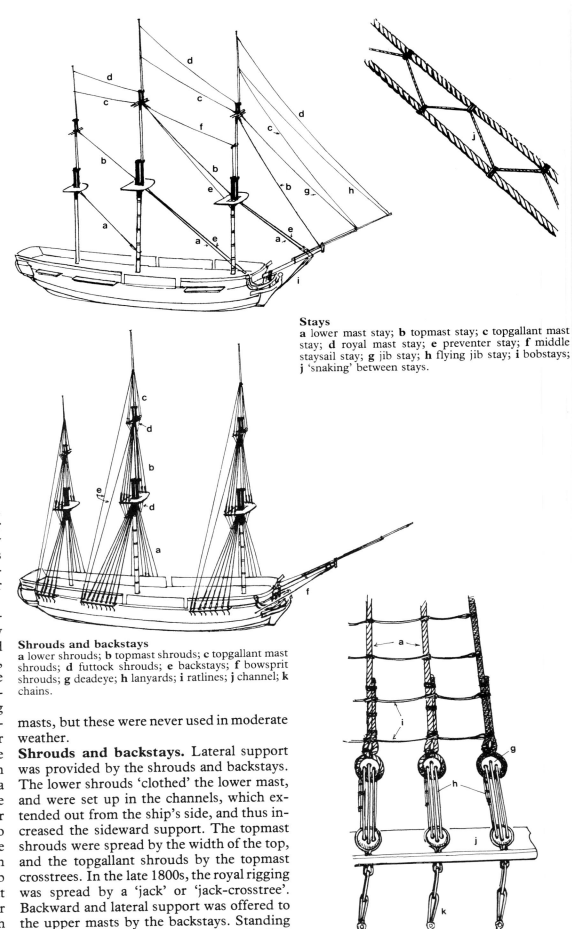

Stays
a lower mast stay; b topmast stay; c topgallant mast stay; d royal mast stay; e preventer stay; f middle staysail stay; g jib stay; h flying jib stay; i bobstays; j 'snaking' between stays.

Shrouds and backstays
a lower shrouds; b topmast shrouds; c topgallant mast shrouds; d futtock shrouds; e backstays; f bowsprit shrouds; g deadeye; h lanyards; i ratlines; j channel; k chains.

masts, but these were never used in moderate weather.

Shrouds and backstays. Lateral support was provided by the shrouds and backstays. The lower shrouds 'clothed' the lower mast, and were set up in the channels, which extended out from the ship's side, and thus increased the sideward support. The topmast shrouds were spread by the width of the top, and the topgallant shrouds by the topmast crosstrees. In the late 1800s, the royal rigging was spread by a 'jack' or 'jack-crosstree'. Backward and lateral support was offered to the upper masts by the backstays. Standing backstays were set up in the channels. The rigging was protected against the weather by

Backstays
A Standing backstays; B breast backstay; C detail of breast backstay outrigger; D travelling backstay.

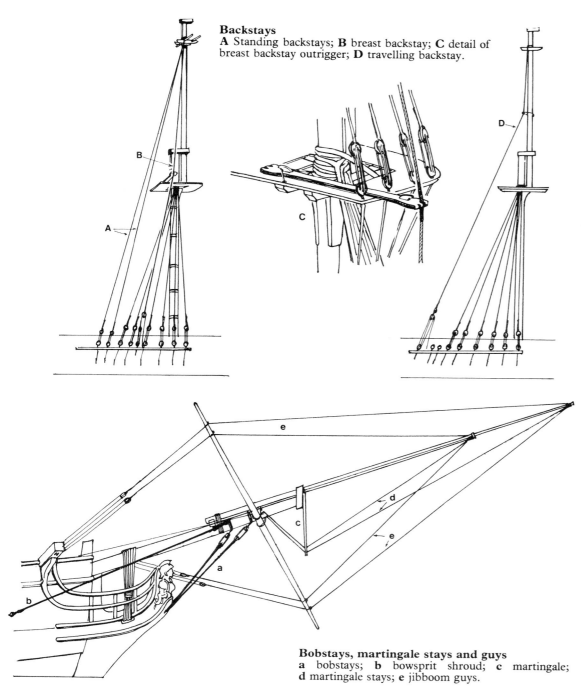

Bobstays, martingale stays and guys
a bobstays; b bowsprit shroud; c martingale; d martingale stays; e jibboom guys.

'blacking down', laying on a hot mixture of coal tar, Stockholm tar, and saltwater.

Breast and travelling backstays. As the name suggests these were set up in the channels abreast the topmasts. When close-hauled, the weather breast backstay was 'crutched' in a notch in the end of the outrigger, and 'borne out' from the top, thus giving the stay a better angle of lateral pull to help support the topmast, and resist the pressure pushing it to leeward. On the other hand, the lee breast backstay had to be 'borne abaft', so that it did not get in the way of the lee quarter of the lower yard. This effective, but clumsy, arrangement remained in use in men-of-war until the late 1800s. In merchantmen, by the

late 1860s, the topgallant backstays were crutched in a spreader at the topgallant crosstrees. This spreader improved the angle of pull both outwards and backwards to the head of the topgallant mast, and unlike the outrigger which fulfilled the same function, it did not have to be shifted every time the vessel went about. The Dutch word for such an outrigger was *doove jut*, and this, I believe, is the origin of the English word 'davit', which initially referred to a piece of timber, with a notched end, thrust out to support the fish-block, in fishing the anchor.

Other supplementary support was offered by various types of shifting or travelling backstays, particularly in small vessels. The

so-called 'travelling backstay' was used in smaller vessels to give support to the topmast, and was particularly useful with reefs taken, since the yard then crossed the mast well below the topmast crosstrees and threw an unduly heavy strain on the mast at this point. They were secured to a traveller which slid on the topmast just above the parrel, and thus applied a backward pull at that point of the topmast where the strain was greatest and the support least. Mossel (II, 240; III, 130) mentions shifting backstays *voor den wind zeilers*, 'before the wind backstays', which were used when sailing for a prolonged period with the wind aft or on the quarter. They were set up on the weather side, to give additional backward support to the mizzen topmast head, which was taking the strain of the main topsail braces.

Bobstays and martingale-stays. The bobstay was a hold-down for the bowsprit, running almost vertically down to the stem of the vessel. The martingale-stays ran from the ends of the jibboom and flying jibboom to the lower end of the dolphin-striker, and thence back up to the bowsprit, or later, to the bows of the vessel itself. There is some confusion between 'martingale' and 'martingale-stay'. The spar, later called a dolphin-striker, and the word 'martingale' to describe it, first appear in 1794. The stays attached to it were the 'martingale-stays'. Once 'dolphin-striker' became the popular English term, the stays began to be referred to simply as the 'martingales'. This had the additional logic that the word, coming to us from French, originally meant – and still does mean – a restraining device for a horse's head, running from the girth between the forelegs up to the bridle. The function of this item of harness matches that of the stays holding down the jibboom. Interestingly enough, *martingale* was re-borrowed into French to describe the dolphin-striker when it first appeared, although later, other terms such as *arcboutant* superseded it. In reading old accounts, therefore, one depends on the context to determine the exact sense in which the word is used. Lateral support was provided by the bowsprit shrouds, and by guys which ran from the jibboom through eyes on top of the spritsail yard. These guys, like the bowsprit shrouds provided lateral support to the jibboom, but had an additional function. The introduction of the dolphin-striker was a great improvement over the earlier means of giving downward support to the jibboom end. Prior to 1800, each time the ship went about, from one tack to the other, the spritsail had to be triced around so that it was shifted over to the 'new' lee side of the bowsprit. The

23

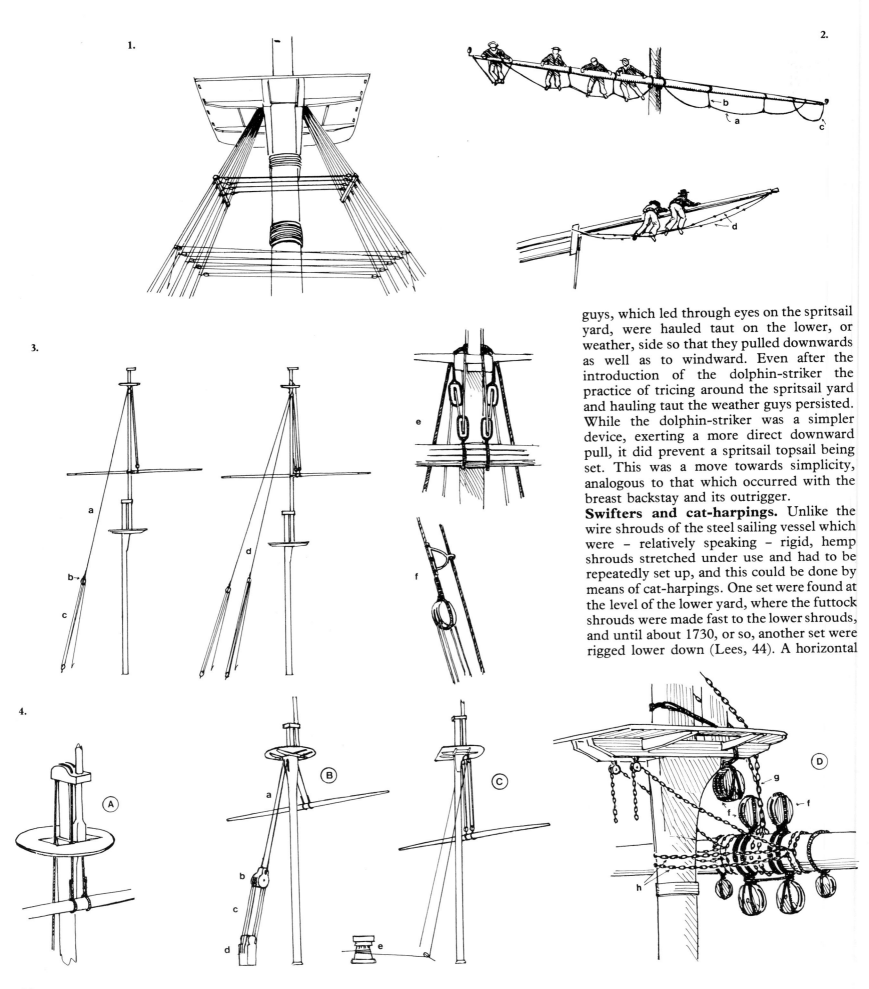

guys, which led through eyes on the spritsail yard, were hauled taut on the lower, or weather, side so that they pulled downwards as well as to windward. Even after the introduction of the dolphin-striker the practice of tricing around the spritsail yard and hauling taut the weather guys persisted. While the dolphin-striker was a simpler device, exerting a more direct downward pull, it did prevent a spritsail topsail being set. This was a move towards simplicity, analogous to that which occurred with the breast backstay and its outrigger.

Swifters and cat-harpings. Unlike the wire shrouds of the steel sailing vessel which were – relatively speaking – rigid, hemp shrouds stretched under use and had to be repeatedly set up, and this could be done by means of cat-harpings. One set were found at the level of the lower yard, where the futtock shrouds were made fast to the lower shrouds, and until about 1730, or so, another set were rigged lower down (Lees, 44). A horizontal

View from aft of catharpins and lower catharpins or swifters.

Footropes and stirrups
a footrope; b stirrup; c Flemish horse; d footrope on jibboom.

Topsail tie and halliards
a topsail yard tie; b fly block; c halliards; d double topsail ties and halliards; e detail of tie blocks on yard and mast; f detail of fly block and traveller on backstay.

Lower yard tie and halliards
A Early lead of ties over lowermast cap; B old style tie; C jeers; D detail of jeer blocks, chain slings and truss (late nineteenth century).
a tie; b ramshead block; c halliards; d knight; e jeer capstan; f jeer blocks; g chain slings; h chain truss.

stave was seized to the shrouds to hold them at the proper distance, and a rope was snaked back and forth from side to side, in such a way that it pulled the shrouds together. Lever (25) calls this rope the 'swifter', but more often the snaking is referred to as the 'cat-harping legs'. Because the foremost shrouds are abreast the mast, they were not cat-harped, since the cat-harping leg would chafe on the mast, but Lever says that in his day, legs were rigged from the after shroud on one side to the foremost shroud on the other. He says these 'cross cat-harpings' are of great use in keeping the lee rigging in, when the vessel rolls. This would also pull the forward shroud in and back, and thus allow the lower yard to be braced up a little more sharply. The forward shroud was exposed to the chafe from the quarter of the lee yard, and lee leech of the course, when close-hauled. Thus both it and the foremost topmast shroud were served throughout their length to protect them from this abrasion. The term 'swifter' was sometimes applied to this foremost lower shroud (Burney, 68; Smyth, 669) but also to the aftermost shroud (Lees, 42; Falconer 285; Steel, 131), and indeed, Hourigan (24) uses it to describe the foremost topmast shroud. The aftermost shroud was also distinctive in that, when rattling down, only every sixth ratline was secured to it.

Footropes or horses. The footropes, upon which the yardmen stood, when working on the yards, are such an accepted feature of later sailing ships that it comes as rather a surprise to realise they were nonexistent before 1642 at the earliest, and probably not till about 1680 on the topsail yards (Lees, 158). Prior to their introduction, the men ran out along the top of the yard and worked, as best they could under these circumstances, standing, strad-dling, or lying, on the lower yards. The yard-arm man when reefing a topsail, sat astride

the yardarm, and a special short footrope or 'flemish horse' was fitted, from about 1760, to give him foothold. Belgian horses were much favoured as draught animals, but the exact connection with Flanders is elusive. The Dutch word for a Flemish horse was *nock-paard*, 'yardarm-horse', the ordinary Dutch word for footropes being *parden*, 'horses'. Röding, in 1793, says that 'in earlier times' *rug-paarden* or *steun-paarden* had been used to give the men working on the yard something to lean their backs against (*rug* means 'back', *steun* means 'support'). Life-lines of this sort, running from the lift to the topsail ties, were, in fact, used in bad weather, long after Röding's time. Beckets, loops of rope hitched to the jackstay, also offered extra handholds to the men on the yards in later days (Underhill, 103). The footropes under the bowsprit and jibboom had knots placed at intervals, to prevent the feet of the men standing on them from slipping.

RUNNING RIGGING
We will first consider those items of gear which controlled the yards, and secondly those which could be classed together as the gear of the sails.

Ties and halliards. The topsail yard was hoisted by a rope which led through a block at the masthead and then down aft to be secured to a tackle. The arrangement was thus a runner and tackle, the runner being called the 'tie' and the tackle the 'halliards'. I am not sure why 'halliards' is, for the most part, used in the plural form, nor why the 'haul-yard' is designated 'tie'. However, in every language one finds a different word for the runner and the tackle, *itague* and *drisse*, in French, *Drehreep* and *Fall*, in German, and so on. When not in use, the halliards were some-times coiled up in tubs to keep them clear for running. In vessels of substantial size, there were two ties and halliards, one leading to each side of the ship. The 'fly-block', to which the tie was fastened, would come down within a few feet of the deck when the yard was hoisted. It was a dangerous missile if a tie should break, and hence was secured to a traveller running on the topmast backstay, or to a lanyard in the top, which would prevent its falling on deck, (Hansen, 21). The traveller also prevented the fly-block twisting, but some officers preferred to depend on a swivel on the lower block of the tackle (Costé, 119).

Double and single purchases. In the mid-1800s, a practice arose of fitting a lighter pur-chase on one side, which would allow the yard to be hoisted quickly with all hands, and

a double purchase on the other, to be used with one watch. When one halliard was being used, the slack of the other had of course to be got down at the same time. At sea, when hoisting topsails, it was usual to haul the weather halliards taking down the slack of those to lee and keeping a turn on, at all times, in case the weather halliards or tie should break (Taunt, 311). Hourigan (25) appears to advocate the reverse practice, but since the wind pressure bears more heavily on the weather rigging, Taunt's advice seems the most seamanlike. Boyd (183) fits the lighter purchase on the port side on fore and mizzen, and to starboard, with the main topsail; Nares (84) does the reverse. The *Leitfaden* (39) rigs the double purchase on alternate sides, but does not specify in which order.

Alternating sides. When hoisting topsails, the fall of the fore topsail halliards was led along one side of the deck running aft, and that of the main led forward on the other. As the yards went up, the hands could run from one side of the deck to the other, and tail on to the fall of the other halliards (Taunt, 311). Mizzen topsail halliards were usually hoisted hand over hand.

Modern authorities indicate that the in-variable rule at sea was to lead the fore topsail halliards to port, the main to starboard, and the mizzen to port. The royal halliards were led to the same side as the topsail halliards, and the topgallant halliards to the opposite sides. This distributed the strain on masts and hull fabric more equitably, and clearly such a convention was useful (Davis, *Block Models*, 53; *Assistant*, 142; McCann, 130). Its use is substantiated by Oderwald (122) and Riesenberg (197), although, it does not seem to have been universally followed in small merchant vessels. For example, af Trolle (102) rigs the fore and main as above, but his mizzen topsail halliards lead to starboard, the topgallant and royal being made fast to port, as on the main masts. Anderson (249) refers to a contemporary model with the mizzen topsail halliards led to starboard, and Longridge (258) mentions the same thing in his model of *Victory*. Hansen (21) belays the mizzen topsail halliards amidships.

With double ties, on the topsail yard, the question does not arise, and it appears that when the topsails had a symmetrical arrange-ment that the fore and mizzen topgallant halliards were led to port, and the main to starboard (Mossel, II, 218). There is rather better agreement that when sending light yards up and down for exercise in harbour, the fore and mizzen topgallants were worked to port, and the main to starborad, and the reverse for the royal yards (Frick, 178; Taunt,

242; Bardenfleth, II, 26; Luce, 369; Pilaar, 215; Ekelöf, 84; Burney, 93). One lacks definite confirmation, however, that the halliards were led to that side of the deck, upon which the yard was worked, but this seems quite probable.

Lower yards. Ties and halliards were at one time used for the lower yards also, until about 1650 in English ships, much later in Dutch vessels (Anderson, 132; Lees, 63). The Dutch practice was to lead the ties over the cap, which in longitudinal section was shaped like a question mark laid on its side. Scores were cut in the convex after part of the cap, which acted like a pair of dumb sheaves. This configuration explains the origin of the Dutch word for a cap, *ezels-hoofd*, 'ass-head' and also the reason why the lift-blocks dependent from it, were called *ezels-ooren*, 'ass-ears'.

The halliards rove through sheaves in the knighthead fixed to the deck, and the ram's-head block, which corresponded to the fly-block of the topsail halliards. The tie, which was double, passed through a hole in the upper part of the ram's-head block, and back up over the cap to the yard. Later, the yard was hoisted by jeers, tackles whose blocks

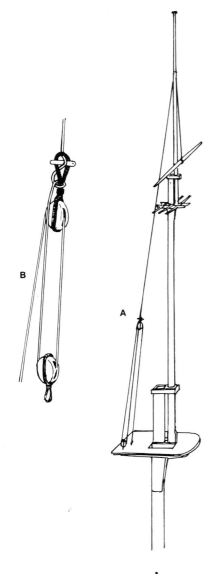

1. Topgallant halliards
A Using yard rope as purchase; **B** detail of toggled halliards.

2. Braces led as in 1800
a counter brace (starboard side only); **b** yard tackle used as preventer brace (shown on port side).

were made fast to the masthead and the slings of the yard. The yards were swayed up by taking the jeer-rope to the jeer-capstan. Smaller than the main-capstan, it was placed between the fore- and mainmasts. From about 1800, it became the usual practice to unreeve the jeers, once the yard was hoisted, and suspend them by a sling. Chain-slings quickly supplanted those made of rope. Still later, the yard was hung by means of a patent truss, which acted as a sort of universal joint, allowing the yard to be traversed by the braces and canted by the lifts, while holding it at a fixed distance from the mast. It supplanted the chain trusses, and was altogether a much better system. It was adopted more quickly in the merchant service than in the navy.

Topgallant and royal halliards. When light yards were sent up and down, for exercise purposes, a simple halliard or 'yard rope' was used. In length this was at least twice the distance from the deck to the sheave-hole in the mast. At sea, the yard had only to travel between the cap and the masthead, and the halliards did not have to be so long. With topgallants and royals, the yard rope could be transformed into a tie and simple purchase, by 'toggling the halliards'. The hauling end of the yard rope was rove through two blocks, which were kept in the top, and had no function when the yard rope was being used to send the yard up from deck. To use it as a halliard, the upper of the two blocks was hooked in the top, to become the lower block of the purchase. The lower block now became the upper block of the purchase. It was fitted with an eye, at its upper end, and through this was passed a bight of the yard rope, a little below the sheave in the mast. A toggle held it in place, thus, in effect, turning the arrangement into a gun-tackle. The royal halliards were often made fast on the weather side, rather than following any strictly alternating pattern.

Staysail halliards. The halliard blocks of the jibs and staysails likewise alternated from side to side of the mast. Frick (184), Burney (75) and Mossel (II, 376) give jib halliards to starboard, flying jib and fore topmast staysail likewise to port, suggesting international agreement on this point. Harold Underhill (142), on the other hand, gives the arrangement in merchant ships with inner and outer jibs, that is to say, four rather than three head sails. The flying jib, and inner jib halliards rove to port, and those for outer jib and fore topmast staysail to starboard.

Braces. Each yard had two braces, by means of which it could be traversed in the horizontal plane. To 'brace up' the yard

1.

3.

2.

4.

1.
Main top of the *Nonsuch* ketch, a modern reconstruction of a small seventeenth century vessel. Note the wooldings around the lower mast, the round top, and the seaman climbing aloft via the futtock shrouds. (Mark Myers' Collection)

2.
Detail of the spritsail and spritsail topsail on a seventeenth century Dutch model. (Author's photo, courtesy Prins Hendrik Maritime Museum, Rotterdam)

3.
Old-fashioned Dutch lowermast cap, holed and scored on each side to take the lower yard ties up over the cap. (Author's photo, courtesy Prins Hendrik Maritime Museum, Rotterdam)

4.
Chain slings and truss on a nineteenth century Swedish warship model. The truss can be slacked off to allow the yard to be braced sharp up. In this ship the topsail sheets are also chain, and run through metal blocks. (Author's photo, courtesy Marinemuseet, Karlskrona)

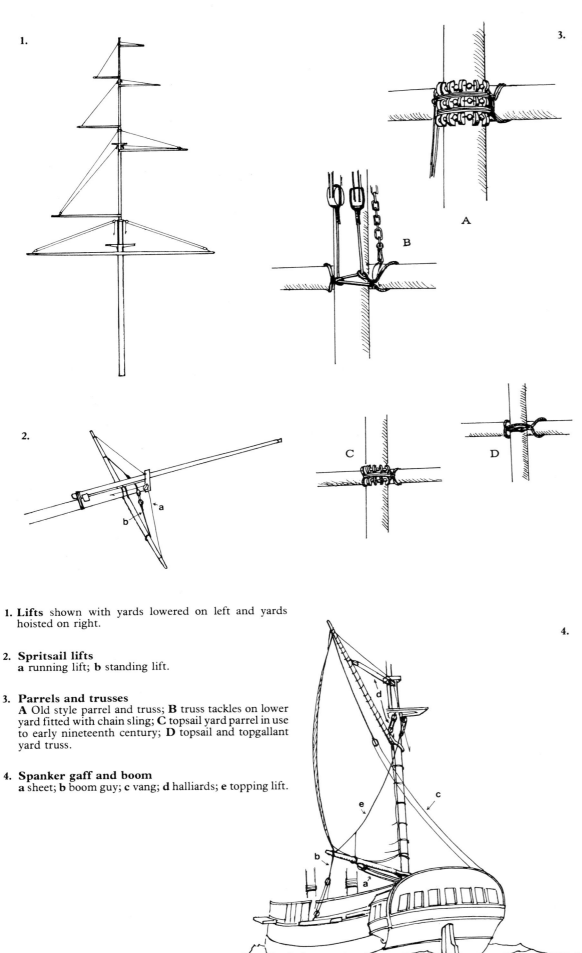

1. Lifts shown with yards lowered on left and yards hoisted on right.

2. Spritsail lifts
a running lift; b standing lift.

3. Parrels and trusses
A Old style parrel and truss; B truss tackles on lower yard fitted with chain sling; C topsail yard parrel in use to early nineteenth century; D topsail and topgallant yard truss.

4. Spanker gaff and boom
a sheet; b boom guy; c vang; d halliards; e topping lift.

meant to swing it into a more acute angle with the keel. To 'brace in' meant to return it towards the square position. The braces were named for the yard they controlled, and further distinguished by specifying whether 'port' or 'starboard', 'lee' or 'weather'. Thus 'lee fore brace', 'port main royal brace', and so on. They led aft from the yards on the fore- and mainmasts, forward from those on the mizzen. One consequence of this was that whenever the main and mizzen yards were to be swung together, as in tacking, the order to haul had to be given in the form 'weather main, lee crossjack braces', so that the yards would swing in the same direction. To avoid this, some naval vessels crossed the crossjack braces abaft the mainmast, so that the hauling part led to the opposite side of the deck. In the late 1800s, the braces of the lower yards were led to a short bumpkin or outrigger, which projected from the ship's side and gave a better angle of pull when the yards were square.

Preventer-braces and counter-braces. When braced sharp up, the lee fore brace exerted its pull horizontally, since it led to the collar of the main stay. The lee main brace on the other hand had a very disadvantageous down lead. It led down to the gunwale, because the mizzen mast was too close to the main, and was itself too ill supported from aft, to allow the brace being led to the mizzen stay. Extra counter-braces were rove through a block at the main yardarms and taken forward to the foremast head, in men-of-war. Hauling the weather counter-brace pulled the weather yardarm forward and swung the lee one aft, and this pull was exerted in a favourable horizontal direction. In tacking, the order 'Mainsail haul!' was given when the after sail was almost becalmed by the fore sails. If the hands 'ran away' with both parts of the lee counter-brace, at the proper moment, the heavy mainyard could be swung easily. If a heavy haul was anticipated, one part could be secured, and the other hauled upon to get the extra purchase necessary. The counter-braces crossed over under the fore top, for the same reason that the mizzen braces crossed. There were thus four braces on the mainyard. To brace in, the after brace was used, and to brace up, the counter-brace (Nares, 251). Nares uses 'preventer-braces' as synonymous with 'counter-braces'. The term 'preventer-brace' also was applied to yard tackles, rigged as extra weather braces, on the lower and topsail yards, and which led downwards and aft as far as possible. They were used in heavy weather, particularly with reefed topsails.

Spritsail tricing lines. The spritsail yards

were not fitted with braces, but with tricing lines, with which they were 'triced around' (Dutch *trijsen*, *omtrijsen*); these led aft up to the fore topmast stay. Sailing by the wind, the lee spritsail yardarm was triced, or canted, up and slightly aft. The later type of spritsail topsail was fitted in a similar fashion, also having tricing lines. The earlier spritsail topsail differed in having simple braces which led aft and worked in the same way as regular braces.

Lower lifts. The lifts canted the yard in the vertical plane. They were attached to the yard at the same point as the brace and were identified by the same names as the corresponding braces. They ran to the lower cap, and hence always exerted an effective upward pull. Sailing close-hauled, the weather leech and tack of the course exerted a tremendous downward pull on the weather yardarm. This was counter-balanced somewhat by hauling taut the weather lift. We have already mentioned the downward pull of the lee main brace when close-hauled. This was opposed by hauling taut the lee lift, but unfortunately, on this very point of sail, the lee lift tended to bind across the foremost topmast shroud and cause unacceptable chafing.

Upper lifts. The topsail yard lifts led through the lower sheave of a sister-block, seized between the two foremost topmast shrouds. The reef-tackle fall rove through the other sheave. The topgallant lifts were rove in an almost identical fashion. When the topsail and topgallant yards were mastheaded, the lifts led almost horizontally and contributed almost nothing in the way of upward support. Their main function, in fact, was to take the weight of the yardarms when the yard was lowered. In reefing topsails, a heavy strain was put on these by the reef-tackle. Later it became customary to fit 'standing lifts' to the upper yards. These supported the yardarms when the yards were lowered, in the same way as the earlier 'running lifts'. When hoisted, the standing lifts hung in a bight abaft the yard and sail. What might be taken for a weather topsail lift leading to the topmast cap, will be seen in paintings showing vessels with weather topmast studdingsails set. This, in fact, represents the halliard of the studdingsail. In men-of-war, light yards were regularly sent up and down. This meant that the eye of the lift and brace had to be slipped on and off the yardarm. To facilitate this, the eye of the lift and the brace were seized together, so that they went on and off as a unit.

Spritsail lifts. These had to be set up each time the yard was triced around. So called 'standing lifts' were fitted close to the slings of the yard. They really functioned as a sort of halliard, the weather one taking the weight of the yard, in the triced up position, the lee one, resisting the upward pull of the weather guys (*Mariner's Mirror* 67, 1981, 60). The Danes called them 'Spanish lifts', the French 'moustaches'.

Trusses and parrels. The light yards were secured to their masts by a simple parrel, which allowed the yard to slide up and down its mast. To send down the yard, the seizing on one side of the parrel was cut, and the yard disengaged for sending down. As mentioned above, the lower yards had originally been hoisted each time sail was set, and a more complicated apparatus, the truss-parrel, had been devised to allow this. An arrangement of trucks and ribs allowed the yard to proceed up and down while holding it against the mast. Truss tackles were fitted so the parrel could be tightened or slackened. In actual use, this contrivance must have been a nightmare, since it was almost certain to bind or stick during hoisting or lowering, if things got slewed. A simpler version, without trusses, was used for the topsail yard. The parrel for the lower yard was dispensed with once it became the practice to keep it more or less permanently suspended by the chain sling, but the necessity for a truss remained. The lower yard was suspended approximately below the heel or lower end of the topmast. As the vessel pitched, it would swing to and fro. When sailing with the wind aft, the truss tackles were hauled taut, and the yard steadied and pulled back towards the mast. When close-hauled, the trusses were let go to allow the yard to be braced up as sharply as possible. This movement was limited, in the case of the foreyard, by the forestay, forward of the yard, and the foremost lee shroud abaft it. After the yard had been braced up, the weather truss was hauled taut, at the same time as the weather lift and brace, and this helped pull the yard clear of both forestay and shroud. This cumbersome apparatus was ultimately replaced by the patent truss which we have already mentioned.

Rolling tackles. As the vessel rolled, the lower yard would oscillate from side to side, and tackles were hooked to the quarters of the yard to impede this movement. In the case of the topsail yard, the parrel would limit such movement, but in heavy weather a tremendous strain came on it with each roll.

Vangs. The vangs or guys were used to steady the head of gaff of the mizzen. The weather one was hauled taut as the sail was taken in, and both of them were set up when it was furled. When the mizzen was set, the sail was allowed to adopt its natural curvature to leeward and the weather vang was not therefore ordinarily hauled taut.

Boom guy. When the mizzen was set with the wind well aft, there was a danger of what we would today refer to as a 'gybe'. The boom was steadied forward by a tackle called a boom guy.

SAILS AND THEIR GEAR

Definitions. 'Plain sail' was the ordinary working sail, excluding studdingsails, and upper staysails, as in the expression 'all plain sail to royals'. In the United States Navy, the fore topmast staysail was not considered part of the plain sail, while a gaff topsail, although rarely used, was. The term is easily confused with 'plane sailing', an expression used in navigation. 'Headsails' were the sails set on the foremast and ahead of it, while 'aftersail' included the canvas spread on the mainmast and everything abaft that. 'Staysails' were those set on stays, sometimes including, and sometimes excluding the flying jib and jib. 'Light sails' included the topgallant staysails, topgallants and royals, which set on the 'light yards' (Taunt, 61).

The sails themselves. These may be conveniently divided into square sails, set on the yards, on the one hand, and fore and aft sails on the other. The named sides and corners of the sails are noted in the accompanying illustrations. It is perhaps worth noting that, contrary to modern practice, the forward edge or leech of a jib was called the 'stay'; that of a trapezoidal staysail the 'bunt', and that of a gaff topsail, the 'mast'. In all three cases today, we would tend to use the word 'luff'. Contrary to what is found in some dictionaries, the upper forward corner rather than the leading edge of a trapezoidal staysail was the 'nock'. The lower forward corner of any fore and aft sail is its 'tack', the after corner being the 'clew'. In the case of a course, the weather clew is sometimes called the 'tack', but in the case of topsails and topgallants, it would simply be 'the weather clew'. In the case of square sails, the term 'weather leech' is used, never 'luff'. The sails were made of flax canvas, supplied in bolts 40 yards long and 24 inches wide, the heaviest being Number 1 for courses, and the lightest Number 8 for royals and studdingsails. A bolt of Number 1 canvas weighed 46 pounds, and with each number it decreased 3 pounds (Kipping, *Sailmaking*, 38). Subsequently, much heavier canvas, Number 00, was used by the Cape Horners. Although the sails were cut as though they would be perfectly flat, the sailmaker was

Sails and their parts
A Square sail; **B** jib and triangular staysail; **C** triangular gaff topsail; **D** gaff sail; **E** trapezoidal staysail
a head; **b** leech; **c** luff; **d** stay; **e** bunt; **f** mast; **g** foot; **h** peak; **i** clew; **j** nock; **k** tack.

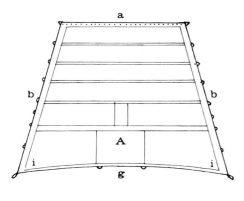
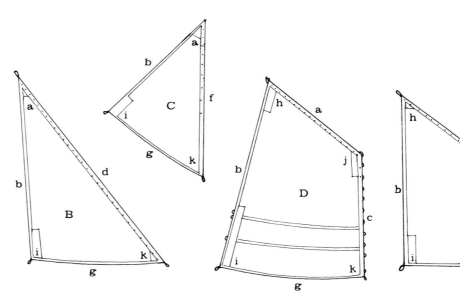

actually contending with a problem in rubber-sheet geometry; the sail, when set and drawing properly, did not form a plane surface. Part of the art of sailmaking was to allow for this. For example, the edges of the jib were curved or roached in a convex fashion. In use, stretched by the wind, the sail can be imagined as a triangular section of the surface of a large sphere, the roached edges now forming the shortest distance between the corners. The boltropes, of tarred Russian hemp, which were sewn along the edges to strengthen the sail, would stretch more than the canvas when the sail was first put into use. Experience guided the expert sailmaker in judging how much slack he should allow in the canvas as he stitched on the boltrope, since a well cut sail could be ruined by bad roping. Boltropes were sewn to the after side of square sails, and by convention, to the port side of fore and aft sails.

Cringles were worked into the boltrope at the corners, and on the leeches to secure bowline bridles, and reef-tackles. The upper corners were made fast to the yard by lengths of rope, the 'head earings', and the head of the sail bent to the yard by means of 'robands'. The first element of this word, *ra*, is an old word for a yard, no longer used in English, but remaining the regular term for yard, in most germanic languages. The headrope thus came directly under the yard, and when the sail was filled by the wind, it tended to pull away, leaving a gap between headrope and yard. A jackstay, initially of rope, later of wire rope, or steel rod, was introduced in 1811 (Lees, 159) to circumvent this problem. The sail was now held well up on the forward upper aspect of the yard. The method of furling the sail changed in parallel with this innovation. Where previously, the

canvas had been hauled up below the yard, it was now furled on top and in front of the yard. I believe the jackstay was an English innovation: at any rate, the word was adopted in other languages, as the accepted technical term, and we find variants like *yackstag*, *Jäckstag*, etc in Dutch and German.

Sheets. The foot of the topsail was spread by hauling home the sheets, which were secured to the clews of the sail. Originally of rope, later of chain, these led from the clew of the sail, down through copper lined sheave-holes at the yardarms, and along through leading blocks under the lower yard, ultimately belaying to the topsail sheet bitts at the foot of the mast.

With the wind aft, the courses were restrained 'betwixt two sheets', as the old Elizabethan sea phrase had it, but sailing close-hauled, only the lee sheet was 'hauled aft', the weather one being idle. The weather clew was held down and forward by a tapered rope called the tack. Upon going about, the other tack was 'got down', and the 'new' lee sheet hauled aft. Thus with the wind on the port side, the port tack was down, and the ship was said to be sailing 'on the port tack'. The tacks and sheets ultimately consisted of tackles rather than the simple tapered ropes which sufficed in Elizabethan times.

Bowlines. Close-hauled, 'sailing on a bowline', as it was sometimes called, the bowlines were hauled or 'steadied out' on the weather side. This held the weather leech taut, and prevented it curling back upon itself. On this point of sail, a great deal of the 'pull' depended on a good set of the weather leech, hence the importance of the bowline. To extend its spread, it was attached to a bridle, which ultimately connected it to three or four bowline cringles on the leech of the

sail. The fore top bowline had a very sharp down lead, and so was nick-named the 'thin man', *magerman*, by the Dutch.

In the latter-day sailing man-of-war, there was just one main bowline, which was fitted with a toggle, so that it could be slipped, and hooked to the other leech of the main course upon going about. Its other end was secured at the foot of the foremast. The fore course had a bowline on each side. Bowlines were occasionally fitted to studdingsails, and to the driver, a sail which extended the mizzen, and thus was distinguished as the only fore and aft sail so fitted.

Clewlines and clewgarnets. In furling the square sails, the clewlines hauled the clews up to the quarters of the yard. They ran from the clew, through quarter blocks and ultimately belayed on deck. Furling, they were hauled in as the sheets were slacked off and overhauled. Setting sail, the procedure was reversed. The term clewgarnet was reserved for the clewlines of the courses. The single clewlines of the light sails were represented by tackles on the topsails and courses. If the sheets were kept fast when the halliards were let go, the clewlines acted as downhauls to 'clew down' the yard. About 1800, there was an alteration in the point on the yard, to which the clew was hauled up. Up to this time, the upper block of the clewgarnet was placed about a third the way out from the slings towards the yardarm. From then on, the upper block was much closer to the centre of the yard. I cannot put an exact date on this change, which reflected a different method of furling the sail. However, Lescallier's plates show the early method as late as 1791, and the new method is found in the illustrations in Lever in 1819, so 1810 would seem about right.

1. **Sail bending gear**
   A Sail bent below yard; **B** sail bent to jackstay on top of yard; **a** earings; **b** robands; **c** jackstay.

2. **Sheets and tacks**
   a topsail sheets; **b** main sheets; **c** main tacks.

3. **Bowlines**
   A Lead of the bowlines *c*1800; **B** detail of bowline bridle; **C** detail of main bowline fitted with sliprope and toggle.

4. **Clewlines** as seen from after side of mast, with sails set on the left and clewed up on right.

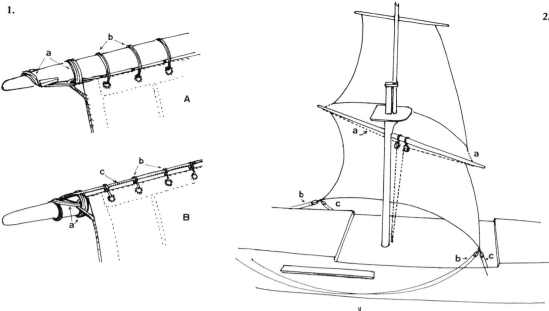

1.

2.

Clewrope. This was a sort of brail running from the clew of a mizzen up to a block at the throat of the sail. By letting go the clew out-haul, and hauling the clew up, at the same time hauling the brails on the lee side, the wind would quickly be spilled from the sail. This came into use in the late 1800s (Knight, 43).

Buntlines. These were secured to the foot of the sail, and were used to haul the central part of the foot straight up in front of the rest of the canvas. Like the clewlines they had to be overhauled when setting sail. At sea, topsail buntlines were rove through 'lizards' hitched to the jackstay. The lizards were short ropes with eyelets spliced in one end. In this case they confined the buntlines in such a way that the foot of the sail came no higher than the jackstay. Upon entering port, they were taken off, so that the foot of the sail could be hauled well up above the yard, preparatory to furling the sail in a 'harbour stow'. Buntline fairleads, were a relatively modern innovation, which vastly increased the power of the buntline to smother the sail (Underhill, 120). They were never used in men-of-war.

Leechlines. These were used to pull the leech in and up to the yard when furling. If they were to function properly, the distance of the leading block on the yard from the head-cringle, should be the same as from the cringle to the upper bowline cringle, to which the leechline was seized. It is this simple geometric relationship which accounts for the fact that single topsails almost never had leechlines, once reefing came into use. As each reef was taken, the effective length of the head of the sail increased, while the leech shortened. Matters could have been arranged to shift the block along the yard, as each reef was turned in, but it was hardly worth the

3.

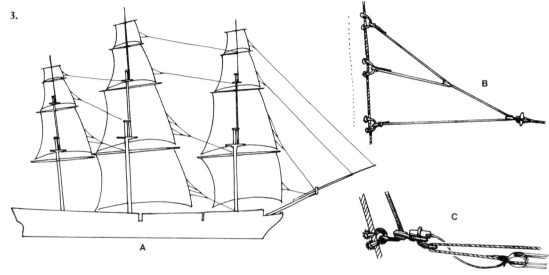

A

B

C

trouble. In the 1600s and 1700s, leechlines were fitted to topsails, and were used to furl them in a particular way, Mainwaring (179) commenting that they were 'used on no other sails'. In his day, 'martnets' were used with the courses, but this cumbersome method was laid aside, and supplanted by the much simpler leechline.

In heavy weather, with the topsails reefed down, extempore leechlines could be rigged, using the topmast studdingsail halliards. They led from the yard abaft the sail, through a bowline cringle, and back up to a block lashed at the corresponding point on the yard forward, thus acting like a double leechline, or 'spilling line'. In the late 1800s, sailing merchantmen fitted leechlines, sometimes an 'outer' and an 'inner', if the course were 'clewed up to the quarters' (Underhill, 188).

Slab lines and spilling lines. Slab lines were similar to buntlines, but fitted on the

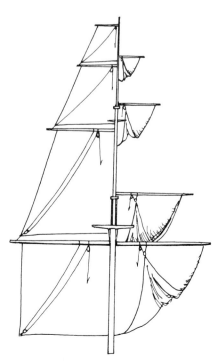

4.

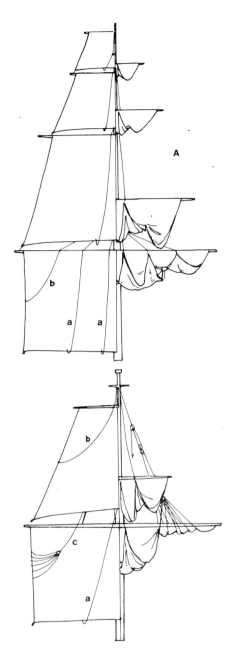

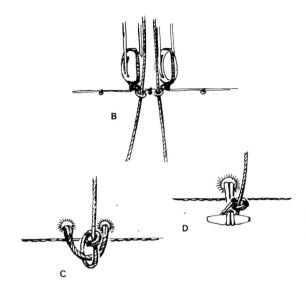

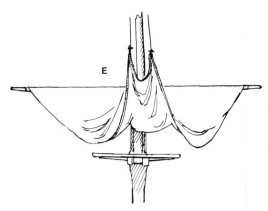

Buntlines and leechlines

A Buntlines (**a**) and leechline (**b**) as seen from forward, with sail set on the left and hauled up by clewlines, buntlines and leechlines on right; **B** detail of buntline lizards on tie blocks; **C** buntline clinched to cringle; **D** buntline with running eye around toggle; **E** buntlines hauled with lizards cast off.

Topsail leechlines and martnets as seen from fore side of the mast, with sails set on the left and hauled up by clewlines, buntlines, leechlines and martnets on the right. **a** buntline; **b** leechline; **c** martnet.

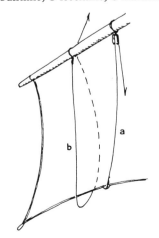

Slablines and spilling lines
a slabline; **b** spilling line.

after side of the course. They were used to lift the foot of the sail, in light weather, to give the helmsman a better view ahead, and to help get the sail subdued, in blowing conditions. Spilling lines, arranged like buntlines and slab lines combined, were a heavy weather arrangement.

Brails. The mizzen course was originally fitted with lines on either side, similar to buntlines, to haul it up to its yard. These were referred to as brails, and on the later gaff mizzen, which used very similar gear, they retained the name brails. Brails are also found on trysails and staysails. Boteler and Mainwaring seem to use 'brail' as synonymous with 'buntlines', and perhaps leechlines also. By Falconer's time, the 'brails' were collectively all the gear that hauled the sail up to the yard, hence expressions like 'the sail hangs in the brails', or it is 'brailed up'. By the late 1800s one would have said that the sail was 'hanging in the gear', the earlier usage having become archaic, and the term brail was limited to those fore and aft sails fitted with them. Since the brails of the latter-day mizzen ran horizontally to the mast rather than up to the gaff, it was usual to say that the sail was 'brailed in', rather than 'up' (Horka).

Gaskets. These were used to furl the sail, and nowadays are made of rope, and seen coiled up neatly, hanging just below the jackstay, when not in use. Mainwaring (121, 146) makes a distinction between 'gaskets' and 'furling lines'. The former, made of sennit, eight or ten on each side of the yard, were used on courses. Staples were driven into the forward upper aspect of the yard, each fitted with two rings. Into one of these, the gasket was spliced, then taken round under the yard to hold up the furled sail, and finally hitched

to the second ring. The longest gaskets were found at the slings, and called 'breast gaskets'. Next in length, came the 'quarter gaskets', securing the sail to the 'quarters' of the yard, namely that section between the slings and a point halfway out towards the yardarm. At the extremities of the yard, where there was even less canvas, yarns were sufficient to confine it. 'Furling lines', also of sennit, were longer, and used on topsails and topgallants. They were secured at the yardarm, and brought in, taking a spiral round the sail and yard, finally being hitched round the ties or the mast.

Mainwaring mentions that the mizzen yard had only one gasket. This started at the peak, and yarns were used to secure the forward part of the sail. Winter's photographs of the Dutch model of 1670, show the staysails fitted with many short gaskets, since they were furled on the stay. Later, they were stowed more compactly, and secured with a single gasket.

Methods did not change radically over the centuries, but there was tremendous variation as to detail. For example, Mossel (II, 24) still describes staples with two rings, but they are now found on the upper after aspect of the yard, because in his day, the sail was no longer furled underneath the yard. When not in use, the gaskets were seized up on the yard out of the way, or at least thrown back, so they did not chafe the sail. They are often to be seen, in 'captains' pictures' either in shallow bights, or made up in 'chain' knots, hanging before the sails, as the vessel enters port.

In the 1800s, naval vessels took to fitting 'harbour gaskets' when at anchor. These were made of sword matting or broad sennit, about three inches wide, lined with duck,

1. Brails
 A Head and foot brails of lateen mizzen; **B** spanker brails with sail set; **C** spanker brailed in.

2. Gaskets (sail set on left side, furled on right).
 A Furling line (on seventeenth century topsail); **B** old style gaskets; **C** harbour gaskets; **D** sea gaskets; **E, F, G, H** different ways of making up gaskets.

3. Bunt gaskets
 A Detail of bunt jigger hooked into glut; **B, C, & D** different forms of bunt gaskets; **E** bunt jigger; **F** bunt whip.

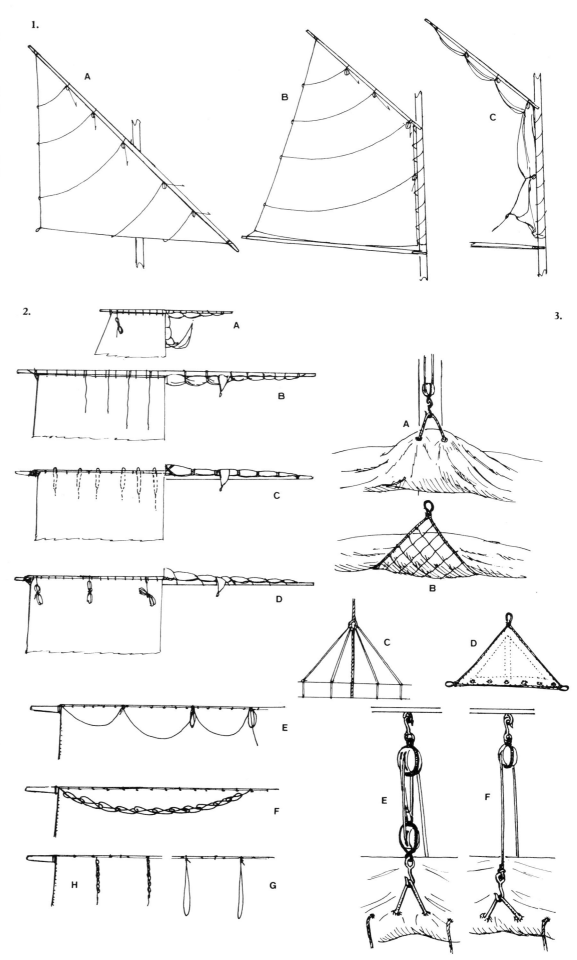

painted black, and fitted every second or third seam. One pattern was made with an eye at one end, and a sennit tail at the other, the body being long enough to encompass the furled sail. The eye was pushed under the jackstay, from forward aft, and seized, so that the eye stuck up, and the gasket hung down between the yard and the sail. When the sail was furled, the tail was taken round it, through the eye, and pushed in between the gasket and sail. With this method, the gasket did not go round the yard (Ballard, 18). 'Bunt gaskets', of which there were two, were longer, and crossed in an 'X', to hold up the heavy bunt. Another popular type was of triangular shape, the space in the centre being filled in with a diamond pattern of rope. 'Sea gaskets' replaced the harbour gaskets, when not in port, and were similar to the earlier pattern of gaskets and furling lines, already described. They were long enough to be taken round booms and all, when furling in bad weather.

Bunt jigger and bunt whip. The change in the method of furling the topsail, in the late 1700s, led to the introduction of the 'bunt jigger', or 'bunt whip'. In the case of the course, the former was a tackle, secured under the top, and hooked to the 'glut', or 'becket', just above the first reef-band, on the after side of the sail. This was done as the last of the canvas was being gathered up, so that the heavy bunt could be hauled up and back on the yard. A second glut was fitted just above the second reef-band, for use if one reef was turned in before furling. Prior to the introduction of a special glut, it had been the practice to knot a couple of reef points together, and hook on to that (Glascock, 27).

A similar scheme was used with the topsail, gluts being fitted above the first three reef-bands. When the close reef was taken, half the canvas was disposed evenly along the yard. Hence, there was no longer a huge bunt to be dealt with, if the topsail should be taken in completely, there was now no necessity for a glut on the close reef-band, on the after side. It was customary, however, to fit one on

33

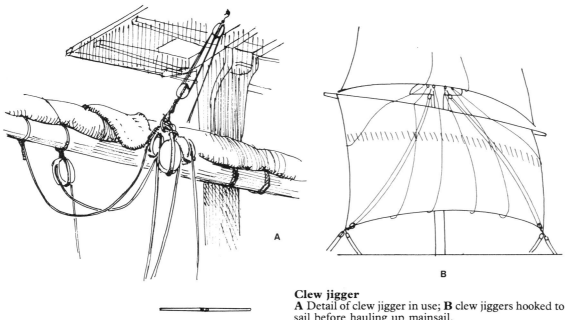

Clew jigger
A Detail of clew jigger in use; **B** clew jiggers hooked to sail before hauling up mainsail.

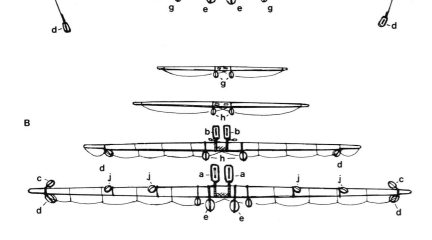

Positions of blocks on the yards
A Late eighteenth century; **B** late nineteenth century.
a jeer block; **b** tie block; **c** lift block; **d** brace block;
e sheet block; **f** double sheet block; **g** clewline (or quarter) block; **h** double sheet and clewline block; **i** buntline block; **j** leechline block.

lengthened if the sail were wet and heavy. The falls were handled in the tops in both cases. This method recommended itself 'in the merchant service, where economy is the secret spring of all action and enterprise', as Murphy puts it.

With courses and topgallants, a single rope, leading through a block, functioning as a 'bunt whip' sufficed. It was often referred to as a 'jigger', to avoid confusion with 'buntline', when hailing aloft (Luce, 197). In port, a whip was often used with topsails also, so that the sail could be run up smartly in sail drill, hauling the fall of the jigger taking too long. Burney rigs a 'long bunt whip', through a block hooked to the heel of the topgallant mast, down forward of the topsail, and up abaft it to the glut. This was used when 'loosed to a bowline', in preparation for whipping the sail up, when the order was given to 'Furl away!' Mossel suggests singling up the topsail buntlines, in port, only one being necessary, and using the other as a bunt whip. The hauling end of the whip was handled on deck, so the men could run away with it.

Clew jigger and clew rope. The clew-garnets hauled the clews up behind the sail. To get a neat harbour stow, however, they had to be hauled forward, on either side of the bunt. The bundle of blocks for tack, sheet, and clewgarnet, the *bouquet*, as the French called it, was no light weight, and the jigger was used to lift the clew and its attached hardware into the furled position. A similar arrangement was used with the topsail, the tackle hooking under the crosstrees, while with the course, it secured under the top. The clew jiggers, doubled as other gear, inner studdingsail halliards, for instance. They were used only in naval vessels, and only in port. In the same way that the bunt whip replaced the bunt jigger, the single 'clew rope' sometimes served instead of a jigger, in a small vessel. 'Clew rope' was also the term used in the United States Navy for a line running from clew to throat of a gaff mizzen, to aid the brails in taking in the sail (Luce, 197, 417; Knight , 42).

Clew hangers. Used on topsails, these are described by Burney (5) as a couple of fathoms of two-inch rope, secured to parrel, truss strop, or jackstay. They were taken under the foot and leech ropes, and through the clew cringle, and made fast to take the weight of the blocks at the clew.

We will later cover in greater detail the gear used for reefing sails, and describe the arrangements for handling studdingsails, when we come to give an account of how these sails were handled.

the fore side of the sail at that point, to which a tackle could be hooked in reefing weather. This had been proposed by Béléguic, the inventor of the French reef, and the practice is endorsed by Hourigan, who calls the tackle, thus used, the 'boss buntline'.

There was great variation in the exact way in which things were managed (Luce, 197; Murphy, 65; Burney, 74; Mossel, II, 363). Murphy prefers a 'long', and a 'short' bunt jigger, the 'long' going to the upper, and the 'short' to the lower glut on the topsail. Alternately, the purchase was rigged as a runner and tackle, the pendant being shortened up to make it function as the 'short' jigger,

1.

East Indiaman lying off Deptford, portrayed in three positions by John Cleveley the Elder, 1755. With sails neatly furled, the masts, spars, standing and running rigging can be clearly seen. Note the long mizzen yard and the vertical stow of the topsail bunts. (Courtesy Richard Green Galleries, London)

2.

Bending sail in the brigantine *Grethe*. The jackstay on the bare foreyard is obvious, as are the buntlines and leechlines which haul up the topsail above it. The short lines hanging from the sail are reef-points. A man stands on the topsail yard to make fast the topgallant sheet to its clew, while three men pass the robands to secure the head of the sail to the topgallant yard. The royal is neatly furled. (Courtesy N V Glassborow)

3.

A frigate close-hauled off Torbay, painted by Thomas Whitcombe, 1810. This shows the classic sail plan of the sailing man-of-war. This ship has fidded royal masts and long poles on which skysails can be set. The mainsail has been hauled up and most of the staysails are furled. (Courtesy Richard Green Galleries, London)

CHAPTER 3
DEVELOPMENT OF THE SAIL PLAN 1580-1900

1580. If we consider the type of vessel familiar to Drake, the principal sails are seen to be the fore and main courses, augmented by small topsails. The spritsail, carried under the bowsprit, and a fore and aft mizzen course serve to balance the sail plan, determining whether bow or stern come into the wind. There are no provisions for reefing, but the area of the three courses can be increased by lacing on a 'bonnet', increasing the hoist by about twenty-five per cent. In making sail, courses and topsails were set by hoisting their respective yards. If the wind increased, the ship was said to be 'blown into her courses'. 'Mare's tails and mackerel scales make lofty ships to carry low sails', runs the old weather rhyme, of a sky presaging wind. That is to say, the basic storm sails were the courses, rather than the topsails, as was the case later on. Sir Alan Moore believed that the great hurricane of 1782 was the last occasion when ships of the Royal Navy attempted to lie to during bad weather under courses (*Mariner's Mirror* 3, 1913, 8). A fourth mast, setting a small 'bonaventure' mizzen was sometimes employed in larger vessels to augment the mizzen. This represented a temporary deviation from the general proposition that the sailing man-of-war never had more than three masts.

1620. At about this date, two further sails were added, a spritsail topsail, set on a little mast perched on the end of the bowsprit, and a square mizzen topsail. The yard spreading the foot of the latter was called the crossjack, the first element of which is also found in the Dutch word for a mizzen topsail, *kruis-zeil*, 'cross-sail'. The topsail was initially an alternative to the mizzen course, rather than an addition, one being set with the wind two points abaft the beam, and the other with the wind forward of that (*Mariner's Mirror* 1, 1911, 207). Topgallants, on fore and main, appear about this time also.

1637. *Sovereign of the Seas* was the finest vessel of her day. The sail plan has extended upwards, topgallants now being set on all three masts, with royals on fore and main above these. The topsails are proportionately

Sail plan c1580.

Sail plan c1620.

larger, relative to the courses, than was the case earlier. With light yards and masts sent down for winter, she would not have looked very different from her predecessors. Royals did not come into general use for a long time after their appearance in this ship.

1760. The most obvious difference from the previous example lies in the introduction of jib and staysails. The spritsail topsail, in its old form, has disappeared, being replaced by a sail, whose yard is run out on the jibboom. It retains the old name of spritsail topsail, and functions as a sort of 'under jib'. A fore topmast staysail sets to the bowsprit and a jib is set on the jibboom. This sail was at first called a 'flying jib', the distinction between 'jib' and 'flying jib' only became necessary, with the introduction of a flying jibboom, in the last decade of the eighteenth century.

About mid-century the mizzen course was

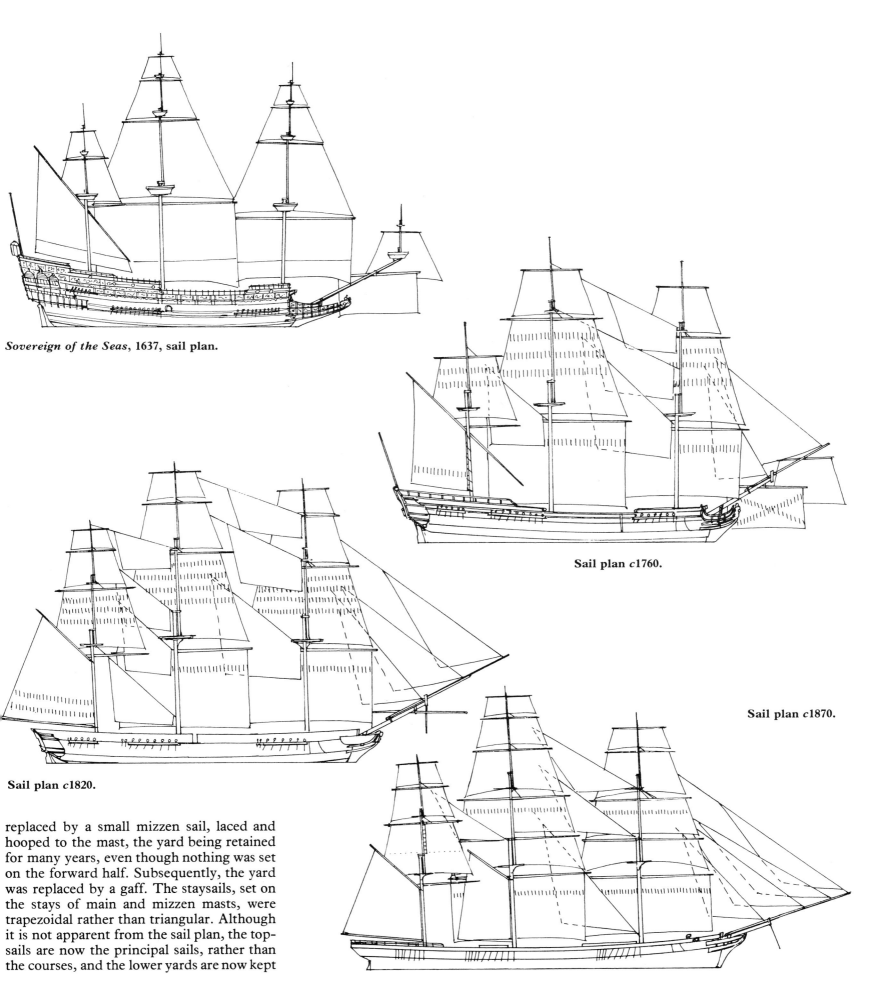

Sovereign of the Seas, 1637, sail plan.

Sail plan *c*1760.

Sail plan *c*1820.

Sail plan *c*1870.

replaced by a small mizzen sail, laced and
hooped to the mast, the yard being retained
for many years, even though nothing was set
on the forward half. Subsequently, the yard
was replaced by a gaff. The staysails, set on
the stays of main and mizzen masts, were
trapezoidal rather than triangular. Although
it is not apparent from the sail plan, the topsails are now the principal sails, rather than
the courses, and the lower yards are now kept

permanently hoisted.

1820. The differences from the preceding example are relatively minor. There is now a flying jib set on the flying jibboom, and the spritsail topsail has disappeared. The spritsail is tending to drop out of use, although the yard is retained. A dolphin-striker points downwards from the outer end of the bowsprit. The mizzen is somewhat larger than before, with a longer gaff, and the foot extended by a boom. If one compares this vessel with the ship of 1580, it will be seen that the foremast has moved aft, allowing increased sail to be carried in the forward triangle bounded by foremast and jibbooms.

1870. Our previous example represents essentially the final form taken by the man-of-war, propelled by sail alone, but it is instructive to follow the further evolution in merchantmen. The staysails are now all triangular, and the large jib has been replaced by two smaller sails, an 'inner-' and 'outer-jib'. The hugh single topsails have been replaced by split topsails. Topsails which can be 'reefed' from deck by rolling the canvas up have also come on the scene.

1890. Split topgallants were introduced in large vessels following the success of split topsails. Four masts were also becoming common in the large merchantmen. Our example is a four-masted full-rigged ship. The topgallant on the fourth, or jigger, mast is single, with split topgallants on the other masts, the so-called 'Belfast rig'. The jibboom and bowsprit are combined in one strong stubby spar, a 'spike bowsprit'. Nothing is carried above the topgallants, and the ship is therefore a 'bald-header'. A sail is set on the crossjack yard, and there is no fore and aft mizzen. The five-masted full-rigged ship *Preussen* was the ultimate in large steel merchantmen, but apart from her greater size and extra mast, does not differ materially from this example.

Sail plan *c*1890.

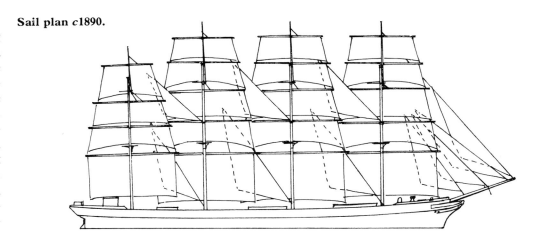

1. Two Dutch warships, engraved in the 1650s by Reiner Nooms, show the basic sail plan of the seventeenth century ship. Topgallant sails were often carried on the fore- and mainmasts of larger ships, though these would be sent down in rough weather. (Author's Collection)

2. A painting by Peter Monamy of an early eighteenth century man-of-war. Note the combination of a small jibboom and a spritsail topmast-like jackstaff. (Courtesy Richard Green Galleries, London)

The *Southwell* frigate by Nicholas Pocock, *c*1760. Note the triangular shape of the staysails. Larger ships than the *Southwell* retained their long mizzen yards for some time after the date of this painting. (Courtesy Bristol Museum and Art Gallery)

The frigate *Norrköping*, last Swedish warship to work under sail alone. This photo was taken in 1892, but the ship's sail plan is the same in proportion and cut as for vessels launched at the beginning of the century. Two small concessions to her time are the spreaders on the bowsprit and the jackline reefs. Note the fore tack bumpkin on the port bow, the topsail leechlines, and the different lengths of the gaskets. (Imperial War Museum, London)

The steel four-masted barque *Pamir*. This ship was launched in 1905, by which time steel masts and yards and wire rigging made possible a massive sail plan spread over more than three masts. The topsails and topgallants are so large that they have been divided into upper and lower halves for more efficient handling, and the spanker is also so treated. Note the one-piece lower and topmasts and spike bowsprit. (Mark Myers' Collection)

1.

2.

3.

39

CHAPTER 4
SOME THEORETICAL PRINCIPLES UNDERLYING SHIPHANDLING

MATHEMATICAL PRINCIPLES

Parallelogram of forces and moment. An understanding of two simple mathematical principles is basic to what follows. The first is the parallelogram of forces, or rather, as it interests us, the rectangle of forces. If we imagine three forces, acting in the directions DA, DB and DC, with magnitudes equal to their length, we have a simple graphical method of allowing us to break down, or 're-solve' force DB into two forces DA DC, at right angles to each other, or to combine DA and DC into a 'resultant' force DB.

The second concept is that of 'moment', 'torque', or turning ability. The turning ability of the force at the end of a pivoted lever, is proportional to the magnitude of the force, the length of the lever, and the direction in which the force is applied relative to it. A four-foot Stillson wrench, in the hands of a muscular man, pulling at right angles to it, is capable of loosening the most recalcitrant nut. Moment is greatest when the force is applied at right angles to the lever, less effective, if exerted at an oblique angle, and zero, if applied along the long axis of the lever. The same principle applies if two forces act, as a 'couple' in opposite directions, at each end of a lever pivoted at an intermediate point, for example the hands of the driver on the steering wheel of a car.

A force, acting in one direction results in instability, unless it is balanced by an equal and opposite force, acting in the same straight line. Thus the mass of the ship, pressing downwards through its centre of gravity, is exactly balanced by the force of flotation, acting upwards through the centre of buoyancy. In the same way, a moment acting in one direction can be balanced exactly by another, acting with equal torque, in the opposite direction, and result in a stable situation. In this case, the opposing forces do not need to be in the same straight line.

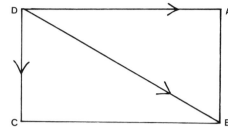

Parallelogram of forces and movement. Forces DA and DC combine in resultant force DB.

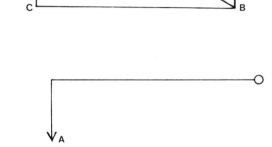

Examples of moment. Force A exerts more effective torque than Force B, Force C than Force D. In the first case, because of direction, and in the second, because of greater leverage. Forces E and F reinforce each other, acting as a 'couple'. Forces G and H make up a balanced couple. Couple IK is balanced by couple JL. Instability results from an unopposed force, M. Stability is restored when there is opposition between two equal and opposite forces, N and O.

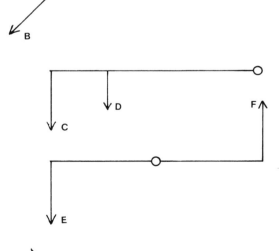

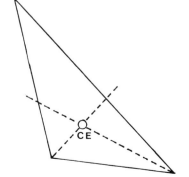

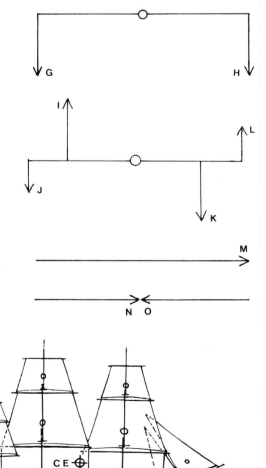

Centre of effort (CE). The CE of a triangular sail is established by bisecting the angles. The CE of a ship's sail plan is established from the collective CE's of all the individual sails.

SOME THEORETICAL CENTRES AND AXES, AND THEIR RELATIONSHIPS.

In physics, it is often useful to pretend that a force acting diffusely on a body, behaves as though its effect were concentrated at one discrete point. For example, the force of gravity is assumed to act at a theoretical 'centre of gravity', at which point the total mass of the body may usefully be assumed to concentrate. Still other theoretical centres are helpful in considering problems in ship stability, buoyancy, trim, and so on, and we will make use of one or two of them here.

Centre of effort of wind on the sail, or CE. Although the particles of air, striking the sail, act at every point of its surface, it is convenient to consider the force as concentrated at a point in the geometric centre of the sail, the centre of effort, or CE. Not only can one fix the CE for the individual sail, but using simple geometric constructions, the theoretical CE of the total sail plan can also be pinpointed. The sail plan, by convention, shows the yards and sails braced up into the fore and aft line. In fact, of course, this cannot be done in practice, but it enables the designer to get an approximate fix on the location of the CE nonetheless, since it is equally unrealistic for all three masts.

Centre of lateral resistance, or CLR. When the submerged part of the hull moves through the water, its progress is resisted by the particles of water which it forces aside. The shape of the hull is such that the resistance to movement is minimal when travelling ahead or astern, and at its maximum when the hull attempts to move directly sideways. This harnesses the force of the wind on the sails, and pushes the hull ahead, while limiting so far as possible the undesirable lateral motion, and might be called the 'orange pip principle' – the pip being of such a shape that, when squeezed between finger and thumb, it is made to shoot out at right angles to the force applied. The resistance may be considered to be concentrated at a theoretical point in the middle of the submerged part of the hull, the centre of lateral resistance, or CLR.

It may not immediately be appreciated that the resistance of the water is a good, rather than a bad, thing. Were it not present, the sailing vessel would be incapable of doing anything other than drift helplessly to leeward. By actually making use of the resistance, she ceases to be totally at the mercy of the wind. With racing hydroplanes, and so on, the resistance of the air to the passage of the boat has to be taken into account also, and

is made use of to provide 'lift'. In our case, this effect can be disregarded, since proportionately it is so much less important than the resistance of the water on the hull. The impedance to either forward or lateral movement varies as the square of the ship's speed.

Centre of gravity, or CG, and centre of buoyancy, or CB. The centre of gravity is the theoretical point at which the downward pressing mass of the vessel may be considered to be concentrated, and will be situated more or less amidships. The centre of buoyancy involves a slightly more difficult concept. It is the theoretical point through which the forces of buoyancy thrust upward, to keep the vessel afloat. It is also the centre of gravity of the water displaced by the submerged part of the hull. If we could imagine the hull plucked from the sea, and the water instantaneously frozen, there would remain a cavity where the hull previously floated. The CB would be at the centre of this void, and hence the old writers on stability sometimes called it the 'centre of cavity'.

Relationship of CE, CLR, CG and CB. The force of the wind acting through the CE can be thought of as trying to push the hull bodily to leeward, and also to heel the vessel over. In the first case, the lateral movement is resisted by an equal and opposite force, acting through the CLR. At least this is true in the idealised situation where there is no leeway. If the CE and CLR are in the same vertical line, as seen from the side, the ship could be forced by the wind directly to leeward but keeping wind at all times directly abeam. If the CE moves ahead of the CLR, the bow will be pushed away from the wind. If the CE moves abaft the CLR, the bow will come up into the wind. In both cases, if unopposed, the ship will eventually come head or stern to wind, with the forces acting through the CE and CLR once more in line.

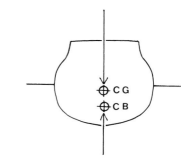

Centre of lateral resistance (CLR). The CLR lies in the middle of the submerged mass of the hull. Resistance is greatest to sideways movement, and least to movement ahead or astern.

Centre of gravity (CG) and centre of buoyancy (CB). The CG is the point where the gravitational mass of the ship may be theoretically considered to be concentrated. The CB lies in the centre of the volume of water displaced by the hull.

Relationship of the CE and CLR. With the CE ahead of the CLR, the bow will fall off from the wind, as in (a). With CE aft of CLR, the bow will come up into the wind (b). In both cases, stability is achieved when the CE and CLR come into the same vertical line.

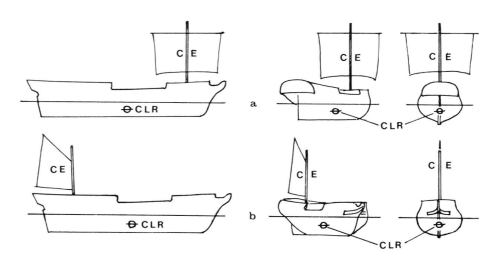

The stability of the relationship can also be disturbed by moving the CLR forward or abaft its original position, while holding the CE stationary. An obvious example would be the shifting of heavy weights forward in the hull, moving the CLR forward. It is perhaps less apparent that most of the square sails exert a similar 'depressing' effect, pushing the bow deeper in the water, having a net effect, similar to moving a weight forward in the hull. If the CLR moves forward, the bow tends to come up into the wind. If it moves aft, the bow falls off. In other words the ship may be thought of as 'weathercocking' around, until the CE and CLR come in the same vertical line.

In the case of the heeling force, the situation is a little different. Looked at from bow on, the CE swings over to leeward, and whether the CLR is thought of as existing on the skin of the vessel, or amidships, the CE could be inclined beyond any possibility of getting one point above the other. Thus we have an unbalanced couple to contend with. The CB and CG lie in the same vertical plane, when the ship is upright, the upward and downward forces being equally balanced. If the ship heels however, the hull is immersed more deeply on the leeward side, and this is accompanied by a shift of the CB to that side. Since the CG does not move, a moment is generated by the forces of buoyancy and gravity, which just balances that caused by wind force acting in the opposite direction to lateral resistance.

If the ship lists because of moving a heavy weight to one side, the CG shifts to that side within the hull, which inclines until the CB comes to lie under the new position of the CG.

In considering CE and CLR, heeling can move the CE out to leeward of the CLR, resulting in an unopposed couple, which will tend to push the bow to windward. This couple can be thought of as working in the horizontal rather than the vertical plane. One way of counteracting this, is to use an opposing couple, one element of which is the turning effect of the rudder, acting at the after end of the hull, and we will return to this a little later. The other correction would be to move the CE and CLR relative to each other, to set up an opposing couple, and hold the bow off the wind.

Rolling, pitching and yawing axes. Let us imagine a styrofoam model of a ship with three straight pieces of wire thrust centrally through it at right angles to each other, one parallel and close to the mainmast, one transversely at the midpoint of the waterline, and one longitudinally between and parallel

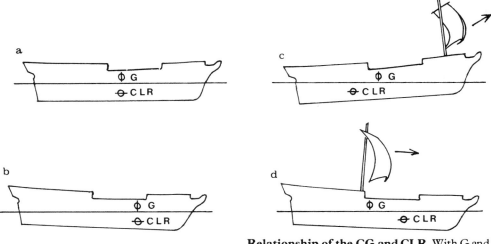

Relationship of the CG and CLR. With G and CLR in line, the ship holds her course (**a**). When the CG is moved forward, CLR moves forward also (**b**). A 'lifting' sail has the effect of moving the CLR aft (**c**), and the bow falls off. A 'depressing' sail has the opposite effect (**d**).

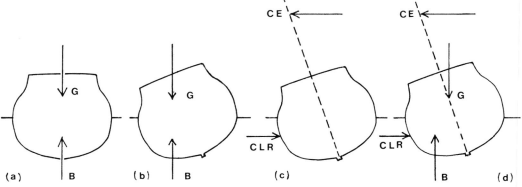

Relationship of CG, CB, CE and CLR. The CB and CG are aligned when the ship is upright (**a**). If the CG shifts to one side, the CB moves in the same direction, as the vessel heels (**b**). The heeling couple, acting through the CE and CLR (**c**) is opposed by a righting couple, acting through the CB and CG (**d**).

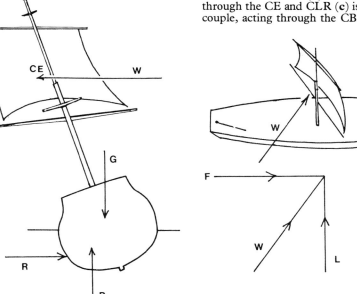

Effect of the wind on the relationship between the CE and CLR. The wind (W) can move the CE to leeward of the CLR. The wind contributes to both leeway L and forward drive F. In the case of a topsail which is inclined to leeward of the hull, F also tends to push the bow into the wind, and weather helm is required.

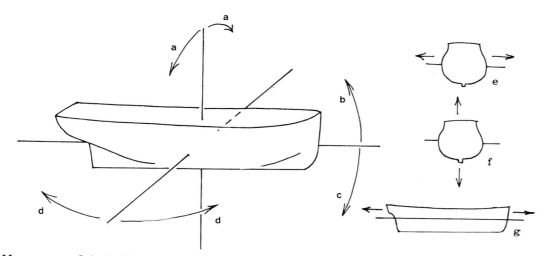

Movements of the hull
a rolling; **b** scending; **c** pitching; **d** yawing; **e** swaying;
f heaving; **g** surging.

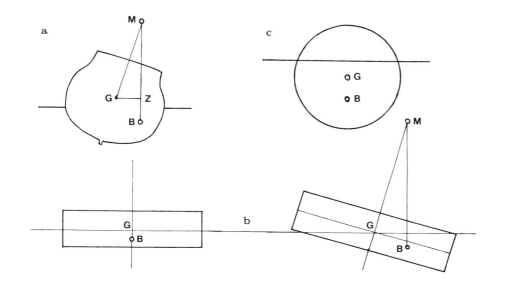

Stability and stiffness. Establishment of the metacentre M and righting arm GZ shown in (**a**). The degree of shift of the CB to the immersed side is dependent on hull shape. It is maximal if the hull is shaped like a flat plank (**b**) and non-existent when it is cylindrical.

FORM OF THE HULL AND STABILITY

Stability and stiffness. If we consider the hull of a sailing ship, heeling over to a breeze, it will be apparent that although the CG has remained stationary, the CB has moved laterally towards the leeward or low side. If we erect a perpendicular through CB, it intersects the midships vertical line, or mast, at a point M, and this is called the 'metacentre'. A perpendicular through G dropped on the line BM, intersects it at Z. The distance GM is called the 'metacentric height', and the distance GZ represents the 'righting arm', or length of the lever about which the force attempting to right the vessel acts. 'Right' is used here in the old sense of 'make erect'. Strictly speaking, the concept of metacentre is true only at small angles of heel (five degrees or so), but the principle is useful in getting a grasp of the idea of stiffness, or large initial stability. When the ship heels, the rapidity with which the CB shifts laterally depends on the hull form of the vessel. If this shift is large, the force of buoyancy acts upwards through B on a long lever, or righting arm, GZ, and the 'righting moment' is large. It will be seen from the diagram that a large GZ is necessarily accompanied by a large metacentric height, or GM. If the torque acting to right, or return the vessel to its normal vertical position is large, the ship is said to be 'stiff'. If the hull form is such that metacentric height, GM and the righting moment, GZ is small, the ship will return to its vertical position less smartly, and she is said to be 'crank' or 'tender'.

If we imagine the ship heeling over to a breeze, the 'heeling moment' or force acting to incline the vessel, is proportional to the strength of the wind acting through the CE, and pivoting about the CLR, and to the height of the CE above the waterline. One notes also that at large angles of heel, the horizontal force of the wind acts at an oblique angle to the heeling arm CE – CLR, and hence loses some of its effect as the ship inclines. Heeling moment is opposed by the forces acting to right the vessel, and in fact the ship will incline to an angle where these two moments are equal and opposite, and a stable situation applies. As we have said, the concept of metacentre really applies only at small angles of heel, but it will be apparent that with greater angles, the righting arm increases rapidly with the angle, up to about 45°, after which it decreases and at a certain critical angle, disappears. This can be expressed graphically as a stability curve (Nicholls, 512).

to keel and waterline. The ship can swing or 'yaw' in a horizontal plane about the first, rather like a weathercock, the bow swinging towards, or away from the wind, 'luffing' and falling off. The bow can 'pitch' downwards, the ship rotating in a vertical plane about its transverse, or athwartships, axis. The opposite rising movement of the bow was referred to as 'scending', that is to say 'ascending', in bygone days. With the more deliberate disturbance due to intentional shifting of weight fore or aft in the hull, movement occurs about this 'tipping', or 'pitching' axis, and the vessel is said to be 'out of trim' – 'down by the head', or 'down by the stern', as the case may be.

Corresponding to the oscillating motion of pitching and the steady more equable disturbance of being out of trim, the ship may 'roll' from side to side about the longitudinal axis. Having the wind on one side, it will incline steadily, heeling to the wind, to the opposite, or leeward side. This inclination is accompanied, and limited, by the concomitant shift of the CB from amidships to the leeward side, which we have already mentioned. 'Roll', 'pitch' and 'yaw' are also used today in virtually the same technical senses when considering the movements of space satellites. Three other oscillatory movements of the hull in a heavy sea are described: 'sway' from side to side; 'surge', forward acceleration and deceleration; and 'heave', up and down. Despite the unpleasant consequences of these gyrations on the semicircular canals of the ear, and the tummy, they are of less interest to us than the other three.

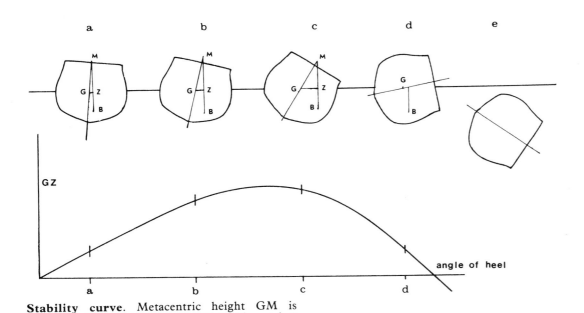

Stability curve. Metacentric height GM is proportional to the righting arm GZ. Plotting against the angle of heel, GZ first increases, then decreases.

BOYD'S TABLE OF WEIGHTS USED IN STABILITY EXPERIMENTS

Class of Vessel and Number of Guns	Length, feet.	Breadth, feet.	Weight to be moved a distance of 40 feet. Tons
1st Rate 120	206	55	112
2nd Rate 84	193	52	90
4th Rate 60	174	44	58
5th Rate 46	160	41	38
6th Rate 28	120	34	22
Sloop 18	112	31	14

Hull form is the main determinant of stiffness or crankness. Two extremes would be exemplified by a long square board, which would be very stable, and a floating log of cylindrical form which would be totally unstable, since the CB is always in the same vertical line as the CG, and no righting arm can be developed. However, the GM, and hence stability, can also be affected by moving the point G up or down. For example stowing heavy weights down low in the hull will lower the CG, and result in a stiffer vessel. Adding topweight high up will make the ship more tender. It was said that the Canadian corvettes could 'roll on wet grass', the reason being the weight of all the extra equipment that was accumulated as the war years passed, which went far beyond the expectation or intention of the designers.

It might at first sight be assumed that great initial stability is intrinsically good, and tenderness inherently bad. This is however, as we shall see, an area where one can have too much of a good thing.

Longitudinal stability. Moving a weight forward or aft will result in the ship being down by the head or the stern. A longitudinal metacentre can be fixed, and a longitudinal GM determined. Because a ship is much longer than it is broad, the longitudinal metacentre is higher than the transverse metacentre, and this is one of the reasons why a ship pitches more slowly than she rolls. Boyd (81) gives a table of the weight in tons which it was necessary to move forty feet forward or aft, to produce an alteration of one foot in the trim of the ship: that is to say, one end of the ship has gone down by six inches, and the other up by an equal amount. For instance, 112 tons in a 206-foot, 120-gun First Rate, 38 tons in a 160-foot, 46-gun Fifth Rate. This type of calculation is nowadays referred to as 'moment altering trim' (Walton, 247). Boyd favoured a device he called a 'trimmer'. This was a leaden U-tube, let in to a deck beam, in a fore and aft line, with a vertical graduated glass tube at each end. This was filled with water, and served to keep track of the trim. 'If the trimmer is consulted, whilst carrying a press of lofty sail before the wind, the ship will be found to be excessively out of trim by the head', as he puts it. I do not know how widespread this device was, but its utility is evident.

It is important to note that the metacentre is not a definite point, in the same sense as are the CG, CB, CE and CLR. It is merely an index of stiffness, derived from a simple geometric construction, and in this cluster of imaginary points, it is more chimerical than the others. Unfortunately, the name suggests that they all fall into the same category, but this is not so. I think the Swedish term *styfhetspunkt*, 'stiffness point', has much to recommend it, for this reason.

Rise of floor, and tumblehome. Although we are not really concerned with eighteenth century naval architecture, it is helpful to devote a little attention to this shape of the hull. This depended to a great extent on the purpose for which the vessel was intended. The flat floors of a collier brig gave maximum carrying capacity rather than speed, and were well adapted to sitting on the mud in a tidal port. Looking at the midship section of a typical man-of-war, it will be seen that the rise of floor, or angle between the floor and the horizontal at the midship frame, is about ten degrees. Above the waterline, the timbers curve inwards or 'tumble home'. When the ship was heeled to ten degrees or so, the floor on the leeward side was almost horizontal, and thus best disposed to provide flotation, since it was the vertical component of water pressure which was paramount in buoying up the hull. At the same time, the keel prevented the ship sagging to leeward since it was free to react with the horizontal pressures generated, if the hull were pushed sideways. If the floor had been flat initially, it would present a less effective inclined surface to the reactive forces of buoyancy upon being heeled. Furthermore, the keel's effectiveness would be diminished because of eddy formation between the turn of the lee bilge and the keel.

'Tumblehome' had the effect of keeping the weight of an upper deck gun, inside the immersed waterline plane. In other words, the side was more or less vertical, when the ship was heeling ten degrees. Were the ship 'wall-sided', a much less stable situation resulted, with the gun, in the run-out position, 'hanging' over the sea, as it were. Furthermore, arciform frames are inherently stronger than straight members of the same size, better adapted to resisting compressive forces. Tumblehome above the waterline also helps keep the CG low. Thus although a section with tumblehome results in a hull with a lower metacentre than one with wall sides, it also results in less topweight and hence a lower CG.

Up to 1740, the fore and main channels of English ships were at the level of the middle deck. With this arrangement, the shrouds could not have led to the mastheads, had it not been for the tumblehome. Anson, after his voyage round the world in the *Centurion* in 1732, recommended that the channels be removed one deck higher, where although they would offer a little less effective support to the shrouds, they would also be less subject to damage from high seas.

Freeboard. It will be obvious that a vessel with too little freeboard could not be heeled without getting into trouble. In the multi-deck man-of-war, freeboard was variable depending on whether the lower gun-ports were open or firmly shut. The loss of the *Royal George* in 1782 occurred when she was purposely inclined – given a 'Parliament heel' – in order to do some work below the waterline. The waves poured in over the sills of the ports on the low side, when a large number of men ran across the deck in a last-ditch attempt to shift the guns back to the other side (Liardet, 114). If the ports had been tightly caulked, the outcome might have been different. The angle of heel at which the ports would have been level with the water, would have been about twenty degrees.

Lines at bow and stern. If the waterline plane increases in area, as the vessel, or part of it, is immersed, flotation increases. This is

the reason why the stem is raked, and why the counter sweeps out, back and up, from the waterline. In fact, if one compares a section near the bow and near the stern, they are quite different, the waterline plane increasing much more at the stern than the bow with each increment of immersion. The lines of the ship and the shape of the hull are such that flotation is greater forward than aft, the centre of buoyancy being forward of the mid-point of the hull. Flotation increases more rapidly aft, if the hull is depressed below the designed waterline. This explains why a vessel which is designed to draw a bit more aft than forward, will float on an even keel when loaded somewhat beyond the proper waterline. 'Flare' is the opposite of tumble-home, and when fast commercial sailing ships were in fashion, they had flared bows which helped deflect the waves and compensate for the poor flotation offered by a

knife-like entry.

Speed. The hull form, of course, also determined the resistance offered to the water and hence the speed. A sharp entry and clean run were the characteristics of a fast hull. The ideal warship hull from Elizabethan times was considered to have a 'cod's head and a mackerel tail', the former for flotation, the latter for speed. The tug, with its powerful engines, can be overdriven, developing a hugh bow wave, and a great trough amidships; but all that fuss and foam under the bow does not indicate speed, merely that despite all kinds of reserve horsepower, she is incapable of exceeding a certain speed, because of her hull contours. The resistance of the water to forward motion may be thought of as active at the bow, and passive at the stern. That is to say, the stern leaves a vacuum behind it, and energy is expended, as it were, sucking water back in to fill this void.

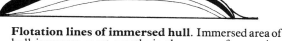

Flotation lines of immersed hull. Immersed area of hull increases most greatly in the upper after section (upper section shown in black).

Deadrise and tumblehome. (**A**) shows deadrise (d) and tumblehome (t). Collier brig midsection (**B**) shows fairly flat floors and little tumblehome, as well as the eddy which may form under the bilge of a flat-floored vessel. Warship hull (**C**) shows greater deadrise and much tumblehome. Large tumblehome enabled early warships to carry their channels (left) lower than was the practice after about 1740 (right).

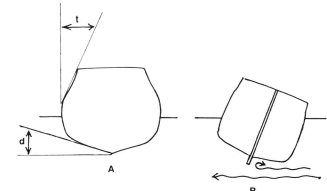

Tug boat at speed develops a large bow wave and trough amidships.

Elizabethan hull form showing fish-like underwater body, fuller forward than aft ('cod's head and mackerel tail').

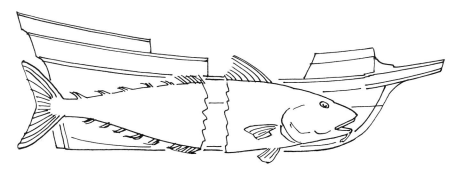

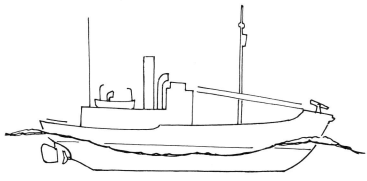

Wave Line Theory. The ship's speed is theoretically limited by the speed of a wave whose length between crests equals that of the vessel.

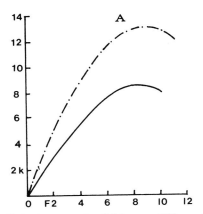
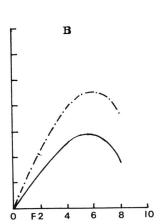
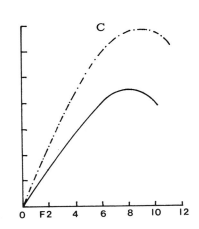
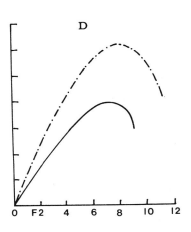

Relative speeds of ships on different points of sail (after M Prager, 1905). The solid line shows the performance of a small wooden barque, the broken line that of a five-masted steel ship. The vertical scale is the ship's speed in knots, the horizontal scale is wind strength on the Beaufort Scale. The best speed is achieved with wind on the quarter, Force 8 to 10, depending on the vessel's size. By the wind, the speed peaks at around Force 6.
A Before the wind; **B** by the wind; **C** in a quartering wind; **D** in a beam wind.

The resemblance between the Dutch word for 'wake', *kiel-zog* or *zog*, and *zuigen*, 'to suck', is no accident.

The top speed of any displacement hull (that is, one that cannot climb up and plane) is related to the square root of the length of the ship. The reason for this was originally analysed by William Froude who developed his Wave Line Theory in the mid-1800s. Incidentally, this should not be confused with the application of Wave Line Theory by John Scott Russell to the design of sailing ship hulls (MacGregor, 190; Kemp, 331, 735). A wave, travelling across the sea, will appear to move at a speed proportional to the square root of the distance between the crests. If we imagine a ship of the same length travelling at the same speed, superimposed on this wave, she will have a crest at her bow, another at her stern and a depression in between. This is comparable to the tug mentioned earlier, which is generating its own waves. However well engined, and however long the displacement hull may be, it will be unable to 'climb up' the bow wave, and this imposes a theoretical limit on the ship's maximum speed. The planing hull is designed to overcome this very problem.

This limitation did not really affect the sailing warship, where 6 knots might be creditable and 8 knots exceptional. Clipper ships, built for speed, might reach 17 knots, at which point the limitation imposed by Wave Line Theory might become significant; but they were, relatively speaking, lightly built racing machines, not required to function as floating gun-batteries.

The most powerful man-of-war was that

with the most guns, of the largest calibre and greatest range, capable of hitting the enemy with the greatest amount of metal. The hull had to be extremely strongly built to withstand the weight of the guns, the shock of their recoil, and the punishment resulting from the enemy's fire. Masts and yards had to be more strongly built than those of a clipper, which was not intended to withstand the shock of collision as one ship 'layed itself aboard' another. Large numbers of men (about one thousand in a First Rate), the drinking water and provisions to sustain them, in addition to the weight of shot and ammunition, account for the generous hull lines necessary to give adequate flotation and stability. Speed was therefore, of necessity, a secondary consideration. Of course, a fast sailer was preferred over a dull one whenever possible.

In comparing the performance of a giant steel windjammer like *Preussen* (407 feet long) with a wooden clipper like *Lightning* (243 feet long), the bigger vessel is theoretically capable of outstripping the smaller by a factor of about 1.3. The term 'windjammer'

suggests, perhaps, that the last commercial sailing ships were slow, lumbering craft, not to be compared with the clippers. It is perfectly true that a clipper could 'ghost' along in the lightest of airs, where the steel windjammer simply ground to a halt, but on the other hand, the latter-day vessels were infinitely more sturdily built, being able to stand up, and make use of a wind that would have forced the clipper to reef right down, if not to lie to. If things were just right, and they found their wind, they were capable of a surprising turn of speed: *Herzogin Cecilie* once logged 20.75 knots (Hurst, *Ships Monthly* I, 1966, 204, 237); and Learmont (*Mariner's Mirror* 43, 1957, 225) felt that the fastest day's run ever was made by *Preussen*, averaging something better than 14 knots, through the water. The day's run is a fairer measure of a ship's speed than the result of heaving the log just one time, provided the affect of current is taken into account. There has been much dispute about whether a day's run of 400 miles was, or was not, possible (*Mariner's Mirror* 43, 1957, 225, 327, 341 and 44, 1958, 64, 141, 328).

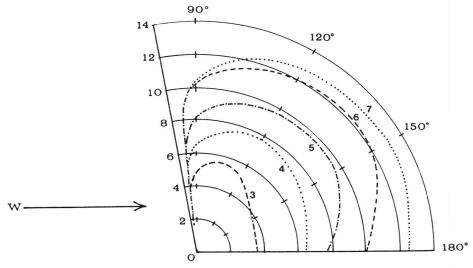

Polar diagram showing performance of the *Gorch Fock* based on observations made by Commander Dr Heinrich Walle FGN, when serving aboard as Sailing Officer. The concentric circles indicate the ship's speed. The broken lines show the speed developed on various points of sail, with wind strengths from Force 3 to Force 7. It can be seen that the best speed is made with the wind quartering, at Force 7.

The form of the hull ultimately had to be a compromise between the need for stability, speed, carrying capacity, strength, etc, and throughout our period of interest, design was much more determined by applying the experience gained in building similar vessels previously, rather than on being based on any very scientific principles. Furthermore, as Frederik af Chapman, the great Swedish designer, put it, 'a ship of the best form will not show her good qualities, except [ie unless] it is, at the same time, well rigged, well stowed, and well worked, by those who command it'.

Rolling. The rolling motion of the ship, in the open sea, is influenced by the GM, and also by the inertial forces which come into play. A stiff ship will incline less than one which is crank, but unfortunately tends to move in a jerky, violent, and uncomfortable fashion, which can make life unpleasant for those aboard. A steadier movement, with a longer period of roll results if the GM is decreased. The rolling ship is the mathematical equivalent of an oscillating pendulum, and as we know, the period of a pendulum is proportional to its length. The 'period' is the time required for the bob to make one complete swing, from left to right, and back again. Looking at the diagram of an inclined vessel, it might, at first sight, be imagined that the GM is somehow analogous to the length of the pendulum. However, for reasons that need not detain us here, the period is actually *inversely* proportional to the GM (Walton, 158, 377).

The other factor which influences the period of roll, and hence the steadiness of the ship, is the moment of inertia. This is not an easy concept, but it can be considered a function of the forces which resist the initiation of the rolling motion, and which exert a damping or smoothing-out effect on the ship's movement, in the same way as a flywheel smooths out the jerky impulsions given to a crankshaft by eight cylinders firing in discrete succession. A simple analogy is the long heavy pole carried by a tightrope walker, reducing the quick jerky movements, which would otherwise result from his progress along the wire. The pole 'wings out' the weight in such a way that the inertia of man and pole, exceeds that of the man alone, his body-weight being concentrated close to his CG.

In the same sort of way, a ship can be made steadier by 'winging out' weights, moving heavy objects from amidships towards the sides. Notice however, that if this is done on both sides, the CG of the ship as a whole has not moved. For example, a man-of-war with guns run out on both sides has an unaltered CG, and GM, but will roll in a less lively fashion. The inertial moment is the sum of the products of each weight multiplied by the *square* of the distance from some central point. It will instantly be objected that moment is generally defined as force multiplied by length of lever, and in the case of inertial moment, the effect is now said to be proportional to the *square* of the lever! This is a matter which is skated over very quickly in the old texts, even Thomas Walton's encyclopedic *Know Your Own Ship* being relatively silent on the matter. Part of the problem is that in the case of inertial matters, we are considering a *moving* force, and 'momentum' would therefore be a better word than 'moment', the former being defined as 'force times velocity'. That a moving force behaves differently from one at rest is a matter of everyday experience. A one-pound weight resting quietly on the toes is almost unnoticed, but dropped from a height, the affect is quite different! In the case of rotating motion, a spinning disc for example, the velocity of a point on the disc is determined by the square of its distance from the centre, the circumference of a circle being related to the square of the radius. Boyd (74) gives this example. Two guns each weighing 5 tons, are placed 40 and 50 feet respectively from the centre of gravity; that is to say in the run-in and run-out positions. The moments of these guns when the ship is at rest, will be 5×40 and 5×50; that is to say they will be in the ratio 200:250, or 4:5. The momenta, when the ship is rolling, will be 5×40^2 and 5×50^2, and they will be in the ratio of 4:6.25, a 25 per cent increase.

Similar considerations apply to moving

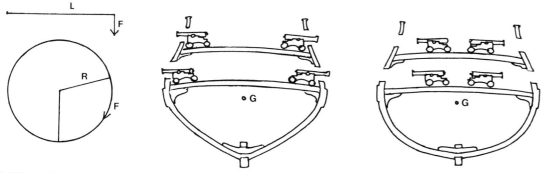

Rolling. Moment is proportional to the Force F and length of the Lever L. Momentum of a Force F, following the circumference of a circle, is proportional to the square of the radius R. Winging out weights, if done equally on both sides, does not alter the CG. The heavy rolling of a tender ship (left) can be eased by winging out the weight of the guns.

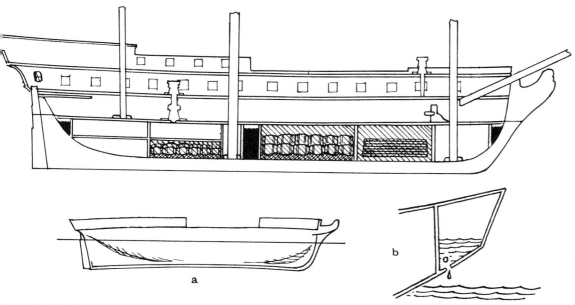

Longitudinal stowage of weights (after Chapman). Heavy casks, cables, etc are stowed in the shaded areas amidships. Lighter stores, sails and gear stowed on white areas, and shot lockers shown in black areas. Note the small shot lockers at bow and stern which could be used to adjust the trim. Heavy weights stowed in the ends of a vessel could produce hogging (**a**). The Chinese developed a semi-watertight bow chamber to mitigate heavy pitching (**b**).

weights towards the ends of the vessel, as it effects pitching. Provided the weights remain on the same deck, and equal weights are moved equal distances fore and aft, the CG, and longitudinal GM remain the same, however, the period of pitching will be increased. In fact, it is rarely necessary to do this, and in a seaway, it is in fact preferable that the ship be capable of lifting her head from the waves in a sufficiently lively manner. Heavy weights stowed at the extreme ends of the vessel, in addition to interfering with buoyancy, exert a savage 'hogging' stress on the fabric of the ship, that is to say they tend to make the bow and stern 'droop'. Hence, they are stored as close to amidships as possible, or at least kept away from the ends. The longitudinal GM can also be increased by striking the weights down lower in the ship's hold. It must be remembered however, that this will also affect the transverse GM, and that if the weight is, at the same time, moved forward or aft, that trim will be altered.

Clearly a heavy weight in the bow interferes with buoyancy, but makes the upward scending motion less violent. To give a practical example of this, Henry Rusk and Harry Dring were, for many years, the co-owners of an ancient Foochow pole junk, which leant a lot of character to the yacht moorage in South San Francisco. This particular craft got the best of both worlds by incorporating a semi-watertight buoyancy chamber in the bow. As the bow pitched down into the sea, this helped resist immersion. Holes of an appropriate size were drilled into the chamber above the waterline, allowing the sea to enter, when the bow was buried, and as it rose once more, the inertia of the contained water slowed the upward movement. The water drained out, and the cycle repeated. A crude but brilliant application of the principle, centuries old!

The sailing ship, incidentally, was steadier in the water than a steamer of comparable size, since the heeling effect of the wind limited the rolling somewhat. Paradoxically, as the wind fell, and the ship wallowed in an 'old' sea, this steadying influence was lost; not entirely however, since even in a dead calm accompanied by a heavy swell, the ship's fore and aft canvas, acted as a sort of 'air-brake' attenuating heavy rolling, if the staysails were sheeted flat aft, and the yards braced up sharp. Even the vestigial canvas of an MFV exerted a definite steadying effect. **The ship as a gun platform.** The ultimate purpose of the sailing man-of-war was to serve as a floating gun platform, and cognisance of this had to be taken in their design. We have already mentioned how this

influenced the form of the hull. Excessive heel was a particular embarrassment in ships whose cannon fired broadside. The formal battle was fought in line ahead, so the admiral could, at once, retain control of the fleet, and allow all ships to concentrate their fire on the enemy, unimpeded by their fellows. He might choose to fight his ships to weather or to leeward of the enemy.

The weather gauge had several traditional advantages, mostly related to the fact that the ships heeled to leeward. The recoil of the lee guns was easier on the breechings, because they recoiled 'uphill'. The smoke from one's own guns drifted down on the enemy leaving the decks clear of smoke, and not obscuring the view of the signals flown by the 'repeating frigates' to windward of the line. As the enemy ship rolled, she exposed her bilges to being 'hulled'. Fireships could be set to drive down on the enemy.

However, there were some disadvantages. The individual enemy ship could break off the action, at will, by dropping to leeward; the men on the upper deck of the weather ship were exposed to fire from sharpshooters in the tops; and most particularly, it might be impossible to open the ports on the gun deck, if heeling was excessive. In the 'Moonlight Battle' of 1780, Rodney chose the lee gauge, to prevent the Spaniards escaping, and because the lowest tier of guns could not be brought into action on the lee side (Padfield, 96). The weapons on the gun deck were the ship's heaviest armament capable of throwing a 32-pound shot almost 2500 yards. However, this required a barrel weighing almost two tons, and so these heavy pieces had to be placed low down in the hull. Even if the ports could be opened, excessive heel could prevent the barrels being elevated sufficiently to fire a shot horizontally at the enemy. The maximum angle of elevation of the barrel was 12°, and hence attempts were made to limit heel to about 7° in a 'whole topsail breeze' (*Admiralty Manual* III, 13). Even making allowances for the English prejudice in favour of battering the enemy's hull, rather than chopping away at his rigging, excessive heel had to be avoided. Bobrik (2517) mentions shifting lead weight to the weather side, prior to action, so the lee guns could be served effectively. This difficulty accounts for the 'girdling' of ships in the seventeenth century, whereby the hull was given extra sheathing at the waterline to increase stability. From what has been said, it might be assumed that a large GM, giving great initial stability, would be sought, and, of course, this could be accomplished by lowering the CG, by removing topweight, or stowing

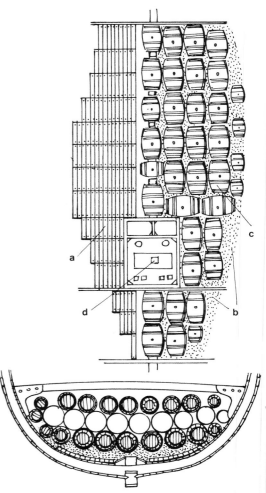

Stowage of ballast and casks (adapted from Blunt) **a** iron pigs; **b** shingle; **c** first layer of casks (shown starboard side only); **d** main mast step.

heavy ballast low down in the hull. In the early 1800s a number of 64-gun frigates were 'razéed' – cut down to 38 guns – by removing the upper deck, and fitting shorter and lighter spars. This resulted in vessels which were so extremely stiff, and which moved in such a jerky lively manner in a seaway, that the violent whipping action sprung the topmasts. The remedy was to increase the topweight by rigging them with longer and heavier spars (*Admiralty Manual Seamanship* III, 11). It was found that the best conditions for serving the guns were obtained, when the CG of the ship was close to the waterline, with a moderate GM between two and four feet, and weight stowed appropriately to give an easy, steady motion in the waves. One reason for wanting a steady rather than a jerky roll was the delay between the gunner's tripping the firelock, the explosion in the chamber, and the flight of the ball. He had to compensate for this lag, by 'firing on the roll'. Firing on the up roll might result in the shot going harmlessly over the enemy, while

Stowage using tanks (after Brady)
A Paint and oil room; **B** general store room; **C** bread room; **D** coal locker; **E** tanks; **F** casks; **G** chain locker; **H** tier gratings; **I** shot locker; **J** shell stores; **K** sail room; **L** spirit room; **M** bread room; **N** slop room; **O** marine stores; **P** magazine; **Q** filling room; **R** light room.

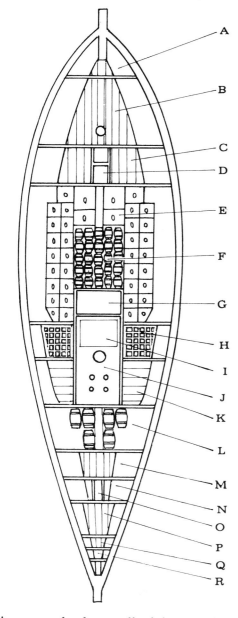

doing so on the down roll might send the projectile into the sea, if misjudged. For an analysis of this, and matters related to eighteenth century naval gunnery generally, Peter Padfield's *Guns at Sea* is unreservedly recommended.

Stowage of ballast. Ballast was carried in the form of shingle and 'kentledge' – cast iron 'pigs', having a hole in each end to allow of their being slung from a hook or dragged about the deck. The largest were 3 feet long and 6 inches square, weighing 320 pounds, and the smallest, 1 foot long by 4 inches square, weighing 56 pounds (Boyd, 83). The commonest sizes used in ships weighed 320 and 160 pounds; the smallest ones were used

for ballasting the ship's launch, and so on. According to Bobrik (2512), scrap iron was also used, in the form of old cannon, condemned anchors, old shot, and so on. Shingle was preferred to sand because it did not work through the ceiling and choke the pumps. Boyd (71) indicates that much less ballast was used in the mid-1800s, than in the late 1700s. He quotes some figures from Fincham, citing the decrease in ballast in a three-decker from about 500 tons in 1783 to somewhere between 100 and 230 tons in 1835. Boyd wonders if the sea-keeping abilities of Nelson's fleet 'Chasing twice across the Atlantic, each ship holding her place' was due to 'the powerful stability resulting from ballast, or merely the consequence of a very high order of seamanship'.

Fordyce (19) offers two rules used in the dockyards to calculate roughly the amount of ballast required. The first was to divide the tonnage by 8, and divide the result by 5; subtracting the two quotients thus obtained gave the number of tons of ballast. The other method was to divide the tonnage by 10. In a brig of 10 guns and 235 tons, the first method would give quotients of 29 and 5, and 24 tons of ballast, while the second rule would give 23.5 tons.

The iron pigs were stowed amidships, either side of the keelson, as shown very well in a plate in Blunt's *Seamanship*. More of the ballast was stowed before the mainmast than abaft it, reflecting the fullness of the body forward. Athwartship wooden battens were nailed on top to prevent the kentledge shifting (Brady, 221). Over this was laid a layer of shingle, and on this the first 'tier' or 'rise' of water casks was placed, sunk one-quarter of their diameter into the shingle. The forward row of casks were placed with their chines, or ends, against the bulkhead, and sitting bung upwards. The bung was always in line with the rivets on the hoops, at either end. The next row was placed abaft the first, chine to chine. The largest casks were 'butts' of 108 imperial gallons, placed amidships. 'Hogsheads' of 54 gallons, and 'half-hogsheads' of 27 gallons were used as 'wingers', out toward the sides of the hold. The ground tier of casks were thoroughly chocked with wedges and firewood, and then covered with shingle, and a second tier laid, so that the casks lay, 'chine and bulge', to the first; that is to say, moved aft half their length, so that each cask was supported by four casks below. The process was then repeated. The lighter shingle, being higher than the kentledge, made rolling easier, and some authorities (for instance Truxtun) thought that, in general, ships should carry about one-half the ballast in this

form (Polland, 100). When iron tanks superseded oak casks, these were placed on a wooden framework over the kentledge, and shingle was no longer needed, wood dunnage between the tanks being sufficient to secure them. The biggest tanks were square and contained 600 gallons. Bilge tanks with one side rounded off were used towards the wings. The tanks had a man-hole in one corner, and were lowered into the hold, using a toggle in this opening. They were placed so that, as far as possible, there were always four man-holes close together, to make filling easier and give more space for storing spare gear between them. 'Wet provisions' (pork, beef, suet, limejuice and vinegar) were stored amidships, while 'dry' provisions (tea, peas, etc) were stored towards the wings. A special 'spirit room' was found aft, for storing rum, sacramental wine, and varnish, the casks being stowed 'bung up and bilge free', chocked so they would not move as the ship rolled.

As provisions were used up, the trim of the vessel would alter. Bobrik (2516) cites a ship of the line using 30–40 tons of powder and shot in a four-hour engagement. He recommends filling the water casks with salt water as they are emptied, and also suggests using small casks filled with lead, and weighing about 60 pounds each, which are kept amidships and used to 'fine tune' the trim. Empty casks were sometimes 'shaken' or knocked down, the staves and hoops being stored so that the ship's cooper could reassemble them as necessary.

ACTION OF WIND ON THE SAILS

Single sail amidships. Let us imagine a ship with a square sail amidships. The wind striking this will have an effect proportional to the square of its velocity and to the area of the sail (Mossel, III, 8). If the wind strikes the sail on its after side, the force (W) can be resolved into two components, a useful one at right angles to the sail (E), and an ineffectual one parallel to it (N). The useful component (E) can further be resolved into two elements. one advantageous, pushing the vessel ahead (F), and another tending to push her directly to leeward (L). It will be seen that the best use is made of the wind when it is dead astern and the sail braced square. There is now no component parallel to the sail, and no tendency to make leeway. Should the wind come from some other angle, the nearer this approaches a right angle to the sail and coming from dead astern the better. Theoretically, the useful force is proportional

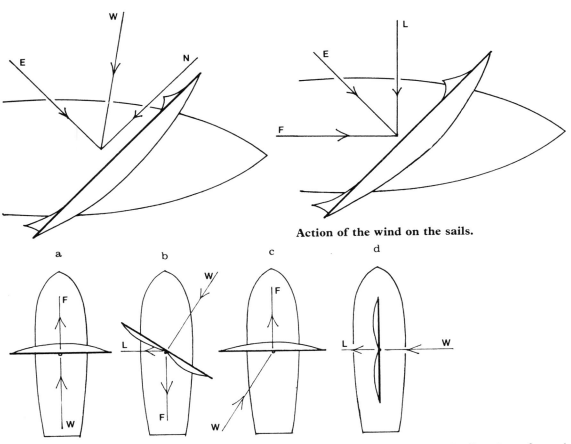

Action of the wind on the sails.

Effect of the wind on one sail. a Wind W striking squared sail from aft produces forward moving Force F and no leeway; **b** striking sail from off the bow produces backward moving force F and some leeway L; **c** Wind on the quarter striking squared sail produces forward movement F and no leeway; **d** Wind striking sail trimmed fore and aft produces sideways moving force L but no headway or sternway.

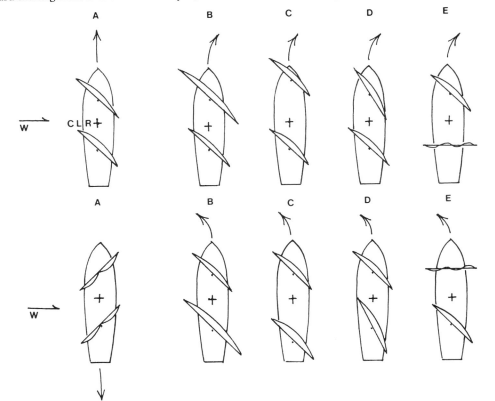

Effect of the wind on two square sails. With beam wind W and sails of equal size and distance from the CLR the ship moves ahead or astern and holds course (**A**). If one of the sails is increased in size (**B**), moved further from the CLR (**C**), braced up more sharply (**D**), or not balanced by another full sail (**E**), the ship will either fall off (top row **B-E**) or come up into the wind (bottom row **B-E**).

to the square of the sine of the angle between wind and sail (Mossel III, 9). If the wind comes from ahead, the force acts to push the ship astern, and to leeward, the exact result depending on the direction of the wind and the angle to which the sail is braced. If the sail were trimmed so that it were exactly in the fore and aft line, and the wind were abeam, the force of the wind would theoretically be totally expended in attempting to push the ship directly to leeward, without producing headway or sternway. If the sail were square, and the wind coming from somewhere on the quarter, the ship would be driven ahead, but would not make leeway, since the lateral component of the wind will slide uselessly past the squared sail.

Two square sails. Let us imagine a vessel with two sails, one placed well before the CLR and the other an equal distance abaft it. If the sails are braced up for the starboard tack, and the wind is on the starboard beam, she will start to move ahead, and will also drive somewhat to leeward. If the wind comes from the other beam, it will start to make sternway and leeway. We are assuming of course, that the sails are of equal size, are trimmed alike, and are the same distance before and abaft the CLR respectively. If the foresail were increased in size, were moved further forward, or were braced up more, a state of balance would no longer exist and the bow would tend to fall off the wind. If the aftersail were increased in size, moved further aft, or braced up more, the ship's head would try to come up to the wind, and the stern would fall off. If the sail is square, or if it lies a-shiver, parallel to the direction of the wind, it will not exert any turning effect on the bow or stern, as the case may be, and the rotational effect of the other sail will be unopposed. The ship will pivot roughly at its mid-point, and if the bow comes to the wind, the stern must fall off. By convention, when considering the ship's motion, we describe what happens to the bow, rather than the stern.

Effect of wind direction on fore- and aftersail. We may consider eight possible situations:

A   Foresail aback. *Ship goes astern and falls off.*
     Aftersail aback. *Ship goes astern and comes to.*
B   Foresail aback. *Ship goes astern and comes to.*
     Aftersail aback. *Ship goes astern and falls off.*
C & F   Sails shivering. *No effect.*
D   Foresail full. *Ship goes ahead and falls off.*

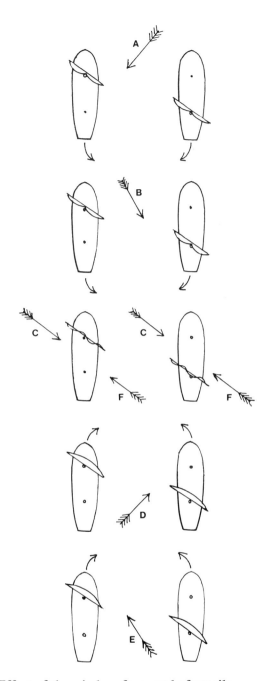

Effect of the wind on fore- and aftersails.

Aftersail full. *Ship goes ahead and comes to.*

E   Foresail full. *Ship goes ahead and comes to.*

Aftersail full. *Ship goes ahead and falls off.*

Conditions B and E are rarely met with in practice and are referred to in Dutch sources as the '*buitengewoon stand*', 'extraordinary situation'. If we disregard them, we may summarise the results thus: a full sail causes the ship to move ahead, while aback it causes her to move astern. Foresail, whether full or aback causes the head to fall off. An aftersail, whether full or aback, causes the ship to come to. A sail braced in square, whether full or aback, has no rotational effect on bow or stern. The effect of shivering a sail is to nullify its ability to influence the ship's movements, in any way whatsoever.

Counterbracing fore and aft. If the sails are inclined in opposite directions, and the wind is on either beam, it will be seen that the sails can be trimmed in such a way that the forward thrust of one is exactly balanced by the after pushing tendency of the other (A). The vessel will neither move ahead or astern, but drive slowly to leeward, and she is said to be 'hove to, fore topsail to the mast' (C), if the wind is on the starboard side, 'main topsail to the mast', if it comes from port (B).

Fore- and aftersail. In the traditional three-masted ship, we are inclined to think of the mainmast as being amidships. In fact, it is always somewhat abaft this, and the sails on the mainmast are part of the aftersail. It is true however, that being closer to the CLR, or pivot point, the turning leverage exerted by these sails is proportionately less than those on the mizzen mast, particularly the mizzen sail itself. It will be noted, that when braced up sharp, the weathermost parts of the sails on the main, particularly the lower

ones, are in fact before the CLR. However, their thrust is transmitted to the ship primarily via the mast, and they remain functionally part of the aftersail. This explains why the main and mizzen yards are swung together in manoeuvres such as going about. Thus the foresail comprises the spritsail topsail and spritsail, the jibs and fore topmast staysail, all the sails on the foremast, and all the main staysails. The aftersail comprises all the square sails on the main and mizzen masts, all the mizzen staysails and the mizzen itself.

The Beaufort Scale. In 1806, Francis Beaufort devised the Wind Scale associated ever since with his name. As Alfred Friendly (143) remarks, it is surprising that no one had previously attempted a similar codification. To be sure, in 1759, John Smeaton, the lighthouse builder, had proposed correlating wind speeds with simple verbal descriptions, but this had never been adopted at sea, and one man's 'small gale' might be a 'whole gale' to someone else. 'When the wind doth not blow too hard, but reasonably, so that a ship may bear her topsails a-trip, we call it, according to the strength of it, either an easy, or a loom gale, which is when it is little wind' (Mainwaring, 154).

> When there is not a breath of wind stirring, it is a Calm, or a Stark Calm. A Breeze is a wind which blows out of the sea, and commonly in fair weather beginneth about nine in the morning, and lasteth till near night. So likewise all night it is from the shore, which is called a Turnado, or a Sea-Turn... A Fresh Gale is that which doth presently blow after a calm, when the wind beginneth to quicken or blow. A Fair Loom Gale is the best to sail in, because the sea goeth not high, and we bear out all our sails. A Stiff Gale is so much wind, as our topsails can endure to bear. It Over-blows when we can bear no topsails. A Flaw of wind is a Gust, which is very violent upon a sudden, but quickly endeth (Smith, 59).

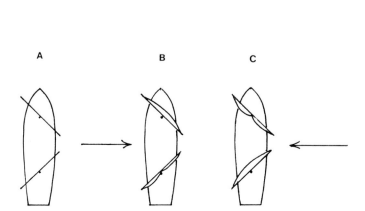

Counterbracing fore and aft.

Fore- and aftersails. The foresails are shaded, aftersails shown in white.

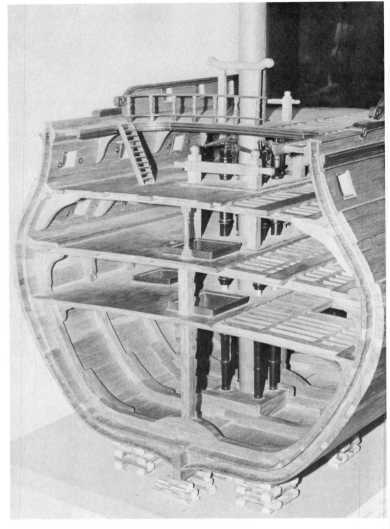

1.

3.

THE BEAUFORT NOTATION TO INDICATE THE FORCE OF THE WIND

Scale	Wind speed in knots	Wind	Sail carried (Bedford & Luce)	Sail carried (Mossel)	State of sea
0	0–1	Calm			Smooth
1	1–3	Light Air	Just sufficient to give steerage way		Ripple
2	3–5	Light Breeze	Speed of 1–2 Knots	Light topgallant Breeze	Wavelets
3	5–10	Gentle Breeze	Speed of 3–4 Knots	Topgallant Breeze	Crests begin to break
4	10–15	Moderate Breeze	Speed of 5–6 Knots	Stiff topgallant Breeze	Crests break frequently
5	15–20	Fresh Breeze	All plain sail to royals	Topsail Breeze	Moderate waves
6	20–25	Strong Breeze	Topgallants over single reefed topsails	Stiff topsail Breeze	Large waves
7	25–35	Moderate Gale	Double reefed topsails	Reefed topsail Breeze	Waves streaked with foam
8	35–40	Fresh Gale	Treble reefed topsails and courses	Double reefed topsail Breeze	Spindrift and much foam
9	40–45	Strong Gale	Close reefed topsails and fore course	Close reefed topsail Breeze	Overhanging crests
10	45–55	Whole Gale (Storm)	Close reefed main topsail and reefed fore course	'Lower sail Breeze'	Sea completely covered with foam
11	55–65	Storm (Great Storm)	Storm staysails		Air filled with flying spray
12	over 65	Hurricane	Can show no canvas		

Our table is a composite of Bedford (73), Kemp (72), Todd & Whall (337), Luce (477) and Mossel (III, 24). The speeds are those which a 'well conditioned man-of-war' would attain, sailing clean full, in smooth water. In the same column, the canvas indicated is that which she could just carry, sailing close-hauled. Mossel and Bedford do not agree completely, on this point, but I do not think the differences are critical. Bedford indicates that at 15 knots, the wind generated a pressure of one pound per square inch on

HMS *Caesar* fitting out at Portsmouth. (*Illustrated London News*, 1854). The accompanying account offers a most instructive breakdown of the weights carried by a 90-gun ship of the period.

Lowermasts, topmasts and yards, 110 tons; standing rigging, 38 tons; running rigging, 46 tons; blocks, 8 tons; sails and spars, 12 tons; cables, hemp, 8 tons; cables, chain, 55 tons; anchors, 22 tons; guns, 290 tons; boats and gear, 12 tons; boatswain's and gunner's stores, 110 tons; powder, 48 tons; shot, 118 tons; shells, 22 tons; small arms, 8 tons; engines, 250 tons; coals, 300 tons; water in casks, 225 tons; tare of casks, 40 tons; provisions, 105 tons; firewood, 3 tons; officers, men, marines and their equipment, 90 tons. (Mark Myers' Collection)

A model showing a section of a vessel with relatively flat floors, illustrating the tumblehome and the disposition of the pumps (Courtesy Kiel Schiffahrtsmuseum: Dr Klaus Grimm)

Weather and lee gauge. This painting by W J Huggins shows the engagement between HMS *Indefatigable* and the French two-decker *Droits de l'Homme* in 1797. (Courtesy N R Omell Gallery, London)

This *Illustrated London News* engraving of the 90-gun ship HMS *St George* in 1861 well suggests the lifting effect of the foresail and jib. (Mark Myers' Collection)

the sails, and this figure doubled at 20, 28, 42, 58 and 80 knots, at which point, the pressure reached 32 pounds per square inch.

Number of masts. Since our interest is limited to the sailing man-of-war, we are concerned primarily with the three-masted ship-rigged vessel. It is of interest however, to analyse the changing relationship of the CE to the masts as we work through the progression from brig to five-masted ship. It will be seen that the sails on the mainmast of a brig have almost as much leverage as those on the fore, particularly the uppermost ones, and that in a four- or five-masted ship, the foresail includes both fore- and mainmasts. Herein also lies the explanation for the peculiar disposition of square yards on the Vinnen schooners, which are found on the first and middle, but not the mainmast.

The historical development of sailing shipping is a constant expansion of the principle that a big sail is better than a small one, but if too big, it becomes unmanageable, and is replaced by two smaller sails. This rule also encompasses the number of masts. The diagram taken from Middendorf correlates the number of masts of sailing merchantmen with gross tonnage, and demonstrates the progression from schooner to five-masted ship. The point at which the designer has to decide whether to add another mast, seems to arrive when the mainyard would exceed approximately one hundred feet in length. Beyond this, the course becomes too large to handle comfortably. The length of the spars was, in the early days, limited by the availability of suitable timber, since they were fashioned in one piece. Subsequently, masts

were built up of several pieces, ingeniously 'coaked' together, and their size was no longer limited by the length of the original trees. Later still, the spars were tubes fabricated of steel plates, and could readily have been made much longer than they actually were. It seems that experience determined the inadvisability of the sail exceeding a certain maximal area. *Victory*'s mainyard is 102 feet long, while the longest yard on Middendorf's plan for a five-masted ship is, in fact, a little shorter.

Why three masts? During the period in which we are interested, the sailing man-of-war was rigged with three masts, something that everybody knows, but nobody questions. Why three? If in the late 1800s ships were being built with four and five masts, why had this not been the case earlier? The answer would seem to be that even the longest sailing man-of-war fell into the range where three masts were still adequate.

Four and five-masted merchantmen. A large merchantman is more economic than two smaller ones, a principle abundantly evidenced nowadays by the rabble of gargantuan Very Large Crude Carriers, or VLCCs, lumbering about the oceans. Therefore, it is not surprising that in the declining days of merchant sail, the experiment was made of building bigger and bigger ships, in the hope that they could somehow make a dollar, where their smaller sisters could not. What with one thing and another, the attempt was not a success, in part because four- and five-masted vessels are inherently less handy than those with three masts, whether ship or barque. This was not as great a disadvantage in the large sailing merchantmen as it would have been in a man-of-war, or small merchant vessel, where the ability to tack readily was very important. I have found almost nothing in print about tacking four- and five-masted vessels, and of course we can plead that this problem lies outside the boundaries of our subject, since it never applied to the sail powered man-of-war. A barque was handier than a ship, because there was one less set of yards to worry about when going about. Certainly it spread less canvas aft, but this was to some extent offset by the fact that, with the wind quartering or further aft than that, the weather half of the mizzen square sails blanketted those on the main, and hence contributed less to forward drive, on this point of sail, than might have been thought. There were examples of vessels cut down from ship to barque, where the sailing ability was quite unaffected, at least with the wind free. In the three-masted ship, the mainmast sail was abaft the CLR,

and pushed the bow into the wind in the early stages of tacking. In the four- or five-masted barque or ship, the mainmast is ahead of the CLR, this lead increasing as one goes through the sequence from four-masted barque to five-masted ship. From first principles, we might expect therefore that the handling of the sails on the main would have been a problem, at least in the early stages of tacking. Wilson-Barker (96) says that 'in a five-masted vessel, fore and main are handled together'. The third mast was called the *Mittel*, 'middle', mast on the German five-masters. Middendorf discusses at length the best names to assign the five masts (20). He preferred the sequence *Fock-, Gross-, Mittel-, Haupt-, Kreuz-mast* for a five-masted ship, substituting *Besahn-mast* for *Kreuz-mast* in a five-masted barque. He follows a similar pattern for four-masted vessels, omitting the *Mittel-mast*. *Gross-* and *Haupt-* are both synonymous with English 'main'. *Kreuz-* and *Besahn-* are identical with English 'mizzen', *Kreuz-* implying however that square sail is involved. The Hamburg firm of F Laeisz sometimes called the fourth mast of a five-master the *Laeisz-mast*, not surprisingly, since they were the only German owners operating such vessels. It was also called the *Achter-mast*, 'after mast'. *Jigger-mast* was sometimes used for the fourth mast of a four-masted barque, just as in English.

Bonaventure mizzen. An exception to the general proposition that large sailing men-of-war had no more than three masts, is offered by the 'bonaventure mizzen' of the early 1600s. In some vessels, the upper works were

Position of the CE in relation to the number of masts in rigs from brig to a five-masted full-rigged ship.

Comparison of the rigs of merchant sailing ships with gross tonnage (after Middendorf).

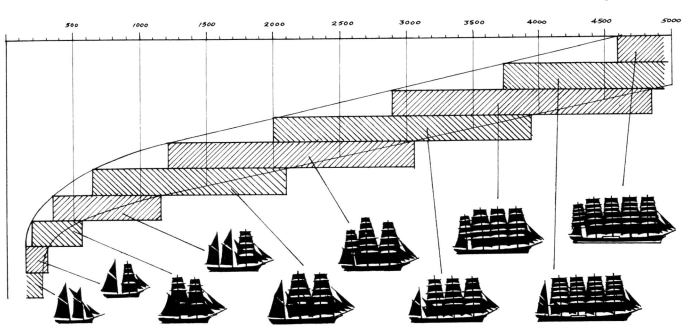

so narrow aloft because of tumblehome, that there was too little spread to support a mizzen mast of adequate height. The mizzen sail therefore, had too small an area to balance the sail plan, and had to be supplemented by a second mizzen, which although smaller, exerted greater leverage because it was further aft and was sheeted out to an 'out-licker' extending aft from the taffrail. An extempore 'ringtail', or light weather sail was sometimes rigged on the taffrail flagpole, even in the very late 1700s.

Relative sizes of masts. Looking at the relative dimensions of the three masts, it will be seen that the proportions of the sails on each mast are about the same. That is to say, the foremast and mizzen masts, with their upper masts and yards, are scaled down versions of the mainmast. The size of the mast is determined by the beam of the vessel at the point where it is stepped. Since the mainmast is placed roughly amidships, its shrouds and backstays have the greatest spread, and the mast can consequently be of greater proportions than the foremast or mizzen mast. It will also be noticed that the backward and lateral support for the foremast occurs at a point where beam is increasing, as one moves aft, while the opposite is true of the mizzen.

Placing of the masts. This varied somewhat, but in a general way, the mainmast was about the midships point, or somewhat aft of this, the foremast placed about the junction of stempost and keel, and the mizzen between the main and stern. It follows that there was a greater space between fore and main, than between main and mizzen. This resulted in an arrangement where there was reasonable balance between the foresail and aftersail, and where there was less blanketting of the fore by the main, with a quartering wind, than if they had been closer together. If the foreyard were swung one way, and the main yard the other, there was a danger that the yardarms might 'lock'. This became less of a problem, the greater the distance between fore- and mainmasts. It would not be true to say that the main and crossjack yards invariably swung together, but this was the case in an operation like tacking, so the problem of locking did not arise. There was some interesting correspondence on this topic in *Le Petit Perroquet*, a few years ago (No 9, 1972, 11).

Anderson (4) points out that during the period 1600–1720, the foremast moved somewhat further aft. Part of this was an illusion, and reflected the way the rake of the stem decreased in the seventeenth century. One reason for moving the foremast aft was the introduction of the fore topmast staysail

Bonaventure mizzen. Elizabethan ship with bonaventure mizzen shaded, (**A**) and eighteenth century ship with temporary sail set on ensign staff (**B**).

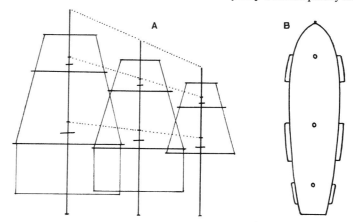

Relative sizes of masts. Main, fore and mizzen masts and yards showing heights from waterline to truck (**A**) and positions of the masts on the deck, showing greatest spread of the channels near the main mast (**B**).

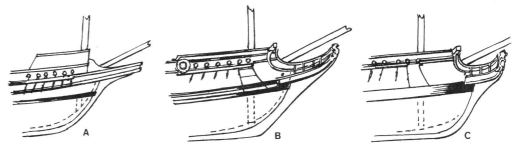

Location of the fore mast showing the way the mast shifted its relative position:
A *c*1580; **B** *c*1680; **C** *c*1780.

and jibs. This increase of sail in the fore triangle meant that the total CE would have moved forward, unless steps were taken to prevent this.

Rake of the masts. The expression 'a rakish looking craft' conjures up a picture of a fast-sailing vessel, engaged in some vaguely piratical enterprise, with masts which rake markedly aft; hence extreme rake of masts is associated in the popular mind with great speed under sail. Actually the word 'rakish' owes a good deal to the idea that a 'rake' or 'rakehell' was a fashionable scoundrel, and therefore impugns the moral character of the

vessel, as it were. In fact, inclining masts have very little to do with the speed of the vessel. It may be done for looks, or to allow a particular internal arrangement in the vessel's hull, but that is about all. Rake was usually related to the waterline, but some authors, for instance Steel, relate it to the keel; in either case since the angle between keel and waterline was for the most part very small, or non-existent, the difference was not substantial. Unless otherwise specified, 'rake' meant to incline aft, while some authorities use 'stay forward' to describe the opposite practice.

If the mast is raked forward, the shrouds

Rake of masts. In an Elizabethan ship (**A**), the *Vasa* (**B**), Two-decker of *c*1800 (**C**), Baltimore clipper schooner (**D**), and steamship *c*1900 (**E**).

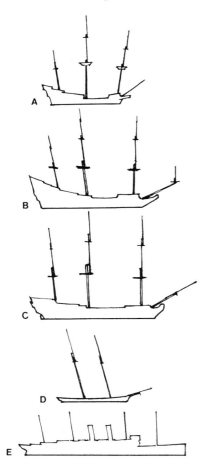

come forward also, and this means that the yard cannot be braced up as sharply as before. The wind in the sails of the foremast, tends to depress the bow, if the mast is raked forward, and this also aggravates pitching. Liardet says (139) that this was sometimes done because it was believed it helped the fore sails catch aback more readily in tacking. He observes however, that it prevented the head coming up into the wind, and the net effect was probably a negative one. As to giving the mizzen mast a pronounced rake aft, he feels it may tend to lift the stern, and give the backstays a better angle of pull, and thus probably does no great harm. Gower (67) considered it aesthetically unpleasing to see 'one mast falling over the taffarel, and another tumbling over the bows'. The *Naval Repository* (39) makes the surprising comment that the mizzen mast differs from the others in being upright, but it is just possible that this results from mistranslating *mât de misaine* as 'mizzen mast' instead of 'foremast'. Some vessels pitch more violently than they scend, and in some ships it was found that raking the masts aft eased their pitching motion considerably.

From a theroetical point of view, the sails are used to best advantage when the masts are vertical, since the wind then strikes the sail at the most advantageous angle. However, it was the usual practice to rake the masts progressively from forward aft. A common method was to have the foremast vertical, or almost so, the main raked aft one or two degrees, and the mizzen one or two degrees more than the main. The result is that the masts spread out like outstretched fingers. That this was done primarily for looks is attested by the fact that it was also the practice in the beautiful multi-masted steamers afloat at the turn of the century. Masts which are truly parallel, give the appearance that they are toppling in towards each other, and this illusion is overcome by having them, in fact, open out slightly. It is sometimes said that this 'fanning' of the masts diminished the blanketting of the upper sails by one another, but in practice this effect must have been inconsequential.

In setting up masts, the pull of the stays had to be evenly counterbalanced by the tension of the shrouds and backstays, if an undue strain was not to be put on the mast. If this rake was to be altered, it was essential that the wedges be knocked out, so the mast was free to move at the 'partners', where it passed through the deck, or else an excessive stress came on it at this point (Brady, 130). If by injudicious staying, the masts were crippled and a permanent warp put in it, a 'belly-guy' was sometimes used to give extra support at this point. This was particularly the case with the mainmast. The backward curve put in it was, probably wrongly, attributed to the pull of the mizzen stay (Griffiths, 246). The same source (239) also points out that the main topsail halliards, which lead relatively further aft than the fore, were exactly contrived to put a tremendous strain on the main topmast, tending to make it belly forward.

Parallelism of yards and horizon. As the ship heeled, the weather yardarm canted up, and the lee one down. This was corrected by hauling the lee lift, and easing off the weather one. If this were not done, the wind striking the sail horizontally, could be thought of as being 'trapped' between the lee half of the yard and the sail, resulting in energy-wasting eddy formation. If the yard is horizontal, the wind can flow smoothly across to leeward (Regan and Johnson, 98). It will be realised, of course, that this cannot be done beyond a certain point without distorting the sail unacceptably.

CE leading the CLR. As we have indicated, the CLR is found roughly amidships, and in fact is taken to be the geometric centre of the plan of the submerged portion of the hull. It can also be considered as the pivot around which the ship swings, either coming up or falling off, as the case may be. Thus, with a beam wind, the CE should be directly over the CLR, if the fore- and aftersail are exactly in balance, and the ship steers her course, neither coming up nor falling off, if the rudder is held dead amidships. If one looks at the rigging plan of a ship, it will be noted that the CE always 'leads' the CLR by a significant amount. This is because the ship, moving ahead, acts as if the CLR had moved ahead also, and as a result comes to lie abreast the CE. As the ship heels, the CE moves out to leeward of the hull, and hence of the CLR. The forward component of the wind force thus acts to push the bow into the wind. Furthermore, the water piling up under the lee bow pushes the forward part of the ship towards the wind also. Another way of looking at it is that as the hull inclines, it is immersed in the water asymetrically, and a greater volume is submerged on the lee side, hence there is greater resistance to forward motion on that side, and therefore the bow is pushed a-weather. To compensate for these effects, the CE is designed to lead the CLR on the sail plan, so that the CE and CLR will actually be in reasonable balance, once the ship is making headway. The amount of lead is greater with the short beamy hull of a tjalk compared, for example, with that of a sharp lined cutter of about the same size (Middendorf, 218), because with a sharp entry the water does not pile up to such an extent under the lee bow. The point around which the ship is actually pivoting is amidships, hence some authorities prefer to call it the 'centre of gravity', arguing that the CLR, has to be a point somewhere on the skin of the submerged part of the hull.

Weather and lee helm. Where a ship is constantly trying to turn up into the wind, and the tendency is corrected by using the rudder to keep her away and on course, she is said to be 'carrying weather helm', 'to be ardent' or 'to be griping'. In the opposite circumstance, where the ship's inclination to fall off is corrected by keeping the rudder a little to weather, she is said to 'carry lee helm' or be 'slack'. In its simplest form, the rudder is controlled by a 'helm' or 'tiller', which is forward of the rudder pivot. Thus if the tiller or helm is turned to port, the rudder goes to starboard. If the helm is put to weather, the rudder is turned to the lee side. Thus when it is necessary to 'carry weather helm', one is actually trying to turn the ship to leeward. Steering commands were traditionally given as 'helm orders', which were thus directly

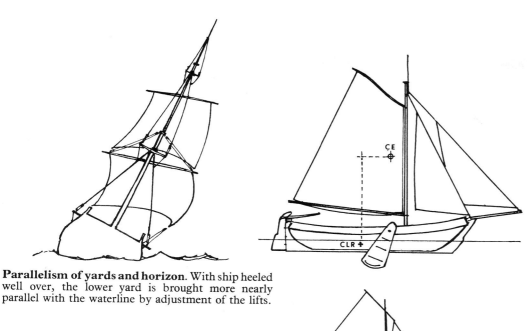

Parallelism of yards and horizon. With ship heeled well over, the lower yard is brought more nearly parallel with the waterline by adjustment of the lifts.

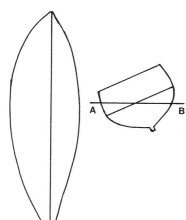

Asymmetrical shape of the hull. When inclined on line AB, the immersed portion of the hull takes on an asymmetrical shape.

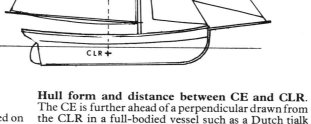

Hull form and distance between CE and CLR. The CE is further ahead of a perpendicular drawn from the CLR in a full-bodied vessel such as a Dutch tjalk (top) than in a fine lined cutter (bottom).

considerate attention of both seamen and builders.' (Fordyce, 21).

If the CLR were too far forward, for example if the vessel was down by the head, she became very difficult to steer, subject to yawing, first one way, then the other, but particularly liable to run up into the wind. This was attributed to the fact that the rudder was higher out of the water, and therefore had a poorer grip on it (Ekelöf, 36). On the other hand, if too much down by the stern, the CLR was too far aft, and tacking became difficult, because the bow continually wanted to fall off. To achieve a balance between these two extremes was the challenge faced by the designer and the commander of the vessel. Ardency increased with speed, and also heel. To some extent, these tend to go together, and in fact this was a situation where shortening sail, particularly taking in lofty sail, sometimes decreased heeling, and resulted paradoxically in an actual increase in speed. An insight into the complexity of judging sail balance is offered by the fact that taking in the fore topgallant, or putting one more reef in the fore topsail than the main, sometimes helped correct excessive weather helm, whereas one would have expected this would have made it worse by shifting the CE aft. The reason was that the depressing effect of the fore topgallant on the bow, and the consequent forward movement of the CLR, outweighed its ability to move the CE forward. Nares (238), says that this is a significant effect when the ship heels more than 12°. He says that although the main topgallant is higher, with greater heeling moment, one chooses to take away the fore 'in the same way as the bow oar of a boat is laid, in preference to an after one'. Similar considerations probably explain why, in many

opposite in intent to orders couched in terms of what the rudder was doing. 'Hard a-starboard!' actually was equivalent to the modern United States Navy's 'Full left rudder!'

It was considered best to have matters organised so the ship was balanced to carry a little bit of weather helm. Carrying too much helm, weather or lee, was bad, because it meant that the resistance of the angled rudder was actually working to slow the ship down. Thus the problem facing the sailing master was to get the CE and CLR in the most favourable relationship.

Effect of sail. Excessive weather helm could be corrected by moving the CE forward, thus increasing the turning moment of the forward sail, by bracing the yards up more sharply, by hauling the sheets of the forward staysails more firmly aft, or by setting additional forward sail. It could be moved aft by comparable manoeuvres to increase the torque of the aftersail. If experience showed that these measures were not sufficient, a forward shift of the CE could be engineered by lessening the rake of the masts, or where drastic measures were needed, stepping them further forward (this was done once, during *Victory*'s long life afloat). Increasing the rake, moved the CE aft.

Effect of trim. The CLR could be shifted forward by appropriate movements of inboard weight forward, and vice versa, thus altering the trim. The general tendency was to design the ships with a little more draught astern. In merchantmen, there was usually little difference between bow and stern (Krogh, 19). 'Trim may be considered one of the most delicate points in the art of navigation, and requires the united and

A brig (after Walters) showing common practice of carrying less sail on the fore than the main to reduce weather helm.

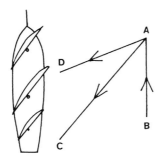 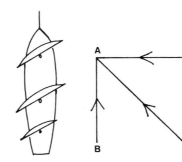

True and apparent wind.

Wind speed is greater aloft than near the waterline, due to the friction between wind and wave at sea level.

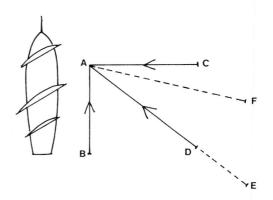

Apparent wind in gusts. When the true wind AD increases to AE during a gust, the apparent wind AC increases to AF and draws aft.

contemporary paintings of brigs, one sees no fore topgallant or royal, while that on the main is set, giving the vessel a rather unbalanced look (*Mariner's Mirror*, 60, 1974, 332).

Boyd gives a couple of examples of what he describes as the 'tender sensibility' of some ships:

> During one of the trials between *Barham* and *Vernon*, the captain, on coming on deck after a very short absence, exclaimed that there was something wrong. It proved that a five-inch hawser, which had been spread on the booms, near the mainmast to dry, had, in the interval, been reeled up, near the bowsprit. On another occasion, when both ships were sailing abreast on a wind, and neither gaining, the men who were lying on the deck round the mainmast were caused to stand up, and instantly *Barham* moved ahead.

In the first case, we are dealing with a movement of weight forward; in the second instance, having a fair number of men upright instead of lying down would raise the CG slightly; but it is not immediately clear to me why this *per se* improved the rate of sailing. Some vessels, because of a subtle lack of total symmetry, sailed better on one tack than the other, and this could prove important, in giving chase, or being chased (Mossel, III, 45).

The remedies for excessive ardency and slackness can be summarised as follows:

SHIP TOO ARDENT

Sail
1. Increase foresail
2. Decrease aftersail
3. Combination

Masts
1. Move one or more masts forward
2. Lessen rake of masts

Trim
1. Move ballast aft
2. Take in fore topgallant
3. Decrease angle of heel by taking in upper light sails

SHIP TOO SLACK

Sail
1. Decrease foresail
2. Increase aftersail
3. Combination

Masts
1. Move one or more masts aft
2. Increase rake of masts

Trim
1. Move ballast forward

Leeway. The vessel sailing close-hauled, worked her way to windward, but also was to some extent pushed sideways. As one looked directly astern, this was betrayed by noting the way the wake angled off slightly to windward, instead of disappearing straight astern. The amount of leeway could be expressed as the angle between the wake and the course – the greater the angle, the greater the leeway. As already stated, the reason the ship did not drift directly to leeward was due to the lateral resistance offered by the hull, and this was to some extent, a function of its shape. A long narrow hull offered proportionately greater resistance to lateral movement than a short beamy hull. Excessive heel resulted in greater leeway, as well as requiring a lot of weather helm (Ekelöf, 17). The most efficient resistance to drifting sideways was offered by the knife-like shape of a centreboard, or leeboard. On the other hand, if a vessel were too long, it became unhandy, and difficult to tack, something that came readily to shorter craft. Mossel considered the ideal beam-to-length ratio to be about 1:5. A vessel which made little leeway was said to 'hold a good wind', or be 'weatherly'. A craft with poor sailing qualities in this regard, was 'leewardly'. The resistance of the water was proportional to the square of the speed, and hence the faster the hull moved through the sea, the less the leeway. Mossel (III, 28) considered that a good ship should make no more than 8° leeway, up to about 6 knots, and beyond 8 knots, leeway should be insignificant. Dick and Kretchmer (II, 169)

thought it should be between 6° and 12°. Waves of a beam sea would tend to increase the leeway (Mossel, III, 33).

Too much sail. When a vessel was 'crowding', or going under too great a press of sail, setting more canvas might decrease, rather than increase, speed. Increased heeling not only caused increased leeway, but also required more weather helm. Sometimes, therefore, furling some of the light sails which had great heeling moment actually improved performance. We have already referred to the reason why taking in the fore topgallant could result in decreasing pressure under the lee bow, and hence decrease the amount of weather helm.

True and apparent wind. Up to this point, we have considered the wind as it appeared to those on board the ship. However, what they experience is the combination of the true wind and the speed of the ship. A steamer heading directly into a 10-knot wind at a speed of 10 knots, will experience an apparent headwind of 20 knots. If it were moving in a true calm, it would create, so to speak, an apparent headwind of 10 knots. If it has the wind directly astern, the smoke goes straight up because it appears as if the air were completely calm. In the case of the sailing ship, it cannot head directly into the wind, but its speed on other courses will result in phenomena similar to the above. At anchor, the true and apparent wind are the same. Otherwise, when the ship makes headway, the apparent wind will be somewhat ahead of the true wind.

Diagrammatically, AB represents the ship's speed, while AD represents true wind. The vector AC represents the apparent wind, and in this case, it is stronger than the true wind, and appears to come from further ahead. With a true wind on the quarter AD, the apparent wind AC is abeam, and of lower speed than the true wind. If the ship's speed remains the same, but the true wind increases, the apparent wind seems to move aft of its original direction. Of course, in moderate wind conditions, increasing the true wind, also increases the speed of the ship. The wind blowing over the sea, however, is impeded at the surface of the water by friction at the interface and slowed by eddy formation. The speed increases in a laminar fashion as one moves upwards through the friction layers, in a very similar fashion to the way a stream flows fastest in the centre of its course, and more slowly

towards the banks. The same thing is true to an even greater degree over land, which explains the finding that, averaged over a year, the wind speed at the top of the Eiffel Tower is four times that at the bottom (Oderwald, 14). One consequence of this effect, is that the wind appears to be 'fairer' aloft; that is to say, the upper sails are trimmed as though the wind were more favourable than is the case with the lower sails. A second consequence is that a gust of wind, coming from the same direction will appear to have drawn aft. This would be assumed to occur at the moment the ship heels over to the gust, but before it has started to move faster through the water, in response to it. Actually the predominant effect may be due to a totally unrelated phenomenon. In the Northern Hemisphere, the wind tends to veer as it gusts; that is, to swing in a clockwise direction. It will be seen that this effect opposes the other one, on the port tack, but is additive on the starboard tack. This need not detain us further here, since this was never the subject of interest during our period, but for anyone interested, there is a detailed analysis of these matters in the early chapters of Alan Watts' *Wind and Sailing Boats*, embodying the results of a great deal of modern research.

In a sailing vessel using auxiliary power, the apparent wind will be even further ahead than when the screw is not being used. In fact, with the true wind a point or so abaft the beam, the sails of a motor fishing vessel needed to be sheeted in, as if close-hauled. In the case of an ice-boat, which can exceed the speed of the true wind, the sheets are hauled tight in, with the wind dead astern, for the same reason. Several contemporary writers,

serving in vessels with auxiliary steam, make the point that under steam and sail, the square sails are almost useless, fore and aft canvas only being practical. Mossel (III, 6) refers to the belief that a ship with the tide under the lee bow will tack more readily than if there is a weather tide, that is to say one setting in the same direction as the wind is blowing. Since, in the first case, the apparent wind is greater the proposition is true, but not because the tide is shoving the bow around. It acts equally on all the submerged parts of the hull.

Lifting and depressing sails. The fore topmast staysail, jibs, staysails of the main, and fore course all tended to raise the bow a little bit, thus requiring less weather helm. The effect of the course was the greatest, and that of the main staysails the least. All square sails, in theory, have the effect of lifting the hull vertically upwards if the masts are markedly raked. The square sails on the main and mizzen tend to lift the after ship which results in depressing the bow, and even the main course has a slight effect in this direction. The staysails between the fore- and mainmasts, could be expected to contribute a little to the lifting of the fore ship, particularly those where the stay ran almost horizontally. All studdingsails were considered depressing sails, the fore and aft mizzen having very little effect either way. Depending on how they were set, the spritsail and both types of spritsail topsail had a depressing effect. This was particularly true of the later pattern of spritsail topsail. With a fresh quartering breeze, and the sheets slacked well off, with the clews well weighted, it is possible to imagine the spritsail setting in such a way as to give a lift.

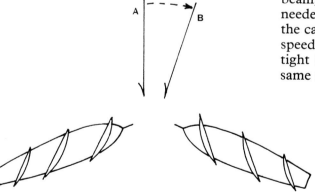

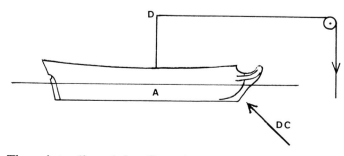

Veering of the wind. As the wind A veers 'with the sun' to B, it scants for the vessel on the port tack and becomes fairer for that on the starboard tack.

The point velique (after Gower).

Lifting and depressing sails. Sails which act to lift the bow are shown in white, and sails which push it down are shown shaded.

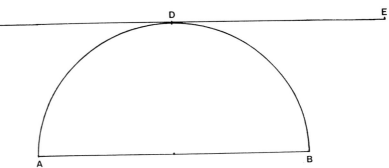

Sail as a curved surface.

Sketch (after Van de Velde) showing the baggy cut of sails in the seventeenth century.

Point velique. The early British authorities, like Steel and Gower, follow Bouguer in stressing the importance of the *point velique*, or velical point (Latin *velum*, 'sail'). The concept involved was as follows: the bow pushing through the water generated a resistance which was partly backward and partly upward; the mean direction of this force intercepted a vertical line drawn through the ship's centre of gravity, at the *point velique*, or 'sail point'. The CE of all the sail set should be at the same horizontal level as this point. If it were higher, the bow would be depressed, if below, the bow would be lifted. In either case, the trim of the vessel would be altered, and her sailing qualities interfered with. Gower proposed determining this point by building a model, and running tank tests, hauling it through the water by means of a falling weight. As can be seen from the accompanying illustration D represents the *point velique*, DC the effective resistance to forward movement, and A the ship's centre of gravity. Later in the century, the idea dropped out of favour, although Bobrik (2521) still alludes to it as late as 1848.

Wind strength and sail. The amount of sail that could be carried prudently was determined by the strength of the wind, and the Beaufort Scale correlated wind strength, sea conditions, with the appropriate canvas which could be set, when sailing by the wind (see earlier section and table). Since the apparent wind is greatest when close-hauled, least when dead astern, the sail indicated on the scale is that considered appropriate to by-the-wind sailing. There was nothing ironclad about this system, since a great deal had to depend on the judgement of the officer, guided by knowledge of the sailing qualities and stability of his ship. The pressure of the

wind on the sail varies more or less as the square of its velocity. The consequence of this is that a sudden doubling of the wind in a squall, increases the heeling moment by a factor of four. Ekelöf (16) says that in winter the air being more dense, the wind's effect is a little greater than a summer wind of the same speed.

Sail as a curved surface. Up to now we have considered the sail as a plane surface, but actually it assumes a curved configuration when properly set. The sail would be most efficient if it were flat, but throughout much of our period, sailmakers persisted in cutting the sails so they acted literally as 'wind-bags' – the billowing topsails which are such a feature of the van de Velde paintings, are more picturesque than efficient. Widespread general appreciation of the virtues of the flat cut sail is usually attributed to the decisive win of the yacht *America* over her British rivals at Cowes in 1851. The pressure of the wind is most effective when it strikes the sail at right angles. To the extent that it hits the canvas obliquely, its effect is by so much diminished. If we compare an imaginary flat sail AB with one shaped like a half-cylinder ADB, one would expect their effectiveness to be about the same, although the former is two-thirds the size of the latter. Put another way, if the sail ABD were flattened out as CDE, it would be one and a half times as effective as AB.

Modern sailing theory compares the sail to an airfoil, Bernouilli's Theorem demonstrating that air flow on the leeward, forward aspect of the sail, generates a negative pressure, which draws the canvas ahead, 'sucking' the ship forward, as it were. It is important to realise that this concept was quite unknown to the seamen of an earlier day.

Asked to explain how a vessel could work to windward, the more scientifically minded would have used the parallelogram of forces and the 'orange pip theory' to explain how the craft was able to do this. In fact, as recently as 1932, this interpretation is still found in the *Admiralty Manual of Seamanship* (II, 198) and whatever its theoretical shortcomings, it explained matters well enough for the practical sailor.

If we consider what happens to a curved sail, it will be found that conditions are not the same at all points on the canvas. If we consider the sail divided into three segments, AB, CB, and CD, it will be seen that they adopt a progressively more acute angle to the wind, as we move aft. The useful part of the wind pressure is that striking the segment at right angles, and it can be seen that the forward thrusting component is greatest in segment AB, and least in segment CD, while the heeling component is greatest in CD and least in AB. In sector CB, intermediate conditions are found. Thus it is the forward part of the sail that contributes most to forward drive, and the after part of the sail is contributing most to leeway. In fact, if the sheet is hauled too far aft, the after leech of the sail will be acting as a 'back sail' impeding, rather than assisting, the vessel's progress. Remember that a sail braced square contributes to headway or sternway, but exerts no turning effect. Turning moment is greatest when the sail is exactly in the fore and aft line, and contributing nothing to forward drive.

Strain on the weather brace. When sailing by the wind, the sail would try to fly fore and aft, if it were not confined by the braces. Looking at a photograph of a sailing ship, on a wind, one is tempted to imagine that the strain is the same on both braces, or possibly that the lee braces are doing most of the work. In fact the strain comes on the weather brace. Sailing close-hauled, the old rule in the French Navy was to brace sharp up, haul the bowlines, and then slack the lee braces (Murphy, 12). The CE of the sail seems to move forward into its weather half. Various explanations can be offered for this phenomenon. The modern sailor would probably explain it by saying that the weather leech was working in 'clean' air, and hence was more effective than the after part of the sail which was disturbed by eddies. Although the yard is pivoting round the centre of the masts, its centre point is well forward of the pivot, and the geometric centre of the sail further forward still, thus setting up a turning moment. An interesting sidelight is cast on this by an experiment carried out by that great innovator, Richard Hall Gower. My copy of his book on seamanship is dated 1808. I think it is worth quoting the extract in full:

> If the wind strike the sail obliquely, the centre of effort will be removed towards the weather leech. This is made evident to seamen, by the strain ever resting upon the weather brace of all square sail; but as it has been improperly accounted for, we shall state an experiment made in the current of the New River, with a view to elucidate the real cause.
>
> AB, Figure 6, represents the upper edge of a thin flat board, about three feet square, nicely swung, by its centre D, upon a pole, in the manner of a parlour fire-screen. The lower end of this pole was forced into the bottom of the river, so that it stood perpendicular. The board or plane, AB, was then immersed in the water, so as to preserve its top edge just below the surface; and at A and B were fastened lines, in the manner of braces to a sail, as represented by AC, BC, to place the plane at any angle with the fluid, which is supposed to be coming in the direction of the arrow. The board being thus circumstanced, it was observed that whenever the plane was given an oblique position to the fluid, the strain rested on the brace AC, which is doing an office similar to the weather brace of a sail. In searching for the cause of this, it was remarked that the fluid which struck the front of the plane followed the course of the dotted lines, while that part of the fluid which passed at the back, to fill up the vacuum took the course of the whole lines, leaving the vacuum more complete towards A than towards B. Consequently the plane was less supported up against the stream at the back towards A than towards B, it naturally would have a tendency to revolve round the pole, and stand immediately across the stream were it not prevented by the brace AC, which bears the preponderating pressure. Now we are of opinion, it may fairly be concluded that the fluid wind will equally take the course of the *dotted* and *whole lines*, and thus account for the strain ever resting on the *weather brace* of a square sail.

The further the pivot point of the yard moved ahead of the mast, the more marked the problem, and the greater the strain on the weather brace. This was why it was important to get the weather truss taut when bracing a lower yard up sharp. The pivot of a lower yard fitted with a 'modern' truss-yoke is always ahead of the mast.

TRIMMING THE SAILS

Bouguer's Theorem. The sail is most effective when the wind strikes it perpendicularly, and the best forward thrust occurs if the yard is square. It is therefore self-evident that, with the wind dead astern, the yard should be square. For other points of sail, however, a compromise position is necessary, bracing the sail in as much as possible, while at the same time allowing the wind to strike it at the most favourable angle; that is, as nearly perpendicular as possible. There must always have been some rough and ready ideas about the best angle to trim the sail, but, so far as I know, Bouguer was the first to attempt to analyse the problem mathematically (297). His book, of some 500 pages, was published in 1757, and attacks this and many other topics of nautical interest, such as stability, true and apparent wind, oscillatory movements, and so on. He concluded that the ship would go fastest when the tangent of the angle between wind and keel, was double that between sail and keel. *Le Manoeuvrier* by Bourdé de Villehuet, published in 1769, incorporates most of Bouguer's ideas, and includes a table (37) incorporating the double tangent idea. Both authors were aware that the principle could only apply when the wind remained forward of one point abaft the beam, or so. When the wind drew still further aft, the after sails blanketted the forward ones and the theoretical increase in speed did not occur. Steel (253) repeats verbatim the proof of Bouguer's Theorem, and reprints the table; Blunt in 1824 (52) reprints the table once more. Richard Hall Gower, (65), observing that the theorem applies over a rather narrow sector, suggests as a rule of thumb,

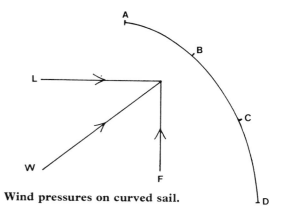

Wind pressures on curved sail.

Angles of the apparent direction of the wind and course.		Angles of the sails with the keel.		Angles of apparent incidence of the wind on the sails.	
D.	M.	D.	M.	D.	M.
180,	00	90,	00	90,	00
176,	15	87,	30	88,	45
174,	87	86,	25	88,	12
172,	30	85,	00	87,	30
168,	44	82,	30	86,	14
164,	58	80,	00	84,	58
161,	10	77,	30	83,	40
157,	22	75,	00	82,	20
153,	33	72,	30	81,	03
149,	41	70,	00	79,	41
145,	48	67,	30	78,	18
141,	53	65,	00	76,	53
137,	55	62,	30	75,	25
133,	54	60,	00	73,	54
129,	50	57,	30	72,	20
125,	42	55,	00	70,	42
121,	31	52,	30	66,	01
127,	14	50,	00	67,	14
112,	53	47,	30	65,	23
108,	26	45,	00	63,	26
. . . .					
103,	53	42,	30	61,	23
99,	13	40,	00	59,	13
94,	25	37,	30	56,	55
89,	28	35,	00	54,	28
84,	23	32,	30	51,	53
79,	05	30,	00	49,	06
73,	39	27,	30	46,	09
68,	00	25,	00	43,	00

Bouguer's table showing best trim of the yards in different wind directions.

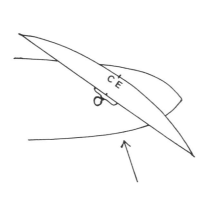

CE of a sail lying forward of the pivot point of the yard.

Gower's experiment conducted to find the relative strain on the weather and lee braces.

that the yards be braced so the angle between the wind and the yard is a point and three-quarters more than the angle between the yard and the ship's head. In fact, this does satisfy Bouguer's rule. Caussé (11) uses a variant of Gower's rule, proposing that the yards be braced in a quarter point, for every two points the wind veers aft. Murphy (12) applies Gower's rule when the wind is abeam. As is often the case following pioneer work, it was later found that a much simpler rule worked pretty well. That is to say, the yards were braced up as sharp as possible when close-hauled, and braced in square with the wind dead astern. In between, as at the extremes, the yard bisected the angle between wind and ship's head. I do not know exactly when Bouguer's Theorem ceased to be accepted gospel. It is quoted by Bonnefoux (65) as late as 1852, but all writers in the later years of the nineteenth century use the simpler rule, Mossel (III, 124) giving a geometric proof to validate it.

Why a square rigger can only sail six points from the wind. The traverse of the foreyard is limited in front by the forestay, and abaft by the lee shrouds. These prevent the yard being braced up any more sharply than three points from the keel line. If the sail is to fill, the wind must be three points further aft; this is because of the curvature of the sail. As the wind hauls ahead of six points from the bow, the weather leech starts to lift, then the weather half of the sail to flap, and finally the sail is 'all in the wind' when the wind is parallel to the yard. Some authors draw a distinction between a shivering sail being 'a little more full than aback' or 'a little more back than full'. When the wind comes from one point ahead of the yard, the sail is thrown back against mast and rigging. Since it cannot belly out aft, in the same way as it does forward, the sail is aback with the wind a mere point ahead, while three points are required to fill it. Six points was about the best that could be managed with a lower yard: slacking off the weather truss, catharping the lee shrouds extra taut, canting the weather yardarm down, and so on might help attain this point, but not exceed it. Many square riggers could not brace up as sharply as mentioned above, and therefore could get no closer to the wind than seven points. The fore braces in a man-of-war led almost horizontally to the knees of the mainmast, underneath the main top; in merchantmen, they led directly to the rail. In all vessels, the main braces led backwards and downwards, and when braced up sharp, this resulted in the lee main brace, which now had an almost

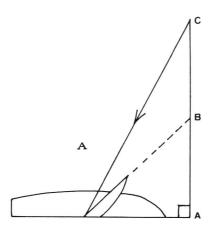

Trim of the sails: (**A**) shows the Double Tangent Rule, which states that the tangent of the angle between the wind and keel AC should be twice that between the yard and keel AB. (**B**) shows Gower's rule, and (**C**) shows the simpler modern practice.

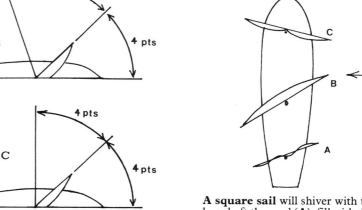
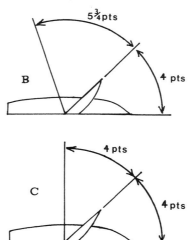
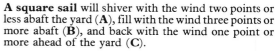

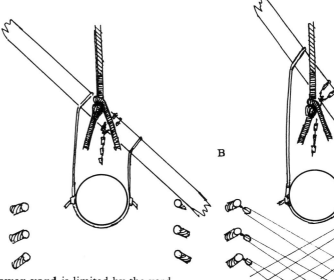

A square sail will shiver with the wind two points or less abaft the yard (**A**), fill with the wind three points or more abaft (**B**), and back with the wind one point or more ahead of the yard (**C**).

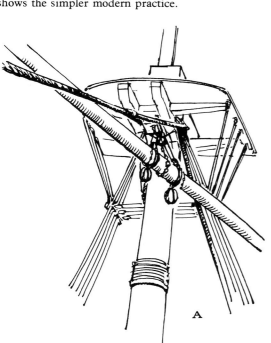

Traverse of the lower yard is limited by the yard coming up against the stay and forward shroud (**A**). It can be increased by slacking off the truss ropes, canting the weather yardarm down and hauling tighter the catharpins (**B**).

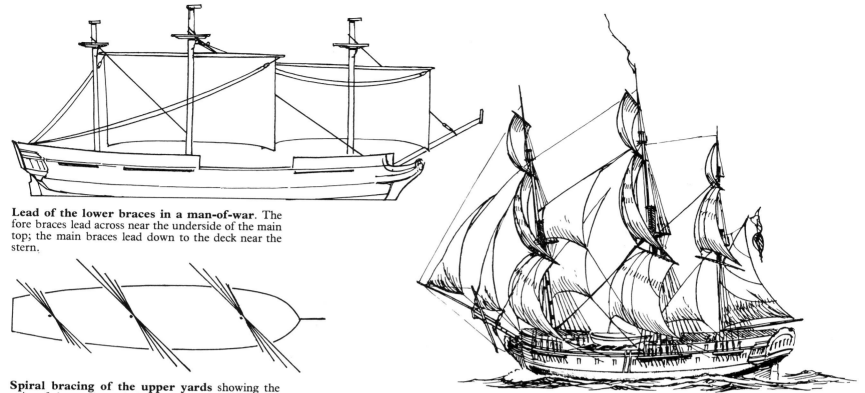

Lead of the lower braces in a man-of-war. The fore braces lead across near the underside of the main top; the main braces lead down to the deck near the stern.

Spiral bracing of the upper yards showing the twist of the yards, each being braced in half a point more than the next below.

Sketch showing appearance of a ship close-hauled, whose yards are braced in a spiral.

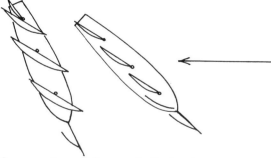

Square rig and fore and aft rig close-hauled. A square-rigged ship can sail to within six points from the wind, a fore and after to within four points.

vertical down lead, tending to cant the lee yardarm downwards. This, in turn, caused the yard to strike the foremost lee shroud at a lower, and hence wider point, and prevent its being braced up fully. The fore and aft sail, of course, filled when the wind was three points on one side. Since they would only start to provide forward drive when the sheet was eased, this meant the mean plane of the sail had to lie a minimum of one point from the keel line. A fore and aft schooner could, therefore, lie about four points from the wind.

Trim of the upper yards. Because of the lesser spread of topmast and topgallant rigging, it would have been mechanically possible to brace the upper yards more sharply than the lower. As a matter of fact, when close-hauled the upper yards were usually braced in, each yard a little more square as

one ascended. Thus the topsail yard was half a point in on the lower, the topgallant half a point more and the royal yet another half point, so that the yards adopted a sort of spiral configuration. This applied to the courses also. On a wind, the tack was forward of the weather yardarm, and the sheet a like amount aft; that is, the foot of the sail was trimmed sharper than the head. The practice of hauling the tack of a four-sided staysail, and the lower corner of a gaff topsail to windward, might be considered exceptions to this general rule. The upper yards were braced in for two reasons. The first was that they exerted the least heeling moment that way, and so were better placed to receive an unexpected gust of wind. The second intention was to adjust the yards so they all pushed together, in a co-ordinated effort rather than in varying directions. At first sight, spiral bracing would seem to defeat this very purpose, since the sails emphatically are not parallel to each other.

Nowadays, we explain matters by citing the dictum 'The wind is fairer aloft', to which we referred when considering true and apparent wind. If the wind draws aft, the yard should, in theory, be braced in, and as we ascend the wind does appear to veer, because it is stronger, so the yards are braced in progressively. Although from the time of Bouguer onwards, the educated officer was

quite cognisant of the difference between true and apparent wind, I do not think there was general recognition that the wind was faster, and therefore fairer, aloft, until the early 1900s. This is surprising in a way, since it was known from about 1800 onwards that the sails could – as distinct from should – be trimmed in a spiral. Secondly, constant observation of tell-tales and weather-vanes from the deck must have provided a clue to a thoughtful officer. Be that as it may, I have come across no references to the concept of apparent wind earlier than 1900 (Oderwald, 14). The ability of the upper sails to set properly closer to the wind was ascribed to their being smaller, with less curvature, and that the foot was better stretched since it sheeted to the yard below (Dick & Kretchmer, II, 174). Hansen (73) ascribes it to the upper sails being of lighter cloth and therefore filling more readily.

Exactly when it became general practice to trim the yards in the spiral fashion is difficult to say. Stibolt in 1800 (24) mentions bracing a reefed topsail yard in more than the lower yard. Steel and Gower do not mention the matter, although this was just the sort of point that would have delighted and intrigued Gower. The 1824 edition of Blunt does not allude to it, but this is not terribly surprising since it is, for the most part, a direct crib from Steel. However, Baudin

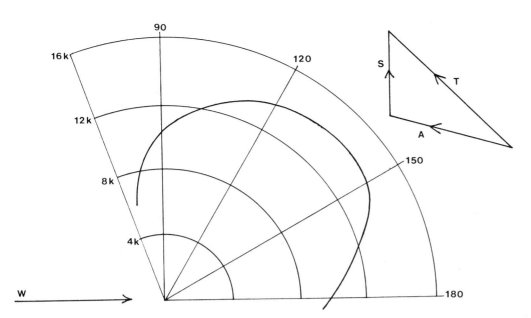

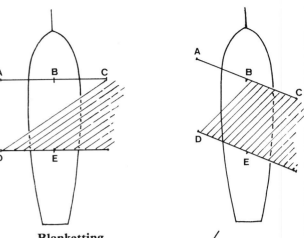

Polar diagram of performance of a representative sailing vessel. Best speed is made in a quartering wind. Note that when the true wind T at 30 knots is on the quarter and the ship's speed is 15 knots, the apparent wind A is two points abaft the beam.

Blanketting.

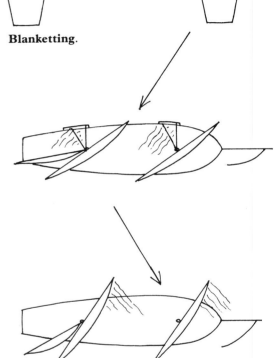

Disruptive effect on clear air flow of weather rigging and weather leech of the sail.

(235) in 1828 says unequivocally, 'In general, when it is blowing fresh, the yards of the upper sails always ought to be a little more braced in than the lower', but offers no further explanation. References from mid-century are plentiful. Totten in 1864 (187) recommends that the upper yards be braced in half a point more than the one below in a fresh breeze, but in a light breeze 'bracing in a very little'. Todd and Whall (69) seem to approve, as might be expected, the spiral trimming of the yards. However, they go on to say that 'although this is sea practice everywhere, scientific experiment seems to prove that, on a wind, the sharper a vessel's yards can be got, the better for both speed and weatherliness; and some very experienced shipmasters recommend getting the lower yards as sharp as possible, and trimming all the upper yards in line with them; of course, only in moderate weather'. They would have braced the upper yards in, with strong winds, as a matter of prudence rather than for better performance. So it was not, it seems, a universally accepted gospel. Massenet (354) trims the upper yards 'over', when actually by the wind, but keeps them braced in as the wind draws all the way aft to the quarter.

Blanketting. It might be supposed that the sailing ship would make her best speed when going directly downwind. Two factors prevent this occurring. The first is the difference between real and apparent wind as already discussed on p58–9. The second difficulty is the fact that as the wind draws aft, the aftersails becalm the fore. It is found, in practice, that the best speed is attained with the true wind anywhere from a point abaft the beam, to about on the quarter, as in the Polar Diagram which is based on the performance of a steel barque. The point at

which blanketting occurs depends, in theory, on the distance between the masts, and the lengths of the fore- and mainyards, or rather the lengths of the head of the courses, the direction of the wind, and the angle to which the yards are trimmed. The yards are furthest apart when they are square, and closest together when they are parallel to each other and braced sharp up. Hourigan (61) suggests using the rigging plan of the ship to estimate the point at which blanketting will start to occur. It would start with the wind about a point abaft the beam if the yards were braced up to any degree, and cannot be avoided, even with the yards square when the wind is parallel to DC (in the accompanying figure); that is on a line joining the weather earing of the mainsail to the lee earring of the foresail. This will turn out to be when the wind is somewhat ahead of the quarter. The rigging plan shows the yard in the 'impossible' fore and aft position, but the yardarms always overlap, and hence we may deduce that AB + DE will always exceed BE, the drift between the masts. The angle ACD will therefore likely be less than 45°, or four points. The angle can be calculated, since it will have the tangent $\frac{BE}{AB+DE}$ where BE is equal to the drift between the masts, AB and DE are half the length of the head of the fore and main courses, respectively.

If the yards are braced up at all, say to six points from the keel, there will be some blanketting of the fore by the main; but if the wind were on the quarter, this is precisely the point to which the bisection theory requires that the yards be trimmed! It can be seen that the lee part of the foresail will inevitably be in the 'wind shadow' of the main. This effect diminishes as the yards are braced in, and is abolished if the yards are square. Just as the

bracing angle is a compromise between the square position which gives maximal forward thrust, and the point where the sail is perpendicular to the wind, so the practical seaman must balance the advantage of trimming the individual sail to make best use of the wind, against the necessity of minimising blanketting.

Revision of the bisection theory. When the yard is braced up sharp, and bisecting the angle between wind and ship's head, the weather part of the sail is effectively a good point further 'in', because it curves forward. Furthermore, as bracing in commences, the wind starts to get cut up by the weather rigging, not striking the canvas cleanly, but

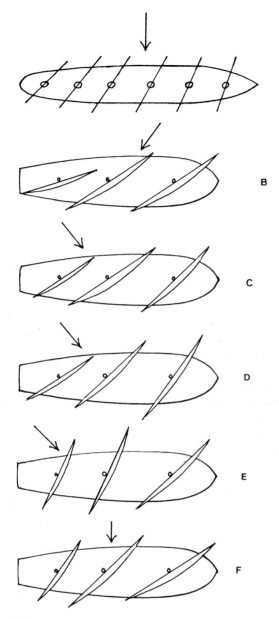

Different bracing of fore- and afteryards showing most advantageous bracing of yards A in *Dynaschiff*; **B** after Hutchinson; **C** after Mossel; **D** after Baudin; **E** after Shultz; **F** after Massenet.

rapidly as the wind draws aft over the next two point sector, so that the yards are square with the wind three points on the quarter. When the wind is three points abaft the beam, the theoretical angle for the yard is five and a half points from the ship's head. This means that the yard will swing two and a half points corresponding to a two point wind shift. Massenet (353) also agrees that the yards should be square before the wind is dead astern, but settles for two points on the quarter, as against Hourigan's three. Cradock (11) uses the following rule: before the beam halve the angle the wind makes with the keel, and brace the yard to that; abaft the beam, halve the same angle but 'round in half a point to allow for badly set sail'.

If the ship were in a seaway, the lee braces, particularly those on the upper yards, had to be left a little slack, to allow for the whipping movement of topmast and topgallant. If they were taut, and there was no 'play', the yard or topgallant mast might be sprung. Nares (261) advocates getting the lower yard in a little, when pitching in a head sea, to avoid damaging the stay, against which the yard would bear. If rolling in a swell, Ekelöf (10) recommends bracing sharper than otherwise. Others recommend the reverse. In the first case mitigation of rolling is the main consideration, whereas in the other case attention is directed towards the heeling moment of the upper sails. To avoid carrying too much weather helm, or to prevent the helmsman jamming the ship too close to the wind, the head yards might be trimmed noticeably sharper than the afteryards by some officers. Cradock (11) says that trimming is strictly a matter of 'judgment and practice'. Hourigan (60) is likewise emphatic that there are no hard and fast rules, recommending the young officer to heave the log before and after trimming sail, if he wants to form an idea of how the ship behaves in different circumstances. Repeated trials will eventually allow him to judge whether the yards are braced up too 'high' or braced in too 'fine'. Much will depend on the surrounding circumstances. The yards should be higher, if the ship is rolling, since this will help ease the motion. With the wind free, the yards can be 'finer' in a fresh than a light breeze. At night, or if the wind is flawy, it is better to be a little too high than too fine. If the yards are a little too high, it will not be any great matter, but if near the wind, and they are too fine, the sails might unexpectedly be thrown aback. Roughly speaking, it may be said that bracing up may be done a little early, but bracing in should be engaged in circumspectly.

Bracing fore and aft differently. In the ordinary way, fore and main were trimmed alike, the officer of the deck laying the main yard himself, and directing the officer in charge of the forecastle to 'lay the fore by the main'. However, this practice was not always followed. Some years ago, when visiting the Hamburg Institut für Schiffbau, Doctor Hans Theime showed me the wind-tunnel where tests had been run on a large model of a four-masted barque, and a model of the six-masted *Dynaschiff* designed by Herr Prölss. Dr Wagner, who ran these trials, found that the best performance resulted when the masts of the *Dynaschiff* were *gestaffelt*, that is to say 'stepped' or 'staggered', namely braced up more sharply in increments of five degrees, as one moved aft. Each mast was assumed to be working in progressively more disturbed, 'dirtier' air, and therefore braced up more sharply. Hutchinson (55) describes sailing on a wind with fore and main braced up to within three points of the keel. He found that the mizzen topsail had to be braced up to a point and a half, to set properly. Thus the foresails were drawing when closer to the wind than the mizzen, and he remarks in passing, that the deep narrow fore topsail of a collier would 'stand without a bowline' for that reason. Heathcote (43) also braces the mizzen half a point sharper than the main. Cradock (11) likewise advises bracing up sharper aft, because the aftersails are affected by the back draught of those forward. Mossel (III, 125) says that, with the wind abaft the beam, the aftersails 'steal the wind out of the forward ones' and so should be braced up more sharply. Murphy (13), Frick (II, 19) and Steel (254) follow Mossel. Baudin (272) says that, sailing large, the main should be a bit sharper than the fore and the mizzen sharper than the main. This agrees with Dr Wagner's finding that the 'staggering' of the inclination of the *Dynaschiff*'s masts was beneficial, even with the wind free. Interestingly enough, some of the old authorities say this is good practice on a wind, others when sailing large. Murphy (12), alone, suggests that it makes sense on most points of sail.

However, we have another equally eminent panel of authorities who subscribe to a different view. Shultz in 1794 says 'when one sails large, it often happens that the aftersails take the wind from the foresails, and the ship becomes ardent, because the influence of the foresails is lessened. So one does well to trim the aftersails somewhat broader, and the foresails are set somewhat sharper so as to receive more wind. This increases the speed and makes steering easier'. This gives some food for thought, and reminds us that the

eddying and whirling about. These two complications make it advisable to keep the yard braced up a little more than the theory suggests. However, once blanketing begins to occur, the yard should be braced in, squarer than the theoretical angle, to increase the distance between the yards, and minimise the becalming effect. The headsails are even closer to the foremast than the latter is to the main, another reason for early bracing in, since this will minimise the becalming effect of the foremast.

Practical trimming. Hourigan (61) suggests keeping the yards somewhat sharper than the theoretical angle until the wind is three points abaft the beam, and bracing in

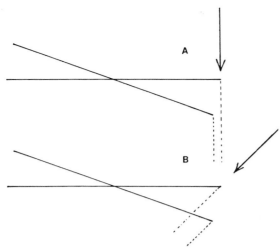

Wind shadow. The limit of wind shadow changes less as the yard is braced around when the wind strikes the yard at right angles (**A**), rather than obliquely (**B**).

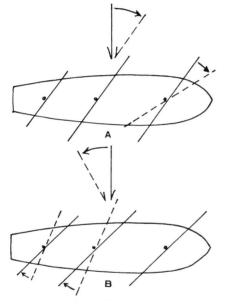

Sequence of bracing. When wind shifts ahead (**A**) the foreyard is braced up first. When wind shifts aft (**B**) the afteryards are the first to be braced in.

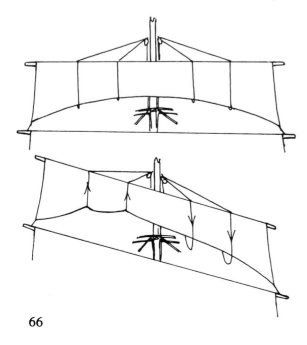

Tourniquet effect of modern topgallant buntlines makes weather buntlines shorten and lee ones lengthen when yard is braced up sharp.

wind-tunnel experiments were not taking into account the increasing ardency that might be expected for the reasons Schultz advances, with the wind well free. Bréart (177) also braces up more forward with the wind well free. Hourigan agrees with him, partly to avoid carrying weather helm, and also to throw the head off the wind, if the ship accidentally comes to, through poor steering. Massenet (353) also recommends keeping the fore a full point sharper with the wind abeam, and even as the wind draws aft, the main and mizzen are braced in more than the fore.

I am pretty sure that the seamen of the day were actually guided by a practical consideration of maintaining fore and after sail in balance, rather than by slavish acceptance of any hard and fast 'rule'. Remember that the more a sail is braced up, the greater its turning effect. Bracing up any aftersail causes the ship to become more ardent, while bracing up the forward sail relieves this. If the forward sail is blanketted, one result may be increased ardency, and bracing up the aftersail, may aggravate, rather than ameliorate this. Furthermore, when the wind is striking the sail almost perpendicularly, the angular change of the yard has to be very substantial before one might expect lessening of the 'wind-shadow'.

Sequence of bracing fore and aft. There was a universal rule that if the wind shifted forward, the forward yards were braced up first. If the wind drew aft, the after yards were braced in first. In other words, the forward sails were kept sharper during the transition, and would cause the head to fall off, if the wind should momentarily shift ahead unexpectedly.

GEOMETRIC PROBLEMS WITH THE RIGGING.

It is evident that hauling taut one item of rigging usually necessitated slacking off another, and *vice versa*. For instance, the topsails could not be sheeted home unless the clewlines were let go. If the tack of the course were let go, the weather yardarm, deprived of the downward pull of the weather leech would cant upwards, unless the lee lift were hauled taut, and so on. This implied that some gear always had to be worked as a unit; for instance weather lift, brace and truss, all

affected each other, and they could not be eased or hauled upon independently. Underhill (178) emphasises that the lead of the upper braces should be upward, rather than downward to their respective yardarms. If not, in letting go the halliards, the braces would 'hang' the yard and prevent it coming down. This was just a matter of good design, but some effects were a little more subtle, and we will take a look at one or two of them now.

Buntlines and bracing. The relatively shallow, wide uppersails of the windjammer are hauled up by four or five buntlines. These run through buntline blocks on the yard, up and in to leading blocks shackled to eyebolts, one on either side of the mast, before running to deck where they are belayed. When the yard is braced up, the distance between the leading block and buntline block increases on the weather side and decreases on the lee side. The geometry is such that if the sail were furled, and the buntlines up chock, swinging the yard would throw a strain on the weather buntlines. To obviate this, the buntlines were slacked off somewhat after furling. Alex Hurst, describes seeing a light royal yard buckled, when it was swung while tacking with buntlines bar taut (*Ships Monthly* 6, 1971, 430). This is not a problem with the sail set, at which time the buntlines have to be slack anyway. The worst that could happen would be a curling up of the foot of the sail where the buntline was hitched. The same sort of thing occurs with standing lifts. The result of bracing up an upper yard, which is hanging in the lifts is to cant the weather yardarm up (Regan and Johnson, 85). This sort of thing was not as big a problem in the man-of-war because the buntlines of the upper sails led much closer to the bunt, or slings, of the yard. Furthermore, in the case of topsails, they were confined to the yard with 'lizards', which allowed quite a bit of play. The leechlines and buntlines of the lower yard were the only items of gear that would require tending for the reason outlined above.

Rather similar considerations apply to the gear, when the lifts were used to cant the yard into a horizontal position, parallel to the horizon, sailing on a wind. The weather outer buntlines and leechlines had to be slacked off on the courses.

In the largest windjammers, the buntlines were of steel wire rope, about two-thirds the size of the corresponding manila gear (Middendorf, 383). To minimise the chafe and fretting of the buntline between the foot of the sail and the buntline block, it was customary to put a rope yarn seizing on the wire at the block. This could be broken by jerking

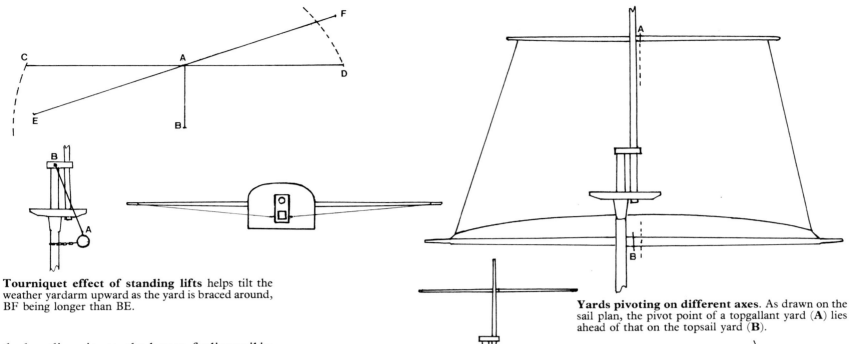

Tourniquet effect of standing lifts helps tilt the weather yardarm upward as the yard is braced around, BF being longer than BE.

Yards pivoting on different axes. As drawn on the sail plan, the pivot point of a topgallant yard (**A**) lies ahead of that on the topsail yard (**B**).

Pivot points of spritsail and spritsail topsail. A shows the arrangement of the yards in a ship with a spritsail topmast, as shown on a sail plan. The sail sets well only when the yards are squared, as even when the yards are arranged so that 'a b' equals 'c d' when braced up, there is serious distortion of the sail. The later style spritsail topsail set from the jibboom (**B**) made for much less distortion, even when the yards were braced perpendicular to the bowsprit.

the buntline vigorously, hence, furling sail in Åland ships was preceded by the order *bräck gårdinger*!, 'Start(break) buntlines!'. The result of repeated seizings, was a gradual accumulation of bits and pieces of ropeyarn at the block, which periodically had to be cut away (Newby, 66, 148, 154). Swedish *bräcka* like German *aufbrechen*, Dutch *inbreken*, and so on, when applied to sails, had the additional special technical meaning of 'flat in', that is, to haul the clew of a jib over to windward to push the ship's head to leeward.

Yards not pivoting on the same axis. By convention, a sail plan represents the yards braced up to the point where they lie in the fore and aft line. This does allow some conclusions to be drawn about the position of the CE, but if one looks at such a plan, it will be discovered that the shape of the upper sails is, in fact, distorted. The forward leech is steeper than the after one, and the distance from the forward head-cringle to after clew is greater than that between forward clew and after head-cringle.

This arises because the centre point of the topgallant yard, for instance, is forward of the centre of the topsail yard, which in turn is due to the topgallant mast being forward of the topmast. For mechanical reasons, the yards cannot actually assume this position, but the tendency is there nonetheless, when they are braced up sharp, and the resulting distortion is real enough. It would tend, in the extreme case, to induce wrinkles running from the forward upper to lower after corner of the sail. Canvas and boltropes are sufficiently forgiving that the effect, while interfering with a 'perfect' set of the sail, is not of overwhelming practical importance. It did milit-

ate against the smooth working of roller reefing gear, which worked best if the yards were square. To reef in storm conditions, however, it was often necessary to brace up and so spill the wind from the sail, which was exactly where this geometric distortion prevented the canvas rolling up evenly.

Spritsail topsail. The same difficulty, in an exaggerated form, applies to the spritsail topsail, whether in its early form, set on the spritsail topsail mast, or in its later form, set under the jibboom. If the braced up yards are to be horizontal, the topsail cannot set properly. In the case of the later spritsail topsail, the problem is solved if the spritsail and spritsail topsail yard are triced up, the lee yardarm, being uppermost, until they are at right angles to the bowsprit and jibboom. I do not believe, however, that it was the usual custom to trice the spritsail yards up to quite such a severe angle, and getting a good set

with the spritsail topsail must have been difficult. The early spritsail topsail had braces, pulling horizontally, and could not be triced up. This meant that it could set properly only with the wind more or less astern, and the spritsail yard square (*Mariner's Mirror*, 63, 1977, 172).

Solution of the problem. So far as I can determine, this difficulty was only addressed seriously by the German builders in the early 1900s (Middendorf, 289). The pivot point of the yard is usually, as one might expect, the centre of the mast. The lower yard, in the sailing man-of-war, was an exception, the pivot being 'moveable', since the chain trusses allowed some fore and aft movement. With both trusses hauled taut, as with the

1.

Armed brig off Liverpool, by Robert Salmon, 1811. The vessel is represented hove to, main topsail to the mast, and mizzen triced up. One can see how fore and after sail are balanced. (Courtesy N R Omell Gallery, London)

2.

East Indiamen of 1750, by Charles Brooking. The vessels are close-hauled on opposite tacks. (Courtesy N R Omell Gallery, London)

3.

Barque *Gorch Fock*. Notice the corkscrew bracing of the yards on the foremast. It was while serving as sailing officer on this vessel, that Cdr Dr Heinrich Walle FGN, made the experiments referred to in the text. (Photo courtesy G Warrener)

1.

2.

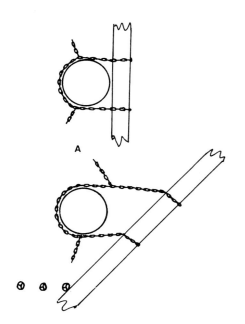

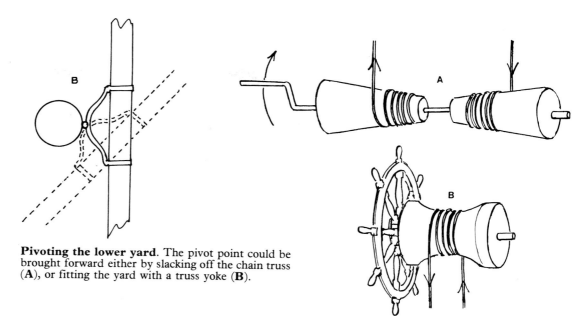

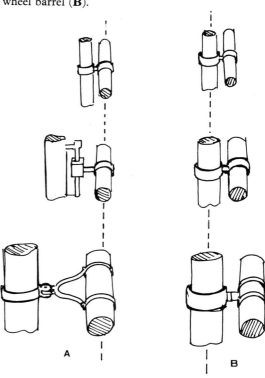

Pivoting the lower yard. The pivot point could be brought forward either by slacking off the chain truss (**A**), or fitting the yard with a truss yoke (**B**).

Unequal traverse of the yardarms called for the use of a brace winch with bi-conical drums (**A**). The same principle had earlier been employed to match the linear movement of the tiller ropes to the circular movement of the tiller end by use of bi-conical steering wheel barrel (**B**).

yard square, the pivot point moved aft. With the weather truss eased, and the yard braced up, the centre point moved forward. With the later form of truss yoke, used universally in merchant sail, the pivot was fixed at the knuckle-joint, just forward of the mast (Underhill, 39). One solution incorporated topsail yards sliding on a vertical steel jack-stay, welded to the fore side of the topmast, with the yards pivoting forward of the mast, in such a way that the turning radii of the three lowermost yards was about the same as that of the topgallant yards with their 'tub' parrels. The turning radius of the topsail yards was shorter, and in the braced up position, the centre of the yard was not so far aft as when tub parrels were used. Another plan used tub parrels for all yards, including the lower one, fitted on a 'pole' mast; that is to say, one built as a one-piece steel tube. The radii were arranged to diminish from below upwards in a steady progression (Midden-dorf, 289).

Unequal traverse of yardarms. Although never used in the sailing man-of-war, the Jarvis Brace Winch is a fitting of significance to anyone interested in sailing ships. Fine examples may be seen on board *Pommern* in the West Harbour at Mariehamn. When a lower yard, for instance, was swung, one brace was paid out and the other hauled in, but it is rather surprising to discover that the amount paid out and the amount hauled in are not equal, except when the yard is nearly square. In the sailing ship this phenomenon was, for the most part, irrelevant, since the braces were hauled separately, and it is doubtful if the average seaman was aware of it. When, however, the attempt was made to operate both braces at once with a winch, the problem became of immediate practical

interest. In this case the kinematic problem is to match the arciform motion of the yardarm to the motion of the winch barrel, which is effectively linear. If one studies the problem graphically, it becomes apparent that an approximate solution is offered by using a winch of bi-conical form, so that 'heave in' and 'pay out' are unequal, except in the middle position. As a matter of fact, exactly the same principle was used, many years earlier, in solving a similar problem with the steering wheel. One way of matching the linear motion of the rope on the steering wheel barrel to the circular motion of the tiller is to use a barrel with sides of bi-concave section. This means that the amount of rope coming off one side is greater than that winding on the other, except when the tiller is nearly amidships.

In any case, the chocks on the Jarvis winch could be set up by the mate, so that a fairly good match was obtained between the two yardarms. Furthermore, matters could be arranged to brace the topsail yards sharper by half a point, as one ascended. Since the cones provide an approximate, rather than a mathematically perfect solution, the residual inequality had to be taken up by a tackle. The three drums were 'nested', the cones on the centre barrel being reversed, to conserve space (*Mariner's Mirror* 58, 1972, 41).

WORKING OF THE RUDDER

Comparing the size of the rudder to the rest of the hull, it is at first sight surprising that so small a device is capable of controlling the movement of the ship. However, we must remember that water is 770 times denser than air, and that the rudder, at the extremity of

Bringing the lower, topsail and topgallant yards into line could be accomplished by the use of a truss yoke and topmast jackstay (**A**) or by use of tub parrels fitted on a pole mast (**B**).

the lever, exerts the greatest possible turning moment about the pivot point at the centre of the hull. In the sailing ship, or the side-wheel steamer, with concurrently acting paddles, the rudder is only effective when the ship has gathered headway or sternway. In the case of a single screw steamer, the situation is different: a 'kick' of the propeller can be

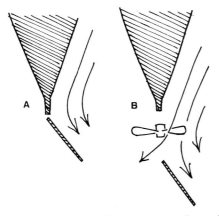

Effectiveness of the rudder was greater in a sailing ship (A) than in an auxiliary steamer with an aperture between the sternpost and rudder (B).

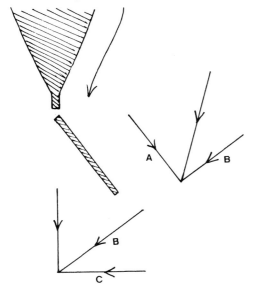

Forces acting on the rudder.

extremely effective in pushing the stern around, even when the ship is not moving ahead or astern. A ship at anchor likewise answers the rudder and sometimes can be so effectively sheered to a strong tide, that the cable comes to lie almost at right angles to the keel line. If the rudder is put over, the stream of water coming along the run, and across the deadwood, strikes the rudder and turns the ship's head in the direction the rudder is inclined. The turning effect is proportional to the square of the velocity of the water and the square of the sine of the angle with which it strikes the rudder blade. Following this line of thinking, Bouguer concluded that the rudder should be so constructed that it could be angled to 54° 44′ from the keel line. Although this figure is repeated by Falconer, Steel, Gower *et alia*, in fact, the practical limit of useful rudder angulation is about 35°. In part, this is because the water striking the upper part of the rudder curves around the lines of the run, and strikes the rudder at a

greater angle than the stream which comes along the keel. Furthermore, the inclined rudder acts like the 'flaps' on an aircraft wing, slowing the vessel down, and hence putting the rudder over beyond a certain angle, interferes with its own effectiveness, which is partly determined by the speed of the ship.

The water striking the rudder at an oblique angle, may be resolved into a component parallel to the rudder (A), and another striking it at right angles (B). This second component resolves into two elements, one of which (C) is at right angles to the fore and aft line, and is the element which actually exercises turning moment. The centre of gravity, or 'centre of lateral resistance' of the inclined rudder blade is indeed displaced to one side of the keel-line, but this contributes very little to the torque exerted, since the lever is so very short. At greater rudder angles, the water may be envisaged as 'piling up' along the deadwood, and thus applying turning moment before it reaches the actual rudder itself. This effect is lost in the auxiliary sailing vessel, since the stream can escape through the screw aperture. Mossel did not feel that this was a great disadvantage, but Hourigan and Nares considered that it interfered disastrously with the vessel's sailing qualities. Nares says that it is almost impossible to *wear* a steamer, unless it be *sailed* round, keeping the main full rather than shivering. A steamer is harder to tack, because the water coming through the screw aperture from leeward, as the stern swings around, interferes with the flow of water along the weather side of the deadwood and onto the rudder. Nares says that if the helm of a steamer is put over to tack, and then let go, it will remain stationary, indicating that it is not doing much good. In the ordinary way, a steamer requires more weather helm because of this escape of water through the screw aperture (Nares, 238).

The rudder's effect was so powerful that it could overwhelm a contrary action due to sail imbalance. Thus a sail could be kept set, its pulling power keeping up the speed, and hence rudder effectiveness, even when its theoretical effect would be contrary. For example, a jib, in the early stage of tacking, should prevent the bow coming up into the wind, but since it increases the speed, it makes the rudder that much more useful (Knight, 397). Nonetheless, it was best if there was a spoke or two of weather helm on. If the helmsman was engaged in a constant struggle to keep the ship off the wind, it meant that the officer of the deck should be looking to the trim of his sails.

Effect of the rudder going astern. If the ship has sternway, putting the rudder to port,

turns the stern to port, while putting the rudder to starboard has the opposite effect. At least, that is what tends to happen in a steamer with a plate rudder, if one discounts the sideward kick of the screw. In the old wooden sailing vessels, the rudder was almost half as thick as it was broad, and the water striking the after surface of the rudder, therefore acted in a precisely contrary manner to the stream striking the face. Furthermore, in going astern, the effect of water gathering between deadwood and rudder was absent. In fact, the dominant element governing the turning movement of a sailing ship making a sternboard, was the fact that the water piling up under the lee quarter tended to throw the stern up into the wind; that is to say, the bow fell off. Even if the foreyards were shivered and the mizzen set and sheeted home, the bow would still fall off. The same thing tends to be true in steamers also, overwhelming other factors like rudder angle or the direc-

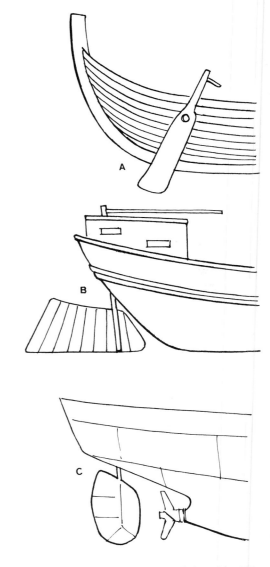

Balanced rudders as seen on a Viking ship (A), a Chinese junk (B), and a modern whalecatcher (C).

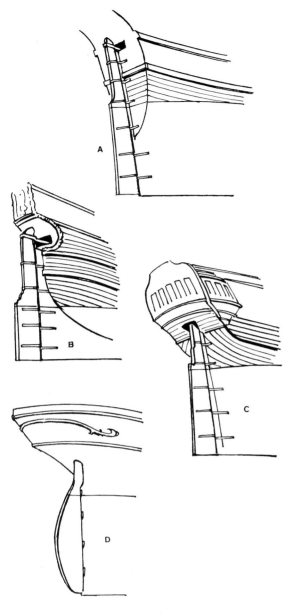

Rudders and tiller apertures as shown in the simple rudder of an Elizabethan ship (**A**), the 'barn door' rudder of a Dutch flute (**B**), the 'rule joint' rudder of a frigate (**C**), and 'plug stock' rudder of a nineteenth century clipper ship.

tion of screw rotation. As a matter of fact, bow rudders do not work very well going ahead. Ships so fitted – for instance the Belfast-Glasgow steamers — used them primarily to manoeuvre when going astern up the channel for a considerable distance. Going astern threw a tremendous strain on the rudder fastenings, the pintles and gudgeons, securing it to the stern post. The wheel had to be carefully watched as stern-way gathered, since if unattended, the wheel would fly hard over. I once had a sharp lesson on this subject, whilst swinging compasses in Table Bay. Going astern rather briskly, I re-ceived a savage crack on the knuckles from the spokes of the steering wheel, and worse still, hopelessly jammed the rod and chain steering gear, with the rudder in the hard over position. It required a couple of hours to repair the consequences of my momentary inattentiveness. 'Twiddling lines' were beckets slipped over the spokes to prevent the wheel 'taking charge' during a sternboard.

Simple and balanced rudders. The hinged rudder, used throughout the sailing man-of-war era, was self-centering. That is to say, left to itself, it would swing into the fore and aft line. The number of turns of rope on the wheel barrel was usually five, or seven in big ships (*Mariner's Mirror* 59, 1972, 41). Accordingly, hard over port to hard over starboard was five or seven turns respect-ively. Sometimes as little as a spoke or two, sometimes as much as a quarter or half turn of weather helm was carried. This required a certain effort on the part of the helmsman, and put a strain on the weather tiller rope. If the task was arduous, the ship was said to 'lie heavy on her helm'. The pivot of a 'balanced' rudder is not at its forward edge, but about a third of the way aft. It is not self-centering, but if left to itself, will adopt one of two more or less stable positions about twenty degrees either side of the midline. It is easier to turn than a hinged rudder of equal size. Gower's experiment with the pivoted board is, in fact, a manifestation of this phenomenon. Despite

the fact that balanced rudders were in use in China for centuries, and that the Vikings used a balanced side rudder of extremely sophisticated design, the hinged rudder was universally used in sailing men-of-war (*Nautical Research Journal*, 1972, 81).

The rudder stock was completely outside the hull in Elizabethan ships. The tiller-port had to be sufficiently wide to allow the tiller to swing from side to side. A very similar arrangement persisted into the 1800s in small ships. Later on, the stock pierced the counter, and a triangular opening, wider aft, was needed to accommodate the movements of the stock. Subsequently the 'plug-stock' rudder was favoured; this allowed the use of a small round hole, the axis of the stock coin-ciding with that of the rudder. With the earlier methods, the opening needed to be made water-tight by nailing a canvas weather-cloth between the edges of the open-ing and the tiller or rudderhead.

Shape of the rudder. This was influenced by the lines of the run. The traditional rudder was broadest as its lowest point, since this was where the water escaping under the re-latively heavy buttocks struck it at the most advantageous angle. In the clippers, the run was much finer and the most effective part of the blade was higher. Designers therefore took to rounding off the heel, accounting for the difference in shape of rudder, of say, *Cutty Sark* and that of *Victory* (Murphy, *Stowage*, 6).

Raking of the sternpost and rudder. Chapelle, (*Navy*, 423) refers to the 'theore-tical advantage of a raking sternpost on steer-ing qualities' but does not elaborate on this. So far as torque goes, the rudder is most ef-fective when its axis is vertical. When a vessel heels, the water strikes the rudder blade obliquely, and hence less effectively. Part of the energy of the inclined rudder is now being expended in raising the stern if the helm is a-weather, and depressing it, if the helm is a-lee. A heeling vessel requires weather helm, and it is important that the ability to apply this be retained. If the helm is put a-weather, when the vessel is heeled over, a vertically placed rudder tends to lift the stern out of the water, giving the rudder a poorer 'grip' on the water, and preventing the bow falling off. If the sternpost is raked, as in a Scottish zulu, the application of marked helm, whether lee or weather, acts to pull the stern more deeply into the water (Krogh, 17; Ekelöf, 32). It was very common for eighteenth century vessels to be built with considerable rake to the sternpost, but I am not certain just how effectively this improved their performance when heeled to the wind.

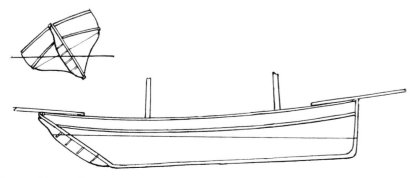

Raking rudder and sternpost as shown in a Scottish Zulu.

CHAPTER 5
SAILS CONSIDERED INDIVIDUALLY

THE COURSES

These originally were the core of the sail plan, the canvas first set, last taken in. In the seventeenth century, their area could be increased by lacing, or 'latching', a bonnet to the foot of the sail. This arrangement was subsequently replaced by larger courses fitted for reefing, from which a corresponding area could be subtracted. Until the late 1600s, the lower yards were raised and lowered much oftener than was the case later on. Subsequently, they were more or less permanently slung aloft, and struck only when riding at anchor, in the very roughest weather. The yard was then said to be carried 'a-portlast' or 'a-portoise'.

Foresail. The fore course was set on all points of sail, and was the only square sail which lifted rather than depressed the bow. This attribute was so esteemed that the reefed fore course would even be set as a storm sail. When braced up, whether full or aback, it threw the bow off the wind, and hence was a key sail in all manoeuvres. In bad weather, it was particularly useful in wearing, partly because of its 'lifting' effect. It would be taken in during a calm, to avoid its slatting about, and in extremely severe weather when scudding, or lying to, under bare poles; but in fact, although it was fairly readily furled, it remained set for the greater part of the time.

Mainsail. This was the largest sail in the ship. Its driving power was most evident when close-hauled, or with the wind abeam. With the wind on the quarter, the weather clew was 'docked up', and if the wind drew even further aft it was hauled up completely, to avoid blanketing the fore course, which was the more useful of the two sails. The mainsail had some particular drawbacks; for instance, Mossel (III, 136) says that some ships simply could not go about with the mainsail set, since it prevented their coming to. An old Dutch term for the main course was *schooverzeil* (Winschooten, 236), which is a worn down form of *schoon-weer-zeil*, literally 'fair weather sail', indicating how it was regarded in the early days.

In a squall, or with the wind chopping about, it was a dangerous matter if the mainsail were thrown aback. Once it was plastered against mast and rigging, it became almost impossible to haul it up with the clewgarnets and buntlines. Since it was part of the aftersail, it would prevent the ship falling off, the very manoeuvre that would have allowed it to fill once more. When aback, it acted to force the ship astern, at the least severely straining the rudder fastenings, at worst tearing the rudder loose, or 'sailing the ship under'. This is the reason why 'mainsail aback' was one of the great bugbears of the eighteenth century sailor. The fore course, in similar circumstances, caused the ship to fall off, and the sail could fill once more, and if necessary, then be taken in.

In men-of-war, the fore braces led almost horizontally to leading blocks underneath the main top. The main braces, on the other hand, led down to the ship's side. This meant that the lee brace had a very unfavourable down lead, when braced up sharp. To com-

Fore and main course
a brace; b counter brace; c sheet; d tack; e clewline; f bowline; g buntline; h leechline.

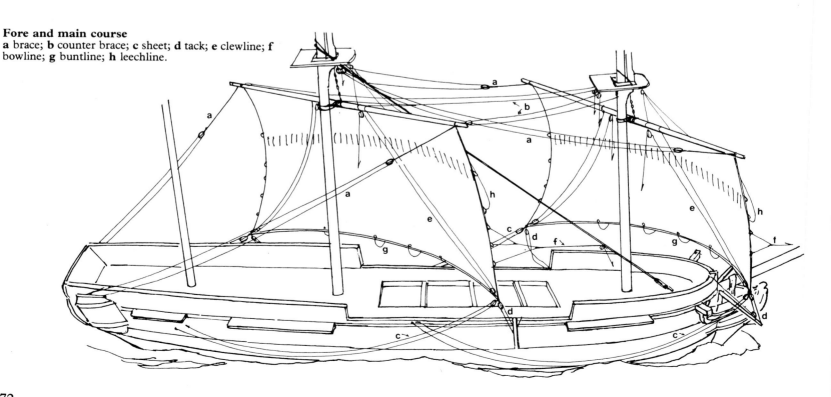

Early practice with courses
A Used as storm canvas, ship working to windward (after C Brooking); **B** riding out a gale a-portlast, with yards lowered (after Van de Velde the Younger).

Foresail used as a lifting sail when running in heavy weather.

pensate for this, and also to assist in swinging the heavy mainyard in tacking, men-of-war were also fitted with counter-braces on the mainyard, leading forward, just under the foretop. There were thus two braces on the fore leading aft, and four on the main, two leading aft and down, and two leading horizontally forward.

Lead of the tacks. The tack was originally a heavy rope, with a wall knot worked in its end to prevent it slipping out of the clew cringle. In the late 1800s, and no doubt earlier, it was tapered, so that the thickest part of the rope was found at the chesstree, or bumpkin (Alston, 63).

Some sort of tack bumpkin for the foresail, called a 'luff', or 'loof', is listed in inventories from the thirteenth to the sixteenth century (Sandahl II, 53). This probably was simply a spar shoved out over the bow, although the word is sometimes used for the rope item we would call the 'tack'. Dutch vessels of the 1600s are shown in contemporary paintings, when by the wind, thrusting a long spar, with a knob on the end, out through the rails of the beakhead, to give the fore tack a better lead. Winshooten (334) calls this an *uitlegger*, 'out lier', hence English 'outlicker', which had the rather similar technical meaning of the outrigger which carried the sheet of the bonaventure. A three-metre long pole of this sort, armed with spikes, was used as a defensive measure in land warfare, and called a *Spaansche ruiter*, or *Friesche ruiter*, 'Spanish' or 'Friesian cavalryman'. The first gave rise to the name the Dutch applied to the dolphin striker, which projected out in a similar manner to the *uitlegger*, and the second is the origin of English and French *cheveaux-de-frise*.

In Mainwaring's day, the fore tack was

taken to the 'comb', a piece of wood with two holes pierced in it, bolted to the beakhead. In the 1700s, the cutwater projected further forward, and the tack led through holes bored in its forward edge. Yet another variation, around 1690, was to use a 'dead block' fitted between the rails of the head (Anderson, 161). None of these methods incorporated blocks or sheaves, the holes being simple fairleads, no doubt leathered and slushed to ease the dead nip, to which the tack was subjected, when in use.

About 1710 or so, English ships began to fit 'tack bumpkins', and these remained in use until the later 1800s. They were sturdy timbers, often exhibiting a slight downward curve, which projected out over the headrail of the beakhead, at an angle of forty-five degrees from the centreline. French ships of the Napoleonic era carried the tack bumpkin at a sharper angle to the midline than their English contemporaries, the intention being to make them more weatherly. When taken into the English service, captured vessels had their bumpkins altered, because it was felt they then tacked more readily than before, the foresail taking aback quicker than when rigged in the French fashion (Griffiths, 180).

Because of the tremendous upward pull of the tack, hold-downs were often fitted, and in some countries, 'shrouds' were also rigged, to

Mainsail
A With weather clew hauled up in quartering wind; **B** mainsail aback.

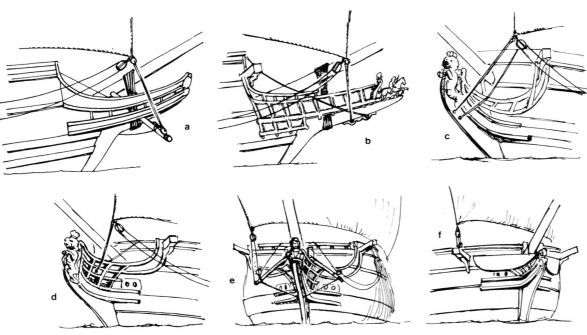

Lead of the fore tack
a to outlicker *c*1600; **b** to comb, *c*1630; **c** to cutwater, *c*1660; **d** to dead block, *c*1710; **e** to bumpkin, *c*1800; **f** to cathead, *c*1860.

give fore and aft support. An associated saw-tooth fitting on the headrail, looks as if its purpose was to allow some adjustment of the position of the bumpkin, but I am pretty certain that it was purely decorative. Bumpkins dropped out of use in the late 1800s, the tack being got down to the cathead, or some other suitable point. The change was related to the concomitant shift of the foremast further aft, relative to the hull. Tacks rove double (that is to say leading through a block at the clew) only came into use late in the 1700s (Lees, 159). Before that time, a tackle was used to get the tack down, hence the term 'luff tackle', still in use today.

French had three terms for 'tack', *amure*, *lof*, and *orse*, the last being primarily used in the Mediterranean, and, like English 'luff', being closely associated with the idea, 'windward side', 'going to windward'. French *porte-lof*, 'tack bumpkin', gives English 'port-luff', and German *Butluf*, and so, in a very corrupted form, survived in the terms 'portlast' and 'a-portice' (Sandahl, II, 86). The main tack was got down to the 'chess-tree', a word related to Old French *chas*, 'the eye of a needle', and hence originally referred to a timber with a hole bored in it.

The fore sheets led aft, almost to the mainmast, while the main sheets were taken to a point under, or just abaft, the mizzen channels; in other words, comparing the points to which tacks and sheets were taken, the former were a shorter distance forward of their respective masts, than the latter were abaft it. This difference in geometry is reflected in the fact that the tacks were 'got down', and 'let rise', while the sheets were 'hauled aft' and 'veered', or 'eased off', the motion in the first case being vertical, and in the second horizontal. Other languages draw a similar distinction, Dutch using *toezetten*, 'set to', and *opsteken*, 'stick up', of the tacks, and *aanhalen*, 'haul in' and *vieren*, 'veer', of the sheets. In French, we have *amurer* and *lever* of the tacks, *border* and *filer* of the sheets. *Amurer* derives from *amure*, the word for 'tack', while *lever* parallels 'let rise', in this particular technical sense. *Border*, literally means 'to board', and is interesting because 'board' is used of the tacks, but never the sheets, in English. There are several synonyms: the tack may be 'got, brought, or hauled (close) aboard', or simply 'boarded'; in Danish, it is 'ridden under'.

Mainwaring (224) says 'When the ship will not fall off from the wind, they flat in the fore sheet, that is pull the sail in flat, as near the the ship's sides as may be.' By the 1900s, this had changed its meaning, although the intention of the order was not dissimilar. 'Flatten in the headsheets! does not mean haul them aft. It means haul them to windward' (Nicholls, 254d).

Alternating tack and sheet. Close-hauled, the course was controlled by the weather tack and lee sheet, the weather sheet and lee tack lying idle. On this point of sail, the weather clew was substantially forward of, and lee clew well abaft, their respective yardarms. The footrope of the sail swept up and back from the tack to the lee clew, in a curve, the boltrope just touching the foremost shroud on the lee side. This meant that the foot of the sail was 'sharper' than the head, and this difference parallels the 'twist' of the upper yards.

By the wind, the sail was said to be 'shrouded', but in the case of the foresail, this could be overdone. 'The lee sheets are hauled close aft, but the lee sheets of the foresail not so much, unless the ship gripe' (Mainwaring, 241). On the same theme, Griffiths (204) says 'However long practice and established custom may sanction shrouding the foresail, there cannot be a doubt but that it is wrong. It is not only unnecessary, in as much as the sail stands well without, but injurious because the eddy wind from the lee leech affects the luff of the mainsail, and also, if hauled more aft than is requisite to make it draw the most, it becomes a badly trimmed sail, and impedes, rather than impels'. The dinghy sailor causes exactly the same condition, by hauling the jib sheet too far aft, and 'back-winding' the mainsail. Shrouding the mainsail was not attended with the same evil consequences, partly because until late in the 1800s, no sail was set on the crossjack yard, and secondly, because the chesstree was much further removed from the centreline, than the end of the bumpkin.

The idle weather sheet and lee tack, would have hung in a long bight, dragging in the water, unless steps were taken to prevent this. 'Tricing lines', or 'beckets' served to hold them up. The slack was secured with a thimble in a lanyard, similar to the tricing line of the spritsail sheet, or secured to a shroud with a knot and eye becket, or just dropped over a cleat seized on the shroud for this purpose. The order to secure the non-functioning items was 'Tacks and sheets in beckets!' (Smyth, 92).

The anchor stocks projected up in such a way that they were likely to foul or chafe the sail and its gear. To prevent this, the hoops were covered with wooden battens, and 'timmynockys', or 'timenoguys', rigged to hinder the tack and sheet slipping down behind the anchor stock.

Before the wind, the mainsail was not set, while the clews of the foresail were controlled by the sheets, the tacks lying idle. 'To sail betwixt two sheets' exactly translates the equivalent French expression *aller entre deux écoutes*, while in Dutch, it was *tusschen twee halsen zeilen*, or *met open halsen zeilen*, 'to sail between', or 'with open tacks'. The foot of the sail curved up and forward, so that the sail acted to raise the bow, as well as drive the vessel forward. With a commanding wind, the clews were by this means pulled towards the sides of the ship, but if the wind were light,

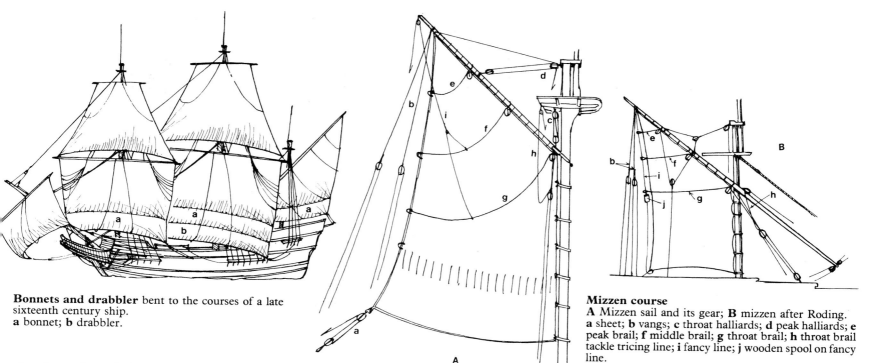

Bonnets and drabbler bent to the courses of a late sixteenth century ship.
a bonnet; b drabbler.

Mizzen course
A Mizzen sail and its gear; B mizzen after Roding.
a sheet; b vangs; c throat halliards; d peak halliards; e peak brail; f middle brail; g throat brail; h throat brail tackle tricing line; i fancy line; j wooden spool on fancy line.

they hung down below the yardarms, well beyond the channels. In this circumstance, the lower stunsails would be set, and the clews could then be 'passareed', hauled out to blocks on the lower booms. With the wind a couple of points free, the clews were just below their respective yardarms, controlled equally by the tack and sheet.

Supplementary tacks and sheets. The arrangement that the tea-clipper sailors called a 'passaree', was called a *Bullentau*, 'bull rope', in German, *fausse amure*, 'false tack', in French. I am unsure of the origin of the word, but in its original form, it has a decidedly Spanish flavour. 'Passarado is a rope wherewith we haul down the sheet block of the main- and foresails, when they are hauled aft, the clew of the mainsail to the cubbridge head of the mainmast, and the clew of the foresail to the cathead, and this is done when the ship goes large' (Mainwaring, 196). Underhill (19) indicates that in the 1900s, it was usual to unshackle the idle tack and sheet, and use a 'lazy tack', or 'tail rope', to secure the clew, while they were being re-attached. 'Preventer tacks' and 'preventer sheets' (*fausses amures* and *fausses ecoutes* in French) were rigged in bad weather and in preparation for going into action. Mainwaring (182) describes a 'loof-hook' as a tackle 'the use whereof is to succour the tack in a great gale, that all the force and stress shall not bear upon the tack, and it is used when we would seize the tack surer, or the like': in other words, it is a combination of 'luff tackle', 'lazy tack', and 'preventer'. The expression 'loof-hook' died out in the 1700s (Sandahl II, 63).

Bonnet and drabbler. The early courses were proportionately quite small sails. Since the technique of reefing square sails had not developed in the late 1500s, the expedient was adopted of adding on canvas to the course, when the wind was light, and removing these supplementary sections, as the wind freshened. The course proper thus corresponded to the reefed course of a ship of 1700. The sail area could be increased by about twenty-five per cent in this way, and all three courses were so fitted.

Tack and sheet were secured to the lower corners of the bonnet, and with both in place, the yard had to be hoisted as high as possible. With the bonnets off, the yard could be lower, and in fact, would set better if so disposed, because the tack could then be got down and the sheet hauled aft. The disadvantage was that the yard now was abreast a broader part of the lower shrouds, and so could not be braced up quite so sharply.

In fact, it was customary to fit two bonnets, one below the other, the first making the sail equivalent to a single reefed course of later days, and with the second bonnet, one had the equivalent of a course with both reefs shaken out.

The first bonnet was called a 'storm bonnet' in most other languages. In English, the second bonnet was called a 'drabbler', based on the idea that it 'drabbled' or 'draggled' on the deck. In Dutch and German, it was called variously *fats, Fatz, Fots*. Bonnet and drabbler were fitted with a series of loops on their upper boltrope, which were passed through

corresponding holes in the foot of the course, and looped successively through each other on the after side of the sail. This arrangement allowed the bonnets to be 'unlatched' very quickly, by letting go the first loop at the appropriate end.

The mizzen course. This sail was the balancing or steering sail, at the after end of the ship, and during three centuries, its appearance changed much more than was the case with the fore and main courses. By 1730, in the largest ships, the proportions of the yard had reached a point where shifting it to the other side of the mast in going about, must have been a problem. In any event, from that time, the yard was kept on the starboard side, and the part of the sail forward of the mast was dispensed with, the forward leech of the attenuated mizzen now being laced to the mast. This innovation spread to smaller ships, and was almost universal in 1750 (Lees, 159). The mizzen staysail was the analogue of the vanished part of the sail. Lees does not give a date for the introduction of this sail, but one would expect it to have followed the change in the mizzen. The mizzen topmast staysail dates from 1709 (Lees, 159).

The yard was retained for a surprisingly long period, even though the part forward of the mast no longer spread any canvas, and so would not appear to have had any useful purpose. This may have been done, in part, because the forward half acted as a counterweight, and also because it was available as a replacement for the foreyard if the latter were damaged (Anderson, 167). Reading Bourdé

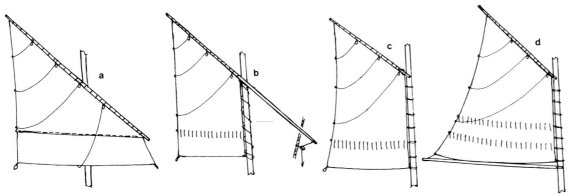

Evolution of the mizzen
a c1600; b c1750; c c1780; d c1800.

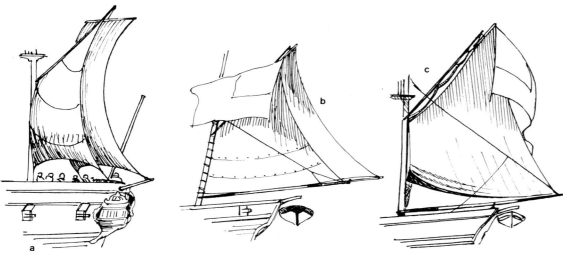

Driver and spanker
a 'square' driver sheeted to outrigger (after N Pocock); b driver set fore and aft (after M F Cornè); c driver or spanker set in place of the mizzen, which is furled. Note the short driver yard (after M F Cornè).

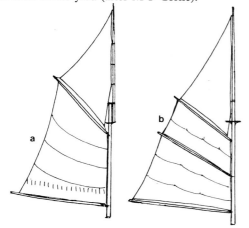

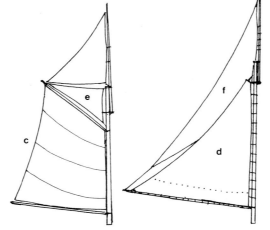

Later development of the spanker
a barque's spanker; b German split spanker; c French split gaff topsails; d Pacific Coast leg-of-mutton spanker; e misère; f ringtail.

de Villehuet (87, 91), suggests that it was at one time the practice, in tacking, to jack the peak of the mizzen out to windward. This was done to get the maximum torque out of the mizzen, although only at the expense of making a back sail out of it. This manoeuvre could readily be managed by hauling the lee mizzen bowlines, but would have been impossible had one depended on hauling the peak of a gaff to windward, with the weather vang (*Mariner's Mirror* 63, 1977, 97).

Ultimately, the clumsy yard was replaced by the much handier gaff, about one half the length, and of smaller circumference than the yard. The peak of the gaff was secured by 'vangs' when the sail was furled. These had not been necessary as long as the forward part of the yard was retained, since the mizzen bowlines fulfilled this function. When the sail was set, the vangs were eased off completely.

The driver. The mizzen could be augmented by a sort of studdingsail called the 'driver', which the Dutch called the *broodwinner*, 'bread-winner'. The head was extended by a short yard, which was run up to the peak, and so effectively extended the gaff. The foot was sheeted out to a boom lashed athwartships to the taffrail. A bowline was sometimes fitted, to give a better set, and judging by the French sources, this sail was sometimes set on its own, with the wind aft, and the mizzen taken in. The boom would then have been thrust out on the lee quarter.

A further refinement was the development of a large sail, comparable to mizzen and driver together, and a swinging boom secured to the mast, to which its clew was extended. This sail was called the 'driver' or 'spanker' and could be set in place of the mizzen in moderate weather. The sail was not laced to the boom, as in a schooner, but set loose footed. The tack could be triced up towards the jaws of the gaff, and this was done when close-hauled, as a means of balancing the sail plan, and easing weather helm. The trim of the sail was controlled by the tackle hooked to the boom, and now designated the 'sheet', while the clew was secured to the boom end, with the 'clew outhaul'.

The introduction of the spanker did not please everyone, as for instance William Nichelson (209), who describes it as 'the most extraordinary, inconvenient, inconsistent, disproportioned, and useless sail that ever was invented by men of sense or reason'. Basically, he objected to the great size of the sail, which made it hard to handle, and necessitated excessive weather helm, in a fresh breeze. He felt that the old-fashioned driver, being a square sail, could be trimmed more effectively with the wind aft, and hence, 'did not lay so much stress on the helm'.

Further evolution after 1900. Although we have outlined the development as it applied to the sailing man-of-war, it is not quite the end of the story, as far as merchant sail was concerned. Although a fore and aft mizzen topsail would have been virtually useless in a ship-rigged vessel, it was very practical in a barque. A number of further changes are apparent, if one looks at merchant sail after 1900. The large German barques split the mizzen, having two gaffs, parallel to each other, into two smaller sails, the lower of which corresponds in area to a reefed mizzen. The French barques of A D Bordes Company liked to split the mizzen topsail horizontally. The lower part, a small sail called the *misère*, was practically always kept set (Randier, 172). Peter Hodges, amongst others, has wondered about the exact usefulness of this little scrap of canvas (*Model Shipwright* 24, 1978, 47). The arrangement did, it is true, eliminate the necessity of shifting the tack to windward, to give a better set to the gaff topsail, upon going about onto a new tack. Henri Picard tells me that the 'handkerchief' of canvas was left aloft, simply because it was too much trouble to stow.

In the Pacific North-West, a 'leg-of-mutton' or 'jib-headed mizzen' was favoured, since this was less complicated and easier to handle than the traditional trapezoidal sail. Above and behind this could be set, from the gaff, a triangular sail, its lower corner sheeted to the boom. Yet another variation, where there was no gaff was the 'ring-tail' topsail. The name 'ring-tail' had been applied, a century earlier to the supplementary driver, the spar extending its foot being the 'ring-tail boom'. An additional extempore sail set on the flag-staff, also went by this name.

Changing the mizzen. Mainwaring in 1625 (187), uses this expression to describe shifting the mizzen to the lee side when going about. The sail was 'spilled' by peaking the yard vertically up and down, and dipping the forward end around the foot of the mast, exactly as in handling the dipping lug of a service boat under sail. To allow of this being done, the parrel was kept quite slack (*Treatise on Rigging*, 59). It must have involved gathering the upper part of the sail in its brails, letting go the tack and mizzen bowlines, and slacking the sheet, then setting everything up anew on the old tack. The mizzen bowlines at this time, according to the *Treatise*, were very simple: a strop, or collar, that could be slipped off the end of the yard would have been a handy arrangement. An interesting feature in this context, is the so-called 'mizzen lift' with its crow's-feet running to the upper end of the yard, and the fall going forward to the main topmast until about 1625, and to the mizzen topmast thereafter. The first lead would have allowed the yard to be hauled right up to the mizzen topmast, whereas the second would not have permitted this (Anderson, 236).

As ships grew larger, this procedure became more and more cumbersome, and was

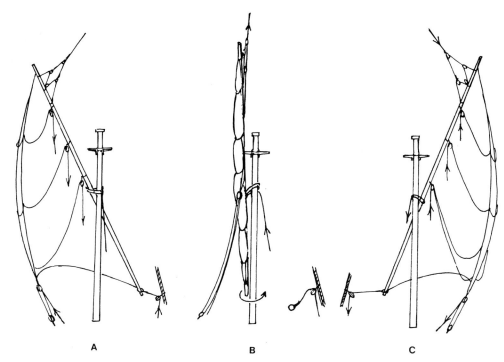

A

B

C

Changing the mizzen
A Slack sheet, brail up, and slack bowline; **B** slack truss, haul on lift, remove bowline and bring heel of yard around behind the mast; **C** slack lift, haul tight truss and weather bowline, let go brails and sheet home.

the cause of the area of the mizzen sail being cut down, to obviate the necessity for 'changing' it. An informative article about the development of the lateen mizzen in Northern Europe, by Peter Hodges, is to be found in *Model Shipwright* (24, 1978, 39).

Goosewinging the mizzen. Mainwaring (155) says, 'when we are going before a wind, or quarter-winds, with a fair fresh gale, we many times, to make more haste, unparrel the mizzen yard, and so launch out the yard and sail over the quarter on the lee side, and so fitting guys at the farther end to keep the yard steady, with a boom, we boom out the sheet of the mizzen sail. This doth help give the ship some way, which otherwise the mizzen sail will not, especially before a wind. The sail so fitted is called a goose-wing.' Boteler (169) says it is also called a 'studdingsail'. The introduction of the square mizzen topsail in 1618 would have removed the necessity for this practice, the topsail being set with the wind quartering, and the mizzen course furled.

Smiting the mizzen. A 'smiting line' was made fast at the forward end of the yard, and made up with the sail, when it was furled with ropeyarns, so that it hung down from the peak. At the order, pulling the line broke the stops successively, allowing the canvas to deploy. The tack, or *hals*, of a course, was often called a *smijt*, in Dutch.

Turning effect of the mizzen. According to Boyd (400), if a vessel were obliged to wear in line, or bear off suddenly, the mizzen, with its after leech out to the crossjack yard, could neutralise the helm, and prevent the stern coming up in the wind. Apart from its lever-

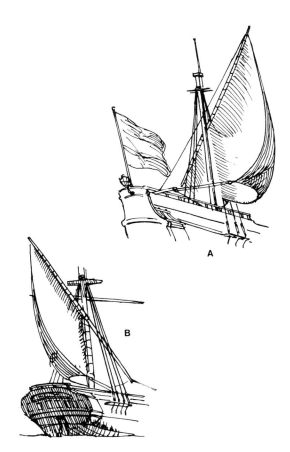

A Goosewinging the mizzen; B bagpiping the mizzen.

Two masted rigs
a Bilander; b snow; c brig; d *langard*.

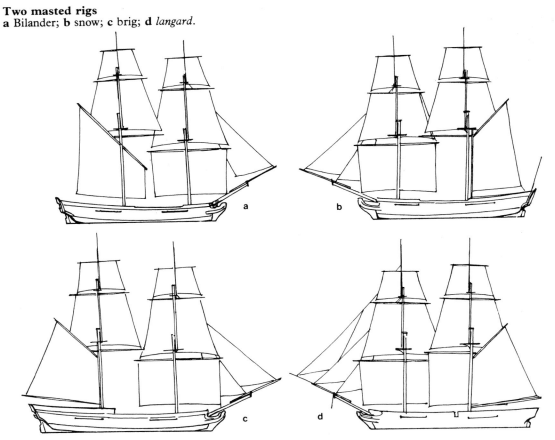

every possible scrap of canvas set. Too much heeling, or carrying too much weather helm, slowed the vessel down, and hence performance was frequently improved by taking away the superfluous canvas, which was serving only to push to bow down in the water. The 'invention' of the crossjack sail, therefore, was not an unqualified success in the full-rigger, whatever its popularity in brigs and snows.

Arrangement of mizzen brails. As might be expected, this changed considerably, during the evolution of the sail. Initially, in the early 1600s, martnets, leading to the mizzen topmast, were used to take in the upper after part of the sail, being replaced by brails about 1650 (Anderson, 240). Subsequently there were two or three brails on both leech and foot, disposed so the sail was brailed up to the yards, as evenly as possible.

In the late 1700s, the smaller mizzen, hooped to the mast, required only three brails, the upper two leading to the gaff, and the lowermost to the throat. Steel, Röding, and Lescallier show nothing below the throat brail, the lower part of the sail hanging up and down the mast, and hence relatively easily secured by its gaskets, when the other brails were hauled. Röding shows the throat brail fitted with a tackle, so it could get an especially solid grip on the sail, in blowing weather. The upper block of this tackle was provided with a tricing line, so it could be fleeted quickly. Röding calls this simply an *Aufholer*, 'up hauler', but it was distinguished by a special name in Swedish namely *dräng*, the literal meaning of which is 'servant lad'. This nicely parallels the English term 'knave line' or 'nave line', used in the sense of 'tricing line of a truss-parrel' (Steel 161); the original meaning of 'knave', of course, rather than 'rogue', was 'boy, servant'.

In many languages, the throat brail itself had a special name, usually identical to the word used for the breeching of a gun. In Swedish, it was called the *brok*, and the order 'Brail up!' was actually given in the form *Gige och broka!* 'Guy up, and breech in!', so to speak. In the 1900s, in fact, some Swedish seamen still called the later horizontal type of brail by the name *brok*, rather than *gigtåg*, as might have been expected (*Longitude* 6, 23).

Sources in the later 1800s, such as L Compte (132), Burney (133) and Boström (Plate 36), show a brail from the leech to the mast, and no tackle on the throat brail. Later still, the head of the sail ran along the gaff on track, and the sail was brailed 'in' to the mast rather than 'up' to the gaff. Knight (43) rigs a 'clew rope', between the clew and the throat

age, due to being so far aft, there was now the additional moment due to the CE of the sail being well out to leeward. The effect, in keeping the head to the wind, was the converse of the action of a weather fore topmast studdingsail holding the bow off the wind.

Snow, brig and langard. The nineteenth century seamen distinguished some types of vessel by the form taken by the mizzen. This was the case with the bilander, snow, brig and langard. The bilander was a small two-masted square rigged vessel setting an old-fashioned mizzen from a full mizzen yard, which I assume, was shifted to go about. Bobrik associates this rig particularly with Sweden, but the name is of Dutch origin, *bijlander* implying a vessel that kept near the land, a 'coaster', as compared with a *binnenlander*, 'in-lander', one which worked the inland waterways. The snow had a small gaff mizzen, loose footed, and set on a 'snow-mast', abaft the mizzen mast, or sometimes a 'horse' serving the same purpose. The brig had a large fore and aft 'mainsail' or 'brig-sail', with a gaff and a long boom. The French seamen called a brig or snow, with a square sail on the mainyard, a *langard*, which was also the name for this square sail. Other languages did not observe this difference, but it seems a useful distinction nonetheless. Today it is usually said that the snow-mast is the thing that separates a snow from a brig.

This is true, but I think originally it was simply a matter or proportion. The eighteenth century seamen would have been able to separate a brig from a snow a mile off, in the same way as he distinguished a ketch from a schooner. The snow mizzen was much smaller, and therefore did not need to be hooped to the mainmast, a small trysail-mast being sufficient, a feature that would only have been obvious close to.

The crossjack. For the greater part of the sailing ship's history, no sail was set on the crossjack yard. It existed only to spread the foot of the mizzen topsail. In the early 1900s some merchant vessels used the crossjack in preference to a fore and aft mizzen. However successful this idea was from a functional point of view, aesthetically, it was a disaster, vessels so rigged reminding one irresistibly of a manx cat. Be that as it may, some American clipper captains introduced the idea of setting a sail on this yard in the 1840s, in addition to the fore and aft mizzen. For the most part it was not a great success, since with the wind free, it interfered with the mainsail, and close-hauled with the mizzen. It is quite striking how many contemporary paintings show the sail bent to the yard, but hauled up and not set. It cannot be over-emphasised that the ship made the best speed with the sail disposed to best advantage, and that, emphatically, did not mean having

3.

1.

East Indiamen riding out a gale under courses. This 1793 painting by Whitcombe shows a relatively late survival of the practice. Note the driver booms carried by both ships in the foreground. (Courtesy Richard Green Galleries, London)

2.

Lateen mizzen of the *Nonsuch*, showing the mizzen bowlines, brails, and parrel. (Mark Myers' Collection)

3.

The spritsail of the *Nonsuch*, drawing well with the wind abeam. The water holes in the foot of the sail show here, and the bonnet latched under the staysail. (Mark Myers' Collection)

4.

The Swedish training ship *Jarramas* working in coastal waters under topsails. The brail on her large jib is interesting and rather uncommon. (Courtesy Marinmuseet, Karlskrona) so that the clew was pulled up, at the same time as the sail was being brailed in.

Fancy lines. To keep the lee brails from interfering with the set of the sail, 'fancy lines' were fitted to haul them up towards the peak (Lees, 109; Steel, 123). Instead of fitting a set on each side, Röding and the early Swedish authors describe an arrangement intended to haul the brails up on both sides of the sail simultaneously. The fancy line ran through a wooden fitting, like a large wooden spool, seized to the after leech of the sail, up through the brail thimbles, then through a block at the gaff peak, similar to that used for the signal halliards, and thence to deck. A knot was worked under the brail thimble of the lowermost brail, allowing the fancy line to haul the brails up to the peak, when the sail was set. Pihlström (219) calls this the *brokup-phalare*, 'throat brail up-hauler'. The wooden chock prevented the throat brail from dropping down too far, when the fancy line was let go. The difficulty I see with this system, is that the brails are not seized to the after leech, as they are with the other methods. This would have caused some difficulty when it came to brailing up in blowing weather. To avoid having the sail 'bag', it was important that the lee brails be manned best, while merely taking down the slack of the weather ones. If the opposite practice were followed, getting the sail in was much more difficult than it need have been (Nares, 95).

Mizzen bowlines and vangs. The upper end, or peak, of the mizzen gaff was steadied by the vangs, when the sail was not set. Under sail, the peak was allowed to swing round to leeward, the sail adopting a natural curve, such that the foot was 'sharper' than the head. If the weather vang were not eased off, or let go, there was danger of the gaff being broken. The lateral movement of the mizzen yard was actually better controlled by the mizzen bowlines, than with the later vangs, the direction of pull in the first case being horizontal, and in the second, all but vertical. This to my mind, explains the survival of the yard, long after the forward part of the sail had been dispensed with. Röding illustrates a mizzen yard with both vangs and mizzen bowlines, while his contemporaries Romme and Lescallier show mizzen bowlines only. I am inclined to think that this latter more closely approaches the truth of actual practice in the late 1700s. When brailing in the mizzen, it was important to steady the gaff with the weather vang, and to brace the crossjack yard in a little. If this were not done, the sail might get foul of the lee crossjack yardarm, perhaps becoming impaled upon it.

Tack tricing line. With a quartering wind, just as the weather clew of the mainsail had to be 'docked up', so the tack of the gaff mizzen needed to be raised, to avoid blanketing the lee clew of the mainsail. This 'tricing up' of the tack was also done to balance the sail plan, when hove to, or to avoid the necessity of carrying excessive weather helm.

Altering the area of the mizzen. The sail area could be increased by latching on a bonnet to the foot of the mizzen course. Since the bonnet was quadrangular, the increase occurred in the same proportions from front to back. When the sail was fitted for reefing on the head, the line of the reef-band runs from a point at the forward upper corner of the sail, to a point substantially down the after leech. The consequence of taking the reef in this way is that proportionately more after sail is taken away, hence balancing the increased pressure under the lee bow, to be expected with the greater heeling effect of a stronger wind.

Bagpiping the mizzen. By hauling the mizzen sheet over to the weather shrouds, or shifting the forward end of the yard over to the lee main shrouds, with the mizzen bowline, a back sail could be made out of the mizzen, and this was referred to as 'bagpiping' it. The procedure which was analogous to 'flatting in afore' was used when it was desired for any reason to luff up, or throw the stern off the wind, as for instance in an emergency manoeuvre, in tending at single anchor, and by some French seamen in tacking.

Bonaventure mizzen. Because of the great height of the Elizabethan aftercastle, associated with marked tumblehome, there was comparatively little spread for the mizzen shrouds. This serves to explain why the mizzen mast of these vessels was so small, and

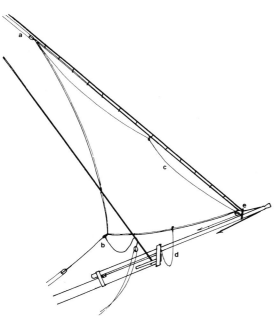

Jib
a halliards; **b** sheets; **c** downhaul; **d** gob rope; **e** traveller.

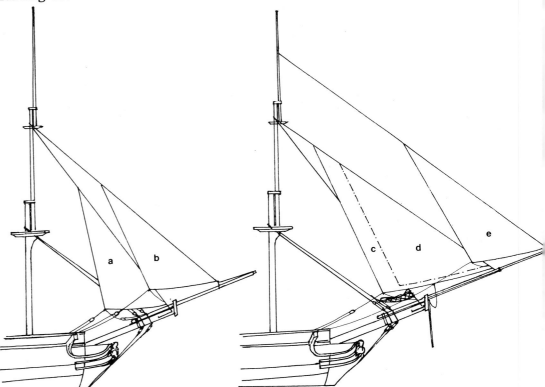

Man-of-war's headsails
a fore topmast staysail; **b** storm jib; **c** large jib; working jib (within broken line); **e** flying jib.

why a second mizzen, on an even smaller scale was sometimes necessary. The clew sheeted home to an 'outlicker', a spar named for the Dutch fitting called an *uitlegger*, used in a similar way, to handle the fore tack. It would have exerted even greater leverage than the regular mizzen, a feature somewhat diminished by its lesser size. With increasing weather, one would expect to see it taken away, when the forward mizzen could continue to stand.

Lateen mizzen topsail. Anderson (231) has comparatively little to say about this sail, which was in use in the late 1500s and early 1600s, although he offers three contemporary representations of it; two of these show the sail on the forward of the two mizzens only. Just how it worked, I am not sure, but it seems certain that it sheeted home to the after end of the mizzen yard, and the 'tack', if one may call it so, was made fast at the other end. It would have been a relatively light weather sail, being so far aft, so high up, and so ill supported by the rigging.

Square mizzen topsail. This 'cross sail', as the Dutch called it, had come into general use by 1618 (Lees, 159). Initially, it was used instead of the lateen mizzen course, being used on the points of sail where the latter was least helpful, namely, from wind quartering to dead aft. With the wind forward of that, it was taken in, and the course set instead. Later on, of course, it became an addition rather than an alternative to the mizzen, and we will return to it further, when considering topsails generally.

The jib. This could be used on all points of sail. By virtue of its position, it exerted a very powerful effect in throwing the bow off the wind, partly because, like the forward staysails, it was a 'lifting' sail, since it pulled both upwards and laterally. In men-of-war, there were usually three jibs, of different sizes, the middle-sized one being used most commonly. The tack was secured to a traveller, which ran out to the end of the jibboom. However, if the weather demanded, the traveller was only run out to half-boom, consequently lessening the leverage of the sail, and the strain on the jibboom. The large jib was only used with the wind quartering, sometimes being set flying, with its fall rove double, instead of being hanked to the stay (Mossel, III, 138). The small jib was substituted in inclement weather. The jib was brought in when the topsails were double reefed, being replaced by the fore topmast staysail. When the spritsail yard was triced around, the weather guys contributed to the support of the jibboom, counteracting the upward and leeward pull of the jib. Thus the

jib could be carried longer in a ship fitted with a spritsail yard. In the late 1800s, the yard went out of fashion in merchantmen, and the bowsprit was not quite as well supported laterally as in men-of-war. Even with spreaders, or half-booms, which replaced the spritsail yard in the latter day warship, the single jib could still be set in fairly brisk weather.

In 1824, Sir Henry Heathcote (74) suggested using an inner and an outer jib, instead of the larger single sail, remarking, presciently, that multiplying the number of weather leeches increases pulling power. His ideas were not found persuasive by the Lords Commissioners of the Admiralty, to whom he addressed himself, but, within a few years, they were almost universally adopted by the merchant service. Splitting the jib did away with the necessity to run the jib-stay out on a traveller, and for substituting jibs of various sizes. The inner jib alone, corresponded to the man-of-war's small jib, set at half-boom.

'More seamen have lost their lives in stowing the jib, than in furling all the rest of the ship's sails put together, and often life has been sacrificed in stowing this sail, when really there was no necessity for doing so' (Todd & Whall, 74). The safety nets to be seen under the bowsprit of the modern sail training ship, are surprisingly, a fairly recent innovation. The bowsprit in the late 1700s steeved up at a considerable angle, the jibboom end being level with the foretop, and Todd and Whall seem to feel that the ships of the late 1800s, with their sharp entry, and relatively less steeply steeving bowsprits, were more dangerous than their predecessors, in this particular regard, since the jibboom and the men on it, were more likely to be plunged into the sea than had been the case in the earlier vessels.

To help in controlling the foot of the huge jib, men-of-war often rigged a 'gob-rope' from the mid-point of the foot of this sail to the cap of the bowsprit, to pull the foot in towards the bowsprit in furling. Although this also occurs as 'gap-rope', the term is an old word for a bridle, and 'gob' in the sense of 'mouth' is still to be heard in many parts of Britain.

Steeve of the bowsprit. This spar was required to 'steeve', or incline upward, if the spritsail, and other headsails were not to be plunged in the water, as the ship pitched into the waves. The modern 'spike' bowsprit angles up at about fifteen degrees, whereas the flying jibboom end, in an East Indiaman, was level with the foretop. Anderson (14) mentions angles of thirty-five and forty degrees, in the 1600s. Griffiths (175), noted

Steeve of the bowsprit
a c1670; b c1745; c c1810; d c1900 (spike bowsprit).

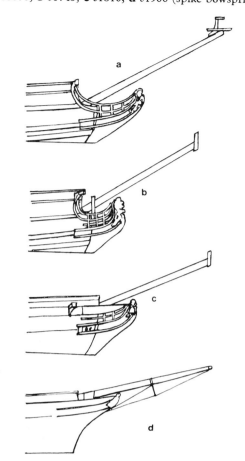

that, in prizes 'which had the French steeve', the foreyard could be braced up more sharply than was the case in English vessels, with their flatter bowsprits. However, since the foresail stood well enough without this excessive steeve, he felt that it was really unnecessary. With a flatter bowsprit, the bobstay exerted its pull at a better angle, and the headsails more effectively obviated the necessity to carry weather helm (Liardet, 49). On the other hand, a well steeved bowsprit gave greater security to the men on the booms in bad weather and the flatter angle of the stays increased the lifting effect of the headsails. The most advantageous angle became a matter of judgment for the sea officer, and the naval architect.

Jib brails. These were not true 'brails', but rather a 'tripping line', or *frihaler*, 'free hauler', as Hansen calls it, used to get the clew over the fore topmast stay, in tacking. It ran from the clew to a block on the stay, down through another at the tack, and thence in to the forecastle.

Jib sheets. These consisted of two pendants, terminating in clump blocks, through which the sheets rove. When the lee sheets were in use, the weather ones rode over the fore topmast stay. In the latter day merchantmen,

Headsails
A Fore topmast staysail set in heavy weather, jibboom steadied by triced up spritsail yard; **B** large jib and flying jib set in light weather.

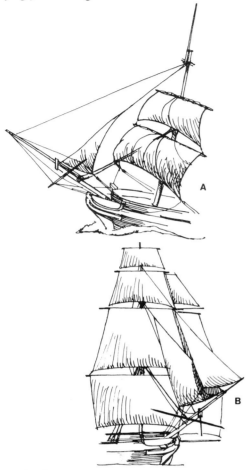

care had to be taken to prevent the wire jib sheet pendants literally 'sawing through' the stay, like an Oropesa cable cutting the tether of a floating mine. Archie Horka advised me that he had seen this particular misadventure occur, through failure to ensure that the rope sheets, rather than the wire pendant, lay across the stay.

Although it was possible to 'flat in' the jib, by bringing the clew over to the weather side, it was simpler to haul across the sheets of the fore topmast staysail, if both were set, because the latter sail did not have to be shifted across a stay. The order to trim the sail anew, after it had been backed in this way, was 'Draw jib!'.

Stowing the jib. With the modern spike bowsprit, the jibs were furled on top of the spar but even in earlier times, the flying jib and jib could be stowed in the same way, if it was intended to reset them shortly. Otherwise, the flying jib came right in, and the jib and fore topmast staysail were stowed in a netting, resembling a little hammock, suspended over the bowsprit. This arrangement permitted the jibboom to be run in, without disturbing the furled sails.

Slacking the jib stay. 'The jib stay is always set up like a harp string. Consequently, when it comes on to blow, both the spray and the rain tend to tauten it yet more. In pitching, it must assist to spring the jibboom, work the bowsprit, and, inasmuch as it resists the free action of the ship, to make her uneasy and constrained in pitching. The unnecessary strain on the rope itself, is enough to induce you on such occasions to slack it. Whenever it blows so fresh that the jib is not likely to be set, let the stay be slacked, by which it will be preserved. Nothing can be easier than to set it up while the jib is loosing' (Griffiths, 226).

The fore topmast staysail. This was set, instead of the jib, in bad weather. Its tack was secured to the bowsprit, a very much sturdier spar than the jibboom. It was not considered part of the 'plain sail', but more as an item of heavy weather canvas, to be kept set as long as possible because of its 'lifting' effect. Mossel says that it was a useful sail, when tending at single anchor, to swing the bow off the wind. In the late 1700s, it was often stowed, like the jib, in a sort of 'hammock', made of netting, which allowed the jibboom to be run in, if necessary under the stowed sail. In merchant sail, during the second half of the nineteenth century, it was quite customary to set it together with the jibs, rather than instead of them.

The flying jib. This was a light weather sail, usually set and taken in with the royals, or sometimes with the topgallants. It would be found set along with the jib, and exerted the same sort of effect in counteracting weather helm, throwing the bow off the wind.

Topsails. In the early seventeenth century, the topsails were thought of as merely adjuncts to the courses. By the end of the 1600s, however, they had become the principal sails of the ship, almost as large as their respective courses, and were the first to be set, and last taken in. They were well supported, at a sufficient height above the water, so that they held the wind, even in the trough of a 'hollow' sea, and were indispensable for all manoeuvres. Reefing topsails appeared about 1680, when first one, and then two reefbands were introduced. Subsequently, the fore and main topsails were fitted for four reefs, the mizzen having one less. When close-reefed, about half the available canvas was deployed. The mizzen topsail was usually furled, when the others required close-reefing: firstly, because its mast was relatively poorly supported, its braces leading forward; secondly, in accordance with the general rule that the ship griped the more it heeled, after canvas had to be taken away, with increasing wind, to compensate

for this. The fore topsail was part of the forward sail, throwing the head off the wind, while the others had the opposite effect. To heave to, one topsail was thrown aback, the other kept full. Thus, one could be hove to, 'main topsail to the mast', or 'fore topsail to the mast'.

The mizzen topsail was used to back the ship away from her anchor when tending at a change of tide. Although it was sometimes backed as a temporary expedient, to pick up a boat, doing so was expressly forbidden when sailing in line. Boyd (394) says that the ship's way may be most readily deadened by squaring the mainsail, which could be done by a very few hands, the lee wheel men and lookouts. All that had to be done was to let go the mainsheet, bowline and braces. Griffiths (249) points out that, on a wind, the crossjack yard cannot be swung away any further than square, else it will 'lock' the braced up mainyard. The mizzen topsail will be aback, but not exerting the turning effect it would exercise if braced right around, as if for the other tack. The unopposed forward sail will now swing the head to leeward.

In severe weather, the fore and mizzen topsails were completely furled while the reefed main topsail could be kept set. Being closer to the middle of the ship, it did not aggravate pitching like the others. Sometimes the main topsail was 'goosewinged', having strong lashings passed to secure the weather half of the sail to the yard, while keeping the lee clew set. However, 'it need hardly be said, that this operation does not do the sail any good. For this reason, instead of goosewinging the main topsail, the majority of seamen would rather take the sail in altogether' (Nicholls, 254).

Topsail sheets. The various ways of rigging these are to be found in many works on seamanship and rigging. Chain topsail sheets came into use about 1840, Costé indicating that the practice was identified particularly with English merchantmen. I am not sure of the exact date or circumstances, but note that Pilaar does not mention chain in 1838, while they are illustrated by Le Compte in 1842. Although rope topsail sheets remained in use in some vessels until the last days of the sailing navy, they were totally superseded by chain in the larger naval vessels and all merchantmen. Chain sheets, which set up with a tackle, were much stronger than those of rope, did not wear out, required less attention when sheeting home, and brought the clew into better approximation with the lower yardarm.

Rope topsail sheets rove through a block at the clew, and then through a 'cheek block' on

Topsail

a brace; **b** tie; **c** sheet; **d** buntline; **e** clewline; **f** bowline; **g** reef-tackle.

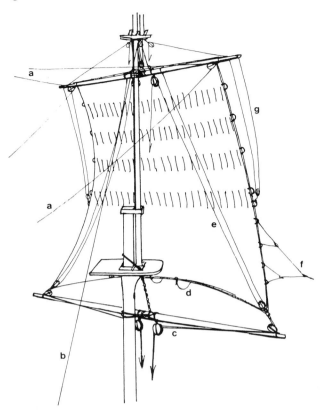

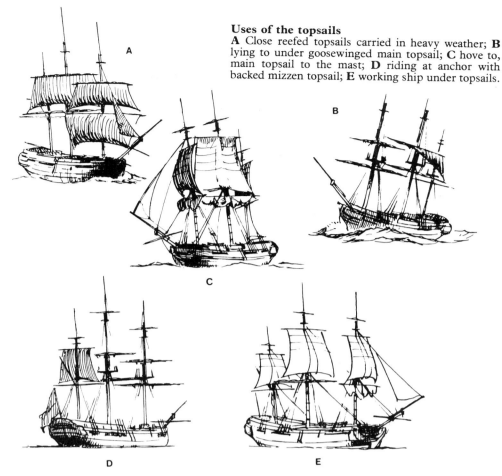

the after side of the yardarm, a 'shoulder block', on top of it, or a sheave actually cut into its substance. If the clewline were not eased down carefully in sheeting home, the rope was dragged into the sheave hole, at a bad angle, and chafed. It was necessary to send the 'topsail sheet man' out to the yardarm, to keep things clear, while setting the topsail. The clew of the sail was held up clear of the yard, by at least the diameter of the sheet block. As a result, the clews of the naval topsail had to be cut differently by the sailmaker, being made shorter than those for merchant vessels (Kipping, 46). A special pair of interlocking 'dog-and-bitch' thimbles were used to prevent the clew developing a half twist, due to the lead of the sheet, and the manner in which the sheet block was stropped (Nares, 61; Glascock, 75).

Topsail clewlines. The clewline blocks on the topsails, like the lower blocks of clew jiggers, were liable to be fouled by the reef points, as the sail was clewed up, and hence they were either 'secret blocks', or were fitted with special thimbles to prevent this accident. The clewlines shared a quarter block with the topgallant sheets, and sometimes the reef tackle fall, multiplying the trouble if the strop of this block carried away. In the latter half of the nineteenth century, it became very common to lead the clewlines

through a block at the cap, rather than to the traditional quarter block. 'The advantage here is, that after having clewed up, the clewline is done with, for nothing of it is lost in lowering the yard. Also the power is nearer the work. The hoist is lighter, for the downhauls are more readily overhauled in hoisting than are clewlines in any other form. The clews are safer in shifting the yard, or when the yard is sprung. The yard itself is more quickly shifted, there being no quarter blocks to cast loose. It takes less rope, and the downhaul is a more effective downhaul, than are the clewlines' (Boyd, 191).

Topgallants. These, being higher up, contributed more to heeling than the topsails. In moderate weather, they were always set, since they added quite a bit to the ship's speed. For the reasons mentioned earlier, they were braced in rather more than the topsails, but they would have to be furled earlier, by the wind, in conditions that might permit them to be used with the wind free. The fore and mizzen topgallants were sometimes taken in, when the main could be left set, to ease the ship's movement in the waves. The topgallants could be carried over a single reefed topsail, and this was frequently done. Reefing the topsails in good time, and setting the topgallants over, meant that when anticipated bad weather finally arrived, the topgal-

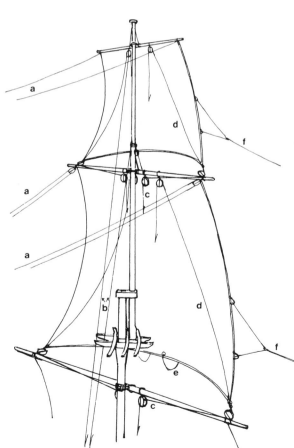

Topgallant and royal
a brace; **b** tie; **c** sheet; **d** clewline; **e** buntline; **f** bowline.

lants could readily be furled, whereas taking a reef in the topsails at that point would have been more arduous.

Royals. These were excellent light weather sails, and the same sort of considerations apply to them as to the topgallants. Small merchantmen sometimes carried only a main royal (Mossel, III, 134), just as some vessels, in the late 1800s, were rigged as 'main skysail yarders'. Exactly the same considerations applied to a main skysail or royal, as to a main topgallant, already alluded to.

Staysails. These filled up the space between the masts and caught the wind, which the square sails allowed to escape, so to speak. Surprising as it may seem, they dropped out of favour in men-of-war, after the first third of the nineteenth century. When a vessel is referred to as getting under way 'with staysails alone', in the early 1800s, 'headsails', jib or perhaps fore topmast staysail are meant (*Mariner's Mirror* 57, 1971, 334). The headsails are the only three staysails mentioned by Mossel (II, 9), although Pilaar, writing some time earlier, and Boom rather later, indicate that 'middle', and 'after' staysails were not unknown in the Dutch service. The difficulty was that they were useful over a rather narrow range of points of sailing, encompassing a sector, from not quite close-hauled, to wind a point or so abaft the beam. Sailing by the wind, they were liable to backwind the square sails abaft them, and with the wind free, they were, in turn, becalmed by the square sails (Wilson-Barker, 93). While Steel (260) seems to think they were useful sails, particularly so 'when the ship gripes much', later authors like Pilaar (256) and Costé (*Supplément*, 6) say that they are little used. 'Some officers object to them, it being a matter of much doubt whether they increase at all the speed of a vessel, or are a useless waste of canvas' says Totten (154). There were dissenting voices: 'Staysails, though very little thought of in the Navy, generally, are often of the most essential service' (Liardet, 189). Mossel, writing in 1865, does not bother to refer to them at all.

The early staysails were trapezoidal, rather than triangular, with a vertical edge, which Lever and his contemporaries referred to as the 'bunt'. Some fairly modern dictionaries call this edge the 'nock' – for instance Anstead (185) – but since *nok* is the term for both 'yardarm' and 'head-cringle of a sail', in the other North Germanic languages, it seems better to restrict the term to the corner, rather than the adjoining edge. Pilaar uses the variant *nek*, 'neck', for the upper forward corner of the staysail, which parallels exactly the term 'throat' for the correspond-

ner of a gaff sail, in English. Danish uses a term, with similar meaning, *kvaerk, qvaerk* (Harboe). The sails were probably of this shape to make them less susceptible to blanketting from the square sails abaft them. In effect, the CE is further forward than that of a triangular sail of the same area. Three sided sails were first advocated by Sir Henry Heathcote in 1824, the full title of his book being *Treatise On Stay-sails For The Purpose Of Intercepting Wind Between The Square-sails Of Ships And Other Square Rigged Vessels*. It includes a short poem describing a vessel rigged with his patent staysails, and another carrying the old-fashioned sails, part of which runs as follows:

> By huge quadrangle, slender stays oppress'd;
> Its baneful lee-way powers appear confess'd;
> Obstructive too, it spoils the sturdier sail,
> Whose favour'd posture courts the growing gale:
> To foil the squall, in vain's the sheet eased off;
> Still doth the noxious plane our labour scoff:
> With lateral force still groans th' endanger'd pine,
> As slowly downward dragg'd, the sails decline:
> At length, relieved of the o'erwhelming load,
> By dint of force the cumbrous mass is stow'd

Sir Henry felt that the then current unpopularity of the staysail could be attributed to the evil effect of its lower half. Remove

this, said he, and all would be well. His triangular staysails did, in fact, recommend themselves to the merchant service, and in fact, they remained part of the working canvas right down to the last days of sail. Nonetheless, they were little used used in men-of-war. Part of the problem was the fact that the old single topsails let little wind go past them. 'Modern' sailing vessels have a sail plan which is relatively 'open', compared to their predecessors, and the staysails were useful over a greater arc, than in the old days.

When used, double staysail sheets were fitted in the Navy, the weather one being left slack like a jibsheet. The upper staysails were frequently fitted with only one sheet in merchant vessels, and subduing a staysail which got to thrashing around could prove a difficult task. For this reason, Todd and Whall recommend that the sheet be led under a bulwark cleat before reaching its pin, so that it can be handled without danger to the fingers. When going about, this arrangement required that the sail be hauled down so that the sheet could be got over to the other side. 'Tripping lines', or brails, were almost essential in handling the sail, with single sheets (Todd & Whall, 87).

The main staysails were part of the forward sail, tending to make the ship fall off. The mizzen staysails were, of course, part of the aftersail. All tended to exert a bit of a lifting effect, on the bow and stern, respectively. The stay of the 'middle staysail' or '*vlieger*', 'flyer', as the Dutch called it, ran from midway up the fore topmast, to the main topgallant masthead, the stay sometimes working on a traveller, or 'jackstay' abaft the topmast. Dutch 'middle' and 'after' staysails set on the main and mizzen masts, respectively.

The main topmast staysail could be a very large sail, but according to Hourigan (40), was, despite its size, relatively easy to handle. Try-sails functioned essentially as staysails set on gaffs replacing the main and mizzen topmast staysails. They were thought, by some, to offer a neater way of arranging things (Totten, 159). Baudin (261) actually calls them 'staysails with gaffs'. They were made of heavy canvas, and could be used instead of storm staysails.

Storm staysails. Sails of heavy canvas were sometimes set on the forestay and mainstay. The mizzen staysail also was sometimes set when lying to in a storm. (We have already referred to the picturesque names given these sails by foreign seamen.) Falls and sheets were extemporised from heavy tackles. They disappeared from the scene with the introduction of gaff trysails which get their name by virtue of their function as storm canvas. A storm mizzen could, with advantage, replace the reefed mizzen. It was secured to the mast with a rawhide lacing, or with 'salamanders', heavy beckets and toggles.

Ring-tail. Besides being used to describe a form of studdingsail attached to the mizzen course, this sometimes meant a supplementary fore and aft sail, set on the tall flagstaff found on the taffrail of a man-of-war. Contemporary illustrations also show it as an occasional sail on snows, contrived, no doubt

Types of staysails.
A Trapezoidal staysails (after Hutchinson, 1777); **B** Sir Henry Heathcote's triangular staysails, 1824, (after A Webb).

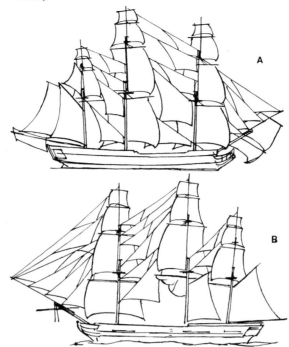

from a boat sail, or something of the sort. The French name, *tapecul*, might *very* freely be translated as 'kick-in-the-rear'; it was applied to other lightly constructed, speedy vehicles such as horse-drawn gigs.

The spritsail. This balanced the sail plan forward, and according to Alan Villiers, one of the few people who have experienced using one, 'was a grand manoeuvring sail' (*Give me a Ship to Sail*, 192), one which 'threw the ship's head off the wind, better than a bowsprit full of jibs'. It could be used by the wind, as well as before it. It was slung on the bowsprit about a third of its length from the end, either before or abaft the forestay. The

Storm staysails
A Ship lying to under lower staysails, fore topmast staysail and mizzen (after Hutchinson, 1777); **B** ship setting main trysail in bad weather (after W Phelps).

1.
Spritsail *c*1650
a halliard; **b** brace; **c** garnet; **d** lift; **e** standing lift; **f** sheet; **g** clewline; **h** water hole; **i** tricing line (*kondwachter*); **j** jibboom guys.

2.
Spritsail *c*1780.

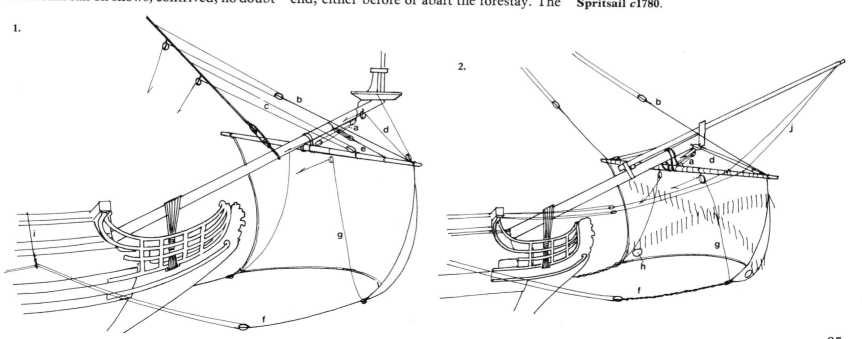

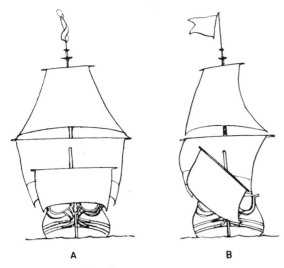

Set of the spritsail
A Yard braced square, before the wind; B yard canted up, on the wind.

Uses of the spritsail
A Reefed spritsail set in bad weather; B ship running under spritsail and studdingsails; C riding to anchor with spritsail set, wind against tide (after Van de Velde the Younger).

slings were loose enough to let it cockbill and traverse, the bowsprit being coppered, and slushed at that point, to allow it to move freely. It is difficult to get much information about how the sail was actually used. Originally it must have been set, by the wind, as well as with the wind quartering or aft. Once there were other headsails, the necessity to use it when close-hauled, would disappear. However, the sail remains in existence for over a century following the introduction of the jib in 1700. *Der Ge-öfnete See-hafen* of 1700 (102) says that it was best used before the wind, or wind abeam, seldom by the wind. It was usually taken in with the topgallants, invariably if the topsails had to be furled, and it was never set at night. Rosvall (42) and Sjöbohm (58), writing a century later, agree that it is best used with the wind free, in moderate weather, furling it at night, at the approach of land, or when sailing in squadron or convoy. It obstructed the sight of the helmsman, and perhaps this explains why it was called the *blind-zeil* in Dutch, and why it was taken in, when it was particularly important to have a clear view ahead. Griffiths (208) describes a hazard, unique to this sail, namely being set on fire by a smoking wad upon firing the vessel's own bow chaser.

When set by the wind, it had a number of disadvantages peculiar to itself. The tack could not be got down, as with the courses, and a bowline could not be rigged. Furthermore, the lower, or weather clew would tend to dip into the sea. To set it, the lee yardarm was cocked up, back, and in. If the sea were rough, the sail was reefed in such a way that only the after half of the sail was set, that is to say the diagonal reef-band running from the lee yardarm to the weather leech was secured to the yard. This transformed the sail into a sort of 'under jib', the lack of a tack and a bowline was now less of a problem, and the sail was clear of the water. The position of the reef-band varied: Romme shows it reaching half way down the leech, while Steel shows it almost down to the clew. In the first case the reefed sail retained a short weather leech, in the second it was essentially reduced to a triangular configuration. If the wind was light enough to deploy the whole sail, weights were hung at the clews to hold them down. The spritsail sheet pendants consisted of two ropes, twisted together, rather than a single pendant, and were secured to the clew by a complicated spritsail sheet knot. This would have resulted in things being extra heavy, the pendant hanging in a short deep catenary, conducive to keeping the clew down. Anderson (223) says that the custom of having long double pendants, which were allowed to become 'cable-laid', by twisting upon themselves, dated from 1690. A weight could have been incorporated in the interstices of the spritsail sheet knot, in the same way that something heavy was sometimes inserted in the 'monkey's fist' of a heaving line (the latter is not a generally recommended practice, by the way). The sheets, which were made fast quite far aft, were held up out of the water by a special laniard, or lizard, called a *kondwachter* in Dutch. This arrangement gave a better spread to the clews, the lizard or 'tricing line', allowing the sheets to lead further out than would have been the case had they simply been made fast in the fore channels. A good sized 'water hole', close to each clew, and sometimes in the middle (Romme), allowed the sail to clear itself, if it were shipping water.

Up to about 1675, the yard was fitted with two sets of lifts: the regular ones ran to the bowsprit end, and then in, and it is easy enough to see how these worked, and why they were necessary; in addition, there were so called 'standing lifts', or 'horses', which were known as 'Spanish lifts' in the Northern European languages, and 'moustaches' in the Romance tongues. These were set up permanently with deadeyes and laniards, and were said by Röding (799) to be 'very troublesome' in tricing the yard. Since the regular lifts doubled as spritsail topsail sheets, the standing lifts clearly were useful with the yard square, and the spritsail topsail set. They also offered a handhold to men working on the yard, and served also as a preventer, if the slings were to part. If the yard were slewed around into a fore and aft position, the weather one would have tautened, and the lee one slackened, this 'tourniquet' action tending to raise the weather half of the yard slightly, hence raising the weather clew a little bit higher above the waves. If the yard were triced up more vertically, the weather lift would have helped support the weight, and the tendency would have been for the lee standing lift to keep the yard close to a right angle with the bowsprit. Since the forestay made an acute angle with the bowsprit, the upper or lee brace pulled the lee yardarm back as well as up. It should, however, have been possible to get the yard in any desired position by appropriate hauling on the lifts and braces.

It will be realised that the spritsail braces,

or tricing lines move the yardarms more or less vertically, while the lifts traverse them almost horizontally, the reverse of their respective functions with all other square sails. In Dutch, in fact, the braces were called *trissen* or *trijsen* rather than *brassen*, reflecting the fact that they 'triced up', rather than 'braced around'. Just as there were 'standing lifts', so there were auxiliary braces called 'garnets'. Although the origin of this word is uncertain, I think there is, inherent in it, the idea of whipping something up; at least this is true with 'garnet-tackle' and 'clew-garnet'. The same thought underlies the Dutch verb *trijsen* and English 'trice'. *Der Ge-öfnete See-hafen* calls the garnets *Triesge*, presumably a variant of *trijsen*, mentioned above, but follows English, in calling the regular braces *Brassen*. Why garnets were necessary early on, and why they disappeared after 1675, is a puzzle which I am unable to answer. Clearly they were helpful in cocking the yard well up, when close-hauled. Once the jib was introduced in 1700, the necessity for setting the spritsail by the wind diminished, but the garnets had disappeared twenty-five years earlier, so there can hardly have been a direct connection between the two events.

Sailing before the wind, the sail hung down almost vertically, with the sheet well slacked off, and weights hung at the clew if necessary. In fact, some contemporary engravings (for example those of Ozanne) give the distinct impression that with a fresh wind, the canvas could swell up and forwards of the yard, so as to give a certain amount of 'lift'; on the other hand, if the clews were hauled too much aft, the sail would tend to form a bag, so placed that it would depress the bow. It was a particularly useful sail, with studdingsails set both sides, since it could draw well on this point of sail, and made steering easier by avoiding yawing, since it 'pulled' the bow, rather than 'pushing' the stern.

Spritsail topsail. We have, in this case, a problem in nomenclature, since this term was successively applied to two different sails. From about 1600 to 1720, it applied to a sail set on the spritsail topmast, disposed at the end of the bowsprit. From 1720 to about 1800, it applied to a sail, analogous to a topsail, which was run out and set under the bowsprit. The same confusion in terminology exists in other languages, although Dutch *schuif-blind*, literally 'shove-spritsail', unequivocally refers to the later sail; even so, *boven-blind*, 'upper spritsail', is applied to both types of sail.

The early spritsail topsail. A few years ago, I submitted a note to *Mariner's Mirror*

Spritsail topsail
A *c*1650; B *c*1780.
  a brace; **b** halliard; **c** lift; **d** sheet; **e** clewline.

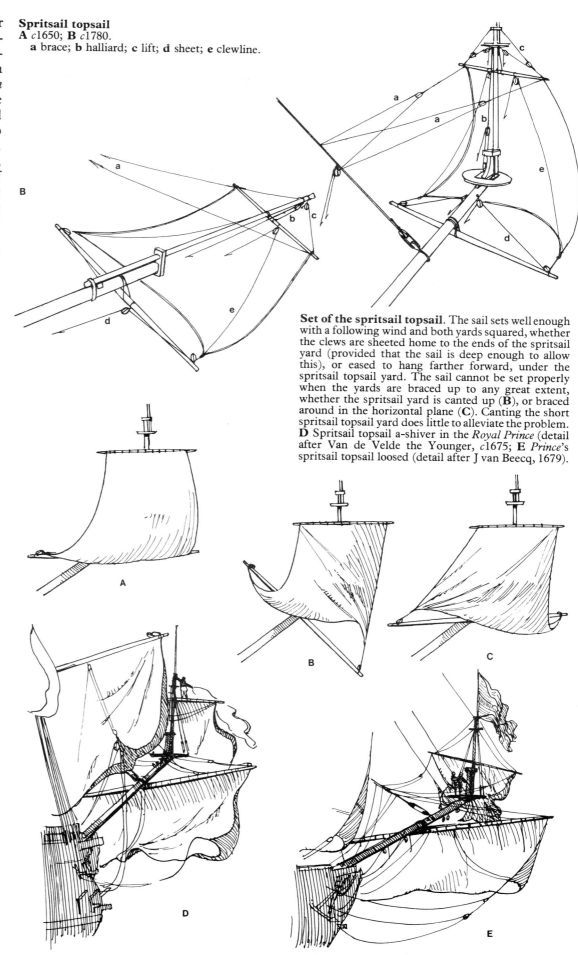

Set of the spritsail topsail. The sail sets well enough with a following wind and both yards squared, whether the clews are sheeted home to the ends of the spritsail yard (provided that the sail is deep enough to allow this), or eased to hang farther forward, under the spritsail topsail yard. The sail cannot be set properly when the yards are braced up to any great extent, whether the spritsail yard is canted up (**B**), or braced around in the horizontal plane (**C**). Canting the short spritsail topsail yard does little to alleviate the problem. **D** Spritsail topsail a-shiver in the *Royal Prince* (detail after Van de Velde the Younger, *c*1675; **E** *Prince*'s spritsail topsail loosed (detail after J van Beecq, 1679).

1. A ship close-hauled in a fresh breeze. This Whitcombe painting shows the usefulness of staysails while sailing on the wind. The amount of square sail set is roughly equalled by the spread of fore and aft canvas. (Courtesy N R Omell Gallery, London)

2. The *Medina* (in three positions) off Portsmouth, 1818. Another Whitcombe portrait, showing the ship setting her lighter sails as she stands out towards the Channel. Notice how she has brailed up the mizzen staysail and hauled down the fore topmast staysail as she brings the wind aft, setting the main staysails, jib and flying jib, spanker and gaff topsail in their place. The studdingsail booms are being run out in the centre portrait. (Courtesy N R Omell Gallery, London)

amount of weather helm needed, and severely strained the ship's fabric in a seaway.

With the wind aft and the yards square, the sail should have worked very well, although it would have been subject to blanketting by the forecourse, something that was not a problem with the spritsail itself. It is often represented on models, sheeted well home to the spritsail yard, with its foot curving backwards right under the top and bowsprit (Winter, *Der Holländische 2 – Decker*, Tafel 4). Apart from the question of chafe, setting the sail in this way would have resulted in exaggerating its depressant effect on the bow. Although I have no concrete evidence how things were actually managed, it would seem best to leave the sheets slacked off, and, if necessary, weight the clews so that the sail would set in the more advantageous vertical position. The mast was raked forward, at least in some vessels, which would help keep the sail clear of the top, if set in the second fashion. A large contemporary model of a Dutch man-of-war, in the Rijks Museum, Amsterdam, shows a spritsail, with sufficient hoist to sheet home to the spritsail yard, but with insufficient gore in the foot, to clear the top. Mr J B Kist told me that they were very sure about the authenticity of the sails on this model. See also, Ketting (121).

The sail is placed so as to exert the greatest possible leverage in throwing the bow off the wind, and this will be most evident, if it is braced up sharp. However, this is exactly where difficulties begin to appear. The braces can pull the hoisted yard virtually fore and aft, but what of the foot? If the spritsail yard is triced up, its lee yardarm is too high, and the weather one too low, to give a good lead to the spritsail topsail sheets. If both yards are horizontal, the weather clew is much closer to the weather yardarm of the spritsail, than is the case with the lee clew and lee yardarm, because the pivots of the two yards are separated by a considerable distance horizontally. In short, the geometry of the sail is very unsatisfactory, except with both yards square.

One can envisage both sails being set with a following wind, in very moderate weather conditions. If suitably weighted and sheeted, they need not depress the bow, and an excess of canvas forward would prevent yawing, whereas it would cause it, if set aft. As to choosing between them, the topsail was smaller, not exposed to the hazard of being ducked in the waves, and did not obstruct the view from the quarterdeck. Thus, with the wind dying down, but a swell still running, it might recommend itself rather than the spritsail. By the wind, the spritsail alone, with a

63, 1977, 172, entitled 'The Riddle of the Spritsail Topsail', embodying a number of questions about this sail, which are recapitulated here.

Contemporary illustrations of the sail actually set are rather uncommon, but it is frequently represented furled, or loosed to dry. It is hardly necessary to underline, however, that a sail would not be carried unless one intended to use it. Furthermore, the advantages would have to exceed its drawbacks which, in this case, are imposing. It required a yard, a top, a knee, a mast, usually with its own superimposed spritsail topgallant mast, in addition to assorted blocks and other hardware. On a model, these items may resemble tooth-picks, but in the prototype, they represented several tons weight, disposed as far forward as possible of the centre of the hull, and hence best calculated to inhibit the brisk rising of the bow as it plunged into the waves. This would also have increased the reef taken, if need be seems much the better sail.

At single anchor, the spritsail topsail is well forward of the cable, around which an anchored vessel pivots. It might have been used to set the vessel ahead, or sheer it while tending anchor at the change of tide. At the moment of weighing, it could have been useful in 'casting' the ship's head one way or the other. Since the anchor was best weighed at slack water, the wind would ordinarily be dead ahead, and until the anchor was out of the ground, the spritsail topsail would be aback. The spritsail itself could not be thrown properly aback, and one has no certain information about how the two sails were handled in tacking. My guess would be that they would be kept set, to keep way on, until the head was coming into the wind, then run up in their gear, before the sails on the foremast flew aback, and the spritsail triced around for the new tack and reset, as soon as it would draw.

It seems astonishing that a sail, with so many apparent drawbacks should have found favour and then survived for almost a century and a half. Its longevity rules out, I believe, two theories which have been advanced to explain its existence: the first, that it was incorporated in the design for aesthetic reasons only; and the second, that the naval architects of the day were initially guided by ignorance, and subsequently governed by stubborn conservatism. The scientific study of the theory of sailing lay, to be sure, well over the horizon, but it is inconceivable that the shipbuilders and seamen of the day, as practical men, would have tolerated the consequences of poor design unless they saw, or thought they saw, some immediate advantage in so doing. However that may be, the old-fashioned spritsail topsail remains, in my view, pretty much an enigma.

The later spritsail topsail. The old-fashioned spritsail topsail managed for some years to survive the introduction of jib and fore topmast staysail. However, by about 1720, it had disappeared. In its place, there developed a square sail set on a yard, run out on a traveller sliding on the jibboom, and functioning as a sort of 'under-jib'. The presence of jib and fore topmast staysail dictated a new lead for the spritsail braces, which now had to be taken up under the foretop, rather than leading to the forestay. A similar lead was used for the new spritsail topsail braces, which thus could trice the yard up, more or less parallel to the spritsail yard. If the sail was to set perfectly, it was necessary, not only that the yards were parallel to each other, but that both were at right angles to the bowsprit

and jibboom. This could be achieved by hauling taut the lee lift as well as the lee brace, which by itself would have pulled the lee yardarm too far aft.

The new sail set better by the wind than the spritsail itself, but in practice, worked best with a quartering wind (Sjöbohm, 58). First principles suggest that it would have exerted downward pressure on the jibboom, but this was not altogether bad, since the jib was pulling upwards, as well as laterally. How it was handled in tacking I am not sure, but it was, unlike its forerunner, capable of being thrown aback, and theoretically at least, could have been used to push the bow off the wind. One suspects that if set during tacking it was just clewed down during the crucial period and then reset. With the advent of the forward staysails, the necessity for a forward square sail, which would function well on the wind pretty well vanished. In the era of flying kites, particularly items like the 'driver', and 'water sail', set as far aft as could be, such a piece of canvas forward must occasionally have proved useful. Forfait (118), however, says that the increased steeve of the bowsprit in the late 1700s, almost nullified its effect in balancing the sail plan.

With the introduction of the jibboom, downward and lateral support was provided by means of guys. These ran from the end of the jibboom through thimbles on the spritsail yard, and thence inboard, to be belayed. When by the wind, the spritsail yard was triced up, even though no sail was actually set, and the guys on the lower, or weather side were hauled taut, thus counteracting the upward, lateral and forward pull of the jib.

About 1794, the flying jib, and the boom upon which it set, began to appear, followed immediately by yet another new fitting, the dolphin-striker. This acted as a jumper-strut, to give a good downward angle of pull to the martingale stay, which was the hold-down for the flying jibboom. At first, this stay made a quick, almost vertical return to the bowsprit, in front of the slings of the spritsail yard, so that it would not prevent the spritsail being set. Later, the return, or 'back-rope', was led aft less steeply, and the spritsail passed into disuse.

Long after the sail had disappeared, part of the drill, in going about, included the order 'Trice around the spritsail yard! Haul taut the weather guys!' The lead of the flying jibboom guys, meant that the spritsail topsail yard had to be canted, willy-nilly with the larger spar, even though the guys were never attached to the spritsail topsail yard. The martingale stay prevented the topsail being set under the jibboom. Thus the spritsail top-

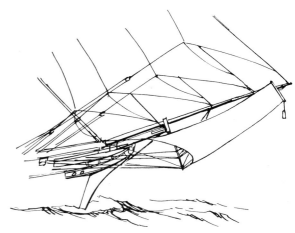

A 'Jemmy Green': later counterpart of the spritsail topsail.

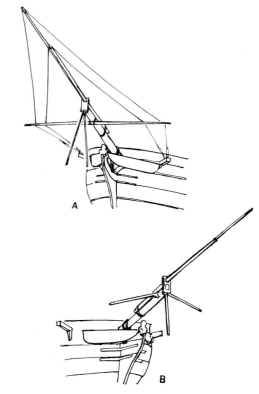

A Double dolphin striker c1815
B Spreaders c1850

sail, whatever its virtues, was doomed to extinction by the dolphin-striker. I have, elsewhere, questioned whether *Victory*, in 1805, really had both a spritsail topsail yard, and a dolphin-striker, but a very eminent Technical Committee decided in 1922, that she should be so represented, and in view of the evidence available, it is not certain how things can be resolved otherwise (*Mariner's Mirror* 63, 1977, 8; 67, 1981, 62).

There are, in fact, a few contemporary illustrations which show both dolphin-striker and spritsail topsail yards, but from 1800 on, a flying jibboom is always accompanied by a dolphin-striker, and the spritsail topsail yard has disappeared. There is, however, no lack of contemporary models, particularly those made by prisoners-of-war, which show both features. What looks well on the mantel-piece, is not, however, necessarily what works well at sea, and the multiplication of contemporary examples of models showing a particular error, does not mean they necessarily reflect practice in the full-sized prototype.

Like many other obsolete items, the recollection of the spritsail topsail lived on in the memories of old seamen, to be resurrected as the 'Jemmy Green' of clippers, attempting to ghost along in light airs. Contrived as a lash-up, using a spare topgallant studdingsail, or something of the sort, it was simply the analogue of the lower half of the spritsail topsail. It was not held in universal high esteem however. The French seamen called it a *haha*, and although Willaumez describes and illustrates it, Bonnefoux & Paris (419) dismiss it as '*une petite voile de fantaisie et d'un usage peu utile*'. Forfait (118) says that the only reason for keeping the yard rigged was that it could be used to set the foot of a triangular *haha*. I have never come across any evidence that this sail was set in English men-of-war of 1800, although it was used, as mentioned, in the clippers, half a century later.

Double dolphin-strikers and spreaders. A forked dolphin-striker was in wide use for the first forty years of the nineteenth century. A study of contemporary paintings suggests that, for some reason, it fell out of favour about 1840. When sailing on a wind, the weather stays were taut, and those on the lee side were relatively slack. The man-of-war in the late 1800s, often used 'half-booms' or 'spreaders' instead of a spritsail yard. These were rigged to point somewhat down and for-

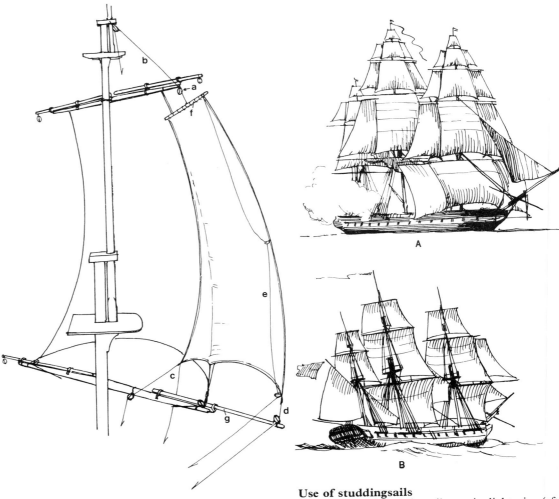

Topmast studdingsail
a jewel block; **b** halliard; **c** sheets; **d** tack; **e** downhaul; **f** studdingsail yard; **g** studdingsail boom.

Use of studdingsails
A Full suit of studdingsails set in light airs (after contemporary print of HMS *Belvidera*); **B** fore topmast studdingsail set in a fresh breeze.

ward, as well as laterally. The weather spreader and the weather half of a double dolphin-striker were, in fact, the functional equivalent of the weather, or lower, half of a triced up spritsail yard and its guys.

Spritsail topgallant sail. Steel (105) lists this along with other rarely used pieces of canvas like royal staysails. It really does not seem a very practical sail, but a yard for it is occasionally represented on prisoner-of-war models. Most likely it would have been set 'flying' (that is to say, without braces) and it would have been handled like a studdingsail, yard and all being taken inboard, when it was not set.

Studdingsails. The fore topmast studdingsail was the most useful of these. It was set on the weather side, in any sort of reasonable conditions, sometimes even with one reef

taken in the topsails. Because of the leverage resulting from its windward situation, it was an excellent sail for easing weather helm, and preventing the helmsman jamming the ship too close to the wind. The main topmast studdingsail could never be set alone, and thus was somewhat less useful. The topgallant studdingsails were strictly light weather canvas. The fore lower studdingsail was an enormous sail, used with the wind almost dead aft, and it was not set as long as the jib would draw. Main lower studdingsails dropped out of use quite early. Main topmast studdingsails also fell out of favour in the Royal Navy, at a time when those on the fore were retained. We will return later to a more detailed examination of how studdingsails were handled.

CHAPTER 6
ORGANISATION OF CREW FOR HANDLING THE SHIP

Watches and part of ship. The crew comprised both seamen, who kept watch, and the day-men or 'idlers', whose duties did not readily permit watchkeeping. The German term was *Freischläfer*, 'free-sleeper'. A distinction was made between 'effective' or 'working idlers', who were artificers, and 'non-effective' or 'excused idlers', who were stewards and the like (Burney, 277). In addition to the sailmakers, armourers, coopers, store-keepers, cooks, stewards, master-at-arms, musicians, and so on, certain officers were also designated idlers: the commanding officer, the first lieutenant, officer of marines, paymaster, surgeon, chaplain, and sometimes others besides (Totten, 257).

The watchkeepers were divided into port and starboard watches. Each watch was further divided into a first and second part, and, in large ships, each part was divided again into quarter-watches, corresponding to the modern RN 'subdivision'. The 'starbolins' worked the starboard side of the ship, and the 'larbolins' the port, when working with the 'hands'. If one watch only was on deck, the first part worked the starboard, the second part the port side, the first and third quarters working to starboard and the second and fourth to port. Incidentally, in some other languages, Dutch *kwartier*, French *quart*, and so on, used in this context, 'quarter' means 'watch' rather than 'quarter-watch'. The Danes sometimes designated the watches 'king's-watch' and 'queen's-watch' (*kongens qvarteer* and *dronningens qvarteer*) instead of starboard and port (Hansen, II, 112). The numbering system allotted the men of the starboard watch, uneven, and those of the port, even numbers. Each man had an 'opposite number' or partner, who assumed the duties of the other if only one were on deck. These partners were in the same mess, stationed at the same gun, and alternated as crew in the same boat.

The hands were allocated a 'part of ship', being designated forecastlemen, foretopmen, maintopmen, mizzentopmen and quarterdeckmen. Until the mid-1800s, the quarterdeckmen were divided into gunners and

afterguard. Subsequently one part of the quarterdeckmen continued to be popularly known as the 'gunners', the first according to Burney (277), the second according to Grenfell (89). Smyth defines the 'afterguard' as 'The men who are stationed on the quarterdeck and poop, to work the after sails. It was generally composed of ordinary seamen, and landsmen, constituting with the waisters the largest part of the crew, on whom the principal drudgery of the ship devolved.' He says the 'waisters' were 'green hands and worn seamen, employed as sweepers and cleaners'. Dick & Kretchmer (289) say that under the German system, the crew were divided into three mast divisions, each consisting of 'topmen' who went aloft, and those remaining on deck, *Kuhlgasten* ('waisters') with the foremast, *Achtergasten* ('afterguard') with the mainmast, and *Schanzgasten* ('quarterdeckmen') with the mizzen mast division; *Backsgasten* ('forecastlemen') were included in the foremast division, although Brommy (385) forms them into a separate forecastle division. Other navies used similar organisational systems.

We have a very fair idea of the way the crew were organised for sail drill in the late 1800s, from sources like Burney and Ulffers, but to what extent the extremely formalised routines of the late Victorian navies reflected the practice of an earlier day, I am not certain. It seems probable that the ritual precision, attainable by a crew of 'continuous service men', would have been difficult to achieve with impressed seamen, during the Napoleonic era.

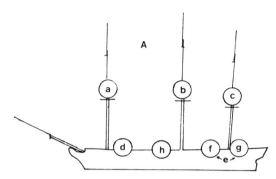
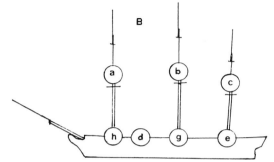

Divisions of the watches
A Royal Navy system (after Burney); **B** German system (after Dick & Kretchmer).
a foretopmen; **b** maintopmen; **c** mizzentopmen; **d** forecastlemen; **e** quarterdeckmen; **f** gunners; **g** afterguard; **h** waisters.

Numbering of crew. Dick & Kretchmer give the German system, whereby the crew were allocated numbers from 1-999. I have no doubt that similar plans were followed in the Royal Navy.

Numbers	
1–99	*Freiwächter* 'idlers'
100–199	forecastlemen
200–399	foretopmen
400–499	waisters
500–699	maintopmen
700–799	afterguard
800–899	mizzentopmen
900–999	quarterdeckmen

Uneven numbers formed the starboard, even numbers the port watch.

Mustering the watch. When the watch came on deck, the practice was to have them 'answer their stations'. This constant repetition meant that in the event, they knew 'in their sleep' as it were, exactly what their job would be in any evolution or exercise. The first lieutenant would assign a specific evolution, in the Night Order Book: 'First Watch, answer to "Furl Sails", Middle Watch answer to "Shifting Topmasts", Morning Watch answer to "Reef topsails in Stays"'. The mate of the watch called out the evolution, and each man responded with his station in that circumstance – 'Reeve fore

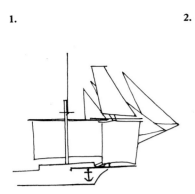

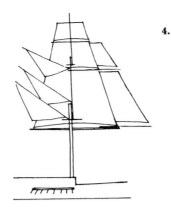

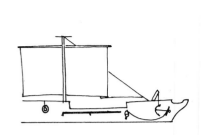

1. **Duties of the forecastlemen.**

2. **Duties of the foretopmen.**

3. **Duties of the maintopmen.**

4. **Duties of the mizzentopmen.**

5. **Duties of the gunners.**

6. **Duties of the afterguard.**

7. **Duties of the marines.**

8. **Duties of the carpenters.**

9. **Deck cleaning duties and stowage of hammocks**
   a foretopmen; b maintopmen; c mizzentopmen; d forecastlemen; e gunners; f afterguard.

top-tackle fall', 'Weather reef-tackle, fore tack, and bowline', or whatever (Glascock, 56).

From the point of view of the individual, the arrangement might work out something as follows, taking, say, Number 53 in a 46-gun frigate (Fordyce, 72).

Watch	First part, starboard watch
Station in watch	Foretop
Quarters	First captain, seventh gun, main deck
Division of boarders and sail trimmers	Second
Assigned as fireman or pumper	No
Arms	Cutlass and pistol
Reefing, furling and loosing sail	Starboard side, fore topsail yard
Making sail from anchorage	After sails are let fall, to deck, to attend fore topsail, topgallant and royal halliards and sheets
Mooring and unmooring	Veers cable on main deck
Weighing	Capstan, purchase, warps, head braces, jib halliards, as ordered
Tacking or wearing, hauling after yards	Raise fore clewgarnet, main tack, or attend main top bowline if mainsail is not set
Hauling headyards	Fore top bowline and fore tack
When tacks are down, and yards up	Set up weather fore topsail lift and fore truss
Making sail...out reefs	On forecastle, set taut reef-tackles and buntlines, hoist sails and haul home sheets
Setting studdingsails	Hook lift-jigger and burton, haul taut, and get ready fore topmast studdingsail

Shortening all sail	Starboard fore topsail clewline
Taking in studdingsails only	Take in starboard fore topmast studdingsail on forecastle
Lowering and squaring yards	Starboard forelift and truss
Crossing yards, loosing or mending sail	Starboard side, fore topsail yard
Boat	Pinnace

DUTIES ALLOTTED TO THE DIFFERENT PARTS OF SHIP

Forecastlemen. These were the biggest, strongest men in the ship. They bent and worked the headsails, fore course, lower and fore topmast studdingsails. They cleared away and secured the anchors, rove the cat-fall and hooked the cat and fish tackles to the anchor. They cleaned the forecastle and stowed the hammocks on the starboard side of the forecastle. They rigged the foremast, foreyard and bowsprit and the corresponding sails, and rigged the swinging boom in harbour. They were divided into 'foreyard loosers and furlers', and 'headsail loosers and stowers'.

Foretopmen. They worked all the masts and yards above the foretop. They bent and worked topsails, topgallants, royals, topgallant studdingsails, main royal, topgallant and topmast staysails, and fore trysails. As on all masts, the smallest men and boys worked on the royal yards, the topsails being looked after by the more robust topmen. In weighing anchor, they passed nippers and stoppers. The royal yardmen looked after and cleaned the fore chains, the topgallant yardmen looked after and cleaned the port booms. Foretopmen cleaned the port side of the main deck, and stowed the hammocks on the port side of the forecastle.

Maintopmen. They rigged and worked the masts and spars above the maintop, bent and worked the corresponding sails, including mizzen staysails, main topgallant studdingsails and, before they fell out of use, main topmast studdingsails. Royal yardmen looked after the main channels, topgallant yardmen looked after the booms on the starboard side. The maintopmen cleaned the

starboard side of the main deck, and stowed starboard quarterdeck hammocks.

Mizzentopmen. Assisted by the second part of the quarterdeckmen, they rigged and worked the mizzen mast and crossjack yard, and themselves rigged and worked spars and sails above the mizzen top, and the mizzen itself. The royal yardmen kept the mizzen channels clean. The mizzentopmen stowed port quarterdeck hammocks.

Gunners, or first part of quarterdeckmen. They rigged and worked the mainmast, mainyard, bent and worked the main course and main staysail. They rigged fish-davit and tackle, bent buoy-rope and streamed the buoy, looked after the life-buoy, rigged the lower booms at sea, and stowed starboard waist hammocks.

Afterguard, or second part of quarterdeckmen. They bent and worked the main trysail and helped the first part with the lower yard of the main. They cleaned the quarterdeck and stowed the port waist hammocks.

Marines. They assisted the quarterdeckmen on deck, were stationed by the life-buoy at sea, and held the reel when heaving the log.

Stokers. In the days of the sail-and-steam navy, they were organised in three watches in the stoke-hole, when at sea, with steam up. If the machinery were not in use, they worked two watches, augmenting the deck force.

Carpenters. Amongst other duties, they rigged the capstan and pumps, and when weighing anchor, stood by the capstan to fleet the turns of the messenger up on the barrel. After the anchor was secured, they fitted the 'jackasses' – canvas bags of a tapered shape, which plugged the hawseholes – and shipped the bucklers, which further secured them. They were also responsible for barring and caulking the lower gunports before going to sea.

Special numbers. Since loosing sail required fewer men than furling, the 'loosers' were usually the watch on deck of 'furlers'. Too many men would simply have got in each other's way. 'Boom tricers' were dependable, experienced topmen, told off to haul up the

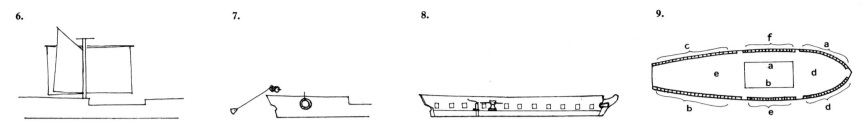

SAIL DRILL AND WORKING SHIP

Going aloft. At one time, the upper yardmen went aloft at the run, at the same time as everyone else. Since they had to climb much further than the lower yardmen, this must have been extremely demanding physically. The damp conditions in the ill-ventilated mess-decks were an ideal setting for the development of rheumatic heart disease, and its complications. In any event, by the mid-1800s, the Admiralty became concerned about the incidence of heart trouble in upper yardmen, and instituted a 'breather' to make the journey aloft less strenuous. Burney (288) says that the upper yardmen should be sent aloft five minutes before the rest of the topmen. Grenfell (93) suggests that the interval was usually somewhat less than this. The intention was that the evolution would appear to be executed in an orderly fashion, the men going aloft together, laying out and laying in together, rather than being allowed to do things at their own time (Engelhart, 68).

Laying out on the yard. When they reached the top, the upper yardmen kept strictly inside the topmast rigging. In preparation for going aloft, the men fell in on deck abreast the lower shrouds. The light yardmen in front, then the topmen and in the rear the lower yardmen. In harbour, and in a calm at sea, they went aloft on both sides. In blowing weather, they went aloft to weather only. From the crosstrees, the men ascended on the Jacob's ladder to the topgallant and royal yards. Sometimes it was necessary for them to use royal lifts, clewlines, and so on, to scramble their way up to the topmast cap, and get onto the topgallant yard in that fashion. The yardarm men often ran out on the topsail and lower yards, holding on to the studdingsail booms. If the yards were braced up sharp, it might be difficult to reach the topsail yard from the weather topmast shrouds, in which case, the men used a Jacob's ladder to reach the yard via the lower cap. The lower yardmen reached the yard

booms. 'Upper bracemen' slipped the topgallant and royal brace and lift on and off, when shifting the light yards. 'Topsail sheetmen' were regarded as important numbers: they worked on the lower yards, and saw to it that the topsail sheets were properly home, overhauled clewlines and other gear of the sail, and were stationed at the yardarm, when setting topmast studdingsails to see they went up clear. Older, experienced, but physically less active seamen were detailed as 'captains of the mast' in charge of handing out and belaying gear at the foot of the mast. They were assisted by the 'mast party', who were sometimes known as 'bittmen' or 'stoppermen'. They passed the stoppers, for example, to hold the topsail halliards, prior to their being belayed. The work aloft was under the charge of the 'captain of the top', assisted by the 'captain of the crosstrees' for the upper yards. The captain of the top worked at the bunt of the topsail yard in furling, and at the weather yardarm when reefing. There was, in addition, a 'midshipman of the top'.

Hands, both watches and the watch. In addition to the seamen, 'all hands' comprised carpenters, idlers, stokers and marines. The hands were turned out in emergency, and in harbour, for any recognised 'hands' evolution. Rather than take the daymen away from their work, it was usual to make do with 'both watches', if that made enough bodies available. At night, the hands would rarely be called, and, if possible, an evolution like reefing topsails, or tacking, would be scheduled at the change of watch, thus causing the least interference with the men's repose. At sea, there was usually a watch evolution at six bells in the forenoon (11.00 hours) and afternoon (15.00 hours) and a hands drill after quarters. In harbour, there was always a watch drill at 08.00 hours, and usually after quarters in the evening (Grenfell, 91).

from the catharpings, or by scrambling out, treading on the weather truss chains. They rarely used the footropes unless it was blowing very hard (Grenfell, 93).

Lifelines. Permanent lifelines were often rigged on the lower yard. Temporary lifelines were invariably rigged in preparation for ceremonial manning of the yards. They ran about four feet above the yard and parallel to it, and the outer ends were bent to the lifts (see section on Squaring, Cockbilling and Manning Yards in the next Chapter).

Bracing. Great care was necessary to see that the yards were properly secured by lifts, braces and rolling-tackles, before the men were allowed to lay out. A sudden unexpected drop of the yard could have disastrous consequences. The braces were not usually touched with men on the yard, but if this was absolutely necessary, they were warned to hold fast beforehand (Krogh, 21).

Tricing up booms. This was done routinely with all sail drill in port, to allow the men room to work. At sea, when loosing sail, it was often omitted, particularly in the case of the topgallant studdingsail booms. Prior to the boom being run up, the inner iron had to be unclasped. The first man at the catharpings ran out, undid the forelock, and lifted the upper half of the hoop, and then returned in. On the lower and topsail yards, 'laying-out marks' were indicated with white paint. The men stayed inside the marks until the order 'Trice up, and lay out!' was given.

Preservation of silence. The mark of a well-drilled crew was the execution of the evolution with no 'singing out' back and forth.

In the execution of evolutionary movements, the strictest silence should be observed. Were the junior lieutenants in their respective stations to indulge less the disposition to hail aloft, duties would be better preserved. On no account should petty officers be permitted to call from deck to the tops or to the masthead. The practice of allowing the foremastmen to hail aloft upon every occasion that a hauling line may be required, speaks little for the in-

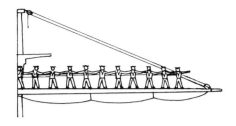

Manning the yards.

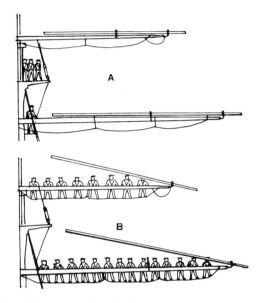

Laying out on the yards
A Standing by; **B** 'Trice up and lay out!'.

ternal discipline of a vessel-of-war. Nor should the topmen's predilection to sing out from aloft, be at all indulged. Ropes are much sooner disengaged on deck by means of a tell-tale shake from overhead, than by individual hails, or shrill shouts from the masthead (Glascock, 317).

'No hailing from aloft is needed, and none should be tolerated', says Luce. The yardman held up his arm when the earing was passed, and other men acted on this signal.

As to the conduct of a midshipman stationed aloft, 'He is not to stand stationary on the top, nor to remain perched like a parrot on the cap, reiterating senseless sounds. Too much unnecessary noise is heard aloft, without the midshipman swelling the clamour. To prevent, or prohibit noise, an officer must himself be an example of silence' (Glascock, 26).

It was preferable that, in all ships, one settled form of order be used, to carry out a particular evolution:

> For example, in shortening sail upon a wind, one lieutenant may indulge in long and loud train of mandatory words, such as 'Let go the bowlines! In topgallants! Up courses! Down jib and staysails!', whilst another officer, less noisy, and more prone to brevity will more effectively achieve the same purpose by the terse phrase 'Shorten sail!' (Glascock, 295).

Orders nonetheless had to be given with sufficient force and accuracy, so they could not be misunderstood, and left no doubt as to their intention.

At the end of an evolution, the pipe 'Haul taut and coil down ropes', sent the men to their stations; the idlers, marines, and so on, fell in at the same time, and if not required to make up sails, were dismissed.

Lay in, lay down from aloft! The men on the yard remained there until this order was given, upon which they returned to deck as speedily as possible, some, according to Mossel (III, 72), choosing to slide down the topsail halliards. If necessary, one or two men were detailed to overhaul the gear, coming down after the others. In harbour, they were known as 'square-yard men' because they did not come down until the yards had been squared to the satisfaction of the boatswain.

Watch bill. Upon commissioning, each member of the crew was given a station for the several duties he might be called upon to

perform during mooring, tacking, shifting topsails, or whatever. It was important to have a sufficiency of force, without having too many people tripping over each other, and to concentrate the numbers where the greatest activity was required. Harbour evolutions would include: bending sail; loosing sail; furling sail; loosing sail to a bowline, or buntline; topgallant and royal yards up and down; topgallant mast up and down; strike topmast; shift topsail yard; shift flying jibboom; shift topsail, course or jib; in and out boats.

Drills at sea included: weigh anchor and make sail; tacking; wearing; trimming sail; setting studdingsails; taking in studdingsails; reefing topsails or courses; shaking reefs out of topsails or courses; shorten sail and come to anchor.

The intention of harbour drills was to improve the efficiency with which similar manoeuvres were carried out at sea. Nonetheless, as we shall see, things were done to expediate matters during drills which would not have been prudent at sea, as for example, the singling of topsail sheets and clewlines, to facilitate handling the sail quickly. The light yards and topgallant masts of a man-of-war worked on similar principles to those of the contemporary merchantmen, but they exhibited many small refinements, unknown in the merchant service, which enabled them to be sent up and down with great facility and expedition.

The boatswain's method of giving the pipe.

> In calling up the hands, or calling the crew to the performance of their duties, the boatswain too often indulges in piercing pipes, and drawling tones of superfluous length. Boatswains have a singular propensity to demonstrate the soundness of their lungs, by an endless protraction of a note on their piercing pipes. They should not be so fond of supplying the place of the sea birds. This is not the worst feature of their taste; for when at last they utter the required summons, they give it forth in tones so drawling, that the first words are often forgotten before the last are out. A-l-l h-a-n-d-s a-b-o-u-t s-h-i-p. This lengthy summons, and a longer winded whistle, and each pipe and phrase three times repeated by the boatswain and his mates, and the ship may be ashore before the leader of the band is convinced how dearly he has paid for his whistle (Brady, 247).

1.

Sailors of the Imperial German Navy going aloft in the armoured corvette *Moltke*. (Imperial War Museum)

2.

Manning the yards at the Jubilee Naval Review, Spithead, 1887. Note the bunt gaskets and the footropes triced up against the yard for neatness. *Illustrated London News*, 1887. (Mark Myers' Collection)

3.

HMS *Edgar* saluting with yards manned at the International Naval Festival, Portsmouth, in 1865. Engraving by Lionel P Smythe in the *Illustrated London News*, 1865. (Mark Myers' Collection)

3.

CHAPTER 7
BENDING, LOOSING AND FURLING SAIL

BENDING SQUARE SAIL

There are very comprehensive accounts of the methods of bending sail from the middle of the 1800s, but only sketchy documentation of the way it was managed earlier. 'Bend' rather than 'bind' remained in use as the technical term for making the sail fast to the yard. Indeed, according to the Oxford English Dictionary, 'bend' is the more ancient form of the two.

Topgallants and royals were bent to their yards on deck, and sent up and down with them. The gear of the courses was overhauled down to the deck, and the sail sent up with buntlines, leechlines, etc, already secured. Topsails were hoisted up with a sail tackle, and the gear was then made fast in the top, before the sail was 'brought to' the yard and bent. As might be expected, there was great variation in detail, as to the exact methods used, and it is only possible to offer a representative account. In the late 1800s, the spare canvas was often stowed in the sail-room 'ready for bending'. Sometimes, however, it was stowed away, so as to take up as little space as possible, made up 'ready for stowing', and before it could be bent, the sail had to be made up on deck. The idea was to have the cringles accessible, so the gear could be toggled on to these eyelets, which were worked in the boltropes, without loosing the whole sail.

In merchantmen, sails were bent prior to proceeding to sea, and replaced only when blown out or badly damaged. However, they were frequently 'shifted', as an exercise, in men-of-war; the topsails, for instance, were unbent, sent down, and replaced by spare sails. To facilitate this, each sail had its own set of gaskets, and was permanently fitted with robands, head-earings, reef-earings, and, in the case of topsails and courses, bending strops. Considerable use was made of beckets and toggles, to avoid having to secure buntlines and the like, to their respective cringles with a proper clinch, which would have taken more time. For harbour sail drill, old, well stretched sails, being lighter and softer were preferred. At sea, especially if heavy weather was expected, better, newer canvas was used, and some changes made in the way the gear was bent to the sail also.

Methods of bending. The head of the sail was made fast to the yard with robands, the head-cringles at the corners being held out and up by the head-earings. The boltrope was sewed on the after side of the sail, so that it, rather than the canvas, was in direct contact with the yard, thus allowing better ventilation of the head of the sail, and helping to avoid the canvas being chafed by the wooden yard. Originally the robands were passed completely around the yard, while later they were secured to the bending jackstay, which was introduced about 1811 (Lees, 159). Light canvas, such as studding-sails, could be laced to their yards, marline hitching the lashing at each turn, or secured with individual sennit stops (Luce, 215).

Robands. The word is not, as it might appear, just a worn-down form of 'rope-band'. The earliest citations indicate that the first element is *ra*, an old word for 'yard', still in use in the other North Germanic tongues (Sandahl, II, 86; *Mariner's Mirror* 16, 1930,

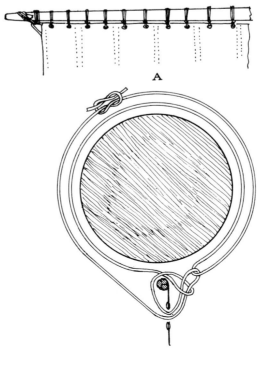

203). There were usually two robands for each cloth, sometimes both placed between the seams, sometimes, one on the seam, and one halfway between (Luce, 206). The 'head-holes' were strengthened by a 'grommet', heavy stitching taken around the hole to prevent the canvas tearing. The robands were of plaited spunyarn, 'sennit', and were secured in various ways (Ashley, 226), two of which will suffice as representative.

Early robands. These completely encircled the yard, and, using the following method, would have been required to exceed twelve feet in length for a lower yard, two feet in diameter. The roband was doubled, leaving uneven ends, and the bight thrust through the head-hole, from aft forward (Anderson, 269; Le Compte, 123). The long end was half-hitched around the bight where it crossed the headrope, and then taken up behind and over the yard, through the bight, back up and over the yard to be square-knotted with the short end. Pihlström (215) takes an extra round turn with the long end around the yard, knotting the ends above the yard and tucking the ends under the round turn. This method uses

Robands
A Early method of passing robands on sail bent below yard; **B** later method of passing robands on sail bent to jackstay.

96

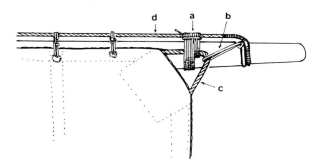

Head earing
a inner turns of head earing; **b** outer turns of head earing; **c** head cringle; **d** jackstay.

Gaskets
A Gaskets in position on yard, with sail loosed; **B and C** methods of passing gaskets; **D** chambrière; **E** sea gaskets; **F** harbour gaskets; **G** bunt gaskets.

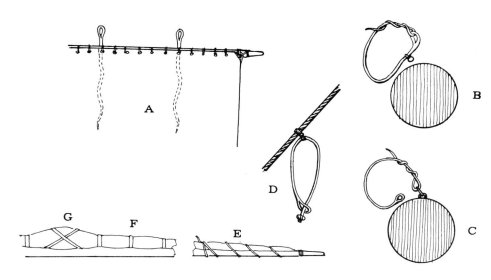

the bight as a sort of pulley, to haul things extra taut. A simpler method was used for light yards. As early as 1700, a perforated bending strip was sometimes nailed underneath the central part of the yard, to serve as a sort of jackstay (Anderson, 58), allowing short robands to be used.

Later methods. With the early method, the headrope came directly under the yard, with the stretching of the robands under use, this actually pulled away somewhat, leaving a gap between the yard and the sail. The introduction of the jackstay, placed on the upper forward aspect of the yard, corrected this problem, and also allowed the sail, when furled, to be got well up on the yard, instead of hanging beneath it, as had been the case earlier. Luce (213) describes the following method of making the robands fast. It was doubled, with uneven ends, and the bight thrust through the head-hole from forward aft. The long end was slipped through the bight and both ends hauled taut, in effect half-hitching the long end to the headrope. To secure to the jackstay, the short end was passed up between the yard and jackstay, while the long end was passed back and down, taking a round turn on the jackstay, whereupon the ends were square-knotted above. The midship roband was distinguished in some way, perhaps being of rope rather than sennit, since it centred the sail on the yard, and was made fast first.

Head-earings. These held the head-cringles out and up. On the lower yards, there were sometimes two earings, an outer, to hold the head out, and an inner, to hold it up. On the upper yards, one earing, passed with inner and outer turns, sufficed. In bending, it was important to get the head on the stretch, and this was accomplished by hooking the reef-tackles or yard-jiggers to the first reef-cringles. Sometimes a special 'bending

cringle' was worked in the boltrope just below the head-cringle for this specific purpose. The tackle could not be hooked in the head-cringle itself since this would have interfered with passing the earing. Getting the headrope taut in a new sail was more difficult than in one stretched by much use. In such a case, the earings and robands were made fast temporarily, and the headrope 'ridden down', the men on the yard leaning or tramping on the bights of headrope to stretch it, after which the headrope was once more hauled taut, and secured properly. There was some division of opinion about the propriety of this practice, some feeling that showing too great a vigour in riding down could permanently ruin the set of the sail (Totten, 127).

Gaskets. These were originally always secured to the yard, and when deployed, lay forward of the sail. Later they were seized to the jackstay, and when not in use, hung behind the sail. In some ships, the gaskets were seized to the headrope rather than the jackstay, a separate set being kept with each sail, being used to secure it when sending it up or down. This facilitated shifting the sail, which otherwise would have required spun-yarn stops, in place of gaskets, to secure the canvas (Ulffers, 121, 221). This type of gasket, about one every third seam, had an eye at the top, seized to the headrope, and projecting above it. The flat plaited body of the gasket was sufficiently long to encircle the furled sail, or sometimes both yard and sail. When the gasket was passed, the tail was taken through the eye, doubled back and tucked in between gaskets and sail. Taunt (78) takes the laniard through a ring secured to the yard further back than the jackstay, to allow getting the sail well up on the yard. Mossel (II, 34) describes a similar arrangement with a staple with two rings on the after

side of the yard. Why there were two rings is not completely clear, but perhaps the gasket eye was secured to the forward one, the gasket going over the sail and the tail bent to the after ring. If the staples were fore and aft, this would have been a neat arrangement.

'Bunt gaskets', were longer than the others, and crossed in an 'X' to hold the heavy bunt up on the yard. Another type of bunt gasket was fashioned like a net, with the upper horizontal side secured to the jackstay, behind the sail, and the point coming round the bunt from below, up and over. 'Sea gaskets' ('long gaskets' as Smyth calls them) or 'furling lines' were of sennit, three to each arm of lower and topsail yards, one to each yardarm of topgallants and royals. They were sufficiently long to be capable of encircling the yard, sail, and if necessary, booms, to confine the canvas in bad weather. They were coiled up and thrown forward of the sail when not deployed, and were taken off in harbour (Taunt, 79).

Chambrières, which literally means 'chamber-maids' were a special type of gasket used in French ships to furl the mizzen and the staysails. They were of square sennit about a fathom long. Four or five were secured at their mid points to the stay, or the after side of the mast. At one end, there was an eye, and at the other a shroud knot, by which they could quickly be made fast, 'buttoning up' the furled sail, so to speak. Incidentally, Röding mentions another form of *chambrière*, without giving an equivalent in any other languages. These were lengths of sennit made fast to the lower shrouds, fitted with stopper knot and eye, which were used to take the weight of the tack and sheet blocks, when the courses were clewed up (Baudin, 252; Willaumez, 139). Perhaps 'clew-hanger', would be the nearest English equivalent.

Bending strop. This was a rope ring, or

Detail of a bending strop.

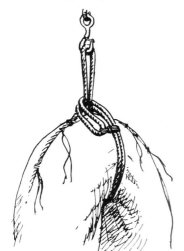

grommet, which encircled the rolled up sail at the slings, as it was sent up for bending, and which was hooked to the sail tackle. In the naval service, it was customary to keep such a strop permanently seized to each course and topsail. One way of fitting it was to make two holes in the sail, close up under the mid-point of the headrope. One end of the rope, which was six to eight feet in length, was taken through one hole from aft forwards, back through the other hole, the opposite way, and the ends of the rope spliced together. The strop was seized to the head-rope, where it pierced the sail, and arranged so a short loop extended about six inches above the headrope, while a long bight hung inconspicuously behind the sail, when it was set. In use, the sail tackle was hooked to the short leg, the long bight going behind and under the rolled up sail, brought up and round behind the short bight forward and then seized to its own parts. When the seizing was cut, the sail fell free of the strop. The reason for securing the strop to the sail was as insurance, in the event the seizing was inadvertantly cut away, before the robands had taken the weight.

Furling a course on deck, ready for bending. The sail was laid on the planking, roping side down, with the headrope stretched fore and aft, hitched to any convenient points, to keep it taut. The foresail was placed on the deck forward, on the starboard side, port head-earing forward, and the main course in the gangway to port, starboard head-earing forward, with the bunts abreast their respective masts. The bending strop and gaskets thus lay underneath the sail, between it and the deck. The sail was gathered down from the head, the first reef-band taken up to the headrope, and the reef cringles stopped to the head-cringles (Luce, 358). The leeches were then laid in along the

headrope towards the bunt, in such a way that the leechline and bowline cringles would be accessible. The lowest part of the leech was folded up at right angles to the headrope, so that the clews lay about six feet above the head, four feet each side of the midship roband. The buntline toggles were brought up in the centre, between the clews, about a foot over the head. The men then extended themselves along the head, facing the foot, and drew the remaining slack sail up as if they were furling the sail on the yard. They then stepped over the sail and knelt down, grasping the double skin formed by the canvas smoothed out between the headrope and the first reef-band, and rolled the sail up in this skin. The gaskets were passed and footed well taut. The clews were taken around over the headrope, under the rolled up sail, brought up, and stopped to the head-rope. The long bight of the bending strop was taken around the sail, looped around the short bight, and seized to its own parts in front of the sail. The head-earings were led in towards the bunt, and stopped to the head-rope, so they could readily be got hold of when the sail was being sent aloft. This arrangement left the robands out and clear, while the clews, buntline-toggles, and so on, were ready for bending the gear, the sail being conveniently rolled up in a long cylinder. The headrope of the course was marked at the points corresponding to the leechline blocks, so that when the leechlines were seized at those points, and the sail was run up to the yard, the leechlines led fair to their leading blocks, and the headrope lined up at its proper place on the yard.

Making up a course for stowing in the sail-room. The sail was laid flat on deck, roping down as before, and with the head rope stretched taut. The first reef-band, second reef-band, belly-band and footrope were successively brought up to the head-rope, thus forming a narrow eight-fold rectangle about two feet across. The clews and bowline-cringles were left out at the ends, and the dog-ears formed by the bights of leech rope with each fold were tucked in out of sight. The hands then rolled up the sail, secured it with the gaskets and stopped the head-earing to the head-rope (Burney, 126).

Furling a topsail ready for bending. The fore topsail was made up on the port side, and the main topsail to starboard (Mossel, III, 51; Luce, 358). The method described by Burney is almost identical with that described for the course, the second reef-band being brought up to the head, to form the skin, and the leeches and clews disposed as mentioned above. This made a heavy bunt,

and kept the yardarms light. The fourth reef-earings were hitched to the third reef-cringle, and the third reef-earings to the second cringle. If the upper earings were secured to the sail, they would have been hitched in a similar manner. British practice was to keep the first two earings permanently secured to the yardarm, rather than the sail, so-called 'bull earings'. The head-earings were stopped to the bunt. Bowline bridles were permanently fitted to each topsail, and kept with the sail. The procedure for readying the sail for stowing in the bins, was analogous to that described for the course, bringing up the third reef-band, belly-band and foot to the headrope (Burney, 126). In fact, some ships always kept the sails in the bins 'ready for bending'.

Bending topgallants and royals. These were bent to their yards on deck, the royals invariably, the topgallants usually. If the topgallants were sent aloft for bending, the buntlines could be used to run them up. To get the additional length, extra rope was bent to the hauling end, so allowing the hitching end to reach the deck. Fore and mizzen topgallant yards were sent up to port, main to starboard, with the royals being handled on the opposite sides.

Bending a course. The sail, 'ready for bending', was brought round to lie on deck beneath the yard. Buntlines, leechlines and clewgarnets were overhauled, so they could reach the deck and be bent on. Tack, sheet and clewgarnet blocks were shackled to the clews, and reef-tackles bent to the first reef-cringle or the bending cringle. A sail-tackle was secured to the top, or the collar of the lower stay, and the lower block hooked to the bending strop. Burney (128) suggests hanging the clew from the strop of the lower block of the sail-tackle, to take the considerable weight of the heavy blocks depending from it. To get the headrope taut, it was necessary to haul the upper corners of the sail out to the yardarms, and this was managed in a variety of ways. Some ships were fitted with a special lower reef-tackle. More often, a reef-pendant was employed, and the reef-burton, intended for hauling this taut, would have served to haul out the head-cringles. Otherwise a yardarm jigger was contrived, using the lower studdingsail inner halliards, or carrying the upper block of the clew-jiggers out to the yardarm from the top, and hooking the lower block to the first reef-cringle, or the specially fitted bending-cringle. The leechlines and buntlines were toggled on to the leech and foot, and then seized to the headrope, so that they would pull the head of the sail up to the appropriate place on the yard. When it had

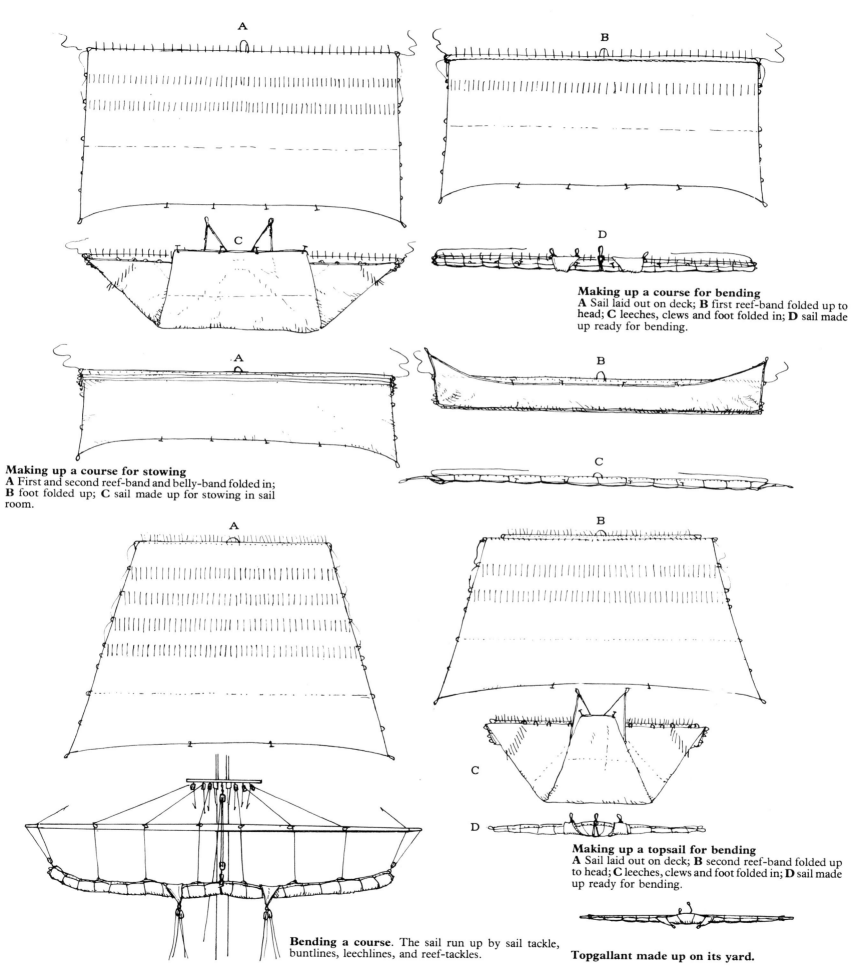

Making up a course for bending
A Sail laid out on deck; **B** first reef-band folded up to head; **C** leeches, clews and foot folded in; **D** sail made up ready for bending.

Making up a course for stowing
A First and second reef-band and belly-band folded in; **B** foot folded up; **C** sail made up for stowing in sail room.

Bending a course. The sail run up by sail tackle, buntlines, leechlines, and reef-tackles.

Making up a topsail for bending
A Sail laid out on deck; **B** second reef-band folded up to head; **C** leeches, clews and foot folded in; **D** sail made up ready for bending.

Topgallant made up on its yard.

been determined that the sail was free of turns, sail-tackle, clewgarnets, buntlines, leechlines and yard-jiggers were hauled, so that the sail went up, more or less horizontally. When high enough, the lower yardmen secured the midship roband, and passed the earings, the starboard side first in harbour, the weather one first at sea (Mossel, III, 50), and subsequently made the remaining robands fast to the jackstay. The seizings on the bending strop and those securing leech and buntlines to the headrope were cut, and the clew-hangers passed (Burney, 128).

Bending topsails in harbour. In the late 1800s, the sail was hauled up by means of a sail tackle depending from the topmast head, or topmast stay, and hooked to the bending strop. The fall was overhauled and the lower block taken down before the lower yard. The sail tackle was just a top burton, with a leading block secured to the strop of the lower block. The fall led through this leading block, and then through a snatch-block on deck, pulling the sail forward, clear of the lower yard and top, as it went aloft. If a common burton were used, a top bowline could be hitched to the bending strop and serve to keep the sail clear. The sail went up, slung by its middle, with the ends hanging down. When the head-earings could be reached in the top, hoisting stopped, sheets were shackled, clewlines, buntlines and bowlines were toggled on. The reef-tackles were temporarily hooked to the first reef-cringles and used to haul the head of the sail taut, thus functioning like the yardarm jiggers of the course. Sometimes they required to be singled, to get the extra length, in bending. The sail was brought to the yard, earings passed, and robands secured as described for the course. The reef-tackle was then rigged properly, if it had been singled, and toggled to the reef-tackle cringle. The seizings holding the bending strop were cut, the gaskets cast off, and the sail-tackle unrigged. If a top burton, it was once again secured to its pendant (Mossel, III, 53).

Bending topsails at sea. Earlier practice is outlined by Pihlström (213), who places the fore and mizzen topsails on the port side of the deck, starboard sides forward, main to starboard, port side forward. The sail was hoisted by means of the buntlines and clewlines, which were stopped to the sail in such a way that it went aloft as a long cylinder, more or less vertically, starboard yardarm first, in the case of the fore topsail. The stops were cut in succession, to allow it to be brought to the yard. Pihlström seems to suggest that this method had become less suitable in 1796, because the clewline blocks had moved in to-

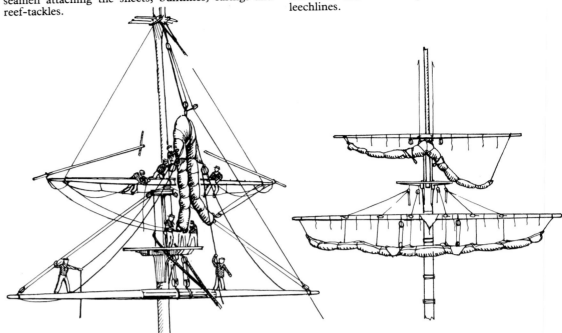

Bending a topsail. The sail run up on the sail tackle, seamen attaching the sheets, buntlines, earings and reef-tackles.

Unbending the lower sails. Topsail sent down by buntlines and course by buntlines, clewlines and leechlines.

wards the slings of the yard: where previously they had been placed a third the distance out toward the yardarm, they were now only one-eighth. The result was that they were a little too close in towards the top, and this made it more difficult to prevent the sail getting foul, as it was being brought to the topsail yard. In a dead calm, the topsail could be sent up forward of all, pretty much as described above. Otherwise, it was sent up abaft the lower yard to weather; that is, on the side upon which the yardarms were braced forward, and hence where more room was to be found (Mossel, III, 53). A burton or other suitable tackle was used to send the sail up. Pihlström (281), describing Swedish practice in 1796, uses the weather topsail halliards. With an arrangement of double halliards, and a single tie block on the yard, the lee halliards were hauled on to pull the upper double block of the weather halliards sufficiently high to allow the topsail to clear the top. The fall of the weather halliards was overhauled in this way, and the lower single block was unhooked from its place in the channels, and secured to the bending strop of the sail. The tie just above the double block, was seized securely to the aftermost topmast shroud, and the lee halliards were hauled taut and belayed. The stanchions on the after rim of the top were removed, as was the lantern, if it were a main topsail, so that the sail would not foul these in going up. The canvas was folded in three parts, with the upper fold being the lee third of the sail. Care was taken to keep turns out of the sail, which was manhandled round the front of the top and brought to the

yard. The weather halliards were subsequently overhauled again, and the lower block hooked once more to its channel eyebolt. The lee halliards were also overhauled, so the upper block was at about the same height as its fellow to weather. This rather clumsy method is illustrated in Lever (54), and alluded to by Mossel, who also suggests using the topmast studdingsail halliards, to help steer the sail clear of obstruction, as it goes up. In blowing weather, it was most important that turns be kept out of the sail, since failure to do so meant the almost certain loss of the sail (Mossel, 54). Boyd (408) remarks that sending a topsail up through the weather lubber's hole, in bad weather, would prevent it being blown to leeward, but was likely to result in getting the sail twisted. He recommends sending down the sail-tackle and buntlines, outside the top, before the weather lower lift, but abaft the lower yard, and the topmast studdingsail halliards abaft everything. The buntlines were toggled and hitched around the sail, somewhat out from the bunt, the sail tackle hooked to the bending strop, care being taken that the sail was facing the right way. The studdingsail halliards were hitched round both legs of the sail, and used to hold it to windward, as it went up. When high enough, the reef-tackles were hauled out, and the studdingsail halliards cast off. Although the weather lower lift was somewhat in the way, doing things in this manner, it was not to be let go to clear the sail; Boyd remarks that to do so 'would be extreme of bad sailoring'.

If the weather were so severe that a topsail

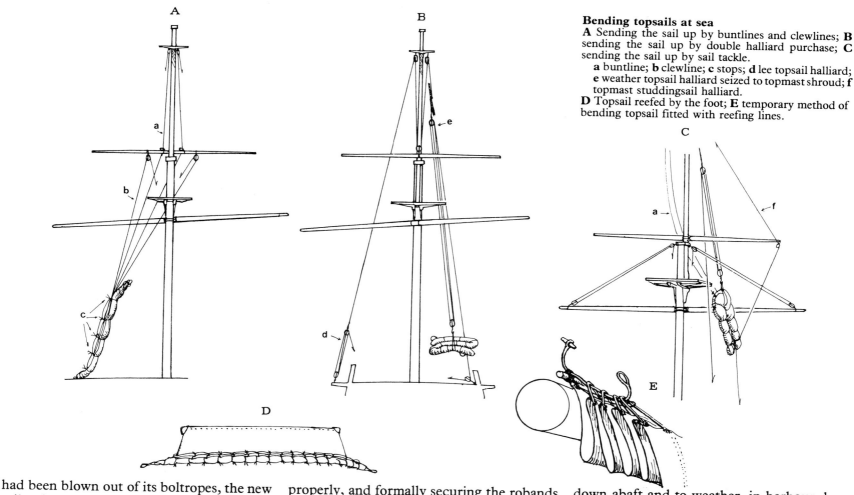

Bending topsails at sea
A Sending the sail up by buntlines and clewlines; **B** sending the sail up by double halliard purchase; **C** sending the sail up by sail tackle.
　　a buntline; **b** clewline; **c** stops; **d** lee topsail halliard; **e** weather topsail halliard seized to topmast shroud; **f** topmast studdingsail halliard.
D Topsail reefed by the foot; **E** temporary method of bending topsail fitted with reefing lines.

had been blown out of its boltropes, the new sail might be 'sent up reefed', the points being made fast on the headrope. This meant that it would be difficult to get the headrope taut initially, and it would require hauling out a second time. Boyd (410) preferred this method, but Liardet (246) believed that the best procedure in a gale was to 'reef by the foot'. The close-reef was stretched taut on deck, and the clews taken as near where they would be hauled up to the yard as possible, and stopped to the foot of the sail. The foot-rope was pulled up to the close-reef and the points passed round the foot, leaving the clews clear. The third, second, and first reef-points were then successively knotted under the foot. The sail thus was set initially, with only the canvas between the headrope and the first reef-band exposed to the weather.

Topsails fitted with reefing beckets were quite readily sent up reefed. Boyd (409) suggests the sail be laid on deck, and the reef-bands brought up to the head, one after another. The robands were slipped through all the reef-lines, and hitched to their own parts. When the sail was brought to the yard, the beckets were slipped through the reef-lines following the robands, and toggled. If there was need to do so, the sail could even be set, until an opportunity offered of bringing it to

properly, and formally securing the robands to the jackstay.

UNBENDING SQUARE SAIL

Canvas not only required to be sent down at the end of a voyage, but also when shifting sails for exercise. It was important, before the sails were stowed in the bins, that they be perfectly dry, especially the boltropes. For this reason, the light sails could be unbent and stowed a day or two earlier than the top-sails and courses, because the thinner bolt-ropes and lighter canvas dried more quickly. Mossel warns that since the sails are the 'salvation of the ship', it is essential they be examined for evidence of mildew and rot, at least once a month, and not be allowed to lie too long, out of sight and out of mind in the sail-room.

In unbending the sail, the men at the yard-arms loosened the earings, keeping the last turn on, until completely ready. The robands were cast off, or cut. The gaskets secured the sail if they were to be sent down with it, otherwise spunyarn stops were used instead, and the gaskets left seized to the jackstay. Topsails could be sent down with the bunt-lines, the courses with leechlines, buntlines and clewlines. At sea, the topsail would go

down abaft and to weather, in harbour, be-fore all. Before the sail was carried below to the bins, the boatswain satisfied himself that all the gear was in order, replacing worn items, so that all would be ready once more for use, immediately it was required.

Shifting sails. This was usually done for exercise, but naturally the practice gained stood the vessel in good stead should it be-come actually necessary while at sea. One topsail was unbent and sent down with a second burton, or just with the buntlines, while the other was being run up with the sail-tackle. Ulffers (121) describes the routine in the German service, where the watch on deck were unbending one sail, while the watch below brought the replacement to the tween deck. In the case of a main topsail, it could be placed below the main hatch, and swung up by a burton hooked to the strop, without the necessity of being manhandled onto the upper deck. At sea, everything would have to be done to weather, and naturally it would take somewhat longer. Mossel (70) estimates that it should take less than ten minutes to shift topsails. Grenfell (89) describes all three topsails being shifted simultaneously, with everything set to royals again, in less than six minutes; this included the time required to strike and rehoist the

Shifting a topsail at sea.

topsail yards! The topgallant yards could be struck and the sails clewed up, or, more usually, the sails could be left set with the sheets slacked off, if the weather permitted (Mossel, III, 69). Ulffers (220) takes the topgallants in, if by the wind, but leaves them set, if before it.

Light yards. To shift topgallants and royals, the yards were struck down on deck. The sails were bent in a similar fashion to the topsails and courses, and we will shortly describe the method of handling the yards themselves. The fore and mizzen topgallants went up to port, the main to starboard, while the royals were handled on the contralateral sides (Mossel, III, 57).

BENDING FORE AND AFT CANVAS

Head sails. The exact technique of bending a jib depended on how it was rigged. The sail secured to the stay with galvanised hanks, or a lacing, which snaked to and fro across the stay, rather than making spiral turns. If the lacing was becketted on, the stay did not have to be unrove to bend the sail. With the old-fashioned metal hanks, the quickest method was to unreeve the stay, pass it down through the hanks, bend a reeving-line to the stay, lead it through the sheave on the jibboom, and haul it taut. The reeving-line was then unhitched, and the stay-tackle set up. Since the jib-sheet pendants, with their clump blocks, were relatively heavy, a 'clew-rope' was substituted, and used to steady the clew, while the sail was being sent out. If the jib had a traveller, it was bent in the 'in' position, up against the bowsprit cap.

The sail was got ready on the forecastle, the forward leech or, as we would say today the 'luff', was snaked down, so the hanks came in their proper order. The stay was got in and run through a few of the hanks from above down. The downhaul was run through a few of the hanks from below up, while the halliards and downhaul were secured to the head of the sail. A bight of the halliards was hitched around the body of the sail, a couple of feet abaft the hanks, or, less commonly a special bending strop was used, and the halliards hooked to this. In harbour, the jib was sent out on the port side of the boom, so that in going out it would not ride on the downhaul, which was always found to starboard. The flying jib went out to starboard for similar reasons, the ring-shaped withe, or boom iron, on the jibboom, through which the flying jib-boom protruded, usually being inclined to that side. At sea, however, both sails invariably went out on the weather side (Taunt, 292).

The halliards were used to raise the sail high enough to clear the forecastle, the downhaul acting as a tack-outhaul, while the clew was steered out with the aid of the clew-rope. The tack was made fast, and the halliards, or bending strop taken off the sail, the halliards being hooked and moused to the head-cringle. The jib-pendants were hooked and the clew-rope removed. The stay was set up taut once more, and finally, the sail furled.

The flying jib and fore topmast staysail were bent in an analogous fashion. Main topmast and main topgallant staysails were handled in the foretop, halliards, downhaul and sheets being bent on. The storm staysails, when required, were secured to their respective stays with beckets (Burney, 131). These beckets, or a rawhide lacing serving the same purpose, were sometimes known as 'salamanders' (*Mariner's Mirror* 53, 1967, 81; 54, 1968, 196).

Unbending and shifting headsails. The sail was hauled down, the stay-tackle and tack-lashing were let go, the reeving-line bent to the inboard end of the stay, while the clew-rope was bent, in place of the sheet-

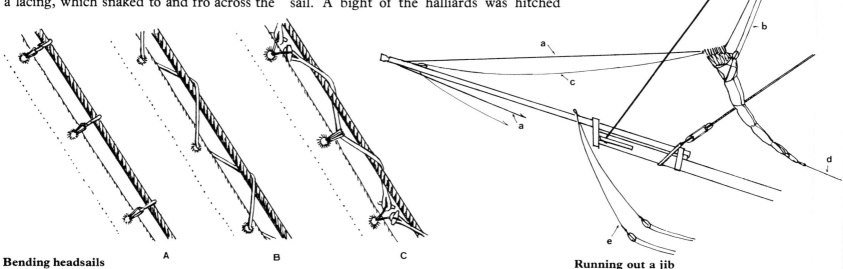

Bending headsails
A Sail hanked to stay; **B** sail laced to stay; **C** sail laced to stay with beckets.

A   B   C

Running out a jib
a jibstay; **b** jib halliards; **c** downhaul; **d** clewrope; **e** sheets.

pendants. The halliards were hitched round the sail, and it was swayed high enough to clear the bulwarks, swung in, and landed on the forecastle, guided by clew-rope and downhaul. The stay was pulled through the hanks and, if shifting sail, rove through those of the new headsail.

Gaff sails. These were rigged in such a variety of ways that one can only indicate the general principles involved. If the head of the sail was laced to the side of the gaff, rather than lying underneath, it was placed to starboard, since the boltrope was always on the port side. The gaff was lowered sufficiently to allow the men to reach it, and steadied with the vangs over to the side upon which the sail lay. The head was hauled up to the throat of the gaff with the clewrope, and to the peak with the head-outhaul. The sail was laced to the gaff, fastened with robands, or seized to rings travelling on the gaff. It was considered poor practice to overstretch the sail, when first bending. 'The disease of "drivers" commences on the taffrail, not in the sail-loft. The Afterguard's jiggers occasion all the perpetual doctoring of spankers, and abuse of our sail cutters,' says Boyd (295). The sheet outhaul, brails, tack tricing-line and clew-rope, were secured to the appropriate places, and the sail seized to the mast hoops. In the Royal Navy mast hoops were used to secure the upper part of the sail only, a lacing of well worn greasy rope being snaked back and forth to confine the luff below the reef-band (Burney, 132).

LOOSING SAILS TO DRY

With a powered vessel once 'Finished with main engines!' was rung down on the engine-room telegraph, the machinery could, in theory, be left idle, until it came time to fire up the boilers and raise steam once more. Nonetheless, to function properly, the machinery needed a certain amount of routine maintenance, and the same consideration had to be extended to the canvas of sailing ships. The primary concern was to prevent mildew and rot developing in damp, poorly ventilated fabric. Riesenberg (218) describes setting the canvas of the auxiliary barque *Frithjof*, and watching it literally melt away, when the sails were loosed and sheeted home. This was the result of protracted failure to air the sails. A few months later, this neglect proved fatal, the vessel being lost, when unable to claw off a lee-shore. The more the airing canvas was spread out the better. However, a ship at anchor might become restless with its canvas fully deployed, 'loosed to a bowline', and hence sometimes the gaskets were cast off, without actually sheeting home the sails, and this was referred to as 'loosing to a buntline'. The method used depended on how wet the canvas was. Mossel remarks that the advent of a squall sometimes

required that sail be shortened prematurely, thus necessitating loosing canvas twice in one day. He felt, however, that the extra exercise this gave the crew was 'bound to be healthy'.

Loosing to a buntline. The booms were triced up and the sail-loosers went aloft and cast off the gaskets, each man holding two gaskets until the command to let fall. The gaskets were then let go, and the bunt whips eased off, allowing the sail to hang loosely in its gear. The gaskets were likewise thrown off headsails and mizzen, the jibs being spread out on the booms, but not hoisted, the canvas hanging in a loose bight. The booms were always left up, the buntlines either being hauled up to the masthead, or 'kept square with the yards'.

Loosing to a bowline. In this case, the canvas was completely deployed, the courses hanging down and being steadied by the tacks and sheets. The royals and topgallants were let fall, and sheeted home so far as practical. The jibs were hoisted, and the mizzen sheet hauled out, the brails being overhauled. The topsails would have overlapped the courses, and therefore the top bowlines were untoggled from their bridles, made fast to the buntline cringles, and used to haul the foot of the sail out and forward. The buntlines and sheets were adjusted so as to spread the sail

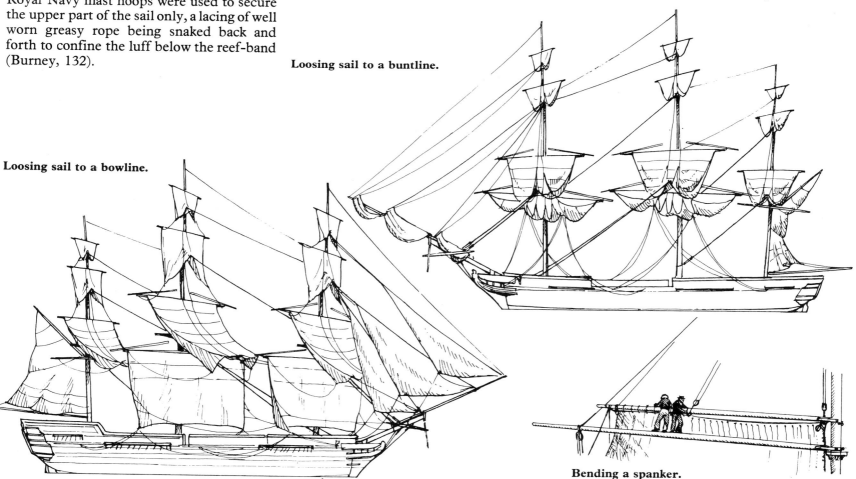

Loosing sail to a buntline.

Loosing sail to a bowline.

Bending a spanker.

Furling a course (handing the sail on the left and passing gaskets on the right).
A Old method; **B** new method.

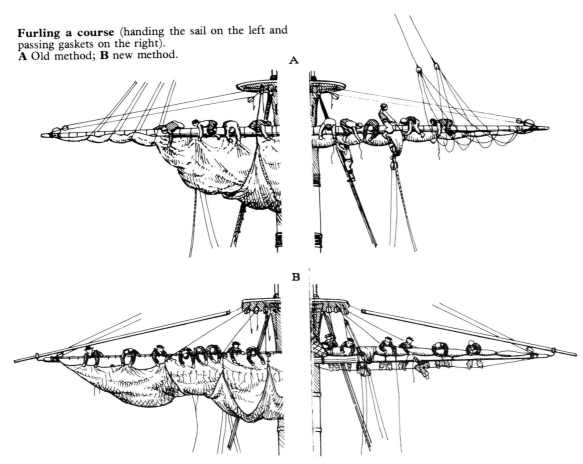

out to best advantage. The topmast and top-gallant studdingsail booms were left triced up, while the canvas was airing. If the light yards and studdingsails were in the rigging, the sails were loosed there (Taunt, 300). Engelhart (68) says that the most suitable time to loose the small sails was after morning divisions, making them fast again at 11.00hrs, 13.00hrs or 15.00hrs, if they were dry. If the light yards were sent up as part of a colour evolution, the sail was loosed just as the yard was canted (Krogh, 23). This would suggest that the loosers would not have been able to get out on the yard, and perhaps some sort of slip-rope was used instead of gaskets to allow the sail to be loosed smartly.

Shortening sail from a bowline. If the ship became uneasy, with so much canvas spread, the order could be given to shorten sail, disposing the sails in the 'loosed to a buntline' configuration. The bowlines were slacked off, the sail clewed up, buntlines hauled until the foot of the sail came level with the yard, jib halliards let go and mizzen brailed up, all gaskets being left unsecured.

FURLING SQUARE SAIL

Earlier and later methods. In the 1700s, the sails were hauled up under the yard, by buntlines, martnets or leechlines, and clew-lines. The gaskets were passed down in front

of and around under the sail, and secured to the grommets on the upper after aspect of the yard. It will be remembered that in the early days there were no footropes, and this would have required the men to sit, or lie rather precariously astraddle the yard. Anderson (152) was puzzled by the fact that footropes first appear on the lower yards in 1642. He considered that they might have been expected to arrive on the scene only with the advent of the reefing topsail in 1655. I think the reason for the innovation may lie in the physical difficulty of passing the gaskets, while lying sprawled out on a yard, which was two feet thick at the slings, and encumbered at that point with jeers, trusses, and so on. At the yardarms, the martnets alone would have served to confine the sail pretty well, when they were hauled taut. They were superseded by the simpler leechlines about 1650 (Anderson, 168), at about the same time as the introduction of footropes. Earlier, the clewgarnet blocks were placed about a third or a half the distance out from the centre of the yard to the yardarm, later moving in almost to the slings of the lower yard. The early configuration is found in Lescallier, as late as 1791, and the later method by 1815, in Lever, I am not sure of the years when this change occurred, but it certainly preceded 1792, the date of William Nichelson's *Treatise*.

Anderson (269) indicates that the head-

ropes were bent underneath the yard, the central part of the sail being secured to a special bending batten, and this remained the usual practice with the course at least until the late 1700s. By 1670, Dutch seamen were bending the headropes of the topsails, and topgallants to the front of the yard (Winter, Plate 4), and within a century, the headrope of the course was shifted upwards in a similar fashion. In 1811, bending jackstays were introduced (Lees, 159), and this corrected the tendency of the robands to slip, causing the headrope to slide underneath the yard. These innovations reflected a distinct change in the manner of 'handing', or furling the sails, and we will now consider how this evolved.

Old method of furling a course. With the headrope under the yard, and the clewlines 'blocked' about a third of the way out towards the yardarm, the sail was run up in its gear, with the canvas fairly evenly distributed across the yard, albeit with some extra cloth in the bunt. The gaskets secured the sail so that the furled canvas was visible under the yard, in a series of scallops, as looked at from the quarterdeck.

New methods of furling the course. In the late 1700s it became customary firstly, to place the clewline blocks much closer to the slings, so furling the sail with more canvas in the bunt, and secondly, to furl the sail on the forward upper aspect of the yard. Boudriot (IV, 100) indicates that the latter practice was being followed in 1780; that is to say, prior to the inward shift of the clewline blocks. The change was primarily motivated by aesthetic considerations, the intention being to make the yardarms appear lighter. However, the purpose of any furl was not only to reduce windage aloft, but also to protect the bulk of the canvas, and shield it from the weather. If the sail were furled under the yard, it was impossible to form a skin, and water inevitably gathered in the pleats of the canvas. The new method allowed one fold to cover all the rest, and shed moisture much more effectively.

In the case of the course, the furled sail and the studdingsail booms came to sit on the front and upper side of the yard. If the clew-line blocks were shifted in, less canvas needed to be stowed towards the yardarms, and the booms could be clamped in closer to the yard. This consideration did not apply as long as the studdingsail booms were carried on the after aspect of the yard, or while the sail was being furled underneath. Although the 'new' method remained popular in men-of-war until the last days of sail, merchantmen in the late nineteenth century commenced clewing the courses up to the yardarms, which distributed the canvas as equally as possible along the yard, and made furling much handier.

Clewing up the sail. As to practice in the 1600s, martnets depending from the topmast head, would have been very effective in subduing the sail ready for furling. Once that was done, they were slacked off, so they hung in a bight under the yards. Actually, it would have been difficult to pass the gaskets before the martnets had been eased off, and just how things were actually managed by the men at the yardarm is not completely clear. At all events, martnets were replaced by the much simpler leechlines in the late 1600s (Anderson). These appear to have been bent to the sail rather lower than one would have imagined; that is to say, when they were hauled up, the leech had to be 'snaked' somewhat, to fit along the yard. The clewgarnets hauled the clews up behind the rest of the sail, and since, as with the leechlines, the distance between clewline block and the head-cringle was less than the length of the leech, the latter hung in a bight below the yard. The buntlines hauled the central part of the sail up to the quarters, with a fairly reasonable spread of the canvas.

With the new position of the clewline blocks, clewlines and buntlines hauled the canvas up closer to the slings. If the clewgarnets alone were hauled, the sail adopted a triangular configuration, point down, with the clews pulled up to the centre of the base of the triangle. Hauling up the leechlines shortened the base of the triangle, and hauling up the buntlines brought the point up to the slings. This is more readily demonstrated by folding a pocket handkerchief, than it can be explained verbally.

Von Littrow (61) gives a very clear description of how the sail was furled, once it was got up in its gear. The topmen were stationed at the bunt, where correct execution was most critical. 'In furling sails, it is the duty of the captains of the tops to be in the bunt, as everything depends how the sail is stowed there, whether it will be a sightly furl or not. A bulky misshaped bunt to a sail, denotes a slovenly set of topmen' (Burney, 137). The section of boltrope between the buntline toggles was snaked down, so that it matched the space available, whereupon the men at the bunt reached down and brought up fold after fold of canvas, until they came to the clews. The topmen kept the canvas up on the yard by standing on it, until they reached the clews. The leech between clew and head-cringle was flaked down alongside the head-rope. All then leant forward over the yard, and brought the rest of the sail up, hand over

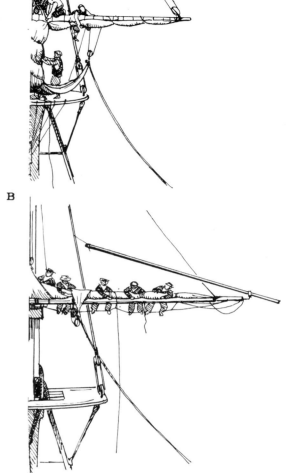

Furling a topsail (handing the sail on the left and passing gaskets on the right).
A Old method; **B** new method.

hand, fold after fold, each fold being held under the breast while reaching for the next handful of canvas. The final fold, or 'skin', formed by the canvas just under the headrope, was flung up bodily on a given signal. The bunt jigger was hooked to its glut, or becket, just above the first reef-band, and hauled to get the heavy bunt up on the yard. The furl being judged satisfactory, the gaskets were passed.

Burney (137) follows a slightly different plan.

At the order 'Lay out!', the outer hands on the yard get hold of the leech as quickly as possible, and pass it in towards the bunt, taking care to form a skin in doing so. The hands on the quarter and bunt of the yard gather the foot of the sail on top of the yard in the bunt, and then they work all the slack sail in between the clews and the yard, towards the bunt on both sides, equalising as much as possible the sail on each quarter of the yard; by doing this the sail will be light at the yardarms, and a good bunt will be formed; as soon as the bunt becket can be

reached, hook the bunt whip, and pull up on it, let go the buntlines, and foot the sail well down in the bunt skin. All hands on the yard look towards the bunt, and give one good skin up together, pass the gaskets, and clew hangers, lay in and down from aloft smartly.

Rosvall (23) suggests stretching the reef-band along the headrope, checking the clewgarnets, and hauling the sail until the foot is got hold of. The footrope and leeches are flaked down as convenient, the sail between first reef and headrope then functions as a skin, and the whole thing is flung up on top of the yard, on the pipe. The bowline bridles are tucked in with the sail, the bowlines emerging just inside the clews at the bunt. Underhill (188) has a useful diagram illustrating merchant service practice around 1900, and offering two alternative methods of clewing up, 'to the quarters' and 'to the yardarms'. With the latter, the sail was simply pulled up like a venetian blind.

The harbour furl. In Mainwaring's day,

1.

3.

5.

6.

Bending a new fore topsail in the brigantine *Grethe*, 1965. The head of the sail is being stretched after the midship robands have been made fast. (Mark Myers' Collection)

Shifting the mizzen topsail at sea, Swedish training ship *Jarramas*. The topgallant has been left clewed up as work on shifting the topsail goes ahead. (Courtesy Marinmuseum, Karlskrona)

HM Brig *Pilot* with sails loosed. The lower and topsail buntline lizards are cast off to haul the bunt well up for furling, and the tack of the spanker is hauled up. (Imperial War Museum, London)

Hands furling sail in HM Brig *Martin*, 1892. The studdingsail booms are triced up and the bunt of the topsails hauled up above the yard. (Imperial War Museum, London)

HMS *Duke of Wellington* with sails drying, loosed to a bowline. (Imperial War Museum, London)

Close view of cadets furling course and topsail in the *Jarramas*. The fourth man from the right supports the clew while another (nearly hidden under the top) passes the bunt in to the middle of the yard. (Courtesy Marinmuseum, Karlskrona)

one suspects that the sails were furled in harbour no differently than at sea. However in the later 1800s, practice in port came to differ in some particulars from the methods used when under sail. In the first case, a handsome appearance aloft, with smartness and celerity in sail drill, were the criteria by which a ship was judged, while in the second, security, speed and ease of execution were all important.

We have already mentioned the use of har-bour gaskets. Engelhart, Brady and Luce all quote a passage, originating I believe with Fordyce, comparing 'low', or 'rolling' bunts, with 'high', or 'French' bunts. The first was the spindle shaped bunt, resulting from the use of bunt gaskets, more particularly one associated with a wider placing of the clewline blocks. The second type of furl resulted when the bunt becket was hauled well up under the top, and as much canvas pushed in behind it as possible. Bunt gaskets were not required with this arrangement, and the time saved in not having to pass them, gave the advantage in competition to ships using this method, hence its popularity. The French bunt sat up like a cocked hat – *en chapeau*, as the French sailors called it – the slack canvas being piled up, so to speak, rather than being spread laterally.

Old method of furling the topsail. The topsail had greater hoist and broader foot, in proportion to its length of head, than either the course or the topgallant, and as a result required to be furled differently. Rosvall (33) gives a very clear description of the method used until the end of the 1700s. The yard being down on the cap, the sail was got up in its gear, clewlines, leechlines and buntlines. A bight of the leechline was taken under the yard, crossed in front of the sail, and made fast to the parrel or mast, while the buntlines were eased off, and the yardarm gaskets passed. This had the effect of draping the canvas into a 'T' shape, or perhaps better the conformation of two 'Js' back to back. If the buntlines were slacked right off, the foot of the sail drooped down over the front of the top. A *förkläde*, or 'apron' was fashioned from a couple of cloths in the centre of the sail, and spread the width of the lower cap by using a pair of reef-points, hitched to the topsail yard. The remaining canvas was then bundled from behind into the 'skin' thus formed, and the whole thing compressed into a neat roll, or cylinder, of sail up and down the foot of the topmast. A spiral gasket secured everything from the slings of the topsail yard to the top. The bowlines were stopped to the top in front of the masts, while the clews were left curling up towards the clewline blocks, like a pair of moustaches. This latter feature is often represented in paintings of the period, but Rosvall did not approve of it aesthetically, preferring to tuck the clews into the apron.

Rosvall comments that 'furling topsail fashion' was only used in harbour, and indeed was pretty well outmoded at the date of writing in 1803. Bonnefoux and Paris describe the use of *couillons*, in association with this method of furling. These provided hand-holds without actually piercing the canvas, and were used, for instance, instead of the reef-points mentioned by Rosvall. They consisted of balls of tow, probably about fist size, which were thrust into the sail from its after side at the desired places, and secured by means of a spunyarn lashing taken tightly round the 'neck', thus forming a sort of button. They helped to make the sail more secure in its gaskets.

New method of furling the topsail. Rosvall (34) says that in smaller vessels, and invariably at sea, the topsail was furled 'topgallant fashion'. The reef tackles were hauled out, and the first reef earing hauled up to bring the reef-band along the headrope. The clews were passed in, and the sail furled using the slack canvas of the first reef as a skin. A couple of reef-points were hitched to the ties, to keep the sail well up on the yard and, when looked at from the quarterdeck, only the clews were visible below the yard, and part of the bunt above.

Anderson (204), describing the various methods of fitting topsails, remarks that there were periods when the sail had either leechlines, or buntlines, but not both. Leechlines are essential with Rosvall's first method, and buntlines with the second, but we must remember that he was describing Swedish practice around 1800, and despite his comment that the first method was not used at sea, paintings of the seventeenth century confirm its use, even during storm conditions, at an earlier date.

Harbour furl of the topsail. This was similar to the practice with the course, already described, in that clew ropes or jiggers were rigged, and the sail was secured with harbour gaskets. The main difference lay in the way the buntlines were handled. The buntline lizards, which ordinarily kept the buntline within a foot or so of the jackstay, were dispensed with, so the foot of the sail could be hauled up almost to the crosstrees; then by slacking the buntlines off bit by bit, the slack sail could be stowed in the bunt. Fordyce reeves the buntlines through lizards at the clew, so that they hauled bunt and clews up together, thus dispensing with clew ropes (Murphy, 2), while Mossel uses only one buntline, as such, employing the other as a long bunt whip.

The sail was furled in a very similar manner to that already described for the course, the leeches being laid in along the yard, and the bunt formed as mentioned above. 'Back cloths' were 'triangular pieces of canvas secured to each quarter of the topsail yard; they are for convenience in stowing the bunt of a topsail' (Taunt, 80). I think the *buikreijers* ('bunt riders') described by Mossel (II, 363) must have worked in a very similar fashion, coming from either side, from aft forward, to compress the sail on the quarters down and forward, on either side of the actual bunt. 'Too much sail should not be left abaft the yard, to be stowed in the back cloths, as when the latter are hauled over, it will give a bunchy, slouchy look about the bunt, when seen from aft' (Taunt, 292).

Burney gives a good description of British practice in 1869. The order was given in the form 'Trice up, lay, out, second reef earing and furl!'. The reef earing was hauled to get the second reef-cringle close to the head-cringle. The yardarm man put his foot on the earing, but did not make it fast. The earing, and first reef-cringle were passed in towards the bunt, together with the reef-points, bowline bridles, and the leech below the second reef-band. The slack sail was pushed into the bunt from behind, and the sail furled as before described. Care had to be taken that the reef earing really was hauled out:

Some hands, with a mistaken idea of smartness, neglect hauling the earing out at all, but commence to pass the leech in at once, the consequence is all the sail is gathered into the bunt, the buntlines are let go, the foot of the sail comes down on the already overfilled bunt. The bunt jigger for a topsail, and the bunt whip for a course is hauled on, and the men in the bunt of the yard endeavour to foot the sail in the skin without success. In all probability during this time, the officer carrying on is hurrying them, and the consequence is the bunt gaskets are passed, and the booms lowered on a badly furled sail, which in nine cases out of ten ends in extra drill. Whereas, if the second reef earing had really been hauled out, and the leech of the sail passed in from the second reef, it would equalise the sail, and give ample room for properly stowing the bunt. Therefore, it should be borne in mind by young beginners that the cause of badly furled topsails commences at the yardarm, and is generally the cause of a badly formed bunt (Burney, 137).

A similar method was popular in the German service, but in the United States Navy, it was not customary to haul out the second reef, a slimmer yardarm being preferred.

With the advent of double topsails, the upper topsail always clewed up to its yardarm, and the lower topsail often followed suit. If the lower were arranged to clew up to the quarters, the buntlines ran out, like an inverted 'V', whereas if the sail were to be clewed straight up, they were more or less vertical.

Contemporary comment. The shift in position of the clewline blocks was not introduced without some protest. In 1792, Nichelson (204) describes it as 'another new-fashioned ridiculous piece of folly, practised by our *Jemmy Seamen*'. With the traditional method, the clewgarnet blocks plumbed just outside the gunwale, so that if clew and its heavy blocks came down accidentally, it would fall clear, and not brain someone standing on the deck. Furthermore, upon the sail being loosed, by the wind, the clews came down outside the lee shrouds. With the new

method, men had to be stationed in the lee rigging, as the sail was set, to push the lee clew clear of obstructions. 'So much for our new *Jemmy* mode of doing things unlike seamen,' growls Nichelson.

Similar considerations applied to the topsail clewline blocks, which before the change, plumbed outside the tops, allowing the clews to fall clear of the rigging, when the sail was set. Nichelson felt that with the new method, 'invented by some *Finical Genius*', it was impossible to furl the sail neatly, the bunt being 'unpleasant to look at, so that the best seaman in the world cannot furl it, or make it look better, or more agreeable to the eye'. Furthermore, when at anchor, or in bad weather at sea, the sail should be 'furled in a body', and this was impossible with the new arrangement. In the event, the opposing school of thought carried the day, whatever the justice in Nichelson's objections.

Expressions used. French *serrer en chemise*, and *en perroquet*, correspond to Rosvall's expressions *beslå topsegelsvis*, and *bramsegelsvis*, 'furling topsail-wise', and 'topgallant-wise'. As to the English equivalents, Mainwaring, indicates that English seamen in 1620, 'furled' (farthelled) the course, but 'stowed' the topsail. The later expressions 'furl in a body', and 'furl in a bunt', I would identify with 'topsail fashion' and 'topgallant fashion', respectively. They may have changed meaning somewhat, over the next century, since Smyth (328) gives:

Furling in a body; a method of rolling up a topsail, only practised in harbour, by gathering all the loose part of the sail into the top, about the heel of the topmast, whereby the yard appears much thinner and lighter than when the sail is furled in the usual manner, which is sometimes termed for distinction 'furled in the bunt'. It is often practised to point the yards, the earings and robins let go, and the whole sail bunted in the top, and covered with tarpaulins

while de Kerchove (326), equates 'furling in a body', with a 'harbour stow'.

French seamen talked of 'furling in a bundle' (*serrer en paquet*), namely any method used at sea to take the sail in, and secure it in a hurry, *sans aucune recherche*, sea gaskets taken round booms and all. *Serrer en chapeau* was the furl taken with a 'high', or 'French' bunt. Bonnefoux says it was so called because the bunt resembled *une sorte de chapeau, dit de Père noble*, and comments that there is little difference between this method and *en perroquet*. *Chapeau*, like *couillard*, was a word used for the bunt gasket. Röding (III, 315) distinguishes the two arrangements, saying that *en perroquet*,

Furling a topgallant (handing the sail on the left and gaskets passed on the right).

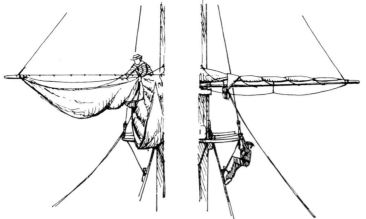

Handing square sails. Details from contemporary paintings by the Van de Veldes show seventeenth century practice in handing a topgallant **A**, a topsail **B**, and a course **C**.

D shows the body of the old-fashioned topsail gathered into the mast by leechlines taken round the sail, the men on the yard passing gaskets and the men in the top making *couillons*.

E Detail of the foot of a furled topsail showing clews leading out and button-like *couillons*.

F Appearance of a later single topsail stowed with sea gaskets in rough weather.

G Appearance of a later single topsail stowed with a harbour furl. **H** Dutch ship with sails clewed up in port, showing appearance of topsails and topgallants with buntline lizards cast off and buntlines hauled home. This was not done at sea (after contemporary painting).

the furl is taken in front of the yard, and *en chapeau*, on top of it.

Mending sail. If the furl were unsatisfactory, the loosers were sent aloft, on the order 'Mend sail!'. The booms were triced up, the gaskets cast off, and the buntlines and clew jiggers run up a little to assist the hands in 'mending' the furl. If the sail had been taken in extremely badly, the furlers went aloft, the sail let fall, and restowed from scratch.

Furling royals and topgallants. Pictorial evidence from the seventeenth century indicates that the topgallants were 'stowed', or 'furled in a body', like the topsails, the clews being either tucked away in the tops, or left pointing out and up. The light sails had less hoist and were made of lighter cloth than the topsails, and no doubt the practice of bending the headrope and furling the sail on the forward side of the yard started with these sails. In a small merchantman, the royal could be furled by one man, and Dana (46) offers a most explicit set of instructions for the green hand, on how to go about it:

> See your yardarm gaskets clear, the best way is to cast them off from the tie, and lay them across between the tie and the mast. This done, stretch out on the weather yardarm, get hold of the weather leech and bring it in to the slings, taut along the yard. Hold the clew up with one hand, and with the other haul all the sail through the clew, letting it fall in the bunt. Bring the weather clew a little over abaft the yard, and put your knee upon it. Then stretch out to leeward, and bring in the lee leech in the same manner, hauling all the sail through the clew, and putting the clew upon the yard, in the same way, and holding it there by your other knee. Then prepare to make up your bunt. First get hold of the footrope and lay it on

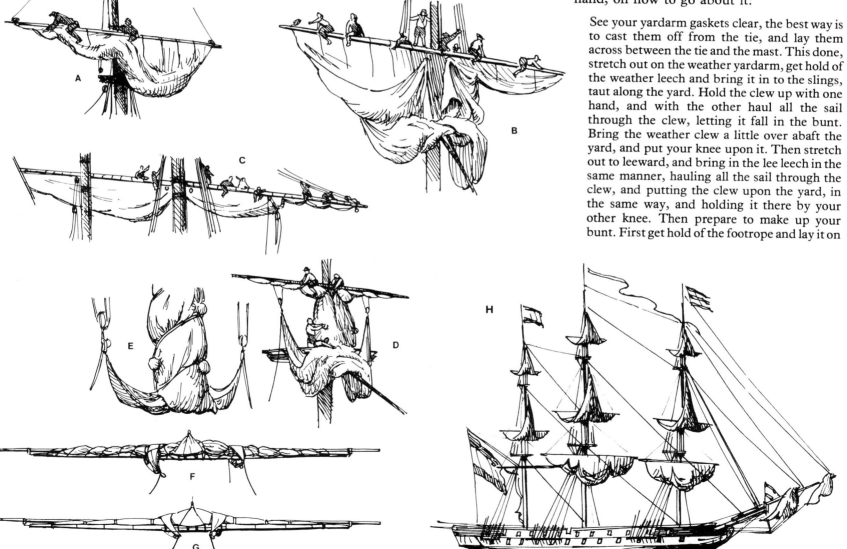

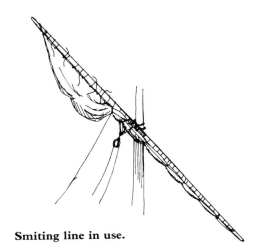

Smiting line in use.

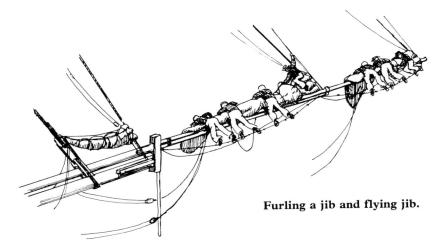

Furling a jib and flying jib.

the yard, seeing that it is all fairly through the clews. Having got all the sail upon the yard, make a skin of the upper part of the body of the sail, large enough to come well down abaft and cover the whole bunt when the sail is furled. Lift the skin up, and put into the bunt the slack of the clews (not too taut), the leech and foot-rope, and the body of the sail; being careful not to let it get forward under or hang down abaft. Then haul your bunt well up on the yard, smoothing the skin and bringing it down well abaft, and make fast the bunt gasket round the mast, and the jigger, if there be one, to the tie. The glut will always come in the middle of the bunt, if it is properly made up. Now take your weather yardarm gasket, and pass it round the yard three or four times, haul taut and make it fast to the mast, then the lee one in the same manner. Never make a long gasket fast to its own part round the yard, for it may work loose and slip out to the yardarm. Always pass a gasket over the yard and down abaft, which will help bring the sail up on the yard.

Lever offers this comment: 'As many vessels in the coasting trade have no buntlines to their topgallant sails, it would be well if the necessity of carrying them were strongly enforced. When it blows fresh, these sails, generally left to the management of boys, are very heavy to hand, and if there be no bunt-lines to spill them, the result may be fatal to those on the lee yardarm, by the sail's blowing over to leeward. Surely the saving of a few fathoms of rope should not be put in competition with the life of a fellow creature!'

In the naval service there were, of course, more men available, and the exact method of managing would have varied a great deal.

LOOSING FORE AND AFT SAIL

Staysails. The jibs and fore topmast stay-sail, were loosed by casting off the gaskets, letting go the downhaul and running up the halliards, while tending the sheets. A man stood by to light up the hanks on the stay, as

the sail went up. The other staysails were loosed in a similar fashion. In men-of-war, the fore and aft sails often had covers, which had to be removed first. Brady (217) says that alternate gaskets were cast off earlier, so that loosing might be accomplished more expeditiously, when loosing as a colour evolution. Loosing to a buntline, the halliards were not hauled, the sail simply being pushed off the boom, so it hung loose in a bight below it.

Mizzen. Mainwaring (228) describes a method of loosing the old-fashioned mizzen using a 'smiting line'. This was made fast at the after yardarm, and made up with the sail, which was furled with ropeyarn stops. By giving a sharp jerk on the line, the stops were snapped successively, and the sail loosed: 'When well executed, this marks the seaman', says Smyth. Loosing to a buntline, the brails on one side were overhauled, and the canvas loosened up, so the wind could blow through it. Frequent airing was necessary to prevent overheating, particularly when the sail was new, and 'the gum had not been shaken out' (Brady, 217). Loosing to a bowline, the brails were let go both sides, and the clew hauled out to spread the sail.

With a boom mizzen, the boom was supported in a crutch of some sort, when the sail was furled. To loose, the weather topping-lift was hauled taut, to top the boom up clear of this; the gaskets were cast off, the brails overhauled, and the clew-outhaul drawn taut.

FURLING FORE AND AFT SAILS

Staysails. The halliards were let go, the downhaul hauled, and the sheets tended. The method of stowing a jib in a harbour furl described by Burney (139) is as follows. The third cloth from the leech was stopped to the stay above the hanks or lacing, and laid in taut along the boom. The first and second cloths hung between the boom and the furlers, and

the fourth and subsequent cloths on the other side. The third cloth was now used to form a skin, the canvas being folded up and pushed under it from either side, so it formed a neat cover, and the gaskets were passed. The sea-gaskets were made fast to the stay and then hitched around sail and boom from forward aft. In harbour, a 'centipede' was sometimes employed. This was a long strip of flat sennit, nailed to the boom, with short gaskets projecting from either side. These were taken over the sail and knotted above. To allow the halliards to be hauled taut, the hanks were pushed down as far as possible on the stay and stopped there. The other staysails were made fast against the fore- and mainmasts in a similar fashion. The middle staysail was pulled down into the foretop and secured there. Other methods, using the foot of the sail, or the aftermost cloths of the leech to form the skin, are described. In port, specially made covers were put on over the furled staysails. We have earlier referred to the way the fore topmast staysail and sometimes the jib were stowed in a net suspended from the forestay.

Mizzen. With a spanker, the topping lift was hauled taut to get the weight off the leech, and then slacked off to crutch the boom. The brails were hauled taut, and the clew hauled up to the jaws of the gaff. A skin was formed with the aftermost cloth, the slack sail was rolled up in this, and the gaskets passed. With a trysail fitted with a lowering gaff, a footrope was contrived by making a rope fast at the throat and peak of the gaff, which was then steadied by the vangs. The clew was hauled up to the jaws, and the leech gathered against the head of the sail. The slack canvas was rolled up from the foot to the head by men standing on the footrope, and the gaskets were passed. Burney (139) says that a brig's boom-mainsail was furled by lowering the gaff down until about three feet above the boom. The men then stood on the boom, and leant over to grasp the sail about four feet below the head, pulling the fold over the gaff, and holding it there with their breasts. The leech was passed in towards the jaws leaving little canvas at the peak, and the slack canvas was gathered up under the gaff, the fold first taken being used as a skin, around which the gaskets were passed. The gaff was then lowered on the boom. The method used in the Canadian Banks Schooners, which also had a very large mainsail, differed in that the gaff remained visible when the sail was furled.

Fordyce (32) claimed that in naval brigs it was best to use a standing gaff for the brig sail in harbour, but employ a 'working gaff' at sea. Shortening and loosing sail for airing canvas in harbour, and when entering and leaving port, it was more convenient to use brails and outhaul. The standing gaff set off the appearance of a small vessel better, and was more practical for displaying the ensign and signals than a taffrail ensign staff. At sea however, the sail was more manageable rigged 'brig fashion'. Rather than taking the sail in when wearing ship, Fordyce (137) suggests dropping the peak, and tricing up the tack. This avoided embarassing the helmsman with a loose and fluttering sail. In a squall, sail could be shortened more briskly by dropping the peak, than by brailing in. Likewise, when heaving to, the peak halliards were settled.

SHIFTING SAILS

Minor damage to sails could often be repaired aloft, provided the canvas could be rendered slack enough. For example, by hauling up the reef-tackles, everything above the close reef-band was no longer on the stretch. There might not be complete agreement on this point between the captain of the top faced with the task of shifting a topsail, and the sailmaker's mate, who might consider it best if he could work with the sail stretched on his bench in the half-deck. Apart from necessity, sails were commonly shifted simply as an exercise. In essence this was just a combination of unbending and bending, but one or two points merit attention. Light sails were shifted on deck, the yards being sent down. While shifting, it was important that sail be balanced. For example, if shifting the fore topsail, the mizzen topgallant, and perhaps topsail, might be clewed up while this was going on. While shifting a topsail, the light sails above it would also be clewed up (Taunt, 340).

Topsail. The halliards were lowered and the sail furled, first of all. In port, the old sail would be sent down on one side with the buntlines, and the new one run up on the other, with the sail-tackle. At sea, the simplest method was to send the old sail down, and run the new one up, to weather, both abaft all. This is the method used by Nares (226), but Hourigan (100) says the old one can be sent down, and the new one taken up to leeward and forward of all, if the course is not bellying forward too much, and rolling is not too violent. Taunt (340) says that it is much better to send down to leeward.

The sail was furled and secured in the gaskets, with several good stops taken for extra security, and sheets and clewlines were unbent. The reef-tackles and first and second bull-earings were unhitched from the reef-cringles. The buntlines were hitched right around the sail near the slings, to ensure that the weight would not come solely on the buntline cringles. Hourigan favoured using the sail-tackle hooked to the bending strop, if sending down to windward. He felt that since the tackle was going to be used anyway, this was the easiest way of overhauling it. Nares uses the weather topmast studdingsail halliards to assist to taking the weight while lowering, and also to keep things out to weather. I found Hourigan's account (102) of how the sail is sent down to leeward somewhat hard to follow. He appears to lower the sail on end, the weight being taken primarily by the buntlines and sail-tackle, but holding up the lee half of the sail by the bunt-whip hooked to the lee earing, and a tripping-line hitched to the lower – that is to say, originally the weather – earing. In a gale, the sail always went down to windward. To start with, a turn of the weather earing was left on, the lee earing was let go and the lee half of the sail roused around the front of the top, and the sail lowered to windward, easing off the weather earing as this was done.

Course. This was a straightforward sequence of unbending the old sail and bending the new, sending the sail down and up with the aid of the leechlines, buntlines and yard-arm jiggers. Taunt (342) says that in a gale, the course is sent down to windward, the lee earing being passed in to the bunt.

Jib. This likewise was a relatively simple matter of unbending one sail and bending another. The fore topmast staysail could be set, if necessary, while this was going on, to balance the sail being carried.

SENDING LIGHT YARDS UP AND DOWN

The royals and topgallant yards were regularly sent up and down in harbour, it being a favourite evolution to send them up in the morning and down at night. The topgallant came down ahead of, and went up after, the royal, but the prettiest effect resulted if they were swayed across and canted together. The facility gained by constant practice meant, of course, that the same task could be carried out readily at sea, although there were significant differences in the way affairs were managed at sea and in harbour. In port, speed and gracefulness were important, and the yards on all three masts would be sent up and down together. At sea it was essential that things be carried out in a workmanlike fashion, and the tops worked independently. We will first consider practice when anchored.

In harbour. The topgallant and royal yards went up and down before all. A yard rope, which had to be about three times as long as the distance between deck and the crossed position of the yard, was used in place of halliards. This arrangement, being a simple whip, allowed the spars to be run up as

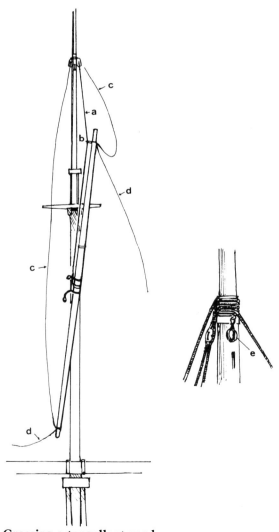

Crossing a topgallant yard
a yard rope; **b** grommet; **c** lift; **d** brace; **e** detail of jackblock.

Stowage of light spars in the main rigging
a royal yard; b topgallant studdingsail; c topgallant yard; d topmast studdingsail.

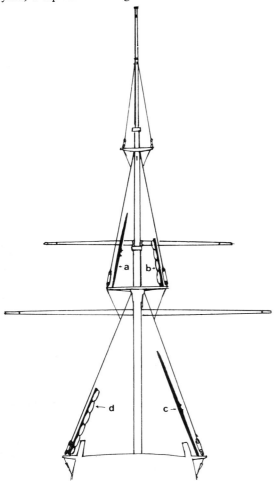

quickly as the men on deck could run away with the hauling end. In fact, the yard rope was simply the same rope as the halliards, but rigged differently, the upper block being un-toggled, and taken down into the top, or completely unrove. The halliards, or rather that part that formed the 'tie', ordinarily rove through sheaves in the topgallant and royal masts, which were made in one piece. The mast itself, was frequently sent down, and since this would have necessitated the yard rope being unrove on each occasion, 'jack-blocks' were shackled to the funnels for the topgallant and royal rigging (Taunt, 330), and used in place of the mast-sheaves, in port. In harbour, old reserve yards were often used, not always having sails bent to them, thus sparing the working yards and sails from wear and tear (Engelhart, 80).

The yard was whipped up more or less vertically, the yard rope being made fast at the slings, and then secured to the upper yardarm by a grommet or, more usually, just a lizard. The yard rope rove through the grommet, which was of a size suitable for jamming down over the upper yardarm, thus confining the yard rope to it. When the command was

given to cross the yard, the lizard was slipped and the yard hauled square by the lower lift and upper brace, the other lift and brace being tended appropriately. The topgallant yard was swayed up until the upper yardarm was level with the crosstrees, and the lower yardarm could be reached by the men in the top, or on the topsail yard. At this juncture, the grommet was slipped off, and the eyes of the brace and lift were slid over the yardarms, and then tended appropriately as the yard was hoisted the rest of the way. The lift and brace went on together, and hence the eyes were seized to form a single unit. It was important that they go on at the correct slew, the lifts leading upwards, and the braces more or less straight backwards. Sometimes the eye-splice was replaced by an iron ring, held in place with a pin through the yardarm.

To facilitate slipping the splices of lift and brace off the lower yardarm, a 'snotter', or 'snorter', of sennit, was fitted to the extreme end of the yardarm. The eyes of lift and brace were slipped over this, when sending the yard up. When the yard was sent down, the upper eye pulled off more or less of itself, and was hauled up to the crosstrees with a 'checking line'. This was a light line rove through a thimble at the crosstrees, and down into the top, where it was worked. Such a fitting was superfluous in harbour, for the other lift and brace which was secured, more or less where it was unrigged. A tripping line was bent to the tail of the snotter, and at the appropriate time, pulling on this slipped the lower eye off the yardarm. The tripping line was then used to steer the lower end of the yard clear of obstruction, in its passage up and down. It led through a leader- or snatch-block on deck, so that it held the yard clear of the topmast and lower stays.

For drill purposes, the fore and mizzen topgallant always went up and down to port, the main to starboard. The royals went up and down on the opposite sides. This allowed the light yards to go up and down virtually together, although the royal had to lead in going up, and lag in coming down. Nares (128) stowed the topgallant yards up and down on the lower mast, and the royals in the topmast rigging, but as we shall see, this was not the only method used.

Since the yard rope was always stopped out on the 'upper' part of the yard, and since the tripping line always was fast to the 'lower' yardarm, this meant that these fittings could be left permanently rigged in port. In the United States Navy, the yard rope was fast at the slings, but permanently stopped out to the quarter-strap on one side; to port on the main topgallant, for instance. It was doubled

back along the yard to the slings, while the tripping line was led in from the other yard-arm to the same point. They were secured here by a toggle, which was drawn at the beginning of the evolution (Luce, 372). This arrangement kept yard rope and tripping line close in to the mast and hence almost in-visible, when not in use. Stratagems of this sort contributed to the 'clean' appearance aloft of these vessels, and the facility with which light yards could be whipped up and down. It will be realised that with this par-ticular expedient, the yard was supported by the lifts and the toggle at the slings, and hence the arrangement was used only when it was not intended to send men out on the yard. If that were to be done, it was important that the yard rope be capable of supporting the weight of the yard at the slings properly. To work as intended, it required the yard being run up a little higher than absolutely neces-sary, so that the lifts could be belayed at their square-marks, and the yard thus fall across in the proper position.

It was common practice to stow the light yards in the rigging, the topgallant resting in a chock in the channels, and confined above to the foremost lower shroud. The yard rope was left rove, but stopped in, so its presence was less obvious. A 'bull rope' was rove from deck through a bull's-eye on the first lower shroud at the level of the catharpings. An eye spliced in its end, was dropped on the upper topgallant yardarm as it passed the lower yard in coming down, and used to haul the yardarm back against the shroud, where it was secured with a 'grab rope' (Luce, 369). The royals were becketted inside the topmast rigging on the opposite side. To balance things up, the topmast studdingsail was stowed in the port lower rigging on the main, and to starboard on the fore. The topgallant studdingsail being stowed in the port topmast rigging on the fore and starboard on the main.

At sea. If the weather were almost a dead calm, the canvas hanging limp, and the lower yards square, the light yards could be sent down, more or less in the same fashion as in port, before all. However, in the more usual circumstance where the sails were drawing and bellying forward, the ship having head-way, the practice was to send them down to weather. The topsail and lower yards being braced up, gave more room on that side. Hourigan (98) says that the royal could be sent down to lee, in front of a close-reefed topsail, if the ship was not rolling too much. This could be useful, if the topgallant were going down at the same time. In sending down only the royals, the weather side would

Shifting topgallant yards at sea
A Sending down the yard.
1 yard rigged with yard rope and tripping line; **2** yard being lowered, sliding down topmast backstay.
B Sending up the yard.
1 hoisting up on yard rope and tripping line; **2** attaching lifts and braces before canting.

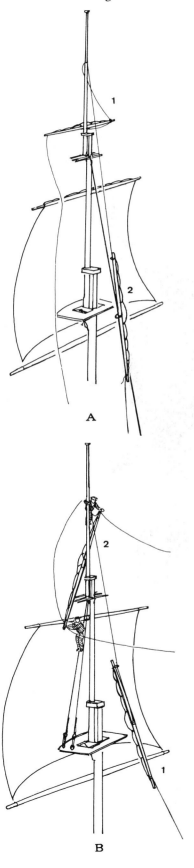

A

B

be preferred. The halliards were untoggled to form a yard rope, which gave sufficient length for the yard to reach the deck, but jackblocks did not have to be rigged, as in port. The tripping line was thrown down to weather, abaft the topsail and lower yards, and before the top, and the yard rope stopped out to lee. The yards could be sent down through the lubber's hole, or if the ship were moving in a seaway, it could be sent down by slipping the parrel round a weather topmast backstay, and using this as a traveller. In good weather, the light yards might be stowed in the rigging, but in a gale, most authorities favoured laying them in the booms, under tarpaulin covers (von Littrow, 94). In the first place, the light sails would usually be set in good weather; secondly, in bad weather the extra windage aloft was unwelcome, and any added strain thrown on the rigging was undesirable, particularly if the ship were rolling heavily; thirdly, the fact that the yards would be going up and down to weather, and therefore not always on the same side, made it difficult for the officer of the deck to keep track of exactly which way the standing part of the yard rope was rove, if they were becketted to the shrouds.

To send up the yard, the yard rope was stopped out on the lee or 'upper', side. The tripping line was snatched on deck abaft, and to weather of, the mast; by keeping it taut, the yard could be run up clear of the lower and topmast yards. It was led through the lubber's hole, if the yard was to follow this route, otherwise it led outside the top. The lee lift and brace were brought around before all and slipped on the upper yardarm, as it came high enough. The weather lift and brace were likewise fitted, to the lower yardarm. It was important that the slack of these was taken down sufficiently to prevent the eye slipping off, of its own weight. The yard was turned so that the canvas of the furled sail faced up and forward. It was crucial that the eye slipped onto the yardarm, on the right slew, and without any twists in the lift and brace. When the yard was hoisted sufficiently high, it was canted across by slacking the lee lift, hauling taut the weather one, and tending the braces appropriately, while the lizard was slipped to release the lee half of the yard from the yard rope. The parrel was then passed. The lashing of the fore and mizzen topgallant parrel was found to starboard, that is to say above, while the yard was still in the canted position, since it was run up on the port side. The lashing of the parrel on the main topgallant was to port (Burney, 66). It seems likely that royal parrels were arranged in the opposite fashion. If it was discovered that the eye of the lift was

foul, or the lift and brace twisted, the remedy was to stop out the yard rope on that side as a temporary lift, to allow a man to lay out and rectify the problem, getting the eye on the right slew (Luce, 372).

The procedure was reversed to send the yard down, the lashing of the parrel being taken off, except for the last turn, which was held until the order to cant the yard was given. In harbour, sometimes the yards might be bare of canvas, but at sea the royal and topgallant sails would always be bent, furled with a low rolling bunt, the clews tucked well in to avoid anything being torn. As to the gear of the sails when the yards were being sent down, the topgallant studdingsail jewel block was seized to the eyes of the lift and brace, and went on and off with them (Luce, 370); the royal sheets were unsnatched from the topgallant yardarms; the quarter-blocks were unhooked from the yard, and hung on eyebolts at the topmast head; the sheets, clewlines and buntlines were untoggled and secured at the topmast cap; the gear of the royal was removed and secured at a slightly higher point, following the same principle. When the yard was sent up again, the gear was rerove.

Disposition of topmen. The plan, suggested by Luce (370), for the royal yards, places one man at the jack-crosstrees, to bend

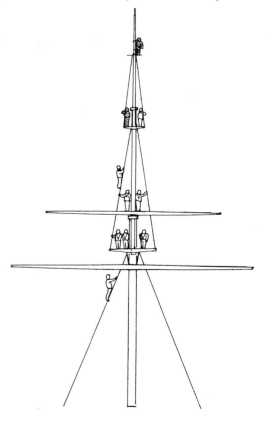

Positions of topmen for sending down light yards (light figures for topgallant yard, shaded figures for royal yard).

and unbend the gear, rig and unrig the upper yardarm, tend the lizard and parrel, slip the toggle of tripping line and yard rope. A second man at the crosstrees bends and unbends the gear, and deals with the lower yardarm. For the topgallant yards, a man at the topmast cap bent and unbent the gear, rigged and unrigged the upper yardarm, handled the lizard and parrel, and drew the toggle of the tripping line. Another man on the crosstrees assisted him in unbending the gear and handling the parrel, overhauled the lower lift and brace down, so it could be rigged by a third man, who stood on the topsail yard. A man in the topmast rigging helped to overhaul the lower topgallant lift, and a hand in the lower rigging cleared away the upper end of the topgallant yard and secured it to the shrouds again, when it was sent down. As it went up and down, the yard was borne off the top and rigging by men stationed in the top. The captain of the top, assisted by a couple of men, sent down the yard ropes, which in harbour were kept coiled up in the top, tended lifts and checking lines, toggled and untoggled the topgallant halliards.

Sending in the spritsail topsail yard. Pihlström (346) outlines how this was managed in 1796. A tail-block was made fast to the bowsprit cap, and an inhauler rove through this, and attached to the slings of the spritsail topsail yard. The clewlines, sheets and buntlines were untoggled, and a second inhauler secured to the weather yardarm. By hauling on the outhauler, and lee lift, the yard was canted around until it was fore and aft. Veering on the outhauler and hauling on the inhauls, the weather yardarm was brought up to rest on the spritsail yard, on the weather side, while the brace and lift were removed. The topsail yard was then brought in further until the lee yardarm was abreast the spritsail yard, allowing the lift and brace to be removed. The yard was then got inboard, sheets, buntlines, lifts, braces and outhauler being secured to the bowsprit cap. In bad weather, the spritsail yard was hauled fore and aft, and lashed to the bowsprit. Taking it in entirely, as described for the spritsail topsail yard, would have been a heavy job at the best of times, and extremely hazardous in gale conditions.

The commands
Up topgallant and royal yards!
Topgallant and royal yardmen in the tops!
Send down the yard ropes!
Way aloft topgallant and royal yardmen!
Set taut! Sway out of the chains!
Sway aloft!

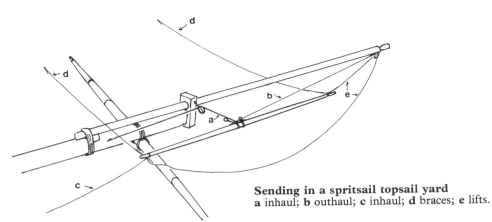

Sending in a spritsail topsail yard
a inhaul; b outhaul; c inhaul; d braces; e lifts.

High enough! (and when the yardarms were rigged), Sway higher!
Tend lifts and braces!
Stand by! Sway across!
Bend the gear!
Haul up the yard ropes!
Lay down from aloft!
Hourigan gives 'Lay aloft! Get the light yards ready for coming down, royals to leeward and forward of all (both yards to windward and abaft all)!'.

SENDING THE TOPGALLANT MASTS UP AND DOWN

Men-of-war of the late nineteenth century were arranged so that this exercise could be carried out very readily, both in port and at sea. Just as with the light yards, the spar was sent down forward of all in harbour, and to weather at sea. In port, it was sometimes stowed on a chock on deck, and lashed vertically forward of the lower mast, when sent down for exercise (Luce, 375). At sea, it was placed in the booms, since the explicit aim of striking the upper masts, in bad weather, was to reduce topweight and windage aloft. The flying jibboom was usually rigged in at the same time.

Fittings. The topgallant and royal masts were made in one piece, the respective stays and backstays being slipped over metal funnels, which allowed the mast to be struck, while leaving the rigging in place on the funnel. The truck with its signal halliards, was lifted off and secured at the topmast cap with the funnels. In the very late 1800s, the truck was fitted with a long sleeve, which slid down inside the royal and topgallant funnels, helping to keep everything steady (Hourigan, 99). The lightning conductor was so fitted so it could be connected and disconnected readily.

Clearance. The rectangular heel of the mast fitted fairly snugly into the square hole, bounded by the crosstrees and trestletrees.

Even as the mast was lowered, there was comparatively little play. In the United States Navy, a 'gate' was fitted on the forward side of the opening, to give a little more room; this was opened as the masthead came down abreast the topmast cap (Luce, 377). The lack of clearance also necessitated that the topsail yard had to be lowered down on the cap, or nearly so, and when sending down to weather, the mast had to be passed through the lubber's hole; that is to say, keeping it, so far as possible, in an almost vertical posture. The topmast cap had to maintain its position at right angles to the topmast. If it drooped forward, the result would be a tendency for the topgallant mast to bind in the aperture. It was for the same reason that cap-shores were fitted on the lower caps, in large vessels.

Ratchet and preventer fid. When sending the mast up, the last foot or so of travel was the most hazardous, due to the risk of the mast rope parting. This was the juncture at which the weight of the royal and topmast funnels, and the extra pressure of stays, shrouds and backstays was now added to the mass of the mast itself. The danger was compounded if something was foul. In English ships, a metal ratchet was fitted to the fore side of the heel of the mast, and engaged a metal pawl on the forward crosstree. Von Littrow appears to consider this arrangement a feature of English masts, and it is illustrated in Dreyer (73, 77). A simpler and commoner arrangement was to have an iron preventer-fid, which slipped into a round hole drilled through the mast 18 inches above the regular fid hole. A lanyard was secured to an eye in one end of the fid, and hitched to the eyes of the topmast rigging.

Fid and lever fids. In its simplest form, the fid holding the mast, was a square or slightly tapered hardwood pin, fitting in a square hole, in the heel of the mast, with either end resting on the trestletrees. A lanyard was secured to one end, to prevent its accidental fall from the top when out, and sometimes another, which was used to pull it through

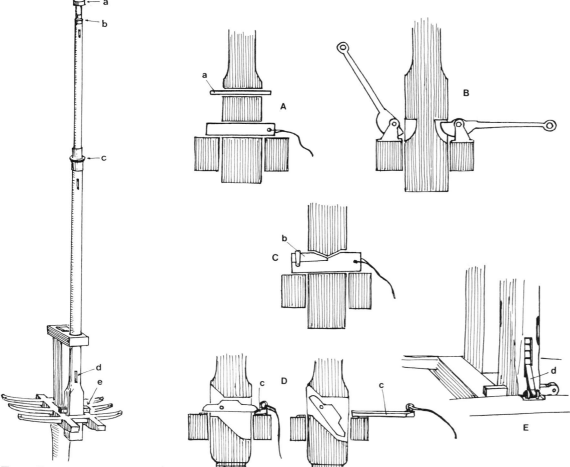

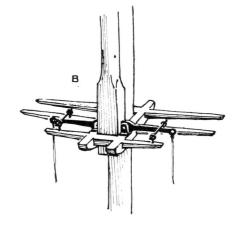

Fids
A Section through heel of mast and trestletrees showing simple fid and preventer fid (**a**); **B** Le Compte's lever fids. The sectional drawing shows the fid engaged on the right and disengaged on the left. When the mast was in place the levers were held down by bolts secured to the crosstrees, as shown by the perspective view; **C** wedge fid: the shoe (**b**) could be removed first, allowing removal of the fid with less difficulty; **D** pivoting fid, shown engaged on the left and capsized on the right. The fid is locked in place when engaged by a pivoting bar (**c**); **E** detail of pawl (**d**) which held the heel in place during the final stages of sending up the mast.

Topgallant mast and its fittings
a truck; **b** funnel for royal rigging; **c** funnel for topgallant rigging; **d** sheave for mast rope; **e** fid.

while fidding the mast (Le Compte, Plate XLI). There were several refinements on this basic principle of which the double lever was the most sophisticated, but while this is mentioned by Mossel, Baudin and von Littrow, I have no evidence that it was used in English or American ships.

Le Compte (Figure 15A, 406) provides the only illustration of the fitting, that I know of. In principle, an iron lever pivoted on an axis resting on the trestletrees. When the levers were engaged, a bolt between the crosstrees secured them in the locked position. In hoisting topgallant masts, the outer ends of the levers were pulled down with tackles to assist the mast rope in raising the mast the last few inches. Von Littrow (24), following Baudin (35), describes a rather complicated procedure, where a temporary fulcrum is used, to allow one lever to engage earlier than the other, and aid in hoisting. The second lever is engaged in its recess, and the pivot point of the first lever is then shifted out to its proper position, and the lever engaged in its notch. The retaining bolts are then passed to secure the outboard ends of both levers.

In addition to their action in jacking up the

mast the last few inches, the lever arrangement had another advantage. To disengage the ordinary type of fid, the mast had to be raised for a few inches before it could be struck. This meant that tackles had to be clapped on the backstays, prior to easing them, and the shrouds and Jacob's ladder had to be eased off along with the royal and topgallant stays. The levers could be eased back without this preliminary raising and, theoretically at least, the standing rigging did not need to be touched. Gower (179) suggested yet another method of arranging things, so the fid could be withdrawn without lifting the mast. He placed a transverse sheave in the fid hole, which rode on the fid, and allowed it to be extracted easily. A fid working on a double wedge principle, as illustrated by Ulffers (Figure 52), should have worked quite well also, only very minimal preliminary raising being necessary to allow unfidding. Burney (182) calls this the 'Sir R Shipping fid'. The upper surface of the mast hole would have required special shaping to conform with the fid. A Swedish arrangement, illustrated in Frick, features a pivoting fid, there is a working model of this at Karlskrona.

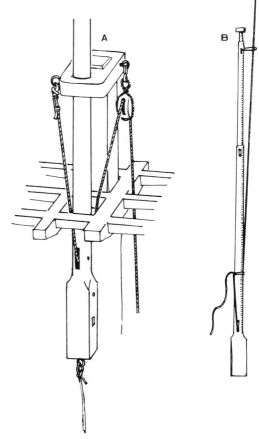

Lead of the mast rope
A Usual lead; **B** mast rope singled and stopped to mast.

Mast rope. The mast rope ran through a leading block on deck, then through a block hooked to one side of the topmast cap, down through a sheave in the heel of the topgallant mast, up once more to the other side of the topmast cap, where it was secured to an eyebolt. The sheave was usually bronze, turning on an iron pin. English practice after 1745 was to run the mortice for the sheave diagonally, from the starboard forward to the after port aspect of the mast. Scores were often cut in the mast to accommodate the mast rope in its passage from sheave to topmast cap. The rope led through the square hole at the crosstrees, during hoisting and lowering. In the late 1800s, an arrangement allowing the mast rope to be snatched, was developed, since this greatly facilitated the handling of the mast for exercise purposes. Accounts of French and British methods can be found in Lees (7) and Boudriot (III, 32).

The mast rope was actually rigged as a double whip, the system having a velocity ratio of two. It had the disadvantage that it required a mast rope about four times as long as the distance between deck and crosstrees, allowing for a sufficiency of slack on deck for the hands to haul upon. The extra power was only needed when the additional weight of the standing rigging was involved; that is to say, when the mast was almost up in its place. Secondly, the mast rope was often really the topgallant yard rope or halliards rigged differently, and as mentioned earlier, this only needed to be treble the distance from crosstrees to deck.

This explains the very common practice of sending the mast up with the mast rope rove singly; that is to say, the rope led from deck, through the block on the cap down through the mast sheave, the end being taken up and half-hitched around the mast higher up. A firm lashing or lizard, through the royal sheave hole, held the 'long' or hauling end of the rope in place. When the head of the mast was engaged at the crosstrees, the 'short' end was unhitched from the mast and secured at the top. The mast rope was thus set up double for the final phase of hoisting.

Yet another variation, used when very short handed, is mentioned by Luce (376). The standing end was taken through a second block at the cap and the top burton secured to this, the lower block being hooked on deck, and the fall belayed. When the mast was nearly up, the hauling end was belayed and the deck force transferred to the burton fall, to get the mast the rest of the way up.

Breeching. I do not know the proper English term for this item – possibly 'preventer top tackle' (Boyd, 412) – but it is called *braguet* by Baudin, and *Brok* by the German authorities, which are the usual words for the breeching of a gun; von Littrow (24) calls it the *Streichreep*, 'strike-rope'; Boudriot's plates (III, 53) show the athwartship groove under the heel of the mast which accommodated it. The breech rope fulfilled the same sort of function as the preventer fid. In the last phase of hoisting, the rope was hitched to the cap, taken down through the lubber's hole, across in the notch under the mast heel, up again through a block on the other side of the cap, straight down to be secured to a breeching tackle, which set up on deck (von Littrow, 24; Dubreuil, 34). This is actually the method of rigging a topmast *braguet*, and I suppose the topgallant breeching, where used, would have worked in a similar fashion.

Lizards. The mast rope was rove through the eye of a lizard between the block at the cap and the sheave in the heel. The end of the lizard went through the royal sheave hole, and round turns were taken to secure the standing part of the mast rope to the masthead. In hoisting, the hauling part of the mast rope could render through the eye of the lizard, the turns of which were cast off once the mast was engaged at the crosstrees. Ulffers illustrates two lizards, one on the standing, one on the hauling end of the mast rope. Hourigan (99) uses the term 'lizard' for another, quite distinct, item. A loop or bight of rope was used as a steadying line, tended by a man on the topsail yard. This encompassed the mast, as it came down, to keep it in line with the mast until it was clear of the funnel.

Heel rope. A rope, hitched to a bail, or eyebolt, in the heel of the mast, served the same purpose as the tripping line of a topgallant yard, in guiding the lower end of the spar in its passage up and down; a very necessary precaution if there was much rolling (Krogh, 105).

Reeving line. If the mast rope had to be rigged from scratch, a light line was dropped down on deck, so the heavier rope could be hauled up (Luce, 376). If the topgallant yard rope was used, or if the mast rope were left rove in port, this would not have been necessary.

Handling in harbour. Practice at sea differed from that in port, just as with the light yards. For drill purposes, an old sprung spar might be used to spare the more serviceable masts, since it would be subjected to little working strain. If shorter stump topgallants had been issued – what were at one time called 'winter poles' – these were preferable to the longer spars used in better weather. At the other extreme, some ships used masts with several feet of 'show pole' above the royal rigging. Liardet (171) is very scathing about this practice, and points out that it complicates unnecessarily the task of handling the topgallant mast.

At anchor, the mast was sent down forward of all, this method being quickest. Since the light yards and topgallant masts were often sent up and down together as an evolution, it was best if the mast went down on the opposite side from the topgallant yard (Krogh, 104). In port, the mast could be stowed vertically on a chock, and lashed to the lower mast. Ulffers (194) says the masthead was seized to the topsail sheets. The light yards had, of course, to be on deck before the mast could be sent down, and the use of jackblocks meant that the yard ropes did not have to be unrove from the sheave holes in the mast.

Handling at sea. In a flat calm, with the sails hanging slack, the mast could be sent down forward as in port. In fact, Boyd (402) mentions squaring the yard, clewing up to weather, and throwing the remainder of the sail aback, to allow the mast to come down forward, while under sail. Much more usually, it would be sent down to weather. The mast was a fairly snug fit in the crosstrees, and hence the butt end could swing out only a limited distance from the topmast, as it came down. To get room, the topsail yard had to be braced up and lying on the cap, and therefore needed to be struck beforehand, unless the topsail were already close-reefed, and hence the yard well down on the topmast. The heel of the mast came down between the topsail ties, and was guided back between them, around the weather side of the topmast, to be landed in the top. This gave an opportunity for singling the mast rope, and

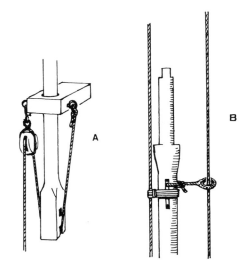

A Detail of braguet.
B Detail of lizard.

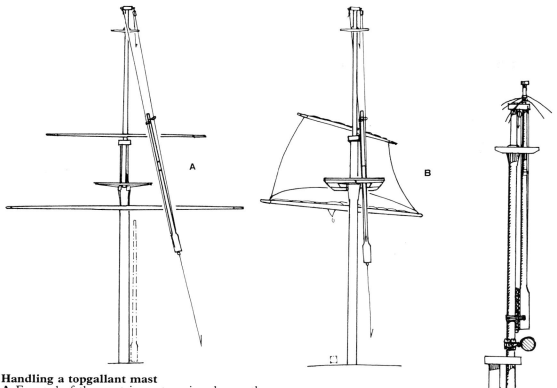

Handling a topgallant mast
A Forward of the mast in port, or in calm weather (stows alongside mast in port); **B** through the weather lubber's hole at sea (stows in booms).

Topgallant mast struck.

Securing the rigging with topgallant mast sent down
a topgallant shrouds; **b** topgallant and royal backstays; **c** topgallant and royal stays; **d** truck; **e** capstan bar lashed to topmast head.

the mast was then lowered through the lubber's hole, and stowed in the booms. Stowing vertically by the mast would not have been practical at sea, since it must have interfered with bracing, and in bad weather have been undesirable for the other reasons already mentioned. Liardet (247) is very insistent that the topgallant masts and yards should always be sent down through the lubber's hole at sea, since accidents occurred frequently when other routes were attempted.

At sea, the yard ropes would always be rove through the regular sheaves in the mast rather than jackblocks, and therefore had to be unrove, before sending the mast down. Liardet (246), however, mentions hauling down on the yard rope, making fast the standing part, to help get a topgallant mast down. An aid of this sort would only have been necessary if the mast were binding in the crosstrees because of the ship heeling well over. Krogh (104) says that if the funnels do not slip off readily, the yard rope is given a vigorous jerk to clear things.

Housing and striking topgallant masts. The mast was not always sent down on deck in bad weather, but rather lowered part way. Boyd (402) draws the distinction between 'down' on deck, 'struck' (lowered to the hounds), and 'housed', the heel being just above the topsail yard, which would, in this context, be in the close-reefed position. When 'struck' the topgallant mast rope was

left rove, and a heavy lashing passed through the fid hole, and around the topmast, with mats interposed between the spars.

Securing the rigging. The stays and backstays were carefully eased, as the mast came down, the tension being released when the funnel landed on the topmast cap. The funnels and truck 'stacked' on the cap, and were secured there. A capstan bar, pushed through everything and lashed, was useful if the topgallant mast was not going aloft again promptly. Injudicious pulling on the rigging could tumble the funnel down, and if the eyes of the rigging came off, the result was a dreadful mess. Hourigan (99) felt that the commonest cause of this catastrophe, apart from imprudent hauling on the backstays, was lack of care in handling the heel rope. The masthead should be allowed to come down clear of the funnels before the heel rope was hauled on vigorously, otherwise the masthead acted as a lever to throw the funnel off centre. Frapping lines were then passed around the slack bights of rigging to keep them snug, and it was particularly important to hang the backstays, and so on, from the crosstrees, rather than allowing the weight to come on the funnel.

Smith, in the *Accidence* (28), in describing how a topmast is struck in a storm, says 'strike your topmasts to the cap, make them sure with your sheeps' feet' Elsewhere (16), he says 'sheeps' feet is a stay in settling a top-

mast', but just what form this took, I am not sure; it may mean that the stays, and so on, were shortened by taking a sheepshank in them. Boteler and Mainwaring do not use this term at all.

Shifting topgallant masts. Boyd (410) brings the old mast down on deck, alongside the new one, with the heels aft, the heads under the lubber's hole, the after sides of the masts uppermost, being particularly careful to get the turns out of the mast rope. When the lizard is cast off, the two parts of the mast rope are held widely separated, so there will be no mix-up, and the rope is snatched in the new mast, and the lizard passed once more, exactly as with the other.

Disposition of force. Ulffers (194) lists the following duties. At the crosstrees: men to overhaul the topgallant shrouds and Jacob's ladder; hitch the eyes of the topgallant brace and lift to the aftermost crosstree; handle the truck and funnels of the topgallant and royal rigging which are secured squarely over the hole in the topmast cap, making sure that the signal halliards are clear, if these were left rigged, through their sheave in the truck; reeve and unreeve the yard ropes; work the lizard which secured the mast rope at the level of the royal sheave hole; handle fid and preventer fid. In the top and on the lower yard, men to fend off the mast, and see that it went up on the right slew. On deck, apart from the hands hauling on the mast rope, men had to be detailed to clap on and tend tackles for the topgallant backstays, easing them off prior to hoisting, subsequently taking down the slack, steadying the mast in the initial stages of the striking process. This was particularly necessary, if there was much rolling at sea.

Topgallant masts abaft topmasts. Some officers preferred to rig the masts in this way, since they could be struck, although not sent completely down, while still allowing a whole topsail to be carried (Hutchinson, 53). Gustav Alexandersson comments that two British merchant vessels *Ben Avon* and *Lawhill*, were found so rigged at the end of the nineteenth century (*Mariner's Mirror* 64, 1978, 192).

The commands.
Down (Up) topgallant masts!
Topgallant and royal yardmen in the tops!
Aloft topgallant and royal yardmen!
Man topgallant mast ropes!
Haul taut!
Sway and unfid!
Lower away together!
Lay down from aloft!
Sway aloft!
Sway and fid!

Shifting flying jibboom. At sea, and sometimes for exercise purposes, this was rigged out and in, as the topgallant masts went up and down. The heel rope of the boom corresponded functionally to the mast rope. It rove from deck through a tail block at the jibboom end, back to the heel of the flying jibboom. The flying jib downhaul, or something similar, was used as an inhaul, and bent to the heel of the spar, which was secured to the jibboom, by a heel lashing just outside the cap,

and a belly lashing half way out to the end of the jibboom (Nares, 55). These had to be let go, and secured once more, when the spars had been shifted.

Jibboom. Before shifting, the flying jibboom had to be in, and the jib unbent. Since the stays would have to be let go, the fore topgallant mast had to be housed beforehand. In calm weather, the topgallant could be kept up, and the fore royal and topgallant yardropes rigged down forward as temporary stays (Luce, 523). The crupper chain holding down the heel of the boom had to be let go, along with the guys, martingale, back ropes, and so on. Various expedients were adopted to raise the spar, while it was coming in. One system used the jib halliards at the outer end, and the fore clew jiggers hooked to the inner end. The heel rope was rove through a block on one side of the cap, back through the sheave in the heel of the spar, and out again to be secured to the cap on the other side. It was eased off, as the spar came in, and was used to send the boom out again in rigging out.

SHIFTING TOPSAIL YARDS

At least one, and usually two spare topsail yards, completely fitted, were kept ready for emergency. All three yards were sometimes shifted for exercise, at the same time (von Littrow, 101; Ulffers, 239). On the other hand, Hourigan (98) indicates that topsail yards were no longer shifted purely for exercise in the United States Navy in 1903. The custom was to keep the spare yard on chocks in the channels or in the booms, the main topsail yard on the starboard side, the fore on the port. We may assume the mizzen topsail yard would have been stowed on the booms to port. Ulffers (239) disapproved of stowage in the chains, feeling that they were less accessible there, and could not be kept fully rigged. Certainly the main topsail yard could be swung out of the chains fairly readily, but, getting the fore would have been less convenient.

In harbour, the yard was lowered forward of the lower yard, the main to starboard, the others to port. At sea, it was sent down to weather, and abaft all. The idea was to secure a tackle to a point about a quarter the way out on one side of the yard, send it down on end, and unrig the yardarms. The lower yardarm was landed on a grating or wooden 'shoe', which allowed the yardarm to slide aft without scoring the deck. The spar was landed on deck, beside the reverse spar, with the weather or 'lower' yardarm aft, in the case of fore and main, forward in the mizzen.

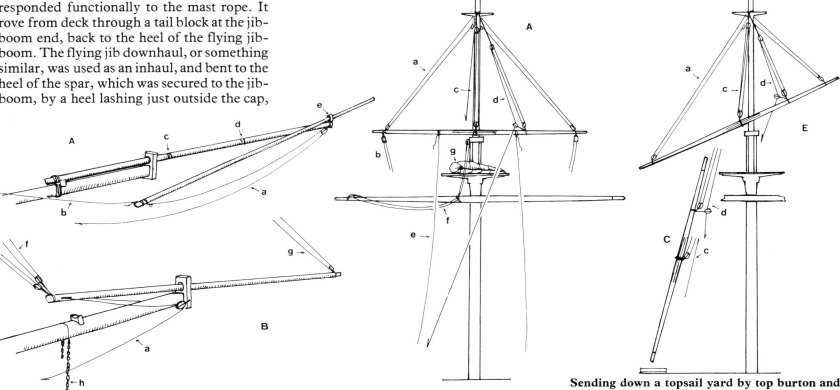

A Shifting a flying jibboom; **B** shifting a jibboom.
a heel rope; **b** inhaul; **c** position of heel lashing; **d** position of belly lashing; **e** flying jibboom iron; **f** clew jiggers; **g** jib halliards; **h** crupper chain.

Sending down a topsail yard by top burton and sail tackle
A Gear rove off ready for lowering; **B** and **C** progressive positions of yard during lowering.
a lifts; **b** braces; **c** burton tackle; **d** sail tackle; **e** bowlines; **f** lower lift stopped to yard; **g** topsail stowed in top.

Preparation. Sail was shortened and 'balanced' beforehand, and the topsail was unbent, being kept in the top ready for bending to the new yard. Some officers preferred to send it on deck completely out of the way (Hourigan, 97). The buntline lizards, topgallant sheets, clewline blocks and reef-tackles had to be cleared away and unrove. The clewlines and sheets could be left in place, bent to the clews. There is no general agreement about the exact method of rigging the lowering tackles. The ties and halliards could not be used, at least as rigged, because the halliard falls were not long enough. Von Littrow (101) uses two topgallant yard ropes, bent to the yard about three feet outside the tie blocks on either side; the 'upper' one was seized to the yard further out, in addition. Krogh (106) uses a 'long tackle', a type of sail tackle, with a fiddle block instead of an ordinary double block above. Nares (228) uses the sail tackle on the 'upper' lowering strop, and the centre burton on the lower. Ulffers (239) uses the sail tackle plus one tie and halliards, with the tie rove singly, that is to say dispensing with the tie block on the yard. Hourigan (97) uses a burton hooked half way out on each side of the yard, and a hawser rigged as a yard rope through a heavy block at the topmast head, and down abaft all. The topgallant studdingsail booms were hauled in, clear of their irons, and hauled up the topmast rigging, butt end first, and made fast there. The top burton could be used to manage the inner end, and the topmast studdingsail halliards the other. Since the lower lift on the side that the yard was shifted would be in the way, it could be let go, and stopped down on the yard, while a preventer lift running from topmast head to lower yardarm was contrived of some other piece of gear, for instance a top burton (Ulffers, 239). A most detailed account of this exercise, and the stationing of the hands to accomplish it can be found in Ulffers, but since the German practice did not necessarily reflect that in other services, it will not be repeated in detail.

Lowering. The lashing of the parrel was taken off, except for the last turn, which was sometimes hitched as a slip-knot, ready to let go on the order. The weight of the yard was transferred to the sail tackle, burton, or whatever, and the tie blocks were unshackled, and seized to the topmast shrouds. By hauling on the upper lift and manning the tackle best on that side, while at the same time easing off on the opposite lift, the yard was tilted into a vertical position. If taking it down abaft the lower yard, the upper brace was eased, and the lower one hauled. The top bowlines were

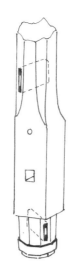
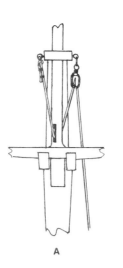

Detail of topmast heel fitted with two sheaves.

Lead of the toprope
A Rigged with one hauling end; **B** rigged with one hauling end led to knight, and other end to top tackle.

often hitched around the yard, and used to control its fore and after movement. When the lower yardarm was within reach of the men on deck, the lift and brace were unshackled, the upper yardarm being unrigged in the top. The lower yardarm was then dropped onto its 'shoe' and slid aft, by further judicious easing of the tackles. Hourigan (98) describes a slightly different technique. Both top bowlines were made fast to the yardarms, and led forward to control the slewing of the yard. In addition, a burton was secured to the slings, to hold the yard forward clear of the top rim. A tripping line, which he refers to as a 'snorter', was used to guide the lower yardarm down, while rolling tackles were fitted to control side to side swaying. The yard was mastheaded and ties, brace and lift blocks unshackled, before canting the yard and lowering it. The course was, for convenience, clewed up while these activities were going on.

Hoisting. The sequence was reversed to get the new yard up in place. At sea, however, getting the parrel secure might be more difficult than letting it go, if there was much rolling. The remedy was to use a rolling tackle to control excessive lateral swinging of the yard. The sail was bent to the yard, the gear rerove, and the sail set once more.

The commands (following Krogh, 106).
Shift topsail yard!
Aloft topmen!
Hoist long tackle!
Man topsail halliards, clewlines, and sheets!
Let go top bowline! Clew up!

Brace in! Haul taut! Let go halliards!
Furl and unbend topsail!
Booms in the rigging!
Standby to sway! Sway!
Lower away!
Stand by to hoist topsail yard!
Sway across! Rig out booms!
Haul out reef-tackle!
Bend topsail!
Standby topsail halliards and sheets!
Hoist away!
Steady out top bowlines!
Send down long tackle!

STRIKING AND SHIFTING TOPMASTS

Differences between topmasts and topgallant masts. In bad weather, topmasts could be struck to reduce topweight, the hounds remaining just above the lower cap, the lower end being secured to the lower mast with a heavy lashing. The topmasts were also shifted for exercise purposes, and since in principle they were just bigger versions of the topgallants, shifting them was just a more complicated variation on the same theme. Von Littrow remarks that, exercise excepted, shifting a badly damaged topmast was likely to occur in a context of general confusion, and hence exact rules could hardly be given to cover all cases, the operation varying greatly with the surrounding circumstances. Whether it was best to lower topmasts in a storm had been questioned from a very early date. Boteler (162) puts it this way: 'And as for the striking of the topmasts in this extremity of tempest, I am of his mind (though many are to the contrary) who holdeth that a ship is the wholesomer in the sea (though it be in a storm or tempest) when her topmasts are up, than when they are struck, and that she hath better way through it; so that when there is sea room enough, it is the safest course not to strike them, neither under the sea nor before.' In the last sentence he means when neither lying to, nor scudding.

One obvious difference between topmast and topgallant, was the presence of the crosstrees and cap on the former. In shifting, these had to be taken off somehow. A second difficulty was the fact that the topmast could not drop past the lower yard without fouling it, unless steps were taken to circumvent this. Whereas the topgallant yards were sent down on deck prior to shifting the topgallant mast, the topsail yard could be lowered onto the top and secured there.

Top-tackle and hawser. Boteler (185) and Mainwaring (216) indicate that the earlier practice was identical to that already described for the topgallant masts. The mast rope, called in this case, a 'top-rope', was secured to the cap, taken down and through a transverse sheave-hole in the mast running on a brass sheave, up through a top-block hanging on the other side of the cap, down once more through a sheave in the knighthead, and thence to the capstan.

A later refinement, which Lees (4) dates from 1675, employed two sheaves in the heel of the mast, at right angles to each other, and two top-blocks. The mizzen topmast, however, always used the simpler method. Sometimes one top-rope was rove through both mast sheaves; sometimes two separate ropes were employed. Ulffers (240) appears to describe a 'hawser' and a 'top-rope', each working in its own sheave. Boyd (117), describing 1860 Royal Navy practice, says that the lower 'dumb' or 'half-sheave' is below the fid hole, and the 'live sheave' above it. In the main topmast, the live sheave runs diagonally from starboard after to port forward aspect, and the reverse in the foremast. This arrangement brings the working top-tackle fall on opposite sides of the deck, on fore and main. In the late 1800s, a top-rope was rigged with two hauling ends. It led from deck through a block on one side of the cap, down through the mast sheave, through a block on the other side of the cap, and was secured to the pendant of a heavy two- or three-fold 'top-tackle', which set up with a swivel block on deck. This is referred to by Nares (230), Taunt (335), and others. In use, the capstan

hove round one end of the hawser or top-rope, in the early stages of hoisting, while to lift the mast for the final fidding or unfidding, the hawser was belayed, and the top-tackle provided the extra power. French and German accounts describe the use of the *braguet* or *Brok*, in the fidding process. Boyd (412) refers to a 'preventer top-tackle', and perhaps this is simply the same thing. This has already been described, when considering striking the topgallant masts.

Topsail yard. The topsail was furled, with the clews tucked well in, to avoid tearing. After unparrelling, the yard was lowered down onto the fore part of the cap, and securely lashed to the foremost topmast shroud chainplates, keeping it clear of the topmast itself. The top bowlines were hitched round the slings to haul the yard forward, clear of the projecting part of the lower cap, on its way down. The yard was lowered by easing away on the halliards and lifts, the topgallant sheets, which were hitched at the crosstrees, and the reef-tackles, had to be eased off at the same time. Ekelöf (90) offers another way of placing the yard in the top, namely fore and aft, outside, or rather on top of the topmast shrouds, which were slacked off so this could be done. Securing the yard in the top would seem to have been the most logical and easiest method, but von Littrow (99), for one, strikes it right down on deck, or rather resting on the gunwales. Taunt (336) gives yet another alternative, when the topmast was partially struck, namely keeping the yard parrelled to the mast, shifted up, of course, near the hounds. By so doing, it could be braced to the wind, if at anchor. Boyd (Figure 216) illustrates ships at anchor, adopting this method.

Clearance. Since the total length of the topmast usually exceeded the distance from deck to the underside of the crosstrees, it was necessary for the heel to dip below deck level, at one point in the evolution. In the case of the mainmast, the main hatch would allow this. A small scuttle was sometimes cut in the deck, just forward of the foremast, to permit shifting the fore topmast. When the mast was lowered sufficiently, the head was hauled forward clear of the top, and it was swayed up once more, so the heel could be landed on deck on its 'shoe' or on a grating, which allowed it to slide across the deck without damaging it. The lower yard was under the topmast, and had to be hauled forward by the top bowlines, or other gear, hitched to the slings, to let the topmast come down, the trusses being slacked off to accomplish this. Ekelöf (91) rigs the jeers to take the weight of the yard, while the chain-slings are let go.

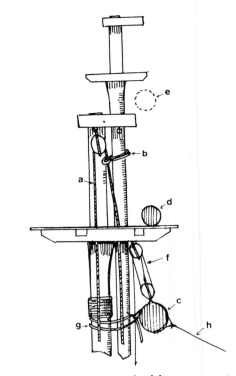

Detail of lower mast head with topmast struck
a toprope; b lizard; c lower yard; d topsail yard; e alternative position of topsail yard; f jeers; g truss; h bowlines.

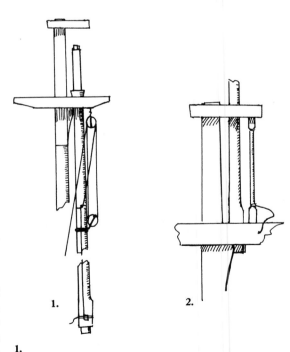

1.
Topmast rigged for sending up with lower jeer.

2.
Details of capshore.

A

B

Masts and yards struck to ride out heavy weather.
A American frigate with topgallant and topmasts struck, lower and topsail yards pointed (after A Roux);
B French frigate with topmasts housed, topsail yards landed in tops and lower yards struck (after F Roux).

The bow of the later patent truss was designed to give sufficient clearance. Liardet (244) cautions that when striking a topmast in heavy weather, with much rolling, the trusses should not be slacked off too soon – in fact, only when the heel of the topmast is just above the lower yard. Furthermore, once it has got below the yard, the trusses should be hauled gently taut once more, to aid the rolling-tackles and braces in keeping the yard as steady as possible. Boyd (411) braces the mainyard sharp up on the starboard tack, the mast being worked on the starboard side of the deck. He does not specifically say so, but it seems likely that the foreyard would have been braced the opposite way, and the mast worked on the port side of the deck. Some accounts suggest that the topmast be lowered on deck heads forward, but at least one authority lands the main topmast head aft.
Jeers. Nares (230), Boyd (411) and Ulffers

(240) rig one of the jeer blocks, to get the new mast up and down. This allowed the new mast to be got ready and partially hoisted, while the old mast was still pointed through the top, and the top-rope still rove. A runner block was lashed to the mast about two-thirds, or three-quarters of the way up. The jeer fall was rove through the foot block on deck, through the upper jeer block, down through the runner block, up again through the jeer block, down to be half-hitched above the runner block, and the end secured by taking it through the fid hole. This arrangement prevented the strop holding the runner block slipping up on the mast. The hauling end led from the footblock to the capstan. My guess is that the starboard jeer block would have been used on the main, and the port on the fore, the blocks being hooked to the collar of the lower stay.
Lizard. The mast rope was rove through a smooth round thimble, that formed the eye of the lizard, which had two tails. These were made fast round the mast below the hounds, each tail taking two round turns, and being knotted to its fellow. In addition, a lashing secured them to the masthead. This arrange-

ment prevented them slipping downwards, while allowing the mastrope to render through the thimble, and confining it to the upper part of the mast, when the masthead was clear of the top. When the mast was hauled up vertically, its foot on the deck, the top-rope was rove and hauled taut, at which time the jeer fall was removed, and the runner block taken off.
Surging. Of necessity, the crosstrees had to be a snug fit on the topmast head, and if they had been in place for a long time, they had to be loosened, by actually dropping the mast with sufficient force to jolt them loose; the usual drop mentioned is six feet. With the crosstrees this distance above the lower cap, the top-rope was stoppered, and the turns slacked up on the capstan, so that about three fathoms was completely loose, and the top-rope was then belayed. Everything being clear, and all hands being out from under, the stopper was slipped, dropping the mast six feet if the 'surge' failed to kick the crosstrees loose, or nine feet if it succeeded (Ulffers, 230). The topmast cap usually could be got off with less trouble. The hammering to which the lower cap was subjected, partly explains the necessity for the capshore, the vertical pillar supporting the fore part of the lower cap, which also served to counteract the downward pull of the top-blocks when these were under strain. The capshore was itself secured by a lanyard, in case it got kicked loose during the surging process (Boyd, 411). If the topmast was so long that it remained protruding through the cap, when the heel was on deck, there was no fear of it falling sideways. Boyd advocates placing coils of rope directly underneath, so that the deck would not be damaged by the heel striking it too vigorously.
Striking topmast and topgallant together. The safest and most logical procedure was to send down the light yards and topgallant mast beforehand. Von Littrow (101) describes a method used when the damage sustained by the masts was of such an extent that it was unsafe for men to go aloft any further than the top, and hence impossible to unfid the topgallant mast. The topmast was struck sufficiently to bring the crosstrees within reach of the men in the top, and then slewed around ninety degrees, so that the topgallant mast was centered over the lubber's hole. The topgallant mastrope was rove, and it was struck down alongside the lower mast.
Execution. The exact details would have varied a great deal. Any studdingsails becketted in the topmast rigging, would be sent down, the topgallant studdingsail booms

1.

1. USS *Portsmouth* at Portsmouth, England, 1882. The upper yards have been sent down in harbour, and may be seen stowed in the rigging. (Imperial War Museum, London)

2. The bustle of activity as a topmast is sent down for exercise. *Illustrated London News*, 1888. (Mark Myers' Collection)

2

might be sent down, or simply lashed securely to the topsail yard, if it was left aloft. Tackles were clapped on the topmast back-stay and the lanyards of the deadeyes loosened. The topmast shrouds also had to be eased up, if a regular fid was used. The lever fids, already described, which were some-times employed in French ships, obviated this step. At sea, the weather backstays were kept taut, as the mast came down. If the fore topmast was being struck, because of bad weather, the jibboom would be run in at the same time, since it lost its upward support, when the stays were slacked away. The top-mast shrouds were stopped down in the top, if striking partially. The eyes of the rigging had to be kept clear to accept the new topmast head in shifting. Blunt (174) describes shift-ing the topmasts and lower yards simul-taneously. He felt, contrary to some con-temporary opinion, that the rigging of the struck topmast did not hold the wind suf-ficiently to counterbalance the beneficial ef-fects of striking, provided it were frapped in closely enough. I have come across no men-tion of preventer fids. However, since hoist-ing was a rather slow process, a crowbar was slipped through the fid hole as soon as it appeared above the top, being withdrawn, as

soon as the fid could be banged in. Ulffers gives a detailed description of how the hands were stationed, but it must have been a situa-tion where much variation occurred.

Commands.
Man the top-tackle!
Sway up! Out fid!
Lower away!
Man the jeers (top-tackle)!
Sway aloft!
Launch-ho! This archaic order is listed by Smyth as being given when the fid is in, and the top-rope is to be let go. It imports 'High enough!'

STRIKING LOWER YARDS

This was sometimes done at the same time as the topmasts were partially struck. The sail might simply be furled, or if necessary un-bent. In the 1600s the practice was very com-mon, while in the late 1800s it was, one imagines, rather rare. Boteler (98, 244) says that, when the yards are struck down, the ship is 'riding a portise', or 'portlast'. He defines the 'portless' [*sic*] as 'the wale or bend that lieth under the portholes of those great guns, which are in the forecastle of the ship'. Krogh (108) describes the procedure thus. The jeers were rove off and hoisted slightly so that the chain slings and truss chains could be unshackled. The yard was then lowered by the jeers and lifts, being steadied by the braces and if necessary hauled somewhat for-ward to hold it clear of the mast. Side to side sallying was prevented by extempore rolling-tackles. When a few feet above the nettings, the jeer falls were belayed, and the yard was

lashed securely to the shrouds, while a heavy lashing was passed around mast and yard.

SQUARING, COCKBILLING AND MANNING YARDS

These activities, although really quite un-related, will be considered together, as a matter of convenience.

Squaring the yards. Upon coming to anchor, and at appropriate intervals there-after, during a protracted stay in harbour, the boatswain had himself rowed around the ship, to check that the yards were square, all lines properly taut, and no loose ends visible. This apparently was not as straightforward as it sounds. 'It may safely be asserted that there are few boatswains to be found, quite com-petent to execute this service, with the nice degree of precision, it requires' (Glascock, 162). Before adjusting the yards, the boat-swain noted that the masts were straight, 'all in one'. Failure to make sure of this, before-hand, might result in the boatswain reporting 'Yards square and all lines taut', then sur-reptitiously getting a pull on something, a topgallant backstay, for instance, and as a re-sult, throwing everything out of line once more. The lower yards were 'trussed to', by hauling both truss tackles taut, the topsail and topgallant yards taken just off the cap, and square by the lifts and braces. It was im-portant that the yard be accurately centred on the mast beforehand, and that, above all, the mistake of hauling both lifts too taut, be avoided. 'There is no professional practice which tends more to disfigure a man-of-war than that of bowing the yards. Moreover, independent of the harm it does, it is seldom indicative of *sea* service' (Glascock, 162).

The traditional method of relaying the boatswain's instructions was to station a boatswain's mate at the jibboom end. However in the late 1800s, flag signals were adopted. Alston offers a simple code, employing flags of different colours for each mast, and indicating the yard to be topped by the way the flag was held. The boatswain's mate raised his arm to indicate that the order was understood, and passed it verbally to the hands manning the lifts. 'This method possesses so many advantages over the general method. It saves the lungs of the boatswain, allows him to go any distance from the ship, is not liable to be misunderstood, is far more expeditious, and in a close harbour, saves all the intolerable bawling that follows the close of any exercise with the fleet' (Alston, 288). 'The most minute and sleepless attention to the squaring of yards is justly held a paramount consideration in a ship of war' (Fordyce, 44).

Cockbilling the yards. This was done as a sign of mourning, ordinarily from daylight to dusk. I do not know how ancient the custom was, but it is mentioned by Engelhart, in 1840. Taunt (427) indicates that cockbilling the yards was the custom in the merchant service, whereas naval vessels usually limited themselves to hoisting the ensign half mast and firing 'minute guns'. On the other hand, Brady (230) describes in detail the way it was executed, so it was not unknown in the United States Navy.

The trusses of the lower yards were slacked off, and if the topsail sheets were of chain, one of them had to be unshackled. The yard was then canted up, until it touched the top rim, with the topsail and topgallant yards topped up parallel to it, their parrels being slacked off, to allow this to be done. The direction of tilt depended on the side the topgallant yards were sent up. For example, if the main topgallant went up to starboard, the yards on the main were canted up to port, those on the fore and mizzen, the opposite way. The peak of the mizzen and trysail gaffs were lowered, and the topping lifts of the lower booms eased off, until the ends of the booms trailed in the water.

Manning the yards. This method of saluting an important visitor involved having the men run out on the yards, remaining standing upright there, for ten minutes or so, while the boat of the VIP passed the ship, or came to the gangway. The men faced either forward or aft towards the approaching boat; in the case of the person honoured coming on board, the men on the mizzen yards faced

forwards, those on the fore and main aft (Brady, 238). Some illustrations show the royal yards manned, others nothing above the topgallants, the royals having been sent down beforehand.

In preparation for the exercise, lifelines were rigged from the ties to the lifts, about four feet above the yard. Fewer men were required to man the yards than to furl the sail, so suitable individuals were selected from the furlers. They were 'sized', placing the tallest men at the yardarm, the smaller ones at the bunt. This was particularly important when the men at the slings had to stand upon canvas slewed up on top of the yard, on either side of the bunt. There was, in addition, the discrepancy existing due to the greater diameter of the yard itself, at the bunt. Engelhart (89) says that the ideal was to have men of the same height on the same yard, the tallest on the lower yard, the smallest on the topgallant.

The saluting party were sent aloft in good time, but kept at the masthead, and inside the 'laying out marks', until the boat was two cables distance away, whereupon they ran out, holding on to the lifeline. The outside man kept his outboard arm outstretched, wound his inner arm round the lifeline, and grasped the jumper of the next man, at the shoulder. Each man, in succession, then supported himself, arm wrapped around the lifeline, and grasping the shoulder of the man next to him. In earlier years, different configurations were employed when honouring a visitor in this particular fashion, such as manning the stays, shrouds and the yards, only on the side the boat approached from.

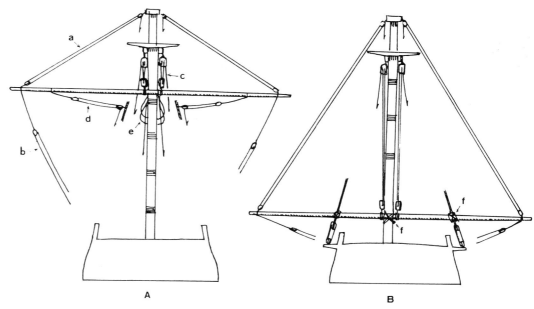

Striking lower yard.
A Yard ready for lowering; **B** yard lowered and secured.
  a lifts; **b** braces; **c** jeers; **d** rolling tackle (if needed); **e** truss; **f** lashings.

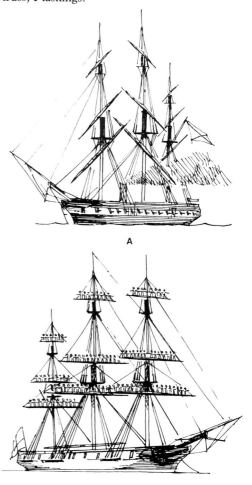

Cockbilling and manning the yards.
A Russian steam frigate with yards cockbilled in mourning (after sketch by Cox, engraved in the *Illustrated London News*, 1865); **B** HMS *Alert* with yards squared and manned (after sketch by Ekelöf, engraved in the *Illustrated London News*, 1868).

CHAPTER 8
MAKING AND SHORTENING SAIL AT SEA

We have considered how sail was loosed and furled in harbour, and of course, things were managed in a very similar fashion at sea. Loosing and furling were similar in that clewlines, buntlines,and so on, were cast off to loose, and hauled to clew up, but there were some significant differences. The sheets of the upper sails were hauled home, and their yards mastheaded when setting at sea, while the yards remained on the caps in harbour.

Although studdingsails were set and taken in, with the other sails, and although reefing was really just a particular way of shortening sail, we have for convenience, considered these topics in separate chapters, and restricted our attention to other matters in this section.

Expressions used. 'Plain sail', as in 'all plain sail to royals', is an expression that does not occur in the dictionaries much before 1900. It meant the ordinary working sail, and did not apply to studdingsails, upper staysails, and flying kites, nor yet to storm canvas. Hourigan comments that, in the United States Navy, 'plain sail' included a gaff topsail (a comparative rarity) but excluded the fore topmast staysail. The term 'plane sailing', referred to a simple method of navigating, and occurs much earlier than 'plain sail'.

The traditional order to increase the amount of canvas was 'Make sail!', and to diminish it, 'Shorten sail!'. Mainwaring (179) talks of 'letting fall' and 'furling' ('farthelling') the courses, 'heaving out' and 'stowing' of the topsails, and 'setting' only of the mizzen course. Similar specialisation of terminology survived into the last days of the sailing navy, Hourigan (921) says that the convention in the United States Navy, was to 'clear away' and 'stow' headsails and staysails; 'loose' and 'furl' all plain square sail; 'clear away' and 'make up' trysail and spanker; 'get ready' and 'make up' studdingsails. I am not certain how widely followed this sequence was. 'Clear away' is acceptable enough for the purposes stated, but 'make up' was used when getting a sail ready for stowing in the sail locker, also when getting it ready for bending, not to mention that studdingsails were 'made up for setting', reflecting the way they were bundled up and sent aloft in a manner totally different from any other sails. Other languages do not seem to draw this type of distinction, German using *beschlagen* and French *serrer*, or *ferler*, for the 'furling' or 'handing' of any sail.

Certain other expressions were used with specific sails, for example the standard form of the order was 'Down jib! In royals and topgallants! Settle the topsail halliards!' The mizzen was 'brailed in' and its clew 'hauled out', when taking in and setting, respectively. 'Douse', or 'dowse', originally implied that a sail was to be hauled *down*, as 'Douse the jib!', and much earlier 'Dowse your Top-Saile to salute him for the Sea!' (Smith, 77). Today, it is sometimes extended to encompass the taking in of any sail, including the courses, which are actually hauled up (Regan & Johnson, 190). Topsails and the light sails could either be 'clewed up' or 'clewed down', depending on the way things were managed, while the courses could only be 'clewed up'. The ship 'set sail', or 'got under sail', by setting the individual sails. Corresponding foreign expressions include Dutch *onder zeil gaan, zeil maaken* ('go under sail', 'make sail'), while in French we have *mettre à la voile*.

ORDER OF MAKING AND SHORTENING SAIL

General remarks. The exact sequence in which canvas was added and taken away depended ultimately on the surrounding circumstances, the character of the vessel, and the judgement of the officer. Although things changed somewhat over the centuries, certain general principles applied. Thus, lofty sail came off first to avoid excessive heeling, and because the light yards and spars were less well supported than the lower ones. Staysails on the mizzen came off before the corresponding items on the main, for two reasons: the mizzen was less sturdy; and secondly, the more a vessel heeled, the greater the amount of weather helm, and the greater the reduction of after sail necessary. On the other hand, lofty sail was sometimes taken off the fore, because it had a greater tendency to depress the bow than the corresponding sails on the main, and this resulted in excessive weather helm.

Exceptions to the taking in of lofty sail are offered by the nineteenth century preference for taking in the courses, and leaving the reefed topsails set. The latter did not lose the wind in the trough of the sea. In the days of the double topsail, it was very common to set the upper topsail first, and take it in last, when leaving, or entering an anchorage. The reason was that, in the first case, the lower topsail could be sheeted home quicker than the upper topsail could be hoisted, and in the second, that the upper topsail halliards could be let go, and the effect of the sail nullified quicker, than the lower topsail could be clewed up. These were considerations that applied with great force in an under-manned merchantman.

With regard to the headsails, in blowing weather, the further out the sail, the sooner it came in, the flying jibboom being lighter, and less well supported than the jibboom. The jib, for similar reasons, was replaced by the fore topmast staysail, as the weather worsened.

As the wind decreased, sail was added in more or less the reverse order, although there was a natural tendency to hang on to sail too long, as the wind increased, and to wait until improvement was well established, before setting it again. The rate of sailing was not invariably improved by adding extra canvas; indeed sometimes things were bettered by getting off some of the upper sails. Furthermore, care had to be taken that a relatively ineffective sail was not taking the wind out of a better one, for instance allowing a lower studdingsail to becalm a jib. On the other hand, it was important not to deprive the vessel of the steadying effect of canvas, if she were rolling heavily. As to the relative difficulty of the tasks, 'There is an old saying amongst seamen that any fool can make sail, but it requires a skilful sailor to take it in' (Todd & Whall, 71).

Sequence of shortening sail c1640.

Sequence of shortening sail c1780.

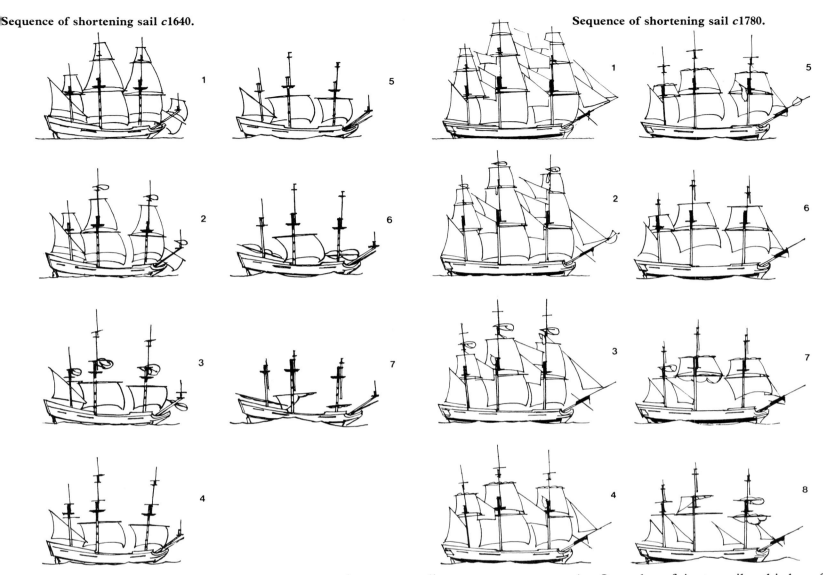

SHORTENING SAIL IN BAD WEATHER

We will consider the case of a vessel sailing by the wind. The wind gradually freshens until it is blowing a gale, and she is 'lying to', or 'lying a-hull' if showing no canvas. In the seventeenth century, a vessel 'lay a-try', or 'tried', while in the nineteenth, it was more customary to say that she 'lay to'. Most authorities 'lie to' for a storm, but 'heave to' for a pilot, but confusion between the two expressions is common enough.

'*Hulling* is when a ship is at sea, and hath taken in all her sails in calm weather. It is done to save the sails from beating out against the mast. But in foul weather, when they are able to bear no sail, the name is no more than taking in all the sail, and tying down the helm to the lee side' (Mainwaring, 167). The following are examples of the order in which things were done at different periods, illustrating the changes in practice over the centuries.

About 1640. Royals and mizzen topgallants were not in use generally.

1. In spritsail topsail, in topgallants, fore topgallant first.

2. Bonnets off courses, lower yards partially struck, in spritsail and topsails.

3. Spritsail topsail yard got inboard, spritsail yard lashed fore and aft.

4. Topgallant masts and yards struck down on deck.

5. Two of the three courses furled, either mainsail or mizzen course left set.

6. Topmasts struck, all sail taken in, except a 'hullock' of mainsail or mizzen. This last corresponds to what was later called a 'goosewing'.

About 1780. The changes in practice are chiefly related to the greater number of upper sails, and the introduction of reefing.

1. In royals, stow flying jib and main royal staysail.

2. In topgallants, set small jib, stow main and mizzen topgallant staysails.

3. First reef in topsails, in middle staysail and mizzen topmast staysail, send down royal yards.

4. Second reef in topsails, third reef in mizzen topsail, stow main topmast staysail and jib, set fore topmast staysail.

5. Reef course, topgallant yards sent down, topgallant masts struck or housed.

6. Close reef fore and main topsail, take in mizzen topsail, set mizzen staysail and storm mizzen.

7. In fore course and fore topsail, stow fore topmast staysail and set fore and main storm staysails, goosewing main topsail.

Late 1800s. Practice remained very similar to the above (Riesenberg, 780; Dick & Kretchmer, II, 300). The main and mizzen staysails were to a great extent replaced by gaff trysails on fore- and mainmasts. In the steel merchantmen of the last part of the century, the fore topmast staysail was carried as part of the plain sail, and the use of double topgallants and double topsails, made reefing much less necessary than had been the case earlier. Studdingsails were never set, and it was most unusual for any of the upper yards to be sent down. Nonetheless, the same principles applied as in earlier years, that is to say,

Handing square sail
A Up to the late seventeenth century, sails were handed by men crawling out along the top of the yard. Courses were often lowered for furling, and topsails handed from the tops where possible (after Bonaventura Peeters).
B Later practice was to hand the sails from footropes rigged under the yard. The lower yards were usually kept aloft, and the sails were more efficiently controlled by their gear (after Pocock).

the outer headsails came off first, along with the upper sails, while the lower topsails did the work of the close reefed topsail of earlier years.

Canvas set depending on point of sail. Assuming the wind to be moderate enough that its direction rather than its strength was the determining factor, attention was directed towards preventing one sail taking the wind out of another more useful one. By the wind, all square canvas, including that later innovation the crossjack sail, could be set. Staysails could be set with the wind just free, and until it drew aft about a point abaft the beam. Once the wind backed round to the quarter, the tack of the mizzen and the weather clew of the mainsail were hauled up, the entire crossjack having been taken in earlier. With the wind more or less dead astern, the mizzen was brailed in, the mainsail hauled up completely, the mizzen topgallant furled, and the mizzen topsail 'scandalised', the yard being settled on the cap, the reef tackles hauled out, but the sheets left home. The sheets of the main topgallant were slacked off, to allow the wind to get at the fore topgallant. The fore topsail, although becalmed on this point of sail, was usually left set. The old-fashioned single main topsail let very little wind past, but in the 'modern' square rigger, the sail plan was much more open, and total blanketting of the fore topsails did not occur. For the same reason, the staysails were useful over a wider arc than suggested above, being kept set until the wind was well round on the quarter, and they commenced to flap about uselessly (Horka).

The fore topmast and topgallant studdingsails could be set to weather, with the wind a point or so free. The lee main topmast and topgallant studdingsails, and perhaps the corresponding sails on the weather side of the main, could be set as the wind drew abeam. The weather lower studdingsail could be set once the wind came round to the quarter. With the wind aft, the studdingsails could be set both sides, but theoretically at least, it was best if these were divided between fore and main. Contemporary illustrations show, for example, the fore lower studdingsail on one side, and the main lower studdingsail on the other. Or, after the main lower studdingsail had become obsolete, one finds various combinations of the upper studdingsails distributing the canvas between the fore- and mainmasts. This usually occurred when the wind had been on the beam and gradually round until it was almost aft. Studdingsails set deliberately to take advantage of a stern wind, usually were set on both sides of the fore.

General remarks on handling square sail. 'In blowing weather, or against a head sea, make sail by degrees, so as to allow the ship to get headway gradually. If you press sail at once, particularly against a head sea, you force her instantly from a way of perhaps three knots, to seven or eight, and thus risk your masts, yards, etc' (Griffiths, 276).

As far as possible, the wind was allowed to help in setting and taking in sail, and at all events, was not allowed to actively hinder the operation. The gear which was tended was just as important as that which was manned, and care was taken that one item of running gear was not 'fighting' another, resulting in a game of 'pull Devil, pull Baker', until something gave way.

In taking in a course, the buntlines and clewlines to lee were more heavily manned than those to weather, and the buntlines were hauled on best, so that the sail was less likely to 'bag', and hold the wind excessively.

The work of securing a wet heavy sail was hard enough if conditions were optimal, and hence it was imperative that the yard be properly laid to the wind, so that the difficulty of the task was ameliorated as much as possible. In light winds, the upper yards were square when being furled, otherwise they were laid, so the wind blew along their length, luffing the ship, if necessary, to accomplish this. There was some difference of opinion about whether the sail should be 'a little more back than full', or 'slightly full', when furling, Krogh (27) and Boyd (396), for example, adhering to the first, and Knight (377) to the second opinion.

In mastheading the topsail and light yards, the lee brace was thrown off, and the weather one tended, to keep the sail lifting as it went up, when setting by the wind. Setting before the wind, both braces were tended, but some were of the opinion that in this circumstance, it was best to luff somewhat, so that the parrel would not bind (Schneider, 146). In very light weather, it was sometimes necessary to haul the lee brace, so that the topgallant bowline could be steadied out or hauled, upon which, the brace was eased off again, to give the topgallant mast some play.

The booms were for the most part not triced up at sea, unless they were in the way of the men working on the yard. If this were done, they were run in a little when the inner iron was unclamped, so that they were triced up more easily. The hands were not allowed on the yards, until these were down on the cap, and steadied as much as possible with braces, lifts, and rolling tackle. As a general rule, the braces were never touched until the yards were cleared, but if this was unavoidable, the men on the yard were cautioned to hold fast while bracing was in progress. Nor were the topsail and light yards ever hoisted with men on them, although at one time, it had been customary for a topman to 'ride' up with the topsail yard, hanging on to the tie, to right up the parrel, and warn when the ties came 'two blocks' (Mossel, III, 97). Hourigan mentions having seen a topman killed in just such a fashion, when the tie parted and the man fell to his death.

When setting a course, the lower rigging and yard were cleared of men if the sail were flapping violently. When topsail sheets were of rope, a 'topsail-sheetman' was detailed to go out on the yardarm to see all clear. It was important that the topsail clewlines be eased down, rather than let go abruptly, firstly so the topsail-sheetman would not be brained by the clew block, and secondly, so that the sheet entered the yardarm sheave hole at the proper angle. If the clewline were slacked off too much, the sheet hung in a bight over the yard, and had to be dragged up and into the sheave. With chain topsail sheets, the topsail-sheetman only went out if something were foul, to avoid being struck with the heavy chain.

The rolling tackle was hauled taut with the yard square, and as a result, came to lie even more tightly as the yard was braced up. The clewlines and buntlines would have interfered with bracing up, if they had been hauled too taut, when the sail was furled. One way of dealing with this, was to seize them at the point where they went through the leading block on the yard. This expedient, while very widely used in twentieth century merchantmen, was not employed in the early days; rather care was taken than the clewgarnets, buntlines, and so on were belayed leaving enough slack to allow the yard being braced around without impediment.

In the 'windjammers', the 'standing lifts' of the upper yards were allowed to hang in a bight abaft the yard, when sail was set, and the same practice was being followed in the Dutch Navy in the mid-1800s, according to Mossel (III, 98). Because of their lead, the lifts do very little to support the yard in the up' position. Photographs of the training ships of the 1900s sometimes show the lifts thrown forward of the sail. This was done, according to Knight (377) so that they would not foul the yards when they were lowered, and would not be in the way of the men going out on the yards. Earlier accounts indicate that the slack of the lifts was taken down, and coiled up on the lower ratlines or seized in the top (Ekelöf, 53; Pihlström, 236; Rosvall, 35). Lift-jiggers were clapped on when the yard-

arms were subjected to extra downward strain, as when studdingsails were set, or the topsail was close reefed.

Sail carried too long. A very spirited account of the consequences of imprudent 'cracking on' is to be found in Boyd (397):

A royal carried too long before, and a topgallant studdingsail carried too long near the wind, are the most difficult jobs that fall to a topman's lot to handle. Beyond a certain pace, these sails set, as above, cannot do the least good. If the trimmer is consulted whilst carrying a press of lofty sail before the wind, the ship will be found to be excessively out of trim by the head. Near the wind, the topgallant studdingsail is fore and aft, bellying to leeward, and taking the wind out of the powerful forward pressing of the topgallant sail. Before the wind, the studdingsail may be becalmed by a spoke of the helm, but the royal has no buntline. Every bound of the sail shakes the topgallant mast like a whip stick, and the men cannot handle it. There is no proper alternative but to let fly the clewlines, and let the sail blow to pieces. If the men have been allowed to go aloft to try and remedy the mischief, they won't come down, and can't be made to hear until they have had a try. It becomes a point of honour with them not to give it up, and at last some bold fellow goes down the lift, and if he is not jerked off, passes the gasket from the yard-arm in.

Weather or lee clew first.

And he who strives the tempest to disarm,
Will never first embrail the lee yardarm.

These lines from Falconer's poem *The Shipwreck* were known to every English seaman in the nineteenth century, and were thought by

many to offer the last word on the best fashion of taking in a course in blowing weather. However, as we shall see, there was not complete agreement on this point. For instance, Boyd (406): 'The most proper way to take in a course during heavy weather has been a matter of controversy since the time of the *Great Harry*. Falconer's oft-quoted maxim was, on his own showing, an innovation upon "long tried practice". The charm of the poetry must not be permitted to cover an error in seamanship.' In Canto II of the poem, the master is preparing to reef the courses, and an argument develops about the best order in which to clew up. The passage runs as follows:

But here the doubtful officers dispute,
Till skill and judgment prejudice confute-
Rodmond, whose genius never soared beyond
The narrow rules of art his youth had conned,
Still to the hostile fury of the wind
Released the sheet, and kept the tack confined;
To long-tried practice obstinately warm,
He doubts conviction, and relies on form;
But the sage master this advice declines;
With whom Arion in opinion joins.-
The watchful seaman, whose sagacious eye
On sure experience may with truth rely,
Who from the reigning cause foretells th' effect,
This barbarous practice ever will reject;
For fluttering loose in air, the rigged sail
Soon flits to ruins in the furious gale;
And he who strives the tempest to disarm,
Will never first embrail the lee yardarm.

The above discussion was focussed on an under sail, taken in during storm conditions. To someone serving in a modern square

Standing lifts. Lift supporting lowered yard on left, and hanging slack behind hoisted yard on right. The broken line shows the disadvantageous lead of a running lift.

Veering the lee sheet. This detail (from a painting by the Younger Van de Velde) illustrates the effect of veering out the sheet of a seventeenth century ship in heavy weather, a practice which Falconer's passage attempted to correct.

1.

Merchant ship shortened down in fresh weather; lithograph by John Ward. Whole topsails are being carried although the topgallants have been furled and the mainsail hauled up. Royal yards have been sent on deck, but their lifts and braces are made fast in the rigging. Note the fore and main spencers. (Courtesy Kingston-upon-Hull Museums and Art Galleries)

2.

The ship in this 1787 painting by Nicholas Pocock is getting in her foresail and main topsail after weathering Portishead Point. The topsail is being clewed up to weather first, with reef-tackles hauled out, while the foresail is being hauled up lee clew first. (Courtesy Bristol Museum and Art Gallery)

3.

The *Golden Fleece* running into Le Havre, taking in her foresail, fore lower topsail and main topgallant. When a ship rigged with double topsails was required to round up and reduce canvas quickly in an anchorage, it was usual to leave the upper topsails set until last – the reverse of the practice at sea. The spanker would also be set and the headsails doused to help her round up smartly. (Courtesy Andrew J Nesdall)

4.

HMS *Cruiser* setting royals and flying jib, 1891. In naval service these sails were usually set and taken in together. (Imperial War Museum, London)

Taking in a course
A Weather clew first; **B** lee clew first.

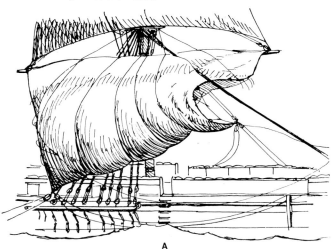

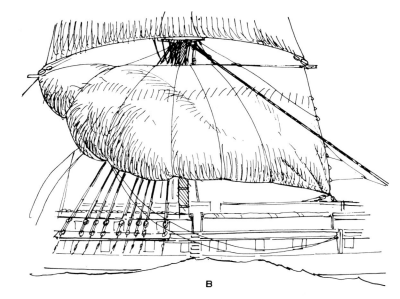

rigged training ship, the argument must seem academic in the extreme. Today's yards and rigging are strong enough to tolerate a great deal of abuse, the gear is much better designed than in earlier days, and there is a sufficient deck force to use it effectively. On the other hand, a wooden yard could be sprung beyond repair, if the tack were suddenly let go, and an old-fashioned sail could blow through the buntlines, or balloon off to leeward of its leechlines, making it difficult to subdue. In modern sailing vessels the buntlines lead through eyelets on the sail, allowing the canvas to be run up almost as readily as a jalousie or a venetian blind, and the clewgarnets lead to the yardarms, rather than to the slings, allowing one to 'throttle' the sail, under almost any conditions.

In the latter-day windjammer, the gear was similar to that just described, but there were barely sufficient hands to man it. Partly for that reason, the traditional sequence was usually followed, the weather side of the course being clewed up first (Tait, 95; Nicholls, 284; Reed, 164).

There was no argument about the necessity of letting go the lee clew in the event that the vessel was in immediate hazard, heeling excessively to the wind. In that case, the sail was sacrificed in the hope of saving the ship. Nor, for that matter, was there any doubt that it was best to take the sail in, one side at a time, rather than running both sides up together as could be done in light weather (Ulffers, 345). However, there were, as we shall see, dissenting voices even here (Liardet, 199).

Weather clew first. The advantage of taking the sail in to weather initially lay in the fact that the lee half of the sail remained full, being steadied by the wind. The disadvantage was that the greater part of the sail was blown to leeward, beyond the stay, so that although the sail could be got up in its gear quite readily, it might be difficult to make it fast properly, because of the balloons of canvas on the lee side of the yard. With the mainsail especially, keeping the leeward, or after, part of the sail full made the ship gripe and lie heavily on her helm. In the case of the mainsail, this part of the sail lay abaft the CLR, but even with the foresail, the lee half of the sail engendered griping, because the CE of the sail was well over to the lee side of the centreline of the vessel, especially if she were heeling much.

Lee clew first. By following this sequence, the heeling pressure on the ship was immediately eased, the tendency to gripe was diminished, and less weather helm was necessary. The canvas was not blown to leeward, the buntlines and leechlines gripped the sail at the proper place, and hauled the canvas tight up to the yard. Nichelson (143), like Falconer, refers to this as 'the old method', but as we shall now see, it never dropped completely out of fashion in some circles.

Contemporary opinions.

In hauling up the weather garnet first, the weather yardarm released from the downward pull of the tack, and bent upwards by the bellying canvas of the course and drag of the topsail sheet, is in great danger of being carried away underneath in the nip of the stay. Moreover, as the bulk of the sail goes bodily over to leeward, the instant the tack is let go, it is not properly embraced by the bunt and leechlines. When all the gear is hauled close up, there remain one or two balloons on the lee side, which throwing themselves backwards over the yards and furlers, as the ship comes nearer the wind, and then leaping forward and bursting with wind, as she falls off, are not to be controlled in any other way than sending men to the yardarm by the lift, and making them work from thence inwards with the sea gaskets.

When it is determined to haul up the weather gear first, the sheet should be slacked off, short of splitting the sail by shaking heavily, and then all the lee gear hauled well taut before starting the tack. In this way the lee leech and buntline will grip the sail nearly at their proper places, and the difficulty we have alluded to be partially diminished.

In hauling the lee clewgarnet up first, the canvas is gripped by the leech and buntlines to *leeward* of their natural places in the first instance, and then, by their pulling inwards as the sail is clewed up, the canvas that would otherwise have been slack is stripped of wind and hauled in taut along the lee yardarm. Whatever canvas may be left slack on the weather side after hauling up the weather gear, is blown into the weather side of the bunt, where it is steadied and bound against the mast and stay, and is easily secured (Boyd, 407).

Another officer who felt the same way was Liardet:

I have continually tried, with the weather and lee clewlines, in taking in square sails when blowing hard, and for several years felt confident that there was nothing like taking in a sail by the weather clew. However, I found this method liable to several objections. In the first place, you are more likely to get the sail over the lee yardarm; secondly, if your weather brace should be carried away in taking in a topsail, your lee rigging would be much endangered. In hauling the lee clewline up first, you have a heavier, but a more steady strain, than when you haul the weather clew up first; with the weather clew, the sail is kept longer shaking, and jerks more, in consequence of which, you try the yard, block strops, and braces more. I have often tried manning all the gear together, then keeping the ship a few points off the wind, and when everything was

A course ballooning through the buntlines. A possible consequence of hauling up the weather clew first (after Baugean).

Taking in topsails
A Main topsail sheets let run and sail blowing out 'en banniere' (after de Sainson); **B** taking in topsails weather clew first (after T Whitcombe).

quite ready, run all the gear up quickly together. I found this plan answer very well, but you cannot do it without plenty of hands. By this way of taking in a sail, every part of the gear bears its proper strain. At the same time, the sail is less exposed to the wind from being taken in, in less than half the time that you can possibly do it, by taking in one clew at a time, and I am inclined to think with less risk to sail and rope (Liardet, 199).

He goes on to quote another unnamed officer:

Let me presume that the lee sheet and weather brace command all square sails. By easing off the lee sheet, the sail is neutralised, spilled, and rendered more manageable. Likewise the weather brace is relieved of the strain, which is not the case with the lee sheet kept fast and the tack let go. In taking in a topsail, I therefore ease off the lee sheet so far as not to shake the sail, and haul up the lee clewline and buntline. Then ease off the weather sheet, and clew all up, attending to the weather brace to humour the sail. By this means, the sail is taken in with scarcely a shake, and the lee clewline and buntline being well up before the weather sheet is started, keep the sail more to windward, and as far as possible prevent it from being blown through the buntlines, which invariably happens if the weather clewline and buntline are hauled up first. I take in a course in the same way. If the topsail is set over the course, you have not such a command over the weather brace, lest the topsail should be brought aback. But the lee clewline being well up, and a good hold of the sail with the lee buntline and lee leechlines, ease away the tack, and haul up together. If the topsail is not set, humour the sail with the weather brace, as in the case of a topsail, or topgallant sail. It is always reckoned bad seamanship, in a gale, to start a tack with the lee sheet hauled aft. I saw a line-of-battle ship's mainyard sprung, from the main tack giving way when under reefed courses. I presume the same thing would have happened,

had it been let go. It has always been an object with me, to have the sail manageable after it has been clewed up, as well as the safety of the canvas in clewing up. You must often have seen the trouble and annoyance in furling a wet mainsail, that has been allowed to blow through the buntlines. In hauling the weather clew up first, without easing the lee sheet, the whole pressure of the wind is still on the sail, and nothing can be done with the weather brace, until the sheet is eased off, and the mischief of the sail being blown to pieces has taken place (Liardet, 200).

Other writers who favour taking in the lee clew first, include Pihlström, Schneider, Bourdé, Baudin and Hansen, while Groeneijk and von Littrow are non-committal, and Kloo and Le Compte avoid the question altogether. Todd & Whall are inclined to favour 'lee clew first', but say that it is 'more customary' to take in the weather side first. On the other hand, I have found about thirty authorities, extending from those like Schultz and Sjöbohm, writing in the late 1700s, to others published in the 1900s, who come down in favour of not 'embrailing the lee yardarm', so the preponderance of opinion, if not consensus, seems to favour the latter method.

Taking in a topsail. Very similar considerations applied in this case, one difference being that the weather part of the sail was not restrained by the stay, when the yard was on the cap, in the same way as the course. Again, both clews could be run up in light weather, but letting go the sheets when blowing hard, would result in the sail being flung out horizontally, *en bannière*, as Dubreuil (160) puts it, thrashing violently about, and endangering the mast and yard. 'Upon the best method of taking in a topsail, in a gale of wind, nautical men are much divided. Some approve clewing up to windward first, and

others to leeward. If the weather side is to be clewed up first, the weather brace must be rounded well in, otherwise the lee rigging will be in danger of being carried away by the great pressure of the lee yardarm. With the weather brace well attended, this is the most advantageous way of taking in a topsail, for thus the sail may be taken in without a shake. But should the weather brace give way, recourse must be had to clewing up to leeward first' (Gower, 112). 'The unanimous opinion of sailors is that it is necessary to clew up a topsail to windward if one wishes to save the sail, and to leeward when the ship is hit by a squall, which occasions a heel, which threatens her stability' (Bréart, 200).

A review of the literature again suggests a heavy preponderance in favour of taking in the topsail weather clew first. This includes Bourdé and Bonnefoux, who prefer to clew up the course to lee, together with Schultz and Mossel, who take in a course in the opposite fashion. Baudin, Hansen, Boyd and Liardet clew up topsails and courses lee side first.

Taking in topgallants and royals. Before the wind, Boyd (396) recommends keeping both sheets fast and clewing down, then clewing up, and 'bracing by': this means the same thing as German *beibrassen*, that is 'brace sharp up', in this case to spill the sail as much as possible. Smyth considers 'bracing by' as synonymous with 'counterbracing', as in heaving to. Not all the texts consulted state a preference for clewing up first on one side or the other, when by the wind. The majority do favour taking the lee clew up first of all, exceptions being offered by Lever and the *Manoeuvrier* of 1903.

Unlike the topsails and courses, the topgallant sails are taken in lee clew first, even against the poetic injunction to him 'who strives the tempest to disarm', for these reasons: firstly the topgallant yardarms are short and bare, compared with those of the topsail, which are long and have the topgallant studdingsail booms further out. So, if the weather topgallant sheet were started first, the sail would belly off to leeward, and rise more than would a topsail of heavier canvas, gear and fittings, and would likely go over its own lee yardarm and be torn. Secondly the question as to possible danger to spars or sails relatively. The topgallant masts are at best, even when outriggers are used, but indifferently supported as compared with the topmasts, and so the strain on them must be relieved first. Most of the strain, it must be remembered, comes when on or near the wind, from the lee part of a square sail. When the lee topgallant sheet is started that is relieved. The weather half is left to slat and the sail endangered, but that is a minor consideration compared to the loss of a spar. The greatest strain on the weather brace also comes from the lee part of the sail, from the down drag of the lee clew itself, which tends to drag the lee yardarm down, and hence strain the weather brace, which has a down lead. The weather brace has a rank lead in also, and being single may part. If this should happen, and the weather clew had been taken in, the yard would immediately fly fore and aft, and everything above the topmast head endangered. All the spars, gear, etc, above the topsail are necessarily lighter, even out of proportion to the relative sizes of the sails. So, all considered, the canvas is risked in the case of a topgallant sail, to spare the spars. In the topsail, the sail is looked to, as the spars, gear, etc, are fitted to stand it (Hourigan 22).

In the case of the light sails, it was always customary to clew down before clewing up, partly because the yards were so insubstantial that there was a tendency for the yard to want to run up the mast on its own if the clewlines were not belayed.

Todd & Whall (75) say that although there was divergence of opinion as to which clew should go up first, all agreed that the weather yardarm should be furled first, and this is confirmed by Ekelöf (44). They further suggest that in furling a royal, a green hand should be sent to the lee yardarm, because the sail flaps about less on that side. In men-of-war, of course, both yardarms were tackled simultaneously.

Setting square sail. In light weather, both sides could be set together. In the case of the upper sails, the clews could be sheeted home more readily, if the halliards were run up at the same time (Knight, 380). There was a difference of opinion whether it was best to sheet home to lee or weather first, in the case of a topsail or a topgallant. Knight (380), Gower (111), Schneider (175), Blunt (165) and Bonnefoux (194), favour sheeting home

to lee first. Bréart (199) favours loosing to leeward first, since the men on the yards would be to windward of the beating canvas, but advocates sheeting home to weather first. However, Dubreuil (163), Pihlström (236), Ekelöf (53), Rosvall (36) and Mossel (III, 99), set the weather clew of the topsails first, especially if light handed. Once the weather clew was home, the sail tended to blow to lee and sheeting home on that side was easier. To get the weather clew down, it was easier if one waited for the weather roll of the ship.

Topgallants and royals might have to be taken in, in bad weather, but would rarely be set again until the weather had moderated sufficiently. For this reason, the exact mode of setting the light sails is virtually never discussed. In the case of the course, getting the tack down properly was more critical than hauling the sheet aft, and was always done first, whatever the order of loosing the sail.

General remarks on fore and aft sail. In setting the spanker, the boom was swung well out to lee, so that the clew outhaul was aided by the wind, in hauling out this sail. In taking in, the lee brails were manned best, the slack of the weather ones being taken down by a few hands, so that the sail would not form a 'bag of wind'.

The vangs were used to steady the gaff when the mizzen was not set or if the sail were flapping about in a light breeze. With a wind of any consequence, the weather vang was eased off as the sail was hauled out, being set hand taut at most: if kept fast, there was a danger of breaking the gaff, were the sail restrained from adopting its natural curve.

The headsails were more easily stowed if they were becalmed by bearing away, giving the ship 'a wipe off the wind', as Todd & Whall call it. Having done so, it was important to remember that the ship would gather speed off the wind, and would be inclined to plunge vigorously into the seas, when she came to once more. This was the juncture at which a man might be washed off the jib-boom. The staysails would run down the stays, without much hauling, if the wind were free, as soon as the halliards were let go (Riesenberg, 786).

HANDLING THE INDIVIDUAL SAILS

The course. This was set by hauling out on the tack or sheet, as appropriate, at the same time overhauling the clewgarnets, buntlines, leechlines and slablines, so they would not 'girt' the sail. In light weather, both clews could be handled simultaneously, but in blowing conditions, the tack was got down

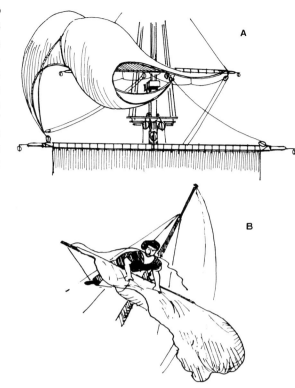

Taking in topgallants and royals
A Lever's illustration of a topgallant clewed up first to weather or sheeted home first to lee (which he advised); **B** 'Furling the Royal', based on a drawing by Edward Haskell in the ship *Tarquin*, 1862–63. Note the gasket clamped firmly in the seaman's mouth while he uses both hands to furl the sail.

promptly before attention was turned to getting the sheet aft and 'shrouding' the foot-rope.

If the ship were by the wind, it might be necessary to brace in a little or haul the weather truss, to get the bunt of the sail clear of the stay, and the lee quarter of the yard off the shrouds, before loosing. Failure to do so might result in a gasket being jammed against the shroud or stay in such a way as to endanger tearing the sail when it was loosed. The loosers cast off the gaskets from the yardarms, working towards the bunt, each man holding on to one or two gaskets, until the order 'Let fall!'. The gear was overhauled, so that the clews could be got down without interruption, a couple of men remaining aloft to see all clear.

To get the tack down, by the wind, it was necessary to ease off the weather lift, possibly also the sheet, clewline and bowline on the weather side of the topsail. In the case of the mainsail, the lee main brace, which angled downward was eased, and the task was made easier by luffing a little (Mossel, III, 99). Once the tack was properly boarded, the other gear mentioned was hauled taut again. By the wind, the tack secured somewhat forward of the weather yardarm, while with the

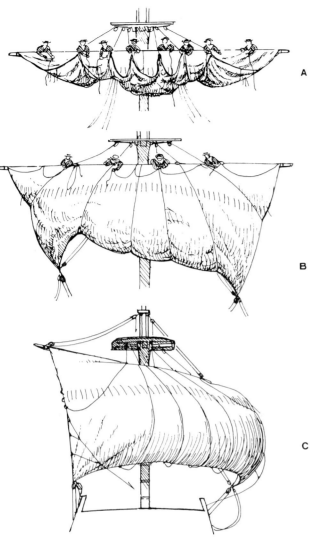

Setting the course
A Sail loosed; **B** sheeting home with the wind aft, the men making up gaskets and overhauling the gear; **C** sheeting home on the wind, the tack got down before hauling aft the sheet.

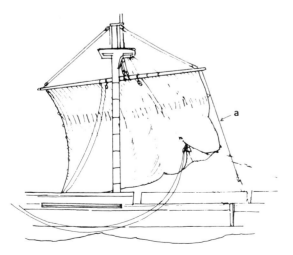

Taking in the course on the wind. In fresh weather a jumper (**a**) was sometimes rigged to steady the yardarm when the tack was let go. The bowline was used to steady the sail while hauling up the clew.

wind large, and the yard braced in a little, it lay directly under the yard. Consequently, it was easier to get the tack down, on the latter point of sail. The gaskets were seized in along the yard, or in later years, were coiled up and flung forward of the jackstay.

When taking in a course in bad weather, it was advisable to have a 'jumper', or hold-down, on the weather yardarm to prevent it snapping violently upward when the tack was let go and the tremendous strain on the weather leech was suddenly released. In getting in the weather side of the sail, the bowline was kept fast until it actually was resisting the efforts of the clewgarnet. In this way the weather leech was steadied, and the sail flapped about much less. In light weather, a man stood in the chains to keep the lee clew clear of the rigging (Krogh, 25).

The topsail. This was set by hoisting the yard, hauling home the sheets, while overhauling clewlines and buntlines. The topgallant sheets and topmast studdingsail halliards were let go while the yard was mastheaded, since they would have resisted the efforts of the halliards. In later years the topsail was mastheaded, but in the 1600s it was often hoisted part way up the topmast. This is commented on by Anderson, and certainly a feature of paintings of that era are the picturesquely ballooning out topsails, which reflected the belief of the day that they 'held more wind' when set in this way. Subsequently, it was realised that the sail functioned much better aerodynamically if it was set flatter, and in fact the first reef ('bag reef') was taken in an old overstretched sail to prevent the topsail bagging, when by the wind (Smyth). Once loosed, the topmen kicked the topsail out of the top, and clear of the inner boom iron, and other obstructions. The clews were more easily sheeted home if the sheet had a straight run at the yardarm sheave, and this was ensured by easing away on the clewlines while hauling on the sheet. In the case of a new sail, the footrope was initially too short and the sheets could not be got home, even with tackles clapped on. In that circumstance, they were got down as close as possible, and alike both sides.

If there were two sets of halliards, the weather ones were used to hoist the sail, when by the wind. Exactly how this was managed depended on the arrangement of ties and halliards. With one tie block and two fly blocks, the weather halliards were fleeted until the fly block was almost at the masthead, coming down as those halliards were hauled. If there were two tie blocks, the weather halliards were heavily manned, and the slack of the other set taken down by a few hands. If the

fore and main topsails were being hoisted together this would have meant manning the halliards on the same side of the deck, instead of the usual fashion, on both sides. Before the wind, the halliards were manned as in harbour, for example in the United States Navy, port fore and starboard main halliards being hauled, and the slack being taken down on starboard fore, and port main (Luce, 364). The mizzen topsail halliards were usually hauled hand over hand, while in the case of fore and main, the men crossed from one side to the other to tail on, as the yards went up. This meant that the yards were supported by the weather halliards, asymmetrically, and if the wind drew aft, and the yards were braced in, the weather halliards were settled a foot or two, so that the strain came equally on both ties, and the yard set squarely on the mast. During hoisting, the downhauls and reef tackles were overhauled if they led along under the yard. The slack of the reef tackle had to be taken down, if it led through sister blocks at the topmast head. The top bowline was 'hauled', if by the wind, or 'steadied out', if a little free, and 'checked', as it was eased off from the first to the second position.

To take in the topsail, the yard had to be got off the lee rigging by bracing in, otherwise it would have scraped down the foremost shroud. The lower lifts were got taut before the halliards were let go, to avoid a sudden jerk on the lower yardarms. Sometimes the lee sheet had to be checked, to allow the weather brace to be hauled. Actually, the topsail was very rarely completely taken in at sea, and then only when already reefed down. It would have been a difficult task overwise since there were no leechlines throughout the nineteenth century. These were fitted in the 1700s, of course, and were essential for furling the topsail 'in a body'. Extempore leechlines were sometimes rigged using the topmast studdingsail halliards (Ulffers, 348). With a close reefed topsail, the weather clew always came in first, because then any advantage to taking it in lee clew first had disappeared (Ulffers, 348).

The topgallant yard rope could be used as a 'preventer' buntline, to assist in taking in a topsail, especially before the wind. If a buntline parted accidentally, a leadline could be dropped down before the sail, got hold of in the top, and passed up behind the sail, to be secured at the slings, and used as an emergency buntline (Ulffers, 329).

The topgallant. These were never set in really bad weather. In light conditions, the clews were sheeted home, the royal sheets let to, and the halliards run up. Taunt (311) hauls the sheets and halliards at the same

Setting the topsails
A Sail loosed but foul of the rim of the top; B weather clew sheeted home, lee sheet and halliards being manned.

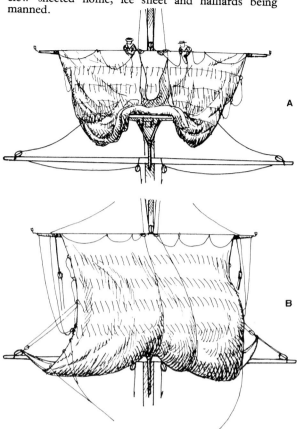

Taking in the topsails (running into harbour)
A Topsails being clewed down to the cap (after A Roux); B topsails being clewed up, then clewed down to the cap (after M F Cornè).

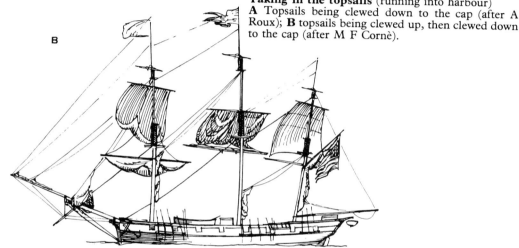

time; Knight (377) gets the sheets home before the halliards are up, but not before they have been started; Dubreuil (159) sheets home to weather first; while Todd & Whall (69), describing merchant practice, run the lee sheet nearly out, then the weather sheet chock home, then finally the lee sheet home properly. The loosers let go the gaskets and hitched the ends to the ties. If there were some kind of bunt gasket, this was kept in hand, by a man at the masthead, and let go just before hoisting. Care had to be taken that neither the footrope, nor the bunt gasket got under the topmast cap, otherwise the topgallant purchase might carry away in futile efforts to get the yard up.

To take in, the halliards were let go, the yard braced in with the weather brace, and the yard clewed down with the weather clewline, the clew on that side being kept fast, while the other side was clewed up. If the weather clew were let go, the yard would have been thrown violently fore and aft, breaking the weather brace, and endangering the sail and yard (Ekelöf, 58). Once down, the clewlines were belayed to prevent the yard trying to run itself up the mast again (Mossel, III, 113). Royals were handled in essentially the same fashion.

It may be remarked here, that it was some-

what easier to shorten sail in a vessel that was close-hauled, than in one that was running free. 'There is less weight of wind to contend with when the ship is close-hauled, than when running before it, and a sail in such cases can be more easily spilled and shaken without danger of splitting it, whereas with a vessel scudding with the wind aft or on the quarter, and increasing to such an extent as to

Taking in topgallants and royals
A Topgallants being furled in progression from aft to forward (after A Roux); B detail of a royal sheeted home but not hoisted.

make it necessary to shorten sail, every precaution must be taken to prevent losing the sail, or worse, springing a yard' (Todd & Whall, 71).

Flying jib. This was run out on its boom with the outhaul, the halliards were run up, the sheets being hauled aft, and the downhaul and inhaul being let go. It was taken in in re-

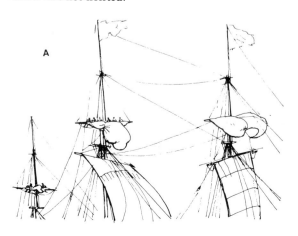

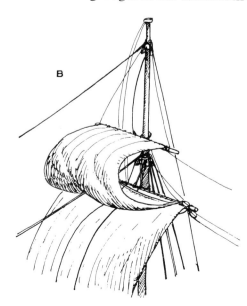

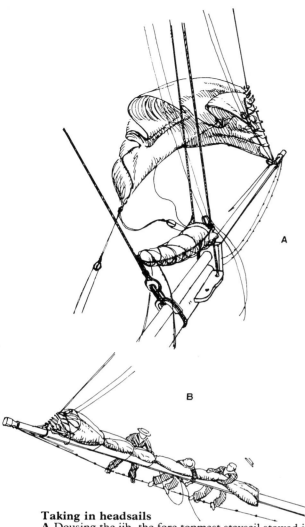

Taking in headsails
A Dousing the jib, the fore topmast staysail stowed in its netting; **B** furling the jib.

verse order, being hauled down first, then in. The sail was taken in to leeward of the boom, the furlers going out on the weather side. If it was planned to set it again shortly, it could be stowed on its boom, otherwise it was got completely in on the forecastle.

Jib. Very similar considerations applied in this case. With a traveller, it was sometimes set at 'half boom', whereas the flying jib was always boom ended. When setting, a hand remained at the tack to light up the hanks. To take in, a 'gob line' was a great aid in getting the foot of the sail in along the boom. The sheets had to be eased off when the head of the sail was two-thirds down, because the clew was closer to the jib stay than it was to the tack. Depending on the circumstances, it could be stowed on the jibboom, or stowed in the fore topmast staysail netting. The gasket was taken round the sail, in a series of half-hitches starting at the tack, and working aft towards the clew. Sail covers were not used at sea. Todd & Whall (71) make this comment: 'A large jib or staysail should never be left shaking heavily, as it puts a great strain on the

masthead, and may damage the spar. In fact, if the sheet gets adrift after the halliards are belayed, the most prudent thing to do, is to down sail at once, and secure the sheet, or else trip it up.'

Fore topmast staysail. In principle, this was handled very much like the other headsails. In the late 1800s, it was used in merchantmen, as part of the working sail, but in men-of-war, it was used as storm canvas, being set instead of, rather than in addition to, the jib.

Staysails. These were handled in a very similar fashion to the headsails, being hoisted with halliards and got down with a downhaul; they sometimes had brails to assist in taking them in. The middle staysail was unique in that the head of the sail set on a stay, while the 'bunt', or as we would say today the 'luff', set on a vertical jackstay. It thus required a halliard to get the 'nock', or upper forward corner, up on the jackstay and a conventional halliard to run the head, or peak of the sail, up the stay. It was taken in by first hauling down the peak and then the nock.

Mizzen course. The Jacobean mizzen course was set by overhauling the brails, casting off the gasket, and trimming the sail with the tack and sheet. The yard was controlled with the mizzen bowlines. The attenuated sail of the late 1800s, was in many respects handled in the same way. The throat brail was fleeted with a special uphauler, or *Dräng*. When set, the lee brails were hauled up with a fancy line, and the yard shifted over to the appropriate position with the mizzen bowlines. To take in the sail, the fancy lines were let go, and the ⌐ails brailed up, the lee brails being manned best, and the gasket passed.

With the gaff mizzen, the sheet was hauled out to the boom end, and the boom was controlled with tackles acting as sheets. The weight of the boom was taken by topping lifts, which lifted the spar clear of its crutch. The lee lift was overhauled, and the weather one eased off, until the leech was just taut, but not subjected to the whole weight of the boom. A lee boom guy served to steady the boom, when running, and prevent it swinging round in an accidental jibe. The sail was brailed 'up' or 'in' according to the way the

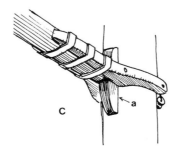

Furling a staysail.

Taking in the mizzen
A Brailing up a lateen mizzen (after Van de Velde the Younger); **B** brailing in a spanker, lee brails first to spil⌐ the wind; **C** detail of a clapper or tumbler (**a**).

brails were rove. To aid in getting it under control quicker, a clew rope, or 'sheet up-hauler', as Krogh calls it, was used to whip the clew up to the throat of the gaff. The lee brails were manned best.

The gaff was steadied by the vangs when the sail was not set, or when it was flapping about indecisively in a light breeze. In the case of a hoisting gaff sail, it was easiest if the gaff went up and down more or less horizontally. To allow this, a 'tumbler' or 'clapper', was fitted in the gaff jaws.

Tacks to weather. Apparently fore and aft sail set better with the foot of the sail as sharp as possible. At all events, the tacks of gaff mizzens, gaff topsails, and quadrilateral staysails were all set up to weather, the first to the windward side of the mast, the second to windward of the gaff, and the third hauled over to the weather rigging, with the wind free. The staysail tack was hauled down amidships, when by the wind (Ekelöf, 47).

DISPOSITION OF CREW FOR MAKING AND SHORTENING SAIL

This is based primarily on Burney, who does not fill in all the blanks in his scheme. Something depended on the arrangements in the particular ship, and the way the running gear was led. For instance, the topsail clewlines might lead to the yard or to the lower cap, or the fore topsail braces be manned in the gangway.

Making plain sail

Aloft	Sail loosers and boom tricers
Topsail sheets and halliards	Fore, main and mizzen mast parties
Opposite halliards	Fore: second part forecastlemen
	Main: first part quarterdeckmen
Topgallant sheets	Topmen, watch below
Topgallant halliards	Marines
Jib halliards (when not hoisted beforehand, for casting)	Carpenters and idlers
Royal sheets (if not led to top)	Upper yardmen, watch below
Royal halliards	Topmen, watch below
Special stations	
Stopper and belay:	
Topsail sheets	Topsail sheetmen, watch below
Topsail halliards, and topgallant sheets	Fore: captain forecastle, and next number, watch below
	Main: gunner's mate, and next number, watch below
	Mizzen: captain mizzen top, watch below
Topgallant halliards	Captains of tops, watch below
Royal halliards	Captains of crosstrees, watch below
Attend:	
Topsail braces	Quartermasters
Upper braces	Upper bracemen

Let go:
Lower buntlines, leechlines slablines, clewgarnets; topsail clewlines, buntlines and bowlines	Main: captains of quarterdeckmen
	Mizzen: captain mizzen top, watch below
Topgallant clewlines	Captains of crosstrees, below
Aloft:	
Light home sheets on lower yards	Topsail sheetmen, watch on deck
At topmast head	Captains of crosstrees, watch on deck

Shortening plain sail, in preparation for anchoring

Aloft	First captains of tops, upper yard and topsail sheetmen of watch on deck, all boom tricers
Clewgarnets	Hands not otherwise stationed
Lower buntlines	Idlers and stokers
Lower leechlines	Fore: first part forecastlemen
	Main: first part quarterdeckmen
Topsail clewlines	Fore, main and mizzen mast parties, not otherwise stationed
Topsail buntlines	Fore, main and mizzen topmen
Topgallant and royal clewlines	Topmen, watch below
Flying jib downhaul	Jib and staysail stowers
Upper braces	Upper brace and yard men, watch below
Jib downhaul	Idlers
Weather lower braces	Fore: first part stokers and marines
	Main, preventer: second part stokers and marines
	Main, after: first part quarterdeckmen, first part carpenters and idlers
	Mizzen: first part mizzen topmen
Weather lower lifts	Fore: second part forecastlemen
	Main: second part quarterdeckmen
Weather trusses	Fore: second part forecastlemen
	Main: second part main topmen
	Mizzen: second part mizzen topmen
Topsail braces, and take down slack of clewlines	Hands specially detailed
Special stations	
Let go and overhaul tacks	Fore: captain of forecastle of side, and fore topsail sheetmen of side, watch below
	Main: gunner's mate of side, and quarterdeck topsail sheetmen of side, watch below
Let go and overhaul sheets	Fore: gunner's mate of side, and topsail sheetmen of side, watch below
	Main: captain maintop, and topsail sheetmen of side, watch below
Stopper and belay clewgarnets	Not given by Burney
Attend:	
Lower braces	Fore: captains of quarterdeckmen
	Main preventer: captain foretop, watch below
Topsail braces	Main: captain maintop, watch below
Upper braces	Upper brace men

Let go:
Topsail sheets	Topsail sheetmen, watch below
Topsail halliards	Fore: captain of forecastle, watch below
	Main: gunner's mate, watch below
	Mizzen: captain of mizzentop, watch below
Topgallant sheets	Captains of crosstrees, watch below
Topgallant halliards	Captains of tops, watch below
Royal sheets and halliards	Royal yardmen, watch below
Flying jib halliards	Not given by Burney
If coming to an anchor	
Let go the anchor	Captain of forecastle, watch on deck, and party specially selected by boatswain
Stream the buoy	Gunner's mates
Attend compressors	Second part of idlers
Veer cable	All carpenters and stokers, first part idlers

Working with the watch. This comprised about a third of the men available with all hands. In setting topsails, the main was hoisted first, followed by fore and mizzen. The courses were not set simultaneously, except in very light winds. The topgallants and royals were sheeted home first, then hoisted. In taking these sails in, the topgallant and royal yardmen helped each other, handling the sails in succession.

THE COMMANDS
To set sail.

Stand by to make sail! Set royals and flying jib!

Lay aloft royal yardmen! Lay out and loose!

Clear away the flying jib!

Man the royal halliards and sheets, flying jib halliards and sheets, weather royal braces!

Haul taut!

Let fall! Sheet home! Hoist away royals and flying jib!

Lay aloft and loose topgallants! Clear away the jib!

Man topgallant halliards and sheets, jib halliards, weather topgallant braces!

Let go topgallant clewlines, lee braces, jib downhaul!

Haul taut! Sheet home! Hoist away topgallants and jib!

Steady out the topgallant bowline!

Lay aloft and loose fore topsail!

Man the weather halliards and topsail sheets!

Let go clewlines and buntlines!

Haul taut! Sheet home to weather! Hoist away the topsail!

Sheet home to lee! Haul out the top bowline!

Lay aloft and loose the mainsail!

Man the tack and sheet! Let go clewgarnets, buntlines and leechlines!

Let fall! Get the tack aboard! Haul aft the sheet!

135

Haul, or steady, out the bowline!

Out spanker!

Let go the brails and lee vang! Man the clew outhaul!

Haul taut! Haul out!

To shorten sail

Shorten sail! Stand by to take in royals and flying jib!

Man royal clewlines, weatherbraces, flying jib downhaul! Stand by royal halliards, flying jib halliards!

In royals! Down flying jib!

Lay aloft to furl royals! Lay out and stow flying jib!

Man topgallant clewlines, buntlines and weather braces, jib downhaul!

Stand by topgallant halliards and sheets, jib halliards!

Let go topgallant bowline! Let go topgallant sheets and halliards! Let go jib halliards!

Clew down! Let go lee sheet!

Let go weather sheet! Clew up!

Stand by to take in mainsail and spanker!

Man clewgarnets, buntlines, leechlines, slablines, spanker brails!

Haul taut! Up mainsail! In spanker!

Lay aloft! Furl mainsail! Furl spanker!

To take in the weather side first, followed by the lee:

Ease away tack and bowline! Haul up to windward!

Ease away the sheet! Haul up to leeward!

Stand by to take in fore topsail!

Man clewlines and buntlines! Haul taut!

Let go top bowline! Let go the halliards! Clew down!

Lay aloft and furl the topsail!

1.
Furling the topgallant in the *Jarramas*. The weather side has been made up first. Note the midship glut holding up the bunt. (Courtesy Marinmuseet, Karlskrona)

2.
Furling gaff topsails in the training ship *Nantucke* Lieut Patrick Hourigan, author of the work c seamanship much quoted in this book, considered ga topsails to be 'of doubtful efficiency, . . . a great deal nuisance'. His comments were written during training cruise in the USS *Alliance*, but he later too command of the *Nantucket*, ex USS *Ranger*, for t Massachusetts Nautical School. (US Navy phot courtesy Giles M S Tod)

CHAPTER 9
REEFING

METHODS OF REEFING
1600-1900

Early practice. Reef points, very similar to those familiar to present day dinghy sailors, were used by the Vikings, and although they were not used in large ships of the early 1600s, they probably remained in continuous use in small craft throughout the centuries and came into favour again with the large topsails of the 1650s (Sandahl, II, 90).

About 1350, additions of extra canvas to the foot of the sail came into use. By 1600, these 'bonnets' – sometimes supplemented by a second bonnet, called a 'drabbler' – were the usual method of increasing the area of the 'course' or body of the sail. Sandahl (II, 22) has pointed out that 'bonnet' has inherent in it the idea that the additional sail is attached to the head of the sail, perhaps in the manner of a raffee topsail. Nonetheless, the only bonnets we can be sure of are known to have been laced, or 'latched', on to the foot of the sail. The word 'drabbler' is closely related to 'draggle', the idea being that the sail is trailing in the wet, like the skirt of a cloak. Sandahl (II, 92) discusses in detail the origin of the term 'reef', which probably arises from an Old Norse root, meaning to 'tear off'. The fourteenth century form 'reef rope' was the same thing as the 'lasket', or 'latchet line', of the bonnet, and indeed, 'reef' may originally have been synonymous with 'bonnet'.

I believe the seaman of the 1600s thought of the courses as the essential basis of the sail plan, the topsails being supplementary. By 1800, on the other hand, the topsails had become the principal sails (first set, last taken in), with the courses, and topgallants having become the adjuncts, so to speak.

The introduction of reef points. About 1660, reef points appear on topsails, which had increased to such a size that some method of lessening their area was needed. Although bonnets must have worked fairly well on courses, provided the yard could be lowered, they would have been less practical with topsails, since the lacing on would have been done in the top, or on the lower yard.

Split topsails. Although the reef point never completely disappeared, a series of innovations, starting in about 1840, offered some improvement on the traditional method. The idea of a double, or split topsail, was arrived at independently by two American ship masters, Robert B Forbes in 1841, and Frederick Howes, in 1853. In the latter year, Howes (whose name is very frequently misspelt 'Howe') fitted his ship, *Climax*, of Boston, with what was the prototype of the familiar double topsail, as used right down to the last days of sail. Howes' initial idea was to lace a light spar across the middle of the topsail: to shorten sail, this was held fast, the halliards were let go, and the upper half of the sail dropped forward into the lee of the lower half, where it was becalmed. The principle was very widely adopted by merchant vessels, modified only to the extent that it became usual to have two separate sails, with the yard of the lower topsail secured to the cap of the lower mast. The lower sail was clewed up to this fixed yard. The upper topsail was secured to its yard, which was lowered, as the sail was clewed down. The same principle was subsequently applied to topgallant sails as well. Forbes, incidentally, referred to the upper of the two sails as the 'topgallant'. Accounts may be found in *The Monthly Nautical Magazine 2*,

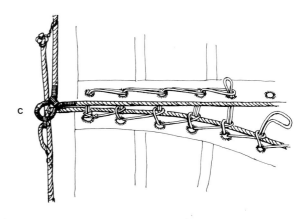

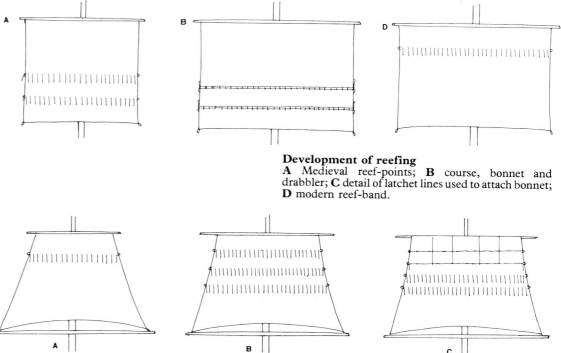

Development of reefing
A Medieval reef-points; **B** course, bonnet and drabbler; **C** detail of latchet lines used to attach bonnet; **D** modern reef-band.

Topsail reef-bands
A Single reef-band, later seventeenth century; **B** three reef-bands, *c*1780; **C** combination of reef-lines and reef-points *c*1850.

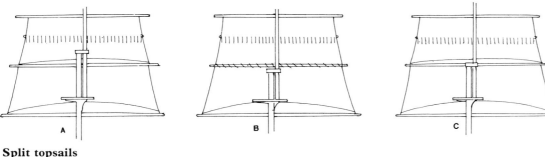

Split topsails
A Forbes' rig; **B** Howes' rig; **C** standard double topsail rig.

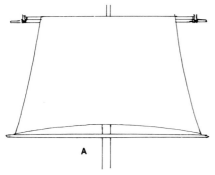

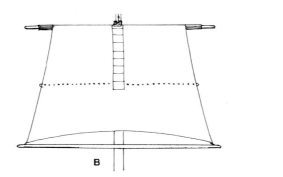

Patent reefing topsails
A Collings & Pinkney's system; **B** Cunningham's system.

1855, 13-23 and 116-122, and in the *US Nautical Magazine* 2, 1845, 303-305.

Patent reefing. Cunningham's patent roller-reefing topsails achieved a certain limited popularity. The tie was used as a parbuckle to roll the sail up on its own yard. This necessitated the presence of a 'bonnet' to cover the centre of the yard, and contemporary paintings of vessels with these sails set, show this characteristic feature. The other type of roller reefing gear, that of Collings and Pinkney, did not have such a bonnet. Excellent detailed descriptions of these two patents may be found elsewhere; for example, in Harold Underhill's *Masting and Rigging*, 127-133, 165, 162. Ingenious as Cunningham's arrangement was, it worked best when the yards were square. This is in part due to the fact that the ideal arrangement, where the pivot point of all the yards lies in the same axis, was only approached in the very last German sailing vessels. Braced by the wind, the Cunningham topsail would have tended to roll unevenly, because the centre of the topsail yard was displaced to windward and forward of the centre of the lower yard. An arrangement where all spars lie with their pivots in the same axis can be found on page 289 of Middendorf's *Bemastung und Takelung der Schiffe*.

Number of reef-bands. Disregarding the actual method used, topsails were usually fitted with three, sometimes four, reefs, so that

when the lowest or close reef was taken, the area of the sail was reduced by about half. Bonnefoux (200) says that the topsail has four reefs, comprising $^3/_7$, or more exactly $^{23}/_{56}$, the depth of the sail; sometimes the first reef is 10-12 inches less than the others. On mainsail and fore course, and topgallants if fitted, the depth is one-quarter that of the sail.

The reef-bands were one-sixth the drop of the sail down from the head of a course, and one-eighth the hoist down from the head of a topsail, according to Steel (78), subsequent reef-bands being worked at the same interval. The mizzen topsail usually had one fewer reef than the fore and main. When the latter were close reefed, the mizzen was taken in entirely. The reason for this was that weather helm increased with increasing wind, hence, under these circumstances, it was necessary to take off proportionately more of the aftersail.

Courses were most often fitted for one reef, but sometimes with a second. In men-of-war, the reef line for the second reef was fitted when very heavy weather was anticipated, for example, rounding the Horn; but usually only one reef was taken. Topgallant reefs were not very common but are occasionally to be seen in paintings of merchant vessels. I am not sure to what extent this was contemporary practice. 'When it blows too fresh to carry a whole topgallant sail over a single reefed topsail, it is time to furl it' (Totten, 165). I believe this reflected the fact that naval vessels rarely reefed topgallants, although Hourigan (28) mentions them being fitted with reef cringles, etc.

The topmast studdingsails were fitted for

one reef so that they could be carried with single reefed topsails. The lower studdingsail was occasionally fitted for a 'rolling reef' as Hourigan calls it. This was so its boom could be topped up, if the vessel were rolling excessively.

In addition to diminishing the sail area, reefing lowered the CE of the sail, causing less heeling, and less strain on the topmast and its rigging. Furthermore, the braces were able to work at a more advantageous angle, with less downward pull. With the close reef, the yard was down almost to the cap, at which point the mast was strongest.

The spritsail was fitted for reefing with diagonal reef-bands, which ran from a couple of feet above the clews to the upper corners. Steel shows the band ending two cloths in from the head-earing, which would appear to guarantee wrinkling of the canvas, and a bag in the leeward part of the sail. When reefed, the sail was almost a triangle. With the yard triced up, the foot of the sail would have been almost parallel with the waterline. According to Pihlström (268), the spritsail topsail could also be reefed, but I have found no confirmation of this.

Reefing fore and aft sail. We find contemporary illustrations of jibs, and occasionally fore topmast staysails, fitted for reefing; this was much more common in small merchantmen than warships. The other staysails were rarely, if ever, reefed. Men-of-war carried three sizes of jibs, using the middle one for moderate weather, and when closehauled. The large one was only used with a quartering wind, and the small one in harder weather. This did away with the necessity for reefing. On headsails, the reef-band was parallel to the foot, and about one-eighth to one-sixth the height of the sail above it. If there was a second band, it was the same interval up again.

Gaff trysails and spankers usually had two, sometimes three, horizontal bands parallel to the foot of the sail. Steel relates the distance from the foot to a proportion of the length of the fore leech. For instance, in his plate showing a brig mainsail, there are three bands, the first nearly halfway up the fore leech and the others spaced equally between that and the foot of the sail. A 'balance reef' was frequently worked in the sail, running from the nock to the after end of the uppermost horizontal reef. When this was turned in, the reefed sail would have been almost triangular, with one point of the triangle being at the lower forward corner, and the adjacent side formed by the gaff cocked up at a very steep angle. One painting in the Peabody Collection at Salem (Brewington, 270),

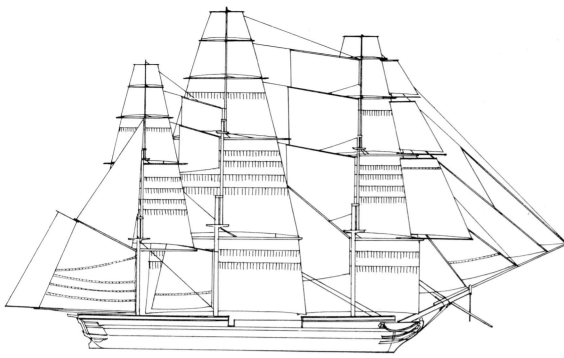

Number of reef-bands. This early nineteenth century American sail plan shows an unusually large number of reef-bands. Foresail and mainsail have two bands and all three topsails are fitted for four reefs. The topgallants, jib, mizzen staysail and fore topmast studdingsail have one reef-band each, the spanker has three normal reef-bands and one for a balance reef. It was unusual to fit topgallant reef-bands and the mizzen topsail had usually one band less than the other topsails.

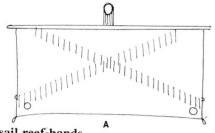
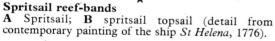

Spritsail reef-bands
A Spritsail; B spritsail topsail (detail from contemporary painting of the ship *St Helena*, 1776).

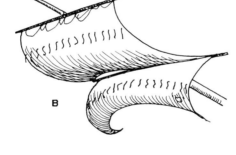

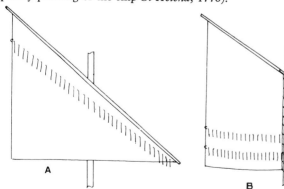
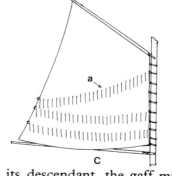

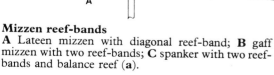

Mizzen reef-bands
A Lateen mizzen with diagonal reef-band; B gaff mizzen with two reef-bands; C spanker with two reef-bands and balance reef (a).

and another of the ship *Malta* in the Sjöhistoriska Museum, Stockholm show mizzens reefed on the after leech. Nonetheless, I find this particular arrangement rather unconvincing. We might expect to find the old-fashioned mizzen course with reefpoints, to reef on the foot, in the same fashion as was done with its descendant, the gaff mizzen. The third row of reef-points on the topsail was being introduced at about the time the mizzen course was disappearing. Lees (Plate 49), reproduces an old draught, showing the mizzen fitted for reefing to the yard. The reef-band is disposed at a shallow angle to the yard, meeting it at its forward end. This is similar to the arrangement used in galleys, and was designed to take off relatively more of the after part of the sail, thus moving the

CE forward, as well as downwards, and lessening the need to carry excessive weather helm. The close reefed gaff mizzen must have been a rather awkward contraption, and, not surprisingly, a triangular storm mizzen was often preferred in its place.

Reefing with reef lines. There is a difficulty with terminology here, since 'reef line' was later used to describe something quite different, but Falconer uses the term 'reef line', and the Swedish sources giving the best description of it, use the Swedish word *lina* (Pihlström, 261). There were four reef lines on the yard, two being one-eighth the way in from the yardarm, and the others three-eighths the way in. When in use, they were middled, so that there were effectively four pairs. Both ends were furnished with pointed metal tips, or 'aiglets', made from large nails, rather on the principle of shoe laces. The sail having been hauled up on the yard, the reef line was inserted from the fore side through a hole in the reef-band. It was then brought up between the yard and the headrope and half-knotted with its fellow over the headrope, thus gathering up the slack of the sail. One end was taken out towards the yardarm, and the other inwards towards the slings, being stuck through each successive hole, from before aft, and marline-hitched on the forward side, after being brought up behind and over the headrope. Where necessary, the reef line was taken zigzag around the robands. This method was used on the courses, but not on topsails.

> Each earing to its station first they bend;
> The reef-band then along the yard extend;
> The circling earings round the extremes entwined;
> By outer and by inner turns they bind.
> From hand to hand, the reef-lines next received;
> Thru eyelet holes and robin-legs were reeved;
> The reef in double folds involved then lay;
> Strain the firm cords, and either end belay.
> Falconer, *The Shipwreck*, Canto II

Old method of reefing with loose points. The points could be kept in the top, and taken out by the topmen when they laid out on the yard. Pihlström gives a good account of these. An overhand knot was cast in the point near its middle. The long end was thrust through the reef-hole from behind and the reef gathered up. The short end was brought up behind the headrope and in front of the yard, and an overhand knot made with both ends, to secure the reefed canvas. The long end, which now pointed backward, was pushed down between the sail and the yard, going under the latter and coming round to be reef-knotted to its fellow. A simpler method was

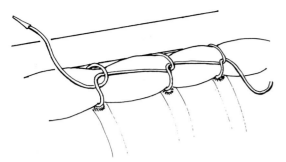

Passing a reef line. The line could also be passed around the yard and sail.

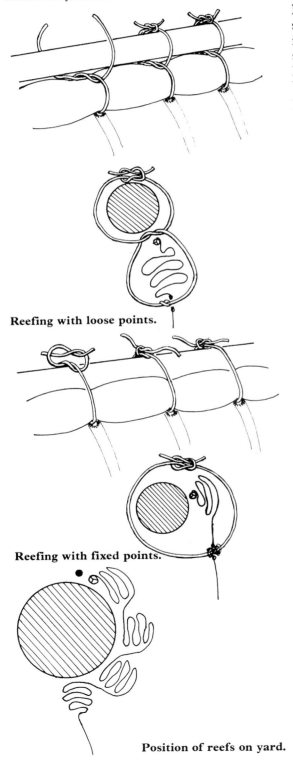

Reefing with loose points.

Reefing with fixed points.

Position of reefs on yard.

to cast a half knot in the loose point, push the short end through from behind, and reef-knot it to the long end which came aft and around under the yard to meet it. Schneider (180) says that if the points are to be left in the sail, they are stuck through from behind, forward, and a half-hitch taken; if not, they are put through from in front, backwards; a second half-hitch would not be needed in this latter case, because they would be secure when reef-knotted, and removed when the reef was shaken out.

Reefing with fixed points. This was essentially the same method as that mentioned in the last paragraph. In turning in a reef, the sail was hauled up first in small and then in larger folds. In the case of the first reef the band was secured on the upper forward aspect of the yard. The after point was brought around the yard to meet the forward point, and reef-knotted with it.

Position of subsequent reefs on the yard. With a topsail, each successive reef-band came a little lower down on the forward side of the yard, the second coming directly forward, the third on the lower forward aspect, and the fourth, or close reef-band, came directly under the yard (Ekelöf, 71). With the first three reefs, nothing of the reefed sail could be seen from the quarter-deck. As a consequence of this method, which distributed the furled sail fairly evenly around the yard, the forward point was, in general, shorter than the after one. Furthermore, the reef-points had to be longer with each successive reef, because more folded up sail had to be encircled. With the close reef the points were the same length because the band lay directly under the yard.

Any method of taking reefs serially ideally avoided having all the reefed canvas bunched up at one point. The above is not the only sequence described. Some texts say that with the first reef, the reef-band should come under the yard (von Littrow, 158; Dubreuil, 236). Sjöbohm (60) goes on to say that the knots of the first reef are pushed forward, so that the second will lie behind, and so on with the third and fourth reef. Caussé says that the first reef-points are hauled taut on the forward side, the second on the rear, the third forward and the fourth to the rear. Generally, the last reef taken should be to the rear. Bonnefoux more or less echoes this, although he also mentions placing the third reef between the first and second (202). He says that the rationale for taking the subsequent reefs behind the others, is that the earlier reef helps hold the subsequent ones up on the yard. A Swedish seaman, af Trolle (138), suggests hauling the forward points best with the first reef, but hauling the after points best with the second reef, so that the first reef-points are hidden. The points usually were tucked up in the folds of the canvas, to keep them out of the way, although Sjöbohm says they were just thrown forward with the gaskets.

Reefing a course. In the smaller classes of naval vessels, it would have been perfectly practical to reef the lower sails in the same way as the topsails, taking the after reef-points back around the yard, and knotting them to their fellows, on the forward side. However, in a First Rate of 1800, the lower yards were about two feet in diameter at the slings, so it would have been very difficult physically for a man on the footrope to get hold of the after leg let alone pass it around the yard; furthermore, it would have been necessary for the after leg to exceed eight or nine feet in length.

Using reef lines was one way of getting round this difficulty. The other method was the use of short points on the fore side of the sail, which made it possible to reef to the jack-stay, and obviate the drawback mentioned above. Brady had this to say about short points: 'some use two, but only one is necessary' (143). The double points were square-knotted around the jackstay, while the single variety hitched to it (Knight, Plate 34; Martelli, 260; Nares, 82, Underhill, 117). It will be realised that this arrangement involved folding the reefed canvas in two, under the reef-band, so that it hung down between the yard and the sail. 'Slab points' were used to haul the slack up, so that it would not thrash about and chafe the sail to bits. The short point had an eye spliced in the end, and this was thrust through the eyelet hole, from before aft. The eyes were held in place with a 'jackline', which traversed the sail, from one leech to the other, along the after side of the reef-band. It was found rather awkward to secure the points to the jackstay, when the sail was bent to it, so the custom developed of fitting a 'reefing jackstay' above the bending jackstay, to make the job easier (Brady, 82).

The French or jackline reef. A completely different method of reefing was invented by a French naval officer named Béléguic, in the early 1800s. It became popular in naval vessels, and remained in use in training ships until the present century.

Not only were there several variations on the basic idea, but there was a great deal of disagreement on the terms used. One essential element of the French reef, the 'reef line' or 'forward jackline', was secured at intervals across the forward side of the topsail, at the level of the reef-band. The other component, the 'reefing becket', was seized to the jackstay. At one end was a toggle, about seven inches long, and towards the other extremity, an eye, which could be slipped over the toggle. To help secure the reefing line, a 'jackline' was run across the after side of the sail. Boyd (282), and Luce (208) illustrate several alternative ways of arranging things.

Underhill calls the two horizontal ropes the 'fore' and 'after jacklines'. Luce calls them the 'jackstays'. Bushell (246) calls the forward one the 'reeving line', the after one the 'jackstay'. Nares calls them, respectively the 'naval line' and the 'jackstay'. I believe that the after rope was sometimes called the 'naval line'. The French seamen called the becket a 'Béléguic', in honour of its inventor. Boyd (283) calls the becket a 'point', and the loop of rope that was used in one variant instead of a reefing line, he refers to as the 'becket'.

The reefing becket, like the old-fashioned point, was made of sennit, plaited down solid for six inches from the toggle, which was secured at its upper end. The eye, about eight inches long, followed, and was in turn finished off with a solid tail of about nine inches, the whole thing being about two feet in length (Bushell, 245). The becket was seized to the jackstay (that is to say, the 'bending jackstay') on the yard, an inch or two below the toggle so that the tail hung down in front of the sail, the toggle projecting up above the jackstay. To avoid throwing the complete strain on the jackstay, the practice developed in Portsmouth Dockyard in the 1850s of taking the becket right round the yard, a method which became general practice in the Royal Navy. This type of becket was plaited solid for four inches in excess of the circumference of the yard, followed by a four-inch eye, then four inches solid, then an eight-inch eye, and a nine-inch tail. Thus, the beckets became shorter towards the yardarms, although the 'functional' length remained constant at a couple of feet. The tail was taken around the yard, through the four-inch eye, and the becket seized to the jackstay, just below the toggle.

When turning in a reef, the tail of the becket was slipped down under the reefing line, brought up in front and toggled. The reef-band then lay confined close to the jackstay, and the reefed sail hung down abaft the sail, as in reefing a course with short points. The second, and subsequent reefs, were taken in the same fashion. To take additional reefs the becket was untoggled, and slipped under the next line, ultimately supporting all four reef lines.

A 'reefing', or 'preventer jackstay', similar to that already described for a course, was

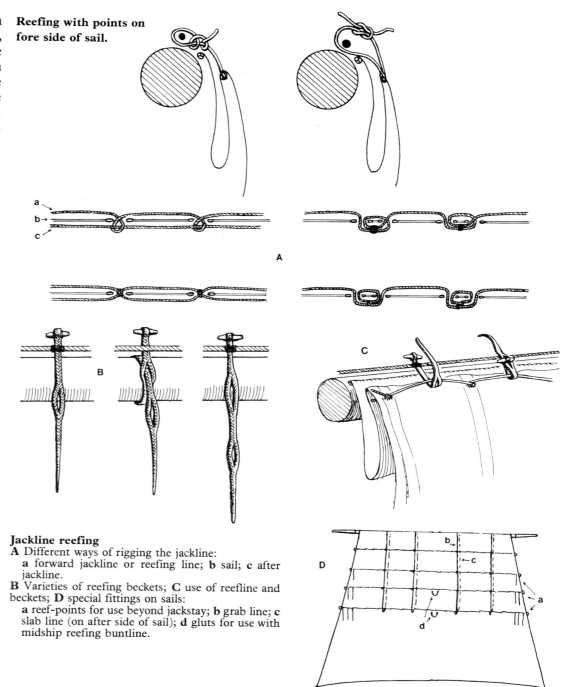

Jackline reefing
A Different ways of rigging the jackline:
 a forward jackline or reefing line; **b** sail; **c** after jackline.
B Varieties of reefing beckets; **C** use of reefline and beckets; **D** special fittings on sails:
 a reef-points for use beyond jackstay; **b** grab line; **c** slab line (on after side of sail); **d** gluts for use with midship reefing buntline.

sometimes fitted abaft the bending jackstay. The beckets were arranged in pairs the first and second reef being taken on the bending jackstay and the third and fourth on the preventer (Bushell, 246); alternatively, the first and third on the bending, second and fourth on the preventer (Burney, 24). If all the beckets were on one jackstay, they could be distinguished by making half of them of rope, the other half of sennit.

A becket with one eye could secure four reef lines, as readily as one, but beckets with two eyes are illustrated by Knight, Luce, and Underhill. While one is not absolutely certain how these worked, it seems likely that they were used with topsail yards fitted with

two jackstays, allowing the second reef to be taken with the second eye, without untoggling the first reef line, as was necessary otherwise.

French and British topsails were fitted with four French reefs, while the United States Navy preferred the traditional reef points on the third and close reef. Since the reef-bands were wider than the jackstay, it was necessary, in any case, to have a few points, at each extremity of the lower bands; for instance, one for the second reef, two for the third, and three for the close reef. These were taken round the yardarms, in the traditional fashion, securing the canvas more snugly than on the yard itself.

One disadvantage of the French reef was the 'slab' of slack canvas, which hung down between the yard and the remaining sail. In the case of a close reefed topsail, there were four of these folds, rubbing against each other, chafing the sail, and exposed to the force of the wind. 'Reef buntlines', 'slab points', or 'slab reef lines', were rigged to pull the canvas up snugly under the headrope, in the same fashion as already described with a reefed course. As in the case of the lower yard, great care had to be taken that all such gear was let go when turning out the reef. Some seamen preferred to secure the slack sail with yarns, which could be relied upon to break, should one inadvertently not have been cut away, when shaking out the reef. If the slab point were not cast loose, a torn sail might be the result. The reefed canvas was too bulky to be totally out of sight, even when slab points were used. C F Sørensen's painting of the frigate *Jylland* under close reefed topsails in 1874, shows this very clearly (Kjølsen, 151).

The merits of the French reef. With beckets, the reef was much quicker turned in than with conventional points, and this gave ships so fitted a tremendous edge in competitive sail drill: Grenfell (103) mentions reefing topsails in 45 seconds with all hands! Mossel (87) gives the time for reefing topsails as four minutes, and presumably this would have been with points. At the other extreme, Todd & Whall refer to a merchantman taking four hours to reef a single topsail. The second advantage was the tremendous reduction in weight aloft: points for the topsail of a First Rate weighed over 12 hundredweight whereas replacing them with beckets and reef lines cut the weight to around 4½ hundredweight (Boyd, 284). As mentioned earlier, the system never caught on in merchantmen, perhaps because they were not interested in reefing against the clock, or perhaps because under the old system a reef-point inadvertently left tied was quickly spotted when turning out a reef, whereas a jammed slabline or becket might go unnoticed, resulting in a torn sail. Another consideration was the ability of the old system to shed water, whereas we may guess that the French reef arrangement allowed pockets of rainwater to collect. The main course of a First Rate weighed about the same as its topsail, that is to say around 15 hundredweight; if we add to that, the half ton of rain water that Boyd says could be held in the bunt of a mainsail (382), and multiply this by the height above the waterline, one can imagine that considerable leverage was exerted (Burney, 24; Nares, 83, 116).

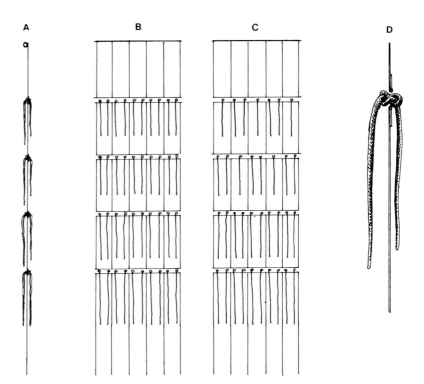

A further advantage was that there was no danger of reefing beckets fouling the sheets of the sail above, as was the case with points. Great care had to be taken to avoid getting the after leg below the topgallant sheets, when reefing.

Length of reef points. Being made of thread or string on a model, these are often a disappointing feature, since they fail to hang in a convincing manner. In naval vessels, the real thing was a substantial affair of plaited sennit, weighing about three-quarters of a pound, although merchantmen in the late 1800s tended to prefer points made of a good grade of manila rope (Kipping, 50). Whether of rope or sennit, the lower reefs of a topsail had longer points, since they were required to encompass more canvas. Theoretically, for the same reason, the points could have shortened towards the yardarms, and Lescallier (189) is one author who suggests this be done. More usually, this was disregarded in making up the points.

Boyd (288), and Bushell (252) offer tables showing the lengths of reefpoints for various classes of vessels, and while not identical in detail, the figures follow similar principles. With the first three reefs in a First Rate's topsail, the forward points of each pair are a foot shorter, while those of the close reef are the same length. Glascock (150), in fact, suggests that the foremost legs of the close reef points should be longer. The difference reflects the way in which the reefed canvas is secured on the forward side of the yard with the upper reefs, but underneath with the close reefband.

Reef points
A Relative length of reef-points (fore side of sail or right); **B** placement of reef-points (after Steel, 1794); **C** placement of reef-points (after Falconer, 1815); **D** detail of reef-points fitted on sail.

Boyd lengthens the forward legs of a First Rate's topsail, in increments of 3, 9, and 12 inches, while Bushell increases them in steps of 6, 6 and 12. In both cases, the points of the first reef are 4 feet 6 inches, and those of the close reef 6 feet 6 inches in length. In smaller vessels, increments of 3 inches were sufficient. Courses were fitted with points reefing to the jackstay – 'half-legged points', as Kipping (57) calls them – and these were 3 feet 6 inches in a First Rate. Reefing beckets were about two feet long, unless they were made to go right round the yard, as was the later English practice.

Number of points. Steel shows two holes to a cloth in courses and topsails. Kipping and Boudriot (III, 78) describe arrangements which alternate one and two holes per cloth. Boyd's tables give figures for all classes of vessels, indicating that the total number of points for a First Rate came to 1678. The course had the same number of points as the first reef of the topsail, 112 in a First Rate's main course and topsail, the succeeding bands having 130, 164, and 176 points respectively. These figures suggest that the third and fourth reefs have the points spaced more closely than the upper two bands. A possible arrangement might be a point per cloth in the course, fore side only; alternating one and two points per cloth, first and second reefs, points both sides; two points per cloth

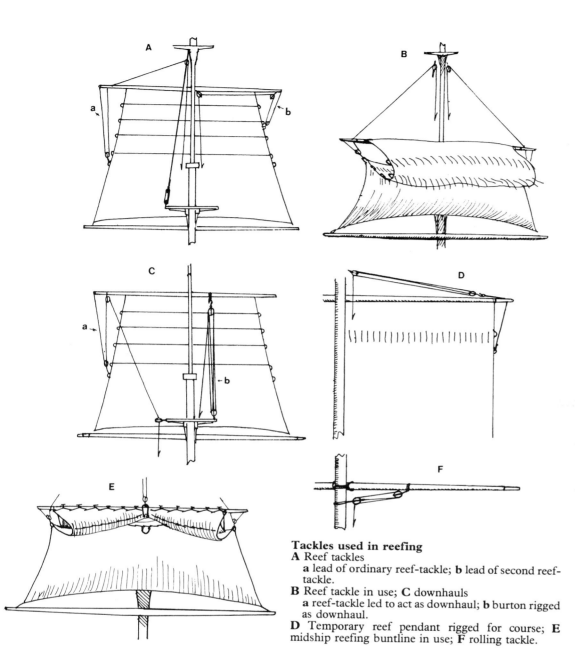

Tackles used in reefing
A Reef tackles
  a lead of ordinary reef-tackle; **b** lead of second reef-tackle.
B Reef tackle in use; **C** downhauls
  a reef-tackle led to act as downhaul; **b** burton rigged as downhaul.
D Temporary reef pendant rigged for course; **E** midship reefing buntline in use; **F** rolling tackle.

in the lower reefs. The head of the topsail was about five-sevenths that of the course, in length. A small increase was necessary from band to band, to take care of the increasing width of the topsail, as one descends.

One man could make up four pairs of points 6 feet 6 inches long in one working day, according to Boyd, who carefully tabulates the numbers of points of various lengths, and the time taken to make them. This was the type of work which engaged the hands during wet weather, when rigging ship, and at other odd moments.

OTHER GEAR USED IN REEFING

Grab lines, spilling lines, or reef lines. Glascock (171) describes these useful fittings, already alluded to, which were used to haul the sail up, and facilitate getting hold of the points, in reefing. Three vertical lines on either side of the topsail yard were hitched to the jackstay above, and the close reef-band below. They were seized either to the eyelet holes of the close reef-point or to the forward jackline. Brady, Glascock, and Boyd, refer to them as 'reef lines', which is a little confusing, at least two other items being so called by other authorities.

Slab reef-points. These, according to Nares (116), were lines spliced to the jackstay and led down forward of the yard, abaft the sail, to be taken through eyelet holes, and secured with an overhand knot. There were the same number as the grab lines on the fore side of the sail.

Reef-tackles. These were always permanently fitted to the topsails. In fact, in later days, there were sometimes two at either yardarm (Luce, 205), one secured below the close reef-band, and a supplementary one below the reef-cringle of the second reef-band. When hauled upon, they pulled the leech of the sail up so that there was slack between the yardarm and the reef-cringle. Ordinarily the fall led down from the yardarm through a block hooked to the reef-cringle, back up through a cheekblock, or through a sheave hole in the yardarm, up through the upper sheave of a sisterblock seized between the two foremost topmast shrouds, and thence to the deck. The lift rove through the lower sheave of the sisterblock. Sometimes instead of passing through the sisterblock, it was led along under the yard going through a trebleblock at the slings. The other sheaves of this accommodated the clewline and the topgallant sheet. In the first arrangement, it was kept taut when the close reef was turned in, and thus helped support the yardarms. With the other arrangement, which was always used for the second reef-tackle, it was helpful in clewing the yard down.

The reef-tackle had to be hauled tighter with each successive reef, to slacken the leech between the reef-cringle and the yardarm. With the close reef, the tackle was 'two blocks'. When taking the third and fourth reefs, the topsail sheets had to be checked sufficiently, to allow the reef-tackle to function properly. If the sheets were not slack enough, the yardarm was subjected to an undue strain and on occasion was wrung off by the tremendous pull of the reef-tackle. The rope became badly worn because it ground across the swallow of the sheave in the yardarm. When led to the eyes of the rigging, as described, they could, by keeping them fast, be made to haul themselves partially taut, as the yard came down. (*Officer of Watch*, 24). Care had to be taken, however, to let them go, otherwise they would 'hang' the yard. If hauled taut, after the reefed sail was set, they helped take some of the strain off the earing.

Downhaul. The topsail yard would ordinarily come down of its own weight, once the halliards were loosed. If, however, the vessel were heeling over, the wind could act to rehoist the yard. Also if the parrel slewed, it might 'hang' the yard, half way down. If this occurred, it was clewed down by hauling on the weather clewline. Later on, a special downhaul was fitted, particularly in squally weather (Lever, 83; Totten, 1164; Bobrik, 2666). As already mentioned, the reef-tackle, if suitably rigged, could also assist in getting the yards down.

Although upper topsails were fitted for reefing, reef-tackles were not used with

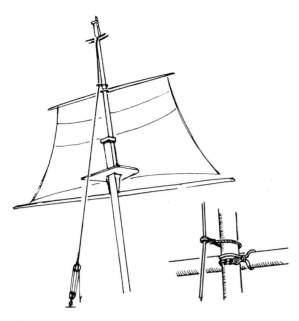

Travelling backstay and detail of grommet.

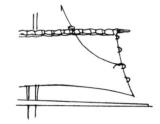

Makeshift topsail leechline.

them. The practice in later days, was to clew the sail up to the yardarm rather than the bunt, and the clewline acted like a reef-tackle. Nor were reef-tackles fitted to topgallants, in those rare cases where they were reefed: they were got up by main force. Some French ships used the reef-tackles as topgallant sheets, a 'vicious habit' according to Bonnefoux (205), since they should always be ready to haul the topsail yard down, and should only be made fast when reefing.

Reef pendants. Reef-tackles were not usually a permanent fitting in courses, at least in the early days. However, if the vessel was expecting heavy weather, they were set up, possibly extemporised from other gear, such as the lower studdingsail halliards. More commonly a reef pendant was used on the course. This was a single rope led through a sheave hole in the yardarm. When needed, a tackle was hooked to it, the top-burton, or the clew-jigger, serving for this purpose.

Midship reefing buntlines. Béléguic's original proposal had included the use of a tackle hooked to a lower reef-band amidships, to aid in hauling up the heavy bunt in reefing. This never found general acceptance, but a 'glut', or becket of rope, was commonly fitted to the fore side of the topsail,

just below the third and fourth reef-bands, and the bunt-jigger could be hooked to this. The 'boss buntline', as Hourigan calls it, acted as a sort of midship reef-tackle, in taking the third and close reef.

Rolling tackles. The purpose of these was to counteract the violent swaying, or 'sallying', of the yard, from side to side. The yard tackle could be hooked to a strop part way down the mast, and hauled taut to act in this fashion. The top-burton could be used, if the yard tackle was not fitted (Cradock, 29) (Pihlström, 259; Sjöbohm, 21). The topsail rolling tackle was fastened to the yard on the weather side, and was hauled taut as the vessel rolled to leeward, thus jamming the yard over at the leeward extreme of its lateral movement. When lowering the topsail yard, the tackle had to be let go, being hauled taut when it was down (Krogh, 85). Lever (55) shows a special method of rigging the topsail reef-tackle in small merchantmen. It led from the yardarm down to the top. When the close reefed sail was taken in and handed, it was hauled taut and acted as a sort of rolling tackle.

Travelling backstay. When the topsail was double reefed, the strain on the yard came at a point on the topmast which was poorly supported by the rigging. A backstay was set up to ride up and down with the yard. It was secured, or confined, by a grommet on the mast above the topsail parrel. A tackle was used to set the lower end up on deck aft, and to the weather side of the mast.

Makeshift topsail leechlines. Although modern marine artists and modelmakers often show leechlines on topsails, they were in fact very rarely fitted during the 1700s and 1800s. The reason was simply this: to work properly, the leading block must be the same distance from the head-cringle as the latter is from the leechline-cringle. In the case of a topsail, this would imply that every time a reef was taken or shaken out, the leading block on the yard would have to be moved. Thus although early topsails had leechlines, once reefing came into fashion, and reef-tackles came into use, leechlines disappeared. However, when the occasion warranted, they could be fashioned from the topmast studdingsail halliards, or from the topgallant sheets, the topgallant yards having been sent down. From a leading block on the yard, the line went to the bowline cringle and was secured there, or led through it, back aft of the sail, to the same point on the yard. This expedient would only have been resorted to, when the third or fourth reef had been turned in (Liardet, 172, 179; Nares, 266). Lescallier shows a main topsail with inner and outer

leechlines, with the inner ones actually crossing at the slings. This would no doubt have been very effective in subduing the sail, but for the reason mentioned, I do not think the practice was very common.

The earing. This important item, sometimes spelt 'earring' was used to secure the reef-cringle at the yardarm. To the early seamen, such as Smith, (29) the term 'earring' was very logically applied to what was later called a 'cringle'. Apparently the name was gradually transferred to the rope that secured the cringle, and this seems to have occurred by about 1700. I have, however, come across the early usage as late as 1762, in the *Naval Repository*. Ulffers says that the earing was six fathoms of 1½ inch rope with an eye spliced in it, so that only two fathoms was single. Boyd says it should be two and a half times the depth of the reef. The reason for having it double, as described by Ulffers, was so the earing would have twice as much frictional holding power, to keep itself up on the yard. Passing the earing properly was a most important part of the reefing process (Dana, 49). There was much variation and discussion about the best way of passing the turns. The 'outer turns' went round the yardarm cleats, and held the cringle *out*, while the 'inner turns' held the cringle *up* on the yard. Murphy says that there should be two outer turns for the first reef, three for the second, and four for the fourth.

The earing was sometimes kept in the top, and taken out by the captain of the top, but more usually those for the first and second reefs were secured to the yard, and when not in use were stopped in along it. Those for the third and fourth reefs were seized to the reef-cringles and hitched to the reef cringle next above when not in use (Ekelöf, 69). If all four earings were made fast to the yards as sometimes done, they were secured further out on the yardarm for each subsequent reef. A 'bull earing' was used for the first and second reefs (Taunt, 306). Illustrations taken from contemporary naval textbooks show stropped thimbles used for the third and fourth reef, which were intended to hold the reef cringle well up. A wire strop with a thimble was likewise used in the latter days of merchant sail reefing to steel yardarms. This gadget was known as a 'bull whanger' (*Sea Breezes*, Vol 17, No 99, page 223; Vol 18, No 106, page 301). A short 'earing-jackstay', a rod with a travelling hook, was also commonly fitted in the latter-day windjammers.

Brady (143) mentions fitting earings, 'on the bight', by which he means that there were two ends, one for the inner, and one for the outer turns. There were also methods of

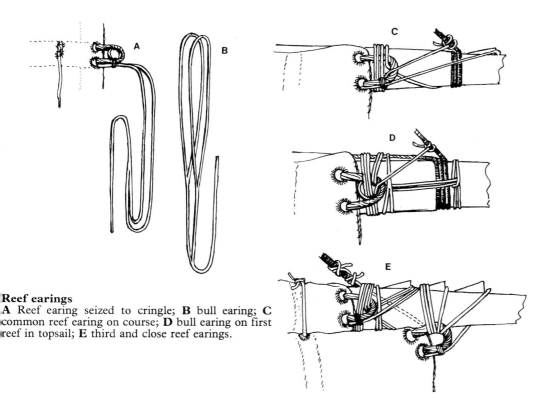

Reef earings
A Reef earing seized to cringle; **B** bull earing; **C** common reef earing on course; **D** bull earing on first reef in topsail; **E** third and close reef earings.

passing the earings, for speed in sail drill, where a loop rather than the end was pushed through the cringle. This also allows extra tension to be applied in hauling it taut. Dubreuil describes 'making a sort of tackle' of the earing, preparatory to hauling up the cringle. I think this must be a similar sort of idea.

TECHNIQUE OF REEFING

Sequence of reefing. Grenfell (106) gives a general idea of the context in which topsails would be reefed. With the first reef, the royals and flying jib came in. In fact, this had usually been done well beforehand. With the second reef, the royal yards were struck down into the tops. With the third reef, the topgallants and jib came in. When it was necessary to close reef, the topgallant masts were housed, the topgallant yards, and all other light spars, were sent down on deck. The fore topmast staysail could be left set with the close reef, if running free: being a 'lifting' sail, it was hung onto, if possible (Hourigan, 28). The mainsail came in with the third reef, if the sea was heavy, but sometimes was left set. The reefed fore course was much more useful, since it helped lift the head and prevented the vessel broaching to.

Reefing a topsail, by the wind. To reef, the yard had to be lowered, and the wind spilled out of the sail. It was important that the vessel be kept under control in the interval, the courses being kept full, and if necessary staysails being set temporarily (Liardet,

178). The steadiness of the yard and proper trim of the sail were crucial. The yard had to be made as stable as possible before the men were sent out on it. To make the work as easy as possible, the sail had to be kept just 'lifting', the wind kept 'blowing in the boltrope', as the French put it, the sail as it were 'cutting the wind in two' (Luce, 470). Dana (49) suggests keeping the sail with a slight 'full', luffing occasionally to shake the sail. Cradock (28) says that the efficiency of reefing a topsail depends entirely on how well the yards were laid. He thought that beginners tended to round in too much, and that the sail should be kept 'a little more full, than aback'. Krogh (83, 85), in contradiction to other authorities, says that the sails should be 'a little more back than full'.

Although there are occasional references to 'reefing at half mast' (Schneider, 178), that is with the yard only half way down, the regular practice was to let go the halliards, and clew the yard down all the way, until it sat firmly on the cap. Since, on the wind, the yard would be pressing against the lee topmast rigging, the weather brace had to be hauled in somewhat, and the top bowline let go, before letting go the halliards roundly. To get the brace in, it was necessary, particularly with the lower reefs, to give a fathom or two of the lee brace, if the course was not set, or to check the lee topsail sheet, if it were. If the halliards were let go, without getting the topsail yard off the lee rigging, it would, in descending, scrape the serving off the foremost shroud. It was important, however, not to brace the top-

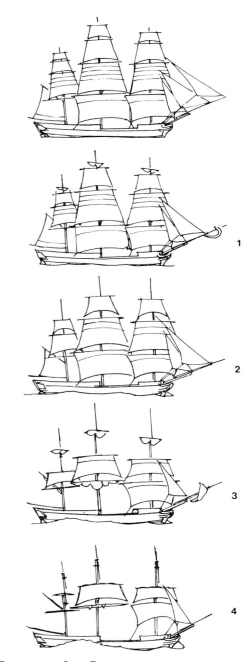

Sequence of reefing.

sail yards so far in that the sail flew aback and caused it to bind against the rigging. When down on the cap, the braces were hauled taut, and if the vessel were rolling heavily, rolling tackles were hooked from a strop on the yard to the mast, so that it would not sway from side to side (Burney, 64). Even though the yard was supported on the cap, the halliards were hauled taut again, since every precaution had to be taken to prevent anything moving once the men laid out on the yard (Liardet, 179). To ensure that the yard did come down firmly on the cap, the halliards were at first settled, and when the yard was at a third, or half mast, the falls were let go. In small ships, and in a stiff breeze, they were let go somewhat earlier (Krogh, 83). The rolling

1.

2.

"CHARLES"

3.

1.
This photo of the training ship *Nantucket* shows a combination of jacklines and reef-points on the topsail. This arrangement was often found in US Navy ships of the late nineteenth century. (US Navy photo, courtesy Giles M S Tod)

2.
The French merchant barque *Charles* carries a spar laced across her topsails at the level of the close reef-band – the system devised by Howes. The upper portion of the sail has two bands fitted for jackline reefing. (Courtesy Alex A Hurst)

3.
HMS *Warrior* with topsails treble reefed in a gale, by F Tudgay, 1863. Although the *Warrior*, Britain's first armoured warship, was launched some two decades after the introduction of jackline reefing in the Royal Navy, this painting shows her with reef-points on her sails. (Courtesy N R Omell Gallery, London)

tackles, if hauled, were let go as the yard came down, and then hauled taut once more. If the topsail yard failed to come down of its own weight, and the parrel slewed and 'hung' the yard, the weather clewline was manned (Ulffers, 332). A special downhaul was used later on, to accomplish this. It was important that the halliards not be loosed if men were working in the crosstrees or on the topgallant yard, since the jar of the yard hitting the cap would shake everything and might send them flying off (Ulffers, 332). They were ordered to remain in the top, or else the halliards were settled carefully all the way down (*Ulffers, Leitfaden*, 114). Mossel, (84) cautions against throwing off the halliards in a light wind, or if the sail was very wet, since the thump of the heavy yard coming down could damage something. Another reason for hauling the halliards taut was so the men working in the centre of the yard could hold on to the ties. If everything were not absolutely secure before the men ventured out on the yard, and subsequently the parrel gave way, dropping the yard a further few inches with a violent jerk, a man could be shaken completely off.

First reef. The first reef was, by custom, taken in men-of-war every evening, when cruising, partly as a precaution to save doing it during darkness, and partly to exercise the hands. The French called this the 'chase reef', *ris de chasse*. Bonnefoux comments that the first reef is always taken in some vessels because the topsails have stretched so badly

146

that they will not set properly otherwise, and wonders why allowance was not made for this beforehand by the sailmaker (Dubreuil, 234; von Littrow, 157). A sail overstretched in this way would have its leeches slack, even when the halliards were completely taut.

Laying the yard. They yard was laid square or nearly so: firstly, this allowed the men to get out on it more easily from the weather rigging (Krogh, 84); secondly, in naval vessels, when reefing more than one topsail at the same time, it was highly desirable that the yards be laid at the same angle, so that all could take advantage of the help offered by the proper use of the helm. The square marks on the braces offered the quickest way of establishing this. If, on the other hand, the fore topsail were braced in less that the main, the hands on the main topsail yard could be having a relatively easy time, with the sail kept just 'lifting' by the helmsman, while those on the fore topsail yard were struggling with a sail still full of wind (Hourigan, 23).

Reef-tackles. As the yard came down, the reef-tackles hauled themselves partly out (*Leitfaden*, 113). They were, in any event, hauled taut enough so that there was plenty of slack leech above the appropriate reef-cringle, the leech adopting a sort of question mark configuration, slack above the reef-cringle, and taut below. Greater effort was required to haul the weather tackle, so this was always hauled first (von Littrow, 157; Bonnefoux, 202). In the case of the third and fourth reefs, the reef-tackle could only be properly hauled, if the topsail sheets were checked. If the course were not set, the strain on the weather reef-tackle could be eased by squaring the lower yard, but this meant getting the braces and trusses taut, and it was much easier to veer the topsail sheet (Blunt, 173). The sail was further controlled by the appropriate use of buntlines and clewlines, and further steadying by hauling on the bowlines if necessary. As noted previously, with a vessel heeling over in a stiff breeze, a strong wind could actually rehoist the yard; the clewlines were belayed to prevent this happening (Bonnefoux, 201).

Trice up! Lay out! Only when the yard was secure, and the reef tackles well up, were the booms triced up, and the men allowed out on the yard. The tackles lifting the inner ends of the topgallant studdingsail booms were worked in the tops. The inner iron, holding the inner end of the boom secure, had to be unclasped to allow the boom to be triced up. The men went out on the footropes, keeping the body fairly straight and the feet pushing down and back on the footropes. If the man's feet swung forward under the yard, his situa-

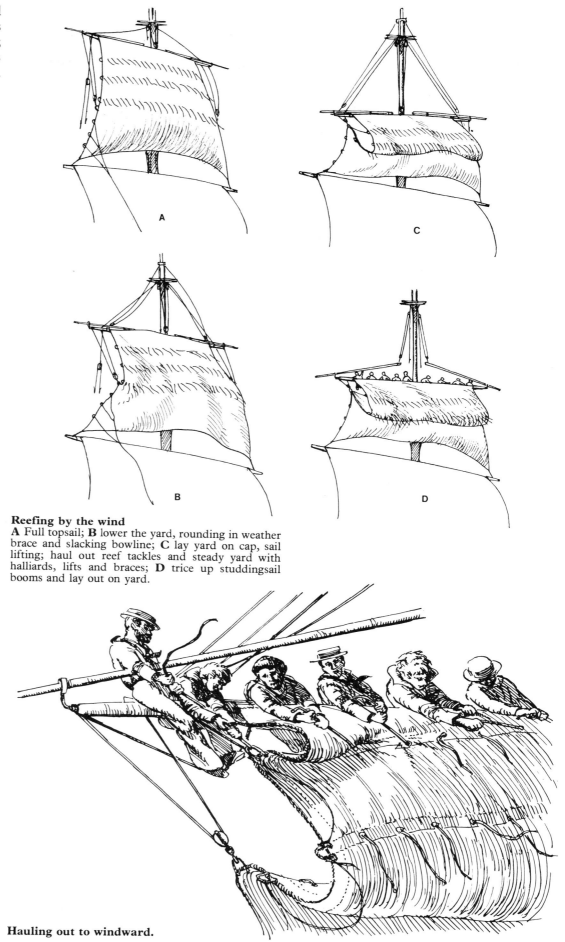

Reefing by the wind
A Full topsail; **B** lower the yard, rounding in weather brace and slacking bowline; **C** lay yard on cap, sail lifting; haul out reef tackles and steady yard with halliards, lifts and braces; **D** trice up studdingsail booms and lay out on yard.

Hauling out to windward.

tion was precarious. The elbows, hands and shoulders were used to hang on to anything available: the old saying went, 'one hand for the ship, the other for yourself'. As they laid out, the gaskets were thrown back over the yard (Ekelöf). The first captain of the top went to the weather yardarm, and the second captain to the lee. In merchant vessels, the weather yardarm – the position of honour, so to speak, when reefing – was taken by the second mate (Dana, 143). It was the duty of the yardarm man to pass the earing, assisted by the man next to him. It was the latter, who rove the earing through the reef-cringle from abaft forward and reached it up to the yard-arm man, who sat astride the yardarm, his feet braced against the 'Flemish horse', and his arm around the lift or studdingsail boom (Ekelöf, 69). The rest of the hands, in the meantime, reached down over the yard and got hold of the reef-points, or reef lines, and the order was given 'Haul out to windward!'. All facing to leeward, pulled the sail up and towards the weather side. This allowed the weather earing to be passed, and when the earing man had passed the turns, or sufficient of them to be secure, he ordered 'Haul out to lee!'. In men-of-war, where shouting aloft was considered undesirable, he indicated that all was secure by holding up his arm. In the French Navy, a midshipman stood between the ties, watching the activities of the captains of the yardarms. Dubreuil (236) mentions a whistle being used, as a signal to haul to windward. All then faced to windward, and hauled out towards the lee side, so the lee earing could be passed. When both were secure, and the reef-band lay taut along the yard, so that the upper fraction of the sail, between the reef-band and the headrope, was now quite slack, the men let go the reef-points and gathered the sail up first in small, then in gradually larger folds, so that the last fold formed a 'skin', to prevent as little water as possible collecting in the folded canvas. Each successive pleat, of which there would be three or four, was temporarily held down by the breast of the man as he leant over to get hold of the next one (Ekelöf, 71). The second man at the yardarm had the job of looking after the 'dog's lug', or 'dog's ear'. He had to fold up the section of reef canvas attached to that bight of leech lying above the reef-cringle. This was of a triangular or cone shape, and had to be laid flat along the yard so that it could be tucked under the succeeding folds of sail. The Dutch expression for this job, was 'breaking the trumpet'. It was important that it be covered by a good fold of sail, so that it could not collect water (Mossel, 85). The reef was held secure with one arm

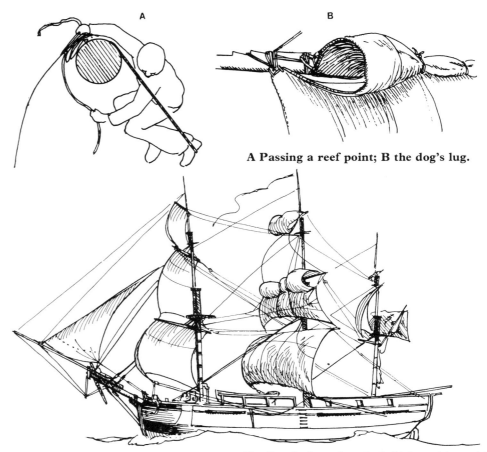

A Passing a reef point; **B** the dog's lug.

Reefing before the wind. Mainyard braced by for reefing topsail, sail controlled by reef-tackles, buntlines and bowlines.

over the yard, holding the forward point, while with the other arm, the man leant under the yard and pulled up the after point, which was square-knotted to its fellow. The ends were tucked between the points and the sail, or sometimes just thrown forward in front of it. Particular care had to be taken to see that the lower point came between the topgallant sheet and the yard, so that in no circumstances would it jam the sheet.

Reefing with beckets was carried out essentially in the same way, as we have already described, but it was a much simpler and faster process. However, the slack reef hung down between the lower part of the sail and the yard, and was visible from the deck, unless steps were taken somehow to pull it up.

When all the points or beckets were secure, the men laid in off the yard and down. The gaskets were cast forward of the sail, the booms lowered, and the inner irons clamped over them. (Ekelöf, 70). The captain of the top looked to see that the points were properly secure, that there were no granny knots, and that they were taking the strain evenly, (Bonnefoux, 23). It goes without saying, that the canvas had to be pleated up as evenly as possible to avoid an unsightly bulge, which the Swedish seamen referred to as 'a calf in

the reef', *kalf i refet* (Sjöbohm, 20).

Reefing before the wind. If possible, one avoided reefing in a squall, or with the wind aft, since it was harder to haul out the reef-tackles with the sail full, and the men risked being knocked backwards by the sail billowing up over the yard. So, if possible, the wind was kept no further aft than abeam. If it was impossible to come to, the weather yardarm was braced back, or 'braced by', so that so far as possible the sail was emptied of wind. The Dutch called this 'reefing topsails under the wind'. It was important to confine the sail as far as possible with buntlines, clewlines and bowlines, clewing it up fully if necessary (Grenfell, 105). Hauling the lee bowline, helped steady the sail, and obviated the potential accident of having it blow up and back over the lee yardarm, perhaps throwing a man off. Reefing in moderate weather, things could be managed very well with the wind aft, much as when close-hauled. When reefing for drill purposes, before a light wind, the custom in the Royal Swedish Navy was to haul out the starboard earing first, unless both could be hauled together (Ekelöf, 71). The old-fashioned buntlines, which ran directly from the bunt up to the buntline blocks, were not nearly as effective in con-

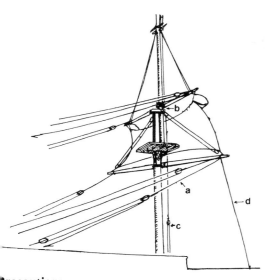

Precautions
a preventer brace; **b** preventer parrel; **c** lift jigger; **d** jumper.

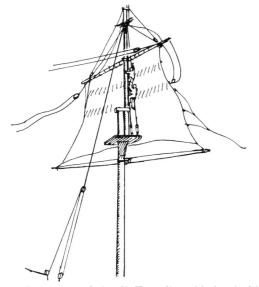

Resetting the reefed sail. Topsail yard hoisted with sail a-shiver and men overhauling the gear; when hoisted, haul taut lifts and weather bowline.

rolling the sails as were the buntlines in the latter day windjammer, which led through fairleads, or eyelets, seized to the fore side of the sail.

Subsequent reefs. These were taken in an essentially similar fashion. As explained earlier, with each successive reef, the reef-tackles had to be hauled up further, until they were chock-a-block with the close reef; with the third and fourth reefs the topsail sheets had to be veered. The task could be eased by bracing the lower yard in a little bit, that is, bringing it more parallel with the topsail yard. It was considered best to take the reefs in their proper order, and even when double reefing topsails, two single reefs were taken. The naval exercise of 'reefing topsails in stays' was an exception to this rule, in that sometimes 'two reefs were taken as one'

(Alston, 232). Pihlström (258) says that in squally weather, all reefs could be taken in one. A large dog's ear then lay all along the yard, but I would think this was probably rather awkward to manage, and taking the reefs singly was better.

In the event that the courses were not set when reefing topsails, it was particularly important that the lower lifts be taut. In fact, Hourigan (27) recommended that a 'jumper' or martingale, be led down from the lower yardarm if the mainsail were not set. This would prevent everything 'cockbilling', if something like a lower lift gave way suddenly aloft.

Preventer braces. When the third, or close reef, was taken, it was usual to rig a preventer brace and preventer parrel. The former was a tackle made fast to the yardarm, and led as far aft as possible (Hourigan, 26). Lower and topsail preventer braces were put on together, on the weather side. Boyd (404) used the sail-tackle for the lower, and the topmast studdingsail halliards for the topsail yard. The preventers were hauled somewhat less taut than the regular braces they were aiding (Ulffers, 339). The preventer parrel was just an extra fitting, much the same as the regular one (*Leitfaden*, 118; Luce, 472). Because of the extreme downward pull of the lee brace, it was usual to haul the lifts extra taut, using special tackles or 'lift-jiggers', with the second, and subsequent reefs (Hourigan, 28). The reef-tackles were slacked off after each reef was taken, but were usually left taut with the close reef, to give some extra support to the earings, and prevent the reef being slewed down under the yard.

Setting a reefed topsail. The halliards were stretched along, and rolling tackles taken off. With double ties, the weather halliards were manned in hoisting, while taking in the slack of the lee ones, but keeping a full round turn on the pin with it. If the weather halliards parted, the lee ones would take the strain, but if a round turn were not in place, someone might be dismembered by the flying coil, according to Hourigan (25). Two men remained aloft, to follow the yard up, and overhaul the buntlines, clewlines, reef-tackle, and so on. The lee brace was thrown off, and the yard was hoisted, the sail being kept just lifting, by controlling the yard, tending it with the weather brace. When up sufficiently, which was judged by the lee leech coming taut, the lifts were hauled taut, and the top bowline hauled. The sail could now be braced up much as before. With standing lifts, as used in the latter part of the 1800s, the lift hung down in a bight abaft the sail. With the full topsail set, and the yard

mastheaded, the lifts gave very little vertical support, but they provided a progressively better pull, as the yard came lower on the topmast with each successive reef. Bonnefoux (205) suggests belaying the lifts before hoisting and seizing the slack on the topmast shrouds in an 'S' form. The lee clew of a reefed topsail, if the sheet had been slacked off, during the reefing process, was hauled home first in setting, because the wind blew the sail to that side. A moment was chosen when the ship fell off the wind a little bit (Bobrik, 2665; Ulffers, 343; Dick & Kretchmer, 303). It was considered best not to 'swig' the halliards up too taut, otherwise the reef might be slewed down under the yard, and have to be turned in afresh (Luce, 471). Moreover, in wet weather, the leech rope would tend to shrink, putting an undue strain on the yard (Ekelöf, 71). The lee brace was belayed, leaving a little slack to allow for the working of the masts, and the play of the yard, particularly in a seaway (Luce, 471; Totten, 162). With the close reef, it was important to hoist the yard clear of the cap, even though it would remain very close to it.

Reefing courses. As mentioned earlier, until the late 1700s, as long as jeers were still fitted, the lower yard was struck a suitable amount after the reef was taken (Sjöbohm, 66). The advantage in lowering the yard was that it was easier to get the tack down, and the sail probably set better. Also there was some improvement because the weight of the yard was lower, and the CE of the sail was brought further down. Rosvall (29) felt that, when scudding, the yards should be rehoisted, since the higher the sail, the better it would hold the wind, in the hollow of the sea. The famous van de Velde picture entitled *The Resolution in a Storm*, gives a very good idea of what an early reefed course must have looked like. When the yard is lowered, it comes abreast the lower rigging on the lee side, at a point where there is greater splay than above, and hence the yard cannot be braced up as sharply; to some extent this could be helped by slacking off the trusses. The CE of a reefed topsail is, of course, lowered in the same way.

Reefing a course required that at some point the tack and sheet had to be started, which would cause the sail to thrash around violently even though it had been held fairly steady by the wind up to that point.

When close-hauled, the lower yard was steadied to some extent, because it bore against the stay forward, and the lee shrouds aft. When it was being braced in, prior to reefing, it lost this support and would begin to sally violently from side to side, also swing-

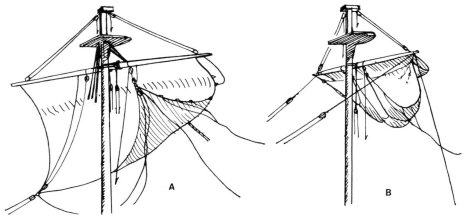

Reefing a course
A Clew up to weather, keeping lee lift well taut; **B** steady yard with truss, braces, lifts and jumper; clew up to leeward; haul out reef-tackles.

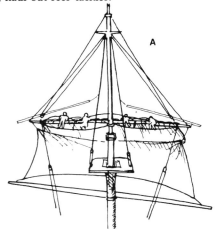

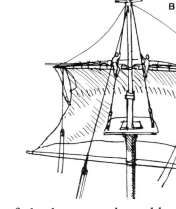

Shaking out reefs
A Settle and steady yard; haul out reef-tackles; trice up booms and lay out on yard to untie points; **B** let go reef-tackles and buntlines; man halliards and tend weather brace, overhauling gear as yard rises.

ing fore and aft, until brought under control by hauling the trusses, which pulled it back against the rigging (Boyd, 406). Under press of sail, pulling the weather truss, slacked the weather brace and vice versa. They had to be hauled together. Hourigan's remark that 'when it's time to reef a mainsail, it's time to take it in' echoed a common sentiment; taking the sail in did not require pointing the yard to the wind, which meant it could be kept under better control than when reefing it. Hourigan suggests reefing the foresail after the third reef in the topsails. The courses were always reefed separately from, and after, the topsails (Boyd, 405), since they kept steerage way on while the topsails were reefed; in fact occasionally staysails were set temporarily for the same purpose. The fore topmast staysail, like the fore course, was kept set as long as possible, to help lift the head. If a course was reefed or taken in, it was important to get the lee lift well taut before the tack was let go, otherwise the weather arm

of the lower yard would cockbill upwards, due to the downward pull of the lee brace. If the lee yardarm was canted down, the yard could not be braced up fully because it would jam against the lee shrouds prematurely in its swing. A martingale or jumper was recommended to hold the weather yardarm down, when the tack was let go. Hourigan (27) suggests using a water-whip from the booms for this purpose.

As mentioned previously, a second reef was sometimes fitted for the fore course, for example if rounding Cape Horn was in prospect (Grenfell, 102), but it was rarely if ever fitted for the mainsail (Burney, 104). The mainsail could be left set, with the third reef in the topsails, if the wind were at any point forward of the quarter. If not, it was usually taken in with the third reef, especially if the sea was heavy, to avoid broaching to (Grenfell). After reefing courses, the leech-line and slabline blocks had to be shifted further out on the yard (Boyd, 405).

Shaking out reefs. This was done by the sail loosers. Too many men would simply have got in each others way, and shaking out a reef was much easier than taking it. Since there were to be fewer men on the yard, and hence much less weight, it was not necessary

to lower the topsail yard right down on th cap, but in fact this was usually done. Th halliards were slacked off, and the ree tackles hauled up enough, so that the leec would be slack. The weather brace wa hauled in, and the yard steadied with lift both braces, halliards, and rolling tackles necessary; the sail was kept just lifting, wit the weather leech shaking. The booms wer triced up, and the men laid out on the yarc Actually, it was not absolutely necessary trice up the booms, to shake out a reef, an this was often omitted (*Officer of the Watc.* 12). If they were in the way, the gaskets wer thrown back over the yard. The first ma capsized each square knot as he came to i and he was followed by the second man wh completed undoing the knot (Schneide 179), or alternatively the first man untie every other knot, and the remainder were ur done by his mate. In any case, the points wer let go starting at the slings, and working tc wards the yardarms, the opposite order which gaskets were cast off. The reef kn lends itself particularly well to the fir method. It was particularly important th every last point be cast off, otherwise ther was the danger of tearing the sail. The san thing applied to the slab reef lines, coming t behind the sail, and perhaps hitched over tr toggles. If the yard was not clear of the k rigging, there was liable to be a problem wil reef-points, since these could be nipped be tween the forward shroud and the yard, c rather the chafing mats placed between then Either the yard had to be braced clear, or tr points had to be cut so that the sail would n be damaged. When all was ready, the captai and second captain of the top glanced alor the yard to see that all points or beckets wer clear, and then the earings were eased off tc gether. The earing was hitched to the cring next above with the third and fourth reefs, c stopped in along the yard with the first an second reef. The topmen laid in, the boon were lowered down again, and clamped, th halliards were led along, and the reef-tackl and buntlines were cast off and overhaulec The lee brace was cast off, and the weath one tended, as the sail was run up until the k leech became taut. One or two men remaine aloft as the sail went up to overhaul the rij ging. Hourigan cautions against allowir topmen to 'ride' the yard up or down. If a t broke, the man would grab for the lift, c other gear, he was tending, and be snatche clear of the yard, and beyond hope of rescu He recommended that they stay abreast tr gear, but safely in the topmast rigging. I taking a reef and shaking one out, the fir man off the quarters of the yard ran up th rigging, to overhaul the reef-tackles (Cradock, 30).

To turn the reef out of a course, the tack was eased off, to allow the reef-tackle to slacken the leech above the point where the reef pendant was attached. Otherwise, the same general principles applied as with a topsail.

Handling topgallants when reefing topsails. The topgallants could be set over single, and even double, reefed topsails. They could be kept set while the first reef was turned in, lowered and clewed up, or clewed up at the masthead while the second reef was taken. Dick and Kretchmer (298) say that the topgallant can be kept set while reefing if the wind was more than two points free, that is abeam, or abaft that. If the wind was forward of the beam, the topgallants should be clewed down. Otherwise the thrashing of the sheets would be a hazard to the men aloft. With the third reef, it was not practical to set them because of the increased distance between the clew and the topsail yardarm. The topgallant halliards could be settled with each reef in the topsail, but the topgallant could not be lowered without having the foot of the sail sawing across the stay. If the topgallant sheets were checked, prior to settling the topsail halliards, care was taken to see that, by adjusting the topgallant clewlines and sheets, nothing was slapping around so as to endanger the men on the yard. The advantage of carrying the topgallant over a single reefed topsail, in anticipation of increasing weather, was the fact that a topgallant could be clewed up, or even clewed down and furled in emergency, more quickly than a topsail could be reefed. A topgallant, set over a single reefed topsail, was more likely to be hung onto in shortening sail, than set in making sail (Hourigan, 35).

According to Murphy (17) the topgallant sheets could be kept fast while the topsail yard was lowered. He claimed to have seen a topsail tie break, and the yard come abruptly down, without injuring the topgallant sheets. On the other hand, the sheets did have to be slackened, when the topsail yard was hoisted (Hourigan, 37).

Middle staysail. The nock of the old-fashioned trapezoidal middle staysail set with a grommet around the topmast, about half way up. This, of course, had to hauled down before the topsail halliards were let go (Lever, 83; Pihlström, 258). If the sail set to a vertical jackstay abaft the topmast, this problem was obviated.

Reefing other light sails. Although reefing topgallants are rarely mentioned by the authors most familiar to me, they were not

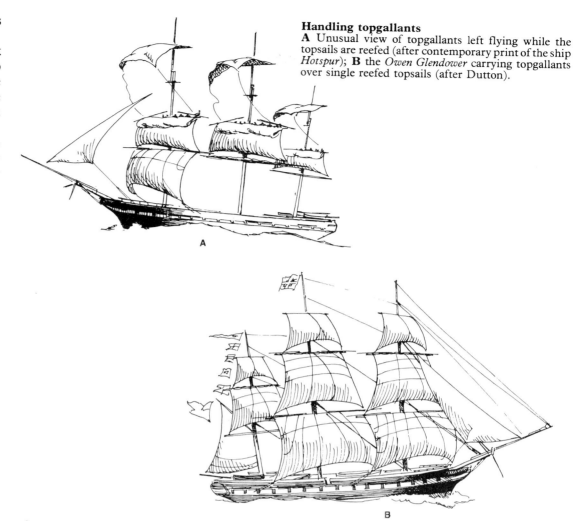

Handling topgallants
A Unusual view of topgallants left flying while the topsails are reefed (after contemporary print of the ship *Hotspur*); **B** the *Owen Glendower* carrying topgallants over single reefed topsails (after Dutton).

unknown. Their existence is attested in contemporary illustrations and some photographs. Bonnefoux says that they could be reefed aloft, but it was better if they were sent down and reefed on deck like studdingsails (208). Some modern artists, where they do show topgallant reef points, depict the reef-band about half way down the sail, whereas one would have expected it would be more like a quarter the distance down from the head. This mistake probably arises because the reef-band is found at half the hoist of an upper split topsail. Upper topsails, fitted for reefing, were quite widely used in smaller merchant vessels. The first reef plus the lower topsail was equivalent to a single reefed topsail, and when the upper sail was taken in completely it was equivalent to a double or treble reefed single topsail. Reefs on lower topsails were not used. It is true that Forbes' lower topsail did carry them, but as we have mentioned he called this the 'topsail', and worked it as such. What we would today call his upper topsail, he called the 'topgallant'. Upper topsails were reefed in the same way as single topsails, but reef-tackles were not used. Once it became customary to clew up to the yardarm, they would have been com-

pletely superfluous. Neither, by the same token, were reef-tackles fitted on topgallants.

Reefing studdingsails. Topgallant studdingsails were never reefed, but topmast and lower studdingsails sometimes were. The reefs were turned in with spunyarn lashings through reef holes over the head or yard of the sail before they were sent up. Yarns were preferred over a single lashing according to Cradock (23). In the case of the topmast studdingsail, the reef corresponded in depth with the first reef of the topsail, so that they could be set together, with one reef taken. The seaman of the 1800s considered the studdingsails, especially the topmast studdingsails, an important part of the working canvas, and this was particularly true of the fore topmast studdingsail, for reasons that we have gone into elsewhere.

Reefing fore and aft sail. In contemporary paintings of small merchantmen, we find examples of jibs, and occasionally fore topmast staysails fitted for reefing. As mentioned earlier, men-of-war, rather than reefing a large jib, substituted the middle or small jib, as appropriate to the weather. Even if the large jib were carried too long, naval vessels had the luxury of having sufficient man-

Reefing various sails
A Reefed studdingsail set with reefed topsail; **B** detail of reefed jib (after Ole Johnson, 1842); **C** second reef in spanker; **D** balance reef in spanker; **E** vertical reef in spanker (after contemporary portrait of ship *Malta*); **F** reefed spritsail; **G** reefed upper topsail (after O Jaburg, 1864).

leech up from the foot. A 'balance reef' was frequently worked in the sail from the nock, the forward upper corner to the after leech just above the reef-cringle for the uppermost horizontal band.

Reefs were taken in fore and aft sail with points, usually one to a cloth, placed on the seam for extra strength. Whether the points were sewed to the grommet of the reef hole, or inserted when required, depended to a certain extent on how often they would be used. For instance one sees examples of the lowest band fitted with permanent points, and those above it not so fitted. Headsails were reefed by tying the points under the foot of the sail. The halliards were slacked off enough to allow this to be done. The tack tackle and clew outhaul were hooked to the spanker reef-cringles, to function in a fashion to the reef-tackles of the topsail, and allow the reef to be turned in. The hooks were 'moused', to prevent accidental disengagement.

In the case of the spanker, and the fore and main trysails, an earing was used at the tack and clew. In the case of the spanker with a clew outhaul and clew rope, the clew earing was passed under the foot of the sail which was protected by wrapping it with canvas. The clew outhaul was sometimes left hooked to the clew, or transferred to the reef-cringle. The points were tied under the foot of the sail, rather than under the boom. This was easier on the sail, and allowed it to be brailed up when necessary. An earing was also used at the tack, to hold down the forward end of the reef-band.

The balance reef was rarely used, but if taken, it left the gaff cocked up at a fairly steep angle. In fact the mizzen was sometimes reefed by keeping fast the head outhaul, and hauling out the clew. The head was further secured by a few turns of the furling line. This was functionally equivalent to a triangular staysail. In fact, it was considered by some preferable to take in the mizzen completely, and replace it with a triangular trysail (Bonnefoux, 208).

Reefing spritsail. Philström (266) is one of the few people who actually describe how this was done. It is reefed with the yard square, secured by hauling taut lifts, tricing lines or braces, and guys. The sail was confined with a couple of turns of the gaskets, and the earing secured on the weather side only. The dog's lug was laid along the yard, and the sail reefed as with the topsail. This leaves a very short weather leech, and the full length of the lee leech. The sail was set by slacking the weather brace, guys, and lee lift. The yard was triced up on the leeward side of the bowsprit, and the foot of the sail now lay parallel

power to subdue it, something that was not the case in the small collier brig. The other staysails were rarely if ever reefed, but rather taken in.

On headsails, the band was parallel to the foot, and about one-eighth to one-sixth the hoist of the sail above it. If there was a second band, it would be the same interval above again.

Gaff trysails and spankers usually had two bands parallel to the foot, again about one-eighth to one-sixth the length of the fore

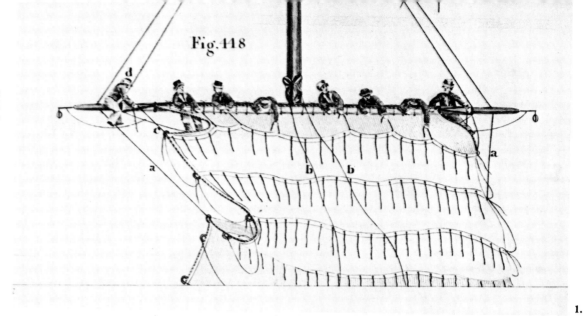

Fig. 118

1.

Reefing a topsail, from Lever's *Young Sea Officer's Sheet Anchor*. The men on the yard are hauling the sail out to windward, where the yardarm man (d) will pass the reef earing (c). (Mark Myers' Collection)

2.

Reefing topails in the *Jarramas*. Although the reef-tackles are hauled out and cadets are busy hauling up the reef, the yard is still some way from the cap. (Courtesy Marinmuseum, Karlskrona)

3.

'On the weather yardarm' by C J Staniland. The men are on the lower yard, apparently being exercised in turning in a reef. Courses were sometimes fitted with reef-points on the fore side of the sail only, due to the girth of the yard. (Mark Myers' Collection)

to the waves. Pihlström also mentions reefing a spritsail topsail, but I have no other confirmation of this practice. To shake out a reefed spritsail, the yard was braced square again. However, if the jib and spritsail topsail were set in a stiff breeze, the reef had to be turned out with the yard canted, because the jibboom required the downward and windward pull of the guys on the lower windward end of the spritsail yard.

Reefing in stays. This was more an example of 'stunt seamanship' rather than a manoeuvre of much practical use. By taking a reef in the topsails at the same time as the vessel tacked, a fancy frigate could demonstrate the crew's facility at smart sail drill. It is mentioned by Ulffers (298), Murphy (18), and Alston (232). Lubbock in the *The Blackwall Frigates* (80) says that the song 'Oh 't is a fine frigate' refers to HMS *Pique* of 1835. There are different versions of this, but the relevant lines run as follows:

And now my brave boys comes the best of the fun,
It's 'Hands about ship, and reef topsails in one!',
So it's 'Lay aloft topmen' as the helm goes down,
And 'Clew down your topsails', as the main yard flies round.
'Trice up and lay out, and take two reefs in one',
For all in a moment, the work must be done.
Then man your head braces, your halliards and all,
And as you 'Hoist away topsails', you 'Let go and haul!'

The watch on deck and idlers reefed topsails, the watch below worked on deck. One supposes that this would only have been attempted with a good working breeze, and a a fairly calm sea, in a ship that turned well to windward. Alston says that it is better to lower topsails when tacks and sheets are

Reefing topsails in stays.

1   2   3

raised, laying the yard square. The mainyard was hauled at the proper time 'regardless of the men on the yard', that is to say the topsail yard, and of course the crossjack yard was hauled at the same time as the main; the topsails were hoisted when the men were off the yard, and the head yards hauled at the usual time.

Ulffers lets go the halliards upon 'Helm a-lee!'; topmen aloft, reef and lay in; then 'Up main tack and sheet!', 'Mainsail haul!' and then hoist main and mizzen topsails. Finally 'Haul of all!' and hoist the fore topsail. Murphy follows a more or less similar plan.

The reefing of the main and mizzen topsails would be facilitated by their being becalmed by the headsails, but I find it a little difficult to visualise how the fore topsail was managed. Once it flew aback, it would be difficult to reef, let alone lower or hoist. Success in tacking was determined by the throwing aback of the square sails on the foremast, but this should not occur too early in the manoeuvre. By squaring the topsail yard, the sail would come aback more quickly than the fore course.

The Commands. In men-of-war, it was usual to reef all three topsails at once. In small, under-manned vessels, this would not have been possible. Reefing could be done by the watch, or all hands might be required. The commands would vary in detail, but the following would be representative for reefing a topsail. Sometimes orders as to booms and so on would not be given from deck, each top being left to look after itself.

Watch, single reef topsails!
Way aloft topmen! Take one reef in topsails!
Man topsail clewlines and buntlines, weather topsail braces!
Hands by the lee braces, bowlines and halliards!
Clear away bowlines, round in weather braces, settle away the topsail halliards!
Clew down!
Haul out the reef tackle! Haul up the buntlines!
Stand by the booms! Trice up! Lay out and take one reef!
Light out to windward! Light out to leeward! Toggle away!

Lay in! Stand by the booms! Down booms!
Lay down from aloft!
Man the topsail halliards! Let go the reef-tackles! Clear away buntlines and clewlines!
Tend the braces! Set taut! Hoist away the topsails!
Belay the topsail halliards!
Steady out the bowlines!
Clear away on deck!

Disposition of crew for reefing topsails.

Aloft	Topsail yard furlers and boom tricers
Unhook topsail lift jiggers	Royal yardmen of watch on deck
Weather topsail braces	Idlers and marines
Topgallant clewlines	Topmen not aloft
Reef tackles and buntlines	Remainder of hands
Stopper and belay topsail buntlines, clewlines, and reef-tackles	Main: captain of quarterdeckmen. Burney does not detail who has this responsibility with fore and mizzen

Otherwise ropes manned and attended, as in making sail.

CHAPTER 10
STUDDINGSAILS

EVOLUTION

Early history of studdingsails. In the absence of any solid evidence, one can only speculate about how the sails evolved prior to 1650. My own guess is that the sequence was somewhat as follows. Perhaps as early as 1550, very likely in the Netherlands, a boom was rigged out on the mainyard, to spread the foot of a jib-headed main topmast studdingsail. This at least, is the arrangement illustrated by Rålamb in 1691. The next logical step would have been to add a triangular lower studdingsail, set point down, the head extended by the boom. However, *Der ge-öffnete Seehafen* (57) indicates that the head of the triangular lower studdingsail was run up to the main yardarm, the foot being set with a boom, with the topmast studdingsail setting 'in a similar fashion'. Smith (39), in 1627, says 'we extend the studdingsail alongst the side of the mainsail, and booms it out with a boom or long pole, which we use also sometimes to the clew of the mainsail, foresail and spritsail, when you go before the wind, or quartering, else not'. Boteler (169) and Mainwaring (106), likewise, indicate that the foot of the sail was boomed out, and in the same context boom out the clews of the lower sails going before the wind. The rope used to haul the clew out in this way was called a 'passaree' or 'passarado' later on, but we may remark in passing, that to the three authors just mentioned, a passarado was a sort of 'false tack' (Romme *Dictionnaire Marine Anglaise*, 214), which held the clew of the foresail down to the cathead, and that of the mainsail to the cubbridge head, when going large. It prevented the clew flying up, when the sheet was slacked off, and is not mentioned in connection with studdingsails or booms.

The development of a square lower studdingsail follows naturally enough, once both topmast studdingsail boom and lower boom are in use. With the introduction of reefing about 1660, the topsail yardarm projected further beyond the head of the topsail than had been the case earlier, and this would rapidly have led to the introduction of a trapezoidal topmast studdingsail.

One imagines that studdingsails developed initially as adjuncts to the sails on the mainmast, where everything was proportionately larger than on the foremast. The ratio of fore to main was about 0.75 in 1600, but by 1700 this had increased to between 0.8 and 0.9 (Anderson, 53). The greater the sail area, the greater the ability of the vessel to 'ghost' in a calm, but it would soon have been realised, that with the wind anywhere between the beam and the quarter, some of the weather fore studdingsails were more useful than the corresponding sails on the mainmast. Fore studdingsails are mentioned as early as 1625 (*Treatise on rigging*, 62)

Later history. Since the main lower studdingsail would blanket the fore course and fore lower studdingsail, it fell into disuse about 1800. Royal studdingsails were popular in the 'flying kite era' in the early 1800s, but dropped out of use later on, although Totten alludes to them as late as 1864. The four studdingsails on the main, and the six on the fore, remained as part of the working canvas into the late 1800's, but some refinements in the gear allowed them to be worked to greater advantage, than the crude lash-ups of two centuries earlier. Note that all the upper studdingsails were suspended from the yardarms, while the lower studdingsails hauled up to the topmast studdingsail booms. In the naval service, main topmast studdingsails disappeared earlier than main topgallant studdingsails (Hourigan, 47; Burney, 187, 264). Burney, in 1869, says that some ships were 'specially fitted' with main topmast studdingsail boom irons: one would guess that these were sail-and-steam vessels with the funnel placed between the fore and main, hence a greater distance relatively between these two masts and correspondingly less blanketting.

Mizzen studdingsails. These were not unknown, and in fact are referred to as late as this century, by Kipping (76). However, I do not think they were ever very popular or practical. Romme (*L'Art de la Voilure*, Plate VI, Fig 39) shows a lower and topmast mizzen studdingsail. Willaumez, as late as 1831, illustrates mizzen topmast, and top-

gallant studdingsails. Apart from the fact that they would have becalmed forward sail, it would have been difficult to lead the tack and boom-brace far enough aft, to give adequate support to the boom.

Studdingsails in the 1900s. As late as 1903, Hourigan (44) explains his prejudice in favour of studdingsails thus: they were no more trouble than the other sails, gave the boys of the Training Squadron excellent practice at sail drill, and the officers experience in organising the efforts of the men. Made of light canvas, with insubstantial gear, they could be sacrificed in any real emergency, such as a man overboard, and, if endangered, were a hazard only to themselves. A snapped boom, although trying to the temper of the officer of the deck, was no great matter, and if the sails were torn, they offered lots of opportunity for the boys to ply needle and palm.

Commercial sail sometimes rigged extempore studdingsails, well into this century. Hourigan mentions seeing a merchantman, with a topmast studdingsail boom rigged out, to set one headsail, head up as a topmast studdingsail, and another, head down, as a lower studdingsail. Gustav Alexandersson has given me a photograph of the *C B Pedersen* setting a triangular lower studdingsail, one corner up, at the fore yardarm, and the foot extended by a boom, in exactly the method described in *Der ge-öffnete Seehafen* two centuries earlier!

The studdingsails 'squared off' the sail plan, in a way that later became unnecessary. Because of the difficulties of adequately supporting the spars higher up, each mast supported, as it were, a tapering pillar of canvas. The French term *phare* for all the sails on one mast, nicely evokes this image, since the literal meaning is 'lighthouse'. The latter day windjammer with its steel spars and wire rigging was 'squarer aloft' than its predecessor; that is to say, the upper yards were more nearly the same length as the lower ones, than had been the case earlier. Hence studdingsails became redundant, even had there been the manpower to handle them (Todd & Whall, 6)

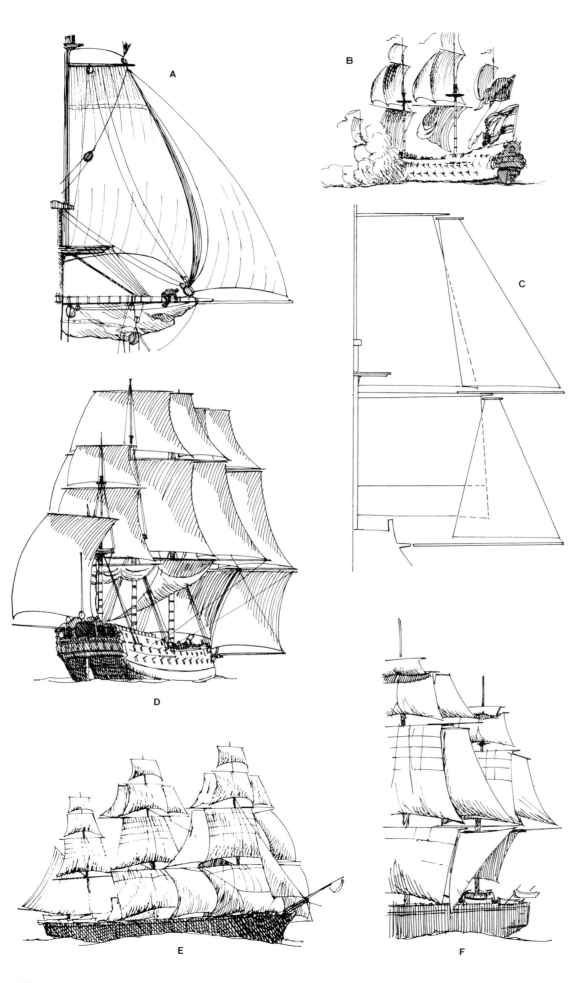

WIND AND WEATHER

Weather conditions obtaining. Ordinarily studdingsails were of most use in good weather, with the wind abeam, or further aft. They would have served best as the wind freshened, while sea remained relatively smooth. In the opposite case – a subsiding wind and the ship rolling heavily in an old sea – the danger of dipping the lower boom, and even, exceptionally, the topmast studdingsail boom, increased (Martelli, 249). They were of the utmost use in the Trade Winds, where they could sometimes be left set for days on end (Mossel, III, 134), but were less useful in changeable conditions, since setting and taking them in required a fair bit of work. Many 'captains' pictures' show small merchantmen, with only the weather fore topmast studdingsail set, and this particular sail was especially useful, since it not only served to prevent the helmsman 'pinching' (trying to keep too close to the wind), but also helped offset the pressure on the lee bow, as the vessel heeled, and meant that less weather helm had to be carried.

I do not know to what extent they could be carried as the wind increased. The only photographs I have seen, show them set in very moderate weather. Montague Dawson's well

Evolution of studdingsails

A Early main topmast studdingsail (after Rålamb, 1691); **B** fore and main topmast studdingsails *c*1675 (after drawing by Van de Velde the Elder); **C** proportions of main lower and topmast studdingsails for *Royal Louis* 1692; **D** fore and main studdingsails and driver, late eighteenth century (after portrait of HMS *Worcester* by Short); **E** late nineteenth century suit of studdingsails (after photograph of HMS *Volage*). The 'save-all' under the foresail is an extempore rig-up; **F** mizzen topmast studdingsail (after photograph of HMS *Active*); **G** combined lower and topmast studdingsail used in Pacific Coast trades *c*1890 (from photograph of brigantine *John D. Spreckles*).

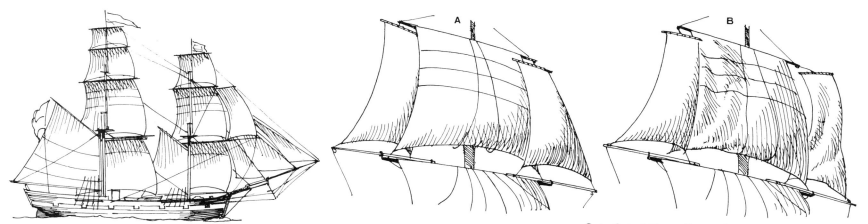

Fore topmast studdingsail set in collier brig (after Jacob Petersen, 1860).

Set of studdingsails on the wind
A Proper set of studdingsails, weather sail abaft, and lee sail before the topsail; **B** improper set of studdingsails, with weather sail backwinding topsail and lee sail backwinded by topsail.

known picture of '*Ariel* and *Taeping*' has seduced succeeding generations of marine artists, by the exhilaration of its turbulent sea, straining booms and ballooning canvas, so that no artist nowadays can afford to paint the scene with less flurry and excitement. However, a contemporary illustration of the selfsame event, (*Sailing Ships*, I, 103), shows the studdingsails drawing nicely, rather than ballooning out inefficiently in such a way as to backwind their principal sails (in this connection, have a look at Dawson's fore topmast studdingsail). On the other hand, John Masefield's *Bird of Dawning* (270) contains a rousing description of a tea clipper setting first a lower, and then a fore topmast, studdingsail as it races up the Channel in very brisk weather, which is a portrayal very much in the mood of Dawson's painting. Masefield no doubt was exercising some artistic licence, but if he had not participated in such activities himself, he must have sailed with men who had.

Direction of the wind. When the wind was a point and a half or so free – that is to say almost abeam – the weather topmast and topgallant studdingsails could be set on the fore. As the wind drew a little further aft, those on the weather side of the main could be set as well. Theoretically, since the 'wind is fairer aloft', the topgallant studdingsail could be set before the topmast studdingsail. With the wind abeam or a little better, the lee main topgallant studdingsail and perhaps topmast studdingsail could be set also. Fordyce (114) indicates that the lower weather studdingsail might stand, with the wind as far forward as one point forward of the beam. Others counselled waiting until the wind was practically on the quarter. The lee fore lower studdingsail was set when the wind had drawn almost dead aft.

STUDDINGSAILS ON DIFFERENT POINTS OF SAIL

Practical considerations. The fact that a sail *could* be set, did not mean that it was necessarily a good idea to do so. A relatively ineffective sail could steal the wind out of one which was more efficient. More sail did not necessarily mean more speed; for example, Bonnefoux (68) speculated that the English frigate *Success* might have escaped capture in 1800, had she not persisted in ill-advised attempts to carry studdingsails, by the wind. Hourigan (51) recounts taking in a lower studdingsail, setting the fore topmast staysail, and seeing the speed increase by almost a knot. He advised, as a practical matter, not setting the upper studdingsails until the wind was a full two points free, and the lower studdingsail only when it was on the quarter, when the jib would no longer draw. Of the two, the jib was the better sail. On the other hand, once set, they could be hung onto a bit longer, as the wind hauled forward. Hourigan's rule of thumb was to take in the lower when the wind was abaft the beam three points, the topgallant studdingsail two points, and the topmast studdingsail when the wind was dead abeam (51). Although the topmast studdingsail could be kept set as the wind drew even further ahead than this, getting it in subsequently might prove difficult. It would tend to blow away to leeward, wrapping itself around the fore topmast stay, once tack and halliards were let go. A most important consideration was that the studdingsails should not interfere with the corresponding principal sail, and 'backwind' it, as a modern yachtsman would say. Thus the weather topmast and topgallant studdingsails were set abaft the weather leech of

the topsail and topgallant sail. If set forward, the wind spilling out of the topmast studdingsail would strike the forward part of the topsail, causing the leech to shake, and the sail to work less well aerodynamically. In turn, if the lee studdingsails were to do any good at all, they were set ahead of the leeches of their respective principal sails. A studdingsail which previously had been set to weather, could by a shift of wind to the opposite quarter, become the lee studdingsail and be 'dipped before all' so as to function more efficiently under the changed circumstance.

The rigging plan would determine, to some extent, the degree of blanketing of one sail by another. Thus the lee main topgallant and topmast studdingsails were very useful in a barque, where there was no mizzen topsail and topgallant to becalm them. The lee fore topgallant studdingsail and topmast studdingsail were prone to be interfered with by the upper sails on the main. I would guess that there was a very narrow sector, from wind just abaft the beam, to somewhere forward of the quarter, in which the lee upper studdingsails were any good, about the same point of sail in which the weather main upper studdingsails were useful. As the wind drew aft, they interfered unacceptably with the sails on the fore. 'It is no manner of use to dip a fore topgallant studdingsail' says Boyd (395). However, the lee main topgallant and topmast studdingsails could be used from when the wind was somewhere forward of the quarter to where it was coming from right aft.

With the wind right astern, or nearly so, it will be seen that the becalming effect of one mast by another was a major problem. The mizzen was taken in, as was the mizzen topgallant, because they would blanket the sails forward. The mizzen topsail was clewed

Studdingsails set with the wind right aft
A and B after Lever; C after Ozanne; D after Baugean (note fore topsail becalmed, main topgallant and royal sheets and halliards eased, mainsail hauled up and spritsail set).

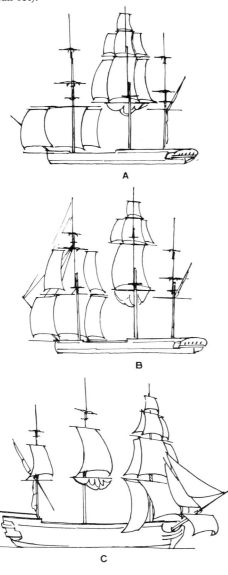

down until the yard rested on the cap, 'scandalising the mizzen topsail' as it was termed. The main course was clewed up, so that it would not steal the wind from the foresail, while the main topsail was left drawing. The sheets of the main topgallant sometimes were veered, and its halliards settled, to allow the wind to fill the fore topgallant. The fore topsail was pretty much becalmed, as can be seen in the contemporary engravings of Ozanne and Baugean, but Mossel (III, 126) says that it was usually left set in men-of-war. Lever's Figure 436 shows the fore course and both lower studdingsails set, with the fore topsail and topgallant furled, and Figure 437, shows the same sails set with the two fore topmast studdingsails in addition; the fore topsail is furled, although its yard is hoisted full up. Lever (82) calls this 'scandalising the fore topsail yard'. This becalming of the fore topsail comes as a bit of a surprise to those familiar with the present day square rigger, where the phenomenon does not seem to be a problem. I think this is because there are a lot more 'holes' in the modern sail plan. At any rate, it is difficult to find photographs showing the aftersail interfering with the forward in this particular way.

On this point of sail, the headsails were of no use, and were accordingly hauled down. The fore topmast staysail was sometimes left set, with both sheets aft, not because it would draw, but because it would help throw the head off the wind in the event of a sudden yaw, or shift of wind forward. The spritsail was left set, since it caught the wind from under the forecourse. Furthermore, it seems to me, that this was one point of sail, where that oddity, the spritsail topsail, would have been really useful. Like the spritsail, it would have pulled the ship along, by the nose, rather than pushing it from behind, and would have been very helpful in keeping it away, in the event of a bad yaw. Regarding the distribution of sail between the fore and main, the fore course, main topsail and topgallant were always set. I would guess that with the wind aft, from about 1660 to 1750, all the studdingsails were set on the main. Whichever course was used, the clews were hauled out by 'passarees' to tail blocks on the lower booms, to give the foot of the sail a better spread.

Later on, the tendency seems to have been to set everything on the fore. Certainly, the main lower studdingsail, although still apparent in Steel's engravings, dropped out of use completely after 1800 or so. At all events, upper studdingsails on the main mask those on the fore, if the wind was dead aft, and if those on the fore were desired, the

corresponding ones on the main would be taken in. Having the wind somewhat on the quarter would change matters, and might allow corresponding sails to draw on both masts. The distribution of sail between fore and main also depended on the 'judgment of the officer', guided by the trim of the vessel according to Lever (82). If down by the head more sail was set aft, and the reverse if down by the stern. All studdingsails would have been 'depressing' sails, pushing the bow deeper in the water, but this would have been more the case with those on the fore than those on the main and more with the upper than the lower studdingsails. This explains the occasional preference for setting the lower studdingsails on the fore, and the uppers on the main. Another determinant governing which sails remained set at a particular moment, was the circumstance immediately preceding. Thus, if it was decided to set studdingsails both sides *de novo*, all could well be set on the foremast. If, however, the weather studdingsails had been set on the fore, and the wind gradually drawing aft, the lee ones were subsequently set on the main, it might well be convenient to leave things that way as the wind drew dead astern. Both Baugean and Ozanne show a main lower and topmast studdingsail on one side, and a fore lower and topmast studdingsail, on the other. Assuming the wind to be slightly on one quarter, the sail on the main would be set to leeward to avoid interfering with the foresail. Despite Lever's illustration, and Masefield's description, of a fore lower studdingsail set alone, I think this was unusual. There was a heavy downward pull on the topmast studdingsail boom, as the lower studdingsail bellied forward. To some extent, this was offset by setting the topmast studdingsail first, and this is the usual sequence in most other accounts familiar to me.

THE SAILS

The lower studdingsail. For most of the studdingsail era, this sail was square in shape. By lacing the yard at a different point on the head, it could be set on the other side (Pihlström, 249). This reversibility was not shared by the upper studdingsails, although Cradock (22), describing the custom in the Royal Navy in 1903, says that all studdingsails 'are roped as port sails'. The thrifty disposition displayed by the Admiralty was echoed in the Training Squadron of the United States Navy, where ships were issued with odds and ends of studdingsails of different shapes and sizes, originally intended for other vessels (Hourigan, 47).

The yard. The sail was made of Number 4 or 5 canvas and a yard was laced to the outer half of the head. The outer halliards were usually hitched to the mid-point of the yard. Hildebrandt (173) says they are secured two feet out from the centre, while Hourigan (49) says 'a little outside the middle'.

Earlier French usage, as described by Romme (*L'Art de la Voilure* 13, 15) was a little different. The fore lower studdingsail had no yard, and the main had the yard on the *inner* half of the sail. This arrangement can be seen in a contemporary drawing by Ozanne. The reason for this reversal of the usual arrangement is obscure. Perhaps the greater spread of the mainyard did not require the extending effect of a yard at the outer end of the studdingsail, and a main lower studdingsail would almost always be set when the course was taken in, and perhaps the placing of the yard at the inner side was in some way related to this. At all events, later French practice followed the more conventional plan.

The halliards. The outer halliards led through a block at the outer end of the topmast studdingsail boom, up through a block secured to a pendant fast to the topmast head, thence down through the lubber's hole, to deck. This lead gave upward support to the boom end. The inner halliards, which sometimes doubled as the clew-jigger, led up to a leading block under the top. This lead meant that the sail could be shifted bodily sideways, to get it over the bulwarks when taking it in, but it gave less effective upward support. To compensate for this deficiency, sometimes a sort of third halliard was rigged to haul up the inner end of the studdingsail yard, once the sail was set (Hildebrandt,174). Von Sterneck (240) led both inner and outer halliards through a double block, on a pendant from the topmast head. The inner halliards were taken through the after sheave.

Tack, clewline and sheets. The tack, or outhauler, led through a block at the boom end, and aft through a leading block near the gangway. Sometimes this latter was a double block, the other sheave of which accommodated the fore sheet (Pilaar, 269). To get the sail under control, when taking it in, a 'clew-line' or 'tripping line' led from the tack, through a bull's eye secured near the mid-point of the body of the sail, up through a block at the inner end of the yard, and thence in towards the mast. Boström (Tab XLII) has the yard block at the middle of the yard. According to Frick (192), the clewline could be forward or abaft the sail: it got a better grip on the canvas if led before, but also was more liable to cause chafe, and for this reason, it

was more usually abaft all. In the Royal Danish Navy, the clewline was called a *nedhaler*, 'downhaul', by analogy with the downhaul of the topmast studdingsails. Of course, it actually hauled the tack upwards.

There were two sheets, one leading through a tail block on the boom or some point nearby, and in through a gunport, while the other led over the nettings, and was only used when getting the sail in. Lescallier (II, 37) fits bowlines, but I do not believe they were widely used.

Reefing lower studdingsails. Steel shows a reef-band parallel to the head of the main, but not the fore lower studdingsail. In fact this type of reef does not seem to have been much used. A century later, Knight illustr-

Lower studdingsails
A Lower studdingsail and its gear:
    a outer halliard; **b** inner halliard; **c** tack; **d** sheet; **e** deck sheet; **f** clewline.
B Detail of studdingsail yard; **C** old French lower studdingsail yard; **D** late eighteenth century lower studdingsail fitted for reefing; **E** lower studdingsail fitted for a rolling reef (after Knight); **F** French lower studdingsail with jackyard (after Bonnefoux & Paris); **G** common jackyard; **H** different methods of bending studdingsail halliards to yard.

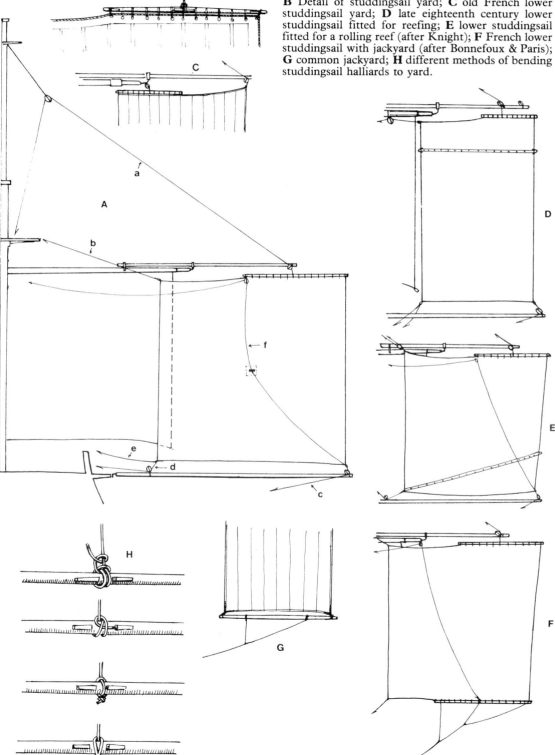

ates a 'rolling reef', running obliquely from the inner clew to one-quarter the height of the outer leech. Taking this reef, allowed the boom to be topped up, if the vessel were rolling heavily. Although the occasional splash in the sea did no harm, there was the likelihood, in the event of a solid 'dig in' of the boom end, that the forward guy would go, and even that the boom would be snapped.

By keeping halliards and sheet fast, veering the tack and hauling in on the clewline, the sail area could be shortened in a rough and ready fashion, reducing the area to an approximately triangular shape, and allowing the boom to be topped up. In the late 1800s, many merchantmen favoured a triangular lower studdingsail, with the lower leech cut in a convex roach, so it would set better. This plan greatly simplified the manner in which the sail was handled.

Lower studdingsail jackyard. Another plan was to lace a light spar or 'jackyard' to the foot of the sail. Costé (188) says this should be two-thirds the length of the foot. This item, which was called a *drijver* by the Dutch, did away with the necessity for a boom, and all its accompanying complications. While it was a handy enough arrangement, it had the disadvantage that it did not work very well with a lee lower studdingsail (Baudin, 272). A bridle led aft, and replaced the tack. Alston (192) mentions setting the sail 'flying', dispensing with the bridle, and simply hanging a deep-sea lead from the outer clew; but he admits that this 'answers imperfectly'.

The jackyard had to be supported in setting and taking in the sail. This was accomplished by a 'tripping line' or *lève-nez* as the French called it, which led from the middle of the jackyard up through a block on the studdingsail yard.

The topmast studdingsail. Like the lower studdingsail, it was made of Number 4 or 5 canvas. The head was secured to the topmast studdingsail yard, and the halliards were usually bent about one-third the length from the inner yardarm, although some authors differ in bending the halliards at the centre of the yard (Costé, 190). The halliards were secured with a studdingsail halliard bend, a fisherman's bend, or a special type of strop. The main thing was to get the yard tight up against the jewel block, with as little drift as possible between them. The halliards led up through the jewel block to a leading block at the topmast head, and thence down to deck. There was a difference of opinion as to whether the best lead was in front of, or behind, the topsail yardarm. The problem was the perennial risk of chafe. Since the

studdingsail yard would mostly be abaft the leech of the topsail, the best arrangement would be to take the halliards abaft the topsail yard also. The opposing school of thought argued that, since the sail bellied forward, when it was actually set, the logical way to lead the halliards was forward of the topsail yard.

The tack led through a block, perched at the end of the topmast studdingsail boom, thence aft to a block secured to the foremost main shroud. There were two sheets, one of which led through a block or bull's eye on the

Topmast and topgallant studdingsails
A Topmast and topgallant studdingsails and their gear: **a** halliard; **b** tack; **c** sheet ('short sheet' on topmast studdingsail); **d** long sheet; **e** downhaul.
B Method of setting topgallant studdingsail without studdingsail boom; **C** detail of inner studdingsail boom iron, or quarter iron; **D** detail of outer studdingsail boom iron; **E** detail of heel lashing, boom run in; **F** detail of heel lashing, boom run out; **G** detail of quarter strop, used in place of inner boom iron for light studdingsail booms; **H** detail of heel-rope, used to run out light booms; **I** detail of boom jigger; **J** boom jigger in use as tricing tackle.

yard, and the other led directly to deck to assist in taking the sail in. In English vessels, the downhaul started at the outer yardarm, through a bull's eye on the outer leech, and then through a block fast to the tack, thence to deck. We will enlarge on this a little later. There was very commonly a reef, at a distance from the head corresponding to the depth of the first reef of the topsail. Pilaar (270) is alone in mentioning two reefs. The purpose was to admit of its being set to weather of a single reefed topsail. Lescallier (II, 37) and Baudin (270) say it was sometimes fitted with a bowline. An especially large topmast studdingsail with its foot extended by a jackyard, is mentioned by Alston (190), but I have no confirmation of this.

Topgallant studdingsail. This was made of Number 6 or 7 canvas, and was of similar trapezoidal shape to the topmast studdingsail. The halliards were secured to the yard, and led up through a block at the topgallant masthead and down to the top, in a manner analogous to the topmast studdingsail halliards. The tack led through a block at the end of the topgallant studdingsail boom, and from there to the after part of the top. Another method, in smaller vessels, dispensed with the topgallant studdingsail boom altogether. The tack, before leading to the top, led through a bull's eye at the outer end of the topmast studdingsail yard, which in turn, was steadied by securing its inner end to the topsail yardarm with a yardarm gasket. Royal studdingsails, when set, were rigged in a similar fashion.

OTHER GEAR USED WITH STUDDINGSAILS

Lower boom or swinging boom. This hooked to the forward end of the channel, and when not in use, swung back along the channel edge and was secured in a metal crane on the ship's side. Pictures of later men-of-war show the boom stowed in this way. However, I have some difficulty visualising just how it would have worked in a First Rate of an earlier day, such as *Victory*. In the first place, a 56-foot boom would have extended well abaft the after end of the channel; secondly, the stock of the sheet anchor would have prevented it being swung in against the channel. Perhaps it was dropped inside this, or perhaps some completely different arrangement was used.

Tangon and back-spira. The English men-of-war, prior to 1745, had the channels set on the hull a full deck lower than was the case later on. Because of this, and the compli-

cation of the sheet anchor, it seems certain that the boom was hooked somewhere else on the hull, or that some other method was used. For example, a boom could have been cantilevered out from the forecastle. While I have no confirmation that this was practised in English ships, it was used elsewhere. Romme's inventory (*L'Art de la Mâture* 82) of the spars of a French man-of-war of 1778, lists and illustrates a hooked boom for the main lower studdingsail (*arcboutant ferré*) and a *tangon* for the fore lower studdingsail. This was a spar, about the same length as the fore topsail yard, tapered at both ends, and of somewhat less diameter than the *arcboutant ferré*. In use, it was rigged out to one side of the forecastle, its inner end being confined by a tackle hooked to the foot of the foremast. Dexter Dennis (*Mariner's Mirror* 52, 1966, 223) felt that the term *tangon* retained this very specific meaning, but in fact later on it was generally applied to the swinging boom. The same sort of thing applies to the Swedish word *back-spira*, 'forecastle-boom'. Rosvall (249) says that a *bom*, 'boom', hooked to the cathead could be used instead of a *back-spira*. This strongly suggests that the latter worked in the same way as the French *tangon*. Later on, *back-spira*, and its equivalent in other languages, was often used to describe a swinging boom. Arguing against its use in English ships, is its absence from the most detailed inventories such as those found in Steel, who carefully catalogues even such things as fire-booms (spars intended to fend off fireships).

Guys and topping lift. These were secured about two-thirds the length of the boom from the ship's side. The topping lift led through a block on a pendant from the masthead, and back to the deck. It supported the weight of the boom, when it was being got in and out. The after guy led back to a block near the gangway. Sometimes this was a treble block, through which led foresheet, lower studdingsail tack, and guy. The forward guy usually led to the bowsprit cap. Various expedients were used to initiate the outward swing of the boom from its stowed position, at which time the forward guy had no leverage. Murphy (50) says that British ships led the topping lift through a bull's eye well out on the yard, and then up to the masthead. He did not think that this was a particularly good idea, and I have no other confirmation of this method. Earlier, Pihlström (251) used the yard tackle, but this would have been a clumsy arrangement. A handy solution was to use a 'lizard'. A line, spliced round a thimble which ran freely on the topping lift, could be taken out to the yardarm and temporarily secured so

that the topping lift exerted a pull in an outward, as well as an upward direction. Some seamen liked to lead the fore guy to the spritsail yard, to achieve the same object.

As the ship rolled to weather, the boom tended to 'unweight', rising and then dropping back with a heavy thump, and so a martingale was sometimes rigged to obviate this (Lever, 81), while others preferred to hang a heavy sandbag on the boom (Hourigan, 53). At anchor, the boom was swung out, and the ship's boats rode to it. For this purpose, it was often hooked lower down, on the wales, to give a more comfortable lead to the boat painters. Costé (189) rigs a boom brace, but this was unusual.

Topmast studdingsail boom. Although on small models, these look like toothpicks, in fact in a First Rate, like *Victory*, they were more like telephone poles, about 51 feet on the main, and 45 feet on the foreyard. They were half as long as their respective yards, and three-fifths of their length projected, when they were run out (Mossel, II, 334). They lay parallel to, somewhat forward and above the yard, so that they were not in the way of men casting off the gaskets, in making sail. To furl, or reef, they could be 'triced up' out of the way.

Contemporary Dutch models of the late 1600s show the booms abaft the yards. In fact, when set to weather, the studdingsails should be abaft the principal sail, so this arrangement is quite logical. This was the era when seamen aloft, lay on, stood on, or sat astride the yard, to do their work. Once footropes were introduced, and the men stood on these, leaning against and over the after side of the yard, the booms had to be moved out of their way. In the third quarter of the nineteenth century, merchantmen experimented with rigging the topmast studdingsail booms under the yard; this plan was followed in *Cutty Sark*, for example. It was an attempt to simplify matters by eliminating the necessity for tricing the booms up. Contemporary opinion was not totally comfortable with this innovation. Murphy (50) says that the booms gave a clumsy look to the yards when in port, and chafed the topsail sheets at sea. Furthermore, passing a heel lashing was more difficult than with the traditional plan.

Studdingsail boom irons. These were the iron hoops on the yards, through which the booms slid. The outer boom iron extended as a gooseneck, or crank, beyond the yardarm. It supported a hoop which incorporated a *lignum vitae* roller on its lower aspect. Murphy (50) refers to it as the 'Pacific iron' in 1849, but this term does not appear to have become popular in the Royal Navy. The

Lower studdingsail boom gear
a topping lift; **b** alternate lead of topping lift through lizard (**c**) when swinging out boom; **d** forward guy; **e** after guy; **f** martingale.

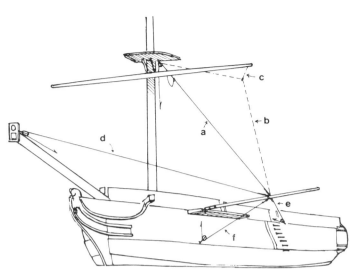

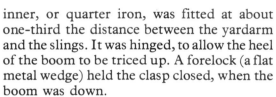

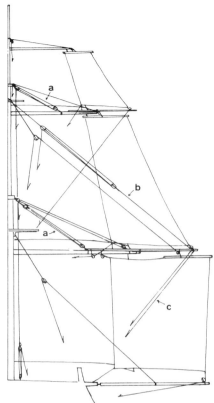

Preventer lifts and boom brace
a burtons rigged as preventer lifts; **b** topmast boom topping lift; **c** boom brace.

inner, or quarter iron, was fitted at about one-third the distance between the yardarm and the slings. It was hinged, to allow the heel of the boom to be triced up. A forelock (a flat metal wedge) held the clasp closed, when the boom was down.

Boom jigger and tricing tackle. To rig the boom out, a tackle was hooked between the heel of the boom and the strap of the inner iron. To run it in again, the block was unhooked from the inner iron and shifted to some convenient point near the slings of the yard. The boom was sometimes 'jumped' in, at the same time as the topmast studdingsail came in. The pull of the tack aided the manoeuvre, and, occasionally, only the hauling part of the tackle was hitched to the boom-heel, the power of the tackle itself being unnecessary. One block of the tricing tackle hooked or toggled underneath the top, and the other hitched to the heel, in such a way that the heel was pulled up under the top when the boom was triced up. There were many variations in the methods of rigging the 'in-and-out jigger', and tricing tackle, but it will be apparent that one tackle could suffice for both jobs. By leading the hauling end through a tail block, or bull's eye, seized to the foremost shroud, at the level of the catharpins, or on the after side of the yard, a fair lead was presented for all three functions.

Heel lashing. Burney (98) describes a short and a long lashing. The first was spliced into an eyebolt in the heel, and secured to the jackstay, when the boom was run in. The long heel lashing had an eye spliced in one end, and beside this a large stopper knot. The other end was led through a hole in the boom about a foot from the end. The stopper knot

prevented the eye slipping through. When the boom was run out, the lashing went round the quarter iron and through the eye, two or three times, to keep the boom from running in. Then two or three frapping turns were taken round boom and jackstay to hold the heel down.

Boom brace. Although the tack of the topmast studdingsail led aft, and thus counteracted the forward pull of the sail on the topmast studdingsail boom, a boombrace was often fitted to supplement this. Both ropes led through a block secured to the foremost main shroud, about ten feet above the nettings. The tail of this block was hitched round the first two or three shrouds, to distribute the pull evenly.

Burtons, preventer-lift and lift-jigger. When studdingsails were set, there was a tremendously increased strain on the yards. Top-burtons were rigged in various ways to counteract this, sometimes to the topmast studdingsail boom, frequently to the lower yard, in which case it was called a 'preventer-lift'. Lift-jiggers were tackles clapped on the topsail yard lifts to get them up bar taut.

Topgallant studdingsail booms. These were fitted in a similar, albeit simpler, fashion. Since they were rather smaller, boom-jiggers were not always used, the booms being rigged in and out by main force.

They were triced up by lines, led from the heel of the boom through a leading block at the crosstrees, and down to the top, where they were manned. Unlike the lower yard, the topsail yard might be at masthead, or down on the cap, when the boom required to be triced up. In harbour, the tricing line led through a bull's eye seized to the foremost topmast shroud at the appropriate height, or the tricing line was led in the usual way to the crosstrees, and a 'boom-back' led through a bull's eye, similar to the above, to pull the boom firmly back against the shrouds.

The outer iron was similar to that on the lower yard, although frequently without a roller. Sometimes the inner one was replaced by a strop, a simple wooden saddle, or a becket and toggle, hitching to the jackstay (Murphy 50).

Heel lashing. Dana (51) takes the lashing back over and behind the yard, pushing a bight up between the yard and the headrope. The end was brought back under the yard through the bight and hauled taut, repeating if necessary. The end was expended around the turns between the yard and the boom. Burney (99) takes the heel lashing through a quarter-strop, then through a strop on the heel of the boom two or three times to hold the boom out, then takes turns around the boom and jackstay to hold it down. When the boom was rigged in, the lashing hung down before the topsail. When the sail was furled, it was passed under the sail, and over the boom to keep the latter down snug.

Surprising as it may seem, from time to time a boom was not properly secured, and as a result rolled right out of its irons and overboard. This was particularly liable to occur after a vessel had been in harbour, and then proceeded to sea, without checking to see that the booms were secure.

Royal studdingsail booms. As we have mentioned, booms were not always used, but if they were in fact employed, they were kept in the top, and taken out on the topgallant yard, when required.

TERMINOLOGY, ENGLISH AND OTHERWISE

Although the word is invariably pronounced 'stuns'l', and hence there is great variability in spelling, we have chosen to use here the standard form 'studdingsail'. Kinship of the word to the Dutch word *stoten* ('to push or nudge') or to the root of the Swedish word *stot*, *stötta* ('a prop or buttress') has been suggested and certainly the early forms of the word, 'stotynge' and so on, would fit. Others, influenced by the spoken form, have suggested a link with the Old French or Norman word *estouin*, which had the same meaning as modern French *étui*, a 'case'. They were, in fact, sometimes called *bonnettes en étui*, that is to say 'studdingsails in cases' (*Mariner's Mirror* 6, 284; 16, 481). In days gone by, they were also known as steering sails, steadying sails, stern sails, storm sails, scudding sails, chase sails and case sails. (Sandahl III, 102)

They had an interesting variety of names in other tongues also. The Dutch called them *lij-zeilen* ('lee-sails'), which is mildly surprising since they were most useful to set to weather. This word was also adopted into Swedish, Danish and German. *Der ge-öffnete See-hafen* also uses the term *Fledermäuse* ('bats') and perhaps the same thought suggested the Spanish term *alas* ('wings'). In passing, we note that to this day, schooner sailors talk about 'winging out' the gaffsails, when they are spread on either side, running before the wind. Boteler (169), describing how a mizzen was boomed out to the side when running says 'and this sail, thus fitted, is termed a goosewing; and sometimes a studdingsail'. The French used *bonnette maillée* ('laced on bonnet') to identify a bonnet under a course, but *bonnette* from 1700 on or so meant simply 'studdingsail'. The Italians had different words for upper and lower studdingsails: the topmast studdingsail and topgallant studdingsail were *cottelazzi* ('cutlasses'), while the lower studdingsail was poetically and beautifully named *scopamare*, 'broom of the sea'. Winshooten in 1681 (139, 349) lists both a *lij-zeil* and a *water-zeil*, and I wonder if 'water sail' may not have been an old Dutch term for lower studdingsail. I think there is some support for this since the Dutch word for the tack of the lower studdingsail was *water-schoot*, 'water-sheet'. Furthermore, the Swedish term for the lower boom, *vater-bom*, clearly is also of Dutch origin and suggests that, although the later Dutch authors do not use this word, it may have been an earlier name for the lower boom in Holland. There is also an indication that 'water sail' was not unknown in English. Romme's *Dictionnaire de le Marine Française* (82) offers the following under the entry for water sails: '*Un Vaisseau a-t-il ses bonnettes basses deployées? On dit qu'il court sous ses bonnettes basses.* In later days, 'water sail' was applied to something quite different, and we will return to this later.

The boom was named for the sail whose foot it spread, that is to say for the sail above it. This is the reason why the Royal Navy, to this day, refer to the boat boom used in harbour as the 'lower boom'. The topgallant studdingsail boom is actually found on the topsail yard, and it will be noted that the lower studdingsail alone is suspended from a boom, the upper studdingsails depend from the yardarms.

We have already alluded to the fact that *tangon* in French, *Back-spier*, in German, etc, originally applied to a boom cantilevered out from the forecastle. Both terms are subsequently used to describe an ordinary swinging boom. The first element of the Danish word *slaeberbom* is the term for a boat's painter, and so may derive from the use to which the lower boom is put in harbour.

In Britain, the outer lower corners of all studdingsails were referred to as 'tacks', but Hourigan follows the American preference for 'outer clew' and 'outhauler' in the case of the lower sail. Dutch, Danish, and German usually refer to the 'inner' and 'outer sheet', although some German authors follow English custom and use *Hals* ('tack') synonymously with 'outer sheet'. As mentioned earlier, a term literally meaning 'water-sheet' is used for the tack of the lower studdingsail in these languages. The early Swedish writers like Sjöbohm follow Dutch practice but for some reason the later ones like Ekelöf and Frick use *hals* ('tack') for 'sheet', and *skot* ('sheet') for 'tack' exactly the opposite to English usage. Frick does designate the tack of the lower studdingsail 'outer sheet'.

The usual technical term for a studdingsail halliard block is 'jewel block'. Although Willaumez in 1831 gives *pendant d'oreille* ('earing'), with the same technical meaning, and Pilaar (269) and Mossel (II, 378) give *oreilje-blok* and *orliët-blok*, these seem to have originated later than the English term. *Orliët-blok* in fact, was originally used to designate a double block below the crosstrees, through which the topsail lifts and topgallant sheets were led. The earlier Dutch equivalent of 'jewel block' was simply *lij-zeils val-blok*, 'studdingsail halliard block'.

Other studdingsails. The 'driver', or 'ringtail', was analogous to a studdingsail. It was used to extend the area of the mizzen in the late 1700s and early 1800s, but gradually dropped out of use as the mizzen became larger, adopting the name 'spanker' or 'driver' in the process. The Dutch called it the *broodwinner*, 'bread-winner'. The German and French terms recognised its resemblance to a studdingsail, calling it *Gaffel-lee-segel* and *bonnette d'artimon*, respectively. A short yard extended its head in line with the gaff. The foot was secured in various ways below – to a boom, an outrigger over the stern, and sometimes one over the

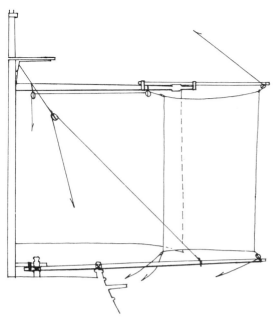

Forecastle boom: *tangon* or *back-spira*.

quarter. It usually had a bowline, and is occasionally represented set, with the mizzen furled (Forfait, Figure 12; Röding, Figure 101). Another short-lived example was the 'water sail', which was found at the same period as the ringtail. It had a short yard which was hauled out to the end of the mizzen boom, the sail setting to leeward and level with the boom, looking like an upper studdingsail on its side. Totten mentions a 'save-all', set under the swinging boom, its clews held down by weights. There are a couple of intriguing references to 'outer' topmast and lower studdingsails, with their own yards, but spread by the same booms. Mossel (II, 334) refers to 'outer topmast studdingsails', *buiten lijzeilen*, but says only that, like royal studdingsails, they were rarely found. A watercolour by Huggins of the East Indiaman *Essex*, shows both outer topmast and lower studdingsails, but the general belief is that these were just a little joke on the artist's part (MacGregor, *Merchant Sailing Ships*, 194; *Mariner's Mirror* 1, 1911, 190, 219, 221, 250; 3, 1914, 318).

SETTING STUDDINGSAILS

Preparations, preventer lifts and lift-jiggers. Prior to setting studdingsails, it was important that the principal sails be trimmed to the best advantage, and everything set up properly. If a lee lower studdingsail was to be set, it was particularly important that everything be perfectly square if the sail were to set properly.

The lower lifts, braces and trusses were hauled as taut as possible. The topgallant

Details of toggle, or squilgee (A) and lizard and slip knot (**B**) used to confine sail while running it aloft.

Other studdingsails. Huggins' *Essex* picture, said to have been painted to amuse his children, shows a scarcely credible variety of kites, including inner and outer lower and topmast studdingsails, royal studdingsails, ringtails, watersail, spritsail topgallant sail, and jib topsail.

clewlines were also set up tight, to give the man on the topsail yardarm an extra handhold. Because of the greatly increased strain on the yards, it was particularly important that these have upward support. In the case of the lower, and sometimes the topsail yard, 'preventer lifts' were rigged. A top-burton hooked to the topmast or topgallant mastcap above, and below to a strop on the yard. A burton was sometimes used to support the topmast studdingsail boom in a similar fashion. 'Lift-jiggers', for the topsail and topgallant lifts, were tackles clapped on the lift a few feet above the nettings, and hooked to a suitable eyebolt on deck. Hauling down on these, set the lift up extra taut.

From about 1870, men-of-war put seizings on the upper lifts in the top, so that they acted like standing lifts; that is to say, the lifts were only taut when the yard was down on the cap for reefing or furling, otherwise they hung in a bight below the yard, and invariably abaft it in merchantmen. It seems, however, that men-of-war often threw them forward of the sail, and indeed this can be seen in some old photographs. This must infallibly have been associated with chafing of the sail, but it is said this was done to ensure the safety of men working on the yard, should the tie break. In that event, a bight hanging abaft the yard would snap taut, as the yard crashed down, perhaps flinging a man off the footropes, as though propelled by a giant sling-shot. The later German authors refer to cutting the lift

seizings before putting on the jiggers, and re-applying them afterwards.

Rotten stops, squilgees and toggles. Setting a studdingsail was in some ways analogous to the exercise of sending up a spinnaker in 'rotten stops' – pieces of yarn strong enough to hold the sail bundled up as it goes aloft, but sufficiently frail that they will easily be broken by a good tug, at the appropriate moment. Rope yarns, sometimes half cut through first, could be used to confine the topmast studdingsail, until it was clear of the lower brace and yard, whereupon the yarns were cut by the topsail sheet man, or in a fresh breeze, the partly sectioned yarn stop could be snapped by jerking the halliards.

Glascock (49) says, 'to dispense with stops below, and knives aloft, sennit or nettle ties should be attached to the studdingsail yard'. These would nonetheless have to be cast off by the man on the yard. Glascock (49) and Brady (144) describe and illustrate the use of a lizard hitched around the sail and yard and secured with a slip knot. Bréart (178) mentions short gaskets, with eyes at each end, seized to the yard at their mid-points. A slip rope was run through the eyes, to confine the sail, and when this was pulled out, the sail fell free.

Another plan used beckets on the yard, similar to those described by Bréart, but they were secured by a wooden toggle, with a lanyard leading to the deck. The toggle was jerked free upon the order 'Out toggle!' or 'Out squilgee!'. Why the US Navy called the 'toggle' a 'squilgee' is not totally clear. It is a variant of 'squeegee', and also referred to a short broom handle with either a mop or a crosspiece fitted with a rubber strip. Others

considered using a sliprope ' a lubberly procedure'. (*Mariner's Mirror* 37, 1951, 244).

The downhauls of the lower and topmast studdingsails were used to gather the sail up, when taking it in, and could also be used in an analogous fashion when setting it. This plan was widely followed, often in association with stops or toggles. Dana (52) hauls the downhaul taut, and makes a double catspaw below the tackblock, slipping the bight of the hauling part through the loops of the catspaw. Hildebrandt coils up a few loops below the block, and takes three or four turns round these, shoving the bight through the loops at one end, much in the way a sea-gasket was made up. In either case, a tug caused everything to fall clear. Hourigan (47, 52), on the other hand, damns this practice, preferring to keep the bights of the downhaul quite slack; otherwise, he says, when the halliards are run up, the downhaul will jam at the tackblock, or the leech bull's eye. It can be imagined that such variation of opinion was common, since this whole business offered so much scope for improvisation and for exercising the ideas of the individual officer.

Setting a fore topmast studdingsail. This sail, set to weather, was the single most useful studdingsail and we will therefore discuss it first. To set it, the sail was hoisted part way, the tack was hauled on, and 'boom-ended', and only subsequently were the halliards got chock up. The trick was to get the sail high enough that it did not have to be wrestled across the lower brace, but not so high that it was difficult to get the tack fully out.

The boom was run out by the boom-jigger. It was essential to have the topmast studdingsail tack, and the lower studdingsail halliards, led through their respective blocks first, since this could not be done once the boom was run out. We have already described how the tack and halliards were led. At this point, the hitching ends had to be thrown down on deck. In both cases, this meant that they would come down inside the lower brace, if the sail were to be sent up abaft all. The sail could be set from before, or abaft all, and although Schneider (153) and Pihlström (247) say it could be set from the top, setting from the deck was both more usual, and more convenient.

Setting abaft all. The sail was got ready on deck, sheets and downhauls cleared away and the tack and halliards bent on. About one-fifth the distance from the outer yardarm, a stop or toggle strop gathered up the halliards, sail and yard. The remainder of the sail was secured with yarns, slip ropes, or whatever. The sail was run up by the halliards, taking in the slack of the tack. A man stood about amidships, letting the downhaul and sheet run through his hands, to prevent the sail twisting as it went up (Hildebrandt, 174). When the bundle was up above the lower yard, and clear of the lower brace, the tack could be brought into effect. The hand on the lower yard cut the stops, or the lanyard was used to jerk the toggle clear, and the sail deployed. The inner leech was gripped by the topsail sheet man, and the sail kept abaft the leech of the topsail and reef-tackle. If this last were hauled taut as the sail ascended, it helped prevent the yard flying forward of the topsail. Once the sail was established, the reef-tackle was once again slacked off to prevent chafing. The inner yardarm of the studdingsail was thus behind the topsail leech, and just below the topsail yard.

Although, as mentioned earlier, the idea was to avoid backwinding the topsail, some seamen nonetheless set the studdingsail clew before that of the topsail, although keeping the yard abaft it. The sails had to be cut, the booms run out, and the halliards bent to the studdingsail yards, to a nicety, if the inner leech of the studdingsail and the weather leech of the topsail were not to saw against each other. In practice, the sails bellied forward, so the leeches were curved rather than straight. Others, such as Bréart (270), preferred to keep everything abaft the topsail, but one advantage of taking the clew forward, was that the topmast studdingsail was then ready to be taken in forward of all.

The manner in which sheets and downhaul were led was determined by the way the sail was to be taken in. If this was to be done forward, the downhaul and long sheet were 'dipped forward'; that is to say, taken forward up over the clew of the topsail, and thrown down to the deck forward of the foresail, where they were made fast. If the sail was taken in abaft all, downhaul and long sheet were made fast on deck aft, being tended as the sail went up. The 'long' or 'deck sheet', was thus essentially another downhaul. Once the sail was set, the topsail sheet man took the 'short' or 'yard sheet' forward or abaft the clew of the topsail, depending on how the inner clew of the studdingsail stood relative to that of the topsail. The sheet passed through a leading block on the yard, and in to the top where it was made fast. The inner clew was thus controlled by the short sheet, when the sail was actually established. The long sheet took over this function when the sail was being sent up, or taken in.

The sail could readily be taken in aft, if the wind was light (Mossel, III, 104; Ekelöf, 62), but the majority of authorities opt for setting abaft, taking in forward (Ulffers, 316; Groeneijk, 20; Krogh, 36; Grenfell, 114).
Setting forward of all. There is a very clear account of one method of managing this by R Curtis Brown in the *Nautical Magazine* (September 1916, 199), which represents

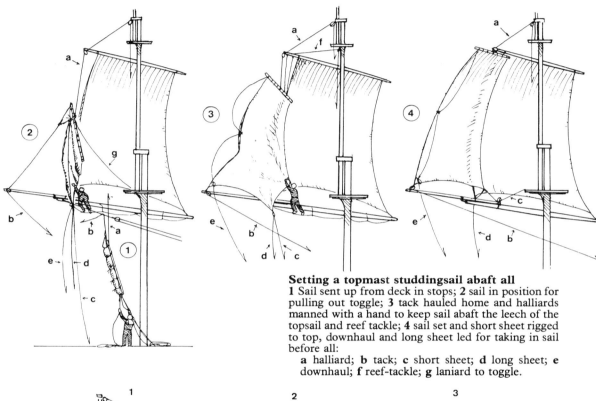

Setting a topmast studdingsail abaft all
1 Sail sent up from deck in stops; 2 sail in position for pulling out toggle; 3 tack hauled home and halliards manned with a hand to keep sail abaft the leech of the topsail and reef tackle; 4 sail set and short sheet rigged to top, downhaul and long sheet led for taking in sail before all:
  a halliard; **b** tack; **c** short sheet; **d** long sheet; **e** downhaul; **f** reef-tackle; **g** laniard to toggle.

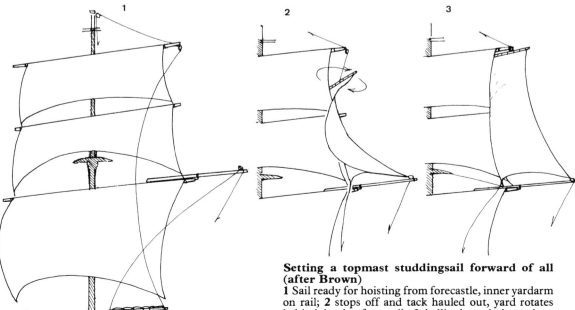

Setting a topmast studdingsail forward of all (after Brown)
1 Sail ready for hoisting from forecastle, inner yardarm on rail; 2 stops off and tack hauled out, yard rotates behind leech of topsail; 3 halliards and short sheet hauled home.

latter-day merchant service custom. The sail was got ready on the forecastle, with the inner yardarm, which was 'much longer than the other', placed on the rail. The sail, thus ascended twisted through 180 degrees. The tack was got out and the halliards up, as before. At the moment the stops broke, the inner yardarm pivoted around the weather leech of the topsail, coming to rest behind it. The sheets and downhaul were handled as already mentioned. Although not actually specified, I am fairly sure Brown is describing a method very suitable for split topsails, where there would be no top bowline to complicate matters forward, and a lower topsail brace to contend with, if the sail were sent up from aft.

Dana (52), Kloo (10), Hansen (III), Schneider (153) and Rosvall (48), all mention setting the sail from forward. Hildebrandt (177) comments that this method was used in the merchant service, but not in the Navy. Of the above, only Hansen implies that the sail is sent up with a twist in it. Dana mentions using this particular trick with a topgallant studdingsail, and we will return to this point later.

Bourdé de Villehuet (174) gives a unique account of a triangular topmast studdingsail set forward. A downhaul leads from the head of the sail to a block near the centre of the lower yard, at the same distance from the yardarm as the length of the outer leech of the studdingsail. To take it in, the tack is kept fast, the halliards slacked off, and the downhaul brings the head of the sail to the lower yard, to which it is made fast with yarns.

Taking in a topmast studdingsail. The downhaul and deck sheet were led through snatch blocks, and used to get the sail down, while tack and halliards were tended. Initially, the short sheet was tended also to prevent the sail being blown too far to leeward. With a well drilled crew, it was possible to get the sail down, and 'jump' the boom in, at the same time, or the boom could be rigged in subsequently. The tack was started, 'to settle the tackblock to its work', as Boyd puts it, then the halliards slacked off. If the tack jammed, the boom was instantly got in, to prevent damage to the irons (Boyd, 395). By slacking the halliards, keeping the tack fast, and pulling the downhaul, the sail was spilled, as its head was pulled down to the tackblock. Finally the tack was let go, and everything hauled down on deck. As already mentioned, it was usually got down forward, and if difficulty was encountered in doing this, a touch of the helm could cast the sail further into the lee of the topsail and foresail, and facilitate the task.

If it were not intended to reset the sail shortly, the gear was unrove, and coiled up in the top, or seized to the futtock shrouds. The downhaul and sheets were made up with the sail. The tack and halliards were frequently left rove, coiled up at the yardarms, or the halliards were hitched to the topgallant clew, and both parts of the tack stopped in along the lower yard, in to the top, and down the shroud. A bight was left slack at the slings of the yard, so there would be no interference when the yard was braced up (Hansen, 107). The sail was rolled up, and becketted up and down, inside the fore shrouds.

Tack, boom brace and martingale. When the lower studdingsail was set, it helped resist the upward pull of the topmast studdingsail tack on the boom end. In its absence, a martingale or 'jumper' was extemporised, using the outer halliards of the lower studdingsail. A toggle was secured with a marlinspike hitch, or something similar, to the hauling end of the lower halliards. By hauling on the hitching end, this toggle was run out to the halliard block where it jammed. The halliards were made fast below and abreast the upper boom, to act as a holddown.

A double block, seized to the foremost two or three main shrouds, accommodated the topmast studdingsail boom brace and tack, which led aft, and were worked together. When the yard was braced in, they had to be hauled, and when it was braced up, they needed to be checked. In practice, this was

not quite as simple as it sounds. The difficulty lay in the fact that the tack, if slacked, would allow the boom end to go forward, only if the outer clew of the topmast studdingsail did not, in turn, pull away from the tackblock. Once this happened, it might be difficult to get the tack down again, without putting an undue strain on the boom. It will be remembered that the rule in setting an upper studdingsail was to get the tack out first, and the halliards taut only secondly. To obviate the problem, many seamen preferred to rely entirely on the boom brace for support in an after direction, and led the tack in along the yard, where it did not need to be touched, in bracing in, or up.

Dipping a topmast studdingsail. As mentioned earlier, when set on the weather side, the studdingsail had to be abaft the principal sail. For similar reasons, if the sail were to be carried to leeward, it had to be 'dipped forward of all', were it not, in turn to be backwinded by the air coming off the lee leech of the topsail. To dip forward, the halliards were slacked well off, until the hands on the lower yard could get hold of the outer leech. They pulled down on this, canting the inner yardarm up, out and forward, shifting it to come on the fore side of the reef-tackle and topsail leech. The halliards were then rehoisted (Alston, 193). Totten (206), on the other hand, advocates pulling down on the inner leech, and certainly this would have been within easier reach. Cradock (22) says this worked best if the breeze were light.

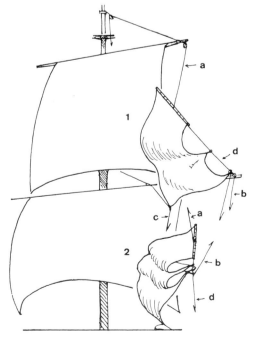

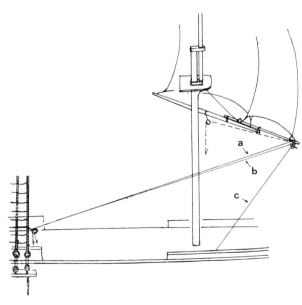

Taking in a topmast studdingsail forward of all
1 Halliards eased and downhaul manned with tack fast; 2 sail pulled down to deck by downhaul and long sheet, slacking tack.

Boom brace and martingale
a tack (alternate lead when boom brace fitted shown by broken line); b boom brace; c martingale.

Others suggest trying both methods (*Officer of the Watch*, 7). One would have thought that the downhaul could also have been used to cant the outer yardarm down.

Boyd (395) says that, in this situation, the wind was liable to spill out of the topsail and keep throwing the inner leech of the studdingsail aft, but by keeping away a little, the helmsman could alleviate this problem. Luce (424) suggests that the sail could be hauled down completely, and then reset before all, first stopping the lee top bowline in along the yard, out of the way. The inner yardarm of a dipped studdingsail was liable to chafe the topsail, and this might indicate the interposition of a hanging mat.

A topmast studdingsail dipped before all, was ready to be taken in forward. The situation was reversed with the topgallant studdingsail, which, if dipped forward, was on the wrong side of the topgallant for getting in. Occasionally, a wind shift to the other quarter, might require that the topmast studdingsail be 'dipped abaft all'. Alston (193) recommends hauling down on the inner leech to achieve this, presumably leaving the clew in a forward position.

Setting a topgallant studdingsail. This was most often done from the top, but sometimes (especially in small merchantmen) from the deck, when it could be sent up forward of all (Hildebrandt, 180; Baudin, 269). The halliards led from the top to the topgallant masthead, thence to the jewel block, from whence the hitching end led in and over the topgallant brace, to the top, where it was bent to the yard. The tack ran from the top, through the tackblock, and down again to be secured to the outer clew of the sail.

A setting stop, or squilgee strap, was placed towards the outer end of the yard, to embrace the sail and halliards, which were run up until the sail was well above the topsail yard. When the lanyard was jerked, the toggle came free, the tack was boom-ended, and the halliards got chock up. The sheet and downhaul were tended in the top as the sail went up. As with setting any upper studdingsail, there was the danger that the sheet might fly loose if not attended, and then everything would have to be lowered so it could be got hold of (Hildebrandt, 173). If the tack parted there was some danger that the men who were rousing the hauling end into the top might tumble off backwards. They were therefore made to sit one behind the other in the top, and haul in this fashion. Everything was belayed in the top, and in the case of the tack and halliards, this was often a matter of hitching them to a suitable topmast shroud,

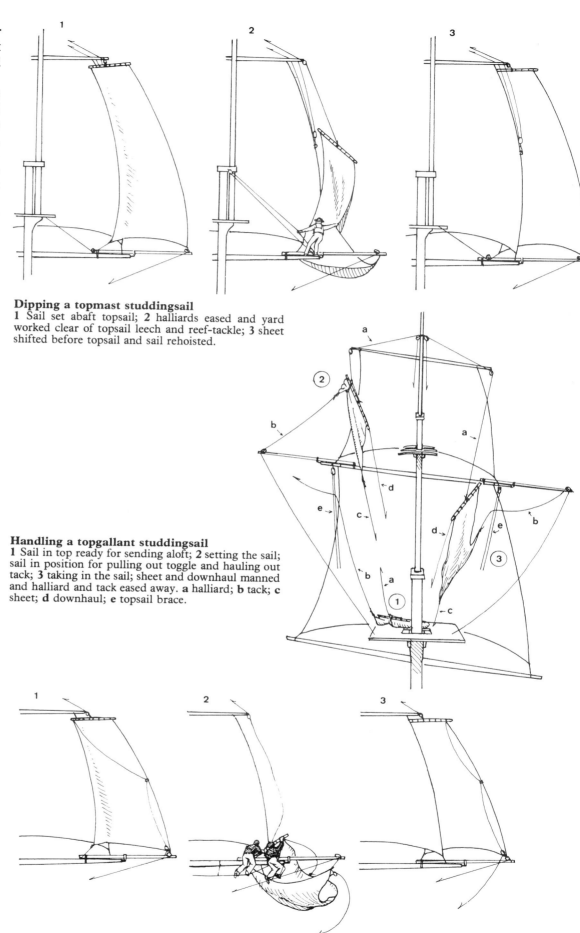

Dipping a topmast studdingsail
1 Sail set abaft topsail; 2 halliards eased and yard worked clear of topsail leech and reef-tackle; 3 sheet shifted before topsail and sail rehoisted.

Handling a topgallant studdingsail
1 Sail in top ready for sending aloft; 2 setting the sail; sail in position for pulling out toggle and hauling out tack; 3 taking in the sail; sheet and downhaul manned and halliard and tack eased away. a halliard; b tack; c sheet; d downhaul; e topsail brace.

Dipping a topgallant studdingsail and changing over the downhaul.

where they were continually coming up, or getting slack, requiring the watch to be continually hauling them taut once more. A cleat seized to the foremost shroud for the halliards, and one nailed to the after part of the top for the tack, remedied this problem (Martelli, 255).

Dipping a topgallant studdingsail. Boyd's (395) comment that 'it is no manner of use to dip a lee fore topgallant studdingsail', arose not only because it was becalmed by the aftersail, but also because, once dipped, it would be that much more difficult to take in. Cradock (23), it is true, says that in these circumstances, it could be handled by passing the sheet and downhaul under the foot of the topgallant sail, and then clawing the studdingsail in over the topsail yard. Certainly, it would be in the lee of the topgallant and topsail, while this was going on, but it does not seem a very elegant way of doing things.

A lee main topgallant studdingsail could be carried with good effect, and Hourigan (52) describes one way of setting it. The yard was capsized in the top, so that the upper part of the sail had a twist in it, the outer yardarm being pulled back and around, so that it now pointed amidships. The halliards were confined by the setting strop towards the end of the inner yardarm, which was now pointing up and out, as the sail was run up above the topsail yard. The toggle was pulled free, the tack got out, and the halliards got up. The inner yardarm pivoted around the leech of the topgallant sail, to come to rest forward of it. The same manoeuvre is described by Murphy (40), and Dana (52).

If already set, the halliards were slacked off and the tack eased, to bring the sail within easy reach of the men on the yard. They transferred the downhaul from the inner to the outer yardarm, from whence it led through a bull's eye on the outer leech, and another at the tack, then to the top. The halliards were then rehoisted and the sail steered up on the forward side of the topgallant.

Taking in a topgallant studdingsail. It was got down into the top by settling the halliards, and veering the tack, so it could be shifted in over the brace block. The sheet and downhaul were hauled into the top and subsequently made up with the sail, which was rolled up, and becketted inside the topmast shrouds. There were various ways of disposing of the tack and halliards. The former could be coiled up and made fast at the topgallant yardarm, or stopped in along the yard and down the foremost topmast shroud, leaving a bight slack to allow the yard to brace up. The halliards could be temporar-

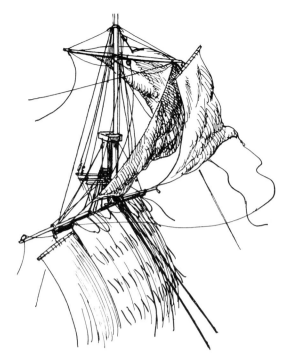

Boyd's topgallant studdingsail carried too long.

ily hitched to the clew of the topgallant sail, or a knot cast in the hitching end, which was then hauled back until it jammed at the block at the crosstrees. Others preferred to unreeve all gear, and coil it away in the top or, in small merchantmen, some other convenient place, such as the longboat (Dana, 52; Hildebrandt 180). The heel lashing was cast off, holding the last turn until the order to rig in, when it was let go, and the boom run in, with the jigger, or by main force, and secured.

Boyd (397) considered a topgallant studdingsail one of the most difficult to take in, if it had been left set too long sailing by the wind:

It is easy for the officer to say 'In royals, haul down!', and to walk the deck as if he had done his share of the work; but ask the men... or get up on the topsail yard, when the studdingsail tack, or halliards, are let go, and you must let go one or the other. The sail flies away to leeward before the topgallant sail, blowing out like a mandarin's streamer, doing all it can, to walk off with the topgallant mast, and bid you goodbye. Then the lee topgallant sheet cannot stand it any longer, and cracks, and the topgallant yard goes fore and aft, and the weather topgallant lift has a jigger on it, and wil not yield. So away goes the whole of it, and it is 'nobody's fault', because the 'right order' was given.

Or else, the weather topgallant brace goes, and we have the same consequences. Or, all the gear holds on, and sail, after an effort, wisps itself round the topmast stay, from whence it is finally cut adrift. The only consolation in the matter is the self-satisfied way with which the epitaph 'Lost overboard by accident', is

written in the log, and the yards of 'number seven', [studdingsails, like royals, were made of Number 7 canvas], which the topmen contrive to save for other than public purposes.

This rousing description explains why the prudent officer got the topgallant studdingsails in, in good time, if he did not wish to contend with a topgallant yard lying fore and aft; in all probability, taking with it, the topgallant stay and mast.

Lead of the downhaul of the upper studdingsails. The English and American sources mostly lead the topmast studdingsail downhaul from the outer yardarm, through a bull's eye about half way down the outer leech, thence through a leading block at the tack, and Boström (Tab XLII) illustrates this method. Costé (192) differs only in offering two bull's eyes on the leech, and Pilaar (270) starts the downhaul from the middle of the yard, but otherwise the same. Many others, however, start the topmast studdingsail downhaul at the *inner* yardarm, over to the bull's eye, and then as before (Kloo, 10; Dana, 52; Frick, 191; Ulffers, Fig. 108; Mossel, II, 383; Sjöbohm, 56).

Frick (191) says that topgallant studdingsails had downhauls, only if they were very large, while Boom (121) and Pilaar (271) say they were not used at all. Luce (422), Murphy (63) and Nares (*Guide*, 65) lead a downhaul from the inner yardarm direct to the top. This had the great merit of simplicity but would not have served if the sail were dipped before the topgallant. Ulffers (figure 112) starts it at the tack, up through a leading

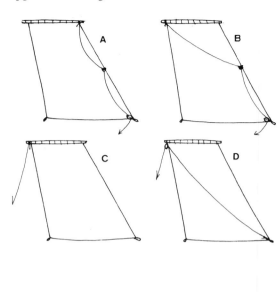

Different leads of upper studdingsail downhauls A or **B** for topmast studdingsails; **B**, **C** or **D** for topgallant studdingsails.

block at the inner yardarm, and down into the top. Frick (191) secures it at the inner yardarm, then through a thimble at the back and thence to the top. I have some misgivings about Alston's (191) lead, from the inner yardarm to a bull's eye on the *inner* leech.

Each method must have had its merits, but I find it a difficult matter to sort out satisfactorily. Having the outer yardarm clew down to the tack would make a neater package to send aloft for setting, and if the halliards and tack were kept fast, while the downhaul was hauled, this would cant the outer yardarm down and allow the inner end of the yard to be dipped. Rigged the other way, the inner yardarm could be canted down to achieve the same result. With the downhaul starting at the inner yardarm, to some extent it would exert a twisting action which might be useful in spilling the sail. Either lead would seem to work, with the sail abaft or forward of the principal sail. Hourigan is the only modern author who makes mention of changing things around before dipping the sail forward.

Since it would seem that different circumstances might well dictate varying the exact lead of the gear, it is surprising to note that, apart from Hourigan, we have to go back to the Swedish accounts of Pihlström (245) and Rosvall (48) to find further reference to this. They state that, with the wind quartering or aft, the topmast studdingsail is set from before. The halliards are secured at the midpoint of the yard or a little inside this. The downhaul leads from the inner yardarm, to the tack, to deck, and is used in hoisting to steer the sail clear of the top bowline, and get the yard abaft the reef-tackle and topsail leech. Conversely, sailing by the wind, the sail is sent up from aft. The halliard is fastened about one-third the way from the inner yardarm. The downhaul is fast now to the *outer* yardarm and is used to manoeuvre the inner yardarm in front of the topsail. A bowline is fitted to the outer leech. It seems to me that there are a couple of pieces missing from the jig-saw puzzle here: for example, if in the second case, they are describing a weather studdingsail, one would expect it to be set *abaft* the topsail. Bending the halliards at two-thirds the way in, would swing the outer yardarm further forward, than if it were made fast at the midpoint. This would also fit better the case of a studdingsail carried abaft the principal sail. A bowline secured to the outer leech, also suggests a weather studdingsail.

Setting a lower studdingsail. As we have mentioned, this was set, for the most part, after the topmast studdingsail, and hence the

topmast studdingsail boom was already rigged out and the outer halliards rove. The boom was swung out, manning the topping lift, lizard and fore guy, tending the after guy; the sail was got ready on deck, and the inner and outer halliards overhauled and bent. As distinct from the upper studdingsails, where the tack was got out first, and then the halliards got up, here the sail was got up and out by the halliards, and the tack got down subsequently. It was an immense sail, of 800-900 square feet in a First Rate and requiring perhaps 50 men on the halliards (Brady, 145). It was kept well up to clear the nettings, in setting and taking in, in effect sliding sideways like a curtain. The only thing it had to avoid fouling, in setting, was the topping lift which, of course, was abaft the sail. The inner leech was always abaft the foresail, and the studdingsail so far as possible was in line with the course. When square, the clew of the foresail was hauled out to the boom with a temporary 'passaree' (Hourigan, 50).

The topping lift was taut, while the sail was being set and taken in, but slackened enough so the outer leech was taut when it was drawing. Similar considerations governed the use of the tripping line, when used with a jackyard. There were two sheets and of these, one, which led over the rail, was used only in getting the sail in; the other was the actual sheet controlling the inner clew and led through a tail block on the boom and in through a gunport. Other descriptions say that one sheet was hauled forward and the other aft.

Taking in a lower studdingsail. To take in this sail the clewline hauled the tack up to the

yard, as tack and outer halliards were tended, and the sail was pulled inwards over the nettings, being dropped down on deck when clear, and made up. Sheets and clewline were made up with the sail which was folded over once, so that it could be rolled up with the yard and stowed against the mast, inside the rigging, or on the booms. If likely to be required again the halliards were stopped in along the yard and down the shroud with the topmast studdingsail tack; otherwise they were unrove.

Studdingsails were sometimes provided with specially made canvas covers, and in fact these were sometimes sewn to the head of the sail (Taunt, 299). 'Centipedes' – lengths of rope with short ties stuck through them – were also used to secure the sails, or else rope yarns.

Boom flying forward. As the yard was braced forward, it was necessary to guy the lower boom forward to an even greater degree, if its end were to remain below that of the topmast studdingsail boom. This meant that the after guy was leading at an increasingly acute, and hence mechanically less efficient angle. Before getting in the lower studdingsail, and losing the after pull of its tack, it was very important to get a good pull on the after guy, so that the boom came more or less square. If this were overlooked, it was possible that the lower boom would swing forward, uncontrollably, when the studdingsail came in. If this happened, one way of dealing with it was to unhook the inner end of the boom, and whip this up with the lower studdingsail halliards. Another method was to take the lower halliards round the boom

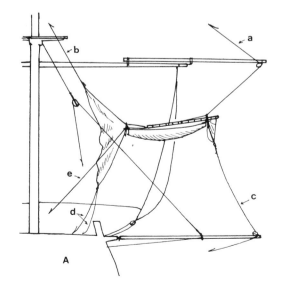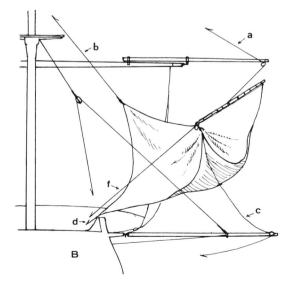

Handling a lower studdingsail
A Setting the sail using beckets and toggles; sail being hauled out; **B** taking in the sail after clewing up:
    a outer halliard; **b** inner halliard; **c** tack; **d** sheets; **e** laniard to toggle; **f** clewline.

1.

2.

3.

1.
HMS *Active* in a quartering wind with topmast studdingsail set on the fore and topgallant studdingsails set on fore and main. It can be seen how spencers, staysails and studdingsails fill up the 'holes' in the sail plan. A spare topgallant is set on the crossjack yard for practice only. (Imperial War Museum, London)

2.
Merchantman running with studdingsails set on fore and main: lithograph by John Ward. Note the way the press of sail has been spread between the masts. The fore topsail has been partially becalmed by the main topsail, while the mizzen topsail yard has been lowered on the cap. (Kingston-upon-Hull Museums and Art Galleries)

3.
HM Brig *Martin* with studdingsails set. This give a clear view from aft of the studdingsails and their ge (Imperial War Museum, London)

with a bowline knot, and use the tack to haul this out to the boom end. This worked best if the topmast studdingsail boom was still rigged out (Luce, 425).

Royal studdingsails. These could be set from the top or the crosstrees. If booms were fitted, these were kept in the top, and only taken aloft, prior to setting the sails. One supposes that some sort of outer iron would be fitted, although no doubt, the boom could simply be lashed into place, or a bull's eye on the topgallant studdingsail yard be made to serve the same purpose. Totten (204) sets the royal studdingsails, with the wind between quartering and dead astern.

Setting and taking in all sails at once. We have described all the above manoeuvres as though they occurred in isolation, but in fact, with a well drilled crew, booms could be rigged out and in at the same time as sail was made or shortened. An idea of the appearance of a large vessel taking in all studdingsails at once, is offered by the picture of the Second Rate *Asia* of 1824, in Anthony Watts' *Pictorial History of the Royal Navy* (77).

In taking in any studdingsail in strong winds, keeping away until the wind was on the opposite quarter would make the sail less full, and therefore easier to handle. It goes without saying that getting a studdingsail aback was very likely to snap the boom (Bardenfleth, I, 184).

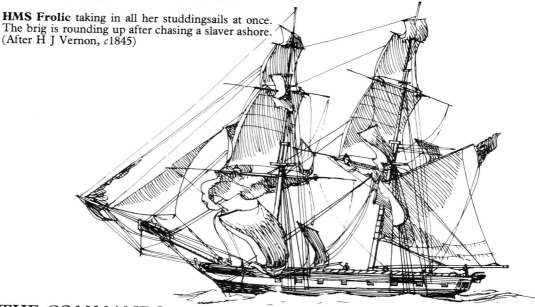

HMS **Frolic** taking in all her studdingsails at once. The brig is rounding up after chasing a slaver ashore. (After H J Vernon, *c*1845)

THE COMMANDS

Get the weather topgallant studdingsail ready for setting!
Haul taut!
Rig out!
Hoist away!

Get the weather topmast studdingsail ready for setting!
Set taut!
Rig out!
Hoist away!
Out squilgee!

Get starboard lower studdingsail ready for setting!
Haul taut!
Hoist away!
Out squilgee!

A merchantman running into Oslo Fjord, painted by V Melbye. Note the starboard studdingsails set on the main, and the port topmast studdingsail on the fore The mainsail is hauled up so as not to interfere with the fore course, and the becalming effect of the after canvas on the upper fore sails can be seen. (Courtesy N R Omell Gallery, London)

Stand by to take in topgallant studdingsails!
Lower away!
Haul down!
Rig in!
Take the jigger off the topgallant lift!
Take the burton off the topsail yard!
Stand by to take in the lower studdingsail!
Ease away the outhaul!
Clew up!
Lower away outer halliards!
Haul in!
Lower away inner halliards!

Man the after guy! Tend the topping lift and forward guy!
Haul taut! Rig in!

DISPOSITION OF CREW FOR HANDLING STUDDINGSAILS

Setting studdingsails both sides on the fore. If this were done on one side only, the individuals of that side would be employed.

Aloft	First captains and first part of topmen, watch on deck, both watches of boom tricers
On foreyard	Fore topsail sheetmen of both watches
On topsail yards, to carry out burtons, rig out booms, etc	First part of topsail yardmen
Clear away topgallant studdingsails	Boom tricers

On deck:
Carry forward lower studdingsails	Marines
Look out for, and bend studdingsail gear	First parts forecastlemen
Clear away topmast studdingsails in rigging, bend gear, reeve tack and boom brace	Second parts forecastlemen, first parts quarterdeckmen
Overhaul topping lift	Headsail stowers
Haul out lizard	Idlers and stokers
Boom topping lift	Idlers, stokers and marines
Haul fore guy, attend after guy	Remainder of hands not otherwise employed

Trice up! Rig out!
Boom jiggers	Mizzen topmen
Inner halliards	Forecastlemen not otherwise employed
Topmast studdingsail halliards	Second parts fore and main topmen, watch below
Topgallant studdingsail halliards	First parts fore and main topmen, watch below
Topmast studdingsail tacks	First parts quarterdeckmen
Topgallant studdingsail tacks	Men in top

Hoist away!
Lower halliards	All stokers and marines
Lower tack	Second parts quarterdeckmen

Stopper and belay:
Lower halliards and tacks	Captains of quarterdeckmen and next numbers
Topmast studdingsail halliards	Captains of fore and main tops, watch below
Topgallant studdingsail halliards	Captains of crosstrees, and next numbers, watch below Gunner's mates
Topmast studdingsail tacks	
Topgallant studdingsail tacks	Men in top

Taking in studdingsails both sides

Aloft	First captains of top, first parts topmen, watch on deck, boom tricers and topsail sheetmen of both watches, and upper yardmen
On topsail yard, to rig in booms	Topsail yardmen of first part
Take in topgallant studdingsails	Boom tricers and topmen aloft, not topsail yardmen

On deck:
Lower studdingsail tripping lines	Second parts quarterdeckmen, after part marines
Inner halliards and sheets	First parts forecastlemen
Topmast studdingsail downhauls	First parts quarterdeckmen
Topmast studdingsail deck sheets	Second parts forecastlemen

Rig in!
Lower boom topping lift	Marines
Topmast studdingsail boom jiggers	First parts quarterdeckmen
After guys	Main and mizzen topmen

Special stations:
Attend lower studdingsail halliards	Captains of quarterdeck, and next numbers
Tend topmast studdingsail halliards	Captains of fore and main top, watch below
Tend topgallant studdingsail halliards	Captains of crosstrees, watch below
Tend topmast studdingsail tacks, and short sheets	Gunner's mates
Tend lower studdingsail tacks	Not given in Burney
Tend burton falls	Captains of quarterdeckmen

HMS *Calypso* with studdingsails set in a good bree[ze] 1898. The topgallant studdingsails have been [set] behind the sail, the port topmast studding sail s[et] before it. The headsail is becalmed. (Imperial W[ar] Museum, London)

CHAPTER 11
STEERING

The helm. Helm was an old word with the meaning 'handle', or 'helve', and by extension, a tiller. Small vessels were steered with a tiller, and this arrangement worked very well at least up to the point where the tiller reached a length of eight or ten feet; the tiller in a First Rate was about thirty feet long, heavy enough to require support at its inboard end, and some other arrangement was necessary. The steering wheel was introduced as late as about 1704, the innovation starting in large ships, and gradually working down to smaller vessels. Elsewhere, we have attempted to explain this surprisingly late arrival of the steering wheel on the scene, and outlined the kinematic problems that beset this particular marriage of the windlass to the lever (*Mariner's Mirror* 58, 1972, 41). Prior to the invention of the wheel, large ships were steered either with tackles hooked to both sides of the tiller, or by means of a whipstaff. It is easy enough to see how the tackles could have been rigged and used to control the tiller movements. A continuous fall would allow one man to handle things quite readily in moderate weather.

The whipstaff or kolder-stok. This was a lever pivoting and sliding in a 'nut' or 'rowle' in the deck, so as to pry the tiller from side to side. 'Whip' embodies the idea of quick movement, while the Dutch word refers to the shaft or 'coulterstick' of a simple plough. The linkage only functioned well when the helm was amidships, or perhaps five degrees either side of that. Jean Boudriot has argued quite convincingly that by pushing the staff after the fashion of a dinghy sailor's 'hiking stick', the helmsman could shove the tiller to twenty degrees or so, although all mechanical advantage disappears at the extremes of motion (*Nautical Research Journal* 26, 1980, 149). Painstaking anatomising of contemporary Dutch models by Herman Ketting and Heinrich Winter confirms what one finds standing at the steering position in *Vasa*, namely that the view of the sails was extremely restricted, and that the helmsman must depend primarily on orders passed to him by the conn.

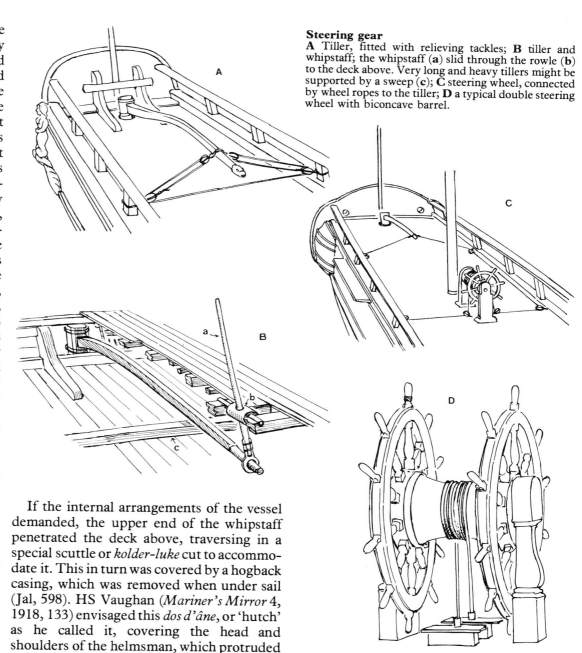

Steering gear
A Tiller, fitted with relieving tackles; **B** tiller and whipstaff; the whipstaff (**a**) slid through the rowle (**b**) to the deck above. Very long and heavy tillers might be supported by a sweep (**c**); **C** steering wheel, connected by wheel ropes to the tiller; **D** a typical double steering wheel with biconcave barrel.

If the internal arrangements of the vessel demanded, the upper end of the whipstaff penetrated the deck above, traversing in a special scuttle or *kolder-luke* cut to accommodate it. This in turn was covered by a hogback casing, which was removed when under sail (Jal, 598). HS Vaughan (*Mariner's Mirror* 4, 1918, 133) envisaged this *dos d'âne*, or 'hutch' as he called it, covering the head and shoulders of the helmsman, which protruded through the deck. We find this idea rather unconvincing, although something of the sort may have been tried in the 1909 reconstruction of Hudson's *Half-moon*.

Although in *Vasa* the helmsman can only stand on the same deck as the 'nut', it is possible that in other vessels he could have been placed on the deck above. Certainly in Ketting's *Prins Willem* model, he could have seen nothing from the lower position, and was in much better communication with the conn, one deck up. In this connection, the *Amaranth* model in Stockholm is of extraordinary interest. The staff is curved backwards, making it easier for the helmsman to grasp it, and a pin is thrust through its upper

Whipstaff

A Reconstruction of helmsman using a whipstaff. In many seventeenth century vessels the helmsman's view of the deck and sails was quite limited by a deck overhead, and his steering was guided by verbal commands and use of the binnacle; **B** sketch showing the action of the whipstaff. The whipstaff is vertical when the helm is amidships (**a**), and slides through the rowle or nut when the helm is put over (**b**). Problems associated with whipstaff steering were the limited travel allowed to the tiller (less than 15° to each side) and the decrease in mechanical advantage encountered when the helm was put hard over.

end, allowing a second man to assist in steering. It may be that these features owe something to the model's restoration by Admiral J Hägg, about seventy years ago, but unfortunately his notes are silent on this point. The pin is the probable basis for R C Leslie's puzzlement as to how the whipstaff operated. He suggested that it worked 'like a Spanish windlass' on tackles hooked to the tiller,

apparently thinking that it was twisted axially (*Old Sea Wings & Words*, 327).

The Steering Wheel. A very common pattern had a wheel at each end of a drum, upon which were wound five and a half turns of rope, with a staple securing the midpoint to the drum. When the tiller was hard over (about forty degrees) to starboard, the turns were all on the forward half of the barrel, and when shifted the opposite way, the turns moved aft. This meant that a full turn of the wheel changed the tiller angle about eighteen to twenty degrees, and a single spoke, of which there were usually sixteen, corresponded to something over a degree of rudder. The uppermost central spoke was specially shaped so it could be distinguished by feel, in the hand of the steersman. It so happens that the earliest patterns of steering wheels were more readily arranged so that the top of the wheel turned in the direction the ship's head was intended to move. With some later designs, it would have been simpler to have them operate the other way, but by that time, the convention was thoroughly established. The tiller ropes were therefore crossed, so that they moved in the accepted fashion.

Axiometer. A helm-indicator was found on the forward standard of the wheel. A pair of gears were arranged so that the rotation of the wheel turned a pointer, indicating how much helm was 'on'. A model at the National Maritime Museum, Greenwich, shows another arrangement, with a pointer travelling to and fro across the quarterdeck.

The compass. 'Binnacle', or 'bittacle', the housing in which the compass was placed, is a word deriving ultimately from Latin *habitaculum*, 'a little house'. There were, at least in latter days, a pair of these, placed so the helmsman always had one in view, no matter upon which side of the wheel he was stationed. The compass bowl was marked on the forward side with the 'lubber's line', which indicated the direction of the ship's head. At night, a lamp in the binnacle lit the card.

The helmsman. Steering was only entrusted to a veteran seaman, and indeed it was found by experience that there were, in any ship's company, only a few truly talented steersmen with a real 'feel' for the job. Not surprisingly, the tendency was to have these men take the wheel to the exclusion of all others. The importance of the task is reflected in the fact that the regular word for the mate of a merchantman is, in many languages, 'steersman', *styrman*, in Swedish, and so on. 'Rudder-man' occurs in *The Complaynt of Scotland*, while 'timoneer', from French *timonier* ('tiller-man'), is given

by Falconer and Smyth. To avoid disturbing the compass, the man divested himself of his knife, before taking the wheel, and always stood on the weather side, his inside hand holding an upper, and the outer a lower spoke. He could be aided by a 'lee helmsman', who took the other side of the wheel, and in bad weather by two more men who stood on either side of the after of the two wheels. These lee helmsmen, or 'blind men', as the Dutch called them, followed the movements of the weather helmsmen, directing their total attention to him, and not watching the compass or the sails. During his 'trick' at the wheel, which usually lasted an hour, the helmsman devoted his total concentration to the matter in hand, casual conversation with him being forbidden. Upon being relieved, he gave his relief the current order, 'Steering full and by, carrying three spokes of weather helm', or whatever. Occasionally when scudding with dangerous following seas, the officer of the deck might choose not to relieve the current helmsman, if he was managing well, and 'had the feel' of the ship. An experienced petty officer, the quartermaster, stood nearby, 'at the conn', and kept a sharp eye on the wheel, under the direction of the officer of the watch. The officer in turn kept a check on the course being steered, how much helm was being carried, and so on: 'How does she head?' – or 'How does she cape?' a yet older variant – to which the helmsmen replied with the course being steered.

A good helmsman was one who did not allow the ship to 'discourse' (Smyth) that is wander to and fro off the course, but who used 'small helm', a spoke or two of wheel, to meet or anticipate the movements of the ship rather than being alternately hard up and hard down, with the vessel yawing heavily. Skill was largely developed by long experience, and knowledge of the vessel's mode of steering, but other factors played a part. An increase in the wind felt on the cheek warned him that with the gust the ship would heel a little more, develop more pressure under the lee bow, and hence tend to run up in the wind, therefore requiring a spoke or two of weather helm.

In blowing weather, if one person can manage the helm, the feel of it in his hand is a nice criterion to judge whether the vessel be coming or falling off; so also is the greater or less noise or whistling of the wind. As the vessel comes against the helm, it will feel heavier; and the wind coming more forward will appear stronger. On the contrary, as she goes off, and gives way to the power of the helm, it eases the hand, and by the wind's drawing aft, appears to lessen. These circumstances to a attentive and nice observer, mark the motion of the vessel sooner than the compass (Gower, 56).

The officer of the watch trimmed the sails if too much helm was being carried. This was relatively easy to manage when sailing with the wind free – the main sheet could be slackened off to relieve a taut weather helm or the jib sheet eased if the helm was too slack. By the wind, things were more difficult: slacking the main sheet might spill the sail, which was already disposed so as to produce the best course and speed (Hourigan, 70). 'The fore topgallant sail, situated as it is, is notoriously a burying sail, and taking it in may ease the helm, resulting in a greater effect on the speed than the sail's pulling power. Some ships are hopeless, and would seem to carry a weather helm with only the flying jib set, and with the sheet to windward' (Hourigan, 70). The fore topgallant phenomenon was an exception to the general rule that taking away forward sail increased the amount of weather helm necessary.

Steering by compass. If the wind was free, and the ship could lay her course, the helmsman was given the course to steer, and he steadied the lubber's line on that point. Since the compasses of the day were rather sluggish, he also checked the ship's head in relation to the horizon, or the sky. 'The helmsman must not pore over the compass, but alternately watch the compass, and the motion of the vessel's head passing the clouds, the sea, or any other object more fixed on the compass, which may happen to present themselves to view' (Gower, 56).

Steering by the wind. When unable to lay the course, and obliged to work to windward, the aim was to keep the ship up to the wind as close as possible without 'pinching' so forcibly as to slow her down unduly. The ideal was to keep 'full and by', that is 'by' the wind, but at the same time the sails well full, and the ship footing along. In a good breeze, the helmsman watched the weather leech of the main course, the cloths of which should just be on the point of shivering. In a light breeze he watched the main royal, going off as it started to shake. Although some officers liked to steer using the mizzen topsail, not all approved:

Seamen are perfectly aware that the mizzen topsails should not be used as a proper sail for conning the ship by; still, as we have often heard it asserted, that as the mizzen topsail is always the first sail to touch when closed-hauled, that it should in consequence, be the proper sail to conn, or guide the ship by. Experience

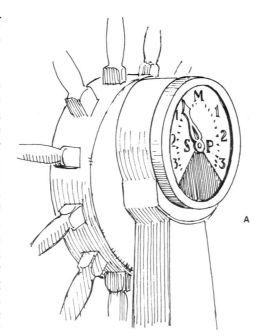

teaches us, that this view of the case is fallacious, and that the touching of the mizzen topsail arises from the mizzen masts unavoidably being so near the mainmast, and that the force of the wind while gliding off such a powerful sail as the main topsail, occasions an eddy wind, which shakes the weather leech of the mizzen topsail. And what proves this more fully is, that the weather leech of the mizzen topsail is sooner shaken in proportion to the strength of the wind. With all plain sail set, the mainsail is generally considered the best sail to steer the ship by; with the mainsail up, the main topgallant sail is then the best sail to steer by; and with topgallant sails handed, the main-topsail. In making long passages, some very good seamen set a small fore topmast studding-sail to steer the ship by, by which means they ensure all of the sails being kept well full; the fore topmast studdingsail being sure to tell tales, if kept too near the wind. We knew a ship where the quartermasters were obliged to steer her by a straight wake closehauled, and a ship of the line which had scuttles cut through her poop deck, that the man at the helm might see to steer the ship by the mizzen topsail. (Liardet, 221).

If the breeze were very light, the helmsman would also be guided by watching a dog-vane, or pennant, at the masthead. Dutch seamen called this vane *verklikker* ('tattle-tale', 'tell-tale') or *Spaansche waker* ('Spanish watchman').

Rudder and helm. Orders to the helmsman were traditionally given in terms of 'helm', that is to say, the position of the tiller rather than the rudder. 'Hard a-starboard!' meant 'Put the tiller (helm) to starboard, so that the ship may go to port!' It will be realised that not only the bow turned to port, but also the rudder, the top of the wheel, and prior to the

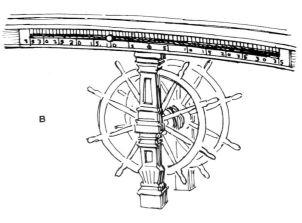

Axiometers
A Axiometer with a circular dial, the needle geared to the barrel of the steering wheel; **B** axiometer with a linear scale (detail from a contemporary model).

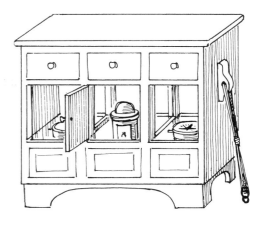

An early binnacle fitted with two compasses and a central lantern compartment to illuminate them.

Helmsmen steering at night. This drawing (after a sketch by Clarkson Stanfield made in the East Indiaman *Warley* in 1815–16) shows two men at the helm, with two lighted binnacles placed by the wheel. Double binnacles were not uncommon on board larger vessels, where even a single helmsman might find a centrally located compass card hard to read.

advent of the steering-wheel, the upper end of the whipstaff. Cogent reasons existed, therefore, for giving the order in what one might call the 'common sense' fashion. The transition to 'rudder' orders was made in many European countries about a century ago, being decreed for example, in the Royal Swedish Navy by General Order 69, of 1872. The change did not proceed smoothly everywhere, since old traditions died extremely hard in the merchant service, even in lands where the new convention was readily imposed in naval vessels. The consequence was at least one serious collision in the German service, the result of misinterpretation of the import of a steering order. In the United Kingdom, the changeover did not occur until 1933, at which time the new regulations were applied to naval and merchant vessels alike. Up to that point, there had always been the worry that a foreign pilot, might instinctively apply the local convention when giving directions on the bridge of a British ship (Reed, 66). Although the United States Navy made the switch from 'Port helm!' to 'Right rudder!' in 1914, practice in American merchant vessels did not change until 1935.

Throughout most of the period in which we are interested, the old system of orders was in use everywhere. Not only that, but the helm convention was so strongly engrained, that the terms 'helm' and 'wheel' are used interchangeably (Luce, 428). Furthermore, the Northern European seamen all used 'rudder' rather than 'helm' in their steering orders; for example German *'Ruder in Lee!'* means 'Helm a-lee!, Down helm!'. Indeed, perhaps this explains the greater readiness of the Northern European nations to make the change. In French vessels, the orders were given in terms of *la barre*, the tiller, *la barre dessous!* 'Down helm!', as in English.

Since the vessel heeled to leeward, the 'high' side was to windward and the helm was put 'up', if shifted in that direction, 'down' if pushed to leeward. The terms 'up', 'down', 'a-lee', and 'a-weather' were not used when steering dead before the wind, or almost so, 'port' and 'starboard' being substituted. Starboard is much the older term, and refers to the fact that the side-rudder was always carried on that quarter, most people being right-handed. The other side was originally called 'backboard', because the helmsman's back faced that way, but in English this word disappeared very early, although it survives as French *babord*, Dutch *bakboord*, etc. 'Larboard' and 'port' are said to arise because they designate the side, unencumbered by the rudder, that was alongside the quay, and

The helmsman's view. A good view aloft was essential in steering by the wind, where the helmsman responded to the action of the wind on the sails.

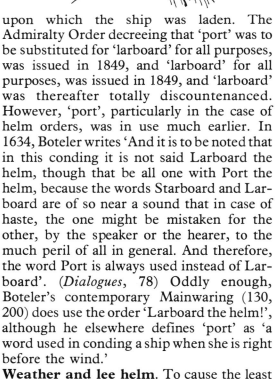

Movements of the rudder and helm
A Tiller (or helm) put to port; rudder and ship's head move to starboard; **B** wheel turned to starboard, tiller goes to port and ship's head moves to starboard.

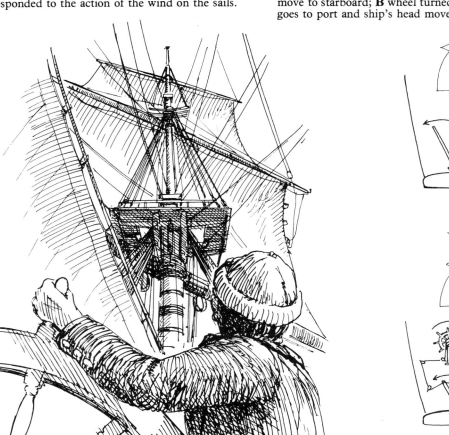

upon which the ship was laden. The Admiralty Order decreeing that 'port' was to be substituted for 'larboard' for all purposes, was issued in 1849, and 'larboard' for all purposes, was issued in 1849, and 'larboard' was thereafter totally discountenanced. However, 'port', particularly in the case of helm orders, was in use much earlier. In 1634, Boteler writes 'And it is to be noted that in this conding it is not said Larboard the helm, though that be all one with Port the helm, because the words Starboard and Larboard are of so near a sound that in case of haste, the one might be mistaken for the other, by the speaker or the hearer, to the much peril of all in general. And therefore, the word Port is always used instead of Larboard'. (*Dialogues*, 78) Oddly enough, Boteler's contemporary Mainwaring (130, 200) does use the order 'Larboard the helm!', although he elsewhere defines 'port' as 'a word used in conding a ship when she is right before the wind.'

Weather and lee helm. To cause the least drag, and hence exert the least adverse effect on speed, the rudder should be carried amidships, or nearly so. If the vessel were out of trim, or the sails were not trimmed properly, the helmsman was obliged to carry a little helm one way or the other. If he had to keep it somewhat a-weather, the ship was said to be 'carrying weather helm'; if he had to keep it a-lee, she was 'carrying lee helm'. In the first case, the ship was 'ardent', her inclination to run up in the wind requiring to be curbed. Ideally the ship was trimmed to carry a spoke or two of weather helm, since in emergency, or in tacking, she would run up into the wind readily. If the vessel sagged continually off to leeward, requiring a lot of lee helm, she held the wind poorly and would be sluggish in stays. The vessel was said to 'gripe' if she periodically lurched to windward, perhaps without requiring the steady application of much weather helm.

Easing the helm. In the ordinary way then, some muscular effort was required to apply weather helm, and hold the helm slightly up. If the wind slackened, the taut weather helm was no longer required, and the wheel was 'eased'. This explains why the order 'Ease down the helm!' was used in tacking, where it refers both to the direction in which the helm is put, and also to the 'easy' or handsome manner in which it is put down. 'Ease up the helm!' or 'Ease the helm up!' are intolerable according to Hourigan, (68). 'Ease her!' was sometimes ordered in the close-hauled vessel, as she was approached by a head sea, with the idea that if the ship's way were deadened by her coming to the wind, she would not strike the opposing sea with so much force. 'It is thought by some that extreme rolling as well as pitching are checked by shifting the helm quickly, thereby changing the direction of the ship's head, and what is technically called "giving her something else to do"' (Smyth). Griffiths, Gower, and Glascock all felt that the theory was fallacious, although it might spare the rudder a little bit:

When a ship is opposed to a head sea, and pitching deep, how customary it is to observe the man at the helm, easing the helm down a few spokes; and the officer of the watch roaring out 'ease her!' Ask the generality *why* they do this, and I think they will either say, to luff her to, or be unable to assign any reason, except, they have always seen it done. Reflect one moment, and ask yourself, from the time the inclination to pitch is observed, till it is actually made, how long elapses? Two, three, or four seconds. Is it possible that such a momentary action of the helm can have any effect? And particularly in a head sea, when from want of fresh way, its action is less powerful.

If a ship is going to pitch deep, and her helm is a-weather at the time, the easing it may, no doubt, be of service. The helm, while a-weather, is a restraint to the free action of the ship, although to keep her out of the wind, it may be necessary. The moment it is amidships, its action is neutralised, and, therefore, in putting it so when making a heavy pitch, it frees the ship of every other restraint, and leaves one end oppressed, instead of both; and the rudder is not liable to be injured by the jerk of the reaction, as she scends down into the sea abaft. On the same principle, it appears idle and useless, if at the time she is carrying a slack helm, to put it any way a-lee (Griffiths, 200).

Effect of stretching the weather wheel rope. Since, sailing by the wind, the weather wheel rope was taking the strain, and stretched somewhat under it, the wheel might show a half turn of weather helm on, and yet the rudder might be only minimally deviated from midships. This stretching had to be considered before engaging in much sail trimming, by the wind. Sailing free, on the other hand, a half turn of the wheel would have resulted in a completely unacceptable amount of rudder drag, the tension on the weather rope being much less. With the mechanical steering arrangements introduced in the mid-nineteenth century, this phenomenon did not have to be considered.

'Ease her when she pitches!' It was an old custom to ease the helm of a ship sailing close-hauled in bad weather when pitching into a heavy sea.

Orders to the helmsman. The form these took changed surprisingly little over the centuries, as we can see from the following excerpt from *The Complaynt of Scotland* (1546), giving the earliest set of helm orders in English. With modernised spelling it runs: 'Then the master cried on the rudder man, mate, keep full and by, a-luff, come no higher, holabar [*haut la barre*!] arruya (*arrivez*!), steer clean up the helm, thus and so'. Apart from the two French commands, both meaning 'Helm a-weather!', the sense is not difficult to follow.

A century later we have this:

In chases and narrow channels, where the course lies not directly upon a point of the compass, there the master, mate, or some other standing aloft doth give direction to him at the helm, and this we call *conding* or *cunning*. Sometimes he who conds the ship will be speaking to him at the helm at every little yaw; which the sea-faring men love not, as being a kind of disgrace to their steerage; then in mockage, they will say *sure the channel is narrow he conds so thick*, whereby you may gather that in narrow channels it is necessary and useful to cond thick, because the points and shelves do lie so near that there cannot a long time be given for a ship to run on, lest she should miss working. Note that according as the ship's sails are trimmed either before or by a wind, so they use several terms in conding; and to use others were improper and ridiculous amongst them. If the ship go before a wind, or as they term it, betwixt two sheets, then he who conds uses these terms to him at the helm: *Starboard, larboard, the helm amidships*. Note that when we say starboard, the meaning is that he must whip the helm to the starboard side, and then the ship will go larboard, for the ship doth ever go contrary to the helm. If the ship

go by a wind, or quarter winds, they say *aloof* or *keep your loof*, or *fall not off, wear no more, keep her to, touch the wind, have a care of the lee-latch*; all these do imply the same in a manner, and are to bid him at the helm to keep her near the wind. *Ease the helm; no nearer (near), bear up*; these words do appoint him to keep her from the wind and make her go more large or right before. Some speeches are common to both; as *steady*, that is, keep the ship from going in and out, but just upon the point that you are to steer, and *as you go*, and such like (Mainwaring, 130).

This is all pretty clear, although the later order 'Nothing Off!' replaced both 'Veer no more!' and 'Have a care of the lee-latch!' - that is 'Don't let her lurch or yaw to leeward!'. Smith (48) offers 'No near, ease the helm!' and 'Be yare at the helm!'. 'No near!' was later replaced by 'No higher!'. 'Yare' meant 'quick' or 'smart'; 'near', by the way, was the comparative form of 'nigh', rather than being a positive form in its own right. Today, we would say 'No nearer (the wind)!'. Nowadays, the quartermaster and the bridge do not actually engage in the type of 'mockage' described by Mainwaring, but should the conning prove too 'thick', it may elicit a certain amount of tooth-sucking from the wheelhouse.

The order was given to the helmsman who repeated it, and if necessary, stated when it had been executed. 'Hard down!' would be followed by 'Hard down, Sir', and then, 'Helm hard a-lee, Sir'. Orders of the form 'Starboard ten!' (Royal Navy), 'Ten degrees right rudder!' (US Navy) were not used during the sailing man-of-war period largely because of the inconstant relationship of the wheel and the tiller movement, using a rope drive. Furthermore, the type of axiometer

1.

2.

3.

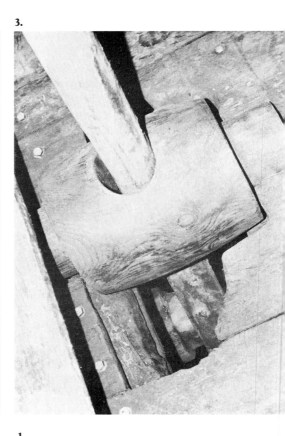

4.

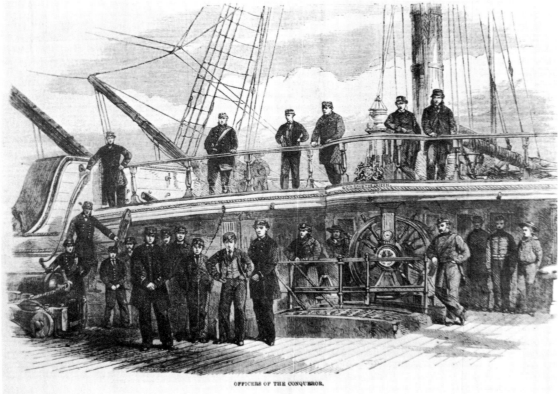

OFFICERS OF THE CONQUEROR.

1.
Tiller steering in the *Nonsuch*. Note the period binnacle lashed to the deck. A turn of rope helped to take the kick out of the 6-foot tiller when heavier seas struck the rudder. Relieving tackles, working on the same principle, were rigged in heavy weather. (Mark Myers' Collection)

2.
Whipstaff on a model in the Sjöhistoriskamuseet Stockholm. This, we think, is a restoration by Admiral Hagg, rather than the original fitting. (Courtesy Sjöhistoriska Museum, Stockholm)

3.
Close-up view of the *Vasa*'s whipstaff, roller, and tiller (Author's photo, courtesy *Vasa* Varvet, Stockholm and Mar Dir Gunnar Schoerner RSN)

4.
The wheel of HMS *Conqueror* (101 guns). Note the helm indicator and the binnacles, two on deck before the wheel and one on the poop. *Illustrated London News* 1862. (Mark Myers' Collection)

5.
Seamanship instruction on the 'swinging model' at the Royal Naval School, Greenwich, 1889. Four boys on the wheel follow the instructor's orders to swing the ship (geared to a track in the floor) to any given course relating to compass points marked on the walls of the room. Nine boys trim the yards and sails accordingly *Illustrated London News*, 1889. (Mark Myers' Collection)

Conning the ship.

Ship sailing before the wind. This helmsman's view of the upper sails is obscured by the awning rigged over the quarterdeck, but as the ship is running before the wind with yards squared and fore lower studdingsail set, he would be receiving his directions from his officers and the compass. (After a painting by Thomas Hearne, 1804, of a voyage in HMS *Deal Castle* in 1775)

used was not within the helmsman's field of view.

Orders used when sailing before the wind. The best accounts of the commands used in conning sailing men-of-war are found in Luce and Hourigan, and form the basis for the following description. In the naval service, some effort would have been made to codify the others, somewhat limiting their number and variation. The following are rep-

resentative. 'Steer West-North-West!', to follow a particular compass course. 'Starboard!', 'Helm a-starboard!' 'Starboard the helm!' to alter course to port; 'Starboard handsomely!' when the turn is to be made circumspectly. 'Give her more helm!', when it was desired to swing more quickly. 'Hard over!', to increase the helm already on, and make the quickest possible swing. 'Steady!' when headed in the desired direction. The

quartermaster reports the course at the moment the order is given, and if satisfactory the order 'Keep her so!' follows. If the ship has gone a little to the right of the desired course, the order 'Steady a-starboard!' might be given, upon which the helm was put a little to starboard, the order 'Steady!' being given, when the required heading was reached. 'Meet her!' was the order given when the vessel was swinging rapidly, nearing the desired heading, and it was necessary to slow the swing. 'Midships!', 'Helm amidships!', 'Right the helm!', all meant to centre the tiller. 'Shift the helm!' was the order to switch from starboard to port, as for example, when starting to make sternway. 'Nothing to the Westward!', if the ship was being steered a little to the west of the desired course. 'Course West-North-West, nothing to the westward!' was caution that the ship must not be allowed to yaw in that direction. 'Mind your starboard helm!' conveyed either a warning that starboard helm would quickly be necessary, or an indication that the ship was going a little to the right of the desired direction, and a little starboard helm was necessary to correct this.

Orders used when steering by the wind. 'Helm up!', 'Hard up!', 'Let her go off!', 'Let her go off handsomely!', all take the ship off the wind. 'Helm down!', 'Hard down!', 'Let her come to!', 'Let her come to handsomely!', 'Bring her to the wind!', 'Luff!', 'Let her luff!', as she is brought to the wind. 'Ease

Ship sailing by the wind. Here, the wheel is managed by four men in blowing weather. The lead helmsman stands on the weather side of the forward wheel, moving the helm in accordance with the officer's directions and his view of the sails set aloft.

down the helm!' is used as an order primarily in tacking. 'Helm's a-lee!' is not a helm order at all, as explained when considering going about. 'Luff and touch her!' was an order to bring the ship up very close to the wind, just shake the sails, and then go off again to the close-hauled point. 'Luff and lie!' is recorded from the mid-1500s, and was similar to the previous order, except that the vessel was to be held up just as close as possible. Later variations include 'Keep her luffing!', 'Hold your luff!', 'Luff, take all you can!'.

'No higher!', 'Earlier, no near!', was given as the ship was brought to the wind, and the desired point was reached, or exceeded, the bow being allowed to drop back a fraction. It would be followed by 'Very well thus!', 'Very well dyce!', 'Steady so!', 'Full and by!', 'Keep her a good full!', 'Let her go her course!'. 'Nothing off!' indicated that the ship was being kept away a little, if anything, and needed to be kept up to it.

'Dyce, no higher!', 'Dyce, nothing off!' meant that the ship had reached the desired point of sail, and was not to be luffed any further in the first case and was not to be allowed to fall off, in the second. Hourigan laments the fact that terms involving 'dyce' had dropped out of use in his day, since these referred to the ship's inclination to the wind and not to the compass. Even 'Steady so' might be misinterpreted, he felt. 'Steady' was only used in reference to the compass heading. The wind could be expected to vary a little bit in direction, hence the need for orders like 'Very well Dyce!'. 'Dyce' also occurring as 'dice', and 'thyst', was an old form of 'thus'. In the latter form it was actually adopted as the personal motto of Sir John Jervis, very much in character for the sailor whose steely-eyed determination to do his duty, cost what it might, is a byword; this was the man who watched the apparently invincible Spanish fleet emerging from the haze, off Cape St Vincent, and declared 'If there be fifty sail, I shall go through them' (Berckman, 247).

'Nothing to windward' or 'Mind your weather helm!', that is, 'you need, or may need, some weather helm', corresponds to 'Nothing to starboard!', 'Mind your starboard helm!' mentioned earlier, or the order might be given, 'Nothing to leeward!', or 'Mind your lee helm!'. 'Mind your steerage' might be a comment on inattention by the helmsman, or merely a warning that the ship was nearing some difficult water in a channel and extra diligence would be required.

CHAPTER 12
TACKING, WEARING AND BOXHAULING

Dutch fluyts tacking (after a drawing by Van de Velde the Elder *c*1672). The vessels to the left and right are in stays; the central fluyt appears to be hauling round her foreyards after paying off on the starboard tack.

Tacking (wind direction follows arrow).

TACKING

The title of this chapter encompasses the three principal methods by which a ship passes from one tack to the other. In the ordinary way, the best method of going about will be by tacking; that is to say, by luffing up to the wind six points, and falling off a further six points onto the new tack. Ideally this will be accomplished by maintaining headway throughout the evolution, gaining to windward the whole time. In fact, dull vessels will only complete the manoeuvre by making a sternboard, the head falling off as they do so, until the after sails can fill and headway develops once more. Theoretically, the ship's head swings through only twelve points, but sometimes she falls off excessively on the new tack, and has to be luffed up again, failing to meet this ideal.

The object was to get the ship moving through the water as fast as possible, and using this momentum, luff up into the wind as far as possible. The headyards came aback, in theory, when the wind was about a point on the weather bow, but in practice, not until the wind was dead ahead, and then acted to force the ship's head further to leeward, continuing the swing initiated in the first phase. The after yards, which were in the lee of the fore, were swung around, so they were braced up, ready for the new tack, filling once

the wind came six points on the 'new' weather bow. Finally, the headyards were swung, and braced up on the new tack. There is an excellent photograph of a man-of-war tacking, in *Mariner's Mirror* 31, 1945, 113, showing HMS *Cruiser*, just prior to 'Mainsail haul'.

To stay, and to be paid. A good working ship, in the proper conditions, could be expected to perform the evolution smartly, and with little fear of failure. If however, the vessel ran up into the wind only so far, and then fell off, the attempt having failed, she was said to have 'missed stays'. If the vessel ran up into the wind, then came to a dead stop, and 'hung' falling of neither on the old tack, or the new, she was said to be 'in irons'. Although ultimately 'pay off' came to mean the falling off to leeward of the ship's head, in the final phase of tacking, the word was used slightly differently in the 1600s. '*Tacke about* is to beare up the helme, and that brings her to *stay*, all her sails lying flat against the shrouds; then, as she turnes, wee say *Shee is Payed*' (Smith, *Grammar*, 53). Boteler (132), however, offers: 'But sometimes the word

Paying, is in use when a ship being to tack about, all her sails are brought a-backstays (that is to say are flatted against the masts and shrouds) for then the sea-saying is the ship is payed'. Mainwaring (197) likewise says that the ship is 'paid' when 'we are sure she will not fall back again'. Once the fore sails came aback, the success of the manoeuvre was assured (von Littrow, 143).

To tack or wear. The best possible conditions for tacking existed when there was a good working breeze and a smooth sea, that is, when the wind was freshening, rather than when it was subsiding. If there were not sufficient wind, adequate momentum was not achieved. If there was a head sea, the waves would tend to knock the bow off again, as she came up to the wind. Proper sail balance and trim was also important. The ideal situation existed when a few spokes of weather helm were being carried, that is to say, when the vessel was trying to run up into the wind spontaneously. If the helm were slack, or lee helm was being carried, it meant that the vessel did not have this inherent tendency to run up into the wind. This could result from too great a press of sail forward, as compared with aft, or the hull being out of trim, down by the stern. These faults were, in the ordinary way, quite easily corrected. The characteristics of the ship had to be learnt by her commander. Some were smart in stays, spinning around like a top; others were dull, requiring a lot of coaxing. The timing of the sequence of manoeuvres within the evolution might require a bit of variation, depending on the surrounding conditions, particularly the strength and state of training of the crew, and the weather conditions obtaining. Thus the considerations applying to a well-manned, smart-working frigate of 1800, and those governing the management of an under-crewed, long-hulled, sluggish Finnish windjammer of 1930, are quite different. 'Surely these varieties of ship require consideration, and at once, decide against any positive commonplace mode. Yet, generally speaking, one plan is used, and if the ship misses stays, *she* bears the blame' (Griffith, 297).

Mossel says that there will be little problem in tacking when the topsails are single reefed, and topgallants are set over. If the topsails are double reefed however, wearing would be the more prudent method of going about. The topsail yards are struck to a point where they cannot be braced up sharp, and when aback, there will be a tremendous strain on the stays. Furthermore, the braces of fore and main lead aft, and hence the yardarms are devoid of proper support when aback. The roughness of the sea, which can be expected to accompany a double reefed topsail breeze, would tend to throw the bow off the wind at the crucial time, and if the ship started to make a sternboard, there would be danger of it smashing in the windows of the stern gallery, damaging the rudder fastenings, and perhaps carrying the rudder away completely (Mossel, III, 236).

When to tack.

In working to windward, the wind frequently 'veers and hauls' three or four points, heading the vessel off, or allowing her to come up. This is particularly the case in the vicinity of land. The proper moment to tack, in such cases, is when the wind is heading her off, for on the other tack you will evidently gain more to windward. By watching attentively, and taking advantage of such slants of wind, keeping the vessel a good full and by the wind, you will gain much more on your course, than if you stood a certain number of miles or hours on each tack (Luce, 430).

In turning to windward, if the ship be in trim, her weights well disposed, her sails not only well

set but judiciously balanced, there will be a lively strain on the weather wheel ropes, yielding to the influence of a single spoke, but challenging again, the ship will not 'bore' or pitch, or flam as if about to beat her head to pieces, or bury her bows in a head sea. Her head will rise and fall in easy graceful undulations; there will be a tremulous motion in the tiller, a sensible pulsation which is said to be an infallible sign of good trim, denoting the amount of life and energy in the whole thing. Like a well mouthed pulling horse, if the wheel be let go at the moment when the pull is strongest, she will dart ardently into the wind, and go round of her own accord (Boyd, 386).

Wind veering or hauling during the evolution. If the wind should draw ahead three points during the actual execution of the manoeuvre, things would be facilitated, the fore would fly aback, and the aftersails would fill, earlier than had been expected. If, on the other hand, the wind drew three points aft, the manoeuvre would almost certainly fail, since headway would have been lost, long before an arc of nine points had been described to windwards. The procedure to follow was to fill once more on the old tack, and, if necessary, attempt the manoeuvre once again (Mossel, III, 235).

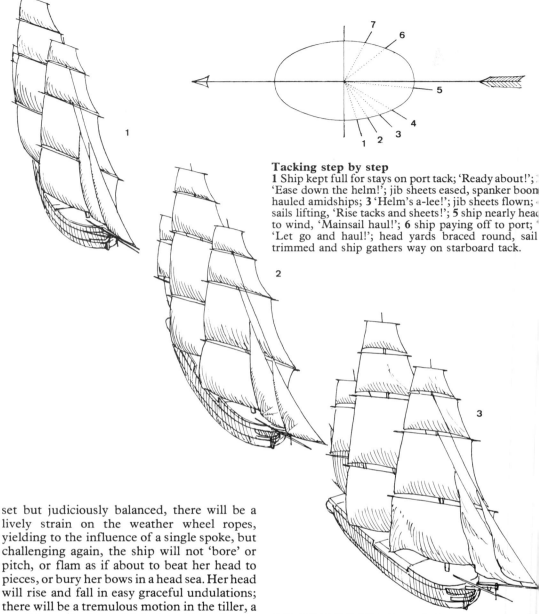

Tacking step by step
1 Ship kept full for stays on port tack; 'Ready about!'; 'Ease down the helm!'; jib sheets eased, spanker boom hauled amidships; **3** 'Helm's a-lee!'; jib sheets flown; sails lifting, 'Rise tacks and sheets!'; **5** ship nearly head to wind, 'Mainsail haul!'; **6** ship paying off to port; 'Let go and haul!'; head yards braced round, sail trimmed and ship gathers way on starboard tack.

SEQUENCE OF COMMANDS

The manoeuvre may be conveniently divided into several stages, defined by the commands used.

First command. 'Ready about! Stations for Stays!'; this was the signal for all to go to their designated position, see everything clear, braces ready for running, and so on. The ship was got moving through the water as briskly as possible, neither jammed up so tight that the weather leeches of the sails were shaking, nor so far off the wind that the arc through which she would have to luff up was increased unnecessarily. The helmsman was instructed to keep the ship 'a good full for stays'.

Second command. 'Ready! Ready! Ease down the helm!' This last order indicated to the helmsman that the wheel should be put down, spoke by spoke rather than being jammed hard a-lee abruptly. Following the

latter practice resulted in tremendous increase in drag, and consequently a slowing of the ship's speed. To aid the luffing, the jib sheets were eased off and the spanker boom hauled amidships, or rather eased in gradually, so that it remained full as long as possible, contributing to headway, as well as turning to windward.

Third command. 'Helm's a-lee!'; this order is a grammatical assertion, rather than an imperative, but in fact was the signal to let go the fore sheet and headsheets. Reading accounts in other languages strongly suggest that at one time in English, the order 'Helm a-lee!' may have corresponded to what I have above rendered as 'Ease down the helm!', as

does *Roret i lae!* in Danish, for example (Bardenfleth, I, 189). The Danish order, by the way, literally translates 'Rudder a-lee!' whereas by convention, English more correctly uses 'Helm a-lee!'. Why there should have been an alteration in the time at which the order was given remains a mystery. Be that as it may, the intention was to lessen the affect of forward sail, and hence allow the bow to swing into the wind. In a very light breeze, the jib and flying jib might be hauled down completely. The sheets were at the very least flowed so that the affect of the sails was nullified. Letting go the foresheet took away the power of the fore course. Since the jibs and foresail were contributing to headway, it was best if the sheets were kept fast as long as the sails were pulling at all.

'Adieu-va!' 'Vaya con dios!' These orders were, respectively, the French and Spanish equivalent of 'Ready! Ease down the Helm!'. According to Willaumez (8) and Bonnefoux (*Dictionnaire*, 11), the custom was to

pronounce the French expression *Adieu-vat!*, to give it emphasis. Both are everyday expressions, of course, and literally mean 'Go with God!'. In this context however, they were prayers reflecting the uncertainty of the outcome attending tacking in the 1600s. A similar tradition underlies the British drifter skipper's invocation 'Heave the nets in the name of the Lord!' or just 'Over in the name of the Lord!', the order to shoot the nets (Elliott, 45). Bonnefoux equates *Adieu-va!* with 'Helm's a-lee!', but I am sure that this reflects the confusion referred to above. Later French practice was to substitute the order *Envoyez!*, which we might translate very freely as 'Away you go!'. *Ree!* was used in Dutch and German merchantmen, and small craft. According to Kluge (653) the original meaning was simply 'Ready!'. The dinghy sailor's 'Lee-Oh!' likewise corresponds more to the second, than the third, command, although of course, the time scale is so compressed, that the distinction is perhaps a little forced.

Bracing to. If the fore could be thrown aback, the success of the evolution was certain, and if the yards were braced in somewhat, the sails would come aback earlier. As the luffing movement continued, the yards were then braced up sharp once more, to maximise the rotational effect. 'Bracing to', as this dodge was known, was accomplished by checking – that is to say, easing off – the lee fore brace and top bowline. The fore bowline, however, was kept fast, because it was needed to steady the weather leech of the fore course, when the fore tack was let go. The fore topgallant bowline was cleared away quite early in the manoeuvre. Bracing to was not approved of by all seamen, because it interfered with the effectiveness of the fore in contributing to headway. Bonnefoux (97) disapproves of the 'English habit' of checking the fore top bowline (*choquer la boulinette*), and letting go the fore sheet. On the other hand, it was the invariable practice of pilots to brace to when tacking in a narrow channel, close to the weather shore, when excessive fore-reaching was inadvisable (Gower, 24).

Fourth command. 'Rise tacks and sheets!'; the intention here was to run the clewgarnets up sufficiently so that the clews of the course would clear the nettings, when the yards were swung. If it were intended to keep the fore tack down, until just prior to hauling the headyards, the command might be given in the form 'Raise maintack and sheets!' (Nares, 242). The lee tack and weather sheet were now shortened in as much as possible, and the lee spanker topping lift hauled taut, while the weather one was let go and overhauled.

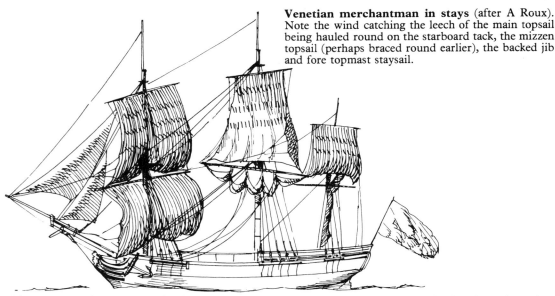

Venetian merchantman in stays (after A Roux). Note the wind catching the leech of the main topsail being hauled round on the starboard tack, the mizzen topsail (perhaps braced round earlier), the backed jib and fore topmast staysail.

This preparation ensured that when the spanker filled on the new tack, the boom would be properly supported by the 'new' weather topping lift.

Fifth command. 'Haul taut! Mainsail haul!'. If the main course were not set, the order was 'Main topsail haul!'. The yards on the main and crossjack were swung around together, as quickly as possible, and braced up sharp on the new tack. The order 'Let go topgallant bowlines!' was given after 'Tacks and Sheets!' (Nares, 242). The lee bowlines were shortened in, along with the lee main tack and weather sheet. The weather main and top bowline were let go.

In the latter day man-of-war, the mainyard was swung, in tacking, by means of the preventer braces, which led forward under the foretop. These were rove through a brace block at the yardarm, and by hauling both parts at once, the swing could be carried out very expeditiously. Initially, a few men grasped the doubled brace, and ran away with it, the remainder of the force 'striking in', or tailing on, as it came in. Pieces of bunting, stuck through the strands of the standing end, indicated the point where it was belayed. Hauling continued on the other end, to get the yard sharp up on the new tack. Boyd (387) recommends seeing the weather preventer brace and lee after brace clear for running, and hung with spunyarn. A kink, jamming the block when the men were running away with the lee preventer, could spring the yard. The swing was assisted by hauling on the tack, main and top bowlines, for which the order was, 'Haul forward the lee main tack and main top bowline!' (Luce, 431). The tack was got down, and the sheet hauled aft. With the foreyard braced sharp up one way, and the mainyard the other, especially with the topmast studdingsail booms projecting bey-

ond the yardarms, care had to be taken that the yardarms did not 'lock'. This meant that fore or main, or both, should not be braced up absolutely sharp, until after 'Haul of all!'. On this point, Griffiths (296) advises against wasting time getting the after yards sharp initially, if a bad haul has been made, since they would brace themselves up sharp once they filled.

Early or late mainsail haul. As the wind drew ahead, the main topsail would start to flap, coming aback from the centre outwards. When the wind was a point, or point and a half, on the weather bow, the weather cloths would be definitely aback, while the lee side was becalmed by the fore topsail. At this juncture, the yards would almost swing themselves around, and it would be easy work running away with the braces. On the other hand, once the whole topsail was in the lee of the fore, it was a dead haul, and much heavier work. If the after yards were swung too early, and the vessel missed stays, a heavy haul was then in prospect to get them braced up once more on the old tack. Too early a swing also tended to deaden headway, and hence a late haul would be considered safer if doubt existed about the certainty of tacking; that is to say with a vessel known to be sluggish in stays, or a swell on the bow (Nicholls, 276; Glascock, 305). At night, judging when to order 'Mainsail haul!' was more difficult, since the officer of the deck might be unable to tell if the weather cloths of the main topsail were aback. Luce (445) says that a decided flap to weather of the spanker would indicate that the proper time had arrived.

Backing mizzen topsail or mizzen. The mizzen topsail, whether full or aback, forces the stern away from, and hence the bow into, the wind. When aback, however, it will mark-

edly diminish headway. In the early stage of tacking, it was usual to haul the mizzen boom amidships, to aid in the luffing process, and by hauling it even further to windward, the turning effect might be increased (Dana, 60). Bréart (181) specifically says that if the boom is hauled to windward, it will result in making a back sail of the mizzen, and by diminishing headway, lessen the effect of the helm.

In the evolution of the mizzen sail, over the centuries, from full mizzen course to a simple gaff mizzen, there was an intermediate stage in the late 1700s, when the forward half of the course was eliminated, the forward leech of the sail being laced to the mast, while the head of the sail set on the after part of the mizzen yard. For thirty years or so, the yard was really serving only as a gaff, and was ultimately replaced by one. In the interim, the redundant forward half of the yard was retained, although apparently quite lacking in function. I have suggested elsewhere that this arrangement permitted the peak of the mizzen to be jacked out to windward, to a degree that could not be duplicated even by hauling the weather vang of the gaff (*Mariner's Mirror*, 63, 1977, 97). Bourdé de Villehuet (91), writing in 1769, advocates hauling the mizzen yard over to the lee main shrouds, so that the mizzen will hold the wind as long as possible, aid in turning the bow to windward, and be trimmed properly for the new tack. I have no other citation supporting this practice, but if this method was widespread, it would serve to explain the reluctance to replace the mizzen yard with a gaff. Along the same lines, there are scattered references to backing the mizzen topsail in the early stages of tacking, rather than swinging the crossjack at mainsail haul (Dick & Kretchmer, 325). A mizzen topsail, whether full or aback, tends to aid luffing. It will not do so when square, or when lifting excessively. Thus, if it was decided to back this sail, it was got around smartly, and not allowed to lie square any longer than necessary. Luce (548) says it was common practice in steamers to brace the crossjack aback when the wind was a couple of points on the bow, before 'Mainsail haul!'. He says that such counterbracing was only adopted when it was taken for granted that the vessel could not be brought around without a sternboard; the point being, that the mizzen topsail aback would destroy headway. Nicholls (276) recommends swinging the crossjack just before the main, even when they are braced around more or less together. In merchant ships with four masts, the jigger topsail was sometimes backed early, simply because there were not enough men to handle mizzen and jigger simultaneously (Todd & Whall, 87; *Mariner's Mirror* 60, 1974, 331).

Sixth command. 'Haul taut! Let go and haul'; the order was also given in the form 'Haul of all!', or, for emphasis, inverted to 'Of all haul!'. The head braces were manned, and the yards swung around smartly onto the other tack. The movement was expedited by hauling on the tack, fore and top bowlines. Foretack, fore top bowline, on the former weather side, and the 'old' lee braces were let go prior to swinging. The tack was got down and the sheet hauled aft.

Early or late haul of headyards. The haul was made when the aftersails had filled on the new tack, and the ship was starting to make headway once more. If the swing were made too quickly, the bow might not continue falling off, requiring the fore be braced in again somewhat. If, however, the haul were delayed too much, the ship fell off too far, and had to be luffed up once more, thus losing ground to leeward (Bréart, 182). If the ship was spinning round well, as would occur in a fresh breeze, the headyards might be swung just before the after yards filled, it being judged that by the time 'Haul of all!' was complete, the ship would have fallen off sufficiently on the new tack, to allow the after canvas to draw (Bréart, 182). The ship might tend to 'hang' in the wind after too early a haul, partly through all the ship's people being on the forward part of the deck, and hence the vessel momentarily out of trim, down by the head (Boyd, 387). In a merchantman, the small crew would not have this effect.

The helm. The wheel was eased down gradually until it was hard over. When carrying a definite weather helm, however, Griffiths (296) advocates putting the helm amidships at once, so as to lessen the drag of the rudder. When the vessel came stationary in the water, the helm was righted, that is to say, put amidships, and if she started to make sternway, put over the other way. 'When tacking with a strong breeze, and a "topping sea", particular attention should be paid to the helm, that it be righted in time, before the ship gathers sternway. The pintles of rudders are constantly damaged in consequence of officers permitting the helm to remain a-lee, instead of righting it amidships, after the vessel has lost her way. If the ship cannot be brought round by the assistance of her sails, it were better to have recourse to the evolution of wearing, than to endanger the efficiency of the rudder by this reprehensible practice' (Glascock, 305). Lever (79) expresses the more usual view when he says 'many seamen object to the helm being put over when going

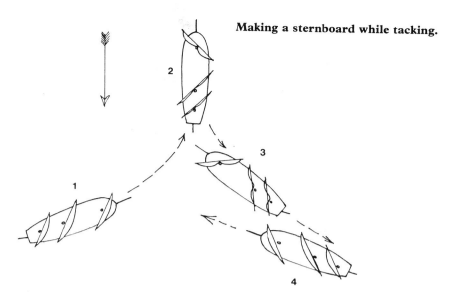

Making a sternboard while tacking.

astern, as a dangerous pressure against the rudder. This can only be objected to when blowing fresh; for in many situations, such as boxhauling a ship, when near a lee shore, making a sternboard etc, it is absolutely necessary to use the helm in sternway.'

With other things on his mind, the officer of the deck might fail to remember to order appropriate changes of helm. Hourigan (74), reflecting practice in the United States Navy around the turn of the century, advocates having the signalman, who is tending the patent log, advise the officer of the watch which way it is trending: up and down, time to right the helm; starting to trend forward, time to shift it.

Making a sternboard. Although, ideally, headway was maintained throughout, gaining to windward every inch of the way, in practice, many vessels were dull in stays, and only completed the manoeuvre by dint of going astern in the final stage. The Dutch expression for this was to let the ship *op zijn gat draaijen*, which we may loosely translate as 'turn on her heel', the literal meaning being a little more earthy (Mossell, III, 235). If the headyards were firmly aback, and the helm reversed, the vessel would come around on her heel, whereupon the after yards filled, and she started to make headway once more, which was the signal to right the helm. In boxhauling, as we shall see, a sternboard was an essential feature of the manoeuvre.

Topsail halliards and breast backstays. With topsail halliards rigged double, that is to say, a separate tie and halliard on each side, the weather one would be taking the strain when close-hauled, because the mast would be leaning somewhat to leeward. In this circumstance, it was prudent to get a good pull on the lee halliards before going about, so they would be up taut afterwards. The opportunity was taken, at the same time,

to get the sheets of the upper sails home, stays taut, and so on (Boyd, 387).

Breast backstays were intended to give lateral support to the topmasts on the weather side. An outrigger, with a leathered fork, or dumb sheave in the end, was used to bear out the backstay from the top. Upon going about, the outrigger was shifted over to the new weather side, the old weather backstay being 'borne abaft', to get it out of the way of the lee quarter of the lower yard. Illustrations showing this feature are rather uncommon, but appear to show outriggers on fore and main only.

Beckets and tricing lines. When close-hauled, several items of running rigging were 'idle', and tended to hang in loose bights, so to keep them out of the way, they were hung in 'beckets'. These were, as the name suggested, loops of rope, with a knot in one end, and an eye in the other, secured to the foremost fore and main shrouds, to secure the lee tacks, and the weather sheets. Sometimes, a simple cleat on the shrouds fulfilled the same purpose (Smyth, 92). As we have indicated, the mainyard was swung by its preventer braces, but once around, the weather after brace took the strain. The after braces were idle during 'Mainsail haul!', but they would have been in danger of getting foul of the davits of the quarter boats, and so on. To obviate this, the lee after main brace was run up out of the way by a tricing line, which consisted of a light rope spliced around a thimble, travelling on the brace. The German term for this fitting was *Leegrossbrass-aufholer*, that is 'lee main brace up-hauler'.

By-the-wind hitches. In small merchantmen, working in a fairway, where frequent tacking was necessary, it was customary to half-hitch, or back-hitch, the weather braces on the pins, in such a way that the yards were

Coaxing a ship around. To help her tack successfully, the ship's headsails have been hauled down, the foreyards braced to, and the mizzen yard hauled over to weather while coming up into the wind.

Lever's figure to illustrate the old method of tacking.

trimmed correctly, the upper a little 'in' on the lower, and so on. Upon going about, the lee braces were thrown off, and ran out until brought up by the hitch. The slack was taken up on the old weather brace, and the coil dropped over the pin and back-hitched, ready for the next tack (*Mariner's Mirror* 62, 1976, 119, 326; 63, 1977, 162). McDonald (*Nautical Research Journal* 18, 1971, 32) says that by-the-wind hitches were only necessary on the upper braces, which had to be checked in their swing. The lower yards were brought up adequately by coming hard against the lee shrouds. He is the only English authority known to me who uses this expression, but it is clearly derived from Danish *bi-de-vind-stik*, or the equivalent in other northern European languages. Hildebrandt (181), writing in 1872, describes the practice, but simply calls it a *Kopfschlag*, which would translate as 'head-hitch'. Massenet (410) makes the hitch about three fathoms short of the by-the-wind mark, so the yards will not come sharp up.

Headsails and fore sheet. The jib and flying jib sheets were eased off, at 'Ease down the helm!', but they were not let go completely, although that may well have been the custom in an earlier day (Groeneijk, 49). The men on the forecastle sometimes created problems by rushing to get their share of the work done as quickly as possible. The order 'Helm's a-lee!' was not given as long as the jibs were drawing. If let go too soon, they flapped about, no longer contributing to headway. The pendants were shifted over the stays only when the wind was dead ahead. If this were done too early, the jibs acted as backsails, impeding, rather than aiding the desired motion. The fore sheet was

traditionally let go with the head sheets, but many seamen preferred to keep it aft as long as it was doing any good, 'tacking with everything fast' as Liardet (243) puts it. Boyd (387) emphasises that 'previousness' on the part of the forecastlemen must be prevented, otherwise they will 'begin shifting the headsheets over, as soon as they have done another piece of mischief, in letting go the fore sheet at the word "Helm's a-lee"'. Hourigan (74) comments on another error, letting go the fore bowline at 'Tacks and sheets!'. If the fore tack were raised by the weather clewgarnet at this point, the bowline would continue to steady the upper part of the weather leech. Even if the tack were to be kept down, the bowline helped keep the weather leech at a better angle, so far as tacking was concerned.

Other staysails. There is little reference to handling these in going about, but certain assumptions may be made. They would be completely in the lee of the headyards during a great part of the manoeuvre, and hence might be better hauled down temporarily, rather than left flapping about. The sheets would have to be shifted over, and like the jibs, that should not be done prematurely. Lever (76) indicates that they were shifted over after 'Rise tacks and sheets!'. If drawing well, the sheets should be kept fast in the early stages of tacking, to help keep way on the ship. The main staysails, as part of the forward sail, would tend to make the bow fall off, hence in luffing, their sheets should be flown, or the sails hauled down. The mizzen staysail, as part of the aftersail, might aid luffing if the sheets were hauled in, in the same sort of way as a mizzen boom hauled amidships. Massenet (410) leaves the staysails set if the breeze is light, but hauls them down, if it is fresh.

Coaxing the ship around. Where the breeze was relatively light, and there was some doubt about the success of the manoeuvre, some extra attention might 'beckon' (*aanwenken*) the ship round, as the Dutch put it. Hauling down the flying jib, and perhaps also the jib, hauling the mizzen boom over to

windward, are mentioned by Mossel (III, 234), who also advises letting go the fore top bowline, and fore sheet, and bracing in the headyards, as an inducement to coming up in the wind, and allowing the headyards to come aback more readily. The German equivalent for bracing to, in this way, was *die Brassen springen lassen*, 'to spring the braces'. Ulffers (295) braces the mizzen topsail aback in the early stages of the manoeuvre (to push the stern to leeward), keeps the tacks of the courses down until the last moment, and makes a late haul of the afteryards. The aim of all these modifications was to allow the sails to swing the ship around in the desired direction, rather than depending, to the usual degree, on the helm. In the chase, or being pursued, with a smooth sea and very light winds, it might be imperative to get onto the other tack. If staying were dubious, a boat could be dropped, to pull the ship's head around (von Littrow, 143).

Ancient method of tacking. Lever (76) makes a point of comparing tacking 'by the method formerly practised', and his own technique for 'tacking expeditiously'. The faults of the old method included jamming the helm hard over and bracing to, both of which diminished headway; shifting the jib sheets too quickly; making a late mainsail haul; and losing ground by falling off too far on the new tack. As I have mentioned, it may also have been common practice to shove the peak of the mizzen over to windward, which is echoed in later references to hauling the mizzen boom over in the same way (Bourdé, 91; Mossel III, 233).

The Dutch accounts of Le Compte (171), and Groeneijk (49) give the second command in the form *Kluiver-en stagzeil-schooten los! Stadig aan lij het roer!*; that is 'Let go jib and fore topmast staysail sheets!, Ease down the helm!'. This suggests that the jib sheet was not eased off, but let go completely, and this may well reflect earlier practice. Groeneijk, who was writing in 1848, says that in his day the jib sheet was kept fast, the helm was put down, and at some point after that, when the vessel had luffed up, the order was given 'Let go fore sheets!', corresponding to 'Helm's a-lee!' in English. Mossel (III, 237), rather surprisingly, omits a command between the equivalents of 'Ease down the Helm!' and 'Rise tacks and sheets!'.

Mainwaring's (234) account, ante-dating as it does, the use of jibs, is of sufficient interest to quote at some length.

Before the ship can be ready to be tacked, she must come *a-stays* or *a-backstays*; that is, when the wind comes in at the bow, which was the lee bow before, and so drives all the sails backward against the shrouds and masts, so that the ship hath no way, but drives with the broad side. the manner of doing it is at one time and together to put down the helm, let fly the sheet of the foresail, and let go the fore bowline, and brace the weather brace of the foresail; the same to the topsail and topgallant sail, only they keep fast their sheets. If the spritsails be out, then they let go the spritsail sheet with the foresheet and brace the weather brace; (the tacks, sheets, braces, bowlines of the mainsail, main topsail and mizzen standing fast as they did). Sometimes by the negligence of him at the helm, sometimes if it be little wind and a head sea on the weather bow, a ship may *miss staying*; that is to fall back and fill again. The best conditioned ships are those which stay with least sails, as with two topsails, or fore topsail and mizzen, but no ship will stay with less sail than those, and few with so little.

The spritsail. Before the advent of the jib, the foremast was stepped quite a bit further forward relative to the keel, than was the case later, and hence, once aback, exerted a proportionately greater effect on pivoting. Apart from Mainwaring, cited above, there is almost nothing to be found on how the spritsails were handled in tacking, although some people such as the late Alan Villiers have actually been shipmates with them in quite recent times, in vessels like *Mayflower II*. In tacking, the spritsail yard had to be triced around, getting the new lee yardarm up and back. The new weather guys were hauled taut to give downward and windward support to the jibboom. Sjöbohm (40) suggests that the spritsail yard was triced around at the very beginning of the manoeuvre, Rosvall (107) as the helm is being put down. It seems much more likely that this was done, in later years, after 'Mainsail haul!', with the wind almost ahead, as indicated by Lever (76). Whether the sail was temporarily clewed up during this procedure is not mentioned; perhaps it depended on circumstances. The yard could be swung almost fore and aft, and hence the sail would have continued drawing almost as long as the jibs, as the ship came up in the wind. That being so, the sheet could have

been kept fast until 'Helm's a-lee!'. In those circumstances where the jib had to be hauled down, the spritsail would best have been clewed up, to help the ship around.

The reefed spritsail offered a special problem, because the reef would have to be shaken out and taken on the other diagonal, each time the ship went about. This must have been rather troublesome, if the ship were tacking frequently. I do not know for certain when the diagonal spritsail reef was introduced, but I would guess in the mid-1700s. *Der ge-öffnete Seehafen* of 1704 is silent on the matter, while definitive double diagonal spritsail reefs are found in Romme, and Lescallier, towards the end of the century. Once jibs were introduced, it seems most likely that the reefed spritsail would only have been set if frequent changes of tack were not in prospect.

The spritsail topsail. The old-fashioned spritsail topmast would not have been set by the wind, for reasons given in considering this particular sail. The later spritsail topsail (set under the jibboom) on the other hand, differed from the spritsail in that it could actually be laid aback, since its clews were steadied out by the spritsail yard. It is just conceivable that this characteristic could have been made use of in tacking, since with the spritsail and spritsail topsail yard triced up almost vertically, a backed spritsail topsail would exert a very powerful leverage in throwing the bow off the wind. This effect, however, would be most apparent when the bow was already through the eye of the wind, when the manoeuvre had succeeded in any case, and as we have indicated, the spritsail and spritsail topsail yards would have been

triced around at this juncture. By the same token, the sail would have held the bow off the wind in the earlier stages of tacking, although in the initial phase it would help contribute to headway. My own guess is that it would have been clewed up or clewed down, by letting go the outhaul, and keeping the sheets fast at 'Helm's a-lee!'. This would have minimised its effect, and best allowed the bow to swing into the wind.

Tacking by hauling of all, swinging all the yards together. This was possible, as a stunt, in a smart working vessel with a strong crew. It was never done when tacking was absolutely necessary; but only to 'try the activity or force of a crew, and the qualities of the vessel' (Totten, 189). The crew were distributed to handle all three masts at once, and the ship was run up into the wind, and allowed to fall five points or so off on the other tack, with everything aback. The order was then given 'Haul taut! Let go and haul!' upon which the yards were swung around together (Dana, 61).

Tacking in squally weather. Boyd (389) says, 'In tacking with a strong breeze, there is danger to the masts from the pressure of the sails when aback, as they are then supported only by the stays. This is sometimes so imminent, that when the sails begin to shake, and are no longer useful in carrying way, the topsails are lowered, and only hoisted again when the ship is round on the other tack'. This was done, of course, to spare the masts and gear, but it was sometimes necessary to let go the topsail halliards if the ship were hit by an unexpected squall, during the evolution, perhaps at an inopportune time. The other occasion when topsails were struck,

Swedish merchantman tacking in squally weather (after Baugean).

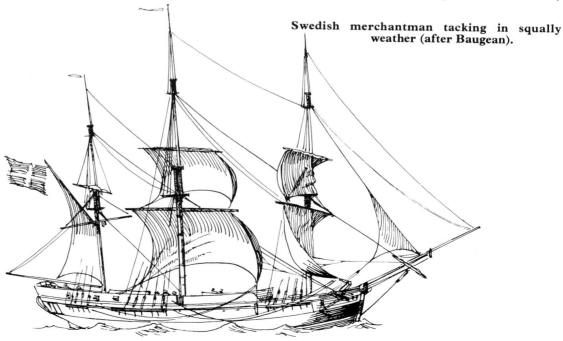

during tacking, was the exercise of 'reefing in stays', which we have considered under Reefing.

If tacking was necessary in squally weather an attempt was made to do so in the interval between squalls. If, nonetheless, the ship was hit by a gust, topgallants and mainsail were clewed up, topsail halliards let go, and jib. hauled down, according to circumstances. If it were judged best to take in the topgallants before tacking, the mainsail might be kept set for the time being, and clewed completely up at 'Rise tacks and sheets!', that is to say, when the wind was blowing pretty well along the yard. The mainsail was extremely dangerous in this kind of weather if it flew aback hard against the mainmast and shrouds. If that happened, it would defy almost all efforts to run it up in its gear. Even if the mainsail were only thrashing around, it would subject the mainmast to unacceptable strain. Ulffers (293) also suggests that the foresheet be kept aft, for the time being, since the vessel might be tending to gripe, because of excessive heeling to the squall, and the foresail would help obviate this problem. If this were done, the command 'Let go foresheet!' which would usually be given, or implied, by 'Helm's a-lee!', would be ordered at the same time as 'Rise tacks and sheets!'.

If things went a-right, the manoeuvre would proceed very quickly because of the tremendous pressure on the backed foremast, and an early mainsail haul might be indicated. If the ship started to make a sternboard, it was crucial that the helm be righted, and then held midships. To shift it, as when tacking in moderate weather, was to risk damage to the rudder fastenings, particularly if the rudder took charge and slammed hard over in either direction. If the ship fell off too rapidly, the headyards were not braced sharp up immediately, and the mainsail was set again if necessary (Ulffers, 294).

Tacking a steamer. Dick & Kretchmer (326) emphasise that in the case of a vessel under both sail and steam, tacking would invariably succeed, since steerage way could always be maintained. Swinging the yards together was therefore perfectly practical in this situation also, and in fact, could be done rather earlier in the turn, than suggested above, since the helm could be depended upon to swing the head round. Swinging everything together would have looked smart, the neatness of the manoeuvre appealing to the military mind.

We have already alluded to Luce's suggestion that the mizzen topsail be backed when tacking a steamer under sail alone. The sailing qualities of steamers are deplored by many writers in the late 1800s, the reason being the unfortunate effect the screw aperture had on the steerage. Water coming along the side of the ship ideally piled up, so to speak, against the side of the rudder, thus causing the stern to move in the opposite direction. Water escaping through the screw aperture, forward of the sternpost, prevented the rudder of the screw steamer exerting its full potential turning effort, and as a matter of fact, because of eddies forming on the wrong side of the rudder, might even reverse the desired effect. The screw was allowed to rotate passively, when under sail alone, since this minimised the drag of the propeller. However, at slow speeds – as would be the case when head to wind in tacking – the screw usually ceased to rotate, and started to drag, further reducing headway (Hourigan, 76).

Tacking a five-masted vessel. There were a few men-of-war, in the days of steam and sail, with five masts, but these were usually square rigged only on the forward three. However, the German merchantmen *Preussen* and *Potosi*, ship and barque respectively, must have offered some special problems in manoeuvring. In a five-masted ship, the forward two masts are ahead of the CLR, the others – middle, mizzen and jigger, by whatever names they are known – are abaft it. This would suggest that the three after masts would be swung at 'Mainsail haul!', and the fore and main, as a unit, at 'Haul of all!', and indeed Wilson-Barker (96) says 'in tacking a ship having five or more masts, the two foremost masts are worked together'. Riesenberg, however, (772) declares that 'A five-master like the barque *France* goes about, swinging the three yards on the after square-rigged masts together'. The foreyards are swung at 'Let go and haul!', as in the case of a three-master; that is, the main is worked with the afteryards, although functionally it appears to be a unit of the forward sail plan. The mainmast would, to some extent, be in the lee of the fore, when head to wind, and this, combined with the shorter lever about which it worked, would reduce its turning ability, once it was aback. The sail plan, being more 'open' with split topsails and split topgallants, the fore would have blanketted the main less effectively than in the days when topsails and topgallants were single pieces of canvas.

Neither Wilson-Barker, nor Riesenberg, had any practical experience themselves in a five-master, but in a most interesting section of *The War with Cape Horn* (275), Alan Villiers records his conversations on this topic with Robert Miethe, once master of the Laeisz five-masted barque *Potosi*. Miethe indicated that the after three square-rigged masts were not swung simultaneously, but rather one after the other, at two-second intervals. A literal reading of the passage suggests that this was done in the order main, middle and mizzen, that is to say sequentially from forward aft. It is said that this interval was necessary because otherwise the yards 'would have got mixed up, because there wasn't room for three masts of them to swing clear at the same time'. This no doubt reflects the practical experience of Miethe, but there are one or two problems with this account that need elucidation. The first is the reason for the two-second interval. The greatest danger of locking the lower yards would exist between fore and main, when one was braced up sharp on the old tack, the other on the new. Swinging three masts precisely together would result in keeping the yards exactly parallel, and hence giving the *least* chance of locking the lower yardarms; so I think we must look further than a mix-up of the yardarms, for an explanation. A two-second interval, by the way, was not a great deal of time, when it is remembered that it took almost half an hour to tack *Potosi*.

The second problem is the order of swinging, from forward aft. We have alluded earlier to the practice of backing the jigger topsail in a four-masted ship, and then handling it as a three-master (Todd & Whall, 87). Furthermore, we have Wilson-Barker's assertion that the main is worked with the fore. These combine to suggest the likelihood that the afteryards might have been swung in the opposite order, that is to say, mizzen, middle and main.

This is confirmed by the account of how a four-masted barque is tacked offered by Massenet (412). After 'Rise tacks and sheets!', the mizzen (*grand phare arrière*) is braced about, and once it is changed, the main (*grand phare devant*) is swung. 'The manoeuvre has the aim of facilitating the bracing about of the masts, because if both were swung at the same time, it would result in the mizzen, blanketted by the main, remaining braced square, and would delay the evolution.' With a four-masted ship, Massenet recommends swinging the jigger as one starts to put down the helm. The check in the rotation of the mizzen yards referred to arises for the same reason as the slow swing resulting from a late mainsail haul, but with the added complication of one extra mast in a four-master, and two in a five-masted barque like *Potosi*. In a man-of-war, the heavy deck force available might well have made light of this problem; in a lightly manned merchantman, even with brace-winches, it was

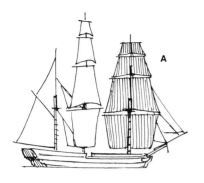
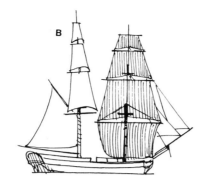

Tacking various square rigged vessels
A Tacking a barque; **B** tacking a brig; **C** tacking a 5-masted barque (after Miethe's description) – yards on mainmast being swung last in 'mainsail haul'.

obviated by initiating the swing of the after-yards early, each mast following in succession, from aft forwards. Presumably the yards reached their final position about the same time, the forward yards helped around by the wind on the weather bow 'catching up' on the others.

Since five-masters were so few in number, and around for such a short period, as compared with the total history of the sailing ship, it may be doubted that this intriguing question can be completely cleared up. Although a vessel like *Preussen* might have been expected to tack less readily than a short beamy three-master, there has to be considered the momentum generated by her great size and weight. That is to say, it would require a lot of effort to get that enormous mass moving through the water, but once it was shifting along, it would have been extremely difficult to stop. To emphasise this point, a liner like the *Queen Mary*, of 80,000 tons gross, travelling at twenty knots, would, if the engines were stopped abruptly, continue to maintain headway for a distance of two or three miles! Hence, perhaps *Preussen*, with her 5000 tons gross could be run up into, and through, the wind more readily than one might have expected. Villiers' account of Miethe's experience in *Potosi* does not indicate whether or not a sternboard was usually needed to finish of the evolution. Since there was so much variation in detail, in the manner of tacking a three-master, it seems possible that there could have been more than one way of tacking a five-master, and perhaps the 'best' way was never actually determined: all in all, a fascinating question, upon which the last word has not yet been said.

Tacking other square-rigged vessels. The mainmast of a four-masted ship or barque was very close to the pivot point,

rather than being part of the aftersail. None-theless it was swung at 'Haul of all!'. A barque was, in fact, simpler to tack than a vessel completely square-rigged, with the same number of masts. The only feature of note was the necessity to shift the tack of the gaff-topsail over to the new weather side. A brig was tacked like a ship, without the complication of crossjack yard and mizzen topsail. The five-masted Vinnen schooners, which had square topsails on the fore and middle masts, but not on the main, presumably swung the yards on the middle at 'Mainsail haul!', and those on the fore at 'Haul of all!' (Underhill, *Deep Water Sail*, 261). This arrangement, although it looks a little odd, was very practical. There was no problem with locking the yards, even when braced up as sharp as could be on opposite tacks. Square sails on the main would have been forward of the pivot point, and been blanketted by those on the fore, when head to wind.

Tacking in line. In men-of-war, consideration had to be given to the fact that it was essential to keep station, when in company with other vessels. The following excerpts from Boyd (388) indicate the problems:

> When performing any evolution in the Line, if sail will not ensure it, do not hesitate to make a sufficiency, even if it should be taken in immediately afterwards. Missing stays, or taking up much time and space in wearing, throws other ships into danger and disorder. You may have been carrying enough sail to keep your station, but it does not follow that you have enough to carry you round, when the signal for an evolution is made. If your leader is dull, but doing his best, and in his station, you must not encroach on him; but you must be handy with your canvas, and sharp in freshening your way with it, just before your own time comes to go about. In every evolution in succession, the eye of the chief is on each performer as he goes around, and when, after a bad one, he asks for the name of the Officer of the Watch, the query is generally followed by an invitation to the flagship, not to dinner... the rule for going about in succession in close order in the Line, is to put the helm down when your next ahead is four points on the

weather bow, in open order five points; in wearing, when he is on your lee bow.

Missing stays. If the ship ran up into the wind, but then fell off on the old tack, the decision had to be made whether to gather speed once more, and make another attempt at tacking, or whether to wear ship. These would be the only options open to a dinghy sailor in the analogous situation (to tack or gybe), but the square-rigger by making a sternboard might be 'boxhauled', a manoeuvre which we will now examine in detail.

BOXHAULING

This implied bracing the fore yards aback, sailing the ship backwards, turning her on her heel through sixteen points, until she was stern to wind, then going ahead while gradually turning up into the wind once more, on the fresh tack. By executing this manoeuvre, less ground was lost to leeward, than by wearing, although more than if the ship had been tacked successfully. I do not know exactly how old this word is, or indeed the practice to which it refers. It is listed by Röding in the late 1700s, but not by Boteler, Mainwaring, and so on, in the mid 1600s. *The Oxford Dictionary of English Etymology* suggests that 'Box the Compass' derives from Spanish *boxar*, *bojar*, 'to sail around', as in *boxar el mundo*, 'to sail around the world'. The young seaman, in preparation for taking his turn at the wheel, had to learn to gabble off the points of the compass, in quarter points, both forwards and backwards. I do not find Luce's (441) suggestion that it arises from the expression 'bracing the headyards abox' of very much help, and in fact I am unsure which term came first. Clearly the idea that the canvas is 'aback' is intimately involved, and this certainly affects the way the word is used, 'brace a-box the fore yard' meaning precisely the same thing as 'brace it aback'.

Not all seamen approved this manoeuvre, involving as it did, considerable strain on the rudder fastenings and the forestays. Bréart (185), for example, does not consider it at all, saying that if the ship miss-stays, the attempt is made again, or the ship wears. In the description which follows, we are relying mainly on the accounts of Luce, Knight and Ekelöf.

Boxhauling, or as Nichelson (133) calls it 'fox-hauling', can be considered either as an evolution in its own right, or as an emergency measure to be used on missing stays. We will consider the latter situation first. Let us suppose that the ship, having been on the port tack, has run up into the wind, the after yards have been swung, and she now hangs in irons, going off neither one way or the other, and it is decided to boxhaul. The headyards are braced right around on the other tack, by hauling on the port braces. The mainsail and spanker are hauled up. The afteryards are squared, and the jib sheet is hauled flat aft. The helm having been put a-lee, that is to say, to starboard, when luffing up, and it is left that way. This configuration of sail will cause the ship to move briskly astern, the headyards and flattened-in jib causing the bow to fall off rapidly to leeward, that is, in this case to starboard. The keel describes an arc of a circle, as the ship moves backwards, 'wearing short round on her heel', in Luce's (439) terminology. The ship will make a circular sternboard, almost retracing her path as she came up into the wind in the first place, until she comes to a stop almost stern to wind. To accomplish this, the afteryards are kept lifting, gradually coming to be braced up sharp on the new tack. This stage will have been reached when the wind is coming from the port quarter, the yards having been square from the start of the sternboard until the wind is abeam. The headyards are squared as sternway is finally lost, and the helm shifted for headway; that is to say, first of all righted, and then shifted to port. The ship gathers way, the head coming up to starboard, and the wind comes on the quarter, the mainsail

and spanker can be set once more, the spanker boom hauled over to port, and the jib sheet flown. As she comes to, the quartermaster meets her with the helm, and the headyards are braced up on the new tack.

It will be realised that the initial dropping astern resembles the movement of a ship when completing a tack by means of a sternboard. the difference is that in the latter case, the headyards remain braced up on the old tack, and that the arc described by the keel, rather than retracing its path in the initial luffing up, is going in the opposite direction. In tacking, with a sternboard, the headyards are braced up as for the old tack, while in boxhauling, they are braced up the opposite way. **Variations on boxhauling after missing stays.** If the ship is in irons, it may be necessary to brace around the headyards, so the bow can fall off sufficiently to allow the ship to continue on the old tack. Another variation is described by Luce (442) under the heading 'Backing a ship around off a lee shore'; Knight (405) does not ascribe it any special name, but refers to the manoeuvre also. The

afteryards having been swung, and the ship having originally been on the port tack, lying in irons, the headyards were braced around, as in boxhauling, so that all three masts were aback, and braced as if for the starboard tack. The helm was kept the same way, so that the keel described a curve backwards, more or less in the path followed when luffing up. When the wind came from aft or well on the port quarter, the headyards were squared, the helm shifted over, and the ship sailed around so as to come to on the starboard tack, when she was met with the helm, and the headyards braced up again on the new tack.

It will be seen that this is really the same procedure described in boxhauling with some differences. All three masts are braced up, as for starboard tack, and the sternboard does not continue until the wind is completely astern, the afteryards not being touched. There is a feature of this method

Boxhauling step by step
1 Ship in irons; foreyards braced round on starboard tack, mainsail and spanker hauled up, afteryards squared and jib sheet flattened in; 2 ship makes a sternboard, head falling off to starboard; 3 wind on the quarter, afteryards braced up; 4 ship nearly stern to wind, foreyards squared and ship gathers way being steered to starboard; 5 ship coming up to her course on starboard tack, foreyards braced up and jib sheet trimmed.

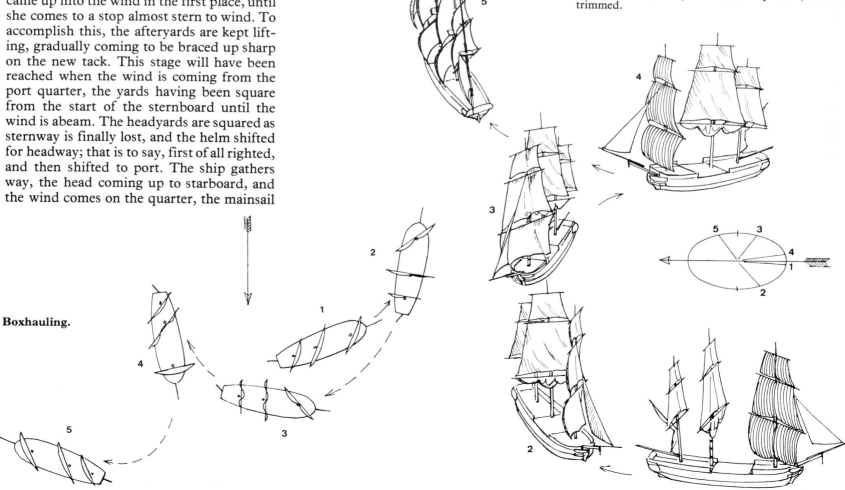

Boxhauling.

which may explain its effectiveness. A vessel going astern, tends to throw the stern up to windward, and this is true of steamers as well as sailing vessels, arising because the water starts to pile up under the lee quarter, thus pushing the stern to windward. The phenomenon is exactly analogous to the banking up of water under the lee bow in the case of a vessel going ahead, with a like tendency to throw the bow into the wind, and a necessity to carry weather helm to counteract this. Whether going ahead or astern, heeling aggravates the problem, and makes the bow or stern fly up into the wind all the quicker. Since in this case, all three masts are braced up sharp, the ship will heel to starboard, and water will quickly pile up under the starboard quarter, causing a rapid falling off of the ship's head to starboard.

Boxhauling as an evolution. This may be performed when working in a narrow channel, the weather shore having been neared, and it is desired to go about without fore reaching as in tacking, while at the same time, the loss to leeward involved in wearing is unacceptable.

With the crew at stations for stays, the ship is run up into the wind. Headway is deadened as much as possible by such devices as jamming the helm down, dropping the jib, bracing to the headyards, letting go the foresheet and so on. At 'Rise tacks and sheets!', the mainsail and spanker are hauled up. The afteryards are squared, the headyards braced abox, and the jib sheets hauled flat aft, when head to wind. Thereafter, proceed as already described.

Wearing short round. This is considered by some authorities, as a variation on boxhauling, or vice versa. Both involve bracing the headyards abox, and both may be said to involve 'wearing on her heel', but boxhauling is initiated by running up into the wind, whereas wearing short round commences by backing the foreyard immediately. While boxhauling may be attempted as an evolution, wearing short round is an emergency manoeuvre only used when danger appears on the lee or weather bow, and makes it necessary to throw everything aback, and stop the ship in her tracks, as it were. Take the case of a shoal on the weather bow, where headreaching, as in tacking or boxhauling would be unacceptable, or imagine a ship close-hauled on the port tack, suddenly discerning through the mists another sailing vessel close to on the weather bow, standing on the opposite, or starboard tack, and hence having the right of way. Here throwing the headyards aback, is better than luffing up. As Hourigan (81) puts it:

Variation on boxhauling with all yards braced aback.

Wearing short round: ship put about to avoid collision with shaded vessel on starboard tack.

the advantage of this manoeuvre to avoid collision is apparent. It declares one's intention immediately, shows the other vessel that she is observed and her right of way conceded. Luffing is bad; you may reach across her bows, when she may keep away to avoid you, increasing the chances of collision when you gather sternboard or if you attempt to wear around, when you again back across her bows. To attempt to tack at close quarters, unless so absolutely close that nothing else is possible, is an unseamanlike *trick*, more becoming the jockeying of a yacht race, where only the loss of the race may be the penalty, than at sea, between two ships, where hundreds of lives may be at stake and where failure would not leave one any pre-text or excuse.

The danger being realised, the helm was put up, the foreyards were backed, the afteryards were squared, the mainsail and spanker hauled up. These measures would bring the ship to a stop in a short distance, and cause the bow to fall off. If the vessel started to move astern, helm was shifted, and had she been on the port tack, the bow would fall off to starboard. When the wind came well round aft on the port quarter, and she started to gain headway, the helm was shifted, and the procedure followed that used in the latter stages of boxhauling. This method would lose less distance to leeward than the usual method of wearing, but rather more than when boxhauling, where the initial luff gained something to windward.

WEARING OR VEERING A SHIP

This was the third method of going about. As in tacking, headway was maintained throughout, but the ship went about stern to wind, and hence to go from one tack to the other, needed to traverse twenty points of the compass to achieve this, first falling off ten points, and then coming to for ten points more. 'Many good officers wear their ships instead of tacking, when they have plenty of sea-room, and the nature of the service will admit. By this means, you save your ropes and sails, and endanger your spars less' (Liardet, 201). This comment embodies the fact that there was greater loss to leeward in wearing than in boxhauling, and especially tacking; in addition a tremendous strain was borne by stays and spars when the canvas was thrown flat aback, and this problem was magnified if weather conditions were bad. Wearing ship, in reasonable weather, had the great merit that it always succeeded in its aim; and the smaller the circle described, the

Wearing.

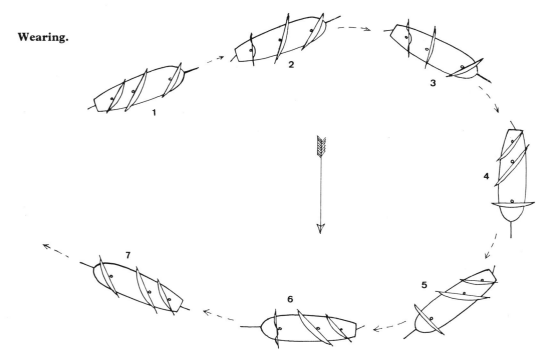

less ground lost to leeward (von Littrow, 146). There was nothing comparable to missing stays, although Steel (265) says that 'ships with a large cutwater veer with difficulty'.

When to wear. As Liardet indicates, some always preferred to wear, if there was room to leeward to allow it. The more general opinion favoured tacking, in the absence of any contra-indication, since the gain to windward was well worth the trouble. Wearing might be necessary because the wind was too light, or on the other hand because there was too much wind or sea on the weather bow. If the vessel were badly out of trim, down by the stern, the bow tended to go off the wind, and she would be carrying lee helm. This meant that tacking would be an uncertain procedure, and hence wearing was best. We will defer consideration of wearing in heavy weather until we review the handling of the vessel in a storm, and confine our attention for the present to wearing in light winds, or moderate weather.

Principle involved. The object was to go off the wind and using the sails on the foremast, sail the ship around until the wind was more or less dead astern. Up to this point in the operation, the aftersail was neutralised, so that the stern could come up to the wind. The spanker and the mainsail were taken in, and the afteryards were trimmed so that the other sails on main and mizzen were all in the wind. The ship was sailed downwind until the wind was coming from the old lee quarter. The afteryards were by that time, braced up sharp for the new tack, and the headyards were now squared, the jib sheets flown, the mainsail set and spanker hauled out. This would allow the wind to fill the aftersail, and cause the ship to come up in the wind, this action being unopposed by the forward canvas. As she came to the wind, the foreyards were braced up, and the luffing movement met by the helm and appropriate trimming of the jibs.

In theory, the main topsail and topgallant being after canvas, should be a-shiver in the early stages of the manoeuvre, but in fact it was more important that the ship have sufficient steerage way to make use of the helm. This being so, most authorities advise keeping the main topsail just full, but not braced sharp up, while the mizzen topsail is kept right in the wind (Liardet, 201). Gower (39), in fact, goes further, and keeps all the aftersails just full, rather than shaking, for the same reason. Ulffers (304) keeps the main course set, rather than clewing it up at once, again to get the best possible headway.

Wearing in a light breeze: First command. 'Stations for wearing ship!'. We may for convenience, divide the evolution into artificial stages, by the sequence of commands, as we did for tacking. Let us suppose, that a ship is close-hauled on the port tack. The crew are stationed as for tacking and the order is given 'Main clewgarnets and buntlines!', 'Spanker brails! Weather main, lee crossjack braces! Everything being manned, Haul taut!'. In a light breeze, when the ship was going downwind, the relative wind speed was at an absolute minimum, and progress might be painfully slow, since the ship would be canvassed for sailing close-hauled.

Second command. 'Up mainsail and spanker! Clear away the after bowlines! Brace in the afteryards! Up helm!'. The main topsail is kept just full, which implies that the wind is coming from at least three points abaft the orientation of the main topsail yard, and the mizzen topsail a-shake. The vessel swings round, so that the wind appears to come from further and further aft, the afteryards being swung gradually as this occurs. As a result, they will be braced up sharp on the new tack, when the wind is fine on the old weather quarter. The lifts are overhauled as the yards are swung from the order 'Overhaul the weather lifts!'. Preparations are made to square the headyards. 'Man the weather headbraces! Rise fore tack and sheet!'.

Third command. 'Clear away the head bowlines! Lay the headyards square! Shift over the headsheets!': these orders will be given when the wind is more or less directly aft. The ship continues to swing to starboard, so that the wind is gradually drawing forward on the starboard side. When the wind is on the starboard quarter, preparations are made to set the mainsail and spanker. 'Man the main tack and sheet! Clear away the rigging! Spanker outhaul! Clear away the brails!'.

Fourth command. 'Haul aboard! Haul out!'; whereupon the spanker is set, the main tack got down, and the main sheet aft. A man aloft overhauls the buntlines, and so on. The ship should now come rapidly to the wind, this movement being unopposed by the squared headyards, and flown jibs. When almost up to the desired point, the headyards are braced up, the jib sheet hauled aft, and the helm righted.

Fifth command. 'Brace up headyards! Overhaul weather lifts! Haul aboard!'; the tack is got down, and the sheet aft. In the case of the foresail, the buntlines had not been hauled, the clews having been lifted with the clewgarnets only at 'Rise tack and sheet!'. It is unnecessary therefore to order 'Clear away the rigging!', as in the case of the main. The jibsheets are hauled aft, the order sometimes given in the form 'Draw jib!'.

Sixth command. 'Steady out the bowlines! Haul taut weather trusses, braces and lifts! Clear away on deck!'; it will be remembered that to get the tacks down, weather lifts, and sometimes weather topsail clewlines must be overhauled. Once the tack is aboard, the lift must be hauled taut, and in fact truss, lift and weather brace must be hauled taut together, since pulling on one may slacken the other. During the evolution several details aloft were attended to consequent on changing tacks. The spritsail yard was triced around, and the weather guys set up. The old weather breast backstays were borne abaft, and those on the new weather side were borne out. The royal weather shrouds were set up, and if necessary the foremost lee shroud was slackened to allow the royal yard to come sharp up. If double topsail ties were in use, the old lee halliards were hauled taut before the ship was on the new tack.

Wearing in a fresh breeze. This was carried out in an essentially similar manner except that it might be possible to shiver the main topsail rather than keeping it full, to maintain steerageway. Luce (438) follows Totten (192) in emphasising that the afteryards must be sharp up on the new tack, before the headyards are touched. Glascock (306) cautioned against putting the helm up before the main brace was rounded in somewhat; doing otherwise meant a heavy haul. In a light breeze the difference would be inconsequential, and it would not matter whether yards or helm were altered first.

English and foreign terms. The English word 'wend', or 'wind' (rhyming with 'bind'), as used by Mainwaring (256) meant 'to turn the ship's head about', but this seems to have been limited to getting the head round by towing with the boat, hauling on a warp, or rowing the vessel round with

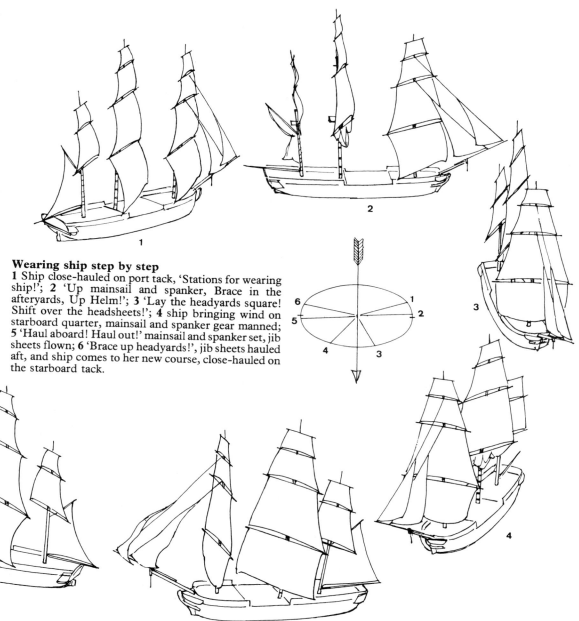

Wearing ship step by step
1 Ship close-hauled on port tack, 'Stations for wearing ship!'; 2 'Up mainsail and spanker, Brace in the afteryards, Up Helm!'; 3 'Lay the headyards square! Shift over the headsheets!'; 4 ship bringing wind on starboard quarter, mainsail and spanker gear manned; 5 'Haul aboard! Haul out!' mainsail and spanker set, jib sheets flown; 6 'Brace up headyards!', jib sheets hauled aft, and ship comes to her new course, close-hauled on the starboard tack.

sweeps. Judging by some of the foreign equivalents, it might earlier have included going about by tacking: at least, German *wenden*, Swedish *vända*, and so on are the usual terms for going about, whether by tacking or wearing, with similar words in other languages. The distinction was made between wending through the wind, or wending before the wind, the former was known as *stagvending*, and the latter as *kovending*, in Danish. 'Staywending' is obvious enough, while 'cow-wending' perhaps suggests that it involved taking the long way around. German *Überstag gehen*, 'go over stay' means 'to tack', but oddly enough, a common German synonym for wearing was *halsen*, which literally means 'tacking', *Hals* being the word for the tack of a sail.

In English, the verb 'to stay' is sometimes

used synonymously with 'to tack' (Smyth, 653), but to Mainwaring, and his contemporaries, it meant the act of running the ship up into the wind, 'to heave her in stays', until the headsails came aback. It occurs also, as we have seen in the expression 'to miss-stay', or 'be slack in stays', said of a vessel in poor trim for tacking.

In French, the expression used for going about was *virer*, which simply means 'to turn', but also has the specific meaning of 'heave in', as in *virer au cabestan*, 'heave in on the capstan'. This comes as a bit of a surprise, when we compare it with English 'veer', which means just the opposite. *Virer vent devant*, ('go about wind ahead') clearly means 'tack' but *virer lof pour lof*, the term for 'wearing', echoes German *halsen*, since it literally means 'go about, tack for tack'.

ORGANISATION OF THE CREW FOR WORKING SHIP

One can get an idea of how this was managed by studying the System for Stationing Crews, to be found in Burney. However, I find this a little hard to follow; in fact, I get a better picture of how things were organised from reading Ulffers, upon which the following is primarily based.

Each quarter had an experienced seaman or petty-officer, in charge, a *Vormann*. This literally means 'foreman', but I have rendered it here as 'captain'. The system is based on how things were done with the watch. If 'all hands', or 'both watches' were called, each worked its own side and there were two men for every job outlined in the schema.

East Indiaman wearing in fresh weather (after N Pocock, 1806).

TO TACK SHIP

Stations for stays! The crew fell in by divisions, special numbers going aloft to clear away the rigging, shift the breast backstays, set up the royal shrouds, and so on. An experienced quartermaster or boatswain's mate took the wheel. Braces and bowlines were thrown off the pins, and flaked down clear for running, under the supervision of the captains of the appropriate part of ship.

Ease down the helm!

Ease off jib sheet	Captain of first quarter forecastlemen
Haul weather mizzen sheet to windward	Weather half mizzentopmen
Tend lee mizzen sheet	Captain third quarter quarterdeckmen

Helm's a-lee!

Let go foresheet	Captains third and fourth quarter waisters
Check lee fore brace	Captain first quarter afterguard
Check fore topbowline	Captain second quarter forecastlemen

Rise tacks and sheets!

Let go fore tack	Captains first & third quarters fore castlemen
Let go main tack	Captains third & fourth quarter of waisters
Lee fore clewgarnet	Foreyardmen of lee side
Main clewgarnets	Mainyardmen
Weather fore sheet	Waisters of weather side
Lee main tack	Afterguard of lee side

Mainsail haul!

Let go main preventer brace and top bowline	Captains third & fourth quarters waisters
Let go main topsail brace	Captain first quarter quarterdeckmen
Let go mizzen braces and bowlines	Captains third & fourth quarters afterguard
Let go main bowline	Captain second quarter waisters
Main preventer brace	Foremast division and forecastlemen
Main topsail brace	Main topsail yardmen of weather side
Main topgallant brace	Main topgallant yardmen of weather side
Crossjack braces	Mizzen topmen and quarterdeckmen (*ie* mizzen mast Division)
Main tack and sheet	Mainmast division of appropriate side, less maintopmen, stationed at the main topsail and topgallant braces
Let go and overhaul main clewgarnets	Captains first & second quarters afterguard

Haul of all!

Let go forebrace	Captain of first quarter afterguard
Let go lee foretopsail brace	Captain second quarter afterguard
Let go and belay lee fore topgallant brace	Captain third quarter afterguard
Let go head bowlines	Captains of forecastlemen, appropriate side
Fore brace	Main lower yardmen, afterguard and quarterdeckmen
Fore topsail brace	Main and mizzen topsail yardmen
Fore topgallant brace	Main and mizzen topgallant yardmen
Fore tack and sheet	Foremast Division
Forebowlines and headsail sheets	Forecastlemen
Fore clewgarnets	Captains of first and second quarters waisters

To Go About Swinging All Masts Together

In this rather showy manoeuvre, which was only done to exercise the crew, the starboard watch looked after main and mizzen, and the larboard watch, the fore.

Afteryards – all are handled by starboard watch

Let go main preventer brace and topbowline	Captain third quarter waisters
Let go main topsail brace	Captain second quarter afterguard
Let go mizzen braces	Captain third quarter afterguard
Let go main bowline	Captain first quarter waisters
Main preventer brace	Foremast division
Main topbowline	Fore topsail yardmen
Main topsail brace	Main topsail yardmen
Main topgallant brace	Main topgallant yardmen
Mizzen braces	Mizzenmast division
Main tack	Second part of mainmast division
Main sheet	Remainder of first part mainmast division

Headyards – all are handled by larboard watch

Let go lee fore brace	Captain of first quarter afterguard
Let go lee foretopsail brace	The same
Let go and belay lee fore topgallant brace	Captain third quarter afterguard
Let go fore bowline	Captains second & fourth quarter forecastlemen
Fore brace	Mainyardmen – afterguard and quarterdeckmen
Fore topsail brace	Main topsail yardmen and mizzen topsail yardmen
Fore topgallant brace	Main and mizzen topgallant yardmen
Fore tack and sheet	Foremast division divided into first & second parts
Fore bowlines and head sheets	Forecastlemen, divided into first & second parts
Let go fore clewgarnets	Captains first & second quarters waisters

Tacking in Squally Weather.

Ulffers (293) considers this eventuality and stations his crew as for stays generally, with the addition of men detailed to take in the topgallant, and take the mainsail in at 'Rise tacks and sheets!' The buntlines are manned as well as the clewgarnets. In this case he has not detailed men to let go the topsail halliards, but this conceivably might be necessary if the squall were severe.

Main clewgarnets	Mainyardmen
Main buntlines	Afterguard
Topgallant clewlines	Topsail yardmen
Weather topgallant braces	Topgallant yardmen
Let go topgallant halliards	Captains first quarters waisters, afterguard, quarterdeckmen
Let go topgallant sheets	Captains second quarters waisters, afterguard, quarterdeckmen

To Wear Ship in Moderate Weather

In spanker, up mainsail!

Lee spanker brails	Lee half mizzenmast division
Weather spanker brails	Weather mizzen topsail yardmen
Weather vang	Weather half quarterdeckmen
Let go and tend spanker outhaul	Captains second quarter quarterdeckmen
Let go main tack	Captains third & fourth quarters waisters
Let go main sheet	Captains third & fourth quarters afterguard
Let go main bowline	Captain second quarter waisters

Main clewgarnets	Main topsail yardmen
Main buntlines	Afterguard

Brace in after yards! Helm up!

Preventer brace	Foremast division
Weather main afterbrace	Main yardmen
Weather main topsail brace	Main topsail yardmen of the side
Lee mizzen braces	Mizzen topsail yardmen of both watches
Weather main truss-tackle fall	Afterguard of the other side
Crossjack truss-tackle fall	Quarterdeckmen
Let go main preventer brace and topbowline	Captains of third & fourth quarters waisters
Let go lee main brace	Captain first quarter afterguard
Let go mizzen braces	Captains third & fourth quarters afterguard
Let go lee truss-tackle fall	Captain third quarter afterguard

Brace headyards square!

Let go fore tack	Captains first & third quarters forcastlemen
Let go fore sheet	Captains third & fourth quarters waisters
Weather fore sheet	Foreyardmen of the side
Lee fore tack	Fore topsail yardmen of the side
Let go bowlines	Captains of forecastlemen of the side
Let go lee truss-tackle fall	Captain third quarter waisters
Shift over foresheets	Forecastlemen
Weather truss-tackle fall	Waisters of the side
Weather fore brace	Afterguard and mainyardmen
Weather fore topsail brace	Main topsail yardmen
Clear away spanker	Mizzenmast division

Disposition of the watch for wearing ship (based on Burney).

For comparison Burney offers the following:

Watch wear ship!
Boom tricers go aloft
Up mainsail; in driver!
Driver brails

Main clewgarnets, buntlines and leechlines	Mizzen topmen and second part quarterdeckmen
Weather after braces!	Men detailed, from quarterdeckmen.
Main preventer brace	Fore part. If necessary to work the after main brace, the fore part man it, leaving the forecastlemen on the preventer.
Main topsail brace	Maintopmen
Main topgallant royal braces	Upper bracemen
Main trusses and lifts	After part of the marines and the quarterdeckmen
Crossjack brace	First part of mizzen topmen
Mizzen topsail brace	Second part of mizzen topmen.
Mizzen upper braces	Mizzen upper bracemen, assisted by upper yardmen
Head braces!	
Fore tack	Fore part, and if not blowing hard, forecastlemen
Fore sheet	Second parts of maintopmen and quarterdeckmen
Fore brace	After part, not otherwise stationed
Fore topsail brace	First part maintopmen
Fore topgallant and royal braces	Fore upper yardmen
Fore trusses and lifts	Manned, if blowing hard, by the forecastlemen

Disposition of crew for tacking (based on Burney).

Watch about ship!
The boom-tricers go aloft to uncrutch the backstays. The mizzen boom is hauled over by the mizzentopmen, and the topping lift shifted by the spanker stowers.
Raise tacks and sheets!
The foretopmen man the weather fore clewgarnet, the maintopmen the main clewgarnet, while the lee clew of the mainsail is hauled up by the second part of the quarterdeckmen.
Mainsail haul!
The captain of the foretop oversees the men of the fore part, not otherwise stationed in handling the preventer brace, while the captain of the forecastle is responsible for watching the first part of the forecastle men shift over the headsails, letting go the main bowline, and seeing the first part of the foretopmen haul the 'new' weather main bowline. The main topsail brace is manned by the first parts of the main topmen, led by the captain of the main top. The main tack is got down by the after part, not otherwise stationed, while the quarterdeck topsail sheet men of the side overhaul the other side, under the direction of the gunner's mate. The main sheet is handled by the second part of the main topmen, and the second part of the quarterdeckmen. The captain supervises the first part of the mizzentopmen haul the crossjack brace, while the second part deal with the mizzen topsail brace. The main and mizzen topgallant braces are hauled by the upper bracemen, assisted if necessary by the upper yardmen, who set up the shifting backstays, led by the captain of the crosstrees.
Let go! Of all haul!
The captain of the forecastle lets go the fore top and topgallant bowlines. He also gets down the fore tack assisted by the fore part not otherwise stationed, while the forecastle topsail sheetmen of the side overhaul the other fore tack. The gunner's mate leads the second part of the main topmen and second part of the quarterdeckmen in hauling aft the fore sheet. Mizzen topmen may also be put on the fore tack and sheet if needed. The fore brace is hauled by the after part, not otherwise stationed, supervised by the captain of the quarterdeckmen. The fore upper bracemen, assisted if necessary by the upper yardmen, haul the topgallant and royal braces.

Organisation in a merchant ship.
For comparison, it is interesting to compare the division of labour in a small merchantman, where there were barely enough hands to manage, even by running from one part of the ship to another. Riesenberg, in *Under Sail*, talks of the ship *A J Fuller*, 2500 tons deadweight, with sixteen men forward. The following is based on Hildebrandt's (183) description of stations for stays in a small German vessel: two or three men, including boatswain, mate or a smart seaman, on the forecastle to handle staysails and fore bowlines; two or three men, including the carpenter or sailmaker, or a smart seaman, to let go and haul main tack and main bowlines; second mate to hitch all the lee braces on one pin for each mast, so they could be let go smartly by one hand, and see all braces ready for running; by-the-wind hitches on the weather braces; one or two men, mizzen sheet and topping lifts; two men, on each side, handle the mizzen braces, while all the others haul the weather braces, clewgarnets, and so on. Dana (59) says it was traditional in American ships for the cook to let go the foresheet, and the steward the main.

CLUBHAULING

This may be considered a special method of tacking. Clubhauling was only resorted to as a measure of desperation in very bad weather, when embayed on a lee shore without room to wear, and where there was no prospect that the vessel could tack successfully because of the sea breaking on the weather bow. As to the name, it appears to use the 'club' of 'clubbing down a river', to make a compound like 'box-haul', I have never found the word 'club' actually used to mean 'anchor'. Other languages had no special term for this procedure.

The lee anchor was cockbilled, the anchor-buoy cleared away, the cable ranged on deck, and stoppered at an appropriate point, depending on the depth of water. A hauling line was led aft from the lee cathead: a hawser was brought out from the aftermost gunport on the lee quarter: the hawser was bent to the line and then hauled forward outside of all. It was made fast to the ring of the anchor to act as a spring, and belayed at something less than the scope of cable outside the stopper. The crew were stationed for stays, with the armourer ready to let go the cable, while the carpenter stood by with an axe ready to cut the hawser on the order.

The helm was put down, and the vessel proceeded to tack. If she stayed successfully, well and good; but if the bow failed to come up in the wind, and it was judged that the ship would mis-stay, the buoy was streamed, the anchor let go, and the cable run out until brought up by the stopper. This would have

Clubhauling step by step
1 Ship close-hauled on port tack, starboard anchor got ready with spring led to quarter; **2** ship fails to stay, anchor let go and ship runs out her cable and spring; **3** spring acts to bring starboard quarter to the wind, then headyards are braced around, cable slipped and spring cut, the ship gathering way; **4** ship brought up close-hauled on the starboard tack.

Diagram of Capt Hayes' Manoeuvre with HMS _Magnificent_.

the effect of swinging the vessel head to wind and throwing the headyards aback. The spring, being shorter than the cable, swung the old lee quarter up towards the wind. The afteryards were swung, and when these filled and the ship started to make headway, the order 'Haul of all!' was given. The cable was slipped, and the spring cut with the axe and let go, a little later than the cable. The vessel was now underway on the other tack, sailing clear of danger. The method could be used even with the rudder lost (Boyd, 417). The lee anchor was used, rather than the weather to avoid allowing the cable to ride across the cutwater. The manoeuvre had expended an anchor, a cable, and a hawser, but it was a worthwhile outlay if it prevented the loss of the ship.

Runciman (34) says that 'keelhauling', as the Blyth seamen called it, was a much talked of plan in his boyhood, some claiming to have actually seen it performed. Clawing off a lee shore, in any event, was a frightening business, requiring the deployment of as much canvas as the vessel would bear, more perhaps than would have been prudent in the open sea. Under these circumstances, the mainsail was set to keep the bow up to the wind, even though there existed considerable risk that it might be thrown aback, with disastrous consequences. One supposes clubhauling would only have succeeded with an extremely well trained and disciplined ship's company, with the addition of equal parts of good timing, seamanship and luck. 'The most gallant example was performed by Captain Hayes in HMS _Magnificent_, 74, in Basque Roads, in 1814, when with lower yards and topmasts struck, he escaped between two reefs from the enemy at Oleron. He bore the name of Magnificent Hayes to the day of his death, for the style in which he executed it' (Smyth, 194). A full account of this exploit is to be found in Glascock (165), and Murphy (10).

Glascock's account reveals that Hayes' exploit was not really clubhauling, as described above, but, if anything, a more heroic feat of seamanship. His ship was anchored to the South of the Ile de Ré, the lee shore running roughly from West-North-West to East-South-East. The wind which had been from the Southwest, swung around to the West, so the vessel lay to her anchors, bow pointing in that direction, but with the old sea continuing to pound the port bow. With the anchors dragging, and the hemp cables disintegrating on the rocky bottom, there was every prospect of the ship being lost. Hayes caused his chair to be placed at the larboard gangway, where he could watch the lead

1.
A squadron of East Indiamen tacking in squally weather, by Nicholas Pocock. This dramatic painting shows ships in all stages of the tacking process: putting the helm down, passing through the wind's eye, paying off with foreyards backed, and filling away on the new tack, reading the scene from right to left. (Courtesy N R Omell Gallery, London)

2.
A frigate in stays, by Thomas Luny, 1805. Her aftersails are lifting, their wind partly stolen by the backed foresails, and it will soon be time for 'mainsail haul'. (Courtesy Richard Green Galleries, London)

3.
This Thomas Luny painting shows a frigate wearing round after reconnoitering the French fleet at Brest. She has weathered the rocks in the foreground and is now bearing away, having hauled up the mainsail, brailed in the spanker, and braced in the afteryards to spill the wind. (Courtesy Richard Green Galleries, London)

4.
HM Brig *Martin* in stays, 1903. Note the foresail with tack and sheet raised, and the men on the forecastle ready to shift over the headsail sheets and tend the bowlines. (Imperial War Museum, London)

The **Magnificent** clawing out of Basque Roads, 1812 (after painting by Gilbert, c1835).

being cast. The lower yards, which had been struck, were hoisted two-thirds the way up, the topmasts remaining struck with the topsail yards working on the caps. The topsails and foresails were secured with spunyarn stops, so they could be set in an instant, the gaskets having been cast off, and the fore- and mainyards braced up for the starboard tack.

A spring was got out on the starboard side, and secured to the anchor cable on that side. Captain Hayes now addressed the men as follows:

'My men, you must, by this time, be sensible that our situation is one which calls for the utmost exertions of all; it is in fact, one of *life* or one of *death*. The orders you are about to receive of me are *new*, and may perhaps, appear *extra-ordinary*. You must, nevertheless, execute them on the instant, without a moment's hesitation; in which case, I trust in God, I may be able to bring the ship into a safe position in a few minutes after the cables are cut. On the other hand, should you unfortunately *hesitate*, or become unsteady, and keep fast sails ordered to be let fall, or let fall those directed to be kept fast, or, in short, not exert yourselves to the utmost in the execution of the orders you will receive, *life* cannot be ours beyond five minutes.' (Glascock, 168).

The original intention was to haul in on the spring, turning the stern towards the reefs on the island, and this is the feature of the story explaining why it was considered an example of clubhauling. If the cables were cut, and the sail set, the yards were already braced on the starboard tack and the ship should be able to sail clear. In the event, when the cables were cut, the cross sea striking the port bow was too much for the spring which parted. On the order, the fore topsail, foresail and fore topmast staysail were set, the two former aback. The helm put a-starboard, and the ship backed round on her heel, initially pointing her head towards the shore. When the wind came abaft the port beam, the mizzen topsail was set, and the helm was shifted. When the wind came aft, the main topsail and mainsail were set, everything braced up for the starboard tack, and the captain exclaimed 'the ship's saved!'. This whole sequence transpired in the space of two minutes. As the ship was plunging desperately, at the point where the bow was closest to the reef, the lead indicated that she had only a foot of water under the keel.

This is altogether a most stirring tale, which not surprisingly made a great impression on Hayes' contemporaries. Nonetheless, one would like to find an account of successfully clubhauling a vessel in the more conventional sense. Under similar circumstances, Bréart (212) recommends dropping a sea-anchor from the weather main chains, as the helm is put down, the hawser leading from the weather hawsehole. He asserts that this will work when one is obliged to tack, and without losing an anchor. Luce mentions that steamers, working in narrow waterways, sometimes drop an anchor, as a temporary pivot, to swing themselves round, picking it up again when they go ahead.

CHAPTER 13
WORKING SHIP IN A TIDEWAY

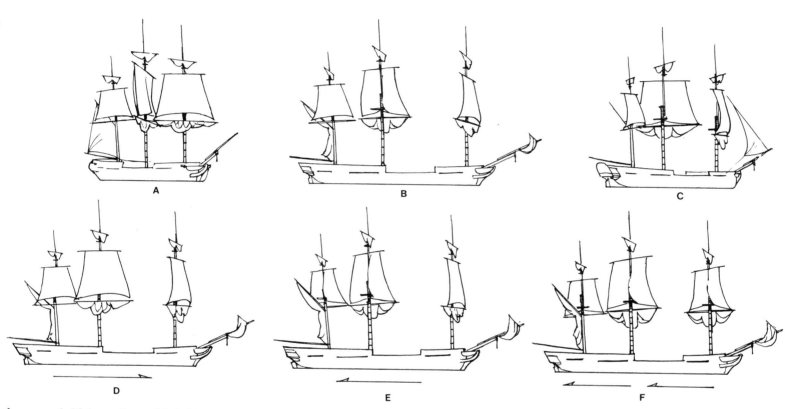

A

B

C

D

E

F

Driving or drifting. In a tidal fairway, a vessel might use the current to go up or down stream, rather than waiting for a fair wind. The Dutch term for this was *drijven*, and Lever similarly calls it 'drifting'. Mainwaring (244) refers to 'tiding it over' or 'up to' a place. Dropping down a river was referred to as 'vailing' in the 1600s; this old word was related to French *avaler*, 'to descend'. If both wind and tide were contrary, the wind blowing in the same direction as the tide was setting (that is, a 'leeward tide'), there was no choice but to 'stop a tide', drop what the Dutch referred to as a *stop-anker*, and wait for the tide to change. If the current was favourable, the set opposing the wind, (namely a 'windward tide'), the vessel could drive up with the tide, using the wind to go backwards and forwards across the current as desired. With a favourable leeward tide, the vessel would reach its objective more quickly, but be much less under control. For instance, in the case of a ship going downwind at exactly the same rate as the current, it would not be

moving through the water at all, hence with no steerage way, and yet be in danger of hitting a fixed obstruction.

Backing and Filling. The best method was to drift broadside with the current, under the topsails, jib and spanker. The main topsail was backed while the fore and mizzen were kept full. If the bow fell off too much, the spanker was hauled out, and if the bow tended to come too much into the wind, the jib or fore topmast staysail were hoisted and the spanker brailed in or triced up. The topgallants and courses 'hung in the brails', ready to be set if needed. The ship was, in fact, hove-to, using the tide to go in the intended direction, and with a strong windward tide, would actually be drifting to weather, rather than making leeway. Easy sail, such as described, was best, fewer braces needing attention, and made the best use of the windward tide.

If it were necessary to shoot ahead, the main topsail was filled, while if too much headway were being made, the mizzen topsail

Backing and filling
A spanker set when bow falls off too far from the wind; **B** ship works broadside to the stream under topsails; **C** jib set when bow comes up too far into the wind; **D** filling all topsails gives headway; **E** backing main and mizzen topsail stops headway, or gives some sternway; **F** backing all topsails gives greater sternway.

was backed in addition to the main. Should it be necessary to go briskly astern, all three topsails could be backed. A vessel in good trim – that is, drawing a little more water aft – tended to keep the bow away from the wind. For this reason, the fore topsail was not braced up too sharply, and sometimes, the mizzen staysail was required, to keep the vessel broadside on to the wind properly. Lever considered that this effect was due to the sternpost being more perpendicular than the stem, which, in effect, was cut away. Making a sternboard markedly aggravated the phenomenon as the pressure under the lee quarter acted to push the stern up into the wind. Going alternately ahead and astern, in this fashion, was described as 'backing and

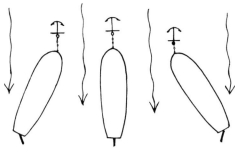

Sheering by the helm in a tideway.

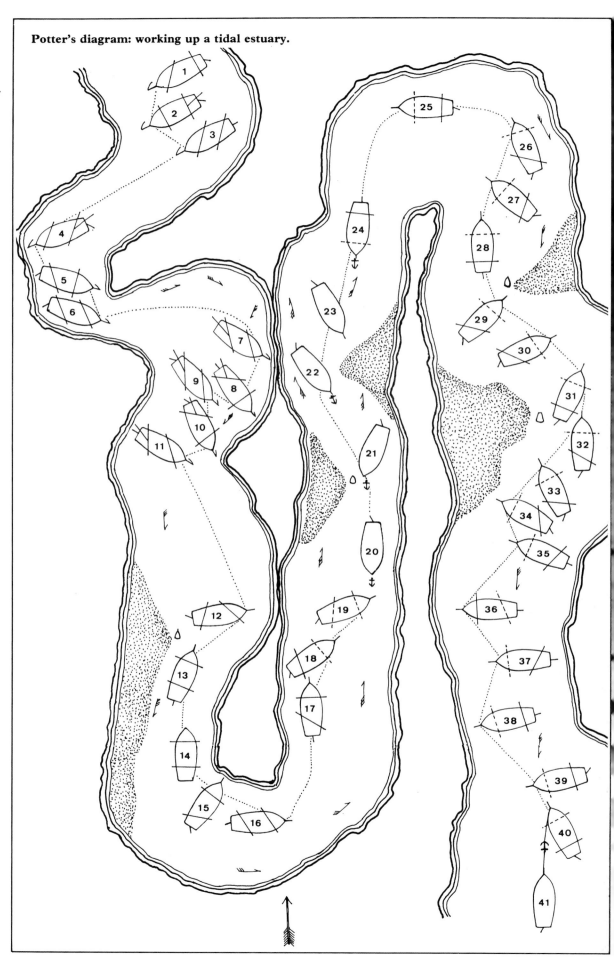

Potter's diagram: working up a tidal estuary.

filling', referring to the way the topsails were handled.

Another method, particularly useful in a very narrow waterway, or in an estuary crowded with other shipping, was to go through stern first, setting just enough sail to give steerageway, and so, breasting the current, drift backwards over the ground while still being able to use the rudder. Mossel (III, 255) calls this 'sailing directly into the current, before the wind with very small sail'. He considers the fore topmast staysail as suitable canvas in a good breeze, with the topsails braced square if the wind were light.

Dredging or clubbing. If the bottom of the channel were silt or sand, an anchor could be used to great advantage, to drop downstream, while keeping the vessel under control. This was termed 'dredging' or 'clubbing'. The comparable German term was *absacken* (Röding), *sacken* having the special technical sense 'to drop astern'. By hauling in, or veering the cable, the speed could be nicely controlled, so that the ship travelled slower than the current, and hence retained steerageway. Mossel refers to this as manoeuvring with a *krabbend anker*, 'a scratching anchor'. The English word 'dredging' arises in the same sort of way, being a variant of dragging. (Uggla uses 'kedging' as a synonym for 'dredging', but I do not believe this usage was widespread; 'kedging' would more usually have implied that the vessel was being warped up against the stream.) By putting the helm over, the vessel could be sheered from one side to the other. If it were desired to sheer to port, the starboard anchor was best, and vice versa. A spring from the quarter, to the cable would enable the vessel to swing herself broadside to the current (Totten, 200).

Wind across the tide. This offered lesser certainty of control, but progress could be made nonetheless. The lee shore had to be approached with circumspection, since missing stays would carry the vessel towards danger. The weather shore, on the other hand, could be approached boldly, since losing way would result in the ship being forced further away from the shallows, and there would be opportunity to boxhaul or wear if she mis-stayed. Manoeuvring in shoal waters of this nature, the lead was in constant use, and an anchor was kept ready to drop, if danger threatened. The anchor was carried a-cockbill, held only by the ring-painter, with the shank-painter already let go. French vessels sometimes carried the anchor *en penau* (that is, cockbilled) but, on occasion, hung it *en galère*, crown upwards, with one of the arms under the bowsprit. This method, apparently stemming from practice in the galleys, may have had some merit. It is still used today by Rhine river tugs.

Working up a tidal estuary. Potter (8) felt that skill in manoeuvring a vessel in tidal waters was the epitome of seamanship, and writing in 1863, felt that the innovations then occurring were bound to result in universal ignorance of this subject.

> The principal cause of that lack of energy and knowledge so apparent in many sailors of late years, is the introduction of steam. The Dutch and the English have always been considered as producing the best seamen; the French never; and for this reason, that neither Dutch nor English could get off their own coasts without being thorough seamen, whilst the French have no such difficulty. The almost universal adoption of steam-tugs in the English ports now, is rapidly reducing the formerly indispensible energy and skill of our seamen to a level with the latter.

This is not really a very fair comment on the demonstrated skills of the French *caboteur* working along the hostile Breton coastline.

Potter, in a most instructive section, details the manoeuvring of a brig through an imaginary meandering tidal waterway, at half-tide. The vessel backs and fills, clubs, sails stern first, and anchors intermittently, as circumstances dictate, and as indicated in the illustration. We will follow Potter's description almost verbatim. It is also to be found reproduced in Luce (609).

> No 1 represents a vessel reaching across the tide with her mainyard aback, to avoid reaching too fast. At No 2, having reached out of the strength of the tide she has thrown her fore-yard aback, and is making a sternboard by which she will fetch No 3, then fill and reach to No 4, where she will tack. The tide sweeping her, while in stays, round the point, but not sufficiently soon to enable her to fill on the starboard tack, the foreyard is therefore kept aback, as in No 5. The tide sets her to No 6 where she fills, the tide in this reach setting to leeward, and she does not make a weatherly course until she meets it running to windward again when she reaches to No 7, where the helm is put a-lee and the mainyard swung, so that she shoots into the position of No 8. She is not permitted to come round, but falls off again, and makes a sternboard to No 9. She fills and reaches ahead as far as she can, and then repeats the manoeuvre of No 7 to No 10, from whence, as before in No 8, she makes a sternboard to No 11. She is now in a fairway, and maintains her position in the strength of the tide, by backing, filling, or shivering the mainyard, or both, until the tide sets her into the position of No 12. She is brought astream of the tide, dropping stern first under better command, through a channel which is too narrow to allow her to drop athwart.
>
> From No 11, she might have reached into the bight, and tacking there have fetched as far to windward as No 13. However there being an eddy tide in the bight, she would perhaps have lost half the tide before she got out of it again, unless she had a commanding breeze.
>
> No 13 being astream of the tide, she drops through the narrow channel to No 14, thence to No 15, where she hauls her wind, on the starboard side to No 16. Sailing along the fairway to No 17, she finds the tide setting to leeward, the fore topsail is clewed up, and she is brought up, there not being sufficient water for her to proceed. The mainyard is therefore braced up to take aback, so that when she rounds to as in No 18, she may not shoot across onto the opposite bank. At No 19, the main topsail being clewed up or down, the anchor is let go, and the vessel swings ahead to wind and tide, as in No 20, waiting until there is sufficient water for her in the next channel. The jibboom is rigged in and the fore topsail furled, as she is coming to a more crowded part of the river, and does not require to reach any distance. When there is sufficient water for her to proceed, known perhaps by the time of tide, or by the water she is riding in, the cable is hove in and she clubs to No 21. The tide here sets into the bight, and she is obliged to sheer broad to port, to prevent her being set in there.
>
> At No 23, the helm is put aport to bring her astream once more, and she dredges to No 24, sets the main topsail again to help her to No 25. The wind being abeam, the main topsail is shivered, or backed, as required, till she arrives where the tide is setting to windward as in No 26. The anchor is hove up, and she drops, filling or shivering the mainyard to No 27, clear of the buoy, is brought astream again as in No 28. She drops to No 29, hauling her wind to cross the tide, as in No 30, where the main topsail being full prevents the tide from setting her upon the sand astern. When she fetches No 31, she is again brought astream, and drops to No 32, where she is layed athwart, and drops fore-reaching a little with her mainyard full, as in No 33. At No 34, the mainyard is laid aback for a sternboard to No 35, from whence, by backing, filling, or shivering the mainyard, either to keep in the best of the tide, or make way for other vessels passing up or down the channel, she arrives at No 39, where she is again laid astream and the main topsail clewed up as in No 40. She drops her anchor and rides to windward or leeward, according to circumstances. At No 41 she is riding to the windward tide. (Potter, 32).

1.

1.
A ship working the tide down the Avon Gorge, painted by Pocock c1785. Five boats are towing at the ship's bows, and she has an interesting combination of sails set to help her down the river. Note the counterbraced fore and mainyards. (Society of Merchant Venturers Collection, courtesy Bristol Museum and Art Gallery)

2.
A Dutch pink driving under backed main topsail, etched by Gerrit Groenewegen, 1789. She is being held athwart the tide by balancing the jib against the mizzen. (Mark Myers' Collection)

2.

CHAPTER 14
TOWING AND WARPING

Brig warping out of harbour.

In convoy, a more powerful sailer might take a sluggish vessel in tow to keep things moving. The necessity might also arise in the event of a vessel sustaining damage, requiring to be pulled out of the line of fire of a fort, and so on.

Warping in harbour. A vessel could be 'warped' about the port, using heavy posts on the quay, or 'dolphins' formed by driving pilings into the mud along the side of the dredged channel. These posts were called *Duc d'Alben* or *dukdalfen* – there are various spellings in Dutch – hence the English term 'dolphin'. Why the Duke of Alava is commemorated in this particular way, I am not sure. The Dutch had little cause to remember him kindly, but whatever the reason, the word dates back to the Spanish occupation of the Netherlands, in the 1500s. The usual German term was similar, but they sometimes called it a 'cat', or 'cat-on-the-land' (*Katt, Katt am Lande*).

By using four warps, hawsers leading obliquely fore and aft to such fixed points, the ship could be shifted ahead, by hauling on the forward, and easing out on the after ropes. As the ship came abreast one post, the eye of the warp was lifted off and taken to the next one. If the pull were against the tide or wind, the forward lines would need to be stronger, while if the wind were from astern, the after lines would be the sturdier. If there were not too much resistance, the hawsers were just walked back. If there was a strong wind, they might require to be taken to the capstan in a large ship, or the windlass in a small vessel. With a wind coming from a-beam, one might imagine that one line from the weather bow, and one from the weather quarter would be adequate. However, once a large vessel got moving, it might take some stopping, because of its momentum. Hence it was always more prudent to have a minimum of four lines.

In narrow channels, such as at Flushing, the warp was taken by boat to the furthest dolphin, and seized to the intervening posts. The seizings were cut as the vessel came abreast them, thus allowing a long, continuous pull on the warp. In getting out of harbour, the final stage of warping might be to a mooring-buoy, a *corps-mort* ('dead body') as it was known to the Dutch and French sailor. Where fixed installations of this sort, did not exist, the vessel had recourse to taking a kedge anchor out in a boat, dropping it and warping up to it.

Camels. Mention of this device arises naturally when considering movement in and out of harbour. In 1691, a Netherlander called Bakker invented the 'camel', and solved the problem, of particular concern in Holland, of moving a large vessel across shoal water to the open sea. The innovation consisted of a pair of specially shaped floats, which ideally were designed to fit that particular vessel. These were placed, semi-submerged, on either side of the hull, chains under the keel holding everything together. They were then pumped dry, thus raising the ship up until she only drew a fathom or so of water. Although originally developed in Holland, they were eventually used elsewhere, including North America. A very detailed contemporary model of one may still be seen in Amsterdam. Why they were named after the 'ship of the desert', I am not certain. Perhaps the reference was to the double-humped Bactrian camel, since they came only in port and starboard pairs. The French term *chameau* also means 'camel'. By employing a series of empty casks strung around the hull, in what the French referred to as a *chapelet*, the draught could be diminished a little, in a sort

Camels
A Eighteenth century Dutch camel; **B** interior shape of a camel; **C** detail of timber supports through gunports, pumps, windlasses and flooding winches; **D** Dutch East Indiaman in camel being towed by a string of 'waterschepen', which were fishing smacks doubling as sailing tugs (after H Kobell); **E** Nantucket whaleship under tow in a camel. The towing and pumping are here powered by steam.

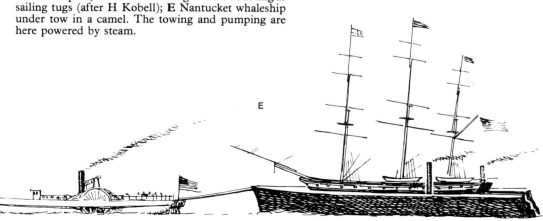

of 'poor man's camel'.

Towing by horses. In the Netherlands, fairly large vessels could be hauled through the canals by means of draught-horses on the tow-path. The Dutch word for this procedure was *jagen*, the tow-rope being a *jaagtross*, and the tow-path the *jaag-pad*. The underlying idea of these words is that of 'chasing'. Although there is not in fact any connection between 'hawser' and 'horse', Dutch *paardelijn* means 'hawser', and literally translates as 'horse-line'. Ten to twenty horses might be required to tow a large vessel, but if the wind were unfavourable, thirty horses might be unable to manage a small one. The tow-rope was secured to the foremast, at an adequate height, the staysail halliards being rigged, so the hawser could be lifted up temporarily, using a *reijer*, 'rider', a leather-covered iron ring, riding on the hawser. Ideally the horses worked on the weather tow-path, if there were one on each side of the canal. If the wind were ahead, the yards were braced up sharp. If it was aft, they could be left square. Every canal had its own regulations about this sort of thing, relating to whether the yards should be topped up, and so on. In the event that two vessels met, going in opposite directions, the larger kept to the outside, and if possible lifted the tow-rope over the mast of the smaller. If this were not practical, the tow-rope was slacked completely off, the smaller craft sailing over it, its team stepping over the line, as it lay on the tow-path.

Towing by boats. In a calm, a sailing man-of-war could put her own boats in the water, and make a knot or so in the desired direction. A tow-line was secured at the bowsprit cap, or end of the jibboom, and a sufficiently long scope paid out, so the pull would be more or less horizontal (Ekelöf, 240). The best arrangement was a towing-post (in Dutch *jaagstut*), about one-third the length of the launch abaft the stem, sufficiently high to allow of the tow-line clearing the heads of the oarsmen. In the absence of this fitting, the line was made fast to the after thwart, that is to say, about a third the length forward of the transom. If several boats were being used, the biggest and heaviest was placed next the ship, and the others in diminishing order of size, further away. Each boat took a line over the stern, and towed the one astern, so to speak. Since the heavier the boat the better, shot or a length of stream cable were sometimes taken on board to increase its effectiveness in pulling the ship ahead.

Steering the boat was not an easy matter; in fact if the tow-line were made fast to the transom, the boat could not be manoeuvred at all. This was the advantage of the towing-post mentioned above. However, in the circumstances where boats were used in this way, it is unlikely that a great deal of steering would have been required. If requested to pull somewhat to starboard, the coxswain steered so that the tow-line moved over to the starboard side of the transom. The opposite if required to pull to port. In changing direction with several boats, the craft nearest the ship turned in the ordinary way, while those ahead slackened the towlines, until they could get in line and pull on the new course (Ekelöf, 240). Boats detailed to pull fire-ships, or a ship on fire, used a length of chain, or grapnels on chains, to secure the towlines to the tow (Luce, 269; Ekelöf, 240).

Towing boats. A boat towed from the taff-rail of a First Rate, the rope coming almost vertically downward, would be in hazard of having its bow lifted by the tow-rope, and hence its after end depressed, perhaps being towed under, as the ship's stern rose and fell to the seas. A better arrangement was to make the tow-rope fast well forward, securing it to the bow slings of the boat; or the rope was slipped through the bow-ring, brought aft with a turn taken round the after thwart, so that the boat-keeper could let it go, in emergency. A boat could be towed under the lee quarter very comfortably in this way (Liardet, 34). Several boats, towed simultaneously, were secured at intervals to a hawser made fast forward, rather than being secured head to stern. The tow-lines were secured to the mast, or a forward thwart rather than the stempost. Since the ship was quite capable of exceeding the boat's normal speed, sail might have to be shortened to keep the smaller craft afloat.

Towing with steam tugs. Since our attention is primarily focussed on men-of-war under sail, we will touch on this only briefly. A sailing vessel could most readily be manoeuvred in confined spaces, like a dock basin, by laying the tug alongside, with springs and breastropes, and interposing a sufficiency of wooden and rope fenders. In a similar fashion, a ship of the line could have been brought up in a calm to engage a shore battery, the towing vessel being secured to the sheltered side. At sea, where abrupt changes of course were not needed, and where the abrasion of two hulls grinding together would have been unacceptable, towing ahead was the more usual method.

A tug, specially designed for towing, could be propelled by either paddles or a screw, the former being particularly well adapted for manoeuvring in confined quarters. In fact, paddle tugs of the *Director* class were built for

Towing by boats
A French ship towing out of port (detail after Vernet, 1754); **B** ship being towed in a calm (after Baugean 1814).

Towing boats
A Two decker towing boats in coastal waters (detail after C Brooking, c1750). Note two lines to first boat; **B** towing a boat at sea (detail after Van de Velde the Younger, c1672).

the Royal Navy in the late 1950s and remained in service until the early 1980s. Towing astern, the hawser was made fast to the tug's towing-hook, which was almost amidships. Like the launch towing-post referred to earlier, this allowed the stern to swing freely from side to side. If necessary, the tow-rope could be temporarily got down on the tug's stern by means of a 'gob-rope'. Keeping this fast, however, prevented manoeuvring smartly, and the tug was said to be 'girt'. The hawser was kept clear of the deck and other obstructions by riding on the tow-rails or beams, which are such a

characteristic feature of the after deck of the steam tug.

A small steam powered man-of-war, such as a gunboat, pulling a ship of the line, might secure the hawser to the mainmast, keeping it up clear by means of an improvised 'rider'. I do not know the English word for this, but it translates Mossel's term *reijer, rijder*. A larger steam man-of-war could employ two tow-ropes, by preference made fast forward, and led through gunports abreast the foremast. Mossel considered that the lines were better secured well forward on the towing vessel, even bringing them to the

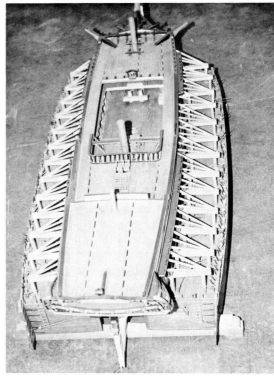

1.
A French corvette warping into harbour, engraved by Jean Beaugean, 1814. Two warps are out ahead and the slack of a third can be seen coming on board just abaft the fore chains. The yards have been braced up to minimise windage aloft. (Mark Myers' Collection)

2.
Dutch model of the ship *Neptunes* in a camel. Note that the two floats do not meet at the keel, but run under the bilges of the ship. Each float has a rudder and is steered by tiller and tackles. The stand supporting the camel is not, of course, part of its original equipment. (Author's photo, courtesy Prins Hendrik Maritime Museum, Rotterdam)

3.
Detail of the camel model, showing the timber supports and braces attached to the ship, the windlasses used to draw the floats together, the discharging pumps, and the handles of the flooding valves. (Author's photo, courtesy Prins Hendrik Maritime Museum, Rotterdam).

4.
A double tow under sail. The *Lady Kennaway* (right) was found abandoned and disabled in the Bay of Biscay by the Danish brig *Industrie* and barque *Najaden*. Here the Danes are briskly towing their prize in line ahead, with studdingsails set. A spar has been rigged out through the *Lady Kennaway*'s stern for a jury rudder, and new sails are being bent. Engraving after a drawing by Condy in the *Illustrated London News*, 1847. (Mark Myers' Collection)

Towing by steamship
A HMS *Hastings* towing into port behind the steam sloop *Rhadamanthus*, whose yards are manned (after C von Brocktorff, 1838); **B** HMS *Retribution* lashed alongside the three decker *Trafalgar* off Sebastopol, 1854 (after sketch by Lieut O'Reilly engraved in *The Illustrated London News*, 1854).

hawseholes, remarking that a horse pulls best, when working against a breast-band. Using two tow-ropes was one way of permitting readier movement of the towing vessel's stern. Another dodge was to rig a 'bridle', the tow being pulled by a single tow-line, which in turn travelled on a bight of rope across the towing vessel's stern. The hawsers were 'keckled', or parcelled, to protect them against abrasion from barnacles, chainplates, and particularly chafing at the angle where they rendered round the gunport. The strength of the tow-rope depended partly on its elasticity. By veering a length of chaincable from the hawsehole of the tow, and making the hawser fast to this, a deeper catenary was produced, moderating the abrupt, jerky movements of the tow-rope.

A manoeuvre of interest to several authors involved the problem of getting a sailing vessel under way from anchor, when the tide was running too strongly for her to get clear by herself. The towing vessel anchored ahead of the tow, which received the towline on board, shortened up its cable, and when ready the towing vessel steamed ahead, both weighed simultaneously, and proceeded on their journey.

One sailing vessel taking another in tow.
This might be necessary where one vessel had sustained grave battle damage, or in convoy as a means of speeding a laggard. Bonnefoux (228) claimed that a man-of-war, or 'better sailer' in the convoy, could tow up to five or six vessels! Much would depend on the surrounding circumstances, the size of the tow-rope required depending on the size of the vessel towed, the speed at which it would be moving, the amount of sea running, and so forth. The bigger the tow, the longer the rope, while a shorter line was used in narrow waters and the lighter the line the better. A

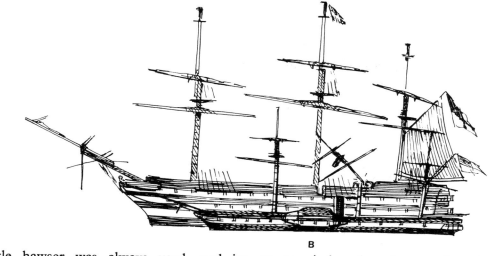

single hawser was always used, and its transfer was effected by getting a light rope across first. This could be managed by using a heaving-line or rocket apparatus, depending on the situation, but the most usual methods appear to have involved either dropping a boat, or drifting a line down to the tow, using an empty water breaker as a float.

To get a heaving-line over, it was necessary to sail close to the tow, which lay hove to, and throw the line across, as the stern of the towing vessel approached the other ship. By passing on the windward side, there was no danger of being becalmed in the lee of the other vessel (Griffiths, 306). This author thought it best for the towing vessels not to heave to, but rather to keep headway on, albeit slowly, as the hawser was paid out. Alternatively, both could heave to, Ulffers (366) suggesting that the towing vessel lie on the weather bow of the tow, and drift the line over with a breaker, or keg. The line was picked up by a man standing on the martingale stay, or by means of a boat-hook. Baudin (325) advocates that the towing vessel heave

to, to windward, main topsail to the mast, while the tow back her fore topsail. Bonnefoux (226) suggests both vessels keep headway on, with the towing vessel lying ahead and to leeward of the other, veering a buoy as above. Once it is picked up, both heave to until the studdingsail halliards, or other like foreganger, has been used to haul the heavier towing hawser over. It is passed through the weather hawsehole, and made fast to the bitts, or taken aft to the jeer capstan. A sufficiency of hawser is got inboard, so it can be 'freshened' as necessary, to avoid all the chafe coming on one spot. The towing vessel always supplies the hawser, because it can be veered out more readily to leeward, and because, once it is slipped, it can be hauled aboard, while still maintaining headway. The cable will pass through one of the stern gunports, or a bridle can be rigged, using two after gunports on the quarters.

All being fast, sail was made, and both vessels got under way. The tow set what canvas she could, but had to beware of shooting forward upon the stern of the towing

Towing under sail
A Frigate *Francesca Themis* (hove to) taking the *Santa Ana* in tow after Trafalgar (after contemporary painting); **B** HMS *Neptune* bearing up for Gibraltar with HMS *Victory* in tow (after C Stanfield).

vessel. If this occurred, the tow sheered to leeward of the other. When a large vessel towed one much smaller, she might have to shorten sail, to avoid travelling dangerously fast. If close-hauled, no attempt was made to hug the wind, but rather a course steered a point or so free, to maintain good steerage way. Both vessels, in general, tried to keep the same compass course, the after following in the wake of the other. If the towing vessel wished to alter course significantly to starboard, the tow initially turned a little to port. This was necessary because the turning-circle of the tow would be of slightly greater diameter, and also because the stern of a ship moves laterally in the opposite direction to the ship's head.

In tacking, the towing vessel luffed up, while the tow bore away four points, thus helping move the stern of the forward ship off the wind. At 'Rise tacks and sheets!', the tow tacked in its turn. To wear, the tow followed in the other's wake, luffing up a little, as the helm of the towing vessel was put up. Ekelöf (212) says that to alter course, the towing vessel should steer somewhat less off the wind than the tow, in falling off, and more off the wind, while coming to. The noise due to the slapping of the water under the bow of the tow made hailing very difficult, and hence Griffiths (308) recommends a predetermined set of signals, flags by day, lanterns by night to signify the following:

Going to fill	You steer badly
Going to heave to	Keep more in the wake
Shorten sail	Cast off the tow rope
Make more sail	Examine service
Going to tack	Freshen hawse
Going to wear	A boat is coming to you
Take in a reef	We are going to reef

In the event of squally or stormy weather or a calm with a heavy swell, it was considered most prudent to slip the tow, rather than risk one ship coming aboard the other. In a windstill the tension of the tow-rope alone would certainly tend to pull the vessels close aboard each other. The towing vessel remained in the vicinity ready to pass the tow once more when conditions improved. When the tow reached the port, roadstead, or whatever the nature of the agreed destination, the hawser was slipped and hauled on board the other vessel.

CHAPTER 15
STORM

Handling the ship during a squall posed difficulties that were, for the most part, relatively short-lived. The ship either luffed through the gust, or bore away, according to circumstances. In a gale, the wind came from more or less the same direction, although it might vary in strength from time to time. If the storm were severe enough to warrant it, the commander had a choice of lying to, or scudding before the wind.

PREPARATIONS

Much of what follows will seem to be unnecessary fussiness to the 'modern' square-rigged sailor, but we must not lose sight of the fact that the latter-day windjammers were more powerfully built, and much better engineered in respect of their ability to withstand foul weather. Hulls and spars of steel and rigging of wire cannot really be compared with the 'sticks and string' used to rig the cockleshells of an earlier era. The degree of security needed would depend on the severity of the bad weather. Many of the following measures were taken, in the ordinary way, when the vessel was made 'in all respects, ready for sea', before leaving port.

The helm. In the gunroom the integrity of the wheelropes was checked, and the gooseneck and sweep greased. Relieving-tackles were hooked to the tiller, and hands detailed to man them, following the movements of the tiller, as it in turn obeyed the wheel on deck. A portable compass was installed, with the lubber line properly oriented to indicate the ship's head, and a lantern prepared, so the compass-card could be read. In the event that the tiller-rope parted, the ship could be steered, after a fashion, with the relieving-tackles, until repairs could be effected. To have the tiller break was an even more serious disaster, against which it was essential to have a spare tiller ready. In a large vessel, such as *Victory*, the rudderhead pierced the deckhead of the gunroom, penetrating to the wardroom, where the spare tiller could be thrust into its mortice in the rudderhead. Suitable relieving-tackles were rigged in the ward room, to be shipped on the spare tiller,

if needed. To secure the rudder, at the time of the accident, large accurately shaped wooden rudder-chocks were wedged into the rudder-port, on either side of the rudderhead, to steady things, and allow the spare tiller to be shipped. These, according to Smyth, were sometimes shipped, as a precaution, when the vessel was going to make sternway rapidly. Mossel (III, 349) describes, at some length, the fitting of 'rudder-tackles', to be used if the tiller broke. Chains secured to the rudder-horn, were becketted along the counter. Tackles were hooked to these, the forward block being made fast under the mizzen channels, and the hauling parts led through a gunport on each side. Since this arrangement resulted in much chafing around the buttocks under the counter, a spare topmast could be used to shift the tackle out clear of the hull. This method does not sound terribly practical under storm conditions, and it receives little attention from the other authorities. However, chains for rudder-tackles are to be seen on quite a few contemporary models.

Securing the guns for bad weather. 'Many a ship has foundered from the mere circumstance of a want of sufficient security in housing the guns. This depends merely on the breeching, tackles and muzzle lashing, nor can any other more direct fastening be applied' (Congreve, 17).

Every seaman must be sensible of the danger resulting from the breaking adrift of a gun in a gale of wind. In two instances, this accident has been witnessed by the author. The first was in a frigate, during a gale of wind, in the Bay of Biscay. In consequence of having previously split the main topsail, the frigate, being deprived of the necessary lofty canvas to steady the ship, became extremely uneasy, and laboured much. The gunner had neglected to examine the condition of the guns, and just as the officer of the watch had despatched a messenger, directing the former to inspect and report their state of security, the weather gun abreast of the fore hatchway drew both breeching bolts, broke away from the tackles, and eventually after several 'sends' between the ship's sides and the coaming of the hatchway,

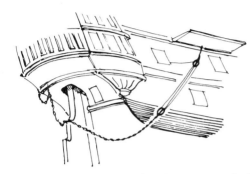

Rudder tackles. Tackle rigged to starboard chain; port chain shown in stops.

by one of which the gunner's mate of the watch lost his leg, and ultimately his life, descended the fore hold, crushing a couple of water butts in the ground tier. The second instance occurred on board a ship of the line, scudding in a heavy gale of wind, homeward bound from Jamaica. The ship was a fast sailer, and, like most fast sailers a 'heavy roller'. The preparatory pipe of 'Stand by hammocks!' had hardly escaped the lips of the boatswain, when the second master, rapidly ascending the quarterdeck ladder, motioned to the first lieutenant to stop the movement, exclaiming 'A lower deck gun adrift, Sir! Let me have two or three hammocks, and I'll endeavour to choke the trucks.' The hammocks were hastily thrown down the hatchways, when, after a heavy lurch had, with fearful force, propelled the gun back into its proper port, the second master succeeded in choking the aftertrucks, and the ship was immediately brought to the wind on that tack which left the unsecured gun on the *lee* side. Had it not been for the presence of mind and activity of this officer, the ship must have suffered most serious, if not fatal, injuries. (Glascock, 210)

Masefield (15) aptly compared the attempt to 'trip' a loose gun-carriage with hammocks, and so on as 'playing leap frog on a see-saw, under a shower bath, with the certainty of death, if you missed your leap'.

The exact method of fitting a gun carriage varied, of course, over the centuries, but in the early 1800s, the carriage was equipped with a gun-tackle on either side, to run the gun out, and a train-tackle, to haul it inboard. The breeching was a heavy rope secured to

Securing the guns
A Securing in the run out position; **B** housing; **C** double breeching; **D** lashing alongside.

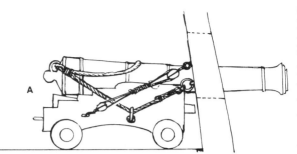

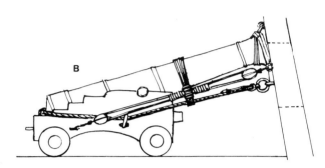

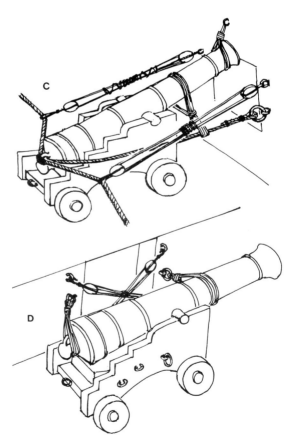

the eyebolts, on either side of the port, passing through large ringbolts, on the side of the carriage, and through an eye cast on the cascabel of the gun, above the 'button'. Boudriot shows a short breeching, which passes through holes in the 'brackets', or 'cheeks' of the carriage. Its purpose was to limit the recoil of the gun, and it was also used to secure the piece, when not in action. The upper deck guns were ordinarily secured in the run-out position. Gunner's wedges, or 'quoins' (French *coins*), were in place under the cascabel, the barrel was more or less horizontal, the gun-tackles were hauled taut, and the superfluous ends were frapped around the turns of the purchase. The breeching was seized securely at the cascabel, and the slack thrown forward on the barrel of the gun (Congreve, Plate 2, Figure 2). Where half-ports were fitted – what the French called *faux-sabords* or *mantelets brisés* – I think the guns would also always have been secured in the run-out position. This arrangement can be seen on the gundeck of *Constitution*. The barrel was accommodated in semi-circular notches in either half of the port, sometimes the fit being made more exact with a lining of felt or sailcloth. In addition to the tompion, plugging the muzzle, painted canvas covers were also fitted to protect the ordnance against the weather, particularly the mouth of the gun and the touch-hole.

Other methods of securing the guns were detailed in the *manuel du Cannonier marin*, and were adopted in different circumstances; these were called 'housing', 'double breeching', or 'lashing fore and aft'. 'Housing' (*amarrage à la serre*, as the French called it) was used if it were desirable to have the lower tier of gunports closed. The cannon was run in, the quoins knocked out to drop the breech, and the muzzle jammed up against the clamp, (*serrebauqière*), above the gunport just under the deckhead, the barrel pointing upwards at an angle of about forty degrees. The muzzle was secured to the eyes of 'housing-bolts', in the clamp, with a secure 'muzzle-lashing', the gun-tackles were hauled taut, and the ends used to form a cross-lashing, frapping both sides of the breeching together, forward of the carriage. The train-tackle was hooked to its bolt, on the rear of the carriage, and to a housing-bolt in the clamp, and hauled taut, the end being expended in turns around the barrel and breeching.

There was some argument about the propriety of cleating or chocking the trucks. On the one hand, it was desirable that the guns should not be allowed to move with the ship's

roll; on the other, each lee-roll brought the weight of the gun and carriage to bear on the ship's side. Multiply that by the number of cannon, and it will be realised that on the down roll, the ship's side was in danger of bursting outwards. Glascock (210) suggests cleating the fore trucks on the lee side, and after trucks to weather. He also proposed rigging 'sea-relieving tackles' (really train-tackles) on the lee side, which were set up to oppose this bursting force on the lee side of the vessel.

'Double breeching' (in French *amarrage à grelin*, that is securing 'hawser-fashion') is described by Liardet (102), and Glascock (210). The spare messenger, or stream cable, was taken over the heel of the bowsprit, and the ends led aft as far as the cabin bulkheads, where the eyes were secured. The messenger was made fast to the cascabel of each gun, and hauled taut. Tackles were hooked to the quarter-bolts, each side of the port, and to strops placed on the messenger. By hauling these taut, the messenger acted to force the guns against the ship's side. Liardet felt that this method had the advantage of allowing the guns to be cleared for action more quickly.

'Lashing alongside' (*amarrage le long du bord*, or *amarrage en vache*, 'cow fashion') gave more room on deck, for example, in a cabin, or when embarking troops. The gun was swung round, and lashed fore and aft against the inside planking, across the port. The gun-tackles were secured to the ship's side, and to the ends of the axles of the trucks, crossing one another, and being made fast with a cross-lashing at the intersection. With any of these later methods, the ports were firmly closed, secured with port-bars, caulked with oakum or felt.

Anchors. When 'catted' and 'fished', these were secured with a ring-painter at the ring, and a shank-painter towards the 'crown', the point where the shank joined the arms. These painters were hauled taut, and, if necessary, preventer painters were clapped on, to give double security. Ulffers recommends unshackling the anchor cable and getting the end inboard if the vessel were off soundings. The advantage of this practice was that tightly fitting plugs could be jammed in the hawseholes, and caulked with greased oakum. If it was necessary to keep the cable shackled on, a special disc-plug was used, with a segment removed to accommodate the link of chain. Conical canvas bags, stuffed with oakum, called 'jackasses' were also used as hawse-plugs. Bonnefoux (124) mentions wedging the capstan, without explaining why this was advisable. Scupper plugs were sometimes necessary on the lee side. The scuppers were, it is true, closed by leather flaps, on their outboard sides, but this would have been far from water-tight, if heeling was excessive and the sea rough.

On deck. The tarpaulin weather-cloths were placed in the weather rigging to give the watch a little shelter from the wind, and life-lines were rigged on the upper deck to give some handhold to the men working there. The hammocks were got out of the nettings, and struck below, so they would not get soaking wet. The old-fashioned wooden quarter-davits were topped up, to get the boat as high as possible, griping it against the mizzen rigging. Since there would be no possibility of launching a boat, should someone be lost overboard, the lifebuoy was made fast to the deep-sea lead-line, and the reel secured aft, so it might offer a last chance to a man in the water. The drain-holes of the boats were checked to see that they were clear, canvas covers put over the boats themselves, and the deck-gripes hauled absolutely taut. The lashings holding the reserve spars in the booms were inspected, and if necessary, side-tackles put on to prevent lateral movement. The cathead lookouts were sent up on the foreyard, where they would be in less danger of being washed away, and furthermore could get a better view. A lee-helmsman backed up the man steering, and if necessary two more hands were detailed to the after wheel. A sea-anchor could be got ready for use if necessary. Some ships were provided with a special collapsible sea-anchor, or 'drogue', comprised of two iron rods, rivetted together in the centre, and disposed cross-wise to support a square canvas drag-sail. A buoy supported the upper corner, and a span secured the rods to a hawser, so the contraption could be thrown overboard, if the need arose. The buoy-rope could be used to draw it back towards the ship, when the emergency had passed. One American author refers to this as a 'parachute drag', reminding us that the word 'parachute' long antedates the heavier-than-air flying machine.

Carpenter. The mast-wedges were carefully inspected to make sure that they were not becoming loose. The pumps were readied, and the pump-wells sounded every hour, while the caulkers got ready the wherewithal to stop leaks. The hatches were 'battened down', the method of doing so, explaining the origin of the expression. The wooden hatch-covers, or gratings, were placed in position and tarpaulins stretched over them. These were made fast to the sides of the coamings by nailing on long laths, or 'battens'. On the topic of hatch-covers,

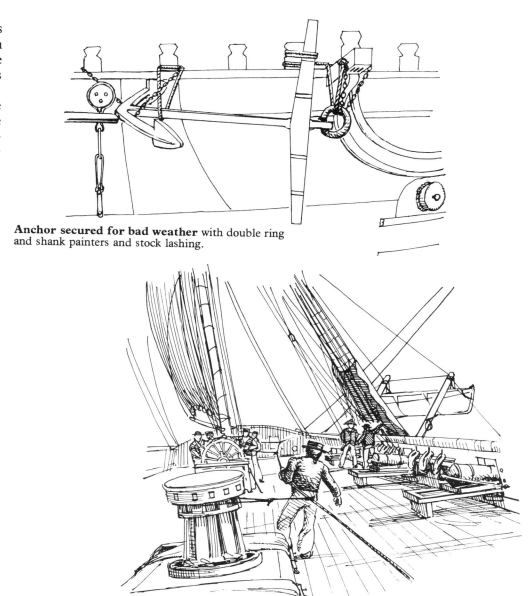

Anchor secured for bad weather with double ring and shank painters and stock lashing.

Deck view of a ship secured for bad weather. Lifelines rigged, hatches battened down, wheel double manned, davits topped up, weather cloth spread in mizzen rigging.

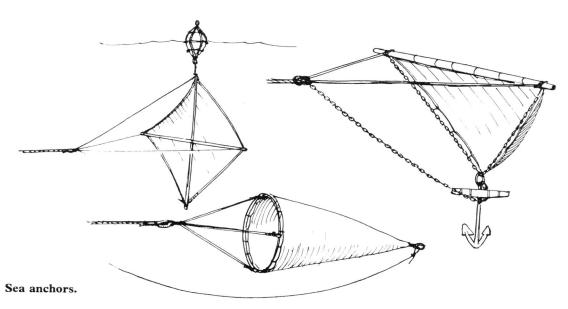

Sea anchors.

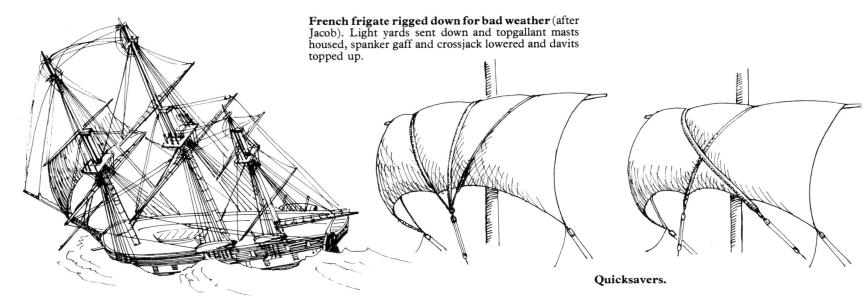

French frigate rigged down for bad weather (after Jacob). Light yards sent down and topgallant masts housed, spanker gaff and crossjack lowered and davits topped up.

Quicksavers.

Liardet (104) complains that they are 'invariably used for every dirty thing that is done, and when needed, are found unserviceable'. One corner of one hatch was left open to allow egress from below, and to get a little fresh air down into the mess-decks. If scudding, this opening would be arranged forward, and if lying-to, aft, to minimise the risk of shipping water.

Aloft. The royals and upper studdingsails were got out of the rigging, and the tops cleared of all extraneous gear. Topgallant yards and masts were sent down. This was facilitated if short topgallant masts ('winter-poles') were shipped instead of the longer spars used in sustained good weather (Bonnefoux, 125). In the 1700s the spritsail yard was swung around, and triced up on the port side of the bowsprit. In later days, the jibboom was run in, and made fast.

Preventer braces were rigged on the weather side of the lower and topsail yards. Some authors mention, in addition, preventer lifts, trusses, slings, clewgarnets, rolling-tackles, and parrels; in fact any gear that might conceivably part, being doubled. Double tacks and sheets were sometimes clapped on the foresail. Reeving the toprope secured the topmast against a fall if fid broke, and was a timely precaution also should it be considered necessary to strike the topmasts (Bréart, 203). The fore topmast staysail sheets were doubled, by taking the weather sheet over the stay, and dividing the strain between both sheets on the lee side. The mizzen gaff was struck, and the boom securely lashed to its crutch amidships. Since the mizzen topsail would never be set in atrocious conditions, sometimes the crossjack yard was struck down on deck, to reduce topweight. Preventer topmast backstays could be contrived from the top-burtons,

galhaubans volants ('flying backstays'), as the French called them. To further support the lower masts, their pendants were crossed abaft the mast, and the side-tackles hooked to them and taken somewhat forward of the foot of the mast.

The shrouds might become loose due to the working of the masts, and this could occur, on the one hand, because the rigging was brand new, or, on the other, after a protracted spell of hard service. Tightening up the lanyards was a fine weather job, which took some time to accomplish properly. As a temporary measure, the stays could be tautened up somewhat, but the resulting forward inclination of the masts would disturb the sailing trim of the vessel. Alternatively, the rigging could be 'swifted', or 'cat-harped' by making fast blocks to each shroud about eight feet up, and criss-crossing a heavy line between the two sides, in the manner of a 'cat's cradle', thus pulling the shrouds taut, and distributing the strain evenly.

When scudding, a 'quicksaver' was set up to prevent the foresail ballooning out too far horizontally. This took various forms, but all worked on similar principles. A broad flat sennit band was secured to the yard, descended in front of the forward side of the sail, and was set up on deck with a tackle. It might have two or three limbs. The French name for it, *croix de Saint-André*, suggests one that was X-shaped, like a St Andrew's cross, and which, therefore, presumably had two lower ends. Rosvall (33) describes the use of a quicksaver rigged on the lee side of a mizzen.

At all times, chafe was the boatswain's great enemy, and this was especially so in bad weather. Extensive use was made of mats and 'rounding' – what would be today called 'baggywrinkle' – at points of chafe. Particularly at hazard were the lower shrouds,

where they were touched by the lower yard when braced sharp up, and sawed upon by the footrope of the course. The topmast shrouds likewise were abraded by the lee lower lift, and topsail yard. The saddle of the latter also ground and chafed the cap, if the topsail halliards were not hauled up specifically to prevent this. The mats were of various types: paunch, sword, thrum, and so on. Smyth says a thrum-mat was similar to the ordinary coconut fibre door-mat. Paunch-mats were used to protect the stay at the point where the bunt of the furled sail impinged on it. The German word for the bunt was *Bauch* ('belly'), a meaning shared by 'paunch'. What were called hanging-mats were usually got out of the rigging in bad weather, being liable to be blown away. Attention to getting points subject to friction well slushed – the parrel of the topsail yard for instance – helped ameliorate the problem.

It was very important that all lifts, trusses, and rolling-tackles be well set up. Braces had to be allowed some play, because of the whipping of the masts. Likewise, Bonnefoux (135) believed that the leeches of the sails set should not be kept unduly taut, otherwise it overstrained both the canvas and the gear generally. The topmen were sent aloft at intervals to check the tops, particularly the condition of the shrouds at the masthead. It was important that the wind not be allowed to get a toehold on the furled canvas. Hence the importance of meticulously tucking in any loose dog-ears, or rope ends. Preventer gaskets, contrived from any spare gear, like studdingsail halliards, could be taken around sail and yard, to make sure nothing came adrift. If thunder were in the offing, the integrity of the lightning conductors was checked. In the sail room, the light sails were stowed away, and the storm sails – fore staysail, main staysail, mizzen staysail and storm mizzen – were cleared away, and got ready in case they were required.

Carrying sail. Mossel remarks that in the modern well-built, well-found men-of-war of his day, bad weather was much less to be feared than in former times, and the consciousness of this gave everyone confidence. Prudence was nonetheless still required. As one writer puts it, 'we have known vessels much risked from officers wishing to have the name of fine fellows for carrying on sail'. The man-of-war was intended as a fighting machine, and tactical circumstances might dictate taking risks which were, in another context, inexcusable. It was also important that the commander keep his vessel, so far as possible, in a condition to engage any enemy that should appear.

It was equally of consequence that sail be made in proportion as the wind moderated, to alleviate rolling, and lessen the working of the masts and guns. 'The ship should not be allowed to tear herself to pieces for want of more sail to steady her', says Liardet (231), who damns the 'idle practice of keeping the ship under low sail in a high sea', as a result of which she may prematurely require recaulking. In this connection, in a stiff, hard-rolling ship, the jerky nature of the oscillation might be aggravated by diminishing the weight aloft. Thus a ship might behave better a few months into a commission, than at the outset, because a substantial amount of stores had been expended in the interval. In some circumstances, it might, for instance, be better to strike the topgallant masts, rather than sending them on deck. (Liardet, 239). Incidentally, Dutch writers of the same period *strijk* ('strike') topgallants on deck, using the verb *schieten* ('shoot') to describe the procedure of partially lowering them (Groeneijk, 151).

Communication. The roar of wind and sea made it more difficult to pass orders. Sometimes two people side by side could hardly hear what the other was saying. As Liardet (109) puts it, 'In gales of wind, or when blowing hard, the voice of the commanding officer can seldom be heard so high as the tops, and continual hailing without being understood only creates confusion aloft, and impedes the duty. In such cases, have two or three smart intelligent sailor boys stationed near the commanding officer to convey his orders aloft, this will save much misunderstanding, hailing, and confusion.'

Apart from the stresses thrown on the fabric of the ship, and her rigging, it need hardly be said, that everyone on board would be having difficulty keeping their foothold, being cold, soaked with rain and spray, and not in the best humour generally.

SCUDDING

In extremely foul weather, the seaman had only two choices: to scud, that is, run before the wind; or to lie to, staying fairly close to the wind, but making headway only very slowly. The greatest danger was to be apprehended if he got broadside on to the wind and sea, particularly if aback, when he was liable to be overwhelmed by the waves, thrown on his beam ends, or lose his rudder if he was unlucky enough to start going astern. Earlier, the terms used were quite different, as is apparent from Mainwaring's definitions:

To spoon is to put a ship right before the wind and the sea, without any sail, and that is called spooning afore. This is done most commonly when, in a great storm, a ship is so weak with age or labouring that we dare not lay her under the sea. For though a ship when she spoons afore do roll more, yet she strains not so much.

But if she be a dangerous rolling ship, then perforce, she must be laid under the sea, for else she will roll her mast by the board, and also it is dangerous, for if a sea should overtake her, when she hath a desperate seel, it may chance to break in and founder her. Sometimes then, to make her go the steadier, they set the foresail, which is called spooning with the foresail. When they do this, they are sure of sea room enough (232)...

Trying is to have no more sail forth, but the mainsail, the tack aboard, the bowline set up, the sheet close aft, and the helm tied down close aboard. Some try with their mizzen only, but that is when it blows so much that they cannot maintain the mainsail. A ship a-try with her mainsail, unless it be an extraordinary grown sea, will make her way two points afore the beam, but with a mizzen not so much. (250).

The equivalent French terms were *fuir devant le temps* ('to fly before the weather'), and to lie *à la cape*, or, as a verb, *capeyer*. The Dutch terms were respectively *lenzen* and *bijleggen* ('lie by'), and similar words were

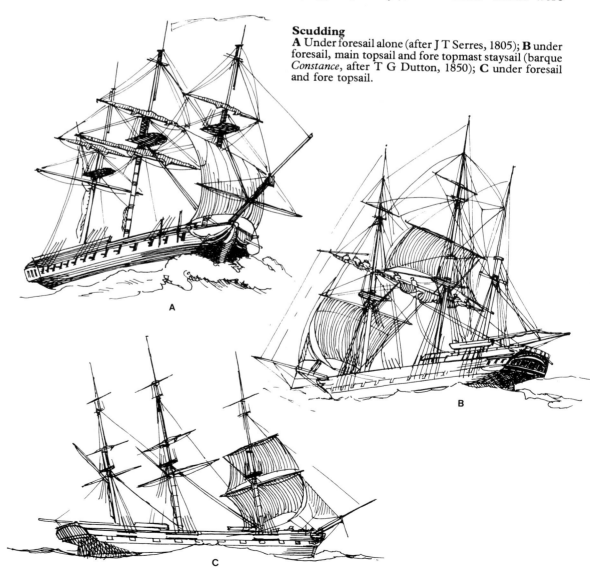

Scudding
A Under foresail alone (after J T Serres, 1805); **B** under foresail, main topsail and fore topmast staysail (barque *Constance*, after T G Dutton, 1850); **C** under foresail and fore topsail.

also used in the other northern European languages. If no sail could be carried, the ship was said to 'scud under bare poles', the Dutch equivalent being *voor top en takel lenzen* ('to scud under top and tackle'), while Bonnefoux speaks of a *cape sèche* ('lying to dry, or bare'). Similarly a vessel lying to was said to 'hull', or 'lie a-hull', or 'strike a-hull', which 'is when they would lie obscurely in the sea, or stay for some consort, lash sure the helm a-lee, and so a good ship lie at ease under the sea, as we term it' (Smith, 51).

Sail used. The intention of the vessel scudding was to reduce the relative wind strength by flying before it. While it was true that more sail could be set than when by the wind, it was not, in fact, possible to outrun the waves, but merely to reduce their impact.

In the 1600s, the foresail without its bonnet was the only canvas used for scudding, and indeed this sail offered some positive features. It was well forward, and hence pulled the bow, rather than pushing the stern. With the sheets eased well off, it exerted a lifting effect on the bow, and this also improved steerage. The forestay, of course, limited the extent to which the sail could be allowed to balloon forward, and this tendency was curbed by using a quicksaver. Murphy (21) rigs the clew-jigger down forward of the sail, so that the clews could more readily be got up, should the sail, by mischance, get aback. However, the courses were prone to lose the wind in the trough of the sea, so causing the vessel to lose speed, and allowing her to be 'pooped' by a following sea – hence the later popularity of the reefed main topsail, which was placed higher above the ocean surface, and supplemented the foresail. The small topsails of the Elizabethan era, would not have served for this purpose in a gale, because they were too ill-supported. The fore topmast staysail, with the sheets hauled aft to hold it amidships, was an excellent sail, since although it held no wind if the vessel were dead before the weather, it exerted a powerful action in throwing the head off the wind in the event of a bad yaw. In the mid-1800s some seamen began to advocate using the fore topsail instead of the main topsail. Murphy (21) recommends that the yard be settled on the cap, and the sheets eased well off, so it will be, to some extent, a lifting sail. Otherwise it would tend, if anything, to depress the bow. Murphy felt that with the combination of fore topmast staysail, reefed foresail, and reefed fore topsail, there was virtually no chance of being brought by the lee. Writing in 1900, Todd & Whall (161) also prefer the fore topsail to the main topsail, this now at a

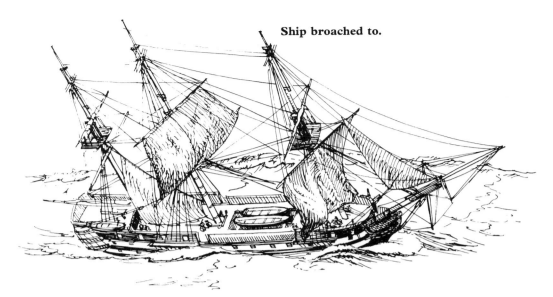

Ship broached to.

time where the foremast was placed relatively further aft than in the Elizabethan vessels. In fact, they say that the main topsail is a poor choice for the purpose, and should not be set along with the fore topsail, because not only is it too far aft, but also because it becalms the fore topsail. This leads them to question its traditional indispensability, which through the early 1800s had become implicit. In their day, the introduction of the split topsails had made scudding somewhat safer than had been the case formerly, when the huge single topsails had to be close-reefed.

Rolling. The vessel running directly before the storm was not properly steadied against rolling by her canvas, and hence many preferred to get the wind two or three points on the quarter, so heeling the ship to leeward, and thus reducing the violence of rolling, and, as a matter of fact, probably increasing the speed. Nonetheless, if the sea was very turbulent, it might be better to keep the wind directly aft (Mossel, III, 352). Much depended on the characteristics of the individual vessel.

Yawing. All scudding vessels yawed more or less, sometimes quite heavily. Rosvall (124) refers to the heavy lurches as 'East Indian yaws'. If the vessel swung towards the wind, inadvertently coming broadside to the sea, it was said to have 'broached to'. If the wind were on the quarter, and through careless steering the stern swung across the wind so that it came on the other side, throwing the maintopsail aback, the ship was said to have been 'brought by the lee'. Two picturesque Swedish expressions are used in the same context: *fanga uggla*, 'to catch an owl'; and *skjuta björn*, 'to shoot a bear' (Ekelöf, 164; Uggla, 66). The consequences were somewhat similar. The seas smashed against the broadside and swept the decks. If the backed sail caused sternway, the rudder fastenings

could be damaged, the tiller broken, and the rudder lost. The vessel could be knocked down 'on her beam ends', and if not recovered, be in immediate danger of foundering. Trailing twenty to thirty fathoms of hawser astern, was one way of lessening the tendency to yaw. Sometimes altering the trim of the vessel by moving heavy objects, shot or chain cables, forward – or more particularly aft – would do the trick, giving the rudder a better grip on the water, so to speak.

Being pooped. It is said that the high sterns of the Elizabethan era reflected the fear of the contemporary seaman of taking a sea over the stern, having it rake the decks, and sweep away all in its path. Certainly, scudding in a flush-decked vessel was considered more dangerous than in one with upperworks aft, but a number of measures could be taken to lessen the danger, breaking the water up astern. The faster the vessel was moving, the greater this surface disturbance, hence, in part, the necessity for keeping enough sail set. Trailing a hawser, or as Bonnefoux (135) advocates, a topsail, had a similar effect. The churning of a steamer's screw partially explained why these vessels were in less danger of shipping a sea over the stern than a sailing vessel similarly situated (Hildebrandt, 191). Somewhat paradoxically, oil could be used with benefit, since it smoothed the surface, preventing the seas breaking; oil bags dragged in the water up forward, formed a slick astern (Knight, 340; Dick & Kretchmer, 342), but surprisingly, all the earlier writers are silent on this matter. The expanse of glass in the stern-galleries of the old men-of-war was also a weak point. Bonnefoux mentions *fausses fenêtres*, 'false windows', also called *mantelets volants* ('flying port lids'), which were installed to protect them, but I do not know the equivalent term in English.

The helmsman. Steering was so critical that

only the best helmsmen were used. Todd & Whall (104), considering the large sailing merchantman with the wheel right aft, recommend keeping the helmsman on for the whole watch, rather than relieving every hour as customary otherwise, if he was getting along nicely. Experience showed that accidents were much more likely to occur at the time of relieving the wheel, while the new hand had not quite got the feel of it (Dick & Kretchmer, 343). The steersman was further strictly enjoined not to look astern, as the sight of a huge sea at his back might break his concentration, and cause him to steer badly. Many seamen hesitated to lash themselves to the wheel, feeling that to do so betrayed a lack of fortitude. Todd & Whall felt that the security offered by a lashing gave the man confidence, and better allowed him to attend to his business.

In this type of vessel, if a sea struck the rudder sufficiently hard, it was possible for the rudder to control the movement of the wheel, despite the heavy gearing-down built into the steering mechanism. Some sort of 'brake' was therfore clearly useful, and the 'relieving-tackle' rigged on merchantmen was an attempt to prevent such sudden abrupt movements of the tiller. This was accomplished by hauling the fall of the tackle taut, which, on the other hand, made steering more arduous, because the wheel would appear 'stiffer'. It will be noted that this 'relieving-tackle' is quite different from that described earlier. A still more sophisticated device was a foot-brake which was fitted in the latter-day big German sailing vessels for the same purpose. If the rudder did indeed take charge, the helmsmen were liable to be seriously injured. On one side, the man was hurled over the wheel as it spun; on the other, the whirling spokes smashed him to the deck. In the large sailing man-of-war rather similar considerations obtained, hence the necessity for assistant helmsmen, or 'blind-men'. If the compass was sluggish, Murphy (21) suggests substituting a light, sensitive compass, and keeping a lantern ready, should the binnacle-lamp blow out. It is interesting to speculate on how things were managed in Elizabethan ships. Mainwaring (256) specifically says that the whipstaff was not used in foul weather, because only one man could handle it. At all times, tackles were used in large vessels of over 500 tons or so. The tackles, incidentally, although a clumsier method, allowed a greater range of tiller motion, than the whipstaff.

LYING TO

The other method of handling the ship in a

Helmsmen thrown by wheel taking charge (after Boyd, 1857).

Ship being pooped.

Lying to
A Under mainsail; **B** under mainsail and foresail, hauled up and backed (after Hutchinson, 1777); **C** under main topsail and staysails (ship *Sea Mew*, after R Salmon, 1835); **D** under mizzen alone (after F Holman).

storm was to hold the ship's head about four points from the wind, and 'try', or 'lie to', going very slowly ahead. The choice of method was often dictated by circumstances. For instance, if the objective lay to leeward, scudding took one in the right direction. If one's destination was more or less to windward, one would lose less ground lying to. The ship could not scud if it were in danger of becoming embayed on a lee shore, and so on. Sometimes, however, having commenced by running before the gale, the weather now worsening and daylight going, it behoved the prudent mariner to lay his vessel to, and have all snug before nightfall. If a vessel, bound to leeward, nonetheless found the going too rough, running before the storm, and perforce had to lie to, until the weather moderated, she was said by the Dutch *van een goed wind, een kwaden maken*, 'to make a bad wind out of a good one' (Mossel, III, 335). Roughly speaking, it could be said that a smaller vessel would be forced to lie to earlier than a large one, and once brought to, she would probably behave somewhat better than a ship of greater size. This would be especially true if she were a lightly built vessel, with a well rounded bow above the waterline, which would rise readily to the waves. The men-of-war of the late 1800s could scud more safely than their predecessors, because of their strongly built round sterns, which lifted the hull clear of the aftercoming seas. Sharply built vessels, especially if rather short, plunged their bows deeply into the water, and did not rise well to the next wave, especially if they were heavily laden, and most particularly if the weight were unevenly distributed towards the bow and stern. Sharply built vessels of greater length behaved rather better, since this form of bow lessened the shock, as it clove into the wave, resulting in less whipping of the masts, straining of the stays, and so on (Mossel III, 355). Notwithstanding what we have said earlier about a vessel running before the wind, 'trying to outrun the waves', and keeping sufficient canvas set to maintain speed there was (as with most facets of this whole business) an opposing school of thought. Todd & Whall (104) recommend that a sailing vessel scudding, and making heavy weather of it, should try shortening sail, if necessary to bare poles, rather than attempt bringing to. This opinion was no doubt influenced by the finding that steamers, whether running before, or lying to, the wind, were often rendered more comfortable simply by reducing the engine revolutions.

Heaving to, lying to and headreaching. As mentioned earlier, we have followed Liardet (III), choosing to 'lie to' in a storm, rather than 'heave to': he considered that the distinction lay in having some canvas aback, when hove to. A distinction was sometimes made between 'headreaching' and 'lying to'. With the former, the ship was making headway, albeit slowly, being considered to be close-hauled under storm canvas, as it were, whereas when laid to, minimal progress was being made (Nicholls, 254).

Choice of sail. The Elizabethan seaman usually 'lay-a-try' under the main course, or occasionally the mizzen. A century later, the common method was to set the reefed mainsail with the backed foresail 'hung in the brails' (Hutchinson, 166), and Rosvall (126) identifies this practice as one used specifically by English seamen. By 1849, however, Liardet (138) comments as follows:

I believe I am right when I assert, that the main topsail of a sailing vessel should be kept set as long as possible, in blowing weather. More particularly when accompanied with a heavy sea. It is the resistance of the main topsail, placed on such a long lever at the mainmast head, which gives the ship that easy motion, which she so generally has when lying by the wind, under that sail. If from any accident, you lose the use of this sail for a short time, the ship will soon convince you of its utility, by her continued heavy rolling until it is set again. The storm sails are not high enough to make sufficient resistance to the rolling of the ship. The shape of the storm staysails prevents their being of much use in steadying the ship in a heavy sea. Besides, all low sails must be liable to the objection of being becalmed in some measure in a heavy sea. How many ships were lost in former times from the practice of heaving to, or lying by the wind under the square mainsail? It must appear wonderful to the seamen of the present day, how this dangerous sail could ever have been used for lying by the wind in heavy gales. This sail, from its central position, and the difficulty of working it, should be furled previous to unsettled threatening weather. If seamen invariably admit that a main topsail is the best sail for steadying a sailing vessel in gales of wind and heavy sea, the same must hold good with steamers. But in a much greater degree is the main topsail required in a steamer than in a sailing vessel. Sailing vessels have their weights more equally divided than steamers, therefore not so likely to strain themselves. The weights in a steamer are so placed that a long steadying lever, in the shape of a main topsail will go far to prevent that heavy jerking motion in a seaway, which strains and disables them so often, when obliged to trust to their sails only, which must be continually the case when employed with fleets or squadrons.'

Although the mainsail balanced the ship quite nicely, it was a desperate matter if it accidentally flew aback, it being all but impossible to haul the canvas up, before the vessel commenced to sail backwards, perhaps tearing off the rudder, and sailing herself under. If it became necessary to bear away, or wear onto the other tack, the sail would make it difficult to get off the wind, a necessary element in wearing. Mossel also considered that it was unacceptably prone to flap about blindly in the trough of the sea, and furthermore caused the ship to make too much headway.

The reefed fore course is mentioned by Bonnefoux, but it was certainly an unusual sail to select, one which was said to result in a lot of lurching to leeward. Lever claimed that it would depress the bow – that is to say when it was braced up sharp – and hence might be useful in a ship that was down by the stern when scudding, of course, it was considered a 'lifting' sail. The reefed main topsail was, like the mainsail, ideally placed near the middle of the ship, but being higher it steadied the vessel better. It could not unfortunately, be braced up as sharp as the mainsail, because when close reefed, its yard was almost on the cap, and therefore touched the lee topmast shrouds at a point where they already had considerable spread. As a result, it was impossible to get as close to the wind as could be done with a mainsail. It could accidentally be thrown aback, but this was not quite such an embarrassment as the analogous situation with the main course, as the topsail could fairly readily be braced around, or taken in (Gower, 50). If even the close reefed main topsail, or main lower topsail, were too much, it could be 'goosewinged', the weather side being made fast, and the lee clew remaining set. A lashing was passed around the weather quarter of the yard, encompassing yard and sail, the latter being protected by parcelling. Everything to windward of this was secured. 'It need hardly be said that this operation does not do the sail any good' (Nicholls, 254). Bonnefoux says that while the combination of reefed foresail and mizzen, or mizzen staysail had been used in the past, it was seen but rarely in his day. The tendency to sheer to leeward, which was a problem with the foresail alone, was abated by adding the mizzen, but the drift to leeward, of the ship as a whole, was accentuated.

The reefed mizzen, or storm mizzen, alone, would seem to have been an excellent choice, holding the bow up to the wind better than any other sail. In fact the vessel rode very uneasily under this canvas, since the bow came almost into the wind, the waves striking it head on, resulting in increased pitching and consequent fatigue of the masts. The vessel which cut across the seas somewhat obliquely, was usually more comfortable than one hammering directly into them. Changing the angle of attack also altered the period of the waves, which might affect the way the vessel rode them out. The ideal was to lie *by* the wind, not *in* the wind. Of the three masts, the mizzen was the least well supported, and even when the vessel lay four points off the wind, the anti-rolling effect was being exerted a long way from the centre of the vessel, where the forces of buoyancy were concentrated. Furthermore, says Lever (89), imagine what would happen if a ship were hove down for careening, using the mizzen mast alone! The mizzen sail was usually fitted for reefing, and if the 'balance-reef' were taken, the throat of the gaff was almost down on the boom, the gaff cocked away up, leaving a rather peculiar looking little triangular sail. The expression 'balance the mizzen' (Smyth, 70) may actually have preceded the balance reef, and earlier referred to a method of reducing area that was unique to this sail. A piece of canvas was wrapped around the sail and gaff, and a lashing passed outside to secure the sail at the throat of the gaff. The Dutch expression for this procedure was *de bezaan bollen* ('to ball the mizzen'), and like 'balance the mizzen' it later became synonymous with 'to reef' this particular sail. A special storm mizzen, becketted securely around the mast, with the sheet hauled aft by a good tackle, was a decided improvement on a reefed down gaff mizzen, since it allowed the mizzen gaff to be got down on deck out of the way.

Other special storm sails were the fore staysail, the main staysail, and the mizzen staysail. These all have commonplace names in English, but not so in other languages: *trinquette*, in French for fore staysail; *pouillouse* in French, *dek-swabber*, in Dutch, for the main staysail; *aap* in Dutch, *carbonero* in Italian, *rabeca* in Portuguese, for the mizzen staysail. 'Deck-swabber' is understandable, but why the Dutch, and other northern European nations, call the mizzen staysail the 'ape', while the Italians called it 'collier', is not immediately obvious; the other terms are even more puzzling. In any case, these sails enjoyed a vogue until the mid-1800s, when the two after ones tended to be replaced by fore and main trysails, or spencers, set on gaffs on the fore and mainmasts. Lever (89) thought the main staysail strained the ship less than any other single sail, because of its position, and its being secured to the strongest mast. Any of these five sails shared the same advantage, namely

that they could not get aback; and the same shortcoming, that they did not take the place of lofty sail in reducing rolling. However by setting two or three storm sails, perhaps with a reefed main topsail, depending on circumstances, the strain could be distributed between the masts, and an appropriate balance of canvas achieved, to suit the individual vessel.

Inventive seamen came up with yet other specially contrived storm sails. Bonnefoux (121) describes a staysail set from the foremast head to the fore tack-bumpkin, presumably the weather one, and sheeted aft on the forecastle. Groeneijk (166) hoists a fore topmast staysail to the mizzen masthead, the tack being secured to the middle of the transom, and the sheet taken forward and to windward to be made fast, thus reversing the usual position of sheet and tack. In extremity, any scrap of canvas might serve as what the Elizabethans referred to as a 'hullock' of a sail. A tarpaulin could be loosed in the mizzen or main rigging, in default of anything better. The tarpaulin was rolled up, taken outside the mizzen rigging, and the wind allowed to unroll it, and subsequently keep it firm against the shrouds (Reed, 264).

The helm. When lying to, steering was not quite so critical as when scudding. The helmsman tried to keep the main topsail just full, but not allowing it to fly aback. The practice of the Elizabethans was to try with the tiller lashed hard a-lee, but later on, it was considered best to tend it rather than keeping it immobile. Bonnefoux suggests that, in his day, in small craft, lashing the tiller a-lee was still traditional. In bad weather, everyone simply went below, hoping for the best, and rode out the storm. The rudder being hard over, was more exposed to the buffeting of the waves, and if, because of a wind shift, the vessel went briskly astern, rudder or tiller might be lost. Too much rudder was avoided for this reason.

Ideally, the sail set balanced so that the ship lay about seven points from the wind, coming up and falling off, with a couple of spokes of lee helm on; that is to say, the inclination of the vessel was to fall off, and she had to be coaxed up to the wind. If the rudder were suddenly swept away, this meant that the ship would go off, rather than come up with her sails aback. In the case of a vessel out of trim, down by the head, it might be necessary to carry a little weather helm, but in such a case, it was best to improve the balance of the sail, so that small lee helm was needed. (Mossel, III, 359). Taking an oncoming wave on the broadside was avoided by having the helmsman put the helm down a

little more. Massenet (316) underlines the importance of the 'smooth', which lay to windward of the vessel, her wake, so to speak, as she drove to leeward. This diminished the force of the waves rolling down from windward, particularly so if oil was used. *Une bonne cape* was achieved when the vessel continuously received the benefit of this flat patch of water. With *une cape molle*, the vessel's head lay about eight points from the wind, and she tended to 'fore-reach' the wind then coming from somewhat ahead of the intended direction. With *une cape ardente*, on the other hand, the ship's head lay seven points from the wind, and she alternately ran ahead, and came up, then went astern and fell off. Thus sometimes the wind came from ahead of, and sometimes astern of the intended direction.

Choice of tack. If close to some danger, such as a lee shore, the tack that would take the ship clear was chosen. Ordinarily, the seas were at right angles to the wind, approaching the ship directly from windward. If, because of a shift, wind and sea were no longer exactly aligned, the best tack kept the ship's head to sea. Thus if the wind drew aft, the vessel would remain on the same tack, but perhaps change her heading so the wind was more abeam, and the waves being taken more on the bow. If, on the other hand, the ship 'broke off' because the wind shifted ahead, it might be necessary to wear and get on the other tack to avoid taking the seas broadside. In either case, it might be that the wind shift would make it more convenient to scud than remain lying by the wind. Local knowledge was of great use also; for instance, in the North Atlantic, experience taught that in a westerly gale, a shift – what the Dutch called an *uitschieter* ('out-shooter') – would probably come from the North, hence the starboard tack was best. The shift, when it came, would be from the quarter, rather than the old lee bow, and hence, there was no danger of getting aback. If the ship were leaking on one side, it was best to keep that side to weather, that is less deeply submerged, than when on the opposite tack.

To wear under a mainsail. In describing the process of wearing, it was noted that this manoeuvre always succeeded – not always the case with tacking. However, in the case of a vessel lying to, particularly under aftersail, such as a reefed main course, it might be difficult to get her to go off beyond a certain point. To get around, the helm was put up, the fore topmast staysail hoisted, and the weather mainbrace hauled, as the wind came further aft. The mizzen yards were pointed to the wind, while the foreyards were braced up

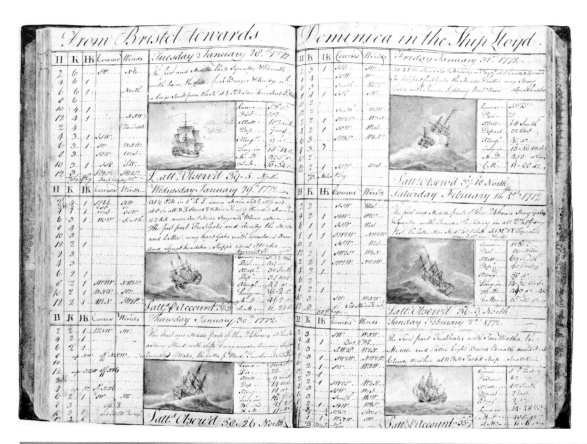

These pages from the logbook of the West India trader *Lloyd* record how she rode out a succession of heavy gales one week after sailing from Bristol for Dominica in January, 1772. The logbook was kept and illustrated by the *Lloyd*'s Master, Nicholas Pocock, who later rose to fame as a marine artist. During the six days recorded here, we see the *Lloyd* in fresh weather with topsails reefed (upper left), her fore and mizzen topgallant masts sent down for the winter passage. On January 29th (middle left) and 31st (top right) she has been blown into her courses; on the 30th (bottom left) she is lying to under bare poles; and on February 1st (middle right) she is riding under foresail alone. The log entries show that during these days Capt Pocock made what sail he could, setting and taking in topsails and staysails as the weather eased and worsened. (Bristol Record Office, courtesy Bristol Museum and Art Gallery)

East Indiaman in a storm, painted by W J Huggins, 1840. This ship is shown in extreme conditions, lying to with topgallant masts struck and all her canvas furled except a reefed spanker, which has just blown out. (N R Omell Gallery, London)

sharp; when the wind was abaft the beam, the main tack was raised, and when the wind was astern, the sheet was raised, and the other tack boarded. Coming up into the wind, the fore topmast staysail was lowered, the foreyards braced in, and the afteryards braced up. If the vessel were reluctant to go off, a hawser, with some sort of drag could be paid over the lee quarter; the weather fore rigging could be manned as thick as possible and the remainder of the crew sent to the weather side of the poop, their bodies, in one case acting as a sail, in the other, to give the stern a little better grip on the water.

To weather coil. 'Weather coil is when a ship is a-hull, to lay her head the other way, without loosing any sail, which is only done by bearing up the helm. It is an excellent condition in a ship, for most ships will not weather coil. The use of it is that when we desire to drive with her head the other way a-hull, then we need not open any sail, wherewith before the ship can come to wear, she will run a great way to leeward, when once she is before the wind and sea under sail' (Mainwaring, 255). The significance of the term would seem to mean 'wearing under bare poles'. However, Smyth (724) gives a totally different definition: 'When a ship has her head brought about, so to lie that way which her stern did before, as by the veering of the wind; or the motion of the helm, the sails remaining trimmed', and also 'when a ship resumes her course after being taken aback; rounding off by a stern-board, and coming up to it again'. Lever (90) describes this procedure, accomplished by filling the foreyards and shivering the after ones, together with the other expedients already described. He remarks that a vessel in proper trim will seldom do it. It will be realised that in high winds, the yards behaved in the same fashion as if the sails were deployed. The could be aback, full, or pointed to the wind. Lever (90) describes boxhauling a vessel under bare poles, when surprised by another vessel bearing down upon her, and not having time to carry out any other manoeuvre. This was a measure of desperation, since although the backed foreyards pushed the bow off the wind, the resulting sternway could be dangerous.

Wearing under staysails and main topsails. If, as tended to be the case in the later 1800s, the ship were not laid to under the mainsail, wearing was a more certain manoeuvre. An excellent description is found in Ulffers (300). We will assume the ship to be lying to under fore topmast staysail, reefed main topsail, reefed mainsail, and reefed mizzen. The principle is the same as desc-

Wearing under mainsail.

Wearing under bare poles.

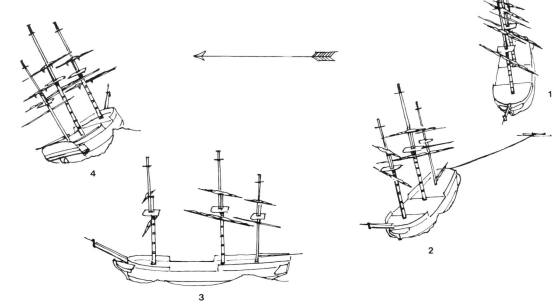

ribed above; that is, after sail is got off, and set again when on the new tack. The mizzen is got in, and the mainsail hauled up. The main topsail is kept just full, hauling in the weather brace, easing away the lee, as the ship falls off. The mizzen topsail and crossjack yards are kept pointed to the wind. Whether the helm should be put up, or the afteryards braced in first, depends on circumstances. It is an easier haul if the yards are braced in while the ship is still close to the wind, and they are being struck by the wind at a more acute angle. If the ship has headway, and is obeying the rudder, the yards may be braced in first. If on the other hand, there is little headway,

the yards must not be braced in first or headway will be further diminished. In the situation described, there is probably adequate forward sail, but if not, the tack of the foresail can be got down, keeping the lee side fast 'goosewinging' it, in a manner of speaking (Totten, 193). As the ship falls off, one continues to brace in the afteryards until they are square, and the ship will now be travelling downwind at a good speed, and the forward yards are also squared. The helm being kept over, the ship now starts to come up on the other tack, the foresail is taken in, the mizzen and mainsail are set once more, the afteryards braced up for the new tack, and when the

Wearing under staysails and main topsail.

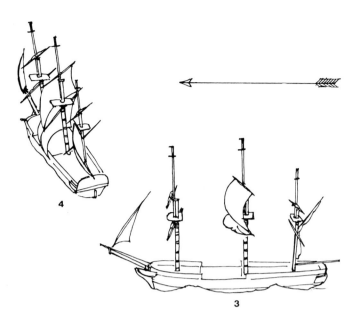

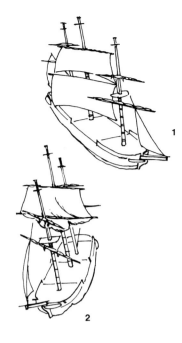

This arrangement refers to a situation where the lee crossjack and weather main braces are worked together, and where the yard-tackles have been rigged as preventer braces or 'jumpers', with the regular main counter or preventer braces leading forward.

Headbraces, up foresail, let go fore bowline!

Fore tack	Captains first & third quarters forecastlemen
Weather fore sheet	Foreyardmen of the side
Fore sheet	Captains third & fourth quarters waisters
Lee fore tack	Foretopmen of the side
Fore bowlines	Captains forecastlemen of the side
Weather fore truss	Waister of the side
Weather fore yard-tackle	Waisters of the other side
Lee fore truss	Captain third quarterwaisters
Lee fore yard-tackle	Captain fourth quarterwaisters
Shift over headsheets	Forecastlemen
Clear away mizzen	Mizzen mast division

The commands.

All hands wear ship!

Main clewgarnets and buntlines, mizzen brails!

In mizzen, up mainsail!

Man weather main, lee crossjack braces!

Stand by to set tack of foresail! Ease down weather clewgarnet!

Down foresail!

Stand by to take in foresail! Weather clewgarnets and buntlines!

Up foresail!

Stand by to set mizzen! Let go the brails, haul out!

Comparison with the organisation for wearing in moderate weather shows few differences, except for the handling of special storm gear. The yard-tackles were rigged either as 'jumpers', or martingales, to steady the lower yards against the jerk, when the tack was let go, or as 'preventer braces' leading aft to the bulwarks. The topsail preventer braces referred to also led aft.

wind is on the quarter, the headyards are braced up. The most dangerous moment during the wearing process occurs when wind and sea are abeam. Thus, efforts are made to avoid having the ship remain in that situation any longer than necessary.

Organisation of the crew. This is an 'all hands' business, and the following is based upon Ulffers' account of German naval practice.

Main clewgarnets and buntlines, mizzen brails!

Lee mizzen brails	Lee mizzen mast division
Weather mizzen brails	Weather mizzen topmen
Weather vang	Weather quarterdeckmen
Mizzen outhaul	Captain second quarter quarterdeckmen
Main clewgarnets	Maintopmen
Main buntlines	Afterguard
Main tack	Captains third & fourth quarters waisters
Main sheet	Captains third & fourth quarters afterguard
Main bowline	Captain second quarter waisters

Weather after braces, after bowlines!

Main preventer brace	Foremast division
Weather main afterbrace	Main yardmen
Weather main topsail brace	Main topsail yardmen of the side
Weather main topsail preventer brace	Main topsail yardmen of the other side
Lee crossjack brace	Mizzen topmen
Weather main tackle fall	Afterguard of the side
Weather main truss	Afterguard of the other side
Crossjack truss	Quarterdeckmen
Tend main preventer brace and main top bowline	Captains third & fourth quarters waisters
Tend lee main brace	Captains third & fourth quarters quarterdeckmen
Tend lee main topsail brace	Captain first quarter quarterdeckmen
Tend lee maintopsail preventer brace	Captain second quarter quarterdeckmen
Let go crossjack braces	Captains third & fourth quarters afterguard
Tend lee main truss	Captain third quarter afterguard
Tend lee yard-tackle fall	Captain fourth quarter afterguard

CHAPTER 16
SQUALLS

'Squalls are invariably to be seen, and it ought to be as settled a maxim in a ship of war never to be overtaken unprepared by one, as never to be surprised by an enemy' (Fordyce, 140).

A squall is a sudden increase in wind strength, occurring in gusts or flaws, which often come in succession, and are of relatively short duration, allowing the sea to settle down between flurries. According to their appearance, they have been described as 'white squalls', 'black squalls', 'thunder squalls', and so on. Bonnefoux considered a squall unaccompanied by cloud, as particularly treacherous, since the only warning was the catspaw on the water as it came in. He called this type a *grain sec*, literally 'dry squall'. Most often, squalls are accompanied by rain, and not infrequently associated with chopping about of the wind, which may change direction by several points, particularly in thundery weather (Hansen, 140). The sequence of wind changes varies: sometimes the squall is preceded by a forerunner; sometimes it comes 'butt end first' – a heavy shower of rain, before the wind; sometimes at the end, it gives a last crack of the whip, the *queue du grain* ('the tail of the squall') as Bonnefoux calls it. The officer of the deck had to keep his eyes peeled for impending squalls, which might hit with little warning, other than the whistle of the wind. Watching the behaviour of other sailing vessels to windward, and seeing the accompanying disturbance of the water might give warning of something in the offing. In daylight, the horizon was continuously scanned for evidence of squall-bearing cloud. A storm cloud with soft diffuse edges was considered less dangerous than one with well defined sharp but ragged edges, especially if scud were breaking away from the periphery. A squall that could be seen through was less dangerous than an opaque black cloud. The relationship of wind and rain was considered significant, but Todd & Whall (76) give many exceptions to the following rule, which is found in many versions:

HMS *Meander* beset by a williwaw in the Straits of Magellan (after engraving by O W Brierly, *Illustrated London News*, 1851).

When the rain's before the wind
Halliards, sheets and braces mind.
When the wind's before the rain,
Hoist the topsails up again.

The wind sometimes has a downward component, and this is particularly the case with gusts blowing through coastal passes, striking a ship sailing along a mountainous coast. The German word for this type of phenomenon was, in fact, *Fallwind*. Todd & Whall (77) caution against this particular hazard in Table Bay, but the danger is well known to people sailing mountain lakes anywhere.

Foreign equivalents. In French, *grain*, *rafale* and *risée* were respectively, gusts (*bourrasques*) of diminishing strength, while the Germanic languages used a word similar to Swedish *by*. Swedish *kastvind*, and similar words, presumably referred to the casting or chopping about of the wind. *Grain* may derive from the association of hail with wind gusts; Spanish *granizada* is a 'hail-squall'.

To luff or bear away. The small boat sailor luffs up in a squall, if it comes from before the beam, and falls off if the gust comes from

abaft it, shortening sail if necessary; some authorities recommend exactly the same procedure for square-riggers (Luce, 457; Dick & Kretchmer, 338). By bearing away, the relative wind speed is reduced and the forward sails are somewhat becalmed by the after ones, allowing canvas to be shortened relatively comfortably. The most dangerous moment occurs when the wind is dead abeam, particularly if way is lost, since the heeling tendency will be most violent at that time. For this reason, if sailing by the wind, and the gust comes directly from windward, falling off may be dangerous, precisely because at some point the wind will come from directly abeam. Hourigan (107) mentions the tendency of the longer ships of his day, in the late 1800s, to 'hang' at this point, refusing to go off, and hence exposing themselves to a knockdown. Nares (274) recommended keeping away in good time: 'If you wait until it is upon you, all the damage will be done long before she commences to pay off.' Todd & Whall (76) also advise giving the ship 'a wipe off before the wind' at an early stage (*Mariner's Mirror* 60, 1974, 32). Luffing up, until the sails just shake, will re-

Vessel caught aback in a squall (after P C Caussé, 1836).

HMS Amazon struck by a squall. Ten of the fourteen sails set in the *Amazon* were blown out by this sudden squall, which came up while the vessel was becalmed (after engraving in *Illustrated London News*, 1852).

lieve the heeling and allow the light sails and topsails to be struck, and the mizzen to be got in more readily, after which the helm may be put up in comparative safety. Murphy (43) says that the merchant service tended to favour luffing through a squall, 'a practice which has withstood the infallible test of successful application for years and years of boisterous servitude'. The afteryards were best kept braced in a little, 'trimmed fine', at this point so they would be shaking before the fore. This also would help keep the head sufficiently off the wind (Murphy, 43). When struck by a squall from windward, the vessel has a powerful tendency to luff in any case, because of the increased pressure under the lee bow, due to heeling. In fact, if the spanker and mainsail are not taken in, it will be difficult to get the vessel to go off at all. The great danger in luffing, is having everything fly aback – particularly so if the wind suddenly hauls forward some points. Not only did this throw a violent strain on the stays and spars, but it was almost impossible to haul up a square sail plastered hard against the rigging, and considerable difficulty might then be experienced in getting the ship to go off the wind, so allowing it to fill once more, and be rendered manageable. Hourigan (107) alludes to another practical point. 'Heavy squalls are, in most instances, accompanied by heavy rain, and if he holds on, to luff through, then *has* to shorten sail, the watch are disconcerted by the rain, (many too, taking more interest in looking about for their oilskins than in manning the weather topsail braces, if they have not already sought cover), and he himself is half blinded by it, as he tries to look aloft to tend the luff or lay the yards.' The mizzen and main course were the two sails most likely to hold the ship's head to the

wind, hence the necessity for getting them in early in the game.

If the vessel were caught relatively unprepared, the squall causing it to heel violently, the halliards of the upper sails were let go, and the main sheet veered, which might relieve the ship sufficiently, and allow it to straighten up somewhat. If that were insufficient to ease the vessel, the lee sheets of the upper sails, and the main sheet, were let go. This could not be done, of course, without causing *un grand désordre*, as Dubreuil puts it, but it might save a vessel on her beam ends.

There was lack of general agreement on the best course of action to follow. Dubreuil (222), for example, says categorically that 'the last means to which one ought to have recourse to receive a squall is to bear away'. He goes on to say that while one may be forced to use this method sometimes, it usually results from a poor appreciation of the squall, or a lack of watchfulness. This judgement seems rather sweeping, and is not echoed by many others. For instance Fordyce (140) felt that bearing up the helm might be the salvation of a vessel, particularly a small one, if lowering topsails, dropping the peak and so on were insufficient. There was general agreement that it was better to shorten sail in good time, receiving the squall under appropriately small canvas. Sometimes this meant losing time, but as Todd & Whall (76) point out, it is much easier to take in a royal unnecessarily, loosing it again when the danger is past, than have to spend hours sending down a sprung yard, or a torn sail. Luce, as mentioned earlier, luffed if the squall came from ahead. Bréart (96) says that to do so, demonstrates *beaucoup de hardiesse*, by which he meant foolhardiness.

Squall to leeward. If the squall came from the lee side, it very often was presaged by a period of calm. If the vessel were closehauled, the inevitable result was to throw everything aback. The afteryards were squared, the mainsail got up, and the spanker in. This resulted in the ship's head being thrown off the wind, unopposed by the aftersail, after which things were managed according to circumstance. It will be seen that the procedure would be very similar to the final phase of tacking. Ulffers (374) suggested that during a calm, in thundery weather, where it is doubtful from which direction the wind may come, a very similar practice be followed. The topsails are struck, reef-tackles got out, fore topmast staysail sheet hauled aft, afteryards square and foreyards braced up on either tack. The wind, when it comes, will then push the bow off, no matter what its direction.

Shortening sail. The most lofty, and the most cumbersome sail was got off first, ideally before the squall hit. Studdingsails (particularly topgallant and lower), royals, flying jib, upper staysails, mainsail and spanker came in. A large jib was replaced by a small one, or the fore topmast staysail was set (Bréart, 95). Studdingsail booms were particularly at risk if the ship were caught unprepared. Hansen (I, 140) says that one may have to luff, even with studdingsails set, because the mainsail and the mizzen prevent the vessel bearing away. To get the upper square sails down, the weather braces had to be hauled, to bring the yard clear of the lee rigging. This also applied to topsails, the halliards being let go, the clewlines, buntlines, and reef-tackles were hauled, to get the yard down on the cap. Particularly if the ship were heeling excessively, there was some

Ship becalmed, preparing for squalls.

Shortening sail in a squall (after 'The White Squall' by J G Evans).

danger that an upper yard, once struck, might masthead itself again, run up by the force of the wind. Hence it was important, that once down, the clewlines were hauled taut and belayed. Getting the mainsail off was vital: if it got aback in a heavy squall, all hands would be unable to get it up, and the ship would not answer her helm and fall off. 'It is here that this sail justifies the respect, sometimes amounting to awe, in which it is held' (Hourigan, 108). With split topsails, only the upper was struck, and there was little use striking a single topsail with three or four reefs in. All that could be done would be to let go the lee sheet. If the ship was slow to pay off, even with the mainsail and spanker gone, the mizzen topsail could be clewed up. The forecourse was kept set because it, along with the fore topmast staysail tended to hold the bow off the wind. Trysails were esteemed as useful canvas in squally weather, because they acted to keep way on, with no risk of coming aback (Luce, 457).

Struck by a squall on the quarter, with all studdingsails set to weather, Hourigan keeps away, easing off the topgallant studdingsail tack and halliards. The other two studding-sails are kept set to help the ship go off. The ship is kept turning away until the wind is brought about a point on the other quarter, which becalms the studdingsails, allowing them to be got in relatively easily.

Officer of the watch. The responsibility for deciding on the proper course of action lay with the officer of the deck. On the one hand, he would not want to get the reputation of being excessively timid; conversely, if he once did sustain a serious knockdown, and lost a topmast, his nerve would be gone for-

ever (Hourigan, 106). It was much more prudent to shorten sail, ready to receive the squall, than to be caught unawares. A squall which passed ahead of the ship was very likely to 'draw' the wind with it, perhaps throwing the sails aback, and in this event, it was much better to be lying under small sail.

'Cracking on' perpetually through everything conveys the idea of 'making a capital passage'. Certainly good runs have occasionally been made under a constant press of sail with continuous breezes, but then experience proves their rarity. How often, after straining every spar, rope and sail, wetting and re-wetting before the men's clothes have had time to dry, do ships wait in stark calms or winds. It is well to reflect on the risk to the ship, and exposure of the crew, caused by a wanton desire to hold on to the last, and drag through a squall when the case is not urgent. If you are reckless enough to carry on without any precautions in threatening weather, or unfeeling enough to do

so with your men standing by, while you in an armour of water-proof, defy the weather, the chances are always in favour of an ugly cloud bringing you wind enough to oblige you to shorten sail. Rain is the general accompaniment, and as the men cannot work in tarpaulins, they are drenched during the operation, and remain so whilst damages are being repaired, which a little common sense might have avoided (Boyd, 391).

HMS *Plyades* caught aback in a Pampero, 1869. The *Plyades* was under all plain sail in a smooth sea when this squall was first seen about 3 miles off. It struck the ship before the orders to shorten sail could be carried out, catching her aback and laying her over until the sea began to pour through the open lower deck ports. She was in danger of driving her stern under until the three topmasts broke at the head and the mainyard buckled. This eased the ship and she was able to run off before the wind, the whole incident lasting less than three minutes. The engraving is by Weedon, after a sketch submitted to the *Illustrated London News* by Lieut W H Lewin. (Mark Myers' Collection)

Hourigan, who gives one of the best analyses of this whole topic, considered it much better to have sail shortened, halliards led along, and the braces and topsail sheets tended, well before the rain hit. There was no need to allow the crew to get soaked unnecessarily. Ulffers in a rather similar vein, advocates getting ready in good time, and then getting non-essential personnel under shelter below deck. The responsibility for making the right judgment lay particularly heavy on the officer of the watch at night, when he might be the only officer on deck, and when he was denied the advantage of many of the omens, which might give warning in daylight.

Waterspouts. These were similar in some respects to squalls, although of a much more limited extent, and visually much more spectacular. A whirlwind generated a column of spray, sometimes accompanied by hail and lightning, which extended from the water up to a low cloud. The upper part was of larger diameter than the lower, and they were said to be capable of engulfing the largest vessels (Baudin, 416). The proper tactic was to steer clear of them, since the accompanying whirlwind could dismast a ship (Ekelöf, 159). If it could not be avoided, sail was shortened, all hands were got out of the rigging, hatches were secured, ready for the onslaught of a large quantity of water on deck. Bréart (971) says that it is best not to take the assault from the beam, presumably because this offers the maximum target. Traditionally, the column of water could be broken by a cannon shot, and Baudin says this has been known to work on more than one occasion.

Commands. Krogh (89) considered that in this type of near-emergency situation, the crew should be accustomed to a short form of command. On the other hand Alston (258) offers this:

> Under ordinary circumstances in squally weather, the invariable cry is 'Hands by the topgallant (or royal) halliards!' Accustomed to the order from long habit, it is repeated without reflection, from a vague notion of safety in the measure, and to be accordance with rule in the event of anything going. As midshipman of a boat, you would not keep the sheet belayed, in breezy weather, and station a hand, in preference, to the halliards. Neither should you do so as officer of the watch, where you know that the heavier the squall is, the firmer the yard will bind, and consequently, that letting go the halliards before the sheet is eased off, will relieve nothing. For the future, then, (if you have hitherto been misled, by custom, to the contrary), place hands by the lee sheets, and let the alarm of 'Hands by the royal halliards!' henceforth die out with you.

It is impossible to list all the orders that might be given, but the following are based on Hourigan. First, to bear away, having been struck by a squall on the weather quarter:

Hard up!

Let go main and spanker sheet, spanker outhaul!

Ease off topgallant studdingsail tack and halliards!

Royal clewlines, topgallant studdingsail downhauls!

Haul taut! Shorten sail!

Topgallant clewlines, main clewgarnets and buntlines, spanker brails!

Up mainsail, in spanker and topgallants! Secondly, to luff through the squall:

Let her luff!

Ease off main and spanker sheets, spanker outhaul!

Royal clewlines, flying jib downhaul, main clewgarnets, buntlines, spanker brails!

Haul taut! shorten sail!

Ease off lee topgallant and topsail sheets!

Topgallant weather braces and clewlines!

Settle away topgallant halliards!

Weather topsail braces, topsail halliards!

Brace in! Settle away!

Haul out reef-tackles! Haul taut buntlines!

Ship *Bloerie Castle* between two waterspouts (after engraving by L Smythe, *Illustrated London News*, 1859).

CHAPTER 17
HEAVING TO

Terminology. 'In bad weather a ship is "lying to" not "hove to", though the confusion of terms is common enough' says Hourigan (30), and we will follow this convention here.

The term 'hove to' we think should be applied when the vessel is really so placed with some sail aback; for instance, a square-rigged vessel with one of her topsails aback, or a fore and aft vessel with one of her sheets hauled to windward. Instead of which, if a vessel have only her main topsail set when blowing hard, and steering by the wind, you will generally see the number of hours she has been so, marked in the log as hove to, and the same when keeping to the wind in gales under storm fore and aft sails. We have often been at a loss to understand why a vessel lying by the wind, and perhaps making merely two or three miles an hour should be called hove to; still, sails aback, or not, this term is indiscriminately used whenever a vessel is under low sail by the wind in blowing weather. We think when it blows so hard that a vessel cannot steer her course, but is brought to the wind under low sail, that she ought then to be called lying by the wind, and not hove to: the term 'hove to' we think would be better applied when a sail or sails are aback. It appears strange that two things so widely different as that of stopping a ship by backing a sail, and that of keeping her to the wind in blowing weather should so long have continued to have the same term. We have not met with any naval work in which the same term is not used indiscriminately for both purposes; still we know well, that most of our best seamen consider it wrong to make use of the term 'hove to' unless with a sail aback; and when a vessel is doing her best to keep her wind under strong sails etc the same seamen make use of the term lying by the wind (Liardet, III).

To heave to, 'lie by', or 'brace by' (Smyth) in moderate weather, the ship was 'brought to' by counterbracing the yards in such a way that she either made headway very slowly, or alternately ranged ahead and dropped astern. ('Bring to!' was also the order from one vessel to another to heave to, as a man-of-war preparing to search a suspected blockade runner.) Gower (46) says, 'When sailing before the wind in moderate weather, a vessel is

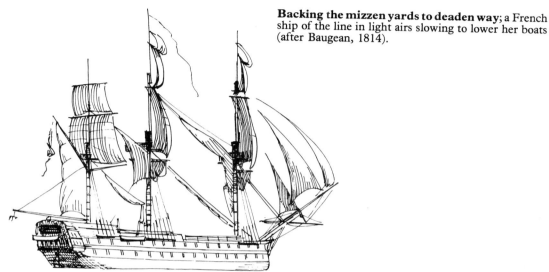

Backing the mizzen yards to deaden way; a French ship of the line in light airs slowing to lower her boats (after Baugean, 1814).

sometimes hove to by hauling up the foresail, and putting the helm either way. This manoeuvre is termed *heaving athwart*.' I have not run across this precise form elsewhere, but a couple of expressions also incorporate the verb 'heave': 'to heave aback' is to suddenly back a topsail to get way off the ship; while 'to heave about' is to go onto the other tack, the context often suggesting that this is done rather abruptly. Sail was shortened until just sufficient remained set to keep the vessel under control, while she lay with the wind on or somewhat forward of the beam, drifting bodily slowly to leeward. Some foreign equivalents are *backbrassen*, *brase bak* in German and Danish, *bijleggen* ('lie by'), *bijdraaien*, ('turn by'), and *stoppen* ('stop'), in Dutch, and *mettre en panne*, in French. The Swedish expression *ligga uppbrassad* ('to lie braced up'), used by Rosvall (129) should be translated as 'braced in' rather than 'braced up', and refers to the squared in yards of the backed topsail. Having been hove to, the vessel 'filled away' by trimming the back sails full once more. 'Fill away' seems the more usual expression, although 'brace full' is given by Bobrik and Romme, it being the literal translation of Dutch *vollbrassen*; the corresponding French term was *faire servir*. The ship could be hove to 'fore topsail to the mast', or 'main topsail to the mast', depend-

ing on the method used. She was said to 'stand on with the mizzen topsail aback' (Totten, 214), or as the French said *en panne courante*, 'a running heave to' (Bréart), moving ahead slowly, as well as driving to leeward. Massenet (389) describes *une panne ardente*, lying seven points from the wind, coming to and falling off, and *une panne molle*, seven and a half to eight points from the wind, with less tendency to yaw, but making a little headway.

To deaden way. Backing the mizzen topsail was one way of doing this, but except where used as a measure to check the speed momentarily, while picking up a boat, for example, the practice was condemned by many authorities. By the wind, the mizzen topsail could only be brought to the square position, otherwise the crossjack yard was liable to foul the main. The result was that the ship tended to fall off, particularly if the jib was set, and might actually pick up speed (Griffith, 249). Boyd (394) also considers backing the mizzen topsail very objectionable, remarking that it was expressly forbidden when sailing in line. The mainyard could be squared on a wind, by letting go the braces, bowlines and main sheet, and this could be done unaided, in a moment, by the lee-wheel and lookout men. Others claimed to be able to regulate the pace of the ship, sail-

Backing main and mizzen yards in action: HMS *Nymphe* engaging the *Cleopatre* (after R Dodd, 1793).

Backing the main topsail to lower a boat: topsails lowered to the cap (after Ozanne).

Backing the fore topsail to pick up a pilot (after C Brooking).

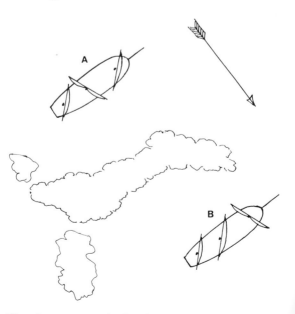

Heaving to near the land
A Ship off a lee shore heaves to maintopsail to the mast on best tack for clearing danger; **B** ship off a weather shore heaves to fore topsail to the mast.

ing in line, by veering or hauling aft the main sheet, to keep their station. Liardet (48) also prefers to brace in the main topsail to slow the ship. However, he points out that this would not be practical with the main course set, and he suggests that if the mizzen topsail is used instead, that the bow be kept up to the wind by bracing it aback as sharp as possible. As mentioned above, this was only practical in vessels where main and mizzen are not too close together.

Reasons for heaving to. This might be done with several objects in view: for example, upon making a landfall at night, to await a convoy, to pick up a pilot, to cast the lead, or to retrieve a man overboard. Sometimes says Bonnefoux (50), it is done to defy an enemy, when one is being chased. He further remarks that this ploy was only advisable when one had the ability to hurl a lot more metal than one's opponent, since in the ordinary way, a vessel under control, moving through the water, was at a distinct advantage over the immobile foe.

Which sail to back. One or more square sails were backed, and practical experience determined the method by which each individual vessel hove to most readily. Backing the main topsail was much the commonest method, mainly because it looked more elegant and hence was preferred by men-of-war (Rosvall, 129). Massenet (389) noted that the main topsail need only be braced around to about a point more than sqaure, while the fore topsail should be braced aback, at least three points. Perhaps for this reason Bréart (170) says that drift to leeward was less with the main topsail back than the fore, although this is contradicted by Totten (212), who claimed the same advantage for a backed fore topsail. The backed topsail threw a heavy strain on the stays, and the main stays were, in fact, better adapted to withstand the

pressure, ascending as they did at a flatter angle than those of the fore. Furthermore, the configuration of the lower yards, main topsail to the mast, was ideal for hoisting out a boom boat, hove to in this way (Bonnefoux, 54). With the main topsail to the mast, the tendency was for the ship to come up to the wind a bit, as it came ahead, then sag off again to leeward as it dropped astern again, the helm being kept a-lee the whole time. With the fore topsail backed, the tendency to yaw was very much less, partly because the vessel would probably be headreaching, and thence under control of the helm. If the forward movement was undesirable, the mizzen topsail could be shivered, or even backed, keeping the main full (Ekelöf, 156). The main topsail being the biggest of the three, it 'balanced' the others, whether fore or aback.

A vessel to weather of an obstruction, hove to with main topsail to the mast, ready to fill away and shoot ahead if necessary. A ship to leeward of a shoal, or other danger, backed the fore topsail, ready, if need be, to fall off clear of the obstruction. A vessel hove to with backed fore topsail, also lay a little closer to the wind, than if the main were backed, and this tendency was increased if the afteryards were braced sharp up. In fact, when it came time to fill away, the vessel might be sluggish in falling off, which might require bracing the foreyards sharper, flatting in the headsails, or shivering the afteryards (Ekelöf, 153).

If it was necessary to heave to, while sailing large, or well before the wind, the ship was brought to by bracing up the afteryards, hauling out the spanker, and putting the helm down smartly. The headyards were left square, and so came aback as she luffed up, heaving to, fore topsail to the mast. By the wind, the vessel was luffed up, main course brailed up, and main topsail square lying aback.

Bonnefoux (56) describes two other methods of heaving to, which do not seem to have enjoyed much popularity, or in any event are not discussed by other authors. Backing all three topsails, and balancing this with fore and aft sail, required that all three masts be attended to, hence it was a rather clumsy arrangement and little used. By appropriate use of the tiller, the ship could be kept under fairly good control, keeping sternway on, and making relatively little leeway. In practice this method was sometimes adopted to back out of a crowded anchorage. The big disadvantage was the great tendency to yaw uncontrollably; as in any manoeuvre going astern, the water pressure developing under the lee quarter quickly forced the stern to windward, and this was greatly aggravated if the vessel was heeling. Shivering the fore topsail, backing the main topsail and keeping the mizzen topsail full, was yet another variant, where the leeway was inconsiderable, although the ship tended to drop astern rather much.

Lying by off a coast, the best practice was to heave to on that tack that would most readily allow the vessel to sail clear. On the wrong tack, the ship might find itself embayed, unable to tack or wear. Bonnefoux describes the fate of the Frenchman *Desaix*, lost at Saint Dominique for lack of this very precaution. Likewise if there were squalls on the horizon, the ship was hove to, so they would hit from the quarter, allowing the ship to bear away, rather than from the bow (Bonnefoux, 53).

In a crowded fairway, where there was a risk of meeting other craft, a vessel hove to on the port tack was obliged to give way to one approaching, sailing on the starboard tack. The only person to address this problem is Krogh (76), who says that the hove to vessel should have the main topsail aback, 'the easier to fall off', to give way to the approaching vessel. It is a pity we have no other comment on this point, because, on first principles, one would have thought that with a backed fore topsail, the afteryards could have been shivered, and allowed the ship to fall off very readily. I think one may further infer that hove to on the starboard tack, a vessel approaching on the port tack would have been obliged to give way.

Whalers heaving to. Murphy (46) agrees with Ekelöf that a vessel will fall off and come to less with the fore topsail aback than with the main, and points out that this was the reason American whalers invariably hove to in this way, when cutting in their catch. The whale was secured alongside, tail forward, always to starboard, hence the windward side. Flensing proceeded while the vessel moved slowly ahead, headreaching, with the aftersails full, and the headyards backed. The upper fore topsail was lowered in front of the lower (Church, 34). The helm was put to starboard, and this along with the backed fore topsail balanced the drag of the whale's carcass, which would have tended to pull the ship's head to starboard. Ranging alternately slowly ahead and astern, would not have been a suitable alternative, since the whale would not have maintained a fixed position relative to the cutting in stage. Under these circumstances, in the open ocean, the direction in which the vessel drifted was not terribly important, but this arrangement would have placed the whaler on the starboard tack, from a right-of-way point of view. Contemporary illustrations indicate that Dutch and English whalers of a century earlier did not invariably secure the whale on the starboard side,

Whalers heaving to
A American practice for cutting in: ship hove to with fore topsail lowered and backed, whale lashed tail forward on starboard side (after W J Huggins); **B** English whaler *William Lee* hove to, cutting in a whale in northern waters (after J Ward, c1831); **C** American whalers *Sea Fox*, *James Allen* and *Commodore Morris* hove to for a gam (after C S Raleigh, 1890).

Heaving to in fresh weather. French barque rigged warship with main topsail to the mast (after Frederic Roux, 1834).

although one hesitates to assert that it was always made fast to port.

Shortening sail. Sail was shortened to topsails, jib and mizzen. The courses were clewed up, and the topgallants clewed up or down as convenient. Totten (213) emphasises that royal and topgallants must be lowered on the cap, or clewed up, especially when the vessel has rapid headway, and is brought to suddenly. If the wind were well free, coming to quickly would result in a rapid increase of the relative wind speed, which, added to the speed of the ship, would throw the light sails heavily back against the topgallant and royal masts, and impose an undue strain on the upper stays and topgallant masts. Thus they came in before luffing was allowed to commence (Ekelöf, 153). The ship's movements were then regulated by trimming the jib and spanker sheets. The jib halliards were often let go, and the tricing line was used to raise the tack of the spanker if necessary. It is not advisable to heave to with reefed topsails says Mossel (III, 246), who advocates either keeping the wind, *aan den wind houden*, or letting go the topsail halliards. The reasoning behind this is not completely clear. It is true that fear of chafe dictated, not only the taking in of the light sails, but also the practice of slacking the topsail halliards, presumably to lessen the abrasion on masts and top rim of the backed sail, and lessen the strain on the mast of those remaining full (Bonnefoux, 57).

To keep a sail full, the wind must come from at least three points abaft the yard, while to throw it aback, the wind need only come from one point ahead. Thus, if close-hauled, it is only necessary to square the main topsail; it need not be braced completely around, sharp up the other way. Keeping the yard square, also minimises the amount the sail is contributing to leeway, the force of the wind being taken up in preventing headway. Leeway was further minimised by checking the lee braces of the full sails; that is to say bracing them in as square as possible without actually shivering (Bonnefoux, 53). With fore and mizzen topsails aback, the ship kept up to the wind better if the fore was braced square aback, and the mizzen sharp aback (Gower, 46). In reading the French accounts, the verb *effacer* is sometimes used of a sail. This does not mean 'efface', but actually implies that the sail is braced sharp up, broadside to the wind, so to speak. It was originally a technical term in fencing, turning one's side toward one's opponent, and hence to turn broadside of a ship, as in preparation for bombarding a fort ashore, or bracing a sail round so the wind struck it more squarely. If fore and mizzen were full on the port tack, the main topsail was aback, and the ship was said to be 'hove to on the port tack'.

Two vessels communicating. This could be done in various ways: heaving to, continuing to sail at slow speed, or by dropping a boat. If both vessels hove to, lying one to leeward of the other, most authorities suggest that the windward vessel back the main topsail, the leeward ship the fore topsail (Groeneijk, 78; Baudin, 303). Baudin felt that if the mizzen, as well as the main topsail were backed, the windward ship would lurch to leeward less. Should a collision be imminent, the windward vessel filled the main topsail and shot ahead, while to lee, the afteryards were shivered, causing the bow to fall of rapidly, under the influence of the unopposed backed headyards. Murphy (46) is alone in suggesting that the fore topsail of the

windward vessel be backed, while the leeward vessel laid its main topsail to the mast. He felt that by following this practice the windward vessel would fall off and come to less. Furthermore, since the fore topsail was smaller than the main, it would fill more readily in the event the windward vessel was obliged to shoot ahead. The leeward vessel shivered her mizzen topsail to fall off. Liardet comments that two vessels close together, even when the sea was like glass, seemed to creep closer, as if impelled by some mysterious mutual attraction. This occurred if their bows were at all inclined towards each other. The explanation lay in the form of the underwater body, which was such that the imperceptible pitching movements which were invariably occurring, tended to move the hull slowly ahead. This was another reason for the lee vessel to back the fore topsail, since this would tend to keep the bow away from the other craft.

In the case of three vessels communicating, the windward and centre ships backed the main topsail, the one to leeward, the fore. Upon the onset of a squall, or other emergency, the weathermost filled away and shot ahead, the centre backed the mizzen topsail and fell astern, while to lee, the afteryards were shivered to allow the vessel to fall off clear of the others.

Other methods. There was some merit in both vessels keeping headway on, albeit slowly, so that they remained under the control of the helm. Krogh (76) suggests that the aftermost vessel remain on the weather quarter of the forward. Ekelöf (153) suggests that the hailing vessel come up on the lee-quarter of the vessel hailed, which seems to contradict Krogh. The practical point was that the leeward vessel might literally have the wind taken out of its sails, especially if the leeward vessel were substantially smaller. Thus to take a pilot on board, the vessel hove

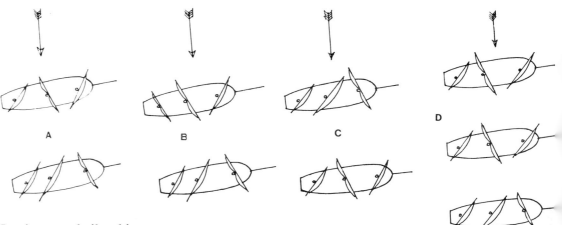

Heaving to to hail a ship
A Usual practice; B Baudin's method; C Murphy's method; D three ships in communication.

to with some headway, to leeward and forward of the pilot boat (Krogh, 77). If there was violent rolling, a small boat becalmed in the lee of a large vessel was in considerable danger of being caught under the projecting channels, sheet anchor, and so on. Mossel suggests that the first ship heave to, and the second sail slowly by, if heaving to were unnecessary.

Mossell (III, 249) describes Dutch practice, when sailing in line ahead, should the admiral desire to personally hail another vessel. If it was one of the foremost ships, it pulled out of the line to weather, and shortened sail so as to drop back, and then keep pace with the flagship, during the communication. She was then supposed to get to leeward, crossing the admiral's stern, make sail, and hasten up the leeward side of the line to regain her station. A ship from the rear, pulled out to weather, made sail to come abreast the admiral, crossed his stern subsequently, and dropped back on the lee side of the line. A steamer in a mixed squadron, hailing the admiral, or indeed any other vessel, approached on their lee quarter, because of the coal smoke. Mossel emphasises the importance of a steamer letting the boiler pressure drop in good time in preparation for hailing. If this was not done,

1.
John Ward lithograph of HMS *Asia* hove to, main topsail to the mast. The jib sheet has been eased to keep her head from falling too far off the wind. (Courtesy Kingston-upon-Hull Museums and Art Galleries)

2.
The West Indiaman *Harvey's Desire* in three positions off Deal, by Thomas Luny, 1795. In the centre of the picture she is hove to with topgallants lowered and courses hauled up to minimise leeway as the pilot's lugger comes alongside. Note that the mainyards need not be braced round very much before the topsail comes aback. (Courtesy N R Omell Gallery, London)

1.

2.

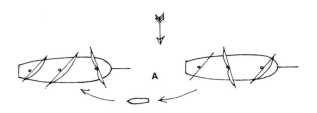

Heaving to to send a boat
A Krogh's method; B usual practice.

A

B

the roar from the waste-steam pipe would drown out any other sound.

Sending a boat. Krogh (76) and Ekelöf (154) agree that if two vessels are to heave to and communicate by boat, they lie on a line at right angles to the wind, one behind the other. Krogh backs the main topsail of the forward, the fore topsail of the after vessel, Ekelöf, exactly the reverse. I find Krogh's recommendation the most persuasive, since the forward vessel could fill away going ahead, while the after one could drop off to leeward.

A fairly widely adopted tactic was for the vessel dropping a boat to get on the weather bow of the craft being communicated with. Once the boat was on its way, the ship headed round it to get on the lee quarter of the other, ready to pick up its boat. This meant that neither coming or going did the boat have a dead pull to windward (Engelhart, 132).

Taking a pilot on board. Rosvall (135) suggests that in moderate weather this is readily accomplished by heaving to, and having the pilot boat come up under the lee quarter, preferably under oars, heaving lines being kept ready in fore and main channels to give aid if necessary. In heavy seas, this would be too dangerous for the reasons outlined above, and he suggests that rather than heave to, headway be kept on, bracing the main topsail square to back it, but keeping the other topsails full, the ship remaining under control of the helm. The pilot boat comes up under the lee quarter, takes a heaving line, and pulls up close enough to allow the pilot to mount a Jacob's ladder dropped to him. Rosvall also describes a heroic measure used in very bad conditions whereby the pilot secures the heaving line about his body, and then casts himself into the water, and is drawn up into the ship.

The general rule for boarding a friendly vessel at sea, in moderate weather, is for the boarding boat to go alongside to leeward, where there is

Heaving to for a pilot
A East Indiaman boarded by a pilot, fore topsail to the mast (after J Askew); B ship *Pitt* heaving to for a pilot (after R Salmon, 1809).

greater facility in ascending the side than to windward. But in boarding a small vessel in bad weather, it is considered best for the boat to go on the weather quarter; for this reason, the vessel laying to drifts faster than the boat alongside, so that if the boat be to leeward, the vessel keeps drifting upon her; whereas, if she be to windward, the vessel keeps drifting clear of her. In the latter case, the main boom is much more out of the way of doing harm (Fordyce, 145).

Fordyce also mentions that a boat shoving off from the lee side of a small vessel is in grave danger of being struck by the fore channels, anchors, and dolphin-striker. He recommends that the vessel should fill and gather way a little, to prevent these accidents.

CHAPTER 18
THE SHIP AT ANCHOR

The ship having finished her voyage, and cast anchor in the roadstead, it might be supposed that the task of the seaman was finished. In fact, the management of the anchored vessel was a most important part of the mariner's art, and we will now turn to a consideration of this subject, first of all having a look at the 'ground-tackle' – 'all the fittings, and furniture, which belong to the anchors'.

Form of the anchor. An excellent review of the development of the anchor by Norman Rubin is to be found in the *Nautical Research Journal* 18, 1971, 230, and also see zu Mondfeld, 179. Throughout the period we are concentrating on, the traditional 'Admiralty pattern' wooden stocked anchor remained in use, more or less unchanged in form. The main piece was the 'shank', at the top of which was the 'ring', and welded to the foot were the 'arms', which terminated in the triangular 'flukes'. The point where arms and shank met was called the 'crown'. The wooden 'stock' was secured just below the ring, at right angles to the plane of the arms. The dimensions of the anchor were related to the length of the shank: the stock was about as long as the shank, or a bit more; the arms were almost as long as the shank, in the 1600s; later, they were shorter and straighter. The ring was one-seventh the shank length in diameter, and padded or 'puddinged' everywhere except where it passed through the shank. When chain was introduced, the large ring was replaced by a small 'Jew's harp' shackle. The stock of English anchors was straight across the top, while the French favoured one curving slightly upwards towards the ends. The stock was, in thickness, about one-twelfth the shank length, at the ends, and one-sixth, in the middle. It was comprised of two oaken sections, held together by driving on four or six square iron hoops. It was at right angles to the arms, so one or other of the latter would be forced to bite into the ground, and it was this feature which made it inherently clumsy to stow. The non-engaged arm projected upwards, and as a result was liable to be fouled by the cable, or even to injure the ship's bottom

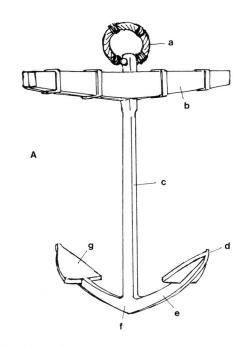

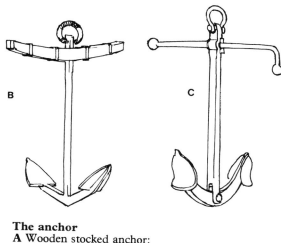

The anchor
A Wooden stocked anchor:
a ring; b stock; c shank; d bill; e arm; f crown; g fluke or palm.
B Old pattern French anchor; C Trotman anchor.

planking, if she 'sat down on it' in shoal water. In the early 1800s, the Royal Navy started to use iron stocks for anchors of the smaller size. These amounted to about twenty per cent the weight of the bare anchor, as compared to 25 per cent with a wooden stock. However the relative buoyancy of the wooden version helped ensure that the anchor landed properly, crown first. The stock had to be heavy enough to ensure that it would lie flat. The design of the flukes was a compromise between one that was big enough to hold in soft ground, while remaining small enough to allow the arm to dig in properly.

In the mid-1800s, intensive search started for ways of improving the form of this anchor, which was not particularly efficient for its weight. One pattern that became popular was the Trotman patent, which was based on earlier designs of Porter and Piper, and weighed two-thirds as much as a comparable Admiralty anchor. These 'portable anchors', featured a folding stock, and removable arms, pivoting on the shank. This meant that they could be stowed more handily, and also that the upper fluke folded back, so that it was unlikely to foul the cable

or injure the ship. We will not concern ourselves with the later development of 'close-stowing' and 'stockless' anchors, which came into use in the late 1800s, since these were mostly used on steamers.

Units of measurement. To make sense of these old accounts, it is important to remember that there were no agreed international standards, prior to the introduction of the metric system. There were for example, 100 pounds in the American, and 112 pounds in the British, hundredweight (cwt). Twenty of each of these made one 'ton', hence the 'short ton' of 2000 pounds, and the 'long' ton of 2240 pounds. The English *fathom*, Dutch *vadem*, and French *brasse*, were only roughly the same length, but there were only five *pieds* in the French *brasse*. There was even less agreement about the length of an 'ell'. In addition to the English unit of that name, there were the Amsterdam, Rhineland, Flemish, Old and Newe Parisian and Netherlands *el*, not to mention similar, but not identical units in each small German principality. The Netherlands *el*, was the metre, just as the Netherlands *pond* was the kilogram. With the introduction of the metric system, many of the old names were adopted into the new system, changing their values. Thus the old 'line', one-twelfth of an inch long (Dutch *streep*, French *ligne*) was now often used to describe one millimetre, and so on. A list of many of these old units will be found in the *Memorandum* (756) and Hildebrandt (157).

Size and weight of the anchor. These were calculated using traditional rules. The bigger the ship, and the greater the top-hamper, the heavier the anchor required to hold it. Because of the reduced windage, a steamer required an anchor two-thirds the weight of a sailing vessel of equal tonnage. The length of the shank, for practical reasons, ideally did not much exceed the distance between the cathead and the waterline. Costé (218) gives the shank length as between three-eighths and four-ninths of the greatest breadth of beam. Mainwaring (88) gives the fraction as one-half.

Anchor weights are often given in hundredweights, abbreviated to 'cwts'. For merchantmen, one rule was, weight of anchor in cwts equals tonnage divided by 20 (Totten, 102). Boyd (227) suggests 4 pounds per ton, that is, somewhat less. A similar Dutch rule was 2 kilograms of anchor per ton in large vessels, and 3 in small vessels. Another rule calculated the weight of the anchor in pounds, by squaring the beam in feet, and multiplying by 3 (Rubin). Totten adds two-thirds the draught loaded, to the greatest breadth of beam, and allows 1cwt for every foot. In men-of-war, the weight of the bower anchor, in cwts, was about the same as the number of guns. The corresponding Dutch rule allowed 50 kilograms per gun; that is, a 44-gun frigate would have a best bower of 2200 kilograms, or just under 44 cwt (Mossell II, 393). A First Rate of 100 guns, like *Victory*, carried a best bower of just under 100cwt (Boyd). *Victory*'s beam is 52 feet; the bower presently found on board weighs 84 cwt, the stock about another 21 cwt.

Other rules related the weight to the dimensions of the anchor and its cable. Bonnefoux (34) cubes the length of the shank in metres, and multiplies by 23 to get the weight in kilograms; that is to say, an anchor 6 metres long, would weigh just under 5000 kilograms. Costé says the anchor should weigh half as much as the corresponding cable, which was 120 fathoms in length. Weights often refer to the anchor without its stock.

The cable. Traditionally, this was 'cable-laid', laid up 'left-handed' from three 'right-hand laid' hemp ropes. The resulting tight compression of the fibres rendered it relatively impervious to moisture, when not in use,

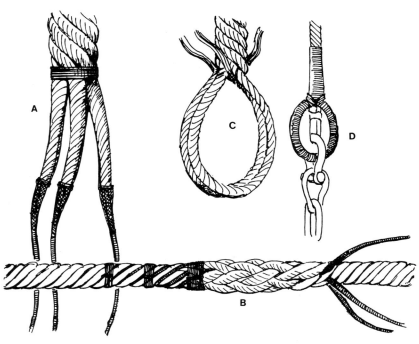

Cable
A Hemp cable with tailed ends; **B** splicing cables together; **C** forming Elliott's eye; **D** hemp and chain cable joined by Elliott's eye.

hence the term 'water-laid'. In 'left-hand laid' cordage, the contlines, or grooves between the large strands, ran down and to the left. As to the confusion between the terms 'cable-laid' and 'hawser-laid', see Ashley (23) and Murphy (83). With regard to size, Costé (217) mentions the widely used rule of half an inch of circumference of cable, per foot of breadth of beam. *Victory*, with a beam of about 50 feet, should therefore have a cable 25 inches in circumference; that presently aboard is actually one inch less. A fathom of such cable would weigh something above an English cwt (Boyd, 140).

Length of a cable. In England, a 'cable's length' as a measure of distance was 100 fathoms, or 183 metres. In France, the *encablure* was 120 *brasse*, or 194.9 metres. In Holland, three *kabellengten* were in use, from 203 to 254 metres long (*Memorandum*, 755). The 'length of a cable' was, in practical terms, governed by the size of the ropewalk, where it was manufactured, about one-third of the initial length of fibre being 'taken up' during the rope-laying process. The length of a hemp cable is variously given as 85 fathoms (Lever), 101 fathoms (Burney), 115 fathoms (Smyth), and 120 fathoms (Totten).

A shot of cable. 'Two cables spliced together make a *shot*, and the use of them is in deep water, and great roads, for a ship doth ride much easier by one shot, than three short cables ahead' (Mainwaring, 225). Totten (110), writing two centuries later, uses the word somewhat differently: '*Shot* is a term used when there are two or more cables spliced together; thus the bower or sheet cable may consist of two or more shots'. The word apparently dropped out of use in England, but is still used today in the United States Navy to describe a length of chain cable – what would be called a 'shackle' in the Royal Navy. Here, I am following Mainwaring's definition.

Joining cables. The outer ends of the cables were 'capped' or 'crowned', or else had a 'ropemaker's eye' worked in the strands, to prevent them unravelling (Totten, 110). Two cables were joined to form a shot, using a 'cable-' or 'drawing-splice', what Sjöbohm (85) calls an 'English splice'. One way of doing this was to tuck the strands twice, as in a short splice, after which they were plaited, or 'tailed', tapered off, sometimes terminating the ends with a short rope. The tailed ends were dogged around the contlines of the cable, a good service being put over all (Ashley, 433). It was necessary to 'draw' the splice in operations like clearing hawse, and the tails made the re-splicing easier. A hemp cable, intended for joining to a length of chain, as in the case of a hempen sheet cable being shackled to the chain foreganger, terminated in an 'Elliott's eye', a special eye-splice, which was made around a metal grommet.

Protection of the cable. The problem besetting hemp cable was the damage it sustained from cuts and chafes. It was particularly exposed to this hazard, both from being dragged across the bottom, and from fretting in the hawsehole, and against the cutwater. As to the first, an effort was made to keep the cable off the bottom if possible, the expedient of buoying it, sometimes even being resorted to (Taylor, 55; Röding, Figure 23). At points where wear and tear were probable the cable was 'served' by wrapping other materials around it. It might be 'wormed', by working oakum along the contlines, then 'parcelled', with strips of canvas, and finally 'served', by wrapping it tightly with used one-inch rope, or something similar. 'Worm and parcel with the lay, turn and serve the other way', went the old saying. 'Platting' was the spiral application of lengths of plaited sennit. 'Keckling' involved worming the cable with spirals of three-inch rope, in an open fashion, as distinct from 'rounding' described above, where the turns were close together. A variation of 'keckling' used close to the anchor, was 'link-worming'; lengths of chain were 'slabbed' or wormed, along the contlines, and secured with seizings. This was much favoured on a rocky bottom (Rosvall, 77). Lever (67) says that the cables of men-of-war should have 7 fathoms of keckling, 4 of rounding, and 4 of platting, extending from the anchor-ring towards the vessel. After having lain at anchor for an extended period, the cable was inspected by 'under-running' it. At slack water, a launch worked its way along the cable, so it could be visually inspected for cuts and fraying, and the service repaired if necessary.

Service at the hawsehole. This was the other spot at which the cable was particularly subject to abrasion. At the hawsehole, a mat of thrummed canvas, in width equal to the circumference of the cable, and three fathoms long, might be laced around the cable, and secured to the headrails (Rosvall, 76), or the cable could be covered with rounding or keckling. A thrummed mat was

one made by sticking short lengths of spun yarn, or oakum, through a piece of canvas. Hutchinson (117) was enthusiastic about the merits of a hide service. A well tanned horse hide was softened by soaking in water, and applied to the cable, beaten on over old canvas parcelling, everything being secured by good lashings. The hide was then well greased, and the cable veered, to put the service in the hawse. There were always areas of maximum chafe, and the damage done at these spots, was alleviated by varying the point of the cable so exposed, veering a little bit from time to time, 'freshening the nip', as it was called.

Windward and leeward service. In the coal trade, where the anchors were in frequent use, 'services' were kept in place semi-permanently. A collier's best bower was bent to a shot of two cables. A 'windward service' was secured at 45 fathoms, a 'second service' at 75 fathoms, and a 'long' or 'leeward service' a few fathoms short of the inboard end, a couple of fakes being left available in the tier to freshen the nip. We will explain the uses of these services when considering the management of the ship at single anchor.

Clinch-service. Glascock (277) recommends that a 'clinch-service' be put on when the cable is first taken on board. Three sheaves are paid down into the tier, whereupon

clap on a racking lashing to the fore beam, previously worming and parcelling in the wake of the lashing; measure then the cable bitted, and clap on a rounding in the wake where the cable would bring up in the hawse in the event of having to veer to the clinch. It is a melancholy fact that more than one frigate during the late war, together with the greater portion of their respective crews, were lost in consequence of

their cables parting in the vicinity of the hawse when veered to the clinch. Few ships adopt the precaution of clapping upon their cables a clinch-service. When too late, the necessity of the practice is discovered.

Chain cable. This was introduced into the Royal Navy in 1811, having been in use in the French service somewhat earlier – Nelson's attack on the invasion craft at Boulogne in 1801, failed precisely because the French were moored with chain (Kemp, 125). The individual links of chain cable were strengthened with 'studs', earlier variously known as 'stays', 'crosspins', or 'spreaders'. Not only did these prevent the kinking to which open-link or 'crane-chain' was subject, but they prevented the links stretching and narrowing, when under strain. The stud was only lightly welded to the link, being held in place primarily by the compression (Knight, 152).

As with hemp, there was considerable variation in the length of a cable. Harboe (22) gives 90 fathoms, Burney (218) 100 fathoms, Brady (328) 150, 165 and 180 fathoms, in the larger classes of American man-of-war, the biggest ships having the longest cables. Costé (222) mentions cables of 180 *brasses* – actually about 160 English fathoms. The cables were made up of a number of shorter lengths shackled together. The Royal Navy traditionally used a 'shackle' of 12½ fathoms, while the United States Navy used a 'shot' of 15 fathoms. Knight (151) described 'shots' of 5 to 40 fathoms in length. It was only in 1949 that the Royal Navy switched to the 15 fathom shackle which had always been in use in the British Merchant service. I think the discrepancy is somehow related to whether one preferred a cable 100 or 120 fathoms in length. The first is comprised of eight short

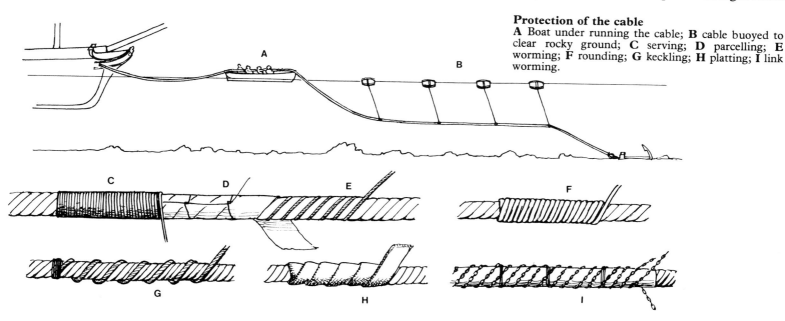

Protection of the cable
A Boat under running the cable; **B** cable buoyed to clear rocky ground; **C** serving; **D** parcelling; **E** worming; **F** rounding; **G** keckling; **H** platting; **I** link worming.

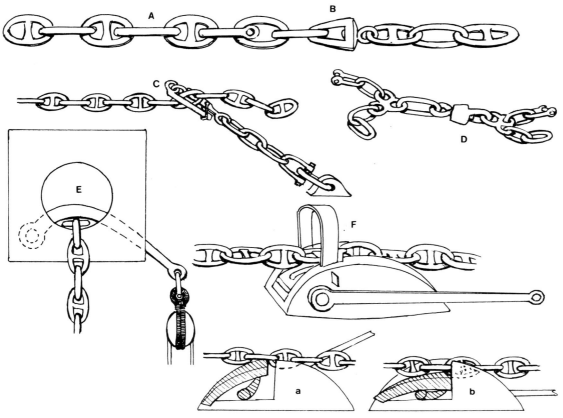

Chain cable
A Stud link chain; B swivel; C blake stopper; D mooring swivel; E compressor; F controller
  a chain runs freely over controller when tongue is raised by handle; b chain is caught by controller when tongue is lowered.

'shackles' of 12½ fathoms, the second of the same number of 15 fathom 'shots'. Swivels were inserted in some of the lengths to prevent the cable twisting up on itself.

The size of the cable was designated by the diameter of the iron rod, from which the links were forged. This was about the same, in inches, as the circumference of the corresponding hemp cable, measured in feet. This means that a First Rate, with a 26-inch hemp cable, would use chain links, 2¼ or 2⅛ inches in diameter; 100 fathoms of such chain would weigh about 240 cwt, while the corresponding 101 fathom hemp cable would weigh about 120 cwt. In general, chain cable weighed about 2–2½ times as much as the corresponding hemp. Boyd (227) determines the weight of a fathom of open-link chain in pounds, by squaring the diameter of the links, expressed in eighths of an inch, studded chain weighing about one-twelfth more. This rule gives substantially higher figures than are given in his accompanying tables.

Hemp and chain cable compared. The advantages of chain cable included those listed below. Most important of all, was its durability and resistance to the abrasion sustained by the cable when lying on the bottom. Since the ship tended to ride to the bight of the chain, not only was the holding power better, but there was less danger of fouling the anchor, and the task of 'tending' when at single anchor was vastly simplified. However, it was still necessary to veer a sufficient quantity of cable. 'It must be in the recollection of many old seamen, who served in the navy before the introduction of chain cables, that we were not in the habit of using a short scope at any time – half a cable, 50 fathoms, was the common quantity' (Murphy, 30). It was possible to veer cable straight from the locker, without the necessity of ranging it on deck beforehand. Chain took up much less space than the comparable hemp cable, and more or less stowed itself, whereas hemp required a lot of handling to get it flaked down properly in the tiers. It was easier to clean, by hosing down, upon weighing, and was not subject to rot. Shackling and unshackling was a very much simpler procedure than splicing and unsplicing hemp. In particular, the task of clearing hawse was managed more easily. In fact, with chain cable, a mooring swivel could be used and the danger of a foul hawse completely obviated. The swivel was just one of several ancillary devices which greatly simplified cable work, such as the Blake slip-stopper, the iron nipper, and the compressor,

which could only be used with chain. There were, in addition, several important advantages in being able to use a chain messenger. The chain engaged positively in the sprocket of a Hartfield-Brown capstan, was in no danger of inadvertent surging or slipping, did not require 'holding off', and did not have to be fleeted up the barrel like a rope messenger.

The disadvantages of iron chain included the following. For cable of equal strength, chain was inconveniently heavy compared with hemp. It was brittle, and the early chains were prone to snap in cold weather. It lacked the elasticity, that was such a valued feature of a hemp cable. Inspection might fail to detect flaws or cracks, whereas damage to a hemp cable was readily apparent. It was harder on the bitts, decks, and woodwork generally. The anchor-rings used with hemp proved to be quite unsuitable when used with chain and had to be replaced by a much smaller and stouter 'Jew's harp shackle', better able to resist the concentration of strain at one point. The extreme weight made any handling of the chain a heavy chore, and there were two circumstances where this was a particular hazard: if the cable were veered too suddenly ('paid cheap') upon first anchoring, the chain pounding down on the anchor was likely to fracture it (Murphy, 29); secondly, in very deep water, it was more difficult to heave in chain than hemp, once the anchor was aweigh.

In Burney's day, although chain had almost totally supplanted hemp, it was still customary to issue both hemp and chain cables for the sheet, and stream anchors. The main reason for issuing the hemp cable was to allow a fairly heavy anchor being laid out, to warp the ship off, in the event of grounding; because of the weight factor, a boat could handle the hemp cable much more comfortably. Liardet (60) thought that hemp cables should be used occasionally, if only to keep the men's hand in at managing them. In particular, he recommended using a hemp cable when anchoring for a short period, either in deep water, or on a steeply shelving shore, where the anchor might inadvertently tumble into deeper water during the weighing process. A ship with 75 fathoms of cable out, and the anchor a-trip, was virtually unmanageable, until the cable was got in. At this juncture, the tremendous weight of the chain, meant a heavy haul to run the anchor up under the bows, whereas with hemp it could have been hove up quite briskly.

The lack of elasticity of the chain was, to some extent, compensated for by the fact that the chain hung in a gentle curve or 'catenary'. (The Latin for 'chain' is *catena*.) The greater

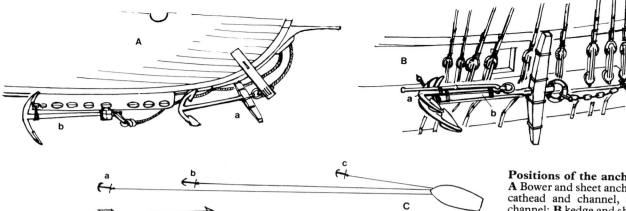

the length, or 'scope', of the cable, the more the violent jerk which accompanied the act of pulling the cable into a straight line, between anchor and hawsehole, was alleviated.

I have no doubt that by far the most numerous cases of parting a chain cable, or breaking the anchor, are caused by a sudden jerk; but a long scope will, in great measure, render such a jerk harmless, as it is only to be dreaded when riding short. Any man in charge of a ship at anchor, with the necessary quantity of chain cable on board, and space astern, to allow him to make use of it, but who neglects to do so, must be considered to be the author of his own misfortune, whether it amount to the loss of his anchor, or the loss of his ship. No excuse can be offered for such neglect, which must originate either in indolence, or in a mistaken notion of the necessity (Murphy, 32).

Naming and disposition of anchors. Inconsistent assigning of names to the several anchors carried, makes this a rather confusing topic. A large English man-of-war of the mid-1800s had at least three, and usually four, heavy anchors. Two were stowed on the bows, hence called 'bower anchors', one being designated 'best bower', the other 'small bower'. Two more were stowed abreast the fore-chains, and called 'sheet anchors'. Sometimes they were stowed abaft, rather than abreast of the channels, and hence often referred to as the 'waist anchors.' Usually, only one was designated as the 'sheet anchor', having a cable permanently bent to it, while the other was referred to as the 'spare anchor'. Costé (221), writing in 1849, indicates that in his day the four largest anchors were of identical size in French ships, the two bowers being collectively *les ancres de poste*, or *de bossoir* ('cathead anchors'), the 'sheet' anchors being called *les ancres de veille*. In French, 'best bower' translates as *ancre de bossoir* (Delbos), or *seconde ancre*; 'small bower' as *seconde ancre* (Delbos), or more usually, *ancre d'affourche*,

that is, 'mooring anchor'; 'spare anchor' could be translated *ancre de reserve*. The Dutch called the bowers *boeg-ankers* ('bow-anchors'), and the 'sheets' were the *rust-ankers*, ('channel-anchors'). The best bower was designated the 'every day', or 'daily anchor' in the northern European languages – *der tägliche Anker* in German, and so on. This is best translated 'working anchor', although in English, this particular term only begins to appear in the twentieth century (Tait, 36). Some authors indicate that the working anchor was actually the lighter of the two bowers. Hildebrandt (148) designates them respectively as the *täglich* and the *schwer* ('heavy') anchor. A similar arrangement is mentioned by Sjöbohm (6), writing in 1791. The working anchor was always that with the longer cable. The German word for the small bower was *Tau-Anker*, *Tey-Anker*, or some like term (Röding). This word arises because the anchor was used in mooring, with a second 'cable', but the form may have been influenced by Dutch *tij*, 'tide', the idea being that, like a *stop-anker*, it was a lesser anchor, suitable for stopping a tide. The term 'stream anchor', arises in just this way. In the later 1800s the stream anchor was stowed on deck, forward of the booms (Ulffers), or vertically against a stanchion in the main hatchway, arms athwartship, stock removed. It could be hoisted out, using the yard and stay tackles, when needed.

Earlier nomenclature varied slightly from the above: traditionally, the heaviest anchor, 'the mainest one of all the rest', was that kept in reserve for the direst emergency. 'That which the seamen call their last hope, and is never used but in great extremity, is called the sheet anchor; this is the true *anchora spei*, for this is their last refuge' (Boteler, 188). The Dutch equivalent was *nood-anker* ('need anchor') or *plegt-anker*, ('plight anchor'). French has several terms, *ancre de miséricorde*, *ancre d'espérance*, *maîtresse*

ancre, grande ancre. Some of these reflect the fact that in earlier days, the sheet was heavier than the bower. Reserving this term for the sheet, results in some confusion as to the meaning of *seconde ancre*. Earlier, it meant the best bower; later on it meant the small bower. Röding (83) lists the heavy anchors in order of weight as follows: *Pflicht*, 'sheet'; *Raum*, 'spare'; *Bug*, 'bow'; *Täglich*, 'working', or 'best bower'; *Tey*, 'small bower'. The literal meaning of '*Raum*' is 'hold', the name clearly implying that it was one stowed below decks as a spare. Röding (111) indicates that the *Bug-anker* was the fourth bow anchor, 'very seldom carried in merchantmen', so this would really translate 'spare anchor', rather than bower anchor. *Tey* and *Tau* have affinities with English 'tow', French *touée* ('length of cable') and *touer* ('to tow' or 'warp'). The literal meaning of *Tau* is 'rope'.

Smaller anchors called 'kedges', were used for 'warping' the ship about in calms, and so forth. In the later 1800s, these were fitted with iron stocks. Stowed in the fore and main channels, with the stock laid alongside the shank, they took up little room, whether lashed against the ship's side, or placed flat on the channel planking. At an earlier date, Blunt (110) indicates that the stream and largest kedge were lashed on top of the spare anchor. It was important that the anchors, including the stream and kedges, be stowed in such a way as to distribute the weight evenly. Smaller 'grapnels', with three or four prongs, were used as boat anchors, and for engaging the rigging of an enemy, prior to boarding.

Disposition of the cables. From the 1600s on, there were four hawseholes, so that it was possible in very bad weather to ride to four anchors, the cables splayed out like the outspread fingers of the hand. Bower cables led in through the inner hawsepipes, on either side of the stem, and the sheet cables through the outer pair. Here is the distribution of chain cables, in the German service in 1870, as given by Ulffers (107): port bower, 150 fathoms; starboard bower, 125 fathoms; port sheet, 50 fathoms; starboard sheet, 50 fathoms. The port bower was let go first, 25 fathoms of cable veered, then the starboard dropped and 50 fathoms more of both cables veered, so that the ship rode 'both anchors ahead' (*en barbe*, as the French called it). The starboard sheet was now dropped, and 25 fathoms veered on all three cables, following which action the port sheet anchor was let go, and all cables veered 'to the clinch', allowing the ship to ride with all four anchors ahead, and all the cable deployed.

In fact, a ship was much safer riding to one anchor by a 'shot' of three cables, than by three anchors, and three cables, one-third the length of the shot. The cables were therefore distributed in a manner such as the following. Three cables were spliced together and bent to the best bower, or 'working anchor'. The Dutch seamen had specific names for each of these lengths of cable, *voorlooper*, *volger* and *legger*, which we may translate 'fore runner', 'follower', and 'sleeper'. One, or if available two, cables were bent to the small bower, while one cable was secured to the sheet anchor. Coste (222) distributes six cables in the following manner: a shot of three form *la première touée*, bent to the best bower, to starboard; two more, *la deuxième touée*, are bent to the sheet anchor, to port; and the sixth is secured to the small bower, also to port.

Sheet cable. In the mid-1800s, chain cables had come into use almost universally, but it remained usual practice to carry two sheet cables, one of hemp, and one of chain. The hemp cable was used when anchoring in very deep water, or where it was necessary to lay out a heavy anchor with the longboat. The chain sheet was used, when dropping a third anchor, during heavy weather, in a relatively shallow anchorage. Rather than expose the hemp sheet cable to the weather, it was

common practice to shackle a length of chain cable to the sheet anchor, and run this along the ship's side, the bights being secured at intervals to eyebolts and then led in through the outer hawsehole. This 'ganger', or 'fore-ganger', was painted the same colour as the ship's side, to render it inconspicuous. Inboard, it could, as necessary, be shackled to the chain, or the hemp sheet cable which was fitted with an Elliott's eye, for this purpose. Prior to the introduction of the chain ganger, the hemp sheet cable was covered with mats and canvas, in an effort to protect it from the weather.

Arrangement of anchors and cables. As indicated above, by the mid-1800s, the bowers were of equal weight, so it was immaterial whether the longer cable was bent to the port or starboard anchor. Earlier, however, it was the practice to bend the longest cable to the best bower, or working anchor; that is, the one which was usually dropped first. The extra length was necessary, as we shall see, when mooring. As the term 'best bower' suggests, the working anchor was usually the heavier of the two bowers. Nonetheless, as we have mentioned, there were exceptions to this rule. Sjöbohm (6) splices five cables together, two and a quarter for the heavier, two and three-quarter cables for the lighter anchor. Pihlström (154) suggests a similar method. By 1803 however, Rosvall (69), also describing Swedish practice, bends the longer part of the cable to the heavier of the two anchors. I believe the merit of this method was that, theoretically, it permitted a shot of almost five cable lengths to be veered. Almost certainly the dividing point of the port and starboard cable was seized to the mast, in some fashion, to take the place of the 'clinch'.

Handling and stowage of hemp cable. The cables were stowed on the orlop, the cable tiers being found on either side, below the main hatch. The 'tierers' were men selected for 'strength, activity and ability', according to Smyth (682). 'This operation is entrusted to the best sailors, because it

demands dexterity, only acquired by long practice' (Coste, 224). The cable was laid down in 'fakes', or 'flakes', starting at the outside and placing each flake inside the preceding one. Another layer, or 'sheave' of flakes was then laid on top, starting from the centre and working out, whereupon the process was repeated. The coil was in the form of an angular ellipse, or rounded of rectangle. At the corners, the cable had to be 'bent and broken in'. 'Look out for a bender' or 'strike out for a bend', are phrases used in coiling cable, according to Smyth (95). To avoid injuring the fibres, by acutely bending the cable, no effort was made to force it into too small a compass, at the centre of the sheave. The space thus left was used to store spare hawsers, nippers, and so on. To prevent rot, it was preferable if the cable were not shot down into the tiers when wet, particularly with fresh water. The cable was stowed on gratings, with battens between the sheaves, to give maximum access of air to the fibres.

Cable, being left-hand laid rope, might have been expected to be coiled down left handed, or 'against the sun'. In practice however, it was usually coiled down 'with the sun' (Boyd, 232; Brady, 105; Totten, 11; Coste, 224). Exceptions to this rule are offered by Griffiths (184), Rosvall (70; Glascock (276) and Boström (143), who coil the cable down 'as bitted', that is to say, the starboard cable with the sun, and the port cable against. Blunt (110) suggests that in smaller merchant ships the starboard cable was bitted, taken round the windlass, or capstan, and coiled down in the tiers, with the sun, while the port cable was coiled in the reverse manner. He says this was not done in the Royal Navy, and remarks that 'a cable coiled against the sun will more easily reverse, and have less grinds or kinks in it, than a cable coiled with the sun'. To avoid bending the cable too sharply, many seamen 'crossed the cables in the hatchway. That is to say the port cable was stowed on the starboard side and vice versa. 'This system tends to facilitate

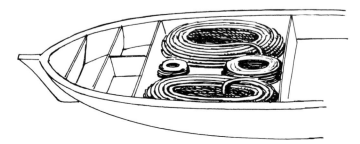

Stowage of cables. The cable fills up the outboard sides of the cable tier, with room for cablets, hawsers, etc between and inside the coils.

Anchor clinch and cable bends (a).

its running out clear, and "bending and breaking in" the fakes, and afford to the tiers in the tier more room for working and coiling the cables' (Glascock, 276). Although this was easier on the rope fibres, it might lead to the cables fouling each other, when one was coming up, and the other was being hove in, as in mooring (Sjöbohm, 6; Totten, 110; Blunt, 110). Costé (223), is one author who stows the cable on the same side as the anchor.

Handling and stowage of chain cable. The early chain cables were at first handled in very much the same way as hemp. In the mid-1800s, hemp and chain cables were found in the same ship, and used interchangeably as required. Thus we find rope nippers, ring-stoppers, and deck-stoppers being used indiscriminately with both hemp and chain. Subsequently these were replaced with the iron nipper, the devil's claw stopper, and the ancestors of the Blake slip. The shifting of chain cable by hand was facilitated by the use of chain hooks – iron rods with a wooden handle at one end and a hook at the other. To lift a bight of chain over the bitts, when bitting or unbitting the cable, a 'hook-rope' was used, rove through a block secured to a beam just above the bitts. Chain cable was bitted in exactly the same way as hemp cable, the bitts being metal sheathed in the wake of the chain. Burney described four chain-lockers, three for the bower cables, and a fourth for the sheet, stream, and messenger. Cable was pretty well self-stowing, and much easier to clean than hemp, simply requiring to be hosed off, as it came up as mentioned previously. The inboard end was secured with a slip to a chain necklace around the mainmast, so that it could be let go in emergency.

Bringing a cable on board. When opening up any brand new coil of rope, the proper method is to start by pulling the end out of the centre of the coil. The cart or wagon, conveying the new cable to the dockside, was therefore provided with a large hole in the bottom, so the cable could be led out through this, free of kinks or 'grinds'. The cable was paid down and coiled with the sun in the lighter, or 'lump', conveying it to the ship. When the lump was alongside, the cable was paid up onto the gundeck through one of the forward gunports, and 'French flaked' fore and aft on the gundeck, as when ranging cable. It was then paid down into the orlop, and coiled down by the tierers (Brady, 105).

Anchor-clinch. Hawsers were bent to the kedges with a fisherman's bend, a round turn and two half-hitches, or something similar. To bend the cable to the anchor-ring of the

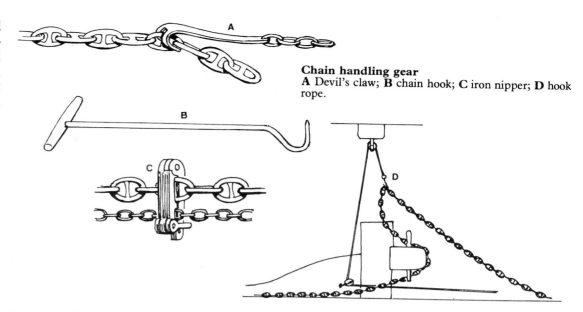

Chain handling gear
A Devil's claw; B chain hook; C iron nipper; D hook rope.

heavy anchors, a special 'clinch', actually a form of running noose, was used. The cable was led through the ring of the starboard anchor, from in out, and an 'inside-clinch' formed with the sun. On the port side, the cable went through the ring from out in (Murphy, 76). The loop of the clinch had to be smaller than the ring of the anchor. The lashings securing the turns of the clinch were called 'cable-bends'.

In a similar fashion, the inboard end of the cable was clinched to the mainmast, orlop beam, or riders. Hence, when all the cable was stuck out, it was said to be 'veered to the clinch'.

Side of the best bower. In the Northern Hemisphere, winds tend to veer, or shift with the sun, moving to the right of the observer, during a gale, so that with a blow starting from the South-West, the wind will tend to swing round until it comes from the North-West. Imagine a vessel riding out such a South-West gale by her port anchor. The wind increases causing her to drop her second anchor and veer on both cables for greater security. If the wind veers round to the North-West, she will swing round until her head points in that direction, and by adjusting the length of the cables, she will lie comfortably to both anchors, with 'open hawse' to the North-West, that is to say, the cables will be 'growing' on the appropriate bows. Had the starboard anchor been down first, the results would have been less happy, since the cables would necessarily have been crossed. Hence the old rule, that in the Northern Hemisphere, the working anchor or best bower, is carried to port, and the small bower to starboard, while in the Southern Hemisphere, the circumstances are reversed (Tait, 37). Stowing the working anchor to port is suggested by Rosvall (69) and Hilde-

brandt (148). The former uses the heavier of the two anchors, the latter the lighter as the working anchor.

Costé (222), Blunt (110), and Smyth (127) however, indicate that French and British ships, in defiance of this rule, stowed the best bower to starboard, small bower and sheet to port. Light is cast on this discrepancy by considering contemporary Dutch practice, which was based on the necessity of keeping open hawse in certain directions. Vessels whose home ports were reached via the Texel, carried the working anchor to port, while those hailing from the Maas estuary carried it to starboard (Groeneijk, 133; Le Compte, 141). In both cases it was desirable that the heavier anchor be to seaward, that is to the westward, since the anchorages were exposed to westerly gales. To the South-South-West, the tide runs, let us say, West-North-West/East-South-East, and the ship is moored with the anchors laid out on that line, the port anchor to the westward. The roadstead is exposed to the North-West, and when a gale comes from that quarter, cable is veered on the port anchor, the ship riding it out with open hawse to the North-West. In the Maas, vessels are sheltered from the North-West, but must be prepared to ride out a gale from the South-West. Accordingly the starboard anchor is dropped to seaward, the ship being moored on the West-South-West/East-North-East line, and will lie with open hawse to a South-West gale (Groeneijk, 133; *Mariner's Mirror* 48, 1962, 138).

Although quite out of period, it is of interest to note that the largest British men-of-war of First World War vintage, carried the sheet or third bower anchor to starboard; that is to say, one anchor to port, two to starboard. Whether riding to the port or the starboard bower, the sheet anchor could be let go, and

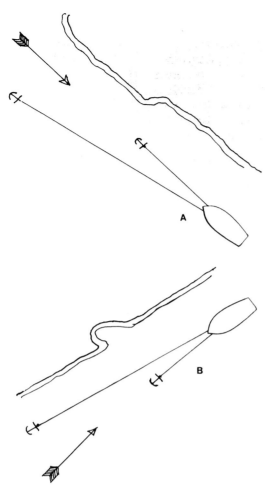

Diagram of anchorage conditions
A In the Texel; **B** in the Maas estuary.

both cables veered, in the assurance that the hawse would be clear, if the wind shifted with the sun. In 1945, The *King George V* rode out a tropical storm in Tokyo Bay, quite securely, in just this fashion (Schofield). HMS *Agincourt*, of 1914, originally laid down for the Brazilian navy, for service in the Southern Hemisphere, carried her sheet anchor to port, and this is understandable on the basis of the Coriolis effect. On the other hand, why some German capital ships of the same era, such as *Goeben*, carried their third bower to port, is a minor mystery. Up to and including the *Nassau* class of 1910, it is carried to starboard. In all later ships, it was transferred to the port side, for what reason I have been unable to determine (Fraider, Heinsius).

Hawseholes and manger. In a large ship, there were four hawseholes, piercing the hawsetimbers, the inner pair being used for the bower cables. A rounded 'bolster' on the outer aspect, blunted the sharp angle which would otherwise have been required of the cable. In rough weather, a lot of water would have been shipped, as the bow plunged into the sea, had it not been for the hawse-plugs

and bucklers. The former, known to the American seamen as 'jackasses', were conical canvas bags thrust into the opening, and backed up by the wooden shield or 'buckler', which was secured to the breast-knees. These were distinguished as 'riding-', or 'blind-bucklers', according to whether they were notched to accommodate the cable or not, the former being used in harbour, the latter at sea.

'The manger' was the space just abaft the hawseholes. 'Its use is to receive the water which bulges through the hawseholes in stormy weather' (*Naval Repository*, 26). It also drained off some of the water coming up with the cable, which rubbed against the manger-boards, as it was hove in. It was drained by large 'manger-scuppers'. The 'manger-boards' formed a partiton about three feet high, and separated the manger from the deck further aft. The Dutch term *pisbak*, literally means 'urinal', no doubt referring to the sloppy, wet condition of the manger. The scuppers could be plugged if necessary.

The riding bitts. A substantial pair of square posts projected vertically above the gundeck, just abaft the foremast. They were supported in front by 'standard-knees', and joined abaft by a heavy cross-piece, the after surface of which was rounded off to form a cushion, and projected quite a bit aft of the vertical members. The whole assembly was known as the 'riding bitts'. In large ships, later on, there were two pairs of bitts, one abaft the other, the after set being a little wider than the forward pair. To 'bitt' the cable, a bight was picked up abaft the bitts, and a loop, or 'cuckold's-neck', made in it, and dropped over the upright, the lower leg pointing forward, and the upper aft. This meant that the cable came aft from the hawsehole, passed outside the knee, under the cross-piece, outside the bitt-post, diagonally back up over the cushion, around the bitt-head, over the cross-piece, and aft again to the main hatch. Thus the starboard cable was bitted in a right-handed loop, 'with the sun', while the port cable bitted 'against the sun'. This 'riding-turn', along with the stoppers, held the inboard end of the cable secure, when riding at anchor. Exactly the same sort of turn was made with a chain cable, the bitts being metal sheathed to withstand the chafe. When veering, the turn was kept on to prevent the cable running out too fast. Stout 'bitt-pins', or 'Normans', could be thrust through holes in the upright, and the cross-piece, to prevent the turns coming off inadvertently. The Norman in the upright was removed when bitting the cable, and

then replaced (Sjöbohm, 10). When heaving in, the turn was taken off the bitt, and the cable rested on the cross-piece, outside the upright, where it was more easily handled by the nippermen. The second or after set of bitts handled the sheet anchors if they were let go.

The cable was 'double bitted' by taking a turn on both sets of bitts. This was done when veering chain, in hard weather, or bringing to anchor in deep water. It reduced the abrasion on the forward bitts (Frick, 220). A cable was 'weather bitted' by taking an extra turn on the upright, the bitt-pin helping to keep it in place. The term was, however, more often used when referring to the windlass (Romme, 361; Falconer, 318).

Any turn of a cable about the bitts is called a 'bitter'. Hence a ship is 'brought up to a bitter' when the cable is allowed to run out to that stop. That part of the cable which is abaft the bitts, and therefore within board when the ship is at anchor is the 'bitter-end'. 'Bend to the bitter end', when they would have that end bent to the anchor, and when a chain or rope is paid out to the bitter-end, no more remains to go. The bitter-end is the clinching end. Sometimes that end is bent to the anchor, because it has never been used, and is more trustworthy (Smyth, 103; *Mariner's Mirror* 38, 1952, 7; 241; *Mariner's Mirror* 61, 1975, 373).

Riding to the bitts.

Ships of war frequently have their cables triced up overhead from the after part of the bitts to the main hatchway, that is when they expect to lay long at their anchors; in such cases there is great danger to the bitts in strong winds. I was in a frigate in Simon's Bay laying at line-of-battle ship's moorings, in a heavy gale from the NorthWest, with yards and topmasts struck and from the moorings being expended round the bitts, instead of being stoppered to the deck-bolts abaft, the bitts were twisted out of the deck by the same process you twist the crown out of a pineapple, and the ship was providentially saved by bringing up with the bower, veered to the clinch. Let it be always borne in mind that the bitts are only veering cleats upon a large scale and that it is always unsafe to ride by them. When the cable is well stoppered abaft of it, they are free of all strain'. (Liardet, 50).

Deck-stoppers. These were used to grip the cable when riding to anchor, and fulfilled the function of the modern Blake-slip, or devil's claw. They consisted of a fathom of rope, half the size of the cable. The lower end was secured to an eyebolt, the deck-plate of which was shouldered, or lengthened towards the bow. These stoppers are the item for which

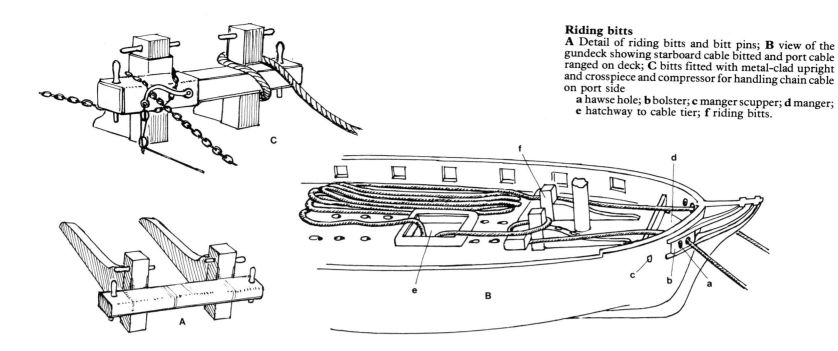

Riding bitts
A Detail of riding bitts and bitt pins; **B** view of the gundeck showing starboard cable bitted and port cable ranged on deck; **C** bitts fitted with metal-clad upright and crosspiece and compressor for handling chain cable on port side
    a hawse hole; **b** bolster; **c** manger scupper; **d** manger; **e** hatchway to cable tier; **f** riding bitts.

'stopper-knots' are named. In the upper end, a wall-knot, Matthew Walker, or something of the sort, was worked from the strands of the rope. The stopper was whipped for about a foot down from the knot, to protect the fibres, and a flexible sennit lanyard, about two or three fathoms in length, was attached by a seizing or running eye, just below the knot. A spunyarn seizing was secured to the lanyard to allow fastening it to the cable once the stopper was passed. There were two or three deck-stoppers directly abaft, and in line with the bitt-post, and a couple on the stand-ard-knee, on the forward side.

To pass the stopper, the knotted end was laid beside the cable, with the lay, that is to say on its starboard side, since the contlines sloped down and to the left. Four or five turns of the lanyard were taken, against the sun, to bind the knot to the cable, and the ba-lance of the lanyard expended by worming it forward along the cable, with the lay, and the end seized (Costé, 234; Totten, 119).

Dog-stoppers. To 'dog' a lanyard, implied taking its tail turns around a larger rope, as just described (Ashley, 599; Smyth, 255). Dog-stoppers were four-fifths the size of their respective cables, but rather than the cablet forming a deck-stopper, they consisted of three or four fathoms of flexible sennit. Costé calls them *bosses à fouet*, 'whip-stoppers'. Unlike the deck-stoppers they were detachable, the lower ends being furn-ished either with a large hook, or knotted so they would hold when slipped through a hole in a timber. Sjöbohm (10) calls them *rund-stoppare*, 'round-stoppers', and says a couple of half-hitches were taken before the end was

expended by dogging it forward along the cable. Similar stoppers were in constant use on deck, to hold braces, tacks, and sheets, etc, steady, while they were belayed. 'Wing-stoppers' were a variant used in the cable-tiers, and were secured to the riders. 'Hatch-' or 'coaming-stoppers' were used to control the cable when veering. The stopper was middled, placed round the cable, and taken through holes of adjoining edges at the for-ward corner of the hatchway. The ends were dogged criss-cross forward along the cable, and seized. It took the place of the lever used with chain cable in the same location, and was accordingly sometimes called a 'compressor'. 'Bitt-stoppers' used around the bitts took various forms. One type, similar to a dog-stopper, was used when riding to anchor in heavy weather. It was middled, and the bight placed over the inboard or upper end of the cable abaft the bitt-post. The ends were taken under the cross-piece, dogged around the cable forward of the bitts, and seized, one end being taken around with the lay, and the other layed crosswise over it against the lay. As the cables stretched, the bitt-stopper jam-med the cable more tightly against the cross-piece. Gower (122) describes a single bitt-stopper, consisting of a length of rope, one end of which was formed into a sennit tail. The first end was slipped through a hole in the knee of the bitts, where it was held by a knot or clinch, on the inner side of the knee, the other end being taken under the cross-piece, over the cable and back around to be dogged forward as before. Another type of bitt-stopper, which was called a *zwakken-hals* in Dutch, consisted of a rope seized so as

to make a large eye, which could be dropped over the upright of the bitts, and hence could be moved from side to side. As illustrated by Le Compte, it terminates in a large stopper-knot, and is fitted with a lanyard. I think it could also have worked like a dog-stopper.

Ring-stopper. This, which Lever calls a 'ring-rope' worked in a rather similar fashion to the bitt-stopper. In its double form, the stopper was clove-hitched to a ringbolt, at its mid-point, and the ends dogged forward around the cable criss-cross; when single, it had only one tail. They could also be used to stop the cable running out in this way. Three loose turns were taken round the cable and stopped up to a deck beam with spunyarn, and the tail wormed along the cable. Upon the tail being jerked taut, the moving cable 'grabbed it', pulled it forward breaking the spunyarn stops, and was itself stopped by the sudden constriction of the turns (Lever, 109). Smyth (575) gives this definition: 'A long piece of rope secured to the after ringbolt, and the loop embracing the cable through the next, and others in succession nip the cable home to each ringbolt in succession. It is a precaution in veering cable in bad weather.' One can see how this works, but I have come across no other reference to this particular method.

Check-stoppers. They could be fashioned of spunyarn and secured to eyebolts, every five fathoms or so. They were light enough to break as the strain came on, just strong enough to slow down the rate at which the cable paid out, as a range was veered.

Chain stoppers. With the introduction of chain cable special devices were introduced

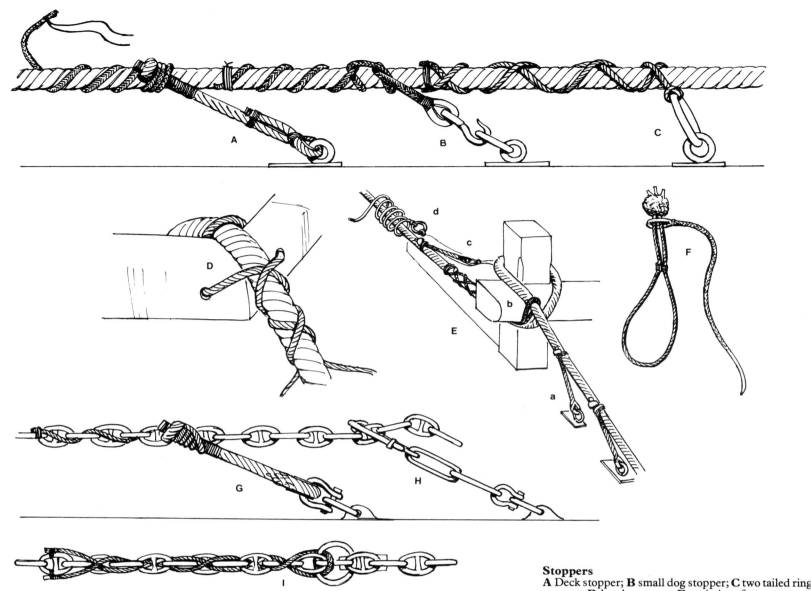

Stoppers
A Deck stopper; B small dog stopper; C two tailed ring stopper; D hatch stopper; E varieties of stoppers: **a** deck stopper; **b** dog stopper; **c** bitt stopper; **d** ring stopper.
F *Zwakkenhals*; G rope stopper on chain; H blake stopper; I ring stopper.

to take the place of the stoppers used with hemp cable. Two of these are still in use today, virtually unaltered, the 'Blake slip', and the 'devil's claw'. Prior to their introduction, rope deck-stoppers were used with both hemp and chain. Since vessels were equipped for a long period with both hemp and chain cables, it is not surprising to find that the old-fashioned deck-stoppers, were also used with chain. Ring-stoppers of a special form were also in use. A length of rope was middled over the chain, the ends taken through a ring large enough to engage a link, and then dogged forward around the chain. Nares (124) suggests that this could be used to check the cable if the compressor carried away.

Names of stoppers. Rosvall (72) gives an interesting list of stoppers used in the Swedish service: *knop-stoppare*, 'knot-stopper', that is 'deck-stopper'; *rund-stoppare*, 'round-stopper', that is 'dog-

stopper'; *hak-stoppare*, 'hook-stopper', that is one fitted with a hook; *stjert-stoppare*, 'tail-stopper', used for clapping on sheets, tacks, etc; *ring-stoppare*, 'ring-stopper', the single-ended version; *stick-stoppare*, 'hitch-stopper', the double-tailed ring-stopper; *lösa beting-stoppare*, 'loose bitt-stopper', the same as the *zwakkenhals*, mentioned above; *fast-beting-stopare*, 'fast bitt-stopper', one thrust through a hole in the standard-knee; *förlorad-stoppare*, 'lost-stopper', that is 'check-stopper'.

Compressor and controller. When veering hemp cable, the movement could be stopped by gripping the cable with a coaming- or ring-stopper. The compressor took the place of this with chain cable. The cable came up over a chafing-piece at the corner of the hatchway, and beside this was placed a curved iron lever. One end pivoted on a vertical bolt, and the other was controlled by a

tackle. To veer, the order was 'Heave back the compressor!'. To check the cable, the order was given 'Bowse to the compressor!', whereupon the lever jammed the chain against the chafing-piece, and so stopped the cable. Bugler describes, and illustrates, the compressors still to be seen aboard *Victory*. Presumably these were fitted to handle chain cables later in her career. Totten (120) refers to 'iron stoppers', which may well be identical with 'compressors', although the context could imply their use with hemp cable.

The controller was a U-shaped casting, with a tumbler, or cam, operated by a lever on the side. When the tumbler was up, the cable could run out unimpeded, through the central groove. When the tumbler was lowered, the vertical links dropped into a fore-

and aft slot, which slowed down, and ultimately stopped the cable. The controller could be thought of as replacing the old-fashioned ring-stopper, which sometimes was used even with chain. A U-shaped bar could be wedged into the casting to prevent the cable jumping out. A transverse bar could be inserted in this to retain the cable in its 'keep'. Dutch and Danish sources call the controller a 'Brown stopper'.

Anchor-buoy. The anchor was buoyed for two reasons: firstly, it simplified the task of keeping a clear anchor, at change of tide, by indicating where the anchor lay; secondly, it offered a means of recovering the anchor if the cable parted, or if circumstances demanded that the vessel slip her cable and leave the anchorage without weighing anchor. Nun-buoys were the most common form, thickest in the middle, tapering towards both ends, and secured with rope slings. They are often described as being shaped like two cones, fixed base to base, but are usually illustrated as having a more rounded appearance, rather like an unshelled pecan nut. In fact, Murphy suggests that this explains the variant 'nut-buoy', but 'nun' was an old word for a child's spinning top, and this more likely is the origin of the term. These buoys were formed of barrel-like staves, hence the Dutch *tonnen-boei* 'tun-buoy', as distinct from 'cork-buoys', those formed of discs of cork. In size, the anchor-buoy was in length one-quarter the length of the anchor shank, in diameter, one-eighth. The buoy-rope was one-third the thickness of the cable (Totten, 124), substantial enough to permit its being used in emergency to weigh the anchor, crown first. A six-inch rope is listed by Steel for First Rates, the

same size as the cat-fall. It was secured to the crown of the anchor with a clove-hitch, and the end seized to the shank. The buoy was stowed in the fore chains, when not in use, its rope coiled up with it. The rope had to be long enough to allow the buoy to float or 'watch', even at high water. If the buoy had leaked, and contained some water, it would not 'watch', and it was necessary to 'bleed' it by draining the water off. 'Watch', by the way, in this technical sense of 'be awash', 'stay afloat, or above water', resembles similar words in other languages, with this basic meaning of 'watch', 'keep vigil', 'stay afloat'; as in French *veiller*, German *wachen*, Swedish *vaka*.

Streaming the buoy. Griffith (174) felt that it was better to hang onto the buoy until the buoy-rope came taut; that is to say, when the anchor was on the bottom, and the ship drifting back with the tide. If the buoy were streamed first, there was a risk that it would be fouled by the cable, and as a result the buoy would not watch. Furthermore, a buoy-rope entangled with the cable materially impeded hooking the fish, upon weighing. Rosvall (73) secures a tail-rope to the top of the buoy, and this runs through a block in the fore chains, being let go when the buoy is to be streamed. This tail-rope, or 'cat's tail' as the Dutch called it, was also used to pick the buoy up, when weighing. Röding (133) secures the tail-rope to the fore shrouds, with a slip-knot, keeping it fast until there comes a tug on the buoy-rope, upon which the slip-knot is let go. Some seamen, on the other hand, gave the order 'Stream the buoy!', just before letting go the anchor. With chain cable, as we shall see, the buoy was a less necessary item, and with the advent of auxi-

liary power, there was the danger of the buoy-rope fouling the propeller (Hansen, I, 131).

GENERAL PREPARATIONS FOR ENTERING HARBOUR AND ANCHORING.

This included some general tasks about the ship, and some specific arrangements regarding the ground-tackle. If a senior officer was already in port, it was determined whether or not his light yards were aloft, or struck, so the newly arrived vessel would be prepared to follow his lead, in this regard.

On deck. The channels were cleaned, the decks holystoned, and the sides washed off with fresh water. The paintwork was touched up, particularly under the beakhead, in the wake of the scuppers and channel-irons, where rust staining was a problem. Clean hammocks were stowed neatly in the nettings, and the boats were got ready for being put in the water. Awnings, wind-sails, and smoke-sails were got up from the sail-room. Wind-sails were canvas trunks, used to direct fresh air below decks, in hot climates, and the smoke-sail was rigged forward of the foremast, to prevent the smoke from the galley floating back on the quarterdeck, when anchored head to wind. The hawse-bucklers were removed, the anchors got off the bows, cables bent, anchor-buoys rigged, bearing in mind the depth of water in which it was proposed to anchor. Lead-lines were readied in the fore-chains, and breast-bands rigged for the leadsmen. The jackstaff, jack and pen-

Anchor buoys
A Different types of anchor buoys; **B** buoy rope hitched and seized to anchor; **C** anchor buoy in use; **D** weighing anchor with buoy rope.

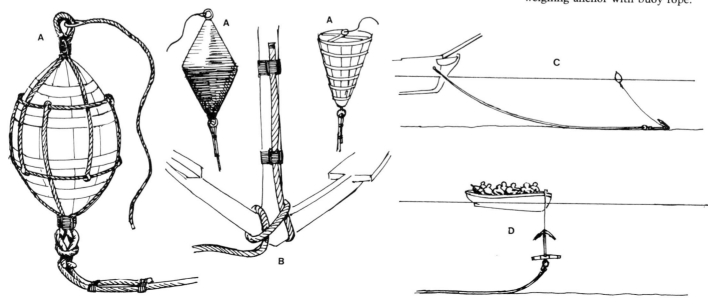

nants were got ready for use. Shot was withdrawn from the saluting cannon, and blank charges substituted, half-ports removed, and the guns squared in the ports. Fordyce (162) suggests that in a brig, the quarter boats should be lowered, and the ship's chronometers protected, to avoid damage from the concussion of the saluting cannon.

Getting the anchor off the bows. At sea during a protracted voyage, the cables were unbent, and the anchor made fast with ring-, shank-, and stock-lashings, hauled in as closely as possible to the ship's side, and cathead. In preparation for coming within soundings, the cables were bent, and the sea-lashings removed, so that the anchor was held only by the singled up ring-stopper, and shank-painter. This operation was referred to as 'getting the anchor off the bows'. The fore pendant-tackle, and the stock-tackle, secured to the upper arm of the stock, were rigged for this purpose. They were hauled taut, the lashings cast off, and the tackles eased off until the anchor was secured only by the ring-stopper and shank painter. Capstan bars were used to pry the inner fluke clear of the

timberhead and the fluke or bill of the anchor was rested on the bill-board, or a wooden 'shoe' to protect the ship's planking.

Aloft. The topmasts were scraped and slushed, and the rigging, tips of the studding-sail booms, and so on, blacked, or painted. All the chafing-gear, brace-mats on the shrouds, hide protectors on the crosstrees, etc, were got down. The studdingsails were got out of the rigging, and their gear unrove. The top-gallant and topmasts were straightened by setting up the shrouds and backstays. Sea-gaskets were removed and newly blacked harbour-gaskets substituted. The topsail buntline lizards were removed from the jack-stay, or tye-blocks, so that the foot of the sail would go well up the mast and facilitate a nice looking harbour-stow. If the weather were light, clewropes and clew-jiggers were rigged forward of the courses and topsails. Sail could be taken in with greater expedition, by 'singling up', such items as topsail sheets, clewgarnets, topsail clewlines, tacks and lower sheets, at least the weather sheet and lee tack. A further refinement, along the same lines, involved unshackling the chain topsail

sheets, and using spunyarn 'rotten stops' to secure the clews of the sail, designed to break when the clewlines were hauled upon.

On the gundeck. The tiers were cleared of all the extra gear that tended to accumulate there while at sea, and sufficient cable 'ranged' on deck, ready for letting go. If it were intended to moor immediately, the messenger was brought to the capstan, and preparations made for heaving in, the boatswain readying nippers, deck-stoppers, etc. With chain cable, the armourer inspected and lubricated the compressor, chain slip-stopper, and so on.

THE MECHANICS OF CASTING ANCHOR.

Letting go the anchor. The ring-stopper was a stout rope, nine inches or more in circumference in First Rates. It had a wall-knot in one end, the adjacent couple of feet being covered in soft leather for protection where it passed through a vertical hole in the cathead, and a good service where it touched the anchor-ring. It passed through the ring,

Anchor releasing gear
A Simple ring stopper; **B** anchor stowed on bow:
  a ring stopper; **b** shank painter.
C Trick stopper secured, holding anchor a-cockbill; **D** trick stopper released, anchor let go; **E** simultaneous release gear for bower anchor; **F** simultaneous release gear for sheet anchor:
  a trip strop; **b** tumblers; **c** painters; **d** tripping bar; **e** fore ganger.

back up over a notch or groove on the cat-head, to be made fast to a timberhead. The shank-painter, of about the same size, had a running eye securing it to a timberhead, from whence it led around the shank, coming up between the latter and the ship's side to be made fast. Practice, in earlier days, was to let go the shank-painter, and use the fore pendant-tackle to ease the shank down into a vertical position, 'cock-billing' the anchor (*faire peneau*, in French), the weight now falling entirely on the ring-stopper. Upon the order 'Let go!', the latter was cast off, and the anchor dropped clear. The forecastle party were in some danger at this particular moment, because the loose end of the stopper came back with a fearsome crack (Costé, 236). 'In passing the stoppers of the anchor, care should be taken that the end which is to unreeve in letting go is brought in *over* the anchor, so that in letting go, this end will be thrown out and down. If passed underneath, it will be thrown up and in as the anchor drops and may swing in with dangerous violence' (Knight, 158). Boström advocates that the petty-officer charged with letting go the stopper, should, upon doing so, immediately hurl himself on deck to avoid injury. This problem led to the development of 'trick-stoppers', as Brady calls them, patent devices which 'let go' by releasing a short chain ring-stopper. The chain was held by a tumbler, which was released by pulling a lanyard, which in turn moved a lever. Le Compte (Figure 513) illustrates Brunton's Patent Anchor trigger, which was widely used. These released the ring-stopper and shank-painter separately. The tumbler was tripped by hauling a many-tailed lanyard, the boatswain calling out 'One, Two, Three, let go!', whereupon the forecastle party hauled on the tails. A further refinement was the invention of a device which released ring and shank simultaneously. 'Letting go stock and fluke' had the advantage that the anchor could be loosed from the rail, without the necessity of first hanging it a-cockbill (Bonnefoux, Plate V; Luce, Figure 432). If the stopper and painter were let go by hand, they were either released simultaneously, or the shank-painter a fraction earlier. Some merchantmen went further than simply cock-billing the anchor, actually hooking the cat, and lowering the anchor down level with the hawsehole, thus ensuring that the stock would not foul the cable in falling (Knight, 158). For the same reason, some seamen ran a rope's end under the cable, hauling it up clear of the stock, the end being let go along with the anchor.

To prevent the cable running out too

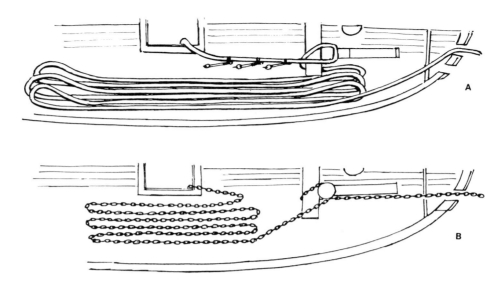

Ranging the cable
A Cable flaked on deck, ready for letting go the anchor; B chain cable flaked on deck, ready for veering over bitts.

rapidly, a turn was taken on the bitts. If it was expected that the ship would drop back rapidly, the cable could be 'double-bitted'. Since the friction of the cable, as it veered, could generate enough heat to set things afire, buckets of water were kept in readiness to extinguish the flame (Groeneijk, 110). If a greater degree of control were necessary, 'check-stoppers' could be put on, or a deck-tackle rigged, abreast the main hatch. Initially, this was set up 'two blocks', one of the blocks being hauled forward, hooked to a strop on the veering cable. This method was sometimes used with chain cable in very deep water (Bardenfleth, I, 214). Actually had it not been for the weight factor, chain cable was rather more manageable than hemp, the compressor and controller, or Brown stopper, offering better command than the ring-stoppers did with hemp.

Letting go a sheet anchor. The sheet anchor was usually secured, stock vertical, against the fore channels, the inner fluke made fast to a timberhead, just abaft the channels. A cable was kept bent to the anchor, so it was ready for letting go in emergency. In the late 1800s, a chain 'ganger', which could be shackled to the hemp or chain sheet cable, was substituted for the hemp. This saved the hemp 'ganger' from exposure to the weather, when the anchor was stowed, which was virtually all the time, and from abrasion on the bottom, in the rare cases when it was put to use. The foreganger was secured at intervals to eyebolts along the bow, with spunyarn stops, which would snap if the anchor were let go.

A simple arrangement was used to throw the anchor out clear of obstruction, when it was let go. This consisted of a U-shaped 'trip-strop' passing under a fore and aft notch in the lower end of the stock, and two 'tumblers', or 'trip-shores', which supported

the shank. These were fastened to the ship's side, by hinges at their lower end. When the painters, or securing chains were let go, the trip-strop and tumblers ensured that the anchor would roll, or tumble, outwards, and fall clear of gun muzzles, port-lids, and so on. Using these devices, a sheet anchor could be let go, almost as easily as a bower. Earlier, it would have required the use of the fish and yard tackles to 'get it off the bows', ready for letting go.

Ranging the cable. As the vessel approached her anchor-berth, sufficient hemp cable was roused up, on the gundeck, from the tier, and 'French flaked or faked' on deck. That is to say, it was laid down serpentine fashion, starting out towards the ship's side, and working inwards, in parallel rows. At the end of each row, the bights were slipped under each other, so they would run out freely. The desired length being on deck, a turn, or 'bitter', was taken on the bitts, and the stoppers passed abaft the bitts. When the anchor was let go, it dragged the outboard end through the hawsehole first, followed by each flake successively. When the jerk came, as the cable 'brought up to the bitter', the last flake was in the same fore and aft line, as the bitts. Had the cable been flaked down in the opposite order, the last turn would have snapped violently across the deck towards midships, as it came taut. Rosvall (73) mentions an alternative method, the cable being roused up and laid down in a series of overlapping loops, starting forward. This meant that the inboard end, and after coils, were on top. To allow the cable to run out freely, the coils were upset, capsized side for side with the part next to the hatchway ending up toward the ship's side. This allowed the coils to pay out one after another, from before aft. With hemp cable, enough was 'ranged before the bitts' to allow the anchor to touch the bottom. The rest of the scope was held in check by the bitt-turn, ranged ready to be veered, as the ship dropped back. Chain cable was also ranged, at least 20 fathoms or so, 'to get things going', as it were. After that amount was out, its own weight would suffice to haul it up from the chain locker. The bights of chain were laid out on deck, in fore and aft rows just as with hemp. Ashley (517) refers to 'long flaking' the chain, the bights of chain being snaked back and forth, lying athwartships. This method corresponds, more or less, to the Rosvall method, mentioned above, used with hemp cable. Ashley comments on the tremendous cloud of dust raised by following this practice. Totten (114) did not approve of ranging chain before the bitts, preferring to have the cable bitted, and the range therefore running out more deliberately. Some officers just let all the chain run out directly from the locker. Totten felt that this should only be done when the chain could be checked with a compressor.

Backing an anchor. If there were doubts about the holding power of a single anchor, it could be 'backed' by dropping another anchor first. A hawser clinched to the ring of the supplementary backing anchor was secured to the crown of the primary anchor, in the same fashion as a buoy-rope, or indeed the buoy-rope was bent to the backing anchor. A suitable length for this hawser was one and a half times the depth of water (Harboe, 204). The Dutch term *katten* has the double meaning of 'to cat', and 'to back' an anchor.

Shoeing an anchor. This was a method used with a very soft muddy bottom, where the grip of the anchor was improved by lashing a wooden disk to each fluke. Mainwaring (90) talks of the merits of 'tallowing' an anchor in such cases, to allow it to sink more quickly. Winschooten (8) says that the Portuguese were reputed to smear the arms of the anchor with fat, when anchoring on a sandy bottom.

VARIOUS METHODS OF COMING TO ANCHOR.

Anchoring man-of-war fashion. It was a measure of the discipline and training of the crew of a man-of-war, if after half an hour at anchor, she looked as though she had been there for a month (Engelhart, 148). Barden-fleth distinguishes two methods of anchoring, respectively, 'man-of-war fashion', and 'merchant service fashion'. Although these terms are not generally recognised, we have used them here for convenience. As to the first method, 'we see it frequently attempted by vessels of war of other nations, and very rarely do we see it performed successfully' (Totten, 240). The second, less spectacular but more seamanlike way, was to come in under topsails, 'feeling one's way, deadening it by checking the braces, or freshening it with some additional canvas' (Luce, 402). Lofty canvas was, however, sometimes necessary to catch a breeze, for instance, where the lower sails were becalmed in the lee of the land. With split topsails, the lowers were clewed up first, since the effect of the uppers could be negated, in a moment, by letting go the halliards at the crucial moment. The first method, however, was the showiest manoeuvre, requiring the ship to charge into the anchorage under full sail, and then, at the last moment, run up into the wind, fire her saluting guns, and take in a cloud of canvas. Upon the smoke clearing, the ship was to be seen lying peacefully at anchor, booms out, and boats in the water. A stunt of this sort could only be attempted by a very well drilled and practised crew, because, of course, it offered more opportunities for things to get fouled up, and required much more forethought and preparation, than when things were done more deliberately. An old print shows Codrington's *Asia*, of 1824, coming to anchor, a pillar of canvas, to royals and studdingsails, collapsing like a pricked balloon, as the saluting gun fires (Watts, I, 77).

Anchoring merchant service fashion. The ship approached the desired spot under easy sail, for example jib, topsails and spanker. The helm was put down and the vessel allowed to headreach up into the wind, while clewing everything up. When headway was completely lost the order was given 'Let go!', and cable was veered allowing the ship to drop back to leeward.

A good anchorage was one protected from the prevailing winds, not too deep, and with good holding ground. Foul ground, encumbered by old wrecks, etc, was avoided. The best types of bottom were, in order, blue clay, mud, sand, stone. A rocky bottom was avoided, because the anchor might become trapped in a crevice, and be impossible to recover, added to which, the stock or fluke might be injured, as the anchor initially hit bottom (Bardenfleth, (I, 214). The quantity of cable stuck out varied from two and a half to six times the depth of water. A shorter scope was needed in moderate weather, or where the anchoring was temporary, as when 'stopping a tide', for instance (Bardenfleth, I, 214; Luce, 402). Leadsmen in both main chains kept calling out the soundings, as the ship came up to her berth. In anchorages, like Madeira, where the ground shelved steeply, it was advisable to have leadsmen in the fore chains, as well.

Once the anchor was on the bottom, the pull of the cable encouraged the fluke to bite, but if there were too much strain the anchor would start to drag or 'come home'. To 'set' the anchor, the vessel had to be moving over the ground. A little movement was essential, but too much undesirable. In a tideway, the vessel stemmed the tide, while if there were no tide, she dropped back head to wind. In light winds, the movement might require the encouragement of a backed mizzen topsail. In the ordinary way, the cable would be 'growing' more or less ahead, as it was veered. In some circumstances, however, it was necessary to run the cable out while continuing to forge ahead. This resulted in the cable dropping straight down beside the cutwater, and endangering the copper sheathing at the bow; hence it was the less favoured method. Furthermore, the chain was acutely angled, at the lip of the hawse-pipe, subjecting it to a severe and unnecessary strain. When anchoring, a second anchor was invariably kept ready for letting go, if the first cable failed to hold the vessel. In the ordinary way, the weather anchor was let go since the cable would then be clear of the cutwater and copper, as the vessel drifted to leeward.

It was preferable that the cable be veered under control, rather than allowed to roar out, and throw a tremendous strain on everything, as the ship brought to, and the cable snapped taut. This could cause the cable to part, or at the very least strain the bitts. Liardet advocated slowing the vessel's drift to leeward, after having dropped the weather anchor, by keeping the ship broadside to the wind, thus increasing the water's resistance to the movement of the hull. 'Too much cannot be said in favour in anchoring broadside to the wind, when circumstances will permit its being so' (Liardet, 19). I am not aware of any other proponent of this technique, although it seems like a good idea. We will now consider some specific cases.

No tide, and light to moderate wind. Standing in, on the wind, the vessel was steered towards a point somewhat to leeward of the desired anchor place. Coming in under jib, topsails and mizzen, the lee lower lifts were slacked away to the squaremarks,

Coming to anchor man-of-war fashion
A HMS *Asia* taking in all (after contemporary painting); B diagram of operation.

Coming to anchor merchant ship fashion
A Diagram of operation; B ship *America* lying to anchor with mizzen topsail backed (after A Roux, 1806); C leadsman in fore chains leaning against breast band.

everything ready for squaring the yards and clewing down the topsails. When almost abreast the desired place, the helm was put down, the yards squared with lifts and braces, and the vessel brought to a standstill, as she came up in the wind. The topsail clewlines were hauled enough to get the clews up above the lower cap, whereupon the halliards were let go, and the yard clewed down. If the yards were squared early, the ship came to a stop more quickly, but clewing up became more difficult, because the canvas was thrown against the rigging; it was easier if the sails were clewed up, while full, or shaking.

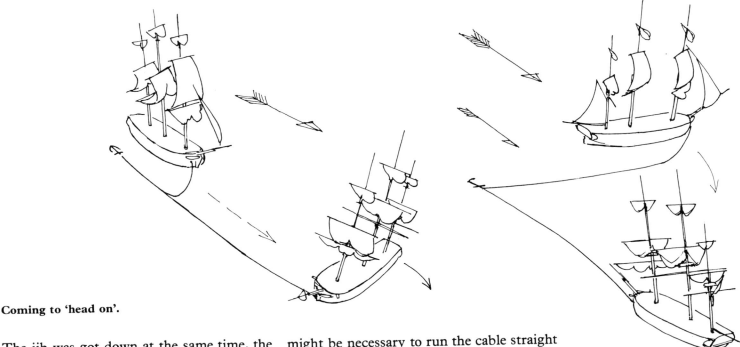

Coming to 'head on'.

Coming to anchor with following wind and tide

The jib was got down at the same time, the mizzen being kept set to aid the luffing movement, and the anchor dropped, as the vessel started to make sternway. The process was essentially similar when coming in, with a 'leading' wind; that is to say, with the wind on the quarter. The vessel had to make a greater circuit to come head to wind, the spanker being set momentarily to help her round, with the boom perhaps hauled somewhat to windward.

Coming to 'head on'. Entering a crowded anchorage, with the wind aft, it might be impossible to round to, as described above, there being insufficient room to make the sweep, and the cable was laid out, while the vessel still had headway. The Dutch referred to this as *met staande zeilen ten anker komen* ('anchoring with standing sails'), while Luce calls it 'anchoring head on'. This method offered greater precision in choosing the exact spot where the anchor was cast, and recommended itself, for instance, in taking up a vacant berth, in a line of moored vessels, where it would be the first to step in making a 'flying moor'. It was also employed as a stratagem, when being chased: if the pursued vessel, running before the wind, were able to drop anchor suddenly, her pursuer might be swept by, dead to leeward, before he could engage properly (Mossel, III, 188). Anchoring head on had the disadvantage that the copper was endangered, and that the ship was liable to be brought up finally with a tremendous crash, when the range had run out, especially if the tide were running in the same direction as the wind. The jerk could be eased by using check-stoppers, double-bitting the cable, and swinging broadside to the wind while veering. With a light wind, it might be necessary to run the cable straight out, rather than around the bitts.

Coming before the wind, and with the tide. This was similar to the earlier cases, but of course the ship had to turn up into the wind earlier. Since the speed of the ship over the ground was considerable, it was particularly important to plan ahead, and not allow the tide to sweep the ship down aboard other vessels already at anchor. Anchoring head on, in this circumstance, was not advisable. Stapert, a Dutch seaman, in such cases, recommended sailing the chain out *across* the tide, laying the bight of the cable out on the bottom at right angles to its ultimate position, the ship gradually hauling it taut as she brought to, astream of her anchor.

Coming before the wind, and against the tide. If the influence of the tide was greater than that of the wind, the vessel could stem the tide, sail directly to the desired spot, take in sail, cast anchor, and drop back with the stream. If the wind were the commanding feature, it might be possible to sail out the cable, perhaps only using the fore topmast staysail (Groeneijk, 118).

Anchoring on a lee shore. The method described for four anchors, was to sail a course parallel to the shore, letting go, in order, the weather sheet, weather bower, lee bower, lee sheet anchors. If the manoeuvre were successful, and the ship managed to sail out the first three cables, they were adjusted so that an equal strain came on all four anchors (Groeneijk, 119; Murphy, 33). The latter author, describes the further expedient of 'backing the anchors with guns'. A hawser was passed under the cables at the hawse-holes, and secured to two or three guns on either bow, a bight of hawser being left slack between each gun. The cannon were then thrown overboard, in the hope that, should the anchors drag, the flukes would catch the hawser, and so be arrested, before the ship went ashore.

The commands. Most of the orders related to shortening sail, and only a general idea can be given.

All hands, bring ship to anchor!
Stand by to take in flying jib, royals, and studdingsails!
Haul taut! Shorten sail! In flying jib, royals and studdingsails!
Man topgallant clewlines, fore (and main) clewgarnets and buntlines!
Haul taut! In topgallants! Up foresail (and mainsail)!
Furl topgallants and royals! Stow the flying jib!
Helm a-lee!
Man topsail clewlines (or clew-jiggers) and buntlines, jib downhaul, spanker outhaul! (The last if spanker is to be set.)
Haul taut! Let go topsail sheets, topbowlines clew up! Down jib!
Haul out the spanker!
Settle away the topsail halliards! Square away!
Stand clear of the starboard (port) cable!
Stream the buoy!
Let go the anchor! Midships!
Man the spanker brails! Brail up the spanker!

MANAGEMENT OF THE SHIP AT SINGLE ANCHOR.

The authorities. Since keeping a clear anchor was much more important in the days of hemp cable, we find that the earlier authors are more interested in the subject. Although Gower, Lever, Taylor, Nichelson, and Hutchinson, all writing around 1800, have a good deal to say, I found much of it very hard to follow, particularly in the case of the last two authors named. Potter's monograph, written in 1862, although totally concerned with chain cable, is considerably easier to understand. Later authorities, like Boyd, either devote little space to the topic, or depend heavily on the early writers: Blunt and Murphy abridge Taylor, Glascock follows Gower and Hutchinson, while Luce depends on Potter. Mossel is one of the few foreign authors consulted who makes an attempt at a systematic account of keeping a clear anchor.

Phraseology. A vessel at anchor, riding to the tide, 'astream' of her anchor, was 'tide-rode', as distinct from her situation at still water, when she lay 'wind-rode'. If influenced by both, she 'lay between wind and tide' (Smyth). If the tide and wind acted together, the ship 'rode leeward tide', while if they opposed one another, she would be 'riding windward tide'. If the wind and tide were parallel, the wind was 'up and down the tide'. If they were at right angles, the wind was 'across', or 'athwart' the tide. The management of the ship at change of tide was referred to as 'tending'. At the end of the lee tide, she was 'tended to windward'. At the end of the windward tide, 'tending to leeward' commenced.

Imagine the tides running East and West, and the wind across the tide, from the North. With helm amidships, the vessel would 'lie astream' of her anchor, due East or West, riding out the tide. It was usual, however, to 'sheer' her one way or the other, by keeping some helm on. If held up to the northward, of the East-West line, she was said to be 'sheered to windward', by a 'check of lee helm', as Lever puts it. If kept down to the southward, she was 'sheered to leeward'. At change of tide, the ship was sheered over to one or other side of the anchor, using helm and sail. If, having been given a sheer, she inadvertently deviated from that situation, the ship was said to 'break her sheer'.

Foul anchor. The anchor lay on the ground, with the lower fluke dug in, the stock flat, and the upper fluke pointing upwards. The lower fluke retained a solid grip of the ground, only as long as the pull of the cable was exerted in a more or less horizontal direction, on the ring, in line with the shank. If the cable were allowed to drag around in such a way as to come foul, making a round turn on the upper arm, the pull would now actually tend to disengage the lower fluke, and the vessel was in danger of 'shouldering' her anchor, and 'walking away with it'. To heave up an anchor foul was accounted the 'seaman's disgrace', particularly in the coal trade, and thus it is surprising to find the Lord High Admiral of England adopting such a fouled anchor as his personal emblem. The entangling cable is added for aesthetic reasons only, to soften the otherwise stark outline of the anchor, and not as a symbolic imputation of fault (Kemp, 323). The chance of a foul anchor somewhat depended on the quality of the ground. If a lower arm once disengaged from the bottom, it might fail to grip again, as the anchor dragged across the ground, the fluke encased in a ball of clay. On the other hand, if the ground were soft ooze, allowing the anchor to sink into it until the upper fluke disappeared below the surface, there was no danger whatsoever of the cable becoming foul.

Keeping a clear anchor. In non-tidal waters, the ship would always ride to leeward of her anchor. If the wind direction changed, the anchor turned in the ground, 'following' the ship, provided the change of direction were not too abrupt, and that there were a steady pull on the cable. The only danger of fouling the anchor arose in periods of calm, if the vessel were allowed to drift over her anchor, and the cable fall slack. The same thing could happen at slack water in tidal waters, and, in addition, the anchor could be fouled if the ship made a complete rotation around the buoy. This may be made clearer by the following example: imagine a ship lying to the flood, to the North of her anchor. When the tide changes, and starts to set to the southward, the ship is not simply allowed to drift down over it, with a slack cable, but set over to the eastward, until she rides to the ebb, that is South of the anchor. At the next change of tide, suppose she is set over to the westward, until she lies tide-rode in her original position, having made a complete circle round the buoy. If the cable were not taut enough during this rotation to oblige the anchor to turn in the ground, there might, at this point, have developed a turn of the cable around the arm, and the anchor will now be liable to drag. This would not occur if the anchor had turned properly in the ground by keeping a pull on the cable; nor would it happen had the vessel been 'tended' on the same side of her anchor, say to the eastward, at each change of tide. This explains why the rules for keeping a clear anchor reduced to two simple precepts: keep a taut cable, and always tend on the same side of the anchor (Totten, 254).

Difference between hemp and chain cable. The seaman of 1800 was rather more preoccupied with his ground-tackle, than was the case later on. He wished to minimise the damage to his hemp cable that arose from allowing it to scrape across the bottom, especially if the latter were rocky. In particular, an effort was made to avoid dragging a bight of cable around, at change of tide. This was yet another reason for keeping a taut cable, the cable being hove in to the windward service, riding the weather tide, and veered again, riding lee tide. If there

Foul anchor
A Anchor fouling on the ground; **B** and **C** anchors coming up foul; **D** how fouling occurs.

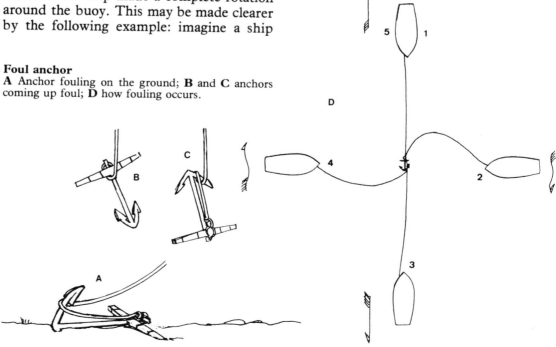

were no wind at slack water, the cable was hove in, until the anchor was a-peak, a temporary canvas service being clapped on the cable, in the hawse. As a matter of fact, the opportunity was usually taken to 'sight the anchor' at this time, making absolutely sure that it was clear, by heaving it up to the bows, and then letting it go again (Lever, 103).

Chain cable was relatively impervious to damage from being dragged across the bottom, and there was not the same necessity for alternately heaving in and veering it, nor was it so necessary to keep a taut cable. It was still advisable, however, that the ship be tended on the same side of the anchor, since the chain otherwise could end up making a loose circle around the upper arm. If this tightened up later, with the onset of blowing weather, the anchor would be pulled out of the ground, and start to drag. With chain, the vessel rode to the point where the cable touched the ground, rather than pivoting round the anchor itself, as was the case with hemp. This explains why an anchor-buoy was considered vitally necessary with a hemp cable, while its use was often omitted with chain.

Wind and tide. Of the two forces, the tide was usually predominant. The outcome depended not only on their relative strengths, but also on the vessel. 'A loaded ship will ride best to windward of her anchor, because she has more hold of the tide, and less of the wind. For the opposite reason, a light ship will not ride to windward at all. In all weathers, a vessel should be kept to leeward of her anchor, so long as she will ride so' (Potter, 12). During the tending process, the ship would very often be heading away from the anchor-buoy, the cable growing on one or other quarter. When firmly wind- or tide-rode, the cable was, almost always, growing ahead or rather on one or other bow.

Wind arrows. In these old accounts, the wind was represented by a fully feathered arrow, and the current by a half-fletched arrow. For the most part, the wind-arrow points in the direction the wind is going. However, some older authorities, for example Potter, chose to show the wind-arrow weather-cock fashion, that is, pointing in the dirction from which the wind is coming. This reflects the fact that a 'North wind' *comes* from the North, while a current 'setting to leeward' goes in that direction.

Scope. The quantity of cable 'veered', or 'stuck out' – the former being much the commoner expression – was called the 'scope', and this would be at least three times the depth of water, and more with strong

tides, or bad weather; too short a scope, and the cable would be pulling upwards, in such a way as to disengage the fluke, and 'start' the anchor. The 'flatter' or more horizontal, the pull on the anchor-ring, the better. Hence, with hemp there was always a minimum of 45 fathoms veered, while with chain, 30 fathoms might be adequate in the same circumstance. The greater the scope, the greater the elastic resiliency of the system, and the flatter the pull.

Riding leeward tide, a hemp cable was veered, until the 'second service' came in the hawse, or the 'leeward service' if the wind were really fresh. Riding windward tide, the cable was under less strain, and to keep it taut, it required to be hove in to the 'windward service', that is about half a cable's length, 45 or 50 fathoms. A taut cable prevented the hemp being cut and chafed on the bottom, and also ensured that the anchor turned in the ground, to lie in the proper direction. Chain cable would not be kept taut, because it was so heavy, and thus, much of the time, the vessel rode to the bight of the cable, rather than the anchor itself. Although chain is inherently non-elastic, it hung down in a curve from the hawse to the bottom, and also often lay in a horizontal curve on the ground. Consequently, as the vessel tended, the first effect of a sudden pull was to straighten out the chain, so easing the jar on the anchor itself.

Giving a sheer. To keep the vessel steady, and the cable taut, she was 'sheered' away from her anchor, using appropriate sail and helm. The cable acted as if it were towing the ship through the water, hence putting the helm to port, sheered the hull over to starboard. It was immaterial whether the bow or stern pointed towards the anchor-buoy. The important thing was to keep the cable on the stretch. Conversely, if too much sheer were applied, an unnecessary strain was put on the cable. (See also the section on 'Breaking the sheer' below).

Wind athwart, or across the tide. In this situation – say wind from the North, tide

setting East and West – there is no distinction between lee and weather tide. With either tide setting, the ship would lie more or less astream of it, and at slack water, she would swing dead to leeward of her anchor, that is, to the South. There was bitter argument about the relative merits of 'sheering to windward', or 'sheering to leeward' during the set of the tide in this situation. To keep the vessel steady, it was best if the cable were kept taut, by giving the ship a sheer, putting the helm over, one way or the other. In the coal trade, it was the custom to 'sheer to windward', by putting the helm somewhat a lee, and so riding out the tide to the northward, or weather side, of the East-West line. Taylor (12) says that this was 'the practice of the most informed seamen'. At the change of tide, the mizzen topsail was sheeted home aback, and the ship swung to leeward keeping a tight cable, 'backing around', as it was called. Nichelson 'bagpipes' the mizzen to the same end; that is to say, the mizzen sheet was hauled forward, and to weather, to make a back sail out of it. If the wind was light, appropriate canvas was set, the most useful sails being the fore topmast staysail and mizzen topsail. If the wind blew hard, the yards were trimmed just as if the corresponding sail were set.

Taylor (13) argued that by sheering to windward, the ship was held steadier, and less liable to break her sheer, pointing out that a ship with unattended rudder has a natural inclination to fly to, rather than fall off: 'Hence, if the helm should be a-weather, or the ship shore to leeward, I cannot conceive how she can lie still for a moment, but will stagger, if I may be allowed to make a low comparison, like a goose cut on the head.' Furthermore, as the ship worked her way towards the wind's eye, in the lulls, the spring acquired by the cable during the sheer to windward, eased the ship when struck by the next gust. Sheered to windward, the bow pointed somewhat in that direction, hence the mizzen topsail would usually take aback at the end of the tide, and could be used

Sheering
a to windward; **b** to leeward.

back the vessel around.

William Hutchinson (108), on the other hand, is equally emphatic that the ship should be 'sheered to leeward', by putting the helm a-weather during the set of the tide, pointing out that this practice results in a swing during the tending process of less than 180 degrees, hence less damage to the cable as it drags around at slack water. Furthermore, he claims that adopting the contrary method often results in the cable getting under the anchor-stock. If sheered to leeward, the stern tended to swing up towards the wind, as the tide slackened, and hence, in tending, rather than backing the mizzen topsail, it was more practical to use the fore topmast staysail to shoot the vessel ahead. As the tide started to turn, the staysail was set, sheet to windward, and, the helm being a-weather, the ship was sheered down directly to leeward of her anchor, gradually swinging round to the next tide, when the sail was stowed (Glascock, 287).

Lever (104) remains neutral, on this point, remarking that sheering to leeward was usual in the Royal Navy: 'It would be endless to relate the disputes which have arisen on the best methods of sheering a ship with the wind right across the tide: men of great experience having given their decided opinions on each side.' Some later opinion (for example Glascock) favours Hutchinson's view, while Potter and Mossel (III, 202) agree with Taylor.

Wind up and down the tide. Lever and Gower give fairly clear descriptions of how things were managed in this circumstance. Let us assume the wind comes from the North, the leeward tide, therefore, setting to the South, and the windward to the North. Riding to leeward tide, there is no danger of breaking the sheer. Even if wind or tide should slacken, the vessel will still ride to a tight cable. During the set of the lee tide, the helm is amidships, the yards braced sharp up, if there is much wind, or left square otherwise.

Tending to windward. As the tide begins to slacken, and the cable commences to be in danger of rubbing on the bottom, it is hove in, so that the weather service is in the hawse, by the time of slack water. In preparation for tending to windward, the ship is given a sheer, either easterly, or westerly, towards the end of the tide, let us say towards the East. This is done by putting the helm a-port, which shifts the vessel bodily to the eastward, and swings the port side towards the wind. The latter tendency can be aided by pointing the afteryards to the wind, backing the head-yards and spritsail yard, and setting the fore

topmast staysail with the sheet to windward. As the tide continues to ease, the vessel, cast for the port tack, is shot ahead and over to the eastward, by bracing all the yards full, and hauling aft the starboard staysail sheet. The anchor-buoy is now on the weather, or port, quarter, the ship bearing, say, East-South-East from it. As the weather tide gathers strength, it pushes the ship further to the northward, and swings the keel over the cable, so that the anchor-buoy comes to lie on the lee, or starboard quarter. At this time, the ship is lying roughly East of the buoy, more or less athwart the tide, with the helm of little use. Lever and Gower shift the helm a-lee, or starboard, just before the stern swings over the cable.

The afteryards are kept full, the headyards being pointed to the wind, and the staysail hauled down. This position of the helm, and configuration of the yards is calculated to allow the bow to approach the wind but this tendency is resisted by the cable and, as the vessel drifts further to the North, the arrangement continues to keep the cable taut.

The sequence could also be explained in this way. As long as the ship is to leeward of the East-West line, the bow is held away from the wind by keeping the helm a-weather, and the fore topmast staysail set. Once the vessel drifts to the weather of this line, the bow is allowed to come to the wind, by putting the helm a-lee, hauling down the staysail, and pointing the headyards to the wind. The aim, in both cases, is to keep the cable on the stretch. The drift to windward continues until the ship lies directly to windward of her anchor. Exactly how far to the eastward and northward the ship lies, depends on her state of lading and the relative strength of wind and tide. With a strong windward tide, she will lie almost to the North of her anchor. If the wind increases, or the tide diminishes, she is forced over to the eastward, and with a very strong wind, she might indeed be kept somewhat to leeward of the anchor-buoy, say bearing East-South-East from it.

Riding to windward. Even though firmly tide-rode during the course of the windward tide, a sheer in one or other direction was necessary for two reasons: firstly, should the wind drop away, in order that the ship would be, at still water, firmly either to East or West of the anchor, and not right on top of it; secondly, with the gusting and lulling of the wind, the vessel would plunge about uneasily from one side to the other if the helm were amidships. In the example given, the bow is pointing something to the East of due South, and hence it will be best if the vessel ride to her starboard cable, helm a-starboard,

sheered to port. This will keep the cable clear of the cutwater, and avoid chafe. If the port anchor were down, it would be best, while tending to windward, if she were shot over to the westward, and sheered to that side during the windward tide.

Tending to leeward. The vessel has ridden the weather tide helm a-starboard, afteryards braced as for the port tack, headyards as for the starboard. As the weather tide slackens, the sheer given the ship by this configuration of yards and helm, and the wind astern, cause her to work over to the eastward, eventually coming something to the leeward of the East-West line. The anchor-buoy initially bears fine on the starboard quarter. A vessel lying to her anchor, in this fashion, with the wind aft, and the cable end-on, is said to be 'riding trade' (Gower, 86; Romme, 246). The Dutch expression *in de lens liggen* is used in the same way. As the tide slackens further, the stern will swing over the cable, bringing the buoy on the weather, or port quarter, and the ship can be set ahead, by bracing full the head-yards, hauling the starboard braces aft, the helm now being put to port. Once she has swung so that the wind is just abaft the beam, the fore topmast staysail can be set, to help shoot her ahead, push the bow off the wind, and keep the cable tight. The lee tide now increasing, the ship continues to swing round

Tending to windward: wind N.

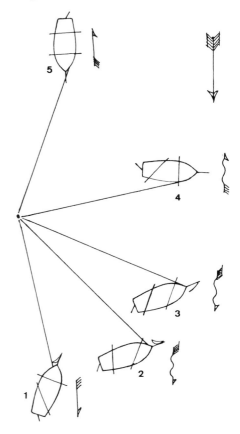

1.

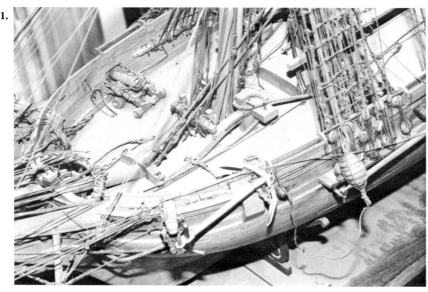

2.

1. Model of a small Dutch warship, showing anchor cathead and anchor buoy, bitts, chain and hemp cab and stoppers. (Courtesy Prins Hendrik Mariti Museum, Rotterdam)

2. Model showing bower and sheet anchors. Note t tumblers for the sheet anchor, and the way the stock painted to match the ship's side. Chain ring and sh painters are fitted to the bower. (Courtesy Nors Marinemuseet, Horten)

3. *Vasa*'s cathead. Note that it projects forward rath than laterally, as was the case later on. (Author's pho courtesy *Vasa* Varvet and Marine Dir Gunn Schoerner RSN)

4. An East Indiaman (in two positions) coming to anch off Penang, painted by Thomas Whitcombe, 1821. T vessel is shown on the right, shortening sail a beginning to round up into the wind. She has anchor on the left, with the hands furling topsails and cours as the backed mizzen topsail assists the veering of t cable. (Courtesy Richard Green Galleries, London

4.

until dead to leeward of her anchor, when the yards are squared, or pointed to the wind, depending on its strength, the staysail hauled down, and the helm righted.

Shift of wind. Should the wind change while riding windward tide, say backing from North to North-West, there will be no difficulty in tending to leeward, keeping the ship over to the eastward of the anchor. Were the wind to veer to North-East, and blow strongly, it might be necessary to tend round to the westward, comforting oneself with the thought that the cable would be well taut, and the anchor turning in the ground (Mossel, III, 200). If the wind were not too violent, it might be possible to sail across the tide, and continue to tend to the eastward, keeping the ship on the same side of the anchor as before. Similar considerations applied to situations where the direction of the tidal current changed during the course of the tide.

Wind a few points across the tide. Potter considers the most common case, where the wind is neither directly athwart, nor yet up and down the tide. Suppose the tides run East and West and the wind is from the North-West. The tide setting to the West is then 'windward' tide, that setting to the East 'leeward'. However, it will be seen that, in tending, the ship may be sheered either round to the southward, that is to 'leeward', or sheered up to the northward, that is to 'windward'. Potter felt the method of handling depended to a great extent upon the weather, and he describes the following four cases.

Riding to leeward, in moderate weather. The ship, riding to the last of the leeward tide, which is setting East, is given a sheer to leeward, by putting the helm a-starboard. When the tide is done, she lies athwart, to the South-East of her anchor. The staysail is set to help her away from the anchor, and when the weather tide makes, and the stern comes over the cable, the helm is shifted a-port, and she gradually comes astream of her anchor, where she is held sheered to leeward by a few spokes of the port helm, during the weather tide. If the current and the action of the helm is not sufficient to maintain the sheer, the staysail in set in addition. When the weather tide is slackening, a broad sheer is given to leeward, by putting the helm hard a-port, and the ship set ahead with the staysail. The stern goes over the cable, as the lee tide makes, and she thwarts the tide, whereupon the helm is shifted to starboard, and she gradually drops astream of her anchor, as before.

It often depended on local knowledge of the quirks of wind and tide, as to the best way of managing things. Potter (23) refers to the fact that in Yarmouth Roads the first of the flood tide sets South-South-West, while the last of the flood sets South. It might seem a matter of indifference which way the helm is put in a vessel riding windward tide, with a South-South-West wind, but with the helm a-starboard she will continue to ride to windward as the tide comes southerly in its after set; with the helm a-port, on the other hand, she would be riding to leeward.

Riding to leeward in heavy weather. If the vessel is riding to the weather tide, and the North-West wind increases, she will, instead of lying to the westward of her anchor, forge ahead, and ride with a broad sheer to the tide, almost due South of it, heading East. The yards are pointed to the wind, that is to say trimmed as if for the starboard tack, and the helm a-port. If the wind increase still further, or the tide slacken, she drives ahead still further, coming South-East of her anchor, heading about East-South-

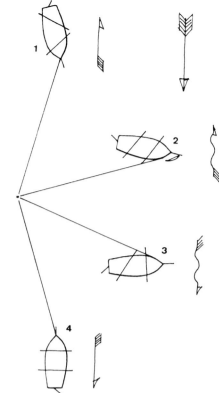

Tending to leeward: wind N.

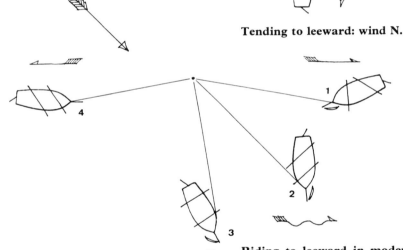

Riding to leeward in moderate weather: wind NW.

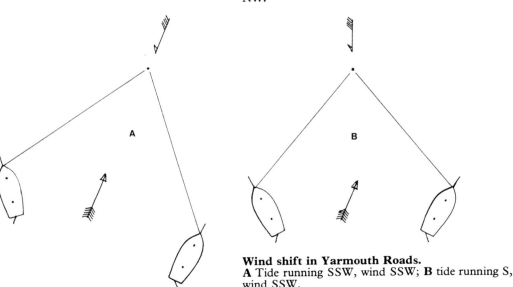

Wind shift in Yarmouth Roads.
A Tide running SSW, wind SSW; **B** tide running S, wind SSW.

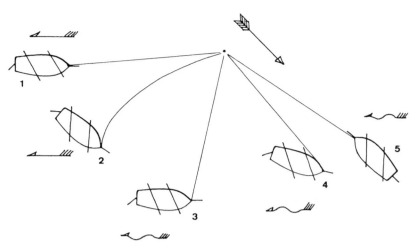

Riding to leeward in heavy weather: wind NW.

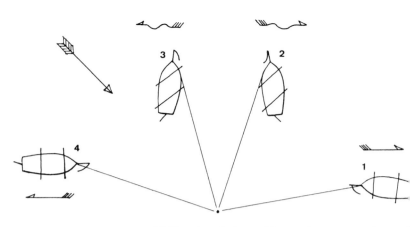

Riding to windward in moderate weather: wi‍ NW.

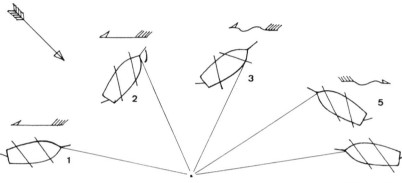

Riding to windward in heavy weather: wind N‍

East, with the wind on the weather quarter. In this position a deeply laden vessel is very likely to break her sheer, fill the yards and go searching off to the South or South-West, taking her anchor with her. A vessel riding high would be less firmly in the grip of the tide, and would swing head to wind.

Riding to windward in moderate weather. Again, imagine the ship riding lee tide. As the tide slackens, the helm is put to port, and the staysail set with the sheet to port, giving her a sheer to windward. The staysail, sheet shifted to starboard, is then used to set her ahead and athwart the current, perhaps adding additional fore and aft canvas to achieve this. When the stream makes to windward, the stern will drift over the cable. The helm is shifted to starboard, and she will gradually fall astream of the anchor, where the helm is eased to allow her to ride with a sheer to windward during the windward tide. If the stream is not strong enough to hold the cable taut, the staysail is kept set during the tide. As the tide slackens, the helm is put hard a-starboard, and she is sheered well up to windward, so that when the lee tide starts to make, she will swing round well to the north-ward of her anchor. Getting her stern over the cable, she gradually falls astream of the anchor to ride out the lee tide.

Riding to windward in heavy weather. Potter indicates a preference for managing things in this way: if the vessel is riding the weather tide, lying astream – that is to the westward of her anchor – and the North-West wind increases in force, she will tend to break her sheer and drift over the anchor; to prevent this, the staysail is set and the yards filled, braced as for the port tack, to sheer her up until she lies roughly North-North-East of the anchor, heading about North-East, helm a-starboard, afteryards filled, braced as for the port tack, forward yards abox. She now lies quite securely, hove to, in a manner

of speaking, the wind on the port beam, the tide on the starboard bow, the cable growing on the starboard quarter, restraining her from shooting ahead, 'considerably eased of its strain by the counteracting effect of wind and tide'. If the wind abates, she will drop back to the westward. When the weather current slackens, the headyards are filled, and when she drifts over her cable, the helm is shifted, and she is allowed to drop back astream of the leeward setting current. Before the tide has reached its maximum strength, the cable is veered to the leeward service. The yards are left braced up, to minimise windage. At the end of the leeward tide, she is given a sheer up to windward, by putting the helm a-port, initially keeping the foreyards pointed to the wind.

This is the time to heave in the cable. While this is being done, it is important that she not break her sheer, and drift towards the anchor, momentarily thwarting in such a way as to get the cable caught on the cutwater or under the keel. 'Getting the rest of the cable in under her bottom, will neither lighten the labour, nor improve the copper.' says Potter.

As the weather tide makes, the yards are filled and the staysail set, to shoot her ahead until she brings the cable on the starboard qu‍arter, when the headyards are backed, and the helm shifted a-starboard. She will now be

in the 'hove-to' position mentioned earli‍ buoy on the starboard quarter and will so ri‍ out the weather tide, as long as the wi‍ continues to blow hard. If it eases, she w‍ fall astream of the weather tide.

The main reason for heaving in a hen‍ cable when riding to windward is to keep‍ taut, and prevent its chafing on the groun‍ With chain cable, the reason for doing so,‍ heavy weather, was somewhat different. T‍ ship could, in the situation just describe‍ ride to a long scope of cable, without harmi‍ it, but not so quietly as when it had be‍ shortened in. With chain, there would not l‍ a fixed point against which the cable cou‍ tighten, the ship riding to the bight of chai‍ rather than directly to the anchor itself.

Breaking the sheer. 'When a ship at anch‍ is forced by the wind or current from th‍ position in which she keeps her anchor mo‍ free of herself, and most firm in the groun‍ so as to endanger the tripping of her anch‍ she is said to break her sheer' (Blunt, 13).‍ the pull of the cable were abruptly exerted‍ right angles to the line of the anchor-shan‍ this might be sufficient to dislodge the low‍ fluke from the ground.

The most obvious example of breaking th‍ sheer occurred if the ship, at change of tid‍ were not tended, but simply allowed‍ 'tumble over her anchor'. Potter offers t‍

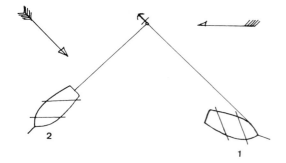

Breaking the sheer: wind NW.

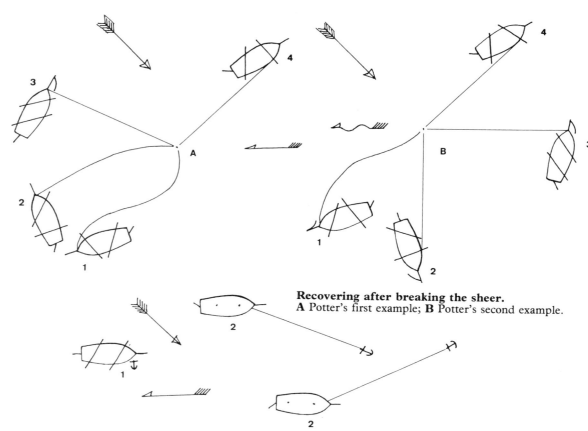

Recovering after breaking the sheer.
A Potter's first example; **B** Potter's second example.

Coming to anchor on a weather tide: wind NW.

following further examples. Suppose the wind from the North-West, the windward tide setting towards the West, the ship, sheered to leeward, is forced ahead by the wind so that she lies South-East of her anchor, heading East-South-East, cable growing under the port quarter, yards braced as for the starboard tack, pointed to the wind, helm a-port. A lightly loaded vessel in this situation would swing bow to wind, and although she would yaw about with the tide under the counter, yet she would be in little danger of breaking her sheer. With a deeply laden vessel, there is danger that she might break her sheer, drift directly westward under the influence of the current, and perhaps come to lie heading South-West, the cable leading directly astern. If this mishap seems imminent, no time is wasted getting the ship up to windward. Suppose her to be heading East, wind and buoy on the port quarter, yards braced to the wind; that is, as for the starboard tack. The helm is shifted, the afteryards swung around, so pushing the stern to leeward and turning the ship so she is heading roughly North-East. The staysail is set, and the headyards swung so that she can be sailed ahead to leeward of the buoy, so that she comes to lie North-East of her anchor.

Should she break her sheer and get down to the South-West of her anchor, Potter (24) suggests two methods of recovery. During the strength of tide, it may be possible to swing her around, head to wind. Suppose the ship heading West-South-West, South-West of the anchor, the headyards are braced to the wind, and the afteryards backed, so that the stern swings round to leeward, and the vessel comes to head North-North-East. She is then sailed up towards the North-East, on the weather side of the buoy, using the staysails, and keeping the yards filled, as for the port tack. Alternatively, the ship is boxed off and 'wore' around, stern to wind. Thus, suppose her South-West of the anchor, the headyards are backed, the afteryards pointed to the wind, and the staysail set aback, to push the head round until she heads South-

East. Then, putting the helm a-starboard and filling the yards as for the port tack, she is sailed up across the tide, on the lee side of the buoy, ending up once more North-East of the anchor. This method would work better if the tide were not so strong. These manoeuvres were difficult with chain, but fairly readily done with a hemp cable, shortened up so that the anchor would turn in the ground, following the movements of the vessel. Taylor (24) offers the following 'Caution respecting the Anchor-Watch':

If at any time, the anchor watch, presuming on their own knowledge, should wind the ship, or suffer her to break her sheer without calling the mate, he should immediately, or the very first opportunity, oblige the crew to heave the anchor in sight; which will prevent the commission of the like fault again: for besides the share of trouble the watch will have, the rest of the crew will blame them for neglecting their duty.

It is surprising that there is no foreign idiom which exactly translates 'break the sheer', an expression in use at least since 1792. 'Sheer' is being used in the sense of 'deviate', or 'swerve', and although probably deriving in the same way as 'shear', 'to cut', it may owe something to Dutch *gieren*, 'to yaw'. Mainwaring (223) refers to 'sheering home the anchors, that is draw them home'; Bobrik talks of 'sheering the ship to her anchor' in

weighing, using sail to sheer the ship up towards her anchor, to facilitate heaving in. **Coming to in a tideway.** Potter considers the situation where the wind is a few points across the tide. Suppose the tide is setting East and West with wind from the North-West. Coming in to anchor, with a weather tide, the decision has to be made whether to sheer to leeward or to windward. Imagine the vessel stemming the weather tide, which is setting to the West, the wind on the port quarter. If to sheer to leeward, the port, or weather anchor is let go, the helm being put hard up and the staysail set sheet to windward. Upon clewing up, she will ride with the helm a-weather, and the cable sheered clear of cutwater and copper. If to sheer to windward, the starboard anchor would be dropped, to keep the cable clear of the bows. The square sails are clewed up, and the staysail kept set after the anchor is gone, sheering the vessel up to windward.

If the lee tide were setting, turning up into the wind might endanger the windlass and risk parting the cable at the moment of bringing to, since the vessel would be swept back under the combined influence of wind and tide. Potter suggests easing the jerk by wearing around, and putting the helm up when the anchor is let go. Suppose the vessel coming in from the West, the helm is put up and

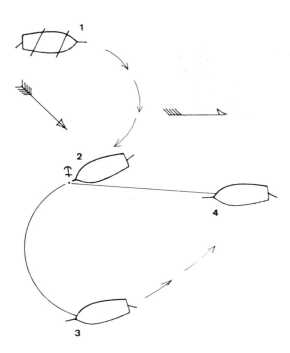

Coming to anchor on a lee tide: wind NW.

she is worn round until heading roughly West-South-West, wind roughly abeam. The starboard anchor is let go, the helm shifted a-starboard, and a good scope of chain is laid out in a bight across the tide. This is straightened out, as the vessel drops back astream of the anchor, without a violent jolt.

MOORING

More than one anchor. It might be supposed that if one anchor was good, several were even better. In fact, in blowing weather, a ship was much safer lying to one anchor with a 'shot' of three cables, rather than three anchors, each with one cable. In the latter case, several factors contributed to the lack of security. Firstly, the strain was likely to come on one anchor at a time, rather than on all three simultaneously, perhaps resulting in that cable parting. Furthermore, the pull was less horizontal, with a short, as compared to a long, cable. Lastly, the elasticity of the cable was proportional to its length, and hence the greater the scope, the better.

Mooring. 'A ship is not said to be *moored*, with less than two anchors aground' (Mainwaring, 189). If a single anchor were dragging, a vessel might drop a second, and have 'two anchors ahead'. This was not usually referred to as 'mooring', this term usually being restricted to this situation where she was anchored 'with a cable each way', riding midway between her anchors. A ship at single anchor took up a great deal of space in an anchorage, since she could swing in a great circle about her anchor, and had to

be 'tended' to avoid fouling her anchor, at still water. By dropping one anchor in the direction of flood, and another in the direction of ebb, the ship being between them, although her bow pointed now this way, now that, the ship herself remained in almost the same position, and this was the best method to follow in a crowded roadstead.

Choice of anchor. In bad weather, it was best if the heavier anchor were laid out towards the point from whence the strongest wind and highest seas were expected. If it became necessary, both cables could be veered away, just as when riding at single anchor. Suppose a vessel were moored with 50 fathoms of cable on each anchor. She can veer away on the windward cable, until she has 130 fathoms out, heaving in, and then veering on the second cable, until she has 30 fathoms of the latter out, both anchors now lying to windward, the longer scope on the best bower, or heavier anchor. Likewise, in an estuary, the best bower was laid upstream, since the river current would augment the ebb, but oppose the flood.

Line of the anchors. If the wind were coming from a point at right angles to the line in which the anchors were laid out, it might, at first sight, be imagined that 'riding to a span' of this sort, with an anchor on either bow, the ship would be safer than if riding to one cable. In fact, experience and theory demonstrated that the ship was more secure riding at long scope to a single anchor, in the appropriate direction, than by two short cables growing very broad on the bows, not in line with the oncoming wind and sea. The tauter the mooring, the worse the situation. A geometric proof of this proposition was offered by Tinmouth, and is quoted with approval by many writers (Murphy, 35; Nicholls, 399; Potter, 26). Imagine a ship subjected to a gale blowing across the line of mooring. If the angle subtended between the cables is 160 degrees, the tension on each cable is three times that which would have

existed in a single cable ahead, one anchor to windward. If cable is veered until the angle is 150 degrees, the tension is twice as great, and if the angle were 120 degrees, the tension is the same. Even in the latter case, the ship is worse off than with one cable, since she is subjected to the weight of two cables dragging her bows down into the sea (Nares, 133).

Dropping the second anchor in a tideway. The vessel might be moored after having ridden at single anchor for some time, or both anchors might be let go immediately upon coming in from sea. In the first case, let us suppose that it was intended to ride to the alternate ebb and flood, 60 fathoms of each cable each way. If we suppose the ebb tide to be setting, and 60 fathoms of cable already out, a further 60 fathoms of the riding cable were ranged on deck, the stoppers were let go, and the additional range veered away round the bitts. Sixty fathoms of the other cable were now ranged on the other side of the deck, and preparations made for dropping the second anchor, and heaving in the first cable. By sheering the vessel one way or the other with the helm, some control could be exercised as to the exact position in which the second was dropped. When the ship lay to a scope of 120 fathoms on the first cable, the second anchor was let go, and the ship warped forward again towards her original position. On one side of the deck, 60 fathoms of the first cable were hove in, while, on the other, 60 fathoms of the second cable were veered. If the current were strong, it might be decided to await the turn of the tide, and make use of the stream, rather than trying to heave in against it. When in the desired location, both cables were bitted and stoppered. If, for some reason, the ship could not be manoeuvred into the proper position to drop the second anchor, by using the tide and helm, it might be necessary to carry the second anchor out with the longboat, or kedge the ship into the appropriate spot. almost a full cable were used on both anchors, so that the splice came between the bitts and

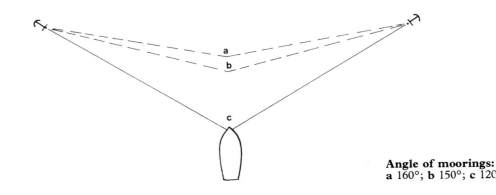

**Angle of moorings:
a** 160°; **b** 150°; **c** 120°

the main hatch, the process of clearing hawse was facilitated, as we shall see. With both anchors down, the sheet cable was bent to the ganger, so that a third anchor was ready for letting go, should some accident befall the other cables.

Running, or flying moor. The best account of the procedure is found in Totten.

Making a flying moor, which is one of those operations requiring great precision and promptness, where the failure in any one part must thwart the whole, and preclude the possibility of its proper performance – I call your attention to, because it may be, and sometimes is resorted to – observing, also, that an officer should never subject himself to the possibility or probability of failing in any manoeuvre, out of the common practice, where the failure may be owing to any other cause than his incapacity or want of judgment. It should never be attempted in a single-decked vessel, where there is not a separate deck to work the cables on. This manoeuvre is sometimes performed by officers, and with brilliant success, even in single-decked ships. I only take this opportunity of recommending to you, as a general rule, never to hazard your professional reputation on the chances of any event so doubtful as the satisfactory performance of this (Totten, 246).

In a single-decked frigate, the decks were already encumbered with braces, topsail halliard falls, and so on, at the moment of coming to anchor, hence the inadvisability of further adding to the confusion with two ranges of cable, the messenger, etc. Even with the cables ranged on the gundeck, clear of the activity on the upper deck, the men holding off the messenger, and the party ranging the second cable were already in each other's way.

Totten (247) describes two methods, the first of which was to approach the anchorage in the usual way, throw everything flat aback, run up into the wind and drop the weather anchor. Then with yards squared, drop back veering away a double range on the first cable, drop the second anchor, and heave in on the first, veering the second until there was an equal scope on each cable. The second method was the real 'flying moor'. The ship came in boldly, both cables ranged on deck, everything was clewed up, the weather anchor was dropped and enough headway kept on to 'sail out' the whole range of the cable, finally running up into the wind, and letting go the lee anchor. The ship then was allowed to drop back, veering the lee cable, heaving in on the weather, until she had an equal scope on both cables. This could be done with the wind and tide aft, or wind

abeam. Clearly this was a spectacular manoeuvre if it came off, but prone for many reasons, to go awry in the execution. Nicholls (391) considered that it was necessary to use this method at slack water, when coming in to moor, with the wind across the tide. If there were a tideway, it was best to drop the upstream anchor first, and drift back, rather than letting go the downstream anchor first, and attempting to sail up against the tide. Boyd (366) felt that the objection to the running moor was the 'great strain which is necessarily brought upon every article concerned in bringing the ship up'.

Anchor bearings. Upon mooring, compass-bearings were taken of prominent seamarks, on the shore, soundings taken and a 'drift-lead' dropped over the side. These precautions were taken in case the vessel should start to drag her anchor, and start dropping astern. In that eventuality, the drift-lead line would tend ahead, and in the case of chain, the vibration of the anchor bumping across the bottom might be transmitted up the cable. Making up one's mind as to whether or not the anchor was dragging or 'coming home', was not always easy, for example if the vessel were sheering about wildly during a gale. As insurance, the sheet anchor was always kept ready to let go if there were any doubt about the bowers. An anchor that had started to drag was less certain to 'bite', than when dropped in the first place. This was particularly true in a heavy clay ground, where the arm could come up 'shod' (encased in a ball of muck). Thus the good seaman always veered a scope of cable adequate enough to obviate the least possibility of the anchor starting to drag, rather than trusting

to its somehow managing to dig in again, the second time around.

Mooring a fleet. Mooring was particularly desirable where a fleet was involved, since the admiral could, in this way, keep his ships closer together, and under better control, than when they lay at single anchor, scattered all over the roadstead, a greater distance apart. The best configuration was to have the line of bearing of the ships at right angles to the prevailing wind; that is to say, if gales were to be expected from the North, the anchors were laid out on a line of mooring running East and West, the ships bearing East and West from the admiral. If it came on to blow, from the North, all could veer away on their cables without fear of fouling the hawse of another vessel. If moored in two lines, the vessels of the second line positioned themselves on the bow or quarter of the corresponding vessels in the first line, so that if cable were veered by a ship in the weather line, she would drop back between two vessels of the leeward line (Nares, 134).

Clear hawse and open hawse. Imagine a ship moored between her starboard anchor lying due South, and her port anchor lying due North, the tides running in a North-South line. Lying to the starboard anchor, the port cable will drop slack, straight down from the hawsepipe. If now, at change of tide, the vessel swings so that the stern points to the West, the cables will be clear of each other, and she will be said to have 'open hawse to the East'. Were she to swing the other way, stern pointing to the East, the keel would swing over the port cable. The cables are now leading the 'wrong' way, and she is said to have 'foul hawse', have a 'cross' in the

Fouling hawse
A open hawse; B foul hawse; C cross in the hawse; D elbow; E round turn; F round turn and an elbow.

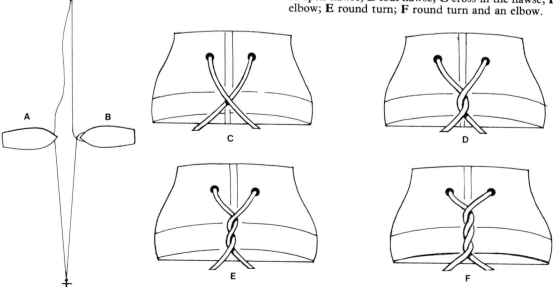

cables, or 'ride cross-hawse' now lying at sixteen points from where she had open hawse. The starboard cable is lying on top, or forward, of the port cable. Continuing the swing another eight points, in the same direction, she will lie to the other tide with almost an 'elbow', which could be cleared by dipping the starboard or non-riding cable under the other one once. If she continues to rotate in the same direction at the next slack water, she will have a 'full elbow', now lying directly opposite to her position when she had a 'cross'; another sixteen points rotation, and she will have a 'round turn', now being in the position where she earlier had a cross; yet another half turn, and she will have a 'round turn and an elbow'; yet another, and she will have 'two round turns', and so on. 'It is not uncommon to see large ships, with two round turns in their cables, a disgusting sight to an active seaman' (Lever, 107). It will be noted that the events in the sequence are named for the situation at slack water, rather than when riding to the next tide.

If one ship drifted down, or anchored, on the bows of a vessel already anchored, the former was said to 'foul the hawse' of the latter. Having been given a 'foul berth', in this way, it was most prudent for the leeward ship to get her anchor up, and find a better spot if the intruder could not be persuaded to move, since, if the weathermost vessel dragged her anchor in a gale, it might occasion the loss of both vessels.

Slack moorings. If there were too great a scope out on the cables, not only would the vessel shift her berth more than necessary at change of tide, but she could get the cables twisted without being aware of it, the turns being taken below the surface. On receiving unexpected orders to get to sea, a 'clear hawse' ship was manifestly in a much better position than with a round turn in her cables. The question 'How's the hawse?' was therefore often put to the officer of the deck. 'I have seen and heard of numberless cases with rather slack moored ships, commencing to clear hawse, as they supposed, to take one turn out of the cables, and finding perhaps four or five, instead of one' (Liardet, 64), the log, during the period the ship was moored, no doubt, indicating that the hawse was at all times 'clear'. Liardet describes a simple telltale which obviated this particular problem. The ends of a piece of silk thread were gummed to the periphery of the compass-card, at the compass-bearings of the anchors, and its mid-point gummed under the centre of the glass cover. As the ship swung round the card, which remained steady, any turns which developed in the cable, were

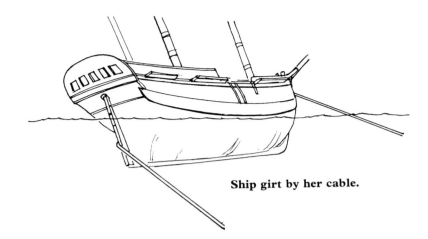

Ship girt by her cable.

reproduced by the twisting of the threads.
Taut mooring. It was also possible for cables to be too tight. The cable that the ship is riding to is unavoidably exposed to the strain of wind and tide. However, if the other cable is also on the stretch, gratuitous additional stress is applied to the riding cable. A vessel moored with an acceptable scope on her cables at low water or half-tide, may find that she is moored too taut at high water. Imagine once more the small bower, or port anchor, to the North, and the ship riding to the best bower, or South anchor, by her starboard cable with a clear hawse, both cables taut, in fairly shallow water. If a breeze springs up from the North-West, on the starboard quarter, the heel, or sternpost, is forced against the port cable, and the stem prevented from swinging over to the eastward, and the ship is brought up all-standing, broadside to the wind, when she is described as being 'girt' (Mainwaring, 155). If the heel works clear, the cable rubs its way along the copper all the way forward to the cutwater. To free the ship, it is not sufficient to veer the port cable slowly, since this will just result in further damage to the copper. Rather, the appropriate length of cable is ranged on deck and let go, all at once, so it will fall straight down clear of the keel (Liardet, 140). It will be seen therefore that, when moored, it was best if the cables were kept neither too taut, nor too slack. In the event of a foul hawse if moored too taut, the turns occur close to the hawseholes, and the nip is very severe. If too slack, the turns occur unnoticed, below the surface, but are not so injurious to the cable (Boyd, 362).
Maintaining a clear hawse. If a moderately fresh breeze blows across the tide, the stern will always swing the other way at slack water. Thus, in the example given above, if the wind blows steadily from the East, the ship will always have a clear hawse. If it blows constantly from the West, she will infallibly get a cross in the hawse. Nowadays

this is not necessarily considered an ev[...] situation, in blowing weather: indeed, it is th[...] basis of the so-called 'hammerlock moor[...] which has the virtue of preventing the shi[...] yawing about as much as she would were th[...] hawse open, whatever devastation is wrough[...] on the paintwork of the bow (Crenshaw, 90[...] However, resuming the study of ou[...] example, if the wind continues from the sam[...] direction, the cross should be taken out at th[...] next tide, since she will swing back to the wa[...] she came. The difficulty is that winds ar[...] prone to shift at the end of the tide, and th[...] ship, rather than taking out the 'cross', migh[...] swing so as to convert it into an 'elbow'. Wit[...] the wind up and down the tide, the ster[...] could be canted in the desired direction wit[...] the helm and her canvas. Suppose the win[...] from the North, anchors North and South, [...] before, riding to the flood tide, the port cab[...] and the North anchor, she will maintain clea[...] hawse if the stern swing to the West. At th[...] end of the tide, sheer the stern in the desire[...] direction by putting the helm somewhat [...] port. In addition, the mizzen topsail is se[...] aback, the starboard yardarm braced som[...] what aft, and the jib hoisted with its she[...] hauled out to the topped up port sprits[...] yardarm, the sail aback. Once the ebb ti[...] commences, the ship swings round, stern [...] the West, and eventually rides to the win[...] ward tide, and the starboard cable. The sa[...] are got in, as soon as she has been cast in t[...] desired direction, and is in the grip of t[...] ebb. To swing her back the same way, at t[...] end of the ebb, the helm is put a-starboa[...] and she is set around with the filled mizz[...] topsail, starboard yardarm trimmed [...] Another method of ensuring the prop[...] swing was to run a line out to a neighbour[...] vessel, a suitable dolphin, or a kedge anch[...] laid out in the appropriate direction.
Mooring with a swivel. From the fo[...] going, it will be realised that the introduc[...] of the mooring-swivel must have been a gr[...] boon. This was a consequence of the gene[...]

usage of chain cable, and was introduced into the Royal Navy early in the nineteenth century, one pattern being known until quite recently as 'Sir Thomas Hardy's Pattern' (*Admiralty Manual of Seamanship* I, 1937). The swivel was attached to two pairs of chains, each a few links long. The method of putting on the swivel was virtually the same as that used today, and is well covered in modern seamanship texts (*Admiralty Manual of Seamanship* II, 1951, 407). The cables were unshackled, and made fast to the two outboard legs of the swivel. The inboard ends of the cables, now referred to as the 'bridles', were then shackled to the inboard legs of the swivel. The bridles were then middled, so that the strain came evenly on both, and veered until the swivel was just above the waterline. Suppose the ship moored and riding to the starboard cable, this was unshackled abaft the bitts and the swivel inserted, shackling one inboard leg, and one outboard leg, to the disconnected cable. A bight of the port cable was then hauled up, through the starboard hawsepipe, unshackled, and secured to the other two legs of the swivel. Both cables and swivel were then veered through the starboard hawsepipe. The cup of the swivel pointed up, so that it could be readily lubricated with tallow. In blowing weather, the swivel was veered away to the bottom, so that the ship rode to this fixed point, the pull on the anchors being almost horizontal. Under these circumstances, it was necessary to 'sight' the swivel from time to time, to clear it of stones and mud, and ensure that it was working properly. Boyd (368) indicates that sometimes only one bridle was used. To avoid unnecessarily encumbering the deck with yet a third cable, the inboard end of the cable left 'spare' was shackled to the ganger of the sheet anchor, in place of the sheet cable.

Swivel with a rope cable. I have one reference to this combination. Gower (96) describes the following method, using a cable 100 fathoms in length. The first anchor is dropped, and veered to 50 fathoms, and an eye lashed in the cable, to which the swivel is attached. A long bridle, perhaps the sheet cable, is brought out through an outer hawsehole, and bent to one of the inboard legs of the swivel. Bridle and cable are veered together, until the inboard end of the cable can be pulled clear of the hawsehole, and bent to the second anchor, which is then let go. The bridle is hove in until the swivel comes under the bows, whereupon a short bridle can be taken out through a hawsepipe on the other side, and secured to the swivel. A buoy-rope is bent to one of the anchors, so it can be

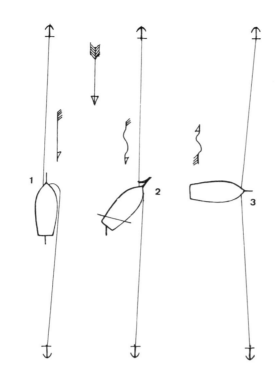

Maintaining a clear hawse: wind N.

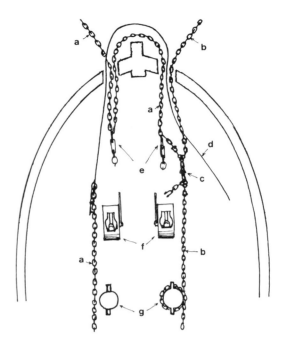

Fitting a mooring swivel.
a port cable; **b** starboard cable; **c** mooring swivel; **d** guide rope; **e** chain stoppers; **f** controllers; **g** chain riding bit.

1

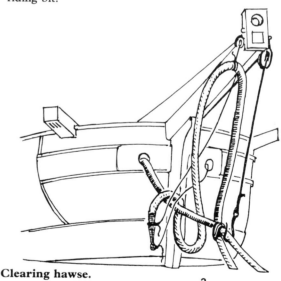

Clearing hawse.

2

weighed subsequently, in order to unmoor. This, says Gower, 'had better be slightly stopped along the cable, so that its end may be got at by under-running the cable, which will put it out of the way of being stolen'.

Clearing hawse. This was best done at slack water, which was in fact the optimum time for cable operations in general. Sometimes, in calm weather, it might be possible to get a turn out by running a hawser over to a neighbouring vessel, or other fixed point, or even by towing the stern around using boats. In an auxiliary powered vessel, by going slow ahead, or astern, the propeller could be used to give the stern a 'kick' around. To clear hawse by swinging, the stern had to go to-

wards the side of the cable that was on top (Knight, 167). Assuming these methods were not practical for some reason or other, it might be possible to insert the swivel, and then get the turns out of the chain, by using levers and whips (Boyd, 363). In the case of hemp cable, this last option was not practical, and it was necessary to engage in the formal operation of 'clearing hawse'.

Since the procedure would only be carried out at slack water, the vessel would be wind-rode, riding to the windward cable, and the clearing manoeuvre was therefore carried out with the lee cable. The cables were hove in until the turns were visible above the water, and a good lashing clapped on, to keep everything steady, preventing the turns riding down below the surface. A hawser was led through a block under the bowsprit, with a large 'fish-hook' bent to its end. This was engaged around the riding cable, just below the turns, and hauled in, to heave the turns well up above the water. If possible, a boat was brought under the bows, to facilitate the operation, otherwise men had to be lowered in clear-hawse breeches, or suspended with bowlines round their bodies. The lee, or non-riding, cable was unspliced, and the outboard end hauled out through its hawsehole, the bight being hauled up and suspended under the bowsprit. If the splice were some distance inboard from the bitts, it might be necessary to hang the extra cable in several bights, or loops, under the bowsprit. The end of the lee cable was dipped around the weather cable the appropriate number of times to get the turns out, then hauled in through its own hawsehole once more, and respliced. The other fore top bowline was used as a 'dip-rope' to guide the clearing cable. The fish-hook was removed, and the lashing cut, which allowed the turns to come out, as the lee cable was hove taut. There was some physical danger to the man actually cutting the lashing, since the cables tended to come apart with great violence, at that juncture. I think modern authorities would council taking the turns out, one at a time, rather than attempting to do so all at once (*Admiralty Manual of Seamanship* I, 1937, 343). All this was easier said than done, but we have tried to give a general idea of the method. Clear, well illustrated accounts are to be found in Lever (107), Le Compte (165), and Knight (168).

Mooring in a river. Mainwaring (188) distinguishes three methods of mooring in this situation, namely: 'alongst', one anchor upstream, the other downstream; 'athwart', or 'across', one anchor towards either shore; and 'water-shot', 'that is, as you would say, quartering, betwixt both, neither across the tide, nor alongst'. An enemy might attempt the destruction of a man-of-war moored in a river, by sending down fire-rafts, attempting to drift a pair of these, connected by a cable, down across the hawse, so that they swept round on either side of their victim, and set her on fire. Defence against this measure included the construction of a boom upstream, anchoring the ship's boats upstream, and adopting the second and third method of mooring referred to above. If moored 'alongst', the ship could depend only on the relatively ineffective influence of the rudder, to sheer herself clear of fire-rafts descending upon her. Moored athwart, she

could take more effective evasive action by hauling herself quickly across the stream.

Unmooring. This was the reverse of the mooring process, and once again involved heaving in one cable, while veering the other at the same time. The weather or riding cable was veered, to bring the ship back a-peak of the other anchor, which was then weighed. If the riding anchor had been weighed first, the ship would have drifted back, completely out of control, until brought up by the lee anchor, perhaps fouling her anchor in the process, and in any case it would have been necessary to heave her up against the wind or tide. Furthermore, by weighing the weather anchor last, the ship started her journey to weather of her position when moored, rather than to leeward. If tide-rode, the anchors would be weighed in whichever order was convenient; that is to say, non-riding anchor first (Nares, 245). In weighing the first anchor, it was important not to dissipate the efforts of the capstan, in hauling taut the riding cable; this would happen, if the latter had not been veered sufficiently. To make sure on this point, it was recommended that several fathoms of the riding cable be veered briskly, just before heaving in on the other cable, at the moment it was considered to be 'up and down' (Glascock, 164).

Disposition of crew for mooring and unmooring (based on Burney). The first and second parts of the forecastlemen rig the fish-davit and overhaul the cat-tackle fall, while the first parts of the quarterdeckmen deal with the fish-tackle. Nippers are applied by the first parts of the foretopmen, carried forward by the topboys, and taken off by the first parts of the maintopmen. If a messenger was not used, the same hands pay down the slack chain. The carpenters are responsible for attending at the capstan, messenger rollers, compressor and controller. The blacksmith attends the slip, and the armourer the pawl. Cable is veered by the second parts of fore and maintopmen. A party selected by the boatswain hoods cat and fish, while the buoy and buoy-rope is handled by the quarterdeck topsail sheet men. The gunner's mate of the side, and the next numbers belay the cat-fall, while it is stoppered by the forecastle topsail sheetmen of the watch below of the side. The same party stopper and belay the fish-fall and the fish-davit topping lift. The caulker and his mate rig and man the pump, while the capstan is manned by hands not otherwise stationed.

GENERAL PREPARATIONS FOR GOING TO SEA.

Full and detailed accounts of these preparations are to be found in Boyd (341), Totten (166), and Ulffers (252). Much depended on the weather to be expected: in light winds, the light yards and studdingsails would quickly be put to use, whereas in bad weather, gear of this sort was got down on deck, storm canvas got up from the sail-room, and every loose item carefully secured, before proceeding to sea, and exposing the vessel to the fury of the elements. Needless to say, sufficient stores, food, water, and munitions had to be aboard for the proposed voyage, the appropriate charts brought up to date by the navigator, and so on. We are however, focussing on those matters that required attention in the hours immediately preceding weighing anchor and putting to sea.

On deck. Braces, lifts, topsail halliards, tacks, sheets, and so on, were coiled down clear for running, with dry stoppers placed ready to aid in belaying them. If the topsail halliards were of new rope, they were well stretched to prevent their becoming 'cable laid', that is to say developing kinks when first used. Square-marks were worked on the lifts and braces, and by-the-wind marks on the braces. The lower booms were swung in and crutched, Jacob's ladders, etc which had been secured to them in harbour, were removed. Awnings, smoke-sail, and wind sails were stowed away in the sail-locker.

The log-line, sand-glass, deep-sea and hand lead-lines were brought on deck and their accuracy verified. In the chains, breast bands were secured for the leadsmen, and leadlines coiled down ready for use. Life buoys, grab-lines, Jacob's ladders were rigged in the mizzen channels, for access to the quarter-boats, and over the taffrail for the stern-boat. Junk-axes were sharpened, and secured in their beckets by the masts along with the life-buoy, and so on.

Aloft. Topgallant masts, topgallant and royal yards were sent up, masts and yards squared by setting up the stays, shrouds and backstays. Parrels, trusses, topmast and topgallant masts were slushed, and the covers were got off the fore and aft sails. Any defective ratlines were repaired so that the topmen could go aloft with confidence. The 'capping' on the ends of the shrouds was checked for signs of rot, and the lanyards of the deadeyes properly set up. Studding gear was rove off, and the studdingsails inspected and becketted in the rigging. The topgallant halliards were 'toggled', and the

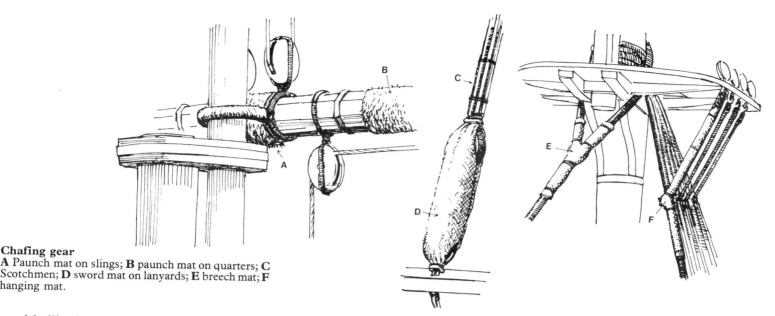

Chafing gear
A Paunch mat on slings; **B** paunch mat on quarters; **C** Scotchmen; **D** sword mat on lanyards; **E** breech mat; **F** hanging mat.

royal halliards set up, on what would be the weather side.

In the tops. The gear was coiled down, making sure that the lubber-hole covers were left clear because through these topgallant masts and yards were sent up and down. Tackles or 'handy-billys', and a heavy mallet (or 'top-maul'), its handle bent to a lanyard, were got ready. Prior to 1800, some seamen seized the foot of the topmast to the lower masthead, with a heel-rope, or *rot-tåg*, as Rosvall (90) calls it. This helped to support the cap in bad weather.

Chafing gear. The following list quote from Alston (178) gives an idea of the measures taken to ameliorate chafing aloft:

Paunch mats on the bunt of all yards between the yard and masts, well greased. A mat on the quarters of the topsail yards in wake of the rigging. Breeches mats on the collars of lower stays, although here and elsewhere, bamboo scotchmen are preferable, when they can be obtained. A mat on lower yards to protect the sail where it takes the stay, when braced up. A mat under each leechline block. Hanging mats, or a hide, on the lower rigging, where the yards bind, on topmast backstays for the same purpose, and in the wake of the staysail pendants, on the foremost swifter of the lower rigging where the foot of the courses take, and on the lanyards, where the sheet chafes, on the crossjack yardarms, for the preservation of the spanker, and on the horns of the crosstrees, for the protection of the topgallant sails. Battens should be permanently fitted on the sheet anchor stocks, to prevent the hoops cutting the fore sheets, or a mat should be laced on.

Paunch mats were placed on topsail and topgallant yards, not on the lower yards, in Nares' day. They were formed by 'thrumming'; that is, thrusting strands of

oakum through canvas, as in making a hooked rug. Earlier, in the days of the truss-parrel, they were found on the lower yards. 'That which we call a *Panch* are broad clouts [cloths] wove of thrums and sennit together, to save things from galling about the fore and main yards, at the ties, and also from the masts. And upon the boltsprit, loof, beakhead, or gunwale, to save the clews of the sails from galling or fretting' (Smith, 30). 'Paunch' here means 'protective covering', rather than 'belly'; like German *Panzer*, it derives ultimately from an Old French word signifying 'belly armour'.

The 'breeches mat' was so called because of its Y-shape, being placed at the collar of the stay, the 'legs' upwards. The 'hanging mat', referred to, covered the foremost futtock and continued downwards to be seized to the upper part of the foremost shroud, or 'swifter', in the wake of the lower yard, when it was braced up sharp. 'Sword mats', got their name because they were formed on a stick called a 'sword'. They were used to cover the deadeyes and lanyards, protecting them from the chafe of the foot of the course, its clew and sheet.

'Scotchmen' were wooden or bamboo laths, or battens, placed on the breast back-stays, and so on. Brady says 'Scotsmen' were more favoured in merchantmen than in men-of-war. Smyth suggests that these fittings were so called because of the notches scored, or 'scotched', in them to accept their seizings, rather than the Scot's reputation for dislike of wastefulness. The Swedish form *skotmatta* might suggest a connection with *skotte* ('Scot'), but I think it is more likely just a corrupt form of Dutch *stootmatte* or German *Stossmatte*, the first element of which means something like 'shock', 'impact'.

A sidelight on the importance of attending to the prevention of chafe is offered by the following item from a letter written by Admiral Collingwood. 'The difference I observe in the expense of sailing the ships is incredible. Some men who have the foresight to discern what our first difficulty will be, support and provide their ships by enchantment, one scarce knows how, while others, less provident, would exhaust a dockyard, and still be in want' (Boyd, 397). To be sure Collingwood's 'unrelaxing spirit of economy' was almost legendary, but his example could, with advantage, have been followed by all officers commanding men-of-war (*Mariner's Mirror* 53, 1967, 98).

Carpenter. The carpenter and his mates sounded the pumpwells, inspected the leather flaps on the scuppers, prepared scupper-plugs, hawse-bucklers, and so on. If the gundeck ports were to be closed, they fitted the splash-boards (Funch, 95), and caulked around the openings as necessary. If need be, tarpaulins and battens were got ready to secure the hatches.

Boats. The boatswain went out ahead of the vessel in a boat, to confirm that the masts and yards were squared, and took the opportunity to record the draught fore and aft. The boats were swung in, or hoisted up on their davits. The yard- and stay-tackles were coiled up in the longboat, or some other convenient place, the boats made secure with chocks and lashings, and the covers put on. The davit-boats were securely griped, boat-ropes led forward outside of all, the quarter-boats being in all respects ready in case of 'Man Overboard'.

Gunner. The muzzle-plugs, or 'tompions', were put in, and muzzle-bags secured to protect the bore against corrosion from salt

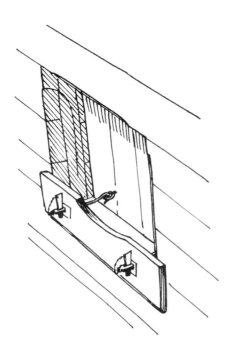

Splash board. Hooks from the splash board were fastened to eyebolts on the inside of the gunport lids.

water. The guns were either run in and secured for sea, or squared in their ports. Boyd (34) gives a long list of supplementary details, which would also have required the attention of the gunner's mates.

Gunroom. The wheel was put from hard-over to hard-over a couple of times, to make sure that the tiller-rope ran freely in the guides, and that the the sweep was clear. If the tiller-ropes were of hide, they were greased; if of white-hemp, they were checked for signs of wear. The availability of the spare tiller, helm-port wedges, and relieving-tackles was verified, and the attachments of the rudder-pendants checked. A rudder preventer rope is described by Rosvall (91) and Le Compte (Figure 554). This was a stout rope with a stopper-knot worked in the end. It was thrust through a hole in the horn of the rudder, from starboard to port, and secured to the counter on the port side.

Preparations for weighing. On deck, the cat- and fish-tackles were rove. On the gun-deck, stanchions were knocked out, and gratings placed to give room for the men at the capstan. The capstan bars were inserted and pinned in place, and the ends 'swiftered'. The messenger was 'brought to', and a sufficiency of nippers placed ready for heaving in.

WEIGHING ANCHOR

Small craft weighed anchor by hand, while merchant vessels up to 400 tons or so, used a horizontal windlass. Sometimes, in small vessels, a tackle was clapped on the cable,

hauled in until 'two blocks', then fleeted and the process repeated. This method could also be used in a launch, when weighing the ship's anchor. As we shall see, a similar technique was also used in large vessels, to assist the capstan in breaking a stubborn anchor out of the ground. Large vessels used the main capstan to weigh anchor, and this most often involved using a 'messenger'. A 'voyal' was similar to a messenger, except that it was taken to the jeer capstan. We will first consider the mechanical details of how the anchor was weighed, first concentrating on the activities on the gundeck, then turning to a consideration of how the anchor was catted, fished, and stowed, finally considering how things were managed aloft.

The early capstan. The design found in *Vasa*, or in the contemporary models of the 1600s (Winter, Ketting,) was more slender and of much smaller circumference than later examples. The spindle was sixteen-sided, buttressed by eight 'whelps', which tapered upwards, so the whole thing formed a truncated cone. The spindle was often decorated with a spiral, or criss-cross pattern, and was pierced through and through by three square holes, at different levels. Three square bars were thrust through these holes,

giving effectively six bars, at three different heights. This arrangement avoided unduly weakening the spindle, and required the tallest men to heave in using the highest pair of bars. The whelps were supported by chocks near their base, and were 'locked' by kicking in horizontal 'pawls'. There were a pair of these abaft the spindle. Sometimes they were made in the form of a horseshoe, having one, rather than two pivots. These 'sliding-pawls', *shuifpallen* as the Dutch called them, remained in use until the 1800s. This type of capstan had completely disappeared from the Royal Navy in Falconer's day, although he remarks that small versions of it, called 'crabs', were sometimes found in small merchantmen.

The later capstan. That found in *Victory* is of much sturdier appearance. As in the earlie version, the whelps taper upwards, usuall with a 'step' to prevent the messenger riding too high. The whelps increased the sweep o circumference of the barrel, without a pro portional increase in weight. The effective diameter was about five times that of th cable handled (Stevens, 107). Iron 'hanging pawls', four in number, drop into a circula cast-iron pawl-rack on the deck. By flippin them over, they work for the opposit

Capstans
A Early seventeenth century capstan:
   a barrel; **b** whelps; **c** capstan bar; **d** sliding pawl; **e** spindle.
B Eighteenth century capstan with hanging pawls (**f**) and removable pawl-rest bolts (**g**); **C** double capstan, the lower one with deckhead hanging pawls; **D** working the capstan: showing the swifter passed through the ends of the bars, the men (most of whom have been omitted for clarity) stepping over the cablet, and one hand fleeting the turns with a mallet.

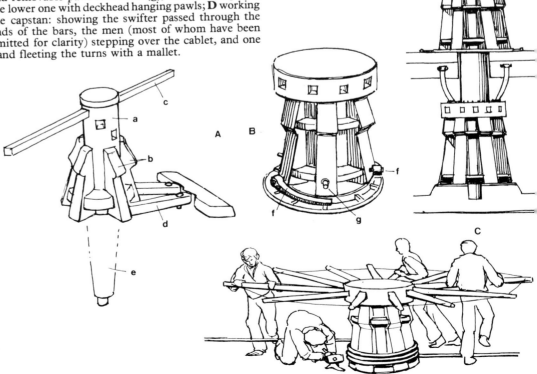

rotation, or when easing back on the load. Another type of hanging-pawl depended from the deckhead, engaging a pawl-rack on top of the drumhead (Falconer, Plate II, Figure 12). Twelve or fourteen bars, made of ash or oak (Harboe), fit into numbered square pigeon-holes on the disc-shaped drumhead, being secured with drop-bolts. In use, the outer ends were 'swifted' (or 'swiftered') by hitching a line, or 'swifter', from one to another. The chocks were made of oak, but the whelps were of fir, which was softer and afforded the messenger a better grip. The whelps were through-bolted in

pairs, and periodically needed to be replaced, as they gave way under use. Pawl-rests were needed to disengage hanging-pawls; pull-out bolts for those at the base, and deck-beam brackets, for those depending from the deck-head.

Two dimensions of the capstan were governed by the physical size of the men heaving upon it: the bars were at breast height, say four and a half feet; while the 'jog' in the whelps was about two feet above the deck. Since the men had to step over the 'high' or holding off end of the messenger, without breaking stride, unless there were a

hatch grating, or improvised ramp, two feet was the maximum practical height.

Double capstans. *Victory*'s capstans are of this variety; that is to say, the capstan on upper and lower gundecks turn on the same spindle, and by engaging drop-pins, or some similar arrangement, are caused to rotate together. This arrangement goes back at least as far as 1691, being described and illustrated by Rålamb. In the case of *Victory*, one capstan has fourteen bars, and that co-axial with it, twelve. With 10 men on each bar, 260 men would have been available to weigh anchor. Allowing for frictional losses, Bugler

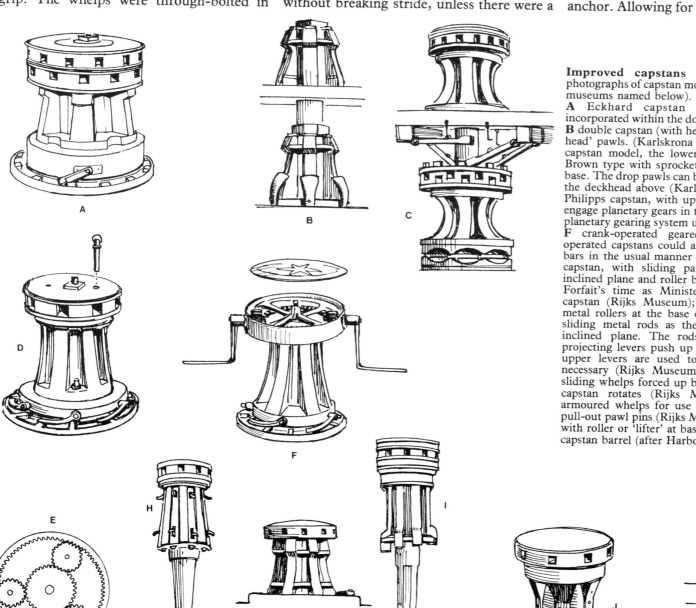

Improved capstans (Based on the author's photographs of capstan models in the collections of the museums named below).
A Eckhard capstan with planetary gearing incorporated within the double heads (Rijks Museum); **B** double capstan (with heads missing) fitted with 'axe head' pawls. (Karlskrona Naval Museum); **C** double capstan model, the lower capstan of the Hartfield-Brown type with sprockets to fit chain messenger at base. The drop pawls can be disengaged and hooked to the deckhead above (Karlskrona Naval Museum); **D** Philipps capstan, with upper and lower drop pins to engage planetary gears in the base (Rijks Museum); **E** planetary gearing system used in the Philipps capstan; **F** crank-operated geared capstan. Some crank-operated capstans could also be worked with capstan bars in the usual manner (Rijks Museum); **G** double capstan, with sliding pawls on upper barrel and inclined plane and roller bearings (introduced during Forfait's time as Minister of the Navy) on lower capstan (Rijks Museum); **H** Du Sahy capstan: the metal rollers at the base of each whelp push up on sliding metal rods as the capstan rotates over the inclined plane. The rods make the lower set of projecting levers push up on the messenger, and the upper levers are used to push the rods down, if necessary (Rijks Museum); **I** Asmus capstan, with sliding whelps forced up by the inclined plane as the capstan rotates (Rijks Museum); **J** capstan with armoured whelps for use with chain messenger and pull-out pawl pins (Rijks Museum); **K** Danish capstan with roller or 'lifter' at base to keep messenger up on capstan barrel (after Harboe, 1839).

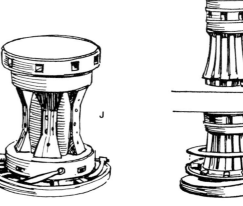

(75) estimates that they should have been able to lift 10 tons, the anchor itself weighing about 5 tons.

Geared capstans. A G Eckhard, a Dutchman, invented a double-headed geared capstan in 1771, and the device was fitted by the Admiralty in the Third Rate HMS *Defiance* the following year. One of the heads contained sun-and-planet gearing, arranged so the spindle could either be driven directly by one head, or geared down about three times, by the other. The heads were counter-rotating, and hence if it were desired to shift from one mode to the other, swifter and bars had to be removed, from one head, reinserted in the other, and the swifter resecured. To overcome this problem, Philipps shifted the gear mechanism below the spindle partners, and used two draw-bolts to connect the drumhead to the barrel, while three more secured the barrel to the outer gears. Thus, to work directly, the upper bolts were pushed down, and the lower ones withdrawn. Reversing the action allowed things to act in the geared-down mode. The bars and swifter did not have to be disturbed, although the men would walk around in the opposite direction from before, to continue heaving in. A practical difficulty with this ingenious arrangement was the rusting of the mechanism resulting from washing down the decks. Small Dutch men-of-war were sometimes fitted with another type of geared capstan, in which a pair of cranks could be substituted for the bars, if desired.

Fleeting the turns. The messenger was taken three and a half turns around the barrel, the inboard end being at the top, the end leading forward to the hawsehole, at the bottom. As the cable was hove in, the turns of the messenger continually tended to 'walk down' the barrel, and had to be 'fleeted' upwards. I am using the term 'fleeting' for this upward shifting of the turns, the process having something in common with fleeting a tackle. The order 'Fleet the messenger!' according to Smyth, was given to shift the eyes of the messenger to the 'inboard' side of the capstan, just prior to the heavy heave required to break the anchor out of the ground. The order 'Surge the messenger!' was given when it was desired to slacken the turns for any reason, including fleeting them up. A couple of men crouched under the bars, and encouraged the turns to shift upwards, by tapping the messenger with a 'commander', or heavy mallet, or using handspikes, *opbrekers* ('up-breakers') in Dutch. Iron crowbars were used if a chain messenger were taken around the whelps (Mossel, II, 412; Le Compte, 147). Murphy

(28) pays particular attention to the eyes of the messenger: 'To prevent surging, the turns ought to be kept close, and steadily up, and hands stationed at the capstan with flattened levers to pry the eyes and lashing up, when passing round the welts (whelps).' Using a windlass, the outboard end of the cable came on the barrel towards midships, and the turns were fleeted laterally, the barrel having taper towards the ship's sides, to facilitate this. To maintain the grip of the rope on barrel, the off-coming end had to be hauled on, 'held off' or 'held on' by men detailed for this purpose – *afhouders* ('off-holders') as they were called in Dutch. By periodically releasing the tension, the messenger was caused to slip or 'surge' momentarily, and because of the upward tapering of the capstan, the turns slipped abruptly upwards, allowing heaving in to continue. 'When the cable is brought too, there is some difficulty in keeping him from rubbing on the deck, which is termed Surging. To assist in this case, there is [*sic*] pieces of wood called nippers, put into straps, that are received in the whelps of the said capstern. And this is the reason the capstern is made tapering upwards, to stop the sliding down of such heavy ropes, if cable may be termed so' (Sutherland's *Shipbuilding Unveil'd*, 1717; also Stevens, 106). The joggle towards the upper end of the whelp prevented the turns jumping up too far.

Holding off was usually done by hand, but one can imagine people using 'jiggers', or a tackle hooked to a strop. Mainwaring and his contemporaries mention using the jeer capstan to 'hold off', although this would only have been practical when it was on the same deck as the main capstan, which was not always the case. 'The jeer capstan hath its name from the jeer, which is ever brought to this capstan to be heaved at by. It stands in the waist, in the hatchway, and serves for many other uses; as to heave upon the viol, or hold off the cable from the main capstan' (Mainwaring, 169).

The messenger. At first sight it would seem simplest to bring the cable directly to the capstan, and no doubt this was done in the 1600s. This would have been perfectly practical with a small cable, such as used with the stream anchor. However, the impossibility of handling with the same ease, a 24-inch cable, like those bent to *Victory*'s bower anchors is obvious: hence the necessity for using a smaller, more flexible 'cablet', to which the cable itself was temporarily 'clutched', as we might say. Apart from handiness and pliability, the messenger was comparitively dry and clean, not covered in

slime and mud, or encrusted with barnacles like the cable.

The non-surging capstan. The ordinary capstan works best if the heavers used by the gunner's mates keep the turns of the messenger inching upwards slowly and steadily. If this fails to happen, the messenger had to be 'surged' upwards: the men at the bars stood to, the pawls were kicked in if necessary, the messenger was stoppered just forward of the capstan, and the men holding off slackened their grip on the messenger; the turns could then be pried up on the barrel, and heaving in recommence. Groignard, writing in 1746, says that all this could waste up to a quarter of an hour. If the operation were carried out without stoppering the messenger, the turns might slip up with a bang, and those holding off have a job getting a good hold on the messenger again. Groignard further says that the shock of sudden surging 'heats, flattens, and frays' the strands of the messenger.

In 1741 the French Academy offered a prize for the best solution to this problem, and M. Philippe Henrat of the French National Archives drew my attention to Folios Marine G. 113, 114 & 115, and the documents therein relating to this search for the ideal *cabestan sans choquer*, or 'non surging capstan'. The resulting entries ranged from the completely potty to the extremely ingenious and the folios referred to are filled with the complaints of those who felt they had been done out of the prize. The devices suggested mostly rely on the principle of the inclined plane, and the method associated with Minister of the Navy Forfait won practical acceptance in Holland as well as France. Through the courtesy of Mr Bas Kist, I was able to examine the beautifully made models of the Forfait capstan, as well as those of du Sahy and Asmus, in the storerooms of the Rijks Museum, Amsterdam. In each case, the inclined plane slopes up and aft, and is equally effective, whichever way the capstan rotates. A simple roller, or 'lifter', is shown by Harboe (140) as being in use in 1839. The introduction of chain cable, or rather the invention of the Brown-Hartfield capstan with its sprocket wheel, meant that further development along these lines ceased to occur.

Situation of the capstans. As the name suggests, the primary purpose of the jeer capstan was to handle the jeers, when hoisting fore- and mainyards. The main capstan was placed abaft the mainmast on the middle gundeck, and, in *Victory*, a second capstan on the upper gundeck is co-axial with it, allow ing both to be worked as a unit. *Victory*'s jeer capstan is found on the gundeck, between the fore and main masts, being virtually identical to the main capstan. In *Vasa*, the main capstan is found on the lower gundeck, while the jeer capstan is on the upper gundeck. A study of cross-sections of contemporary vessels suggests that this was, in fact, a common arrangement in the 1600s, meaning that in such cases a voyal (or viol) could not be used nor could the jeer capstan serve to hold off.

Windlass. Although this was more characteristic of the small merchantman, and hence of less interest to us, than the capstan, it was used in smaller men of war and the device merits some mention. The barrel was supported at either end by 'windlass-bitts', or 'carrick-bitts'. From these, long knees projected forward, analogous in fact in structure and function to the knees of the riding-bitts, since the cable was 'bitted' to the windlass, as well as being hove in by it. The barrel was eight-sided, and in these surfaces square holes were pierced, to take the hand-spikes, or heavers, by which the machine was rotated. Forward of the centre of the barrel stood the stout pawl-bitt, from which depended one or two hanging pawls, which engaged in holes or notches in the centre of the barrel. The pawl notches were found in each face of the barrel; that is to say, it would 'catch' every one-eighth of a turn. The holes for the handspikes sometimes were offset, from one face to the next, to avoid undue weakening of the barrel. Sometimes, holes were not placed on adjoining faces, but rather on every other face, Studies of contemporary models sometimes show the barrel tapered from the centre down towards the ends, where they pierce the carrick-bitts, while other examples exhibit no taper whatsoever. The carrick-bitts were sometimes joined by a strong cross-piece, which served as a belaying-pin rack, for the head-sheets, etc. On the inside of the carrick-bitts were found cleats, to hang one cable on, while the other was being hove in. Röding (389) calls this cleat a *Nordman*, 'Norman'. A square peg, called a *kattenkopf* ('cathead') by Röding, but known as a 'Norman' in English, could be thrust into one of the heaver-holes, and used to secure the cable, when there was not too much strain on it. The cable was taken three times around the barrel, the turns coming off the top, the inboard part being kept to the outer end, to facilitate fleeting the turns. When riding at anchor, the windlass barrel fulfilled the same function as the bitts. The cable was seized to a Norman-pin thrust into the barrel, further secured by deck-stoppers,

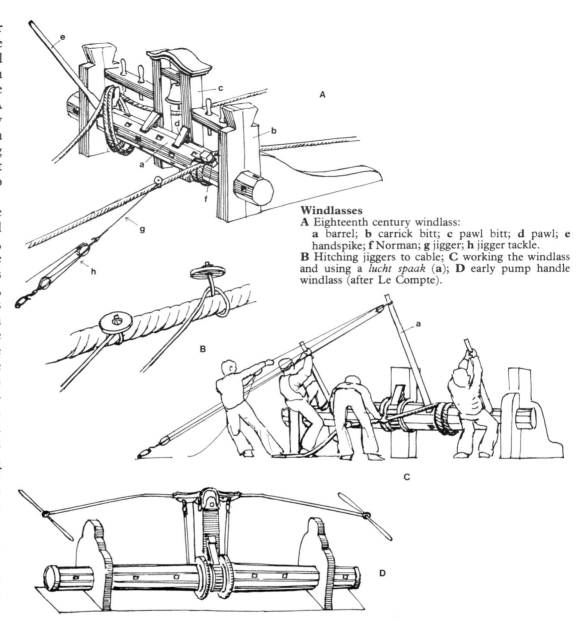

Windlasses
A Eighteenth century windlass:
  a barrel; **b** carrick bitt; **c** pawl bitt; **d** pawl; **e** handspike; **f** Norman; **g** jigger; **h** jigger tackle.
B Hitching jiggers to cable; **C** working the windlass and using a *lucht spaak* (**a**); **D** early pump handle windlass (after Le Compte).

and by heavers jammed in on the forward side of the barrel, so they were forced against the deck and prevented the cable paying out. The cable was 'weather-bitted' by taking an extra turn around the barrel outside the carrick-bitts. The Dutch referred to this extra turn as an *Enkhuizer*, named after the town of Enkhuizen. Perhaps the name arose because the warping drum of the windlass resembled a dummy 'wooden cannon', otherwise known as an *Enkhuizer* (as related to me by Brongers).

To heave up the anchor, several men, working simultaneously, stuck handspikes vertically into holes on top of the barrel, and hauled them down and back, until they lay horizontal, thus causing the barrel to rotate a quarter of a turn, two 'clicks' of the pawls. For a heavy heave, the handspikes could be double-manned, and perhaps move through a shorter stroke, rotating the barrel only one-

eighth of a turn. According to Röding, the men of the Northumberland colliers were reputed to be the best seamen of all, when it came to heaving up anchor. Hutchinson (138) tells of hiring seven men from a collier, to shift the berth of his ship. They 'hove up the anchor by two brisk motions, for each square of the windlass, in a quarter of the time that it used to be done by eighteen men, and this difference was entirely owing to their dexterity, learned by great practice; they rise with their handspikes and heave exactly to-gether with a regular brisk motion, which unites their powers into one'. I wonder if each of the 'two brisk motions' corresponded to a one-eighth turn of the barrel, or whether the second was the return to the original position. The operation of such a windlass was not without danger, even though it was safer than a capstan, if the ship were weakly manned. If, in heaving, the men just failed to get the next pawl to catch, they were in danger of being thrown violently over the bows, as the ship rose to the next sea. This was one reason why Hutchinson (138) considered the introduction of pawls which engaged every sixteenth of a turn such a great improvement. At moments requiring an especially vigorous heave, an extra long handspike was inserted in the barrel. A tackle, secured to a notch at its upper end, was used to haul it down and back. Rosvall (88) calls this a *bräckbom* ('break-boom'), Le Compte (149) a *lucht-spaak*, 'spoke-in-the-air'.

The relative efficiency of the windlass is attested to by its survival, almost unchanged into this century, examples being found in coasting vessels still extant. These modern examples exhibit two refinements which are described as early as 1842 by Le Compte, namely a pawl-rack with 32 teeth, and a simple arrangement permitting two men to turn the barrel by pumping up and down on handles, similar to those found on a railroad 'speeder'. Up to four pawls came into use later on.

Jigger and jigger-tackle. To maintain the friction between the cable and the windlass or capstan, it was necessary to 'hold off', or 'hold on' (Falconer), by hauling on the inboard end. In the case of a small cable, coming off a windlass, this could be done by hand. If the weather were so cold that the cable was icing up, or if the rope was slippery because of a coating of slime, some help was needed. A simple gadget was used for this purpose, consisting of a fathom of rope with a stopper-knot in one end, thrust through a sheave. The sheave was dipped under the cable, and a half turn taken with the bight around the rope and under the sheave. By taking a turn around his body with the rope's end, the man could now keep a grip on the cable and, by backing away as it came in, could manage to 'hold off', even when the hawser was slippery. The English seaman

called this contrivance a 'jigger' (that is, 'thingamajig'), while the Dutch called it a *woid* or *wuit* ('reel'), the reference being to the sheave. For extra purchase, an eye was worked in the inboard end of the rope, and a 'jigger-tackle' was hooked to it (Lever, 119). When the jigger had been walked well aft, or when the jigger-tackle came 'two blocks', the man hauling on it called 'Fleet the jigger!', whereupon, a man at the windlass 'fixed his handspike between the deck and the cable, so as to jam the latter to the windlass, and prevent it from running out, till the jigger is replaced on the cable near the windlass' (Smyth, 412).

Deck-tackle. This was called a *marguerite* in French, and an 'anchor-tackle' in most of the northern European languages. Röding, probably mistakenly, gives the English equivalent as 'messenger'. It could be thought of as a variant of the jigger, although it actually was used to assist the messenger when a particularly heavy heave was in prospect, as for breaking an anchor out of very stiff ground. In its simplest form, it was virtually the same thing as a voyal; a rope was clapped on the cable near the hawse, and the end taken to the jeer-capstan. The effectiveness was greatly increased by securing the standing end well aft, leading the rope through a large block stropped to the cable, and back to the jeer capstan. Rosvall (87) describes a more powerful variant, rigged 'trumpet-fashion'. The hawser was secured to the cable just within the hawse, led through a block close to a gunport, abreast the jeer capstan, then through a block stropped to the cable close abaft the bitts, thence to the jeer capstan. More powerful tackles could be used, and Willaumez (384) remarks that nothing can withstand the power of such an arrangement, 'rather the arm of the anchor will break, or the cable part'. It seems possible that the deck-tackle was sometimes called a 'collier's purchase'. However, Murphy (28) uses this term for a somewhat

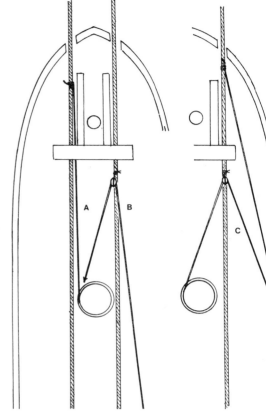

Deck tackles
A Deck tackle; B deck tackle rove through block, tackle rigged 'trumpet fashion'.

Messengers
A Messenger rigged for heaving in cable:
  a cable; b messenger; c mousing; d seizing.
B Different ways of joining the ends of the messenger.
C mousing; D Turk's head mousing.

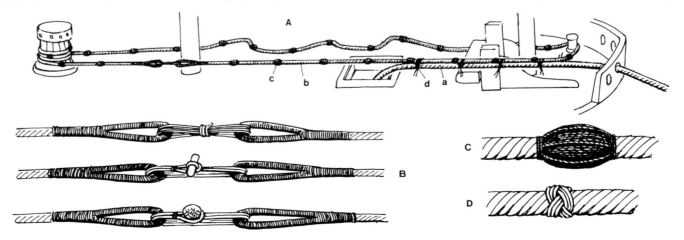

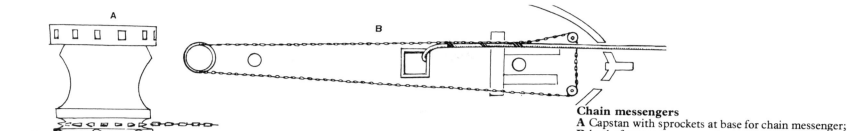

Chain messengers
A Capstan with sprockets at base for chain messenger;
B lead of messenger around capstan and rollers.

different method of assisting the capstan. If the weather were calm, the cat-fall was fleeted, and the block hooked to a strop on the cable close to the water's edge. The force of the cat could then be used to aid in the heavy heave. Nares (126) describes the use of a runner and tackle to get an extra heave on chain cable, indicating that the technique remained in use into the late 1860s.

Messenger. It may be that the voyal antedated the messenger, but both worked on the same principle. As ships increased in size, the thickness of the cable reached a point where it was no longer practical to wrap the cable round the capstan. The messenger was a small hawser, 'clutched' to the cable with nippers, and taken to the capstan, in the cable's stead. It was a 'cablet', or scaled-down cable, of hemp, three-fifths the size of the cable. The eyes at the ends were secured together either with a seizing, or a strop and toggle. Ashley (271) illustrates one form of this, using a spritsail-sheet knot. With a seizing, the eyes were about a fathom apart. In use, the messenger was secured to the cable, at the bitts, by the nippermen, led aft, and taken three and a half turns around the capstan, then run forward around vertical rollers, just abaft the manger, and so brought round by the bitts once more. The Dutch and French terms were, respectively, *kabelaring* and *tournevire*. It will be realised that there were some bights of slack, *trompete* Sjöbohm calls it, snaking about, on the side opposite to the incoming anchor cable. This was fleeted forward by a few hands, the *kabelaring-afschakers* ('messenger-fleeters') as Mossel calls them. The men holding off sat on deck facing aft, the messenger passing through their hands (Totten, 121). No one else mentions the sitting posture.

'Mousings' were formed on the messenger about a fathom apart, so that the nippers would be less liable to slip. Costé (229) offers a very detailed description of how these were made. *Pommes*, or *fusées*, as the French called them, were in length equal to the circumference of the messenger, and at their widest point, exactly twice its diameter. The Germans called them *Mäuse* ('mice'), and Swedes *kuntor*, *sjömanskuntor* (Rosvall, 85;

Sjöbohm, 11). Harboe (186), writing in 1839, still considers them to be worthwhile, but Costé, at about the same date, indicates that they were falling out of fashion in France, since not only did they flatten and disintegrate under use, but some seamen felt they prevented the capstan getting the best grip on the messenger. Costé felt that Turk's-heads made of ratline, worked nearly as well, or indeed, taking a couple of turns with a light cord, hitching and worming this around the messenger, 'English fashion', would suffice. In fact, Lever's illustrations do not show mousings on the messenger, and I suspect that either they were never popular in British vessels, or fell out of use quite early.

The messenger was taken round the capstan, so the hauling end, which was nippered to the cable was at the bottom. Thus, to heave up the starboard anchor, the turns were put on 'with the sun'. To heave in the port cable, the lashing or toggle, had to be let go, and the eye dipped through the turns, reversing them, and bringing the hauling end to the bottom. On those occasions when the capstan was being used to lower a heavy weight, after having raised it, the turns required to be reversed, so the end supporting the load came off the top. I am pretty sure that, when not in use, the messenger was usually triced up to the deck-head; Stibolt (4) talks of 'giving down the messenger', and the model of the Dutch two-decker described by Winter, shows the messenger stowed in this way. Preparing for a long sea-voyage, it would of course have been struck down into the cable-tier.

Chain messenger. It will be easiest to deal with the chain version, at this point. Prior to the introduction of steam-driven cable-holders, chain cable was hove up by nippering it to a chain messenger. This was originally handled by taking the chain round the capstan, hemp messenger fashion, iron-faced whelps being required to accept the chain (*Memorandum*, 139). Subsequently, capstans were designed specifically to handle chain. Chain messengers were introduced by a British firm in 1828, according to Le Compte, who pointed out the following advantages compard to one made of hemp. It

did not wear out, did not slip, and hence did not need to be fleeted or surged. It led the cable straight to the chain-pipe, leading down to the cable-locker. It did not need to be held off, or lighted along on the opposite side of the deck, and, if the other cable needed to be hove in, it did not need to be unspliced and dipped. Messenger chain was made with square open links, alternately long and short, the ends being joined by a 'peculiar splicing shackle' (Boyd, 229). The base of the Hartfield-Brown capstan was fitted with a sprocket, the teeth of which engaged the long links of the messenger, which made a half turn around it. The cable and messenger were gripped together with rope nippers, strops, or iron nippers. One significant difference between rope and chain messenger was the fact that the chain had to be kept taut, throughout its length, so it could not disengage from the sprocket. To accomplish this, the vertical rollers, abaft the manger, were laterally adjustable, to allow taking up the slack, and there were no loose bights on the 'return' side of the deck. With a rope messenger, rollers are really superfluous.

Viol or voyal.

When the anchor is in such stiff ground that we cannot weigh it, or else the sea goes so high that the main capstan cannot purchase in the cable, then for more help, we take a hawser and open one strand, and so put into it nippers, some seven or eight, a fathom distance from each other, and with these nippers we bind fast the hawser to the cable; and so bring this hawser to the jeer capstan, and heave upon it, and this will purchase more than the main capstan can. The viol is fastened together at both ends with an eye and a wale knot, or else two eyes seized together (Mainwaring, 251).

Smith & Boteler give more or less garbled versions of this passage. None of them mention the use of a 'messenger', and although some later authors (for example Falconer and Steel) seem to equate this with a voyal, I think the two items were distinct, the voyal being used with the jeer capstan and viol-block, while the messenger was used with the main capstan (Blunt, 141; Romme, 349).

Voyal
A Lead of the voyal to viol block and capstan; **B** detail of viol block.

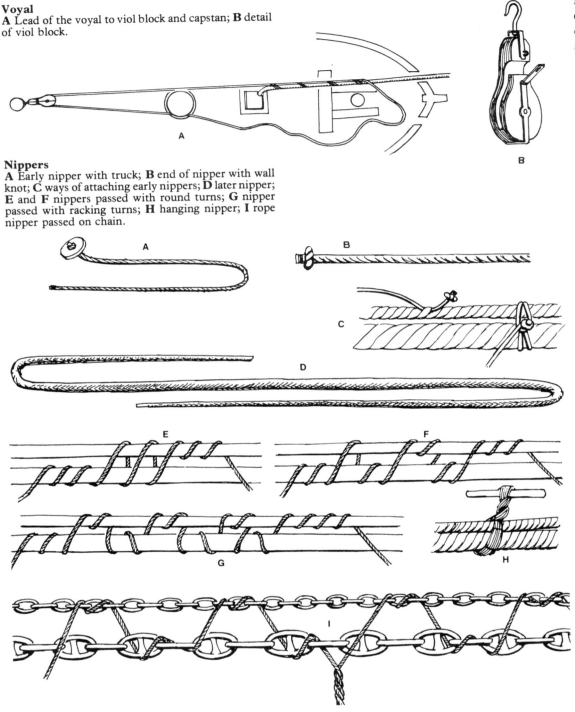

Nippers
A Early nipper with truck; **B** end of nipper with wall knot; **C** ways of attaching early nippers; **D** later nipper; **E** and **F** nippers passed with round turns; **G** nipper passed with racking turns; **H** hanging nipper; **I** rope nipper passed on chain.

resistance faced by a French officer who devised a capstan with recesses in the base, designed to accept the links of the cable. This arrangement was named *Barbotin* after its inventor, and was objected to by other officers, precisely because the jerks of the cable were now transmitted directly to the capstan, instead of indirectly by way of the messenger (Frick, 214).

Early nippers. The nipper was the device used to seize the messenger to the cable, and it took several forms. In Mainwaring's day, they were 'Small ropes, about a fathom and a half, or two fathoms long, with a little truck at one end, or some have only a wale knot, the use whereof is to hold off the cable from the main capstan, or the jeer capstan, when the cable is either so slippy, or so great that they cannot strain it, to hold it off with their hands only' (Mainwaring, 191). It will be seen that these are identical with what were later called 'jiggers', which we have already described. As mentioned earlier, when discussing the viol, the nippers are thrust under a strand of the hawser, and used to bind viol and cable together. This particular method would not have worked if the messenger, which wound steadily round the capstan, was required for more than a short heave. However, it would have worked well enough for the latter purpose.

It seems possible that nippers of this sort could have been used to hold messenger and cable together, without the necessity of actually opening up a strand of the former. Gower (128) appears to refer to them when he says that 'the nippers mostly made use of with a knot in one end, are very subject to jam'. I am not entirely clear exactly how they were used, but the most likely method would have been to take a 'cow-hitch' around cable and messenger, so that both the wall-knot and the free end pointed towards the nipper man, who hauled the end taut, and walked aft with it. Blunt (141), as late as 1826, describes a longer version: 'another method, when the strain is great is to have nippers with an over hand knot made at one end, and with that end, a turn is taken around the cable and viol leaving three or four feet of the end. Then with the other end, take three or four racking turns, and expend nearly the remainder with round turns round the cable and viol, laying the knotted end under and over each of the last turns.' The turns rode against the knot which prevented them slipping along the cable. Falconer's reference to nippers on six or eight feet in length, suggests that this too, is thinking of this early type, terminating in a wall-knot.

Later nippers. There is a great deal more

The voyal may have got its name from the viol-block, a fitting not actually mentioned by Mainwaring, but quite certainly in use in his day. This was a very large snatch-block secured to the foot of the mainmast, its shape perhaps reminding the viewer of a musical instrument such as the violin-cello. I would envisage the voyal as a hawser temporarily nippered to the cable abaft the bitts, passing aft to be snatched in the viol-block, then led forward to take three and a half turns round the jeer capstan, before being taken forward round the foremast and riding-bitts. Its ends were secured either with a seizing or a toggle,

working button-hole fashion. It will be realised that using the viol-block does not increase, in the least, the mechanical advantage, but it allows the viol to pull almost straight aft, rather than directly towards the jeer capstan, and hence allows more nippers to be applied at one time than would have been the case otherwise. The disadvantage of the frictional losses is more than compensated for by the fact that the strain is applied to the block, rather than directly to the capstan. This would have been particularly appreciated if the ship were rising and falling to a head sea. Analogous reasoning explains the information about the way these were handled. Sjöbohm (11) says they were of sennit, plaited about three fingers broad in the middle, tapering towards the ends, and five or six fathoms in length. If this seems rather long, we must remember that one turn on *Victory*'s cable requires two feet of nipper. Gower (129) and Lever (109) illustrate, very clearly, different methods of casting them on. One common method was to take two or three round turns around the messenger, followed by two or three turns around the messenger and cable, ending with two or three turns around the cable alone. The turns went on with the lay of the heavier ropes, those on the messenger alone, being aft, those on the cable alone, forward. This configuration served to draw cable and messenger together, as the capstan was hove around, while at the same time separating the turns lengthwise, so preventing jamming. If there were a very heavy heave, 'racking' turns could be taken, criss-crossing between cable and messenger, and constricting the two tightly together. This method was liable, however, to result in the turns jamming, requiring that the nipper be cut, and interfering with the steady activity of the men at the bars. 'Nothing is more tedious than the need to stop the capstan frequently' (Rosvall, 86). 'The captain of the foretop should be ordered, after the ship gets underweigh, to dry all the nippers, make them up, and return them to the captain of the hold, as they would otherwise rot, and if not taken care of, would be appropriated to every idle purpose' (Blunt, 169).

Selvagee strops, or hanging nippers. The northern European languages distinguished two kinds of nippers: those just described, which they refer to as 'seizings', Swedish *sejsingar*, etc; and 'strops', which they call 'nippers', Swedish *knipare*, etc. The latter were 'skeins of untwisted spunyarn, marled together into a "selvagee".' In use, the strop was passed around messenger and cable, a heaver was thrust through the eyes, and twisted back, up, and towards the topman, who then held it, as he walked aft (Rosvall, 86; Sjöbohm, 10). Brady (111) indicates that, in his day, some American ships had reverted to this method, when handling chain cable. Each man provided two selvagees and a heaver, in addition to an iron pin, which was thrust through a link of chain, to prevent it slipping through the strop. Totten (118) calls the selvagees 'hanging nippers', 'much used in heavy heaving, and found very useful because of the facility with which they are applied and removed'. He indicates that they were some-

times applied over the ordinary nippers, to get an extra grip, when the cable came up slippery. With either type of nipper, if the ship were plunging in a seaway, the men hauled them taut, as the bow dropped, and the strain on the cable eased momentarily, holding fast, as the ship rose once more (Sjöbohm, 13).

Nippers with chain cable. It is rather surprising to find that long sennit nippers were used, even when cable and messenger were of chain, being passed in the same fashion, as with a hemp cable. A much more effective device was the iron nipper. This was a specially shaped hinged shackle, designed to grip one link of the messenger together with one link of the cable. Since no slippage was possible, only one iron nipper needed to be in place at a time, as against four or five rope nippers.

CATTING, FISHING, AND STOWING THE ANCHOR

Once the anchor had been hove up, the stock was just above the water, and it then had to be 'stowed'. It was first 'catted', by hauling the ring up under the cathead, after which it was 'fished', hauling the shank up until horizontal, and the inboard fluke secured to a timberhead. To stow it for sea, it was 'second catted', and the stock hove upright with the stock-tackle, secured with ring-, and shank-painters, and stock-lashing.

Cat-tackle. A widely accepted explanation for the origin of this term is that it is named for the cathead, which traditionally was ornamented with a lion mask. This would be a little more convincing if many other languages did not also call the tackle the 'cat', while using a different word for the cathead. For example, in German we have the verb

katten, and the nouns *Katlaufer* ('-fall'), *Kat-gien* ('-tackle'), *Kat-block*, etc, while the cat-head is *Krahn-balken* ('crane-beam'). *Katten-kopf*, which literally means 'cat-head', on the other hand, was the term for a 'Norman', a square peg pushed into a hole in the windlass barrel, to which the cable was seized. The French used *capon* for the cat-tackle; this with the parallel verb *caponner*, obviously arises in a totally different fashion from *bossoir*, the word for the cathead. Other words for the cathead such as Italian *grua*, French *grue*, German *Krahn*, all derive, like English 'crane', from Latin *grus*.

The cat-block was a very large triple block, 26 inches across in a First Rate according to Steel, having a large hook, about two feet long, secured to its lower end. The fall, of six-inch rope in a First Rate, was secured on one side of the cathead, and rove alternately through the sheaves of the cat-block, and the sheaves in the cathead, then inboard through a leading block, where it was belayed to a timberhead.

Catting the anchor. The fall was overhauled, and the cat-hook was engaged in the ring of the anchor, from out in, guided by lines attached to the block and the back of the hook. These were called the 'cat-back', and 'second cat-back', and were tended from the forecastle and beakhead. If the ring could not be hooked by these means, a man could be lowered through a trap in the beakhead, wearing 'clear-hawse breeches', or suspended in a bowline.

Fish-tackle. The anchor having been catted, it was then 'fished'. The fish-tackle did not need to be as strong as the cat, because it did not have to take the full weight of the anchor. Steel lists a double-block, 18 inches across, with a five-inch fall, in a First Rate. The flukes were hauled up, and the inner one

Catting the anchor
A Catting the anchor; **B** detail of cat tackle
  a cathead; **b** cat block; **c** cat back; **d** second cat back.

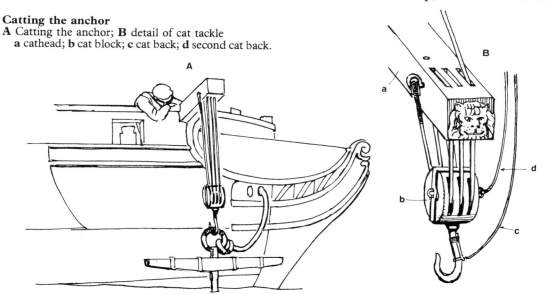

secured to a timberhead just forward of the fore chains, leaving the shank horizontal. In the 1600s, and 'anchor-lining' or 'bill-board' – the 'bill' was the point of the fluke – fitted at or just forward of the fore channels, protected the ship's side from damage as the annchor was hauled up. Another device used to save the side was a specially shaped wooden fender, or 'shoe' (French *semmelle*, *savatte*), which engaged the fluke, and was hauled up with it. The fish-hook was engaged on the inner arm, from out in, between the crown of the anchor, and the fluke, the manoeuvre being assisted by a 'fish-back', a line secured to the hook, analogous to the cat-back in function. The hook slid out along the arm until stopped by the fluke.

There were a great many variations in the method used to rig the purchase. It could be accomplished using the foremast tackle, but the task was simplified if some sort of 'fish-davit' were rigged to allow the tackle to plumb the fluke, when the anchor had been catted. Up to about 1780, the davit was a long squared baulk of timber lying athwart the forecastle, being manhandled from side to side as required. Iron bands called 'span-shackles' acted as hold-downs, and can be seen fitted to some contemporary models (Lees, 35, 128). From about 1770 on, the davit was shorter, and fitted in a shoe, or socket, in the fore channels, or just forward of it. If there was a topping-lift, or if the davit were adequately secured in some other fashion, the fish-tackle could be led aft to the main channels, rather than being up and down the foremast. The short fish-davit was steadied by fore and aft guys, a topping-lift

and a martingale. The fish-tackle usually secured to a 'fish-pendant', to which the 'fish-hook' was secured. A special variety of pendant was the *traversière*, which we will deal with separately.

The foreign terminology offers some interesting features. The Dutch verb *kippen* having the technical sense of 'to fish the anchor', was adopted in several other languages. It has the base meaning of 'tip up', or 'cowp' as they say in Ulster. Since Dutch *kip* also means 'chicken', it may have influenced French *capon*, which meant the cat-tackle. French *traverser* was the technical term for 'fishing' the anchor, the basic idea being that the anchor is 'got across'. The 'fish-davit', was called *devis*, *davis*, *daevis* in Danish, and *dävert* in Swedish. Röding gives the French equivalent as *davit*, but we also find *homme de bois* for one type of fish-davit, and *petit bossoir*, for a smaller version. Spanish *pescante* clearly is somehow derived from the idea of 'fishing'. The first element of the Dutch synonym *penter-balk* ('painter-baulk'), is, I think, analogous to English 'shank-painter' and 'ring-painter'. According to Kluge (611), *penter* is ultimately related to French *porteur* ('carrier', 'bearer'), although *pendant* ('hanging pendant') would seem just as likely.

Traversière. The advantage of using a fish-davit was that the anchor was held out, clear of the ship's side, during the fishing process. Röding (107) indicates that in his day the French, Spanish, and possibly the Danes, used the fore pendant-tackle with no davit, perhaps holding the anchor clear of the side with the fore yard-tackle. The use of a 'fish-

hook' seems to have been universal in English ships, but in some French ports, a special kind of 'anchor-strop', the *traversière*, or *traversin*, was used. Clear illustrations are to be found in Röding (Fig 37) and Lescallier (Plate XV). A similar fitting is described by Sjöbohm (14), and Rosvall (73), confirming its use in Swedish ships. The *traversières* consisted of a pair of stout ropes, secured to the arms just inside the fluke with a running eye, and having a thimble in the other end, with which they were seized to opposite sides of the stock at its centre, when not in use. A lighter line was seized to the *traversière*, perhaps serving as a grab-line (Lescallier, Plate XV).

In use, whichever *traversière* faced inboard and aft, could be got hold of as soon as the stock broke the surface, and the fore-pendant tackle hook engaged, by lowering a man down on the stock (Lescallier, 287). This would have been much quicker than the traditional method of hooking the fish, and particularly useful if one were obliged to fish an anchor to leeward, with the ship heeling over to that side. Contemporary illustrations indicate that, in some ships, the anchor crown was still below the surface, even when the cat was run up 'two blocks'. An excellent description of the *traversière*, based on Costé (226), is to be found in Boudriot (III, 209). Exactly how well the *traversière* fared when the anchor was on the bottom is a problem, and explains why it was later fashioned of chain rather than rope (Bréart, 142). Earlier writers, such as Bourdé, use the term *cantonnière* as a synonym, but this term was obsolete by 1820. A short strop, or *coude*, secured to the crown of the anchor, is illustrated by Röding and Lescallier, and also served to hook the fish. It would not have had the advantages of the *traversière* mentioned above. Lescallier (287) says the *coude* was not in use in all French ports. He further states, quite definitely, that the English did not use the *traversière*, but one or two models of English origin, in the Rogers Collection at Annapolis do, in fact show this fitting. It is possible that this feature is not original, however.

Second catting. When the cat-tackle was hauled 'two blocks' with the cathead, the ring of the anchor was still quite some distance below the cathead, separated from it by the length of the hook, plus the diameter of the cat-block. The anchor was got fully up by 'catting for the second time', or 'ringing up' (Knight). The weight was temporarily transferred to the ringstopper, and the cat-block hooked to a strop secured to the shank below the stock, and the anchor hauled up so

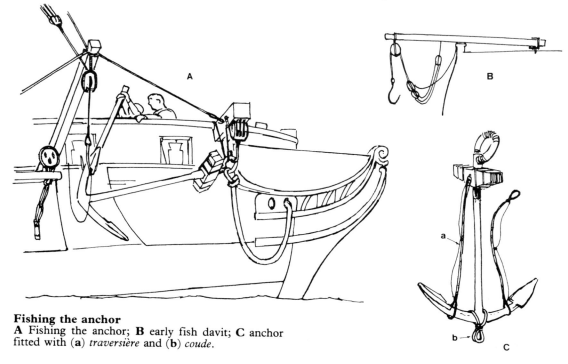

Fishing the anchor
A Fishing the anchor; **B** early fish davit; **C** anchor fitted with (**a**) *traversière* and (**b**) *coude*.

the ring was close to the cathead, where it was secured for good with the ring-stopper. Burney (230) refers to one method of second catting as 'Spanish catting': the cat-fall, or a shorter rope substituted for it, was rove alternately through the sheaves in the cat-head, and the ring of the anchor, hauling the anchor close up, the ring functioning as the lower set of 'sheaves' of the tackle.

Stock-tackle. When the anchor was catted and fished, the upper fluke was secured in the channels, while the lower arm canted down and outwards from the ship's side. In consequence, the stock lay with its lower end pointing down and in, and in some danger of scraping up the ship's planking during the operation of second catting. Smyth, Nares, Burney and Boyd describe the use of a 'stock-tackle', secured to a strop on the upper end of the stock. Hauling on this, canted the stock into a vertical position, and, at the same time, pulled the upper end of the shank in closer to the forecastle, when stowing the anchor for sea. If the stock-tackle were not used, the lower end of the stock was liable to come foul of the cable and bind (Boyd, 370).

Stowing for sea. The anchor having been catted and fished, and the stock pulled upright, it was made fast with ring-stopper, shank-painter, and stock-lashing, all of which were made fast to suitable timber-heads. Once clear of soundings, when emergency use of the anchor was no longer in prospect, the cable-bends were cast off, the clinch undone, and the cable unbent, and stowed below.

HEAVING IN

On the gundeck. We will consider first how hemp cable was handled, and then turn to chain. The messenger was got ready, taken round the rollers, and led aft to take three and a half turns on the capstan, the holding off end uppermost, the eyes being lashed or toggled together. The boatswain supplied fresh dry nippers and readied sand and ashes by the bitts. He saw jiggers available for holding off, the deck-tackle rigged if necessary, and the deck sanded, if it were wet, to afford good foothold. To allow the men to work the capstan, gratings were placed in the hatch-ways, and any obstructing stanchions knocked out. The bars were inserted in the pigeon-holes, secured with drop-pins, and swifter. One or two men crouched down below the bars, armed with heavers and mauls, to fleet the turns up the barrel, and set the pawls as required. To heave in, the stop-pers were taken off abaft the bitts, and the cable unbitted. The cable and messenger were then boosted up on the cavil, or cross-

piece of the bitts, outside the upright, the messenger lying outside the cable, and the vertical bitt-pin dropped in its hole.

Passing the nippers. This was done by the foretopmen before, and the maintopmen abaft, the bitts. The 'nippermen' stood on either side of the cable, which was supported about waist height above the deck by the manger-boards, and the cross-piece of the riding-bitts. Burney (226) gives the following description of how the nippers were passed:

> The messenger is brought to a cable, as a cable cannot be brought to a messenger. This is done by taking two round turns with the after or in-board end of the nipper round the messenger by one of the inside hands, the coil, or remain-ing part of the nipper, is then passed over the cable to one of the outside hands, who facing aft, passes it round the messenger and cable, with the sun on the port side, and against the sun on the starboard side, rousing each turn taut, keeping the messenger on top of the cable, dogging the end round the cable and round the end of the next nipper, to prevent it from slipp-ing; it is held by one of the topmen, who walks aft with it. When far enough aft, and the cable is secured by other nippers following in a similar way, he starts the nipper he is holding and passes it forward again, the nippers are constantly being passed in this way as the cable comes in at the hawseholes. When there is much sea on, or a great strain, racking turns are passed.

Another method was to middle the nipper

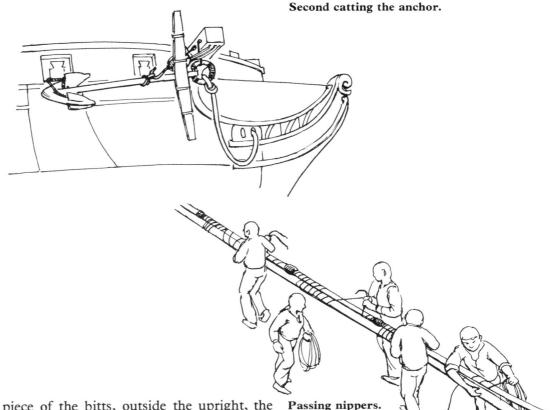

Second catting the anchor.

Passing nippers.

and work towards the ends. I am not completely clear why Burney suggests oppo-site rotation on the starboard side. The after turns were on the messenger, the forward ones on the cable, and all contemporary illustrations show them as taken with the lay, which implies taking the turns always 'with the sun', if the cable and messenger are assumed to be moving aft and the turns on the messenger are taken first. Falconer and Lever confirm that the lighter task of walking aft, holding the twisted ends of two succes-sive nippers was entrusted to the ship's boys. It is sometimes claimed that this practice explains the origin of the term 'nipper' in the sense 'smart young lad', but this is a very dubious proposition. A detailed analysis of that particular question is to be found in *Mariner's Mirror* 37, 1951, 238. Bitt-stoppers, ring-stoppers, and coaming-stoppers were kept ready during heaving in, to be applied, in emergency, should the pawls give way.

Voyal. In ships taking a voyal to the jeer capstan, the arrangements were essentially similar, except that the voyal lay inside the cable, and was snatched in the viol-block, which was secured to the mainmast. 'The jeer capstan hath its name from the jeer, which is ever brought to the capstan to be heaved at by. It stands in the waist in the hatchway, and serves for many other uses, as to heave upon the viol, or hold off the cable from the main capstan' (Mainwaring 169). Rees, writing in 1820, but probably describing earlier practice, says the voyal was only used in the largest ships of the Royal Navy. Blunt (141) says 'when the strain is too great for the messenger alone, the viol is used'. This appears to imply that messenger and voyal were used together, but I find it hard to accept the practicability of nippering the three separate items together. Mainwaring does not mention a messenger at all, and indicates that the voyal was used only on occasion. The question arises, therefore, whether the cable itself was taken to the main capstan. While this seems quite possible, there are some complications associated with doing so. Assume that the starboard cable is being hove in, it will be coming off the capstan on the port side of the deck, abaft the mainmast. To stow in in the orlop, the holding off end would have to be led back to the opposite side of the deck, to prevent a bight being left abaft the mainmast, at the end of the heaving in process.

Cleaning the cable. As mentioned in the section on tending at single anchor, an effort was made to keep the cable clear of the ground. With a muddy bottom, however, it was difficult to avoid having it come inboard covered in slime, not offering a solid grip for the nippers. In such cases, fresh dry nippers were kept handy, and sand, ashes and broom-straws were scattered on the cable and whelps of the capstan to improve the traction. Care had to be taken not to choke the pawl-rack of the capstan with sand, in such circumstances.

Chain cable. The chain messenger was led around the rollers, and over its guides by means of a hook-rope. A hook-rope was also used to unbitt the cable. It was run through a bitt-block, in a deck beam over the bitt upright. The end was taken through a leading block on deck, and by hitching it to the messenger when this was first hove in, the cable was unbitted. Cable and messenger lay on top of the cross-piece when heaving in. The chain cable and messenger were nippered in exactly the same way as those made of hemp. Rope nippers were later replaced by iron nippers, which were simpler and more efficient. Although chain was heavier than the corresponding hemp cable, it was simply dropped into the cable-locker, being in a manner of speaking 'self-stowing', and this did away with the heavy work of tiering the cable. The compressor-tackles were manned during weighing, and bowsed to immediately if the capstan-pawls gave way, so checking the cable.

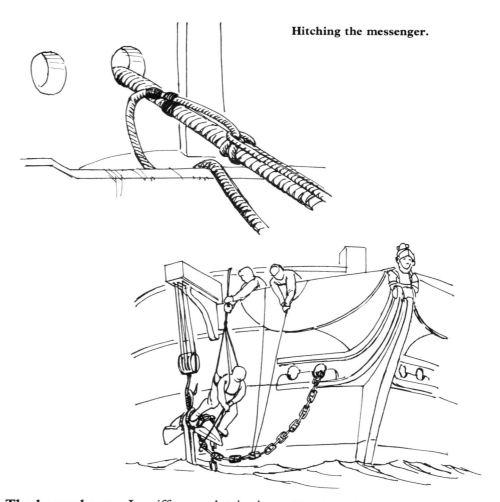

Hitching the messenger.

Clearing a foul anchor: seaman working in 'clea hawse breeches'.

The heavy heave. In stiff ground, tripping the anchor out of the bottom might be difficult, and special methods were needed to apply the necessary extra force to the cable. It must be emphasised that only a fathom or two of cable would come in, during this heavy lift. Once the anchor was a-weigh, it could be run up relatively quickly, and several dodges were used to get the extra pull, at the critical juncture. We have already mentioned the use of the voyal, and the deck-tackle, in this situation. Another expedient was 'hitching the messenger': 'When the nippers are insufficient, the messenger may be hitched thus: The bight of the messenger is fastened round the cable at the manger with a rolling hitch, and the bight seized round the cable before the hitch. This practice is by no means so good as the others' (Blunt, 142). As in heaving in, at any time, if the ship were pitching, both in nippering and heaving on the capstan, it was a case of 'get all you can', as the bow pitched downwards, 'holding on' as it rose again. If the anchor were reluctant to trip, in calm weather it could be encouraged to do so by ordering all available hands forward, and heaving in as much as possible. The crew then moved aft in a body, thus raising the bow. This effect could be multiplied by having every man carry a 32-pound shot in

his arms. Similarly, heaving the cable as ta as possible, at slack water, just before t flood, would cause the incoming tide to the vessel, and loosen things up.

Weighing in a heavy head sea. 'When y have room, and are pitching, it will be best get the anchor up before making sail. By doing, you will ease the chain, nippe capstan, messenger, etcetera' (Boyd, 385)

When obliged to weigh with a heavy head s do not make sail, if you can help it, until anchor is up, as under these circumstanc such sudden jerks are continually brought the capstan, as to require all the palls to down; and even then, the cable is sometin hove in with great danger to the men at t bars; but when you add to this, the force of t sails in a fresh or strong breeze, pulling agai the bars, the danger is then much increase We have, unfortunately, known several m much hurt in this manner, when sail mig have been set quite as well, after the anchor up. But if you are obliged to set topsails befo weighing the anchor, they had better be ke on the caps, the yards laid for casting, and t sails hoisted as soon as possible after the anch is up (Liardet, 261).

Heaving through all. This was the term used, when because of slipperiness the nippers failed to hold, or the messenger surged on the capstan. Sand and ashes were thrown on the cable, and 'fresh nippers, thick and dry for weighing', were called for (Smyth, 680). Selvagee strops were sometimes put on over the regular nippers, and Rosvall (86) suggests making a sort of temporary mousing by half-hitching a length of dry sennit around the cable, the ends being hauled taut, on either side. Hitching the messenger might also be resorted to in this circumstance.

Anchor comes up foul. Bréart (146) considers that the most difficult case arose when the arm was foul, and the anchor came up crown first. He suggests hooking the cat to the crown, or to a strop on the shank, walking it up until the crown was close to the cathead. The ring-painter was passed under the crown and belayed, the cable cleared, the cat cased down, disengaged, and looked to the ring. The ring-painter was then eased off to allow the anchor to be catted properly. If the stock were foul, the cable could usually be got off with ropes worked from forecastle and beakhead. Boyd (370) remarks:

We seldom get over a foul anchor without having a man overboard. Sailors will not be slung in a bowline-knot unless forced, and even when so slung, cannot work efficiently. Clear-hawse breeches are inexpressibly useful. Make them of painted canvas, roomy, and wooden-soled at the feet, well roped, and fitted with two spans, long enough to clear a man's head, when taut to a rope. In these, men can work dry, effectively and safely.

On the forecastle. The cat- and fish-tackles were rigged, and their falls led aft. When the anchor ring appeared above the water, the cable was stoppered, and the cat was hooked, from without in. The cat fall being manned, or taken to the jeer capstan, the order 'Walk away with the cat!', was given and when the tackle was 'two blocks', 'Well the cat!' followed; the ring-painter was passed, the cat eased off, and the cable stoppered for good. Once the weight was taken by the cat, it was necessary to unstopper the cable, to allow enough slack for the ring to approach the cathead. Bitt-stoppers, or compressor, were kept ready to catch the cable, if something carried away during the catting process.

The fish-tackle was overhauled, and the hook engaged from forward aft, or without in, on the inner arm, just below the fluke, upon which 'Walk away with the fish!' was ordered; the anchor was hauled up until the shank was more or less horizontal and shank-painter passed. The fish was then eased off,

disengaged and unrigged. As mentioned earlier, using the *traversière*, the fish-tackle could be hooked at an earlier stage in the proceedings.

GETTING UNDER WAY FROM SINGLE ANCHOR

General remarks. It would be imprudent to weigh anchor unless there were sufficient wind to give steerage way, and in a confined anchorage, only when the wind was 'fair' for sailing out. Weighing anchor against a strong tide made the work unnecessarily heavy, the ideal time being at slack water; at any rate, not at the strength of the tide. This implies that, most usually – though, as we shall see, not always – the ship was wind-rode while weighing, and the wind dead ahead.

It must have been a scene of some confusion in a small single-decked vessel, when getting under way. Braces, halliards, and so on, had to be off the pins, and led along on deck. Forward, the falls of the cat and fish had to be handled, and the forecastlemen walking these back, would have got in the way of the men manning the topsail halliards. Add to this, the cable-party, nippermen, and so on, and we have the making of a fine muddle. The advantage of having the cable, and if necessary a spring, handled on a separate deck is obvious. How things were managed is best envisaged by quoting directly from contemporary authorities.

Order of setting sail.

When about to get underway, the ship being tide-rode, and the wind aft, the comparative strength of wind and tide must be well considered before coming to the decision to make sail and weigh, or to weigh first and to make sail afterwards. For it looks ill to see a ship under canvas forging ahead over her anchor, tearing the copper off her bottom, breaking the nippers, and sheering unmanageably about, before breaking ground. And it is

equally bad management, when the anchor is hove up, and the ship is drifted by the tide without steerage way. If the wind were light, it might be necessary to make nearly all sail before breaking ground, or if moderate, merely to loose them. If it were blowing strong, the ship might stem the tide without any sail, but in this latter case, it would be well to have a headsail set, so as to prevent the possibility of breaking the sheer, whilst stowing the anchor (Boyd, 385).

'In general, it is much more seamanlike to cast a ship under her square canvas. With a perfectly clear road out, it can be done under the fore and aft sails, but the ship is all but unmanageable excepting to turn, and it is by no means a pretty manoeuvre, excepting when the necessity is obvious' (Hourigan, 90). The most usual sequence was to heave to short stay, pawl the capstan, stopper the cable, loose, sheet home and hoist topsails, and if necessary topgallants, keeping the courses confined in their gear. Then the bars were manned once more, the anchor was weighed and the ship made sail.

In casting with the square sails set, ships invariably gather sternway, the moment that the anchor breaks ground. On this account, and under the circumstances, it is considered a good general rule, in the case of a foul wind, to cast with the head towards the nearest of the neighbouring dangers, to make a sternboard while the anchor is being catted, then to fill and make sail enough to ensure going about in stays when requisite. When there is not room enough to admit of going much astern, set the mainsail before starting the anchor, and have a purchase all ready to clap on the cable the moment that the anchor promises to give a heavy heave. Otherwise, the ship may go tripp-

Casting ship under square or fore and aft sail
A HMS *Thetis* ready for casting under square sail (after N M Condy, *Illustrated London News*, 1847); **B** frigate casting under jib, with sails loosed and starboard anchor being catted.

ing it astern into shoaler water, and certainly will be unmanageable until the anchor is at the bows (Boyd, 384).

'The topsails ought to be hoisted together, and smartly, topgallants the same, and royals the same. It is excessively slovenly and unbecoming a ship of war to have the sails creep up one after the other, without system, uniformity, or alacrity' (Fordyce, 112).

Casting under headsails alone. Not everyone agreed with Hourigan on this point: 'When there is plenty of sea room, and the wind is fair, it is best to cast under the headsails, and make sail when before the wind' (Boyd, 384). This method is mentioned by Bréart (166) and approved of by Liardet (260) with a free wind:

> If you have no danger in your way, instead of making all sail for casting, when you have a long stay, it will generally be found much easier to weigh the anchor, and run the ship under the jib, until you have catted and fished the anchor. By this means, all your square sails will be set much easier than when the wind is right ahead, as it saves the incessant footing the sails out of the tops, clews of the topgallant sails getting foul of the crosstrees, sails binding against the caps, and thereby endangering their splitting, etcetera, are avoided. I have always been under the impression that you can weigh your anchor much easier, and cat and fish it better, before making sail, than by the contrary practice; and that the sails are set with less hands, and quicker, when the ship is before the wind, than can ever be done while riding head to wind'.

For some further discussion, see *Mariner's Mirror* 57, 1971, 334.

Spunyarn stops. Bonnefoux thought it was a pretty manoeuvre to deploy all the canvas at once, which could be accomplished by mastheading the topsail and topgallant yards before setting the sails. His contemporary Dubreuil (194), on the contrary, considered this the method of a show-off rather than a good seaman. The sails were loosed, the gaskets cast off, and replaced with lashings of spunyarn, partially cut through – what one would today call 'rotten-stops' – so that they were weak enough to break, when the sheets were hauled home. In addition, hands remained aloft, ready to cast off the buntgaskets on the order. Dubreuil felt that the sails, set in this fashion, blew out almost horizontally, and were difficult to get sheeted home quickly, the vessel meanwhile not being properly under command.

Disposition of the crew. When weighing anchor, the watch on deck handled the canvas, catted and fished the anchor, while the idlers and watch below worked the cables

and manned the capstan. The forecastlemen rigged the cat-tackle while the gunners rigged the fish-tackle; the forecastlemen hooked the cat, and the captain of the forecastle the fish. The fore- and maintopmen of the watch below cast on the nippers, the former before, and the latter abaft, the bitts. When anchoring, the forecastlemen cleared away the anchors, ready for letting go, the carpenters removed the bucklers and hawseplugs, the fore- and maintopmen ranged the cables, the gunners streamed the buoy, and the boatswain gave the signal to the forecastlemen to let go the ring- and shankpainters. On the gundeck, the armourer looked after the chain cable Blake stopper, while the idlers manned the compressortackle.

Commands. These representative orders may be divided into those heard on the forecastle, those on the gundeck, and those concerned with making sail.

Up Anchor!
All hands up anchor for home! (this was a traditional phrase, according to Hourigan, when the destination was the vessel's home port.)
Rig the capstan!
Bring to the messenger!
Man the bars!
Ready for heaving around!
Heave round!
Heave cheerily!
Heave and pawl!
One more pawl!
Get all you can!
Fresh and dry nippers for the heavy heave!
Fleet the messenger!
Surge-ho!
Hold on!
Avast heaving!
Rig the cat!
Hook the cat!
Grapple the buoy!
Man the cat! Haul taut!
Walk away with the cat! Belay!
Rig the fish!
Hook the fish!
Man the fish! Haul taut!
Walk away with the fish! Belay!
Unrig the fish! Ring up the anchor!

Make sail!
Aloft sail loosers!
Lead along topsail sheets and halliards, jib halliards!
Lay out and loose!
Stand by! Let fall!
Lay in and down from aloft!
Man topsail sheets and halliards! Tend the braces!

Sheet home and hoist away topsails!
Lay aft to the braces, port head, starboard main, port crossjack!
Haul taut! Brace abox! Brace up!
Man the jib halliards!
Clear away the downhaul! Hoist away!
Starboard head braces!
Brace around the headyards!
Shift over the headsheets!

An interesting sidelight on earlier practice is offered by this excerpt from Smith (48):

> The master and company being aboard, he commands them to get the sailes to the yards, and about your geare, or worke on, all hands, stretch forward your maine halliards, hoise your sailes halfe mast high. Predy!, or, Make ready to set saile. Crosse your yards, bring your cable to the capsterne. Boatswaine, fetch an anchor aboard. Breake ground, or Weigh anchor! Heave ahead! Men into the tops! Men upon the yards! Come, is the anchor a-pike? That is, to heave the hawse of the ship right over the anchor. What, is the anchor away? Yea, Yea! Let fall your foresail. Tally! That is, hale off the sheets. Who is at the helme there? Coile your cables in small fakes! Hale the cat! A bitter, belay, loose fast your anchor with your shank-painter! Stow the boat!

Methods of getting underway. It is impossible to detail every possible circumstance, but the following examples will suggest the general principles used. Of course, the technical problem was sometimes solved by having the ship's boats tow the vessel to sea. Sailing 'tugs' were sometimes used by the Dutch, and the arrival on the scene of the steam tug, rendered the congregation of large numbers of vessels in the Downs, waiting a favourable slant of wind, a thing of the past.

Weather anchor. The exact method adopted rather depended on the known qualities of the vessel, such as whether she paid off easily with the headyards backed, went astern readily, gathered headway quickly, and so on. The basic rule was to 'cast away from the anchor, and towards the nearest danger' (Hourigan, 90). It was desirable to have the anchor cable growing to weather, rather than to lee. In the latter case, the ship would be drifting towards the cable, and the anchor fluke was liable to foul the cutwater, as it came up, and subject the copper to damage from the cable; furthermore, the buoy-rope might become foul of the sternpost and rudder (Dubreuil, 192). If the vessel were heeling, the crown of the anchor might be so far below the surface, that hooking the fish was impossible. This consideration was so paramount that if the ship had, for some reason, to be cast towards her anchor, it was best to get her on the other tack before catting and fishing. On the other point, the bow was cast *toward* the most proximate danger, because this would result in the ship backing *away* from it, as she dropped astern. While weighing one anchor, a second was always kept ready for letting go, in the event some unforeseen circumstance required immediate re-anchoring.

Wind ahead, no tide, no nearby obstructions. The cable was hove short, and the vessel cast away from, say, the port anchor, the afteryards braced as for the port tack, the headyards abox, and the headsheets hauled over to port. The anchor being aweigh, the helm was put to starboard, and this combination of helm and canvas caused the stern to back around to port as she gathered sternway. Eventually, the afteryards filled and she gathered headway, whereupon the helm was righted, headsheets hauled over, and the spanker set. When the anchor was catted and fished, topgallants, courses and other sails were set as appropriate, the ship continuing on her way, close-hauled on the port tack. If the object was to end up going downwind, the casting movement could be continued, as in boxhauling; that is, the afteryards were kept shivering, instead of being allowed to fill, so that the stern ran up into the wind, the helm being kept a-starboard. When the wind was well aft, the headyards were squared, the helm righted, and the ship started on her way downwind. Gower (108) remarks, however, that a ship will not wear very well, until the anchor is up under the bows. A third variation was to remain hove to, fore topsail to the mast, while the anchor was catted and fished. The same method could be used when there was an obstruction ahead, or on one quarter, casting towards the latter, and then backing away from it.

Backing out. If there were obstructions on either beam, and ahead, the ship could make a sternboard straight back, by keeping the helm amidships, and the yards square. This method is described by Murphy. Other seamen preferred to back all three topsails, say by hauling aft the port braces and keeping the helm a-port. This configuration of canvas pushed the bow to starboard, but the helm prevented it falling too far off the wind. Some control could also be exerted by having the ship's people move to one side, causing the vessel to heel; the bow moved in the same direction as the side on which the crew stood.

Wind ahead, leeward tide. This was similar to the case mentioned earlier, with the exception that the helm could be used to sheer the vessel, and initiate the casting process. The helm had to be shifted the

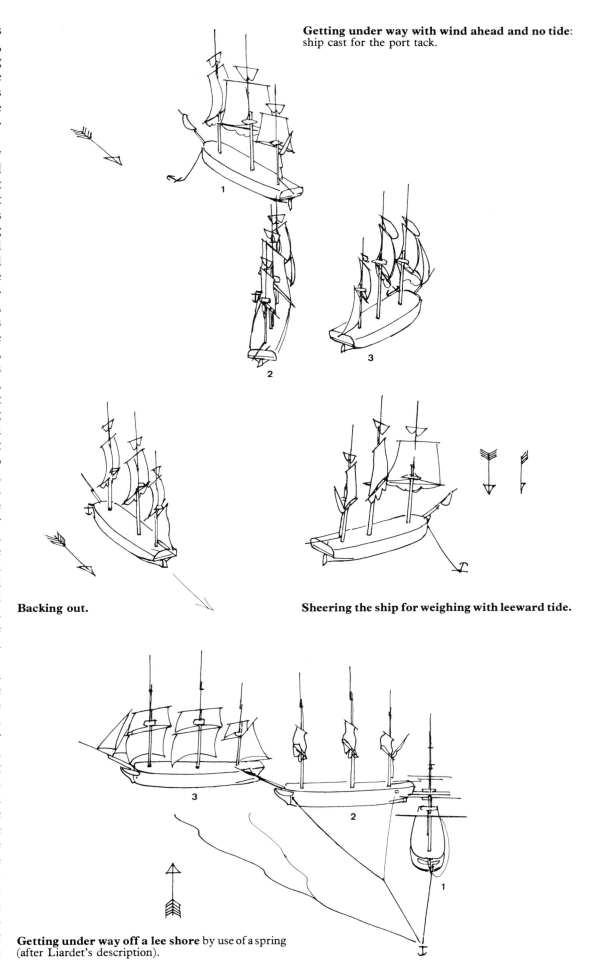

Getting under way with wind ahead and no tide: ship cast for the port tack.

Backing out.

Sheering the ship for weighing with leeward tide.

Getting under way off a lee shore by use of a spring (after Liardet's description).

1.
Ship tending at single anchor, using the headsails and braced up foreyards. Title page of Lever's *Young Sea Officer's Sheet Anchor*. (Mark Myers' Collection)

2.
'A view of a Ship of War clearing hawse and making the Signal to Unmoor' by Nicholas Pocock, 1762. She has an 'elbow' in her cables. (Courtesy Bristol Museum & Art Gallery)

3.
Vasa's jeer capstan. The pawls would have been placed on its after side. (Author's photo, courtesy *Vasa* Varvet and Marine Dir Gunnar Schoerner RSN)

4.
Boy seamen running round the capstan in the training ship *Mercury*. This could be done once the anchor was broken out of the ground, and it was simply a matter of running it up under the bows. The original caption refers to the boys' practice of swinging their feet off the deck and riding the bars over hatchways or other obstructions. The swifter is clearly shown. *Illustrated London News*, 1888. (Mark Myers' Collection)

1.

'Heave Together!' French and British sailors manning the capstan on board a French warship. Notice how the proportions of the capstan are determined by the need for the capstan bars to be at chest height, and that the barrel must be shaped so that the inboard, or 'high' end of the cable can be stepped over. The men are grasping the bars in the approved fashion, hands in front, thumbs outwards. Apparently, men at the inner ends of the bars were so close to each other that they could not lean so far forward, and stood more upright, pushing with their hands. *Illustrated London News*, 1891. (Mark Myers' Collection)

2.

HMS *Duke of Wellington* weighing anchor with topgallants set over reefed topsails. The original caption to this 1854 engraving in the *Illustrated London News* states that the sounds of the boatswain's pipe and the sailors at work on the capstan to the fifer's tune could be clearly heard over the water, and that the anchor was at the bows only ten minutes after beginning to weigh. (Mark Myers' Collection)

3.

Merchantman getting under way at the mouth of the Avon, by Joseph Walter. Of interest here is the cat-tackle which has just been hooked on to the anchor ring, and the motion of the ship as she pays off from the wind. The boat under the lee quarter is keeping well clear. (Courtesy Bristol Museum and Art Gallery)

4.

Catting the anchor in the ship *Cumberland*, painted by Nicholas Pocock, 1778. The hands are tailing onto the cat tackle falls, and the yards braced for casting ship. (Courtesy Bristol Museum and Art Gallery)

instant the vessel started to make sternway. If the ship were tide-rode, and the wind a couple of points on the weather bow, casting was facilitated. With the wind on the lee bow, it was more difficult, and getting under way might require the use of a spring.

Leading wind, ship tide-rode. A 'leading' wind was one on the beam or quarter, that is to say, 'fair'. If the vessel were anchored in a narrow channel, or crowded anchorage, the authorities agree that it was best to weigh on the weather tide, that is to say, the flood. In this case, the ship would not be obliged to cast, since her bow would be pointing to seaward. By setting sail, she could stem the tide, as the cable was hove in, and then proceed to sea.

Wind across the tide. In a narrow channel, similar considerations applied as in the previous case. If there were enough room, the ship could either stand directly out to sea upon weighing, or do so after going about. Otherwise it might be necessary to use a spring.

Use of a spring. A 'spring' was a hawser used to cast the vessel in a particular direction. It was usually led out of one of the after gunports, since the greatest leverage was exerted furthest from the bow. A simple example of the sort of situation where it was useful would be the preceding one, where the wind was across the tide, the vessel lying wind-rode athwart a fairly narrow channel, running East-West, with the wind North. There is no room to back astern, but by using a spring she can be cast in the appropriate direction, and lose nothing to leeward. A dolphin, or kedge-anchor, laid out in the required direction, acted as a fixed point, about which the stern could pivot. In the former case, the hawser could be rigged as a 'slip-rope'; in the second, a boat was kept in the water to recover the kedge, when it had served its purpose. By leading such a hawser in through a sheet hawse-hole, and running away with it, it was possible, in mild weather to get the ship moving fast enough ahead, that she never slipped back, even when the anchor was aweigh (Hourigan, 93). With a shoal astern, and no room to cast in the ordinary way, the ship might be warped ahead to a kedge laid out ahead of the anchor, and perhaps, by this means, give herself enough sea room astern to cast in the ordinary fashion.

A spring could also be hitched to the riding-cable, and used to cant the vessel in the desired direction. We have earlier described how this method was used to rescue the *Magnificent* in Basque Roads. Liardet (196) gives yet another vivid description of how a vessel was got under sail, after having dragged her anchor on a lee shore:

> It was blowing too hard to attempt to warp her off shore, and the ship was too near the rocks to make sail from, therefore, between the squalls, we agreed to try the following plan – with the stream-cable, we made a spring from aft on the port side, to the riding cable; a sufficient number of men were sent aloft to have the double-reefed topsails, and the courses ready for letting fall at a moment's warning; the topsail sheets and halliards were all well manned, and taut for a run; the spring was hauled taut, and secured to the mainmast; the yards were all laid perfectly square, the cable was then veered gently during one of the greatest lulls, until the wind was right on the port beam. The riding cable was then instantly well stoppered, and ready for slipping with the damaged cable of the anchor, and at the same instant, for cutting the stream cable; at this moment, the topsails were sheeted home, and hoisted at the same time, and from the wind being right abeam, and the yards square, of course little or no increased strain was brought on the spring or bower cable. When the topsails were up, braces, tacks, sheets, driver outhauler, and a jib halliards all well manned, the preparative word given to insure everything being taut, the next minute the yards were braced sharp up, and topsails, courses, jibs, and driver all well set. By this means, we insured the ship getting way previous to slipping the cables, and cutting the spring, when the ship had sheered her cables taut, and brought her head within seven points of the wind. Consequently, she had felt and sprung to her canvas. The bower cables were then slipped, and the stream cable cut at the same instant. In less than ten minutes, she was tacked, and in about two hours worked completely out of danger (Liardet, 196).

Getting under way from fixed moorings. These were found in narrow fairways, and crowded harbours; consequently, the vessel would usually cast off with a leading wind. Letting go was even simpler than weighing anchor. A slip-rope was led from a hawsehole through the ring of the mooring-buoy, and back in to be belayed. Upon the command 'Let go!', the end was cast off, and the slip-rope hauled aboard. A spring, rigged in a similar fashion, could be led from an after gunport, around outside of all. The vessel could be cast in exactly the same way as already described, the exact method depending upon the state of the tide, and so on.

Phraseology. In preparation for weighing, the cable was 'hove short'. When it was in line with the mainstay, the ship was 'at long stay'; when in line with the forestay, it was 'at short stay', 'short stay apeak' (Smyth). The latter condition, by the way, corresponds to *à long pic*, in French. This was the juncture at which sail was set, after which the cable was hove in further, until it was 'up and down', the anchor now being 'apeak', *à pic*, in French. Once it was broken out of the ground, the anchor was 'atrip', or 'aweigh', and the ship 'underway'. Brady and Hourigan, in common with many other writers in the 1800s, use the spelling 'under weigh', and indeed talk of the anchor being 'a-way', but modern practice mostly tends to favour Gower's 'under way'. The anchor was 'in sight', when it could be descried under the surface, the first indication being the cloud of muddy water around it. It was 'a-wash', when the ring surfaced. Arising from these, developed the encouraging cries to the men at the capstan, 'Heave and a-weigh!', 'Heave and in sight!' and 'Heave and a-wash!'. 'Heave and rally!', 'Heave cheerly!' were the orders when a special effort was needed to break the anchor out of the ground. 'Heave and stand to your bars!', 'Heave and pawl!' were used in the same circumstances, with the bow rising and falling to the sea, the cable being hove taut, and the anchor tripped, as she rose to the next sea. The old-fashioned horizontal pawls had to be knocked in and out requir-ing an order 'In pawl!, Out pawl!', or something of the sort, whereas the later 'drop-pawls' functioned automatically. Harboe and Uggla offer exhortations to 'Get the last pawl!', 'One more pawl!', under these circumstances. Smyth uses the spelling 'paul', while Totten's choice of 'pall' exactly follows German *Pall*. Other orders that might be given while weighing, include 'Heave round!', 'Avast heaving!', 'Surge the messenger!', 'Surge-ho!'. 'Avast heaving!' corresponded to the order 'Belay!' when hauling on other ropes. It was given when a nipper jammed, or someone's fingers were trapped. 'Surge-ho!' was the warning that the men 'holding off' were to be ready to slacken their grip, allowing the messenger to surge, and the turns to fleet up on the capstan barrel. Upon the stoppers being passed, the pawls were knocked out, and the messenger and cable eased back until the strain was taken by the stoppers.

Slipping the cable. Occasionally it might be necessary to put to sea without having time to weigh the anchor. This might arise from some tactical necessity, or because of the weather. In either case, some thought was given to the subsequent recovery of the anchor, and its cable. Even if there was an anchor-buoy, it was worthwhile buoying the cable also. A buoy-rope was led in through the hawsepipe, and bent to the end of the cable, or chain due to be slipped. When it was let go, cable and buoy-rope ran out together. The cable could be slipped most readily if a shackle or splice were placed close abaft the bitts. In the event that the chain cable was veered 'to the clinch' – that is to the point where it was secured round the mainmast – it was best if the cable were secured with a lashing, since this could be cut more readily than the pin of a shackle could be knocked out. In emergency, it might be necessary to cut through a hemp cable with an axe, when no time was available to unsplice and buoy the cable.

Dana (78) describes a method of slipping, employing a 'slip-rope' as a spring, to cast the vessel the desired way. This was taken out through an after gunport, led along, outside of all, and bent to the cable, just outside the hawsepipe. This was done on the port side, if it was intended to cast to starboard. A buoy-rope was led in through the hawsepipe, and three turns taken round the windlass barrel, the opposite way to the three turns made by the cable. The buoy-rope was bent to the end of the cable, where it had been unshackled. In this way, when the cable and buoy-rope were let go, they cleared themselves of the windlass barrel.

LAYING OUT AN ANCHOR

Terminology. A small 'kedge anchor' and hawser were used to 'warp' the ship, in certain circumstances. 'Kedge' derives from Middle English *caggen*, 'to draw, or fasten'; both the French term *ancre à jet*, and Dutch *werpanker*, have the connotation 'throw-anchor', and presumably are related to the small craft practice of throwing a grapnel out ahead, and hauling up to it. English 'warp', for that matter, also has the basic meaning of 'to throw', although in this particular sense, it probably came into English from Dutch *werfen*. The same basic thought underlies the traditional phrase 'to cast anchor', which is synonymous with 'to anchor'.

Available anchors. For shifting berth in an anchorage, running out a line to keep a clear hawse, or to warp through a narrow channel in a calm, a kedge anchor was adequate. Luce (286) lists four kedges, weighing respectively one-seventh, one-eighth, one-tenth, and one-fourteenth the weight of the best bower, while Boyd (225) indicates an establishment of two kedges, respectively one-eighth, and one-fourteenth the weight of the bower. Merchant ships, according to Murphy, rarely carried kedge anchors. If the ship had run aground, it would be necessary to lay out a heavier anchor, say the stream, or even a bower.

Longboat fitted for anchor-work. The longboat or launch of a First Rate was a substantial craft, perhaps 34 feet long, fitted with a windlass amidships, rollers, which could be placed on the transom and stempost, and a curved davit, which was secured aft and projected over the transom. In the mid-1800s, an English shipwright named Cow started fitting launches with 'trunks'. These were vertical pipes, which screwed into brass plates in the bottom, and extended above the waterline, directly underneath the windlass (Luce, 340). These greatly simplified suspending heavy items, like guns or a bower anchor, directly under the keel of the launch, since the rope supporting them could be taken directly to the windlass through the bottom of the boat (May, 13).

Methods of carrying out anchors. In a transom-sterned boat, the greatest flotation is aft, hence the anchors were carried in the sternsheets, hung on the transom, or suspended under the after part of the hull. The longboat was ordinarily of such a size that it could support the weight of the bower anchor, but if the flotation were in doubt, two pairs of empty water-butts were lashed together, and the boat lowered on to them, to get the extra buoyancy. Other methods employed two boats, suspending the anchor between them, either as they lay side by side, or stern to stern. If the anchor were hung off the stern, the French seamen described it as being *en cravatte*, or *en bandoulière*, hung 'necktie-', or 'bandoleer-fashion'. The usual method was to suspend it by the ring, rigging a toggle with which it could be slipped (Knight, 181). It might be suspended with

Boats for anchor work
A Boat fitted for anchor work with
  a windlass; **b** trunk; **c** davit.
B Kedge carried in sternsheets; **C** anchor slung fore and aft beneath boat; **D** anchor carried between boats in line; **E** anchor slung fore and aft, chain stopped to gunwales; **F** anchor slung athwartships beneath boat; **G** anchor carried between two boats abreast; **H** Casks used to give extra buoyancy.

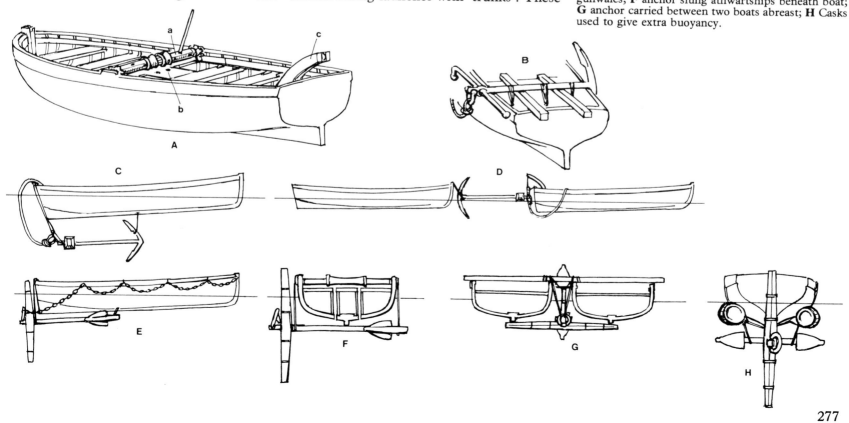

the shank horizontal, hung from its 'balance-point', the arms on one side of the boat, and the stock on the other (Bourdé, I, 153); or where the boat was used to weigh a larger anchor by the buoy-rope, it remained hanging under the davit, crown uppermost.

If the anchor were carried in the stern-sheets, two capstan bars were laid fore and aft, resting on a thwart across the gunwales, and the transom. The anchor was laid transversely on these, stock on one side, arms on the other, or the arms could be slid forward on the bars and thwart, the stock remaining abaft the transom, pointing up and down.

Laying out. It will be realised that although great distances were not involved, there was some guesswork as to whether the hawser would reach or not. Perhaps this explains the origin of the term 'guess warp'; an old French term used in the same context was *mouiller en créance*, which we might translate as 'anchoring on trust' (Willaumez, 192). The boat's distance from the ship could be estimated by eye, by using a sextant, or by running out a light rope of known length, for example the deep-sea leadline. If wind and sea were running towards the spot were the anchor was to be dropped, the boat rowed in that direction, and the hawser was paid out after it. If the opposite condition obtained, it was better to pay the whole hawser down into the boat, drop the anchor, and bring the end of the hawser back to the ship. In this circumstance, it was imperative that the anchor end of the hawser be placed in the boat last of all, since it went overboard first.

The depths of water involved were never great, in the ordinary way being less than the draught of the parent vessel. A boat leadline was used to determine the depth exactly. When chain cable was used, the initial length was usually suspended in bights around the boat, outside the gunwale, so that when the anchor was let go, there would be sufficient chain to reach the bottom. Any further chain in the boat was secured with check-stoppers of spunyarn, so it would not run out too violently. The men in the boat must have been at some hazard when this was going on; one authority suggests that they lie under the thwarts, while the chain ran out. A hawser, or stream cable, of hemp, was much lighter, and usually preferred, in this circumstance.

It will be apparent that when laying out a stream anchor and a substantial length of cable, there was no room left for the oarsmen. The boat was then towed by the cutters to the desired place, or hauled there by warping on a small kedge laid out beforehand, a steering oar being used in place of the rudder.

Weighing anchor by means of the

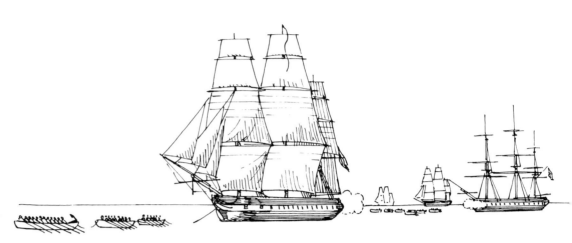

Kedging. USS *Constitution* kedging away from HMS *Belvidera* (right) note anchor in sternsheets of boat at left (after T Birch, c1830).

launch. A kedge offered no great problem. If it was not buoyed, the hawser was under-run, starting at the ship, rowing the boat and pulling the hawser in over the bow roller, paying it out over the stern, until the anchor was reached and weighed. The same method could be adopted even with the largest anchors. In fact, under-running the cable, in this way, was also undertaken to inspect and clean a hemp cable which had been in the water for a protracted period. To weigh a heavy anchor, two luff-tackles were carried in the boat. The single blocks were hooked to ringbolts aft, and the double blocks to strops around the cable, at the davit. One tackle was fleeted, as the other was hauled upon. In the event of a heavy heave, the double block of one could be clapped on the fall of the other, 'luff upon luff'. If the tackle failed to break the anchor loose, the crew moved to the end of the boat, got all they could and belayed. They then went to the other end of the boat and jumped up and down together (Boström, 147).

The other technique was to weigh using the buoy-rope. Several authors suggest rigging this in a special way when there was the prospect of weighing anchor with the launch. A block was stropped to the crown of the anchor, and the buoy-rope rove through this, and both ends being secured to the buoy. This arrangement greatly facilitated the task of the men in the boat, when it came time to lift the anchor.

Warping in chase, in shoal water. Here is a vivid contemporary account of this operation:

This is a scene of the greatest possible animation. You are in chase of a vessel nearly your own force. At any rate, she is too great a force to attempt carrying her with the boats. You have every possible sail set, but just as you are within a few miles of the land, the wind dies away, until at last it becomes a perfect calm. Suppose the chasing ship a frigate, the water from twelve to fifteen fathoms. Hoist out and lower down all boats. Have two of your heaviest kedges ready for your boats to run out as guess warps. Form them into two divisions for towing out the kedges, which should be boated if possible. Send the first division of boats away immediately in what you consider the best direction. Have everything quite ready on both sides of the main deck for warping ship, cabin bulkheads down, sampson's posts close aft as you can, deck well sanded, fiddler and fifer all ready to strike up any favourite tune amongst the ship's company. The moment the end of each hawser enters the hawsehole, away with it, strike up fiddler or fifer, and make a clear run fore and aft the deck, until you get in the slack. Then proportion your force to insure the holding of the anchor. The second division of boats should start the moment the first hawser reaches the spot, and so continue working the kedges out and in. In the *Belvidera*, when the squadron under Sir Philip Broke, in the *Shannon*, chased the United States frigate *Constitution*, this chase was on soundings, and kedging was had recourse to by the squadron, and the American frigate also. This is a case in point, which clearly proves, that in calm weather, the sails should be furled, or as little exposed as possible, as the sails create a resistance in proportion to the ship's velocity through the water (Liardet, 64).

Recovering an anchor by sweeping. If the cable parted, and the buoy failed to 'watch', an attempt was made to mark the anchor by dropping an extempore marker-buoy, for example a breaker with sufficient line wrapped round it to keep it afloat; this was 'unreeled' by a weight secured to the other end. A hawser, a weighted one-inch line, and two boats were needed to 'sweep', or

Sweeping for an anchor
A Diagram of an anchor being recovered by sweeping with two boats; **B** detail of boats and weighted line used in sweeping (after Röding, 1793).

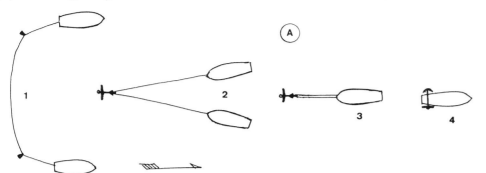

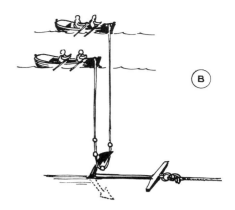

'creep' for the lost anchor. Assume the tide setting from the marker-buoy towards the presumed direction of the anchor. Each boat rode out at right angles to the tide, paying out its end of the light line, until a total of 50 fathoms or so was deployed. Deep-sea leads were made fast at this point, and allowed to take the line to the bottom, sufficient line having been retained in the boat to allow this being done. Both boats pulled, or drifted, down with the tide, feeling the lead, as it bumped over the bottom. If successful, the line caught on the upper arm, and the boats were swung together by the force of the tide. The lines were then married, and hauled in, until almost up and down. One end of the line was secured to the hawser, which was coiled down in the sternsheets of one of the boats, and the line used to pull the hawser down round the arm, the fluke preventing it coming off. When both ends of the hawser

were finally secured in one boat, a light line was bent to a large shackle, which was secured round both parts, and allowed to slide down towards the anchor, after the fashion of a 'sentinel', or 'kellet'. This 'jewel', as Liardet calls it, bound the two parts of the hawser securely to the arm below the fluke, and permitted the anchor to be weighed by the boat, or possibly the ship. If a marker-buoy was not dropped, the anchor might be located by the cross-bearing taken when it was dropped, or by making repeated sweeps in its supposed situation. It was best of course if the sweeping line approached from the direction of the shank, since this offered the greatest chance of hooking the arm. Dragging for a cable was done using a 'creeper', or grapnel, *chatte* as it was called in French. The sweep was carried out at right angles to the presumed lie of the cable, since this would offer the best chance of snagging it. Smyth

suggests that when something drops overboard in shallow water while in harbour, it was a good idea to throw a white plate or something of similar high visibility after it, to allow it to be located quickly.

The sweeping for anchors is carried on to a very great extent about the mouth of the Thames by large fishing vessels not immediately in employ. These vessels get acquainted with the loss of anchors sustained by gales of wind, and take the opportunity of fine weather to sweep for them. They situate themselves tideward of the anchor, and each taking an end of the sweep-rope, they separate a considerable distance by putting themselves upon opposite sheers, to preserve which, a spring is fixed to the sweep-rope, and so they drift with the tide. It is amazing the quantity of ground these vessels will sweep over in the course of a day! (Gower, 174).

CHAPTER 19
SHIFTING HEAVY WEIGHTS

The methods used for hoisting boats in and out from the booms are examined in detail in the next chapter, but in essence, this was done using the stay-tackles and triatic stay, assisted by the yard-tackles. The yards had to be supported to withstand the heavy strains involved. Rather similar methods were used for shifting other heavy items, such as guns and stores, and we will deal with these now.

Winding-tackle. This was ordinarily the heaviest purchase available. Mainwaring describes one having an upper block with three sheaves, and a lower block with two, although even heavier versions were used. The upper block was secured to a whip which ran through a heavy block stropped to the main-stay, or hooked to the masthead pendant. The lower block was hooked to the sling around the load, the fall leading through a snatch-block, so it could, if necessary, be taken to the capstan. The French called it a *caliorne*, the Germans a *Mantel-Takel*, or *Spanisches-Takel*, meaning 'tie-tackle' or 'Spanish-tackle'. The word *Mantel*, is said to derive from the Spanish *amante*, with the same technical meaning. Röding gives the English equivalent as 'tie', but 'whip' would probably be better. In German, there were two words for 'tackle': *Takel* meaning a heavy purchase, and *Talje*, a light one.

Garnet-tackle. For lighter tasks, a less powerful purchase was used. It will be realised that the heaviest tackle was also the slowest, and hence not suitable for lesser weights. The word 'garnet', with which we are more familiar as an element of 'clew-garnet', is related to Dutch *granaat*. Pilaar gives the variant *karnaat* for a mizzen side-tackle, but it usually occurs as *stag-granaat*, 'stay-tackle'. I think the word somehow arose because of a fancied resemblance of the tackle-block to a pomegranate. The name of the fruit in turn, is of French origin – *pom(m)e*, and a word *granate*, implying that it is like an apple with seeds. From it we also get the name of a jewel and a colour, 'garnet', a weapon 'grenade', and the solder who uses it 'grenadier'. The French actually called this tackle the *bredindin*, while the usual German term was *Französisches-Takel*, 'French-

Detail of a Baugean engraving of a British transport loading military stores in a Mediterranean port, 1814. A gun is being hoisted on board by the main tackle and yard tackle as the ship lies drying her sails. The mainsail has been left furled with its sheet and tack unrove to keep clear of the tackles. (Mark Myers' Collection)

tackle'.

Wien-Takel. Röding illustrates three versions of what literally translates 'Vienna-tackle', but perhaps it owes something to English 'winding-tackle'. It is identical, in one variation, with what would usually be called a double Spanish burton. 'Burton', incidentally, is thought to arise because the English seaman at one time distinguished a particular type of purchase as a 'Breton tackle', in the same way as the Germans talked of French and Spanish tackles.

Mast-tackles. Tackles hooked to the mast pendants were distinguished as 'fore-tackle', and 'main-tackle'. They were called 'side-tackles' (*Seiten-Takel*) in German, and *candelette* in French. The fore-tackle was

called the 'fish-tackle' when it was used to 'fish' the anchor. The mast-tackles were also used as the stay-tackles is handling the boat. A purchase hooked to the collar of the main-stay was called the *hondefok* ('dog-foresail') in Dutch, because it also served as the halliard for a main staysail of the same name.

Other tackles. We have mentioned Mainwaring's reference to 'boat-tackles', and touched on the use of 'long-tackles' and 'sail-tackles', when shifting sails. A 'water-whip' consisting of two light tackles, rigged as 'yard' and 'stay' was often kept rigged semi-permanently for lifting lighter articles in and out. It was more complicated than a simple whip, but got its name because it was used to shift water casks.

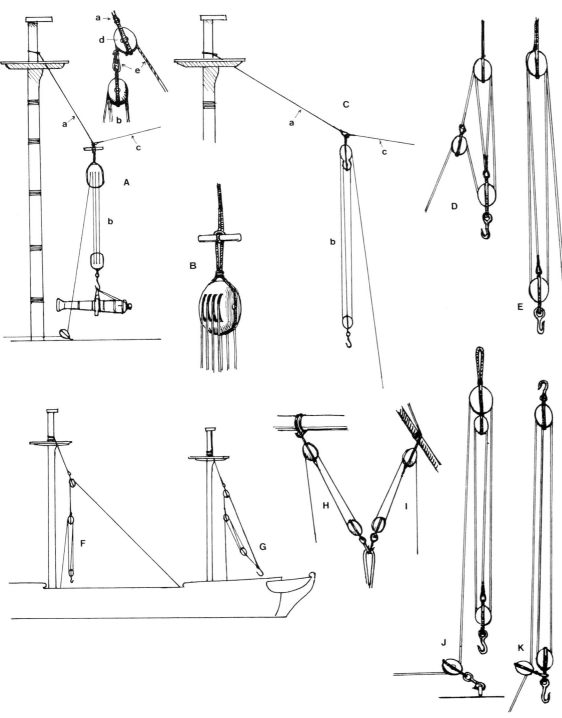

Tackles used in shifting weights
A Winding tackle:
　a pendant; **b** winding tackle; **c** guy; **d** tie block; **e** whip.
B Detail of winding tackle block toggled to pendant; **C** garnet:
　a pendant; **b** tackle; **c** guy.
D Double Spanish burton; **E** top burton; **F** main tackle; **G** fore tackle rigged as fish tackle; **H** water whip yard tackle; **I** water whip stay tackle; **J** long tackle; **K** sail tackle.

CHAPTER 20

LOWERING AND HOISTING IN BOATS

Until about 1800, all the boats were stowed on the booms amidship, sometimes nested one inside the other. There was tremendous variation in the number and size of boats carried, depending on the size of the ship, and so on. Falconer lists the boats of a man-of-war in order of size, as longboat or launch, pinnace, cutter and yawl. In addition there might be a barge, somewhat larger than a pinnace, used in harbour for transporting flag officers. A shorter version of the yawl, was known as a gig. A galley was appropriated for the captain's use, and was rather larger than a gig (Smyth). Detailed tables of the specifications of the boats supplied to different classes of ship are to found in Nares (191) and Mossel (I, 454).

Names of boats. Most of the terms came into English from other languages, with the ultimate origins remaining quite obscure. Launch is from Spanish *lancha*, which is thought to be derived from a Malay word meaning 'quick, nimble'. *Pinnace*, and a similar word in French, descend from older versions like French *spinace* and Anglo-Norman *espynasse*. An ultimate Indo-Portuguese origin has been proposed for cutter, but it may simply be related to the idea of 'cutting through the water'. Yawl has close equivalents in most other languages, such as French *yole*, Dutch *jol*, German *Jolle*. These latter remind one of 'jollyboat', which was the same as a yawl, but the original forms this took, 'jollywat', 'gellywatte', and so on, seem to have derived separately. Barge arises from Old French *barge*, and etymologists have suggested that it shares similar origins with both 'barque' and 'barrico' (breaker). 'Gig' may be native English, and was adopted not only into Dutch as *giek*, but other languages as well. The basic sense is to 'spin like a top', or to spin along, as a lightly built boat, or horse-drawn vehicle.

Dutch and French terms. The equivalent were as follows:

Longboat	Barkas	Chaloupe
Pinnace	Werksloep	Pinnace

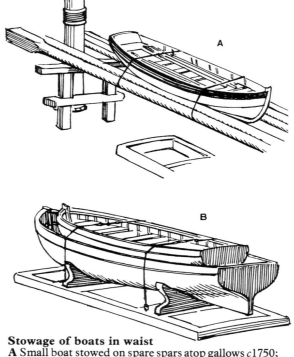

Stowage of boats in waist
A Small boat stowed on spare spars atop gallows c1750;
B boats nested on chocks over hatch c1850.

Typical range of man-of-war's boats c1800
A Long-boat; B pinnace; C cutter; D yawl.

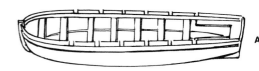

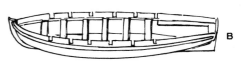

Hoisting gear
a Main stay tackle pendant; b fore stay tackle pendant; c triatic stay; d main stay tackle; e fore stay tackle; f main yard tackle; g fore yard tackle; h top burton; i rolling tackle; j guys.

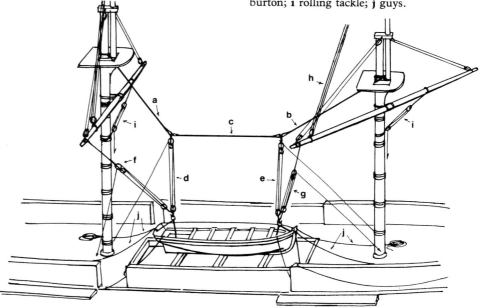

Cutter	Kotter	Coutre
Barge	Kapiteins-Sloep	Canot de parade
Yawl	Jol	Yole
Gig	Giek	Gigue, Youyou

In French the general term for 'ship's boat' was *canot*, hence of course our word 'canoe'. The word *embarcation* appears to have been limited to larger boats, over 18 metres or so (Bonnefoux). Dutch *sloep* and French *chaloupe* explain the origin respectively of 'sloop' and 'shallop'. I have never actually come across the form 'work-boat' in English, or *travaille-chaloupe* in French, but the latter may have existed at one time, since a very similar form is used in Danish. In any event, a boat was required for general purposes, as distinct from ceremonial use, fetching stores, and so on (what the French referred to as *la poste aux choux*, 'cabbage-stations').

Hoisting out a boat from the booms. At sea, the vessel hove to, and the boat was swung out to leeward. At anchor, it was usually hoisted out to port, but if tide-rode, and the wind across the tide, to leeward (Krogh, 167). Because the aftermost forward shrouds came down well abaft the foremast, while the foremost main shroud was abreast the mainmast, the boat was swung out over the rail, closer to the mainmast than the fore. For this reason, the ship always hove to, main topsail to the mast, that is to say, with the mainyard almost square, and the lee fore yardarm hauled aft.

With the larger boats, it was necessary to give extra support to the yards, which involved rigging a rolling-tackle on the weather side to steady the yard over to lee, clapping on lift-jiggers, and fitting a preventer lift on the lee side, devised from a top-burton, or something similar, to support the lee half of the yard. In addition, all braces and trusses were hauled taut, the lee yardarms were topped up a little, the lee lifts and lee topsail clewlines being hauled taut alike, to distribute the strain.

Tackles and guys. The boat was initially raised using the stay-tackles amidships, the yardarm-tackles subsequently taking the strain as the boat was swung out over the railing, and then being eased off to lower the boat into the water. The inner purchases, the 'side-' or 'stay-tackles' depended from the masthead pendants; these were permanent fixtures, which were of the same thickness as the shrouds, and fitted at the same time when placing the standing rigging. A large thimble was eye-spliced into their lower ends, and they went on as a pair, so that one hung on either side of the mast.

The pendants were held away from the masts, when hoisting a boat, by means of a span, the same length as the boat, the pendants and span together forming the 'triatic stay'. Sometimes a special one-piece triatic stay was rigged, half-hitched to fore and main mastheads, the stay-tackles hooking to thimbles on the bight. The stay was, in any event, comprised of three parts, and this no doubt explains how the word arises; but it does not account for the early variants 'skiatic' or 'skyatic', alluded to by Steel and Totten. The upper blocks of the stay-tackles had to be whipped up, to allow them to be hooked. The yard-tackle – or as it was known in German, etc, *Nock-Takel*, that is, 'yardarm-tackle' – was sometimes kept up on the yard. The lower block and fall were hauled up by tricing lines, and then everything stopped neatly along the yard out of the way. This explains why the elements of a 'union purchase' used today in off-loading a merchantman are still called the 'yard' and the 'stay', the former plumbing the quayside, and the latter the hold. According to Mainwaring and Boteler, there were special 'boat-tackles' secured to the aftermost foremast shroud and the foremost mainmast shroud. There is no further explanation, and the exact method of securing these tackles is a little puzzling, since they plumb the boat neither in its stowed position, nor when it was alongside. Presumably it was used in association with yard-tackle.

The stay- and yard-tackles, between them took the weight in the fashion described above. In addition, the boat was steadied by guys, or tackles acting as guys. As many as six are described, two each on the bow and stern, to steer the boat sideways, and two to prevent 'sallying' fore and aft. Essentially the same arrangements were used for hoisting the boat in, when it came time to do so.

Further preparation. If the vessel were rolling heavily, it might be necessary to run in the guns, and close the gunports. Old haw-

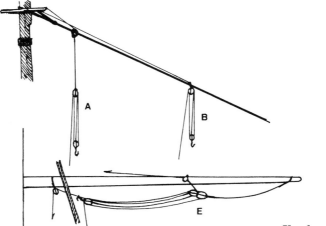

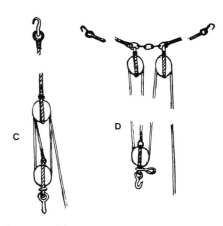

Yard and stay tackles
A Main stay tackle *c*1790 (after Steel); **B** fore stay tackle *c*1790 (after Steel); **C** main stay tackle *c*1890 (after Nares); **D** fore stay tackle *c*1890 (after Nares); **E** yard tackle triced up to yard.

sers dropped over the side, and wooden fenders, helped protect the boat as it went over. Krogh (167) advocates holding the boat against the ship's side, with inhaulers, passed out through the ports, and allowing it to slide up and down against long wooden skids, when rolling was particularly heavy. A painter, or boat-rope was taken well forward from the boat's bow, and if pitching back and forth were a problem, fore and after guys were passed from ports on the middle deck. The coxswain kept a sharp eye on the drain-plug, when hoisting out or setting in any boat. Needless to say the plug had to be securely in, before the boat hit the water. In hoisting, it was knocked loose, as soon as the boat lifted clear of the surface, and the water drained out readily, particularly if the after tackle were raised somewhat less than the forward one.

When raising and lowering the boat, all excess weight was removed; mast, sails, oars, water-cask, thwarts, and so on, were taken out before it was hoisted. Two or three men remained in the boat, to hook and unhook the tackles, fend off from the ship's side with boat-hooks, and so on. The falls of the tackles were led through footblocks, and arranged so that at no time were the men hauling upon them underneath the boat. This precaution was necessary to avoid serious injury, if something gave way, and the boat crashed down unexpectedly.

Disposition of force. Luce (221) stations the men thus: in the boat, the coxswain and a couple of hands; on deck, fore- and maintop-men clear away the booms to receive the boat; aloft on the fore, forecastlemen take clew-jigger out on the foreyard to trice up the yard-tackle, if not permanently fitted, and rig it as

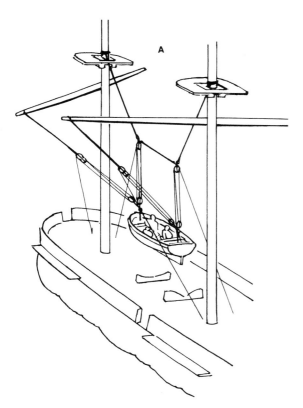

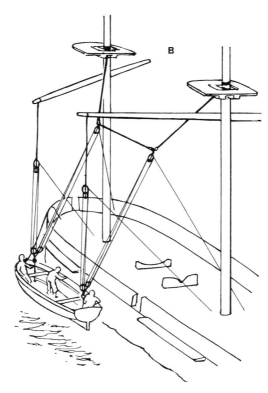

Hoisting out a boat
A Stay tackles used to lift boat off chocks; **B** yard tackles used to move boat outboard, tackles lowered away together to drop boat in water.

a lift-jigger, hook burton to the burton-strap as a preventer lift; foretopmen, overhaul the burtons, send the falls on deck, send down the fore topsail clew-jigger as a tricing line to haul up the triatic stay and upper block of the fore stay-tackle. On the main, the gunner's mates look after the yard-tackle and rig the main lift-jigger; main topmen, haul up the after end of the triatic stay, and upper block of the main stay-tackle, overhaul the burton, sending the falls down on deck.

Luce (222) suggests leading the falls of the four tackles thus: that of the foreyard, through a snatch-block hooked by the fore fiferail; that of the mainyard, through a foot-block by the main fiferail, and both led aft. The fore and main stay-tackle falls were similarly led through blocks by their respective fiferails, on the opposite side of the deck, and likewise led aft.

Procedure. The order being given, the men lay aloft, and when ordered lay out on the yard. When ready, the tackles are triced up and the yards braced as needed. This would usually mean bracing the fore yardarm aft, and the main yardarm somewhat forward of square.

The yard-tackles are manned and walked away, until high enough, when a turn is taken, and the stay-tackles are hauled, a turn being taken on the stays. Eventually they will be lowered together. After the boats are hoisted in, the men detailed lay out, clear away the burtons, and so on. The stay-tackles and triatic stays are lowered on deck, and the yards squared.

Orders.

Lay aloft! Lay out!
Trice up! Brace in!
Man the yards!
Walk away with the yards, take down the slack of the stays! (that is to say when hoisting in; the stays would be hauled first when hoisting out.)
Well the yards!
Man the stays! Walk away with the stays!
Well the stays!
Lower away of all!
Avast hoisting!
Stand by to lower away together! (To lower triatic stay)
Haul taut! Square away!
Lay down from aloft!

Boats on davits. About, or a little before 1800, the custom arose of stowing boats on davits over the taffrail, and on the quarters. Baudin (Plate 2) shows a quarter-boat abreast the mizzen channels, while other sources show the davits placed between main and mizzen channels. The French seamen referred to these boats as being *en porte-manteau* ('on the coat-rack'), and for the same reason, the stern-boat was by extension sometimes simply called *le porte-manteau*. A boat stowed outside the mizzen channels was *un canot de porte-haubans* (Bonnefoux, 59). Vessels engaged in the Greenland whale fishery, had of course been in the habit of carrying boats in this way from the early 1600s, and in a way it is surprising that the innovation came so late to the man-of-war. Davits varied greatly in form, from squared baulks of timber used in the early 1800s, to curved iron davits in the later men-of-war, very similar to those still occasionally seen today. The word came into English from Dutch: *doove jut* originally was the term for the outrigger used with a breast backstay, or the anchor davit which was sometimes shipped in the launch. The characteristic feature of these fittings was that they projected or 'jutted' out, and had a dumb-sheave, fork, or something similar at the outboard end. *Doove* literally means 'deaf', rather than 'dumb', but I think the latter word best suggests the underlying idea. As a matter of fact, English 'davit' was re-adopted into Dutch and German, although the old forms were also in use in their original technical meanings.

Fixed davits projecting over the taffrail were used to suspend a small yawl or gig. Besides this, a boat was carried on either quarter. The original clumsy arrangement can be seen in *Victory*, where baulks 10 inches square are pivoted at the fore and after ends of the mizzen channels. A jackstay connects the outboard ends, which are further steadied by fore and aft guys and topping-lifts. The lifts form a span, which is controlled by a fall leading through a block under the mizzen top. Sheaves are let into the outer ends of the davits, forming the upper elements of the tackles. Depending on the size of the boat, these might be luffs, four-fold tackles, or something even more substantial. The falls were stowed so they were clear for running, on reels or flaked down in a special rack.

Lowering gear. The tackles were needed to hoist the boat up, but in fact impeded the rapid lowering in emergency. For this reason, a 'runner' was often rove when the boat was hoisted up. One method, of many used to rig this, secured a stout rope to the davit head, down through the eyebolt to which the tackle hooked, over a fairlead at the davit head, and made fast to a cleat at the inboard end of the davit. This took the weight of the boat, and the tackles were then unhooked. To lower, the runners were eased away, and when ready, let go, unreeving from the boat of themselves. Sometimes they were arranged so that they could be handled, and let go, by the boat's crew. 'No mechanical contrivance can or does excel a simple well handled runner for lowering boats. There is no complication in a clear rope's end and a large round thimble, and this is all that is required for dropping a boat at full speed' (Boyd, 356). On the other hand, the falls had, in any case, to be overhauled down in preparation for hoisting in, and some preferred to lower on the falls, if there was no urgency, thus dropping the boat and fleeting the purchase at the same time. The lower block was hooked to an eyebolt near the waterline, and the fall hauled taut, ready for rehoisting.

Clifford's lowering gear. I do not know when this was introduced, but apparently prior to 1861, since it is illustrated in Bréart. This allowed the boat to be lowered by one man, and kept the craft absolutely level as he did so. An excellent description of it is to be found in Nares.

Robinson's disengaging gear. This is described in the 1897, but not the 1862 edition of Nares, so presumably was introduced in the interim. Of about the same vintage is Wood's detaching apparatus, described by Luce (278). If a quarter-boat were dropped with a fair bit of way on, it might be swept back, at the moment it struck the water, making it difficult to unhook the lower block. To some extent, this was obviated by keeping the sea-painter taut, but it helps explain Boyd's liking for a runner. Real disaster overtook the boat, in a seaway, if the forward fall were let go first, since the boat would then swing violently round end for end. Disengaging gear let go both ends simultaneously, and sometimes was arranged so that it could only be activated when the boat was waterborne. The Robinson gear could be slipped when the weight was still on the falls, dropping the final few inches. The command was given from the deck, watching the roll of the ship and the passage of the waves under the boat. Manifestly, it was undesirable to drop the boat heavily. Apart from any question of damage to the structure, the boat's crew would find the impact anything but pleasant, especially if seated. A very comprehensive account of Robinson's gear, which is still in use today, can be found in the *Admiralty Manual of Seamanship* I, 1964, 272.

Stern davits. Ideally, way was completely off when the stern-boat, usually the gig, was lowered. If there was sternway on, it was unsafe to drop the boat, because it would undoubtedly have fouled the rudder, or jammed under the counter. Using runners, the stern was allowed to reach the water first. If there was headway on, it then swung around, with the boat-rope and forward runner, or falls, taking the strain. Likewise when hooking on to rehoist, no attempt was made to lay the

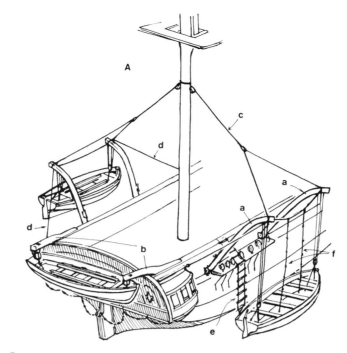

Stern and quarter boats
A View of vessel with a stern boat and two quarter boats:
a quarter davit; **b** stern davit; **c** davit topping lift; **d** davit guy; **e** Jacob's ladder; **f** lifelines.
B Old style quarter davits; **C** curved iron davits.

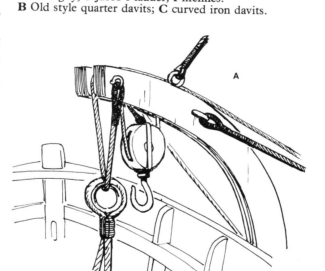

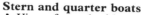

boat across the stern. Rather it was manoeuvred up to the forward falls, which were hooked and hoisted a foot or so. The after purchase was overhauled sufficiently to hook on aft, and then by hauling in the boat gradually swung broadside on.

Jackstays and lizards. The jackstay was a rope leading from the davit head to the waterline, and travelling on it, a lizard, the tail of which was held taut in the boat. This was an excellent device to prevent lateral sway, in hoisting or lowering.

Lifelines. These depended from the span between the davit heads, and had Turk's-

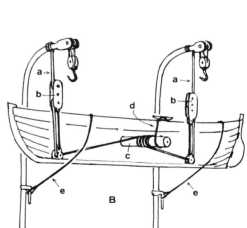

Boat lowering gear
A Tackle unhooked and runner rove off for lowering boat; **B** Clifford's lowering gear (cutaway view of boat): lowering ropes (**a**) are led through 3-sheave friction blocks (**b**) and leading blocks to roller (**c**). When lanyard (**d**) is let go, the ropes unwind from the roller and the boat lowers. The lower eyes of the gripes (**e**) slip off their pins as the boat descends.

heads worked on them at intervals to give handhold. When the boat was raised or lowered, the crew took the weight off the boat by supporting themselves by hanging on to the lifelines.

Sea-painter or boat-rope. This was made fast to the bow, and if the ship had headway, gave steerage way to the boat. The rudder of the sea-boat was always kept shipped, with

285

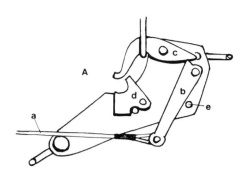

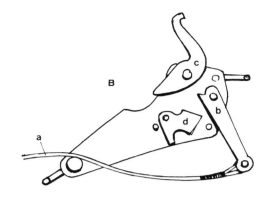

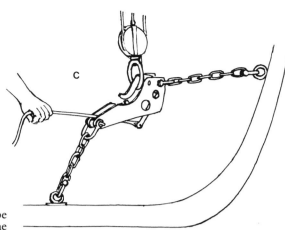

Robinson's disengaging gear
A Interior view of releasing hook in locked position; **B** interior view of releasing hook in open position. As long as lanyard (**a**) is held taut, lever (**b**) locks the tumbling hook (**c**) in place. A hinged mousing (**d**) prevents the ring from slipping off the hook, and a safety pin can be inserted in hole (**e**) to lock the mechanism; **C** the Robinson gear in use. The bow and stern lanyards may be connected by a short tackle, releasing both hooks simultaneously when let run.

Lowering a stern boat
A Boat is lowered so that stern reaches the water first; **B** stern tackle is unhooked, then bow tackle, and boat rides to sea painter.

the tiller over towards the ship's side, secured with spunyarn, or the coxswain pushed the helm in that direction, so that on entering the water the boat immediately sheered out from the vessel's side, allowing the oars to be shipped immediately. The boat being under control, the boat-rope was cast off, and coiled up on board, ready for the boat's return. Some preferred to use a steering oar, whale-boat style, as offering more leverage.

Gripes. These secured the boat when it was hoisted. One at either end of the boat, they were made of canvas, or flat sennit, and ran vertically downwards from the davit head around the boat, to be set up in the channels. Later on, the very practical method of crossing them diagonally was introduced, and the slips used today, were originally preceded by lashings, which had to be cut or cast off, when the gripes were let go prior to lowering. Clifford's patent included an arrangement to slip the gripes automatically. The hold-downs used to secure the boats on the booms, were also known as gripes.

Lowering the boat. The boat was cleared away by the coxswain and crew, the cover taken off, plug pushed in, with oars, rudder, water-cask, compass, lantern, and flares on board. The usual practice was to keep the quarter-boats ready in all respects, so that they could be lowered on the run, in the event of a man being lost overboard. To take off the cover was the work of a moment. This was in place if the weather were very hot, or if the vessel were under steam, and usually was removed at night. The gripes were slipped, and when ready, the boat, held against the jack-stays by men tending the lizards, was lowered with the runners. The sea-painter was kept taut, and when ready, the after runner was let go, then the forward one. If lowered on the falls, the procedure was very similar. In the event that inadvertently the boat was dropped with sternway on, the order of letting go was reversed.

Hoisting the boat. This would ideally be done with a little headway. The boat-rope was thrown down, and made fast, the forward fall hooked, then the after. The man looking after this had to hold the block upright, so it would not capsize and tangle the falls. The boat's crew, with two or three exceptions, went up the Jacob's-ladder into the channels. Boyd advocates this practice rather than have the men climb the lifelines. In any event, the extra weight was got out of the boat. The falls were manned on deck, leading in the same direction, half the men on one fall, and facing them, the other half grasping the other fall. The falls were hauled taut and hoisted, initially independently. If necessary, the boat was canted stern downwards a little, to clear the bilges, when the plug was removed. When level, the order was given to 'marry'

the falls, and the men ran away with both ropes held together. When near the top, they walked the last bit up, and the falls were belayed. The lifelines were sometimes used as a stopper, passed through the hoisting eyebolt, and over the davit head, to take the weight off the tackles. The sea-painter was taken forward as far as possible, stopped in to the channels with split yarn, and the gripes were passed, care being taken to see they were free of turns.

Orders.

Clear away the starboard lifeboat!
Quarterdeckmen [the watch, or whoever] muster aft!
Let go the gripes!
Stretch along the falls!
Walk back the falls! Lower away!
Lower away aft! Let go aft!
Lower away forward! Let go forward!
Cast off boat-rope!

Orders to hoist.

Man the falls!
Haul taut singly!
Marry!
Hoist away!
Walk!
High enough!
Separate the falls!
Ease to the stoppers!
Belay the falls! On gripes!

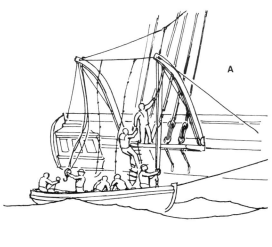

Hoisting in a quarter boat
A Boat comes alongside, painter is secured forward and tackles hooked on, bow tackle first. Loose gear and most of boat's crew are got on board ship; **B** boat is hoisted up, somewhat down by the stern to drain out water. Boat tenders hang on lifelines to lighten the boat; **C** boat is hoisted home and secured in position with gripes and boat rope.

British frigate lowering her boats (detail after P Ozanne, 1801). Here the waist boat is being hoisted out on yard and stay tackles with a few men in the boat and in the rigging to send her clear. The stern boat has already been lowered and is still hooked on to the davit tackles. The stern boat's crew are boarding by laying out along the spanker boom and down a Jacob's ladder made fast to it.

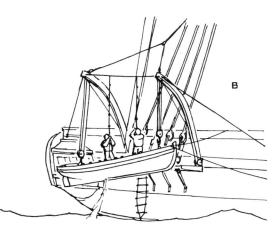

A French armed brig hoisting in a boat at sea (detail from an engraving by Baugean, 1814). With fore and mainyards counterbraced, the yard tackles are in position above the boat. All the boat's crew have left save two men to fend it off the ship's side and stow the gear. (Mark Myers' Collection)

Model of the Dutch armed brig *De Onderzoeker, c*1814, showing the ship's boat stowed on chocks in the waist. Note the spars lashed to the gallows, the portable galley, and the special opening in the foreward hatch to take the cable below. (Courtesy Prins Hendrik Maritime Museum, Rotterdam)

Swedish corvette *Eugenie* with tackles rigged for hoisting in a boat. The yards have extra tackles to steady them, and the stay tackles and triatic stay show up well. (Courtesy Marinmuseum, Karlskrona)

CHAPTER 21
MAN OVERBOARD

This emergency does not receive much attention from the early writers, and yet it was a situation demanding the display of the greatest possible coolness, seamanship, and quick thinking, if the man were to be recovered. The later authorities however considered it a most important topic, devoting a good deal of space to it. The officer of the deck had to make two crucial decisions: firstly, whether to launch a boat at all; secondly, how best to bring the vessel to the wind, and drop the cutter. This was one of the questions he ran through in his mind upon taking over the watch, so that, in the event, the correct orders would be uttered instinctively. A well fitted ship's boat could live in quite heavy seas, but the most dangerous moment occurred when it was dropped or being recovered. The decision whether or not to risk the lives of a whole boat crew in the hope of saving one man, depended on the weather conditions. If launching a cutter was out of the question, the ship would be got about, in the hope of somehow getting near enough to the man to heave him a line and haul him aboard.

Lifebuoy. At the cry of 'Man Overboard!', one or more buoys were dropped by the lifebuoy lookout. Ekelöf (259) says this should be done immediately at night, only upon the order, by day. The familiar doughnut shaped lifebuoy, whether of sheet copper, or cork, was a substantial affair, and the aim was to drop it close to the man, but not on top of him, since although the buoy floated, it was quite heavy enough to cause serious injury. Sometimes two buoys were dropped, one with, the other without a line. If the man in the water got hold of the second, he could be pulled inboard, fairly readily. Gratings, or anything else that would float, could also be used in emergency; net bags full of corks were to be found on deck in training ships, since they were used when the boys were over the side swimming. Rather than trying to climb up on the buoy, the man pushed his head up through the centre, or capsized it so it came back over his head, and he then supported himself on his elbows. Some forms of buoy

'**The Rescue**' (after T Luny, 1832). As the ship's boat nears the man clinging to a hatch grating, the ship drives slowly to leeward. The weather is rough and the ship shortened down – conditions which made it a matter of fine judgement whether to lower a boat or not.

provided a frame, on which he could sit. Considerable ingenuity was exercised in improving the simple lifebuoy. In the German Navy, cans filled with oil-soaked oakum were attached to the buoy, to help smooth the surrounding sea, while the Franklin Lifebuoy, used in the United States Navy, had two cal-

Lifebuoys
A Standard ship's lifebuoy; **B** early nineteenth century lifebuoy fitted with hanging grab lines; **C** the Franklin lifebuoy: the swinging upright tubes contained calcium phosphide flares which ignited on contact with water. The chain inside the buoy provided a seat for the man awaiting rescue; **D** lifebuoys carried on athwartships boom on taffrail; **E** lifebuoy carried at end of spanker boom.

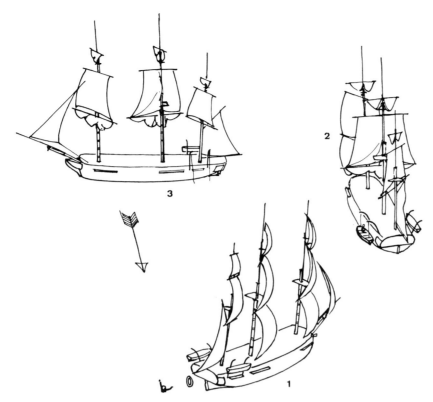

Man overboard manoeuvre, ship by the wind
1 Lifebuoy thrown to man in water, hands called to stations, helm put down; **2** ship put in stays, mainyard squared and quarter boat lowered; **3** ship heaves to on new tack, to windward of man in the water.

''Man overboard' from HMS St Jean d'Acre in the Baltic in 1854' (after Sir O Brierly). A rescue in fresh weather: the ship appears to have tacked before heaving to, and lies up to windward of the man in the water.

cium phosphide flares, which ignited on contact with the water, thus rendering the buoy visible at night for twenty minutes or so (Ekelöf, 259). Apparently these flares, or the similar Holmes' Storm and Danger Signal Lights, gave off highly obnoxious fumes, which could disturb the man in the water, but greatly increased the visibility of the buoy. Other types of flares were ignited by a friction device, working on the match-box principle, as the buoy went over.

To go about or not. Griffiths (214) says:

> If the ship be on a wind, instead of squaring the main yards directly, turn hands up, about ship, squaring the mainyard and lowering the boat, while in stays. By this mode, the attention of the ship's company is called to a particular duty, you prevent the hurry and confusion which otherwise generally prevails, and the ship instead of having the man on the weather quarter, and increasing her distance from him, has him, when about, three or four points on the lee bow, dropping towards him.

In the same vein, another English officer, Basil Hall, is quoted with approval by Glascock (304), and Murphy (38):

> The best authorities recommend that, if possible, the ship should not only be hove aback, when a man falls overboard, but that she should be brought completely round on the other tack. Of course, sails should be shortened in stays, and the mainyard left square. This plan implies the ship being on a wind, or from that position to having the wind not above two points abaft the beam. The great merit of such a method of proceeding is, that, if the evolution succeeds, the ship, when round, will drift right down towards the man. And, although there may be some small risk in lowering the boat in stays, from the ship having, at one period, sternway, there will in fact be little time lost if the boat be not lowered till the ship be well round, and the sternway at an end. There is more mischief done generally by lowering the boat too soon, than by waiting till the fittest moment arrives for doing it coolly.

To stop the vessel as quickly as possible, it was run up into the wind, and then allowed to drop astern, squaring the main topsail, and so heaving to on the same tack, main topsail to the mast. Initially, the man would be on the weather quarter, and just after heaving to, on the lee quarter. Since the ship dropped directly to leeward, he would eventually come to lie on the weather quarter once more, as the ship drifted further away. By going about before heaving to, it was hoped to place the ship almost dead to windward of the man, and therefore drifting down towards him.

The later writers, while not disagreeing with the theoretical merits of this plan, felt that the latter-day sailing warships, particularly those with a screw aperture, simply were not sure enough in stays to risk going about. They therefore favoured heaving to on the same tack (Hourigan, 110; Luce, 462; Dick & Kretchmer, 330).

Sailing with the wind free. With the wind dead aft, it was immaterial which way the ship was rounded to, although perhaps turning to the side on which the man had fallen, would be slightly better. With the wind on the quarter, the ship was most quickly hove to by putting the helm down, and turning to windward. To expedite this, the weather after braces were let go, so the afteryards would tend to fly round, and allow the main and mizzen topsails to be braced up, which would cause the ship to luff more rapidly. The headyards were kept square, so that when the wind came abeam, or just ahead of that, the ship was hove to, fore topsail to the mast, almost dead to leeward of the man. The boat would have to pull away on the weather beam. This was the point of sail upon which studdingsails were likely to be set on the weather side, and in emergency, there was no hesitation in sacrificing the light gear, if it meant the life of the man. The lookouts on the yards were warned to hold on, the upper studdingsail tacks and sheets were let fly, and the lower studdingsail clewed up with its spilling line, resulting in a jumble of canvas, snapped booms, and so on, to windward. Furthermore, the leverage exerted by the studdingsails would tend to prevent the ship coming to the wind. For this reason, it was advised (at least when the wind was only a point or two on the stern) to go round the long way, which brought studdingsails on the leeward side when hove to, hence out of the way, and furthermore allowed them to aid rather than hinder the action of the helm (Hourigan, 113). The halliards of the lee studdingsails were then let go to settle the studdingsail yards down on the brace-blocks. With studdingsails set both sides, the ship was rounded to either way. Since the headyards were left square, the studdingsails did not greatly interfere with them. In the case of the mainmast, it was important not to forget the topmast and topgallant studdingsail tacks, since they could prevent the mainyards being braced up, unless they were tended.

Lookouts. It was the task of the lifebuoy lookout, to keep the man in the water, or at least the lifebuoy, in sight. Two men were subsequently detailed to ascend the mizzen rigging for the same purpose. A compass bearing at the time of the accident was another useful datum. By means of flag signals, one meaning 'Steer to your starboard!', one

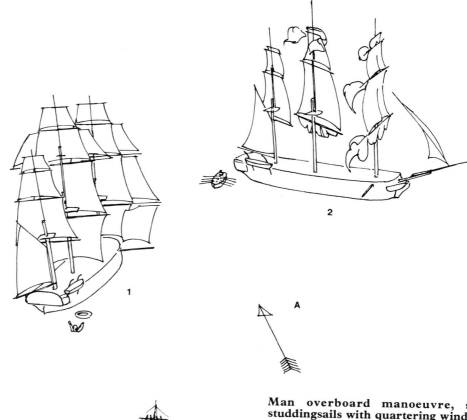

Man overboard manoeuvre, ship under studdingsails with quartering wind
A 1 Lifebuoy thrown to man in water, helm put down and hands called to stations; **2** afteryards braced up, studdingsail tacks and sheets let go, ship heaves to, fore topsail to the mast and quarter boat is lowered; **B** ship taking in studdingsails and lowering a boat to a man overboard (after vignette on title page of Capt Kynaston's *Review of the New Methods of Lowering and Disconnecting Boats At Sea*, 1857).

meaning 'Steer to your port!', and a third meaning 'So you go well!', the coxswain of the boat was directed in the desired direction. One advantage of using oil, in association with the lifebuoy, was the high visibility of the slick so produced. At night, in addition to the lifebuoy flares already mentioned, a lantern was run up to the peak of the gaff, to indicate the ship's position to the boat, which itself carried a lantern, and a box of flares. A pair of canvas 'shapes' by day, or a pair of lanterns by night, could be lined up to indicate the probable bearing of the man, or the course the ship had been steering at the time of the accident (Ekelöf, 261). 'Blue lights'

(also called 'Bengal Lights') or rockets, were got ready to indicate the ship's position to the boat, if necessary.

Dropping the boat. Assuming there to be a boat hung on davits on each quarter, the lee boat was cleared away, and dropped when the vessel's speed had been sufficiently reduced, but before it had gathered sternway. In the event that it was planned to go about, and heave to on the opposite tack, the order would be given to clear away the weather boat, which would, after the manoeuvre, be on the lee side. Ekelöf (260) advocates dropping the 'old' lee boat, although he remarks that many authorities prefer the 'new' lee

'The Lifebuoy Is Recovered' (after H af Sillen, 1890). A 'Man Overboard' exercise in the Swedish Navy. The ship, perhaps an auxiliary steamer, appears to have been hove to without tacking and lies to leeward of the lifebuoy.

boat. Since the boat would be dropped while the ship was almost head to wind, this probably was only of importance when it came to hoist it again, being best done to leeward. The boat could be dropped when speed had reduced to four or five knots, under favourable conditions, and if the vessel were turning up into the wind, or tacking, the stern would still be swinging to leeward, hence the merit of using the weather boat, with a relatively smooth sea, and a smart working ship. However, as the ship heeled to leeward, the lee boat was closer to the water (Bardenfleth, I, 222). If sailing free, say with the wind on the starboard quarter, the order might be given in the form 'Clear away the second cutter!', which was stowed to port (Dick & Kretchmer, 330). The boat being cleared away and the crew wearing cork vests, the coxswain was given directions by the officer of the deck as to the direction in which to pull, based on his estimation of where the man was to be found: 'Steer two points to starboard of the moon!', 'Pull dead to leeward!', a specified compass course, or whatever.

The boat could be lowered when headway was reduced to about four knots (certainly before sternway developed), care being taken

to let go aft first. Just before 1900, various kinds of quick-release gear began to appear, the forerunners of those still used today. Sailing in squadron, the prearranged 'accident' signal was hoisted, and at night, position lights were hoisted, so that other vessels could either keep clear, or lower boats themselves, as circumstances dictated (Luce, 462). If necessary, the second quarter-boat could be lowered to assist in the rescue efforts, and would ordinarily be cleared away in any case. The judicious use of oil, to smooth the sea could be helpful.

I do not know exactly when it became the universal custom to carry cutters rigged as sea-boats on the quarter, but probably in the first third of the nineteenth century. Prior to that, a yawl carried on davits projecting over the taffrail would have been used, or the launch swung out to leeward, using yard and stay tackles. Preparations were immediately made for rehoisting the boat on its return, the ship ordinarily remaining hove to, in the meantime. If the weather was bad enough to warrant it, the ship wore short round and ran down to leeward of the boat, heaving to on the same tack as before (Hourigan).

Organisation on deck. The cry 'Man overboard!' was all too likely to result in the hands

all rushing aft, only too anxious to do something to rescue their comrade. It was paramount for the officer of the watch to prevent things degenerating into total confusion and panic. Hourigan orders, 'Part of ship everybody!', 'Silence fore and aft!'. Since the first task was to heave to, perhaps going about first, 'Stations for stays!' was a useful command. For the same reason, the boats' crews were primarily drawn from the forecastlemen since by the wind, or sailing free, the fore-yards did not need to be touched. The lifebuoy lookout and the men chosen to go aloft in the mizzen rigging would have been detailed when the watch came on deck and was mustered. The boat lantern was brought aft each night, and kept by the binnacle, or some other place known to the boat's crew. At night the surgeon would have to be called, so he could resuscitate the victim of the accident, when brought on board.

Orders, sailing by the wind, to heave to.

Hard down!
Let go the lifebuoy!
Silence fore and aft!
Flow head sheets!
Haul in spanker boom!
Let go lee main braces, main tack and sheet!

Clear away main bowlines!
Clear away the lee lifeboat!
Main clewgarnets and buntlines!
Up mainsail!
Brace aback!

The headsails and spanker are used to aid the action of the helm in luffing up. The main clewgarnets can only be used before the mainsail is hard aback against the rigging. Once that has occurred, only the buntlines and leechlines can be used. In bracing round, letting fly, and so on, the yardarm lookouts must be warned beforehand to watch out for themselves.

Orders, sailing by the wind, to go about and heave to.

Let go the lifebuoy!
Ready about!
Stations for stays!
Clear away the weather lifeboat!

Proceed as in tacking, making a late main topsail haul, and leaving the mainyards square. The main course should be up before it is thrown flat aback, and the boat lowered before headway is lost.

Orders, sailing with the wind on the quarter, studdingsails set to starboard.

Hard down! or Hard a-port!
Let go the lifebuoy!
Silence fore and aft!
Clear away the port lifeboat (second cutter)!
Lee main, weather crossjack braces!
Brace up!
Let fly studdingsail tacks and sheets!
Clew up lower studdingsail!
Fore and main clewgarnets and buntlines!
Up courses!

With the wind aft, 'port' and 'starboard' are less likely to confuse the men, than 'lee' and 'weather', especially for the watch below, rushing up on deck to help.

Man overboard exercise in a British three-decker, c1860. A new type of simultaneous releasing gear was being tried out on the quarter boat on this occasion, and it was found that the boat could be safely dropped, fully loaded, from a height of six feet above the water while the ship was sailing at eight or nine knots. Engraving by Edward Weedon, *Illustrated London News*, 1860. (Mark Myers' Collection)

CHAPTER 22
ACCIDENTS

Accidents were sometimes the result of not going about things in the most workmanlike fashion, or a failure to keep spars and rigging in top shape, rather than mere happenstance. However, the skilfulness of a seaman could be demonstrated by his manner of dealing with a problem, when struck with undeserved disaster. Liardet, that thoughtful observer of shipboard affairs, makes a couple of interesting comments that are relevant. In the first place, the zeal of the first lieutenant to keep a smart ship should not be permitted to endanger its safety.

> The loss, or endangering of some of Her Majesty's vessels, it is to be feared, may be attributed to the over anxiety of many officers to have clean and white decks, when going into port. As this object in some ships, is made to outweigh the consideration of the vicinity of land, rocks, shoals, etc, a time when every rope ought to be coiled down clear for running, and the watch kept continually on the move, instead of which ropes are coiled up, and decks often holy-stoned under such circumstances, before daylight. No ship, when washing decks, can be so ready to perform any sudden evolution that may be required, with her ropes triced up, buckets, brooms, holy-stones; and if you add to this, the hurry of throwing down the ropes, the chances of a few tracing beckets being left on the running ropes, by which blocks may be choked, and yards stopped in their bracing, or sails retarded in setting, or taking in, etc. With the above, and numerous reasons that might be given, it does not appear right to risk any of Her Majesty's vessels, for the sake of her upper deck losing its usual whiteness for one or more days. The evil does not always rest here, for the attention of the officer of the watch is more often taken up with the decks, than the situation of the ship ought to justify. On such occasions, we have known the pilot to be asked to wait until the sand was washed off the decks, or until they were swabbed, or ropes coiled down, before complying with the pilot's wishes (175).

This deferment of a necessary activity such as tacking could have serious consequences, and as Liardet says, 'if the ship gets into danger, then all is confusion and hurry, because nothing is prepared'.

Yet another source of danger arose from misguided efforts to increase the ship's speed. Liardet (250) damns the

> practice of loosening vessels at all points, so as to give the decks, upper works, masts etc as much play as possible while in chase. To give this supposed desirable advantage, stanchions are removed from supporting the decks, mast-wedges are taken out, rigging often slacked, and sometimes a butt of water suspended between the fore- and mainmast. Hammocks are hung up, and the watch below desired to turn in, with a shot or two as bedfellows. Then, shot-boxes, bags, etc, to be suspended between the decks. This is all done with the intention of accelerating the vessel's speed. But some officers during our late wars, when in chase, have done most extraordinary things with the view to increase the speed of their vessels, such as sawing beams, timbers, or planks in two, etc.

ACCIDENTS TO RUNNING RIGGING

The parting of running gear could be minimised, although never totally eliminated, by careful attention to preventing chafe, constantly 'freshening of the nip', so that the same part of a rope was not acutely twisted or kinked as it passed through a block, changing ropes end for end, and so on. This was much more important in the days of hemp rigging and wooden spars, than was the case in the steel windjammers, where everything was much stronger than absolutely necessary. Hemp rope shrank considerably in cold or wet weather, and had to be slackened under the circumstances. The longer the rope, the more it 'took up', and hence gear like royal and topgallant studdingsail halliards, was particularly liable to carry away for this reason (Nares, 275; Liardet, 229). The greatest strain came on the gear in bad rather than good weather; hence effecting repairs was often enormously complicated by the pitching of the vessel. It was of the greatest importance not to make matters any worse, causing further damage, bearing in mind that the canvas and light running rigging were less

important than the major spars. 'In choosing the remedy, select that which is most likely to save the endangered spars, even at the risk of lost or split canvas' (Luce, 515). One of the most systematic accounts of accidents, and their remedies is found in Ulffers, upon which much of the following relies.

Jib halliard parts. This will occur while hoisting the jib, which will be halfway up the stay. It is retrieved with the downhaul, and if needed in a hurry, replaced by the fore topmast staysail halliard.

Parting of jib downhaul. This may occur during setting, if a kink jams in the fairlead and the halliard does not go first, or while the jib is being taken in. In the first case, the sail is set in the usual way, while in the second, it is run up all the way, and the sheet slacked off, so the sail remains just full enough to prevent its beating itself to pieces. Depending on circumstances, the men on the jibboom might be able to manhandle the canvas down, or use the broken end of the downhaul to reach a hank a couple of feet above the jib-boom, and get the sail down a bit at a time. By untoggling the lee topgallant bowline, and making a bowline round the jibstay, the jib could be hauled down using the topgallant bowline as an emergency downhaul, the loop sliding down the stay. The topgallant bowline led almost parallel to the jibstay.

Parting of jibstay. This accident results in the whole strain coming on the forward leech of the jib. The sheet is carefully eased off, as far as possible, without actually letting the sail thrash about, and the helm is put up, to becalm the sail as much as possible while it is taken in. If it is necessary to hold the wind, the fore topmast staysail is set instead while the damaged stay is replaced. If there is no room to keep away, the ship goes about and takes in the jib when head to wind (Nares, 276).

Parting of jib tack and jib sheet. The tack would run up the stay a little, and the sail was simply hauled down. If the lee sheet goes, the sail may be got under control with the weather sheet. If however, the jib pendant parts, the sail will be uncontrollable until the vessel falls off, and becalms the jib in the lee of the other sails. If necessary, the fore topmast staysail can be set while repairs are effected. Similar considerations apply to accidents occurring to the gear of the other headsails. In any circumstance where the effectiveness of such forward canvas is suddenly removed due to the abrupt parting of the running gear, the ship will immediately start to turn up into the wind, and therefore the quartermaster is immediately given the order 'Mind your weather helm!'. 'A quartermaster who knew his duty, would drop the peak, or let fly the mizzen topsail sheets, without waiting for orders, while the officer was occupied in saving the yard' (Boyd, 403).

Parting of weather topgallant brace. When by the wind, the strain is on the weather brace, and the lee brace should always be checked somewhat, so that it will not be snapped by the 'whipping' of the masts as the vessel pitches. If the weather brace goes, when by the wind, the yard will immediately fly fore and aft, coming to rest against the topgallant stay, and throwing a tremendous strain on the parrel and the weather topgallant rigging. It is imperative that the topgallant mast be relieved of this lateral pressure, and to this end, the lee sheet, lee brace, halliards, and weather bowline are let go. The lee part of the sail will fly round in front of the weather half, immediately easing the strain. The weather sheet is never let go, because the sail must be clewed down with the weather clewline. The bowline is let go to allow the weather half of the sail to come aback, which it tends to do as the yard comes 'in', with the lee quarter of the yard sliding down the lee topgallant rigging. Once the sail is down and aback, lying relatively quietly against the rigging, the weather quarter of the yard is lashed securely to the weather topgallant shrouds, and men can be sent out to furl the sail and repair the brace.

If the brace parts with the wind on the quarter, the weather leech restrains the sail so that it will not blow forward quite so much. Nonetheless, it will beat to and fro in such a violent fashion, that the topgallant mast will be endangered. The lee sheet is let go and the sail is hauled down with the weather clewline, and the lee quarter of the yard is lashed to the lee topgallant rigging. To get the weather quarter of the yard back against the weather topgallant shrouds, the lee topgallant bowline is hitched around the lee yardarm, as far out as one can reach from the crosstrees. By hauling on the bowline, easing off the lee brace, and shroud-lashing, the yard pivots at the parrel and permits the weather quarter of

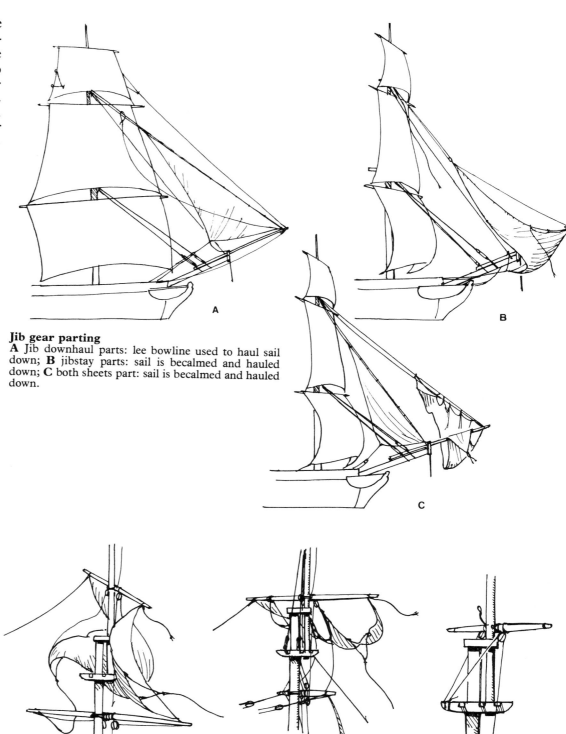

Jib gear parting
A Jib downhaul parts: lee bowline used to haul sail down; **B** jibstay parts: sail is becalmed and hauled down; **C** both sheets part: sail is becalmed and hauled down.

Topgallant brace or parrel parting
A Weather brace parts: lee sheet eased and sail clewed down; **B** lee bowline hitched to yard and used to square yard; **C** parrel parts: clewlines made fast to trestletrees and used to confine yard at the slings.

the yard to be got back against the rigging, and the weather side to be secured sufficiently to allow of hands laying out to repair the damage.

Topgallant parrel carried away. Before the wind, the braces act to hold the yard back against the mast. By the wind, however, the yard can blow well over to leeward, the brace simply acting to pull it aft, and throwing an enormous stress on the masthead. By the wind, the sail is thrown aback and lowered. Before the wind, the yard is braced by, to spill

Topsail brace or parrel parting
A Weather brace parts: sail brought aback and lowered, yard lashed to topmast shrouds and new brace rove; **B** parrel parts: sail tackle and strop used to confine yard at slings.

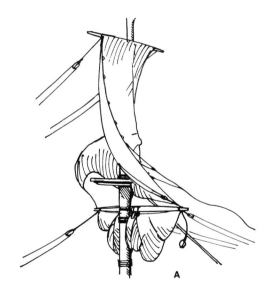

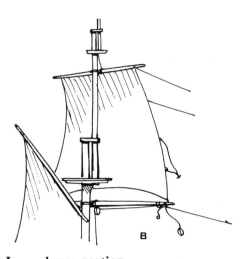

Lower brace parting
A Weather mainbrace parts: lee topsail sheet eased, mainsail hauled up and topsail backed, main yard worked by preventer braces until new brace rove; **B** weather crossjack brace parts: weather topsail bowline hitched to yardarm as makeshift brace.

the sail, and lowered. The sheets are not let go, so preventing the sail flying up and entangling itself on the stay (Liardet, 165). The expedient of unbending the clewlines from the clews, and securing them abaft the trestletrees, and using them to pull the yard back against the mast, is mentioned by Liardet.

Topsail yard parrel carried away. Rather similar principles apply if the weather is moderate, but throwing the topsail aback would bring the yard back with an unpleasantly heavy thump in bad weather. Spare parrels are kept in each top.

Parting of weather topgallant brace and parrel. Not only will the yard fly fore and aft, but it will swing heavily to and fro, so as to immediately endanger the topgallant mast. The lee sheet is thrown off, and everything

thrown aback. Once the sail is comparatively quiet, laid against the topgallant mast and rigging, the lee sheet is hauled home once more, and both clewlines used to clew the yard down, whereupon it is lashed to the shrouds, and the damage made good.

Parting of weather topsail brace. The yardarm is checked in its forward movement by the weather leech of the topsail, but it will ultimately press against the topmast stay. To allow backing the sail, and so relieve the pressure on the stay and topmast, the topgallant and course are got in, and the lee topsail sheet eased off. In the case of the fore topsail, both courses will have to come in, since the mainsail would unbalance the sail plan, if it were unopposed by the fore course. Once the sail is aback, the halliards are let go, the reef-tackles hauled out, and the weather yardarm lashed

to the weather topmast shrouds. In bad weather, a topsail preventer brace was rigged to take some of the strain off the weather brace. With several reefs taken, and the yard almost down on the cap, the preventer had quite an effective lead. It would not have worked well, with the yard mastheaded, because the downlead would have been too steep to allow an effective pull aft.

Parting of weather topsail brace and parrel. The consequence of this double accident is identical with the loss of the brace, except that in addition the yard can sally violently to and fro, bringing the topmast and everything above it in danger. The ship is allowed to fall off, to becalm the sail, and the lee sheet eased a little, although not so much as to allow the canvas to thrash about dangerously. Liardet recommends getting the wind on the opposite quarter to spill the sail as much as possible. The strop of the sail-tackle is taken up to the topmast head, placed around the ties and mast, and hooked to itself. The sail-tackle is then set up to an eyebolt on deck to weather, as far aft as possible, and upon the halliards being let go, the strop slides down the topmast, holding the yard against the mast, as the sail-tackle is hauled. Once down, the weather side of the yard is lashed to the topmast rigging, and the brace rigged anew.

Parting of topsail parrel. The helm is put up, and the ship got before the wind. There are then two options, either use the sail-tackle as described above, or haul the halliards up, as taut as possible, which will bring the yard very close to the mast, so that a temporary parrel may be rigged, allowing the yard to be struck on the cap, where permanent repairs can be effected. Brady (217) recommends that topsail parrels be made of curb-chain, for greater strength.

Parting of main brace. By the wind, the yard would fly forward hard against the lower stay, and this pressure is relieved by easing off the lee main topsail sheet, hauling up the course, getting in the topgallant, and backing the topsail. Preventer braces are rigged until the regular brace is replaced. Since men-of-war usually had preventer- or counter-braces already in place, the loss of the brace was no great matter.

Since 'Splice the main brace!' is usually thought of, in the Royal Navy, as a fictional command, resulting in a double issue of rum, the question has arisen, from time to time, whether the actual rope was ever actually spliced, rather than being completely replaced. Certainly a 'long splice' would render quite readily through the braceblock, and Bardenfleth (II, 52), for one, refers to the actual practice. Incidentally, the Dutch order 'Bezaans-schoot aan!', 'Haul the mizzen sheet!', as a call to the hands to muster aft for a tot, as a reward upon the completion of some particularly arduous task, dates from at least 1723, much earlier than 'Splice the main brace!' in this particular context. Likewise, in the other Germanic languages, extra effort was rewarded by 'Hauling the mizzen sheet', rather than 'Splicing the main brace'. It is true that today 'Splitsa storebrassen!' a literal translation of the English expression has crept into modern Swedish, but this was not the traditional phrase.

Parting of weather fore brace. The same principles apply here, as with the main brace, but attention has to be given to the consequences of taking away forward sail, balancing this by taking in after sail, if necessary. Ulffers (387) considered that the lower stay and yard were in less danger if the brace went, than was the case with the topmast stay upon the parting of the topsail brace. In bracing up sharp, in the ordinary way, the lower braces were cast off completely, while the weather topsail braces were veered more cautiously, precisely because of the greater relative strength of the lower stays.

Parting of weather crossjack brace. The yard is braced in with the other brace, both leading forward, it will be remembered. The weather mizzen top bowline is untoggled and hitched to the crossjack yardarm, to act as a temporary brace, while the new one is fitted.

Parting of weather preventer main brace. This can occur when trying to jam the yard sharp up, after tacking. The yard is braced up with the lee after brace, hauling on the main top bowline and main tack, at the same time. The lee main brace, which has a down lead must be slacked off, to allow the tack to be got down. Failure to do so may spring the yard (Nares, 279).

Parting of weather topgallant sheet. The sail will fly against the stay, and remain full. It will not immediately respond to hauling the weather clewline, and in fact the latter item may break, if it is tugged at too vigorously. The weather bowline is hauled, to clear the sail from the stay, and the lee sheet eased off. Then, by hauling the weather brace, letting go the halliards, and easing off on the bowline, and lee brace, the sail is got down and aback, whereupon it is clewed up.

Parting of weather topgallant sheet and clewline. If by the wind, the sail is got aback by easing away the lee brace and bowline, hauling on the weather brace, and the lee clew is manhandled into the crosstrees. Before the wind, it is necessary to heave the sail aback, perhaps requiring an alteration of course.

Parting of weather topsail sheet. The same sort of considerations apply as with the topgallant sail. Since the sail is deeper proportionately than the topgallant, the bowline is of great help in studying the weather leech. Easing off the lee sheet, and hauling the weather brace, the halliards are let go, and the sail got down, the reef-tackles hauled out and the sail clewed up.

Parting of weather topsail sheet and clewline. The sail is steadied as described above, backed and the yard struck. The weather clew will lie against the lower lift, and when the buntlines are hauled, it can be reached from the top.

Parting of lee topsail sheet and clewline. It will first be necessary to back the sail and strike the yard, and this is accomplished by hauling on the weather brace, easing off the bowline, and letting go the halliards. Sailing with the wind on the quarter, the ship is brought to the wind, so the sail can be backed. The weather clew is got up, the buntlines are hauled to allow the lee clew to be reached, and pulled into the top.

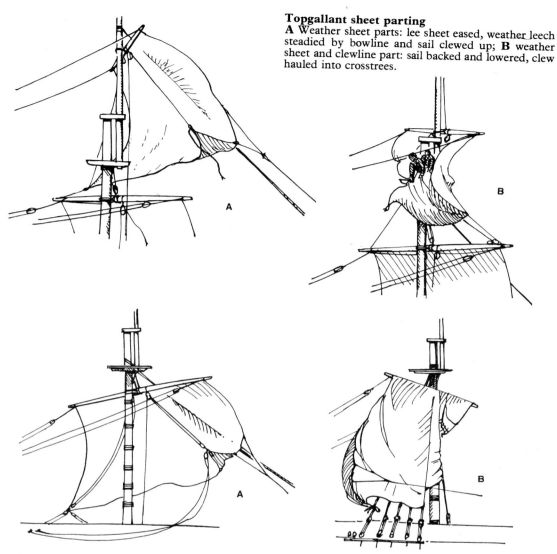

Topgallant sheet parting
A Weather sheet parts: lee sheet eased, weather leech steadied by bowline and sail clewed up; **B** weather sheet and clewline part: sail backed and lowered, clew hauled into crosstrees.

Lower tack or sheet parting
A Tack parts: weather leech steadied by bowline and clew hauled up; **B** tack, sheet and clewline part: sail brought aback and clew temporarily lashed to lower rigging.

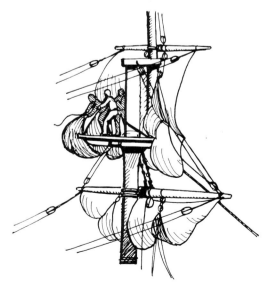

Topsail sheet and clewline parting with sail backed and lowered, clew manhandled into top.

Seaman lowered down the leech of a sail attaching bowline to bridle.

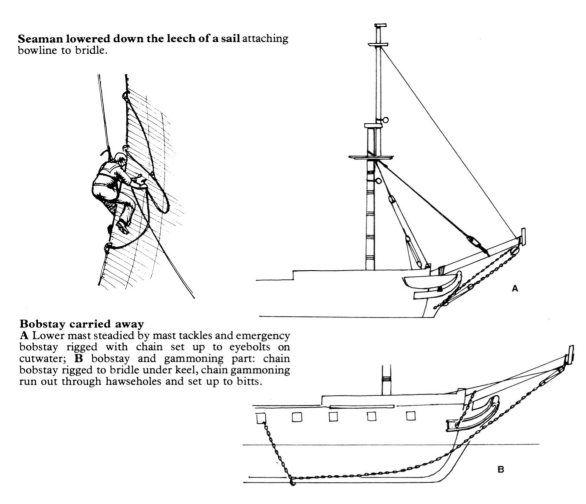

Bobstay carried away
A Lower mast steadied by mast tackles and emergency bobstay rigged with chain set up to eyebolts on cutwater; **B** bobstay and gammoning part: chain bobstay rigged to bridle under keel, chain gammoning run out through hawseholes and set up to bitts.

Parting of weather reef-tackle. This usually occurs when reefing topsails, due to the yard not being properly laid. The men are got off the yard while the weather side of the sail is clewed up, so the leech can be hauled into the top, and a new fall rove. Bardenfleth suggests lowering a man from the yardarm in a boatswain's chair, but this would not be practical in reefing weather, when the necessity was likely to occur.
Parting of tack of a course. The weather clew will fly up, and wrap itself around the stay, unless the leech is steadied by the bowline. Clew up to weather, then to lee, and repair.
Parting of sheet of a course. If the ship is by the wind, the lee clew will flap about out of control. By keeping away, the lee tack can be used to steady it out forward, and the sail can then be clewed up. If the shackle holding clewgarnet, sheet and tack breaks, there is no choice but to throw the sail aback, and lash the lee clew to the rigging until the shackle is replaced. Bracing aback is carried out carefully, striking the corresponding topsail, and hauling out its reef-tackles, hauling up the weather clew of the course, and buntlines.
Parting of bowline or bowline-bridle. In the case of a topsail or course, keep away to

hold the sail full. If the weather permits, a man may be lowered from the yardarm to repair the damage. If not, the sail must be got in, and the work done on the yard (Ekelöf, 219).

ACCIDENTS TO STANDING RIGGING

Before the wind, the strain on the standing rigging comes on the shrouds and backstays; with the sails aback, all the strain comes on the stays. The strain is distributed between stays, weather shrouds, and backstays with the ship by the wind. When the ship is pitching, the strain alternates, as the masts whip fore and aft. If one item of standing rigging carries away, attention must be given to the remote, as well as the immediate consequences. Thus the loss of the bobstay endangers not only the bowsprit, but also the foremast, main topmast, and mizzen topgallant mast, all of which ultimately depend for their security on the integrity of the bowsprit and forestay.
Bobstay carried away. This can occur either when everything is suddenly thrown aback, when sailing by the wind, or when pitching violently. The more free the wind, the less the strain, and with the wind aft,

there would be none, were it not for pitching motion. The remedy, therefore, is to bear away, take in jib and fore topmast staysail, and shorten sail, particularly taking off the fore and main topsails and topgallants, to minimise pitching. The fore topgallant mast is struck, and the jibboom and flying jibboom run in. The foremast pendants are cleared away, and set up to the knightheads, with tackles to take the strain off the forestay. Liardet considered it a pernicious habit to have the pendants tucked away 'neatly' under the tops. This not only subjected the ropes to unnecessary kinking, but also resulted in rot. Ths worming and parcelling was designed to shed water when the pendant hung vertically down; twisted up under the top, it resulted only in the local collection of water, and the destruction of the fibres. He therefore felt that the pendants were more properly disposed up and down, stopped inside the shrouds.
Ulffers (392) describes two methods of rigging an emergency bobstay. The cutwater was sometimes fitted with eyebolts, for use specifically in this eventuality. To one was shackled the end of a length of chain stream-cable, which was rove through a clump block stropped to the bowsprit, and set up with a tackle to the eyebolt of the other side. The other more complicated method is described by several authors, so apparently was quite well known. It utilised four lengths of stream-cable, each consisting of 12½ or 15 fathoms of chain. Two were taken out through opposite gunports, fairly far aft, to act as a strop. The ends were manhandled forward to the beakhead, and shackled together. The other two cables were shackled on either side of the junction, about a keel's breadth apart. The inboard ends of the chains forming the strop were then hauled in, and the other cables veered until the strop was up and down under the keel, with the forward chains leading along the keel, and up on either side of the stem. They were set up to the bowsprit with tackles, or deadeyes and lanyards.
Bowsprit gammoning carried away. This could occur if the bobstay had become loose. Ulffers uses a stream anchor cable as jury gammoning, leading an end out of one hawsehole, up over the bowsprit, down through the other hawsehole, and setting up taut with the cable secured to the bitts. Similar precautions as to bearing away, and shortening sail, as with a parted bobstay, had, of course, to be taken first.
Forestay carried away. Immediate danger to the masts is relieved by bearing away, and setting up the fore mast-tackles and pend-

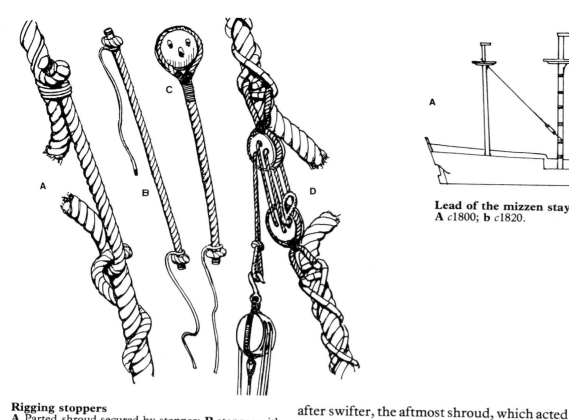

Rigging stoppers
A Parted shroud secured by stopper; **B** stopper with knots and laniards at each end; **C** stopper with single tail and deadeye; **D** parted shroud being set up with fighting stoppers.

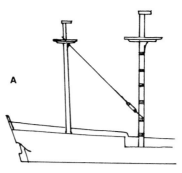

Lead of the mizzen stay
A c1800; b c1820.

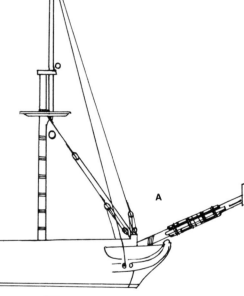

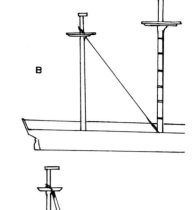

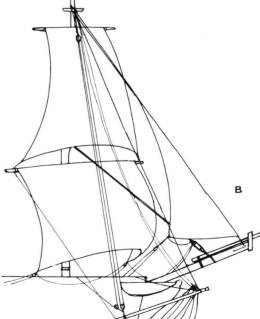

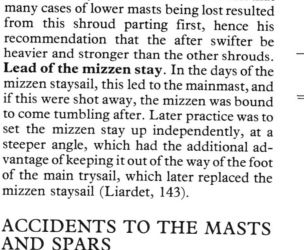

ants. A reserve forestay is rigged by taking a hawser up through the lubber's hole, round the lower masthead, down on the other side, and both ends led forward. The hawser is cut to a suitable length, and the ends spliced together. A large deadeye is worked into the bight, and set up to the knightheads, making sure that the strain comes evenly on both sides at the masthead (Ekelöf, 219).

Parting of shrouds. The strain on shrouds or backstays could be relieved immediately by going about on the other tack, or failing that, getting the sail aback on the affected mast. Men-of-war were equipped with rigging stoppers, specifically to allow the quick repair of a shroud shot away in action. The stoppers were lengths of hawser with a stopper knot, wall-and-crown, or similar, worked in one end, and a lanyard so the stopper could be secured to the ruptured shrouds. Some had a stopper knot and lanyard at either end, some had a deadeye spliced in one end, and a stopper knot at the other. Nares illustrates 'fighting stoppers', consisting of a pair of stoppers with deadeyes, which are hauled together with a lanyard and tackle. The lanyard was fitted with beckets, so either end could be used as the 'standing end'. The exact method used depended on the site of the damage. Liardet (211) felt that the most important lower shroud was the

after swifter, the aftmost shroud, which acted as the backstay of the lower mast. He felt that many cases of lower masts being lost resulted from this shroud parting first, hence his recommendation that the after swifter be heavier and stronger than the other shrouds.

Lead of the mizzen stay. In the days of the mizzen staysail, this led to the mainmast, and if this were shot away, the mizzen was bound to come tumbling after. Later practice was to set the mizzen stay up independently, at a steeper angle, which had the additional advantage of keeping it out of the way of the foot of the main trysail, which later replaced the mizzen staysail (Liardet, 143).

ACCIDENTS TO THE MASTS AND SPARS

Bowsprit sprung. Brady (180) brings the topmast breast-backstays over the topsail yard, and sets them up to the knightheads, to support everything on the fore. The pendant tackles are also set up on either side. The fore topmast stays are unrove, taken through the hawseholes, and set up on the gundeck. The jibboom is run in, and once the bowsprit is free of the strain, the bowsprit is fished, and the rigging set up properly once more.

Broken jibboom. This may occur if the weather guy or martingale parts. The wreckage will lie under the bowsprit, in the water to leeward. Keep away, furl the fore topgallant and send down the fore topgallant mast which is in immediate danger because its forward support is gone. Once the fore topmast

Accidents to bowsprit and jibboom
A Bowsprit sprung: lowermast secured by mast tackles, topmast secured by breast backstays and topmast stays led through hawseholes, bowsprit fished; **B** jibboom broken: spar recovered by jib downhaul or topgallant bowline and sail tackle.

staysail is set, the jib should lie comfortably in its lee until it can be cut free. The outer end of the boom can be retrieved with the jib downhaul, and the other piece can be raised with the sail-tackle, sent down from the crosstrees, before all. Fore buntlines and the inner lower studdingsail halliards can also be used to recover the spar and gear. A heel-rope is rove, to get the stump inboard, and the boom is replaced by a spare, if available.

Lower mast sprung. This is a dangerous matter, since if the mast breaks, everything above must go, and very likely the topmast next abaft. Warships carried, among the spare spars, 'fishes', specially hollowed out for the particular purpose of splinting a damaged lower mast. The word derives from French *fiche*, *ficher*, here in the sense of 'fix', although the actual technical term used by French seamen for this particular item, was *jumelle*, the underlying idea being that it 'doubles' or 'twins' the sprung mast. The fishes, along with other spars, if necessary, were nailed above and below the injured part, woolded with a heavy hawser, and the lashings further secured by driving wedges under them. Similar wooden fishes could be prepared for the lower yards, but Ulffers prefers special iron fishes, which were stronger, and less clumsy, in that application. Brady suggests using spare anchor-stock pieces, in an emergency. The anchor-stock was composed of two longitudinal sections, held together with square iron hoops, when in use on the anchor.

If the mast, let us say the fore, was sprung close up under the top, it could not be fished as described above. All the sail on the fore had to be got in, and the main staysail set to provide some forward canvas. The ship was kept away, the main topmast was steadied with its own breast-backstays, brought forward. The topgallants were sent down, and the fore topmast housed sufficiently that the heel came well below the crack. This required striking the lower yard, rigging the top-rope, and so on. The topmast was then supported by its top-rope, and a chain through the fid-hole. It was used to splint the lower mast, lashing and wedging the two together very firmly, chocks being inserted in the interval between them. The topmast was then wedged in the cap, and the lower yard rigged, so it rode on the topmast. The reefed topsail and course could then be set. The topmast rigging had to be shortened up, either by cutting or sheep-shanking it. If the lower cap were sprung, it could be woolded and wedged, but usually a spare cap was carried, kept in two halves for convenience, and bolted together, before being hoisted aloft.

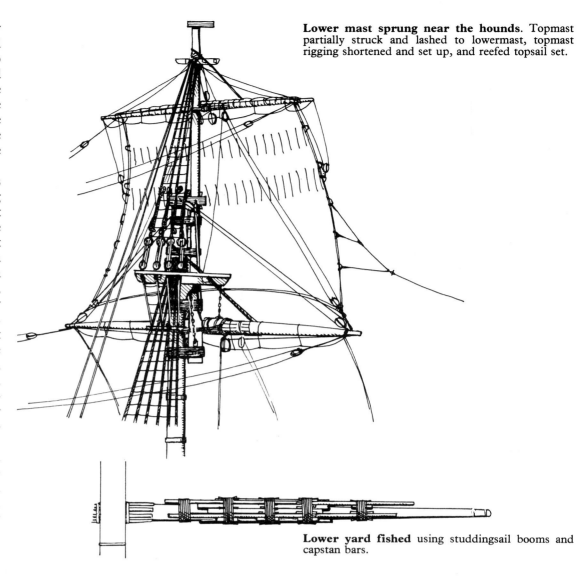

Lower mast sprung near the hounds. Topmast partially struck and lashed to lowermast, topmast rigging shortened and set up, and reefed topsail set.

Lower yard fished using studdingsail booms and capstan bars.

Topmast sprung. If the crack were near the heel, the expedient described for a sprung lower mast would serve equally well, but the obvious remedy was to replace the damaged topmast with a spare one. A damaged topgallant mast was invariably replaced.

Lower foreyard carried away. The ship is got before the wind, the foresail got in, and the fore topsail clewed up. Sufficient mizzen canvas is furled at the same time, to balance what is taken away forward. Using the jeers, top-burtons, lifts and pendant-tackle, the yard is got down on deck. It is fished if possible, replaced by a spare one in the event that one is carried, or the topsail yard is rigged in its place. In the interim, the ship can be got on course again, unreeving the topsail sheets, and making them fast on deck.

Jury rig. 'Jury' as in 'jury mast', derives from Old French *ajurie*, 'aid'. The Dutch word was *noodmast* ('mast of necessity'), and in French it was *mât de fortune*. A spare topmast was most useful for rigging a jury lower mast, while in a brig, the main boom

could be used. In the event of losing the foremast, it might be practical to shift the mizzen up in its stead (Brady, 220). A topmast studdingsail boom, with its sail as a lug would make quite an effective mizzen. A jibboom could serve as a topsail yard. Brady remarks that it is often surprising how well vessels manage to keep their speed, under jury-rig. Sails could be made smaller by taking some cloths from the middle, and by reefing at the head. It was still important to maintain the balance of the sail plan. For this reason, the loss of the foremast posed a bigger problem than the loss of the main. In the latter case, it was a simple matter to counterbalance fore and after canvas.

In cutting away the wreckage of spars, it was important to save as much as possible for jury use. At the same time it was necessary to cut the jumble of spars and rigging clear, if there was a danger that the stumps might pound a hole in the ship's side, were a sea running. Junk-axes were kept sharpened, and becketted on the upper deck, ready for

Jury rig
A French ship of the line under jury rig, steering by means of a spar towed astern (after P Ozanne, c1778); **B** American frigate *Macedonian* under jury rig in 1818 (after contemporary painting). The foreyard appears to be intact with a full foresail bent, although the mainsail and fore topsail would seem to be spare topsails bent to the smaller jury yards. The main topsail appears to be a spare topgallant; **C** British warship being towed under jury rig (after contemporary painting). Note the stumps of the fore- and mainmasts to which the jury masts are lashed.

Emergency steering gear
a parted tiller rope; b relieving tackles; c wedge for jamming rudder trunk; d spare tiller.

emergency (Liardet, 120).

Frapping, or girdling the hull. This was: 'The act of passing four or five turns of a large cable-laid rope round a ship's hull, when it is apprehended that she is not strong enough to resist the violence of the sea. This expedient is only made use of for very old ships, which their owners venture to send to sea as long as possible, insuring them deeply. Such are termed, not unaptly, floating coffins, as were the old ten-gun brigs, or any vessel deemed doubtful as to seaworthiness' (Smyth, 321).

ACCIDENTS TO WHEEL AND RUDDER

Wheel-rope parts. The ropes were constantly inspected by the navigator to determine if they required replacement. The hide ropes which were substituted for untarred hemp in the mid-1800s, stood up to continued use quite well. When sailing by the wind, the strain was on the weather rope, and this would be the one that gave way. The helm was instantly put down, and the vessel tacked, or the ship was hove to on the other tack, with the fore topsail to the mast. It was also possible to steer the ship by trimming the sails appropriately, while repairs were made. Nares sends all the men to the weather side, thereby lessening the pressure under the lee bow, and reducing the amount of weather helm carried. The important thing was to prevent the vessel going astern, or allowing the rudder to beat from side to side. Sailing before the wind, either wheel-rope could go, and the ship was brought to the wind by putting the helm over, using the remaining rope. Scudding in bad weather, the relieving tackles were hooked to each side of the tiller, so it could be got under control immediately, if a wheel-rope parted. A source of confusion is the fact that the term 'relieving-tackle' was subsequently used for a purchase with an endless fall, which rode across the iron tiller, in later merchant ships. Some of the largest

Hull frapped with a hawser with the turns set up with a Spanish windlass.

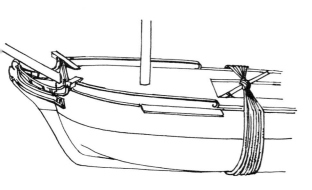

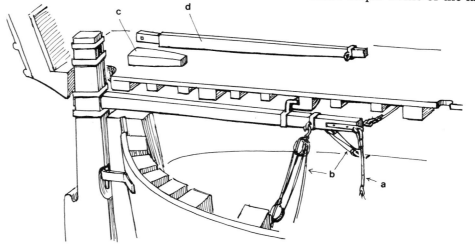

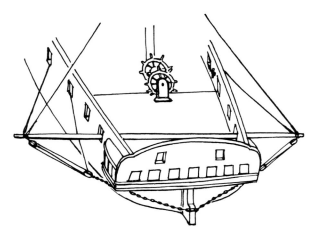

Steering with rudder chains; the falls of the tackles led to the wheel.

windjammers had a foot-pedal which allowed the helmsman to apply a brake to the wheel. The steering apparatus was intended to control the rudder, not the other way around. However, a cross-sea might strike the rudder, and cause the wheel to 'take charge', hurling the unfortunate helmsman over it.

Tiller or rudderhead fractures. Large men-of-war had provision for shipping a spare tiller, one deck above the tiller-flat, and this reserve helm was shipped, if the other were damaged. Heavy wedges were kept ready in the gunroom and jammed on either side of the rudderhead, to steady it temporarily, if the tiller were broken.

Rudder chains. If the rudderhead were wrung off, the ship could be steered using the rudder chains. These were shackled to a stout metal strap bolted to the rudder-horn, the upper after corner of the afterpiece of the rudder, just above the waterline. The chain was becketted loosely round the counter, to allow the rudder sufficient play, and to the forward ends were spliced rudder-pendants, which were made fast in the mizzen channels. The main purpose of the rudder chains was to secure the rudder, should it be jarred loose from going aground. In addition, by rigging tackles on the pendants, they could, at a pinch, be used to steer. The leverage offered would seem to have been barely adequate for the task, but a rather similar method was used in small vessels, the San Francisco Bay scow-schooners, for example. Several types of jury-steering contrive to use the wheel. Mossel (III, 393), for example, lays a spar across the quarterdeck, or jutting out through the port on a lower deck. The ends project twelve feet out from the side, and are supported with 'lifts' to the mizzen mast, and guys running forward. The double block of a tackle is hooked to the rudder-pendant, the single block to the end of the spar. The fall is taken through a leading block on the spar, up through the fairleads under the wheel, and the turns taken round the barrel. By leading the fall to the appropriate end of the barrel, the wheel can be arranged to turn in the direction the ship's head is intended to go. It will be realised that the rudder chains operate as though there were an after-pointing tiller, the rudder-horn projecting backwards. The fall is cut off at a suitable length, and seized to the staple at the mid-point of the drum, leaving an extra foot or so with a half-hitch at its end. Two half-hitches are temporarily seized, so that they may be hauled on, as the fall stretches, and develops too much play.

Rudder carried away. The rudder was too heavy to allow of a spare being carried. A rudder-mould, or pattern, was kept on board however. This was made of laths, and indicated the position of each pintle, so allowing another rudder to be made, with the assurance that it would fit the gudgeons on the sternpost properly. To lift the new rudder into place, a tackle was hooked above the rudderpost, and secured to a strop in the tiller-hole, and the rudder lifted sufficiently high to allow the upper pintle, which was the longest, to engage in its gudgeon. The rudder, being held close against the sternpost with rudder chains, was then carefully lowered to engage the other rudder irons, and the wood-lock spiked on, to prevent its rising inadvertently (Davis, 201). The exact method used would vary so much, that it is impossible to give any better representative description than the above.

Steering using a hawser. The old seamanship books offer a great variety of lash-ups, most of which had been used for jury-steering, at some time or other. One method used a light rope, which was middled, and clove-hitched, and through the hitch about 50 fathoms of heavier hawser was veered. The clove-hitch was then hauled taut, and a further 50 fathoms of hawser was veered. The lighter ropes were taken through leading blocks on a spar, on either side, as described earlier, and brought to the steering wheel. By hauling in on the starboard rope, the hawser was pulled to that side, acting as a drag, and causing the ship to turn to starboard. She could be inclined to port by heaving in on the other side. Other methods are described which use lengths of junk, old cable, secured in a wooden frame, and weighted to float these improvised rudders upright (Mossel, III, 394).

Methods using a spar. A French pilot named Olivier, or Ollivier, described a jury-rudder using two pairs of gun-carriages secured to a heavy spar. This depended on the sides of the carriages being kept vertical, and this was achieved by weighting the lower pair with kentledge (Baudin, 391). In smaller vessels, something resembling a scull, or steering oar, could be constructed, and would function quite well, if the weather were moderate. The jury-rudders invented by Peat, and one identified with the corvette *Le Duc de Chartres*, were in this category (Mossel, III, 400).

Rudders using a wooden frame. Bassière employed the partioning from the wings and pump-well to construct a snowshoe-shaped panel, which pivoted on a rope hauled up the rudder-hole, a bridle with guys hauling it forward. Bassière is also credited with using a contraption, made of two gun-carriages, as a drag to allow a vessel with jury-rig and no rudder to go about (Baudin, 381, 389). Robiné's rudder was elliptical, formed of boards nailed criss-cross. A towing-bridle was secured to three holes in the forward edge. Three similar holes in the after edge took the steering ropes. A hole in the top could be used for an inhaul. Stareich used a rectangular frame with two studdingsail boom-irons bolted to its leading edge. A topmast studdingsail boom was passed through these, and then up through the rudder-hole. The lower end of the boom was held forward by guys. Steering ropes were attached to the after edge of the jury-rudder. Captain Marco Stareich sailed the Austrian brig *Norma* for thirty days with this arrangement, which received favourable comment from Bréart (307), Bardenfleth (II, 61), and Hansen (I, 171). It had the great advantage that no major spars were required to construct it. If the breeze were light, it worked best raised almost to the surface, with a moderate breeze, about half way down, and with a strong breeze, lowered to its full extent.

Steering apparatus using casks. A French officer, Captain Quoniam of the *Pallas*, lost his ship's rudder near the Cape of Good Hope, and successfully steered his ship with the following arrangement. Casks were sawn in two, so as to form a pair of tubs. These, being hooped securely, were fitted with a bridle on the open end and an 'inhaul' on the bottom. The inhauls were used to tow the casks bottom upwards, on either side of the ship. The 'bridle' ropes were secured to the barrel of the steering wheel, so that when the wheel was turned to port, the port cask was pulled round hollow side forward. This would cause the ship to turn to port. It will be seen that canvas drogues would serve the purpose even better. Bardenfleth (II, 60) describes another arrangement using four half-casks or tubs. Outriggers are placed forward, amidships, and aft, suitably guyed, and supported by lifts. Four-point bridles are secured to the 'open' ends, and bridle ropes are hitched to the outboard ends of the forward and middle outriggers. In the bottom of the tubs an inhaul is fastened, taken through a leading block at the end of the spar immediately abaft, led inboard and belayed. If it is desired to turn the ship to port, one or both port casks are lowered into the water, the drag having the desired effect. Although more tedious to use in actual service than the Quoniam system, this arrangement had the merit that there is no impediment to movement, except when the necessity arises to alter course. This was successfully used in the French steamer *Cachemire* (Dick & Kretchmer, II, 361).

Edward Pakenham's rudder. A description of this is to be found in practically every seamanship text of the nineteenth century. The rudder was formed primarily of a square topmast, a spare lower cap, an anchor stock, a mast cheek, or bibb, and other lighter planking. The topmast, cut off to the appropriate length, formed the stock of the rudder. The square hole of the lower cap was cut away, so it formed a deep slot, wide enough to embrace the sternpost. The round hole of the cap was slipped over the topmast. The remainder of the topmast was sawn into two pieces, a long one above the cap, and a short piece below it, which were spiked to the stock. Abaft this, in successsion, were secured a piece of jibboom, and the cheek of the lower mast. These pieces were through-bolted, and further secured with fore and aft planking. The stock came up through the rudder-trunk, an improvised tiller being slipped through the fid-hole, which was uppermost. The half anchor-stock was placed transversely abaft the improvised rudder-stock, hollowed out to allow the latter to turn readily, and secured with guys, to hold the upper end against the sternpost. The rudder thus pivoted in the rudder trunk, the anchor-stock, and the round hole of the cap. Although Totten (228) says that this was 'the most approved way of preparing a temporary rudder', other authors, Bréart and Mossel, for example, felt that it was difficult to make, structurally weak, and clumsy in operation.

Dusseuil's jury-rudder. This employed a specially prepared rudder-stock with three pintles. In addition a combined pintle and gudgeon-brace was used to haul the lower end of the stock against the sternpost. The stock was built out with other spars, weighted with kentledge and shipped like a regular rudder. This pattern was adopted by the Admiralty in 1839, and a specially made jury-

stock was prepared for each ship. This, together with the pintle-gudgeon brace was carried on board for use if needed. With the plug-stock rudder, the rudder aperture angled forward, just above the port, which explains the inclination of the Dusseuil rudder.

There were still other jury-rudders, but the above will give an idea of the possibilities. Bonnefoux (231) mentions several other arrangements which had been proposed, or even subjected to practical trial.

LEAKS

Causes of leak. Besides sustaining an overt breech of the ship's fabric by striking on a rock, wooden ships were prone to develop small leaks, due to the fastening of the planks giving way, or caulking becoming loose in the seams. The 'hood-ends' of the planks, where the strakes of the side met the stem, was a spot particularly prone to springing leaks. In the tropics, the relentless beating down of the sun on one side of the vessel, as when moored head and stern, or when sailing day after day on the same course in the Trades, could cause havoc. 'In tropical climates, the sun has such power from constantly striking in the same place, that the pitch is soon melted out of the

seams, the oakum becomes dry and rotten, or at any rate of little use in keeping out the water in a seaway, and it will not take many weeks before a well-caulked and tight ship becomes a leaky one' (Liardet, 128). Men-of-war were usually careful to spread awnings, to protect the deck, but paid less attention to the side of the vessel. The captain of a merchantman, faced with the possibility of damage to a valuable cargo, would be more concerned, and would attempt to shade the side of his ship. A vessel that was 'spitting oakum' leaked progressively more and more. Hutchinson (253) talks of a vessel rolling, 'hauling under the chains', the strain of the shrouds causing the side planking to open and close. Iron vessels were not immune either, leaking from loose rivets, or in the neighbourhood of the underwater inlet of a force-pump, for example.

Site of the leak. Certain deductions could be made depending upon the rate at which the ship made water. If it increased with headway, the leak was in the bow, while if it decreased, the problem was in the stern. If it increased on one tack, more than the other, the opening was on the lee side. The pressure of the water increases proportionately to the square root of the depth. Hence, 'if a ship

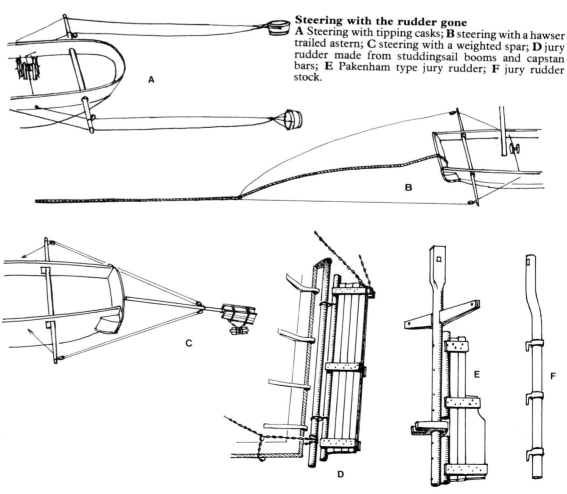

Steering with the rudder gone
A Steering with tipping casks; **B** steering with a hawser trailed astern; **C** steering with a weighted spar; **D** jury rudder made from studdingsail booms and capstan bars; **E** Pakenham type jury rudder; **F** jury rudder stock.

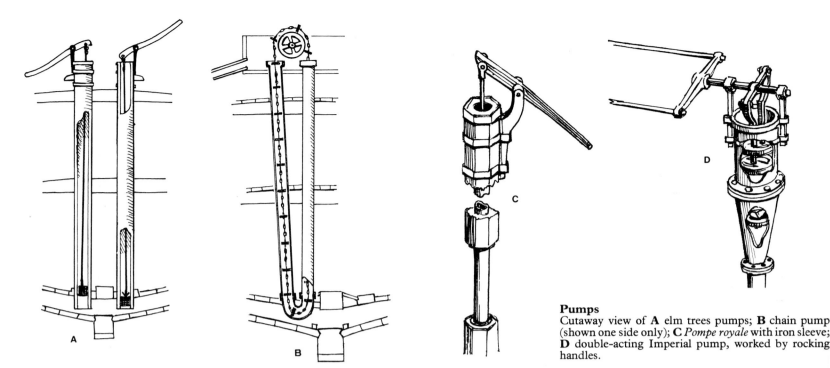

Pumps
Cutaway view of **A** elm trees pumps; **B** chain pump (shown one side only); **C** *Pompe royale* with iron sleeve; **D** double-acting Imperial pump, worked by rocking handles.

spring a leak under her bottom, although the water should increase upon the pumps at first, yet after it has risen to a certain height above the leak, the pumps will then be able to prevent its rising higher' (Gower, 150). The point of this comment was that while it might appear initially that the pumps could not control the inflow, and the vessel must necessarily sink, as the water rose, the people at the pumps would be able to keep things under control: as the Irish lieutenant reassured the captain of a leaking vessel, 'Don't be uneasy Sir – the more that comes in, the less there will be' (Glascock, 114).

In calm weather, one method of finding the leak was to row around the outside of the ship, placing one end of a pole against the waterline, and pressing the ear against the other. It was asserted that in the neighbourhood of a leak, a murmuring sound would be heard, due to the vibration of the hull, as the water flowed through the leaking seam (Gower, 151). In clear water, watching the movement of a piece of bunting on a pole was another method proposed.

Temporary repair of a leak. If the site of a single leak were known, one method of stopping it was to place a sail over it. A doubled up topsail, for instance, was suspended from the fore and main yardarms, lines run under the keel from the two lower corners. Whips securing the upper corners were then slacked away so that the sail could be placed snugly over the source of the trouble, the water pressure holding it in place. Actually, it was difficult to hold an exterior canvas patch of this sort in position, once the ship had headway, but the method was used with success

from time to time. If the patch were made with a proper collision mat, by 'thrumming' the canvas, with short pieces of oakum, after the fashion of a hooked rug, so much the better. If there were insufficient time to get such a thrummed mat ready, tar was poured on the canvas, and chopped up oakum scattered thickly on this. Some leaks close to the waterline could be tackled from within, although care had to be taken not to loosen the ship's skin planking further, in attempts to plug the hole.

Pumps. Given the difficulties in maintaining watertight integrity referred to above, it will be realised that the ability to keep the hold clear of water was vital to the ship's survival. The best modern description of these old pumps, with excellent illustrations, is found in Boudriot (II, 145). Dutch methods are detailed by Rijk (253) and Mossel (I, 278). Chain-pumps were not used in the 1800s by the Dutch or the French, but can be seen in *Victory*, and in fact date back to the 1600s, being mentioned by Mainwaring (92). Bugler (79) concluded that about thirty men could be stationed at *Victory*'s pumps, to deliver about 120 tons of water per hour. Hutchinson claimed, from personal experience, that working on the chain-pumps was much less tiring than handling the older elm-tree pumps.

The elm-tree pump was much older, and considerably modified, remained in use well into the 1800s. Bugler felt that in *Victory*, they were only used to pump sea-water up for washing down decks, and as a back-up for the fire-pump. However, historically they were also used as bilge-pumps. Since the piston

tended to wear out the wooden cylinder, the French replaced the wooden casing with a cast-metal cylinder, this being an essential feature of what was called a *pompe royale*. Boudriot illustrates a refinement of the simple pump handle. Fitted with a many-tailed whip, called a *martinet*, it allowed fourteen men to tail onto the end of the lever.

Various improvements on the suction- and force-pump were tried out, such as double-acting pumps where one piston was on the downstroke, as the other was on the upstroke. Chain-pumps were liable to failure of the links, and the leather discs. Elm-tree pumps could choke up at the bottom, even though fitted with a 'rose box', to filter out the dirt. The pump-rod could be withdrawn vertically upwards through a small scuttle in the deckhead if necessary, and a metal pump-hook could be slipped down the cylinder to withdraw the lower pump-box if its valve needed replacement. The depth of water could be sounded by dropping an iron rod, on a line down a leaden sounding-tube close by the pumps. It was dried off after use, if necessary by being rubbed with ashes if another sounding were to be made shortly. There were never less than two pumps, and four in a large vessel, placed to plumb the pump-well, around the step of the mainmast. The bilge water drained through the shingle ballast to reach the well, which was clear of obstruction. Having pumps on each side of the keel, meant that at least one would be on the 'low' side, if the vessel were listing. To prevent water collecting between the first futtocks of the frames, adjacent to the keelson, a limber passage was contrived. This consisted of a line of holes in the futtocks, beside the keelson. A chain passed through them, and by jerking this 'limber-clearer' to-and-fro, the holes could be kept clear, allowing the water to reach the pump-well.

Ship in danger of sinking. Richard Hall Gower (153), in 1808, gives a very sound analysis of what to do in a sinking vessel. The problem with free water in the hull, is not simply its weight, but the fact that the centre of gravity of the water always shifts to the low side, thus aggravating both rolling and listing. He suggests striking down all unnecessary tophamper from aloft, stowing heavy weights such as guns and shot low in the hold, jettisoning everything from the upper deck, not necessary for life, and filling the orlop deck with as many bunged-up empty casks as possible. Brady (184) describes the technique of throwing a lower deck gun overboard. The bad-weather lashings securing the gun, with its muzzle up against the clamp were removed, a breech-tackle was secured round the pommelion on the breech, and hooked to the housing-bolt on the clamp. The quoins were pushed under the breech, the capsquares, holding the trunnions to the carriage were opened, and the breech further raised with handspikes, so the gun would not fall back into the carriage. The breeching was unrove, side-, port-, and breech-tackles were manned. Then watching the roll, the port was hauled up, and the gun hurled out on the down roll, by hauling on the breech-tackle and lifting the cascabel with handspikes, whereupon the port lid was shut as quickly as possible. Gower records that 'it has frequently happened that ships have been left by their crews, because the water gained upon the pumps, and that the same vessels have been met with afterwards, and brought into port'.

RUNNING AGROUND

The German seaman wished no more for his vessel than that she 'should always keep a foot of water under the keel'. Neglect in observing this precaution, could result in the ship touching the ground. Amongst the reasons for this accident could be cited piloting errors like failure to appreciate tidal change, the effect of an onshore current, having an anchor drag in a roadstead, or being forced ashore while being pursued by an enemy. Obvious signs of impending danger might be offered by the colour of the water becoming paler, or seeing the breakers over a shoal and the results varied from a momentary retardation to loss of the ship.

The surrounding circumstances influenced the outcome to a great degree.

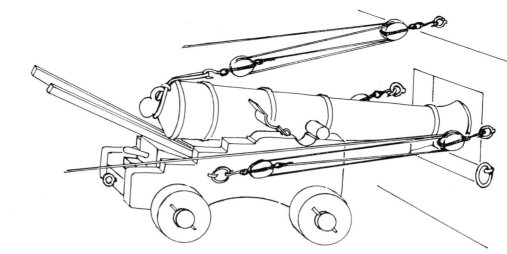

Cannon ready to be jettisoned.

French brig *L'Eclair* chased ashore on Guadaloupe (after A Roux, 1809).

Going aground during the flood tide, the vessel had every prospect of getting off successfully, while on the ebb, she would have to wait for the succeeding flood. In this circumstance, a marked fall of the tide, would result in greater evil than a small drop. The worst time to be stranded was at high-water of a spring tide, when there might be a long wait before the next springs. A flat bottomed ship was calculated to sit comfortable high and dry on a shoal, more or less upright, where one with a greater rise of floor would infallibly have fallen over on its side. On the other hand, a vessel of fine underwater form was safer on the rocks, provided it was shored upright, there being less danger of its being bilged, than one with a flat bottom. Going ashore in a calm was manifestly less dangerous, than when a heavy sea was running.

Taking the ground on a shoal. French *talonner* was a special word for a momentary touching of the ground, arising because the *talon* was the after extremity of the keel.

Since most vessels drew more water aft than forward, this was the most likely part of the ship to touch the ground on a sandbar. Collier brigs, working the Thames estuary, were trimmed so that the keel was horizontal, relying on the resulting six inches or so reduction in draught, to bump their way over the occasional sandbank, in 'fleet' water. If the vessel were not lucky enough to sail her way over the bank, it would come to a dead stop. By bracing the yards around, so they came aback, it might be possible to back the ship off, if she had been sailing by the wind. Before the wind of course this option did not exist, and everything had to be furled. An anchor was laid out astern, firstly, so that the ship would not drive further up on the shoal and secondly, to be used in warping the vessel off. Mossel (III, 430) says that one is sometimes hesitant to run a warp out aft, through the stern windows, because this results in destroying the captain's quarters. With a flood tide, it might only be necessary to wait a while, for the rising water to float the ship off.

If waiting alone were insufficient, all the other boats were put in the water, to lighten the ship, in addition to that used to lay out the kedge-anchor. Gower (168) hauls the ship off a steep sandy shoal, using 'stop-waters', or drogues, made of casks, sawn in half, after the fashion of sea-anchors. This would not work if the ship were heavily aground. The navigator sounded all around the ship, to form a better picture of the situation, and decide on how she was best got off.

Soft muddy bottom. This was the easiest to get clear of, but offered the poorest holding ground for the kedge. The grip of the anchor was improved by securing 'shoes' made of flat boards to its flukes, to increase their area, and by backing the first anchor with a second kedge, laid out in the same line. A vessel in soft ooze tended to dig a 'bed' for itself, as it rocked under the influence of the waves. Mossel refers to a ship thus placed as being *geboied* ('fettered', or, as one might say, 'in irons'). To loosen the grip of the silt under these conditions, the ship could be 'sallied', or rocked, by sending the men aloft, and

having them shake the rigging in unison, or by having them move together from side to side of the deck, by drum beat, or the stroke of a bell. Carrying weights such as 32-pound shots enhanced this effect. The nature of the bottom had a bearing on things also. Mossel (III, 424) considered that if a ship was embedded 'even an inch' in sand, there was no prospect of warping it off, whereas, in soft mud, it might be managed. On the whole, it was usually better to wait for the tide to come in, and the water to rise sufficiently, rather than trying to kedge the vessel off prematurely by main force.

Lightening the ship. If the vessel floated higher in the water, obviously it could swim off more readily. Swinging out the boats, all the heavy spars from the booms, along with the topgallant masts and upper yards, would

Ship aground on a shoal with sails backed and kedge run out astern to back ship off, hands lightening ship.

result in considerable weight reduction. In addition, the fresh water casks could be started, the boilers of a steamer drained, and the pumps then used to clear the water out of the bilges. Shot could be cast over the side, followed by the guns, which were best dropped on the shoreward side (Mossel, III, 429). Jettisoning all this material was naturally only undertaken when in dire straits. If only the bow of the vessel were aground, shifting weight aft might suffice to allow it to float, or be warped off. Spare anchors, cannon, etc, were buoyed for later recovery, and cross-bearings taken to mark their position. Furthermore, care had to be taken where they were dropped, bearing in mind that they should never be placed where the ship could 'sit on them', at some later stage of the salvage operation. 'Many ships have been lost through striking on their own guns or anchors' (Liardet, 191). For the same reason, it was considered bad practice to drop a bower anchor under foot from the cathead, immediately upon stranding, because it would lie in just that position where one of the arms might subsequently impale the bow timbers. If there were danger that the rudder fastenings might be torn loose, the rudder-chains were cleared away, so that the rudder itself would not be lost.

Shoring up the vessel. If the ship rolled over, the incoming tide would quickly fill the hull with water and mud, making recovery impossible, hence the importance of keeping the hull more or less upright. The spare top-masts and lower yards made the most suitable shores. If the bottom were soft, a 'shoe' had to be contrived, to act like the basket on a ski-pole, so that the lower end would not simply disappear into the ooze. On a firm bottom this was not necessary. If the ship were listing well over to one side, the shores were secured

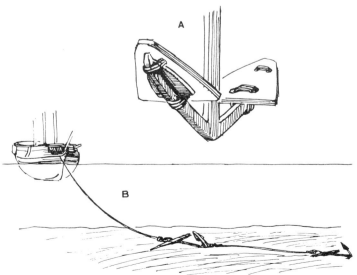

Holding in soft ground
A Shoeing an anchor; **B** backing an anchor.

L'Astrolabe **aground on a reef in Tonga** (after contemporary print). The boats have been hoisted out to lighten ship, which is pounding in a heavy sea. A shore has been rigged on the quarter.

on the low side; if she remained upright, props were fastened on both sides. Bréart (272) gives a detailed description of shoring up, using the mainyard. Let us suppose the vessel was listing to port. The sail was unbent, the clewgarnets, buntlines, leech-lines, etc, unrove, and the booms sent down on deck. The toprope was rove through the top-block on the port side of the lower cap, and the end hitched to the middle of the lower yard. The jeers were rove and hoisted sufficiently to let go the slings. The topsail yard was carefully secured with braces and lifts, a tackle being rigged as a preventer-lift on the port side. A heavy tackle, the *caliorne*, was secured to the port topsail yardarm, and its lower block hooked to the starboard yardarm of the lower yard. Tackles rigged as guys were made fast to the port main yardarm, and by easing away on the jeers, toprope, and port lift, the yard was peaked up to starboard, lowered, and guided over the side, eventually hanging by the tackle from the port topsail yardarm. When firmly on the bottom, and steadied by the guys, it was secured by a lashing running between two adjoining gunports. The heavy tackle, which had been used to lower it, was then unhooked from aloft, and set up on deck, so it acted to prevent the ship sliding down the spar, so to speak. A shore could also be fastened using a spare topmast, lifting it from the booms, by means of the yard and stay-tackles, and shifting it over the side, so its foot rested on the ground. Guys, and cross-lashings were rigged in the same fashion as described above. An anchor laid out on the 'high' side of a listing ship could also be of help in keeping the hull steady, the cable being winched taut, using the deck capstan.

Raising the ship. Various expedients are described to actually lift the bow off the bottom, in the case of a ship sitting aground forward. Sheers rigged above the forecastle, in the same sort of way as described for shores, could be used as a basis for lifting the bow with a heavy tackle. The ideal solution would have been a custom-made pair of 'camels', and in fact extempore floats were successfully used on occasion. One celebrated salvage was that of HMS *Gorgon*, which ran firmly aground off Montevideo but succeeded in getting herself off with home-made pontoons primarily contrived from her own emptied boilers. A ring of empty casks could be made to serve the same purpose. Bréart describes ballasting these initially, to get them lower in the water, before making them fast, so increasing their effective buoyancy, when the weights were removed. The French authors refer to casks

Sending down the mainyard to use as a shore.

Raising the ship sheers rigged over forecastle and a string of casks submerged to lift bows off the ground.

employed in this way, as a *chapelet*, ('chaplet'), since they resembled a string of beads. Luce (578) tells of another method using a pontoon, which depended on the fact that a ship, when careened with her keel out of the water, draws less than when upright: a stranded vessel, believed beyond recovery, was sold for a pittance to a salvor, who got a pontoon alongside, hove the ship down as if careening, and floated both free. Liardet uses the same principle to reduce the draught by a few inches, in a ship just touching the ground The 'weather' guns are run in, and the crew all move over to the 'lee' side, so that the lee bilge, rather than the keel, is the lowest point. A ship with a bad leak would not float off with the incoming tide, since the hold would simply fill with water. If possible, therefore,

at low tide, the leak was caulked or patched, or covered with a thrummed canvas mat.

Raising a ship which had rolled over. Bréart describes a technique using pontoons secured on both sides, or anchored securely. Chains are secured on the weather side of the hull, passed under the keel and made fast to the pontoons with tackles, shorter ones to the lee pontoon, longer ones to the weather pontoons, passing up the lee side of the ship and across its deck. The weather pontoons are used to raise the vessel up, the chains working as a sort of parbuckle. The chains to the lee pontoon, keep it up, once raised. When the lee pontoons are initially secured, ballast is placed on the side towards the ship. Once made fast, the ballast is shifted over to the other side of the pontoon. Bréart (274)

1.
A brig off Plymouth breakwater with her fore topsail sheet parted, painted by N M Condy. Hands are going aloft to get the wildly thrashing sail stowed. (Courtesy N R Omell Gallery, London)

2.
HMS *Calcutta* in a gale. Her mainyard has broken and the mainsail blown out. (Imperial War Museum, London)

3.
A British 74, badly damaged in battle, making repairs to her rigging at sea. Note the lifebuoy dangling from the spanker boom, which is of a typically French pattern. Engraving by Baugean, 1814. (Mark Myers' Collection)

4.
The *Ripon*, a P & O steamer, had her rudder damaged in a gale. This engraving shows the boatswain securing the rudder chains, by means of which the ship was steered with the quarterdeck capstan. *Illustrated London News*, 1846. (Mark Myers' Collection)

5.
Detail of a contemporary model of the Dutch East Indiaman *Vergelijking* of 1780, showing a sophisticated jury rig above the stump of the foremast. (Author's photo, courtesy Rijksmuseum, Amsterdam, and Bas Kist and Herman Ketting)

6.
Vasa's elm tree pump. This was placed in the mid-line, just forward of the steering position on the upper gundeck. One imagines there must have been a canvas hose to convey the water to the pump-scupper in the ship's side (Author's photo, courtesy *Vasa* Varvet and Marine Dir Gunnar Schoerner RSN)

7.
Sectional view of a man-of-war, showing the elm tree pumps and Dutch 'Imperial' double-acting pumps. (Author's photo, courtesy Nederlands Scheepvaart Museum, Amsterdam, and H Hazelhoff-Roelfzema)

8.
Lord Howe's fleet returning to Spithead under jury rig after the battle of the 'Glorious First of June', 1794. Many of the ships have lost their topmasts, and some, all of their lower masts. The least damaged ships are towing the lame ducks. (Courtesy N R Omell Gallery, London)

5.

6.

7.

8.

HMS _Amazon_ capsized off Mauritius, 1780 (after D Serres).

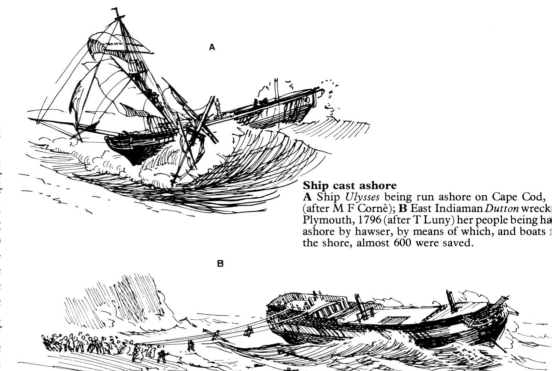

Ship cast ashore
A Ship _Ulysses_ being run ashore on Cape Cod, (after M F Cornè); **B** East Indiaman _Dutton_ wreck Plymouth, 1796 (after T Luny) her people being ha ashore by hawser, by means of which, and boats the shore, almost 600 were saved.

claims that this method was successfully used to salvage a ship at Brest.

Shipwreck. The ancient English term was actually 'ship-break', and this is long out of use, although it survives as German _Schiff bruch_, and French _naufrage_, both having this identical meaning, the latter word deriving from medieval Latin. If there were no prospects of saving a ship trapped on a lee-shore, all efforts were directed to saving the lives of her company. In the worst case, the vessel would sink 'with all hands', or as the Dutch put it, _met man en muis vergaan_, ('perish with man and mouse'). If circumstances permitted, it might at least be possible to choose where the vessel would actually strike the shoreline. A steep shelving beach, with no off-lying reef was obviously better than a rocky shore. The aim was to get the ship as far up the beach as possible, and if she could be lightened beforehand by throwing overboard the guns, etc, so much the better (Bréart, 276). If striking bow on, everyone was got aft, since the likelihood was that the masts would snap and pitch forward, at the moment of impact. It would often be best to remain on board, until the weather moderated, but if the vessel started to break up, the crew would have to struggle ashore as best they could.

Depending on circumstances, the where-abouts of the wreck, and so on, rafts were constructed, a breeches-buoy contrived, muskets and stores landed if possible. Mossel emphasises the importance of maintaining discipline in this situation, and recommends that the key of the spirit-room be in the commander's pocket, and if necessary let the rum casks be stove in, rather than add the complication of drunken crew-members. Traditionally, the commanding officer was the last person to leave the stricken vessel, taking with him the ship's log, which might perhaps be helpful in defending him against a subsequent charge of having unnecessarily hazarded his vessel.

FIRE

'Fire on board ship is one of the most bewildering casualties to which human beings are subject; but to allay the terror consequent upon the first announcement of the calamity, nothing can be so effectual as a knowledge, not only that measures to meet the evil are already systematized, but that every man, having a specific duty to perform, is less at leisure to give way to apprehension' (Glascock, 335).

Causes of fire. One cause of fire aloft was a lightning strike during a thunder squall. Having observed, at close quarters, a ponderosa pine light up like a torch, after having been struck, one can well imagine an equally spectacular response in the rigging of a sailing ship. Actually, if the lightning conductors were in good repair, the various sections firmly in contact with each other, and ultimately with the ocean, there was little danger. In thundery weather, tubs filled with water were placed in the tops and channels, and the courses were brailed up; it was an old sea-belief that the down draught from the

lower sails enhanced the chance of a st (Ekelöf, 263). Fire in the rigging was al danger during action. The magazines, fi as they were, with explosive material, v illuminated only from a contiguous 'li room', and the gunner's men working t wore special clothing to minimise the da from static electricity. Smoking was allowed when permission had been giver the 'smoking lantern' to be lit; and at ni lanterns and candles were issued only to p officers having specific need of them – w not in use, they were hung up in s particular place (Liardet, 135).

Fire bill.

The propriety of 'beating to quarters' upor sudden alarm of fire may be disputed; certainly there are objections to the adoptic prevalent practice.... Again, admitting the men assemble quietly at quar considerable delay ensues as a double ope ion of first mustering the people, and dispatching detached parties to collect t implements necessary to extinguish the fir If a specific duty be assigned to e individual borne on the books, the moment the alarm of the fire be given, and the alarm should be conveyed, instanter, through the medium of a rapid and peculiarly-marked movement of the bell, every soul on board has then only to repair to his assigned station; and those whose duty it is to provide the appropriate implements will procure them, and proceed forthwith to their respective posts, without awaiting the orders of officers. The fire bill should be so formed, and each man so stationed, as to meet contingencies incidental to fire afloat, whether happening in harbour, or occurring at sea. For example a ship moored in a crowded anchorage may have to slip her cables, to avoid endangering others ... But the first consideration should be to ascertain promptly the precise position of the fire; and this duty should be entrusted to the first lieutenant, at the head of a party of petty officers and leading men, to be designated fire-searchers (Glascock, 335).

Fire-fighting. Wet mattresses, hammocks, blankets and so on, might be enough to put out a small fire; otherwise, buckets of water were passed from hand to hand, and the wash-deck hoses were used. A description of a ship's fire-engine, found in Mossel (I, 288) is representative of practice in the mid-1800s. The apparatus had a beam, with transverse handles at either end, rather like a railroad 'speeder'. Two cylinders worked into a reservoir to operate up to three hoses. Mossel claims that the largest version was capable of shooting a jet 17 metres vertically upwards, and delivering 20,000 litres per hour. The hoses were tubular lengths of canvas, measuring 16 metres, connected with copper junctions, and equipped with a metre long branch-pipe or nozzle, the whole arrangement being very similar to that still in use today. By opening the sea-cocks, and letting water pour into the bilges, the ship's pumps could also be brought into use in a fire-fighting capacity (Bréart, 279); this did not apply to chain-pumps which did not lift water under pressure. The fire-engine was under the charge of the carpenter, who reported the engine ready, and the force-pumps ready for use, to the officer of the deck at sunset (Glascock, 107).

Fire aloft. If this broke out, the important thing was to reduce as much as possible the relative wind speed. If the fire were forward, the ship was got before the wind; if aft, it was hove to. In the case of a fore topsail afire, the sail was clewed up, the ship got before the wind, the fore topmast staysail got down, and the fore course cut away from the yard, and dropped on deck. The yard was then struck, and an attempt made, by men in the top to put the fire out. If the main topsail were alight, the ship was hove to under the fore topmast staysail and mizzen, everything else being taken in. It might become necessary to cut away the mast, starting on the lee rigging, finishing with the stays and weather shrouds. An effort was made to leave a good stump, so that a jury-mast could be lashed to it.

Fire in the hull. Some cargoes – coal, hemp, and cotton, for example – were liable to ignite spontaneously. If the exact location of the fire were known, it might be possible to plug the scuppers, flood the upper deck to a depth of eight inches, and bore augur-holes through the deck, to dump water directly on the fire, without letting air in at the same time. A refinement of this method was to build a trough at the appropriate point on the upper deck. Todd & Whall (114) describe how the crew of the American ship *John Kay* extinguished a fire in the hold, by boring holes along the waterline, then going about, thus submerging them, on the other tack. Bréart (280) points out that even when the fire is extinguished, the lower part of the mast, or the planking where the chain plates are secured, may be charred, and the integrity of the mast compromised. He emphasises that such damage should always be suspected, and suggests securing the mast with extra struts, made of studdingsail yards, capstan bars, etc, and girdling the ship with hawsers, under the keel, to back up the chain plates.

In a man-of-war, spontaneous combustion was an unlikely event, but fire was a disaster nonetheless. The cross-draught through the gunports would have fanned the flames, to a degree that did not occur in the hold of a merchantman, so all ports, scuttles, and hatches were closed, as far as possible and windsails and ventilators taken down. In the event that the fire were on one side of the deck, the ship was got onto the other tack, to keep the conflagration on the lee side.

HMS *Fisguard* struck by lightning (after engraving in the *Illustrated London News*, 1847). The ship was fitted with a lightning conductor and suffered no damage from the bolt.

HMS *Bombay* on fire (after engraving in the *Illustrated London News*, 1865).

The ultimate catastrophe in a warship was explosion in the magazines, and these were accordingly flooded if the fire threatened to ignite the powder. Fire having broken out, it might also become necessary to jettison spirits and other combustible materials like paint and varnish.

Fordyce (82) organises the crew into groups as follows: the lumbermen, or wreck-clearers, were ready with axes and crowbars to break down bulkheads, scuttle decks, as necessary to get at the fire, and cut away masts and rigging, if the fire was aloft. The fire party, at the site of the conflagration, used buckets and hoses, together with wetted swabs and hammocks, passed to them by the hatchway men. The pumpers, manned the pumps to supply water to the engine, which was manned by the fire-engine men. The firemen drew water from over the side in buckets, and together with the water-drawers, who rigged whips from the yard-arms, supplied the hatchway men with tubs and buckets. The smothering party were responsible for closing gunports, laying on tarpaulins over hatchway gratings, as necessary to cut the air off from the fire, and passed wet hammocks to the hatchway men. The ship's police were responsible for the spirit room, and the gunner took charge of the magazines, ready to flood them if neces-sary. The carpenter rigged the chain and wash-deck pumps. The captains of the guns saw that their guns were unshotted and the charges withdrawn, and collected up powder horns, rockets, and so on on deck. The caulker stood by ready to open the sea-cock and flood the ship, if ordered. Armed sentries were detailed off to prevent any unauthorised meddling with the boats or leaving of the ship.

Magazine exploding in the Dutch warship *Alphen* at Curacao, 1778 (after H Kobell).

BIBLIOGRAPHY

BOOKS RELATING TO RIGGING AND SEAMANSHIP

W Abell. *The Shipwright's Trade*. London, 1948.
Admiralty Manual of Seamanship. Various volumes published in London in 1908, 1915, 1937, 1951 and 1964.
A H Alston. *Seamanship*, 2nd edition. Portsmouth, 1871.
A H Alston. *Seamanship*, 4th edition. Portsmouth, 1902.
R C Anderson. *Rigging of Ships 1600-1720*. Salem, 1927.
R & R C Anderson. *The Sailing Ship*. New York, 1947.
R C Anderson. *17th Century Rigging*. London, 1955.
E H H Archibald. *The Wooden Fighting Ship in the Royal Navy*. London, 1968.
E H H Archibald. *The Metal Fighting Ship in the Royal Navy*. London, 1971.
C W Ashley. *The Book of Knots*. New York, 1944.
Anonymous. Published by J D Potter. *The Anchor Watch*, 4th edition. London, 1863.
Anonymous. *Der ge-öffnete Seehafen*. Hamburg, 1705.
Anonymous. *Manuel du Gabier*, 6th edition. Paris, 1918.
Anonymous. *Masts, Spars, Rigging & Stores of the Navy of the United States*. Washington, 1826.
Anonymous. *The Naval Repository*. London, 1762.
Anonymous. *The Officer of the Watch*. Portsmouth, 1883.
Anonymous. *Seamanship & Navigation for the Officers in charge of the Marine Schools*. Ottawa, 1903.
Anonymous. *Svenska Flottans Historia*, Volumes I-III. Stockholm, 1942.

G A Ballard. *The Black Battlefleet*. Lymington & Greenwich, 1980.
F C C Bardenfleth. *Laerebog i Sømandskab*, Volumes I & II. Copenhagen, 1899.
D W Barker. *Elementary Seamanship*, 10th edition. London, 1929.
L S Baudin. *Manuel du Jeune Marin*. Toulon, 1828.
F G D Bedford. *Sailor's Pocket Book*, 2nd edition. Portsea, 1875.
J van Beylen. *Schepen van de Nederlanden*. Amsterdam, 1970.
G Biddlecombe. *The Art of Rigging*. Salem, 1925.
G Block. *Bootsdienst*. Hamburg, 1925.
E M Blunt. *Seamanship*, 2nd edition. New York, 1824.
E Bobrik. *Handbuch der praktischen Seefartskunde*. Leipzig, 1848 (Reprint 1978).
P M J de Bonnefoux. *Manoeuvrier Complet*. Paris, 1852.
D J Boom. *Het Tuig & het Op-& Aftuigen*. Den Helder, 1888.
A Boström. *Handbok uti Tackling*. Karlskrona, 1840.
Ph M Bosscher. *Een Nuchter Volk en de Zee*. Amsterdam, 1979.
J Boudriot. *Le Vaisseau de 74 Canons*, Volumes I-IV. Grenoble, 1973-1977.
Bourdé de Villehuet. *Le Manoeuvrier*. Paris, 1769.
J M Boyd. *Manual for Naval Cadets*. London, 1857.
W Brady. *The Kedge Anchor*, 6th edition. New York, 1852.
W Brady. *The Kedge Anchor*, 18th edition. New York, 1876 (Reprint 1970).
E Bréart. *Manuel du Gréement et de la Manoeuvre*. Paris, 1861.
R Brommy & H von Littrow *Die Marine*, 3rd edition. Leipzig and Vienna, 1878.
A Bugler. *HMS Victory. Building, Restoration & Repair*. London. 1966.
C Burney. *Young Seaman's Manual*. Jersey, 1869.
C Bushell. *The Rigger's Guide & Seaman's Assistant*, 4th edition. Landsport, 1859.

C Canby. *History of Ships and Seafaring*. New York, 1963.
A Challamel. *Manuel du Manoeuvrier*, 3rd edition. Paris, 1903.
H I Chapelle. *History of American Sailing Ships*. New York, 1935.
H I Chapelle. *History of the American Sailing Navy*. New York, 1949.
H I Chapelle. *The Search for Speed under Sail, 1700-1855*. New York, 1967.
F af Chapman. *Architectura Navalis Mercatoria*. Stockholm, 1968.
E K Chatterton. *The Ship Under Sail*. London, 1926.
G S L Clowes. *Sailing Ships*. Part I, London, 1932.
G S L Clowes. *Sailing Ships*, Part II. London, 1936.
W Congreve. *Elementary Treatise on Mounting Naval Ordnance*. London, 1811 (Reprint, c1970)
F A Costé. *Manuel de Gréement*, 2nd edition. Paris, 1849.
F A Costé. *Notes supplémentaires au Manuel de Gréement*. Paris, 1837.
C Cradock. *Wrinkles in Seamanship*. Portsmouth, 1884.
R S Crenshaw. *Naval Shiphandling.*, 2nd edition. Annapolis, 1960.

O Curti. *Libro completo dell'Attrezzatura navale*. Milan, 1979.
O Curti. *Het Scheepsmodel. Romp, Constructie & Bouw*. Bussum, 1975.

R H Dana. *The Seaman's Manual*, 2nd edition. London, 1844.
C G Davis. *Ship Model Builder's Assistant*. New York, 1926 (Reprint, 1960).
G Devillers. *Manuel de Matelotage & de la Voilerie*. Paris, 1971.
C Dick & O Kretchmer. *Handbuch der Seemannschaft*. Berlin, 1902.
F C Dreyer. *How to get a First Class in Seamanship*. Portsmouth, 1900.
M P -J Dubreuil. *Manuel de Matelotage et de la Manoeuvre*, 3rd edition. Paris, 1844.

C Engelhart. *Tjenstutöfningen ombord å Krigsskep*. Karlskrona, 1840. (A translation from Fordyce's *Outlines of Naval Routine*. London, 1837.)
A Ekelöf. *Lärobok i Skeppsmanöver*. Stockholm, 1881.

W Falconer. The *Shipwreck*. Falmouth, 1815.
D Fordyce. *Outlines of Naval Routine*. London, 1837.
P Forfait. *Traité élémentaire de la Mâture des Vaisseaux*. Paris, 1788 (Reprint 1979).
P Forfait. *Traité élémentaire de la Mâture des Vaisseaux*, 2nd edition, Paris, 1815.
R Foulerton. *Letter to the Admiralty on the Ship Manoeuvrer*. London, 1846.
F Fox. *Great Ships: The Battlefleet of King Charles II*. London, 1980.
C Frick. *Manöver med Segelfartyg*. Stockholm, 1867.
C G Frick. *Lärobok i Sjömanskap*. Stockholm, 1872.
J Furttenbach. *Architectura Navalis*. Frankfurt, 1629 (Reprint, 1968).

S C Gilfillan. *Inventing the Ship*. Chicago, 1935.
W N Glascock. *Naval Officer's Manual*, 2nd edition. London, 1848.
R H Gower. *Theory & Practice of Seamanship*, 3rd edition. London, 1808.
R Grenfell. Notes on Sail in the 19th Century. *Mariner's Mirror* 19 (1933) 89.
A J Griffiths. *Observations on some Points of Seamanship*. Portsmouth, 1828.
J P L Groeneijk. *Besturing van het Schip*. Amsterdam, 1848.
P de Gunthelberg. *Söe-Krigs-og Orlogs-mands Haand-bog*. Copenhagen, 1768.

H J Hansen. *The Ships of the German Fleet 1848-1945*. New York, 1975.
C P V Hansen. *Laerebog i Sømandskab*. Parts I & II. Copenhagen, 1884.
H Heathcote. Treatise on Staysails. London, 1824.
O Hildebrandt. *Praktisches Lehrbuch für junge Seeleute*. Danzig, 1863.
O Hildebrandt. *Praktisches Lehrbuch für junge Seeleute*, 2nd edition. Danzig, 1872.
R Hoeckel. *Modellbau von Schiffen des 16 u. 17 Jahrhunderts*. Bielefeld, 1971.
I Hogg & J Batchelor. *The Naval Gun*. London, 1978.
P W Hourigan. *Manual of Seamanship for the Officer of the Deck: Ship Under Sail Alone*. Baltimore, 1903 (Reprint 1980).
F Howard. *Sailing Ships of War 1400-1860*. London, 1979.
W Hubatsch. *Die Erste Deutsche Flotte 1848-1853*. Herford, 1981.
W Hutchinson. *Treatise on Naval Architecture*. Liverpool, 1794.

J K Jenson. *Haandbog i Praktisk Sømandsskab*, 4th edition. Nivaa, 1924 (Reprint, 1971).
J Jobé. *Great Age of Sail*. Lausanne, 1967.

G Kåhre. *The Last Tall Ships*. London, 1978.
E Karlsson. *Pully-Haul. The Story of a Voyage*. London, 1966.
E Karlsson. *Mother Sea*. London, 1964.
H Ketting. *Prins Willem. En 17de Eeuwse Oostindievaarder*. Bussum, 1979.
B Kihlberg. *The Lore of Ships* (English translation of 1963 edition) Gothenburg, 1972.
R Kipping. *Sails and Sailmaking*, 2nd edition. London, undated.
R Kipping. *Masting, Mastmaking & Rigging of Ships*, 11th edition. London, 1868.
F H Kjølsen. *Fregatten fortaeller*. Copenhagen, 1962.
A Kloo. *Kort Utdrag af Skepps-Manövern*. Malmö, 1849.
A Kloo. *Kort Utdrag af Skepps-Taklingen*. Malmö, 1854.
A M Knight. *Modern Seamanship*, 3rd edition. New York, 1903.
H Konow. *Haandbog for Matroskorpet*. Copenhagen, 1907.
F G Krogh. *Laerebog i Sømandskab*. Horten, 1883.

B Landström. *Sailing Ships*, New York, 1969.
B Landström. *The Ship*. London, 1961.
B Landström. *Regelskeppet VASAN*. Stockholm, 1980.
B Lavery. *Deane's Doctrine of Naval Architecture 1670*. London, 1981.
P Le Compte. *Practicale Zeevaartkunde*. Amsterdam, 1842.
J Lees. *Masting & Rigging of English Ships of War 1625-1860*. London, 1979.
D Lescallier. *Traité Pratique du Gréement des Vaisseaux*, Paris 1791 (Reprint 1968).
R C Leslie. *Old Sea Wings, Ways & Words*. London, 1890.
D Lever. *Young Sea Officer's Sheet Anchor*, 2nd edition. London, 1819 (Reprint 1955).
F Liardet. *Professional Recollections on Points of Seamanship*. Portsea, 1849.
H von Littrow. *Handbuch der Seemannschaft*. Vienna, 1859.
N Longridge. *Anatomy of Nelson's Ships*. London, 1955.

F A Macdonald. The Handling of a Square Rigger At Sea. Article in *Nautical Research Journal* 18 (1971) 31.
D Macintyre. *The Adventure of Sail 1520-1914*. London, 1979.
D Macintyre and B W Bathe. *Man-of-War*. London, 1969.
A McGowan. *The Ship. The Century before Steam*. London, 1980.
A McGowan. *The Ship. Tiller & Whipstaff*. London, 1981.
D R Macgregor. *The Tea Clippers*. London, 1972.
D R Macgregor. *Fast Sailing Ships 1775-1875*. Lymington, 1973.
D R Macgregor. *Square Rigged Sailing Ships*. London, 1977.
D R Macgregor. *Clipper Ships*. London, 1979.
H Manhoudt. *Zeilschepen en hun Tuigage*. Bussum, 1980.
A Martelli. *Seaman's Guide for preparing Ships for Sea*. London, 1848.
G Massenet, J Vallerey and A LeTalle. *Gréement, Manoeuvre et Conduite du Navire*, 2nd edition. Paris, 1915.
A H May. *French Sea Terms of Northern Origin*. Mariner's Mirror 26 (1940) 144-157.
F L Middendorf. *Bemastung & Tekelung der Schiffe*. Berlin, 1903 (Reprint Kassel, 1971).
E Moberg. *För Fulla Segel*. Stockholm, 1957.
W zu Mondfeld. *Historische Schiffsmodelle*. Munich, 1978.
A Moore. *Sailing Ships of War 1800-1860*. London, 1826.
Manual of Seamanship for Boys & Seamen of the Royal Navy. London, 1904.
G P J Mossel. *Het Schip*. Amsterdam, 1859.
G P J Mossel. *Het Tuig, de Masten, Zeilen, enz. van het Schip*. Amsterdam, 1858.
G P J Mossel. *Manoeuvres met Zeil-, en Stoomschepen*. Amsterdam, 1865.
(For convenience these have been designated Mossel I, II and III.)
A Mühleisen. *Handbuch der Seemannschaft*. Bremen, 1893. (Translation of Todd and Whall)
W Mountaine. *The Seaman's Vade-Mecum*. London, 1756 (Reprint 1971).
C G D Müller. *Seewissenschaft*. Berlin & Stettin, 1794.
J M Murphy and W N Jeffers. *Nautical Routine & Stowage*. New York, 1849.

G S Nares. *Naval Cadet's Guide*. London, 1860.
G S Nares. *Seamanship*, 2nd edition. Portsmouth, 1862 (Reprint 1979).
G S Nares. *Seamanship*, 7th edition. Portsmouth, 1879.
E Newby. *The Last Grain Race*. Cambridge, Massachusetts, 1956.
W Nichelson. *Practical Navigation & Seamanship*. London, 1792.
Nicholls's Seamanship & Nautical Knowledge, 12th edition. London, 1905.
Nicholls's Seamanship & Nautical Knowledge, 18th edition, Glasgow, 1938.

J Oderwald. *Handboekje bij de practische Oefeningen*, 2nd edition. Amsterdam, 1926.

P Padfield. *Guns at Sea*. London, 1973.
E W Petrejus. *Modell van de Oorlogsbrik IRENE*. Hengelo, no date.
E W Petrejus. *Modelling the Brig-of-war IRENE*. Hengelo, 1974.
E W Petrejus. *Oude Zeilschepen en hun Modellen*. Bussum, 1971.
E W Petrejus. *Nederlandse Zeilschepen in 19de Eeuw*. Utrecht, 1974.
C Pihlström. *Skepps Aflöpning, Förmasting och Uptakling*. Karlskrona, 1796.
J C Pilaar. *Het Schip en dezelfs Tuig*. Medemblik, 1838.

J Randier. *Grands Voiliers Français 1880-1930*. Grenoble, 1974.
Reed's Seamanship & Nautical Knowledge, 27th edition. Sunderland, 1930.
P M Regan and P H Johnson. *Eagle Seamanship*, 2nd edition. Annapolis, 1979.
J C Rijk. *Scheepsbouw*. Rotterdam, 1822.
F Riesenberg. *Standard Seamanship for the Merchant Service*, 2nd edition. New York, 1936.
F Roder. *Von der Sprache der Seeleute*. Hamburg, 1973.
C Romme. *L'Art de la Voilure*. Paris, 1781 (Reprint 1972).
C Romme. *Description de l'Art de la Mâture*. Paris 1778 (Reprint 1972).
F C Rosvall. *Skepps-Manövern*. Stockholm, 1803.
W Runciman. *Collier Brigs and their Sailors*. London, 1926.
A C Rålamb. *Skeps Byggerij*. Stockholm, 1695 (Reprint, 1943).

K O B Sandahl. *Middle English Sea Terms*. Volumes I-III. Uppsala, 1951, 1958 & 1982.
G Schoerner. *Regalskeppet*. Stockholm, 1964.
J C Schneider. *Beiledning i Sømandskabet*. Copenhagen, 1826.

P W Schultz. *Unge Søemands-Haandbog*. Copenhagen, 1795.
F Sjöbohm. *Skepps-Takling*. Karlskrona, 1792.
F Sjöbohm. *Sjö-Manoeuvern*. Stockholm, 1787, and Karlskrona, 1791.
J Smith. *Accidence for Young Seamen*. London, 1626 (Reprint, 1907).
J Smith. *A Sea-Grammar*. London, 1627 (Reprint 1970).
H Warington Smyth. *Mast & Sail in Europe and Asia*. Edinburgh & London, 1929.
D Steel. *Art of Rigging*. London, 1818 (Reprint, Brighton, 1974).
D Steel. *Mastmaking, Sailmaking & Rigging*. London, 1794 (Reprint 1932).
D Steel. *Rigging & Seamanship*. London, 1794.
Freiherr von Sterneck. *Takelung u. Ankerkunde*. Vienna, 1873.
T E Stibolt. *Fordeling og Commando ved et 3-Mastet Skib*. Copenhagen, 1800.
Eva-Marie Stolt. Revised plans of *Vasa*. Statens Sjöhistoriska Museet, 1980.
H Szymanski. *Deutsche Segelschiffe*. Norderstedt, 1972.

J Tait. *New Seamanship*, 5th edition. Glasgow, 1913.
J Tait. *New Seamanship*, 14th edition. Glasgow, 1940.
E H Taunt. *Young Sailor's Assistant*. Washington, 1883.
H Taylor. *Instruction for Young Mariners*. London, 1792.
W Timm. *Kapitänsbilder. Schiffsporträts seit 1782*. Bielefeld, 1971.
G M S Tod. *Last Sail Down East*. Barre, 1965.
J Todd and W B Whall. *Practical Seamanship*, 5th edition. London, 1903.
B J Totten. *Naval Text Book*, 2nd edition. New York, 1864.

Probably F Ulffers. *Leitfaden für den Unterricht in Seemannschaft*. Kiel, 1868.
F Ulffers. *Handbuch der Seemannschaft*. Berlin, 1872 (Reprint Kassel, 1981).
H A Underhill. *Masting & Rigging the Clipper Ship & Ocean Carrier*. Glasgow, 1946.
H A Underhill. *Sailing Ships and Rigging*. Glasgow, 1938.

A Villiers. *Voyaging with the Wind*. London, 1975.
A Villiers. *Give me a Ship to Sail*. London, 1958.
A Villiers. *The Way of a Ship*. New York, 1953.

B Wagner. *Windkanalversuche für einen 6-mastigen Segler nach Prölss*, and *Windkanalversuche mit dem Takelagemodell einer 4-Mastbark. Schiff und Hafen*, Hefts I & III, 1967. Pages 13-20, and 165-172.
H Walle. Dissertation. *Der Einfluss meteorologischer Navigation auf die Entwicklung der deutschen transozeanischen Segelschiffahrt 1868-1914*. Bonn, 1979.
A Watts. *Wind and Sailing Boats*. London, 1965.
A J Watts. *Pictorial History of the Royal Navy 1816-1880*. London, 1970.
R Werner. *Das Buch von der Norddeutchen Flotte*. Bielefeld & Leipzig, 1869.
C White. *The End of the Sailing Navy*. London, 1981.
G R C Worcester. *Junks & Sampans of the Yangste*. Annapolis, 1971.

C van Yk. *De Nederlandsche Scheepbouw Kunst*. Amsterdam, 1697 (Reprint, 1979).

In addition to the articles listed by title as being particularly useful, many snippets of information were culled from the pages of: *The Mariner's Mirror*, the quarterly journal for the Society for Nautical Research; *Nautical Research Journal*, quarterly journal for the Nautical Research Guild; *Das Logbuch*, quarterly journal of the Arbeitskreis für historischer Schiffbau e V.

Museum year-books were extremely useful, particularly those published by Bergens Sjofartsmuseet, and Handels-og Sofartsmuseet på Kronborg; *Model Shipwright*, published quarterly in London; *Model Ship Builder*, published bimonthly in Wisconsin; *Sea Breezes*, published monthly in Liverpool; *Le Petit Perroquet*, formerly published quarterly in Grenoble; *Longitude*, published in Stockholm.

DICTIONARIES

A Ansted. *Dictionary of Sea Terms*. Glasgow, 1944.
P M J de Bonnefoux. *Dictionnaire abrégé de Marine*. Paris, 1834.
P M J de Bonnefoux and Paris. *Dictionnaire de Marine à Voiles & à Vapeur*. Paris, 1848.
Bourdé. *Manuel des Marins*. L'Orient, 1773.
G Bradford. *Glossary of Sea Terms*. New York, 1927.
G Bradford. *The Mariner's Dictionary*. New York, 1952.
G Bradford. *Glossary of Sea Terms*. British edition. London, 1954.
A R Bradshaw. *English-French Naval Terms*. London, 1932.
F H Burgess. *Dictionary of Sailing*. London, 1961.
J C Colcord. *Sea Language comes Ashore*. New York, 1945.
Country Life Book of Nautical Terms. London, 1978.
L Delbos. *Nautical Terms in English and French*. London, 1902.
W Falconer. *Universal Dictionary of the Marine*. London, 1780 (Reprint, 1970).
D H Funch. *Danske Marine Ordbog*. Copenhagen, 1846 (Reprint 1976).
E von Gegerfelt. *Sjöspråk*. Stockholm, 1922.
R Gruss. *Petit Dictionnaire de Marine*, 3rd edition. Paris, 1963.
C L L Harboe. *Dansk Marine Ordbog*. Copenhagen, 1839 (Reprint 1979).
P Kemp. *Oxford Companion to the Sea*. London, 1976.
F Kluge. *Seemannsprache*. Berlin, 1911 (Reprint Kassel, 1973).
C W T Layton. *Dictionary of Nautical Words and Terms*. Glasgow, 1955.

J Lecompte. *Dictionnaire Pittoresque de Marine*. Paris, 1835 (Reprint 1981).
D Lescallier. *Vocabularie des Termes de Marine Anglais et François*, 2nd edition. London, 1783.
W A McEwen and A H Lewis. *Encyclopedia of Nautical Knowledge*. Cambridge, Md. 1953.
G E Manwaring and W G Perrin. *Life & Works of Sir Henry Mainwaring*. Vol 2. London, 1921.
W G Perrin. *Boteler's Dialogues*. London, 1929.
W Pirrie. *Dictionary of Sea Terms, Phrases & Words. English & French*. London, 1895.
C Romme. *Dictionnaire de la Marine Anglaise*. Paris, 1804.
C Romme. *Dictionnaire de la Marine Française*, 2nd edition. Paris, 1813.
W C Russell. *Sailor's Language*. London, 1883.
G Smyth. *Universal Military Dictionary*. London, 1799 (Reprint 1969).
W H Smyth. *The Sailor's Word-Book*. London, 1867.
N W Thomas. *The Naval Wordbook*. Kiel & Leipzig, 1899.
Th Uggla. *Engelskt-Svenskt Sjö- och Handelslexikon*. Gävle, 1878.
J-B-P Willaumez. *Dictionnaire de Marine*, 3rd edition. Paris, 1831.
A Young. *Nautical Dictionary*. Dundee, 1846.

MULTILINGUAL DICTIONARIES

E Bobrik. *Nautisches Wörterbuch*. Leipzig, 1858.
D J Boom. *Zeemans Woordenboek in Vier Talen*. Den Haag, 1888.
A Jal. *Glossaire Nautique*. Paris, 1848.
Handbuch für den Verkehr mit den ausländischen Marinen. Berlin, 1935.
R de Kerchove. *International Maritime Dictionary*, 2nd edition, New York, 1961.
A C Littleton. *Vocabulary of Sea Words*. Portsmouth, 1879.
H Paasch. *From Keel to Truck*. Antwerp, 1885.
K P ter Reehorst. *The Mariner's Friend*. London, 1865.
J H Röding. *Allgemeines Wörterbuch der Marine*. Hamburg, 1793 (Reprint Leiden, 1969).

REFERENCES WHICH ARE PRIMARILY ICONOGRAPHIC

Baugean. *Bâtiments de Guerre et Marchands*. Paris, 1814 (Reprint Grenoble, 1971).
H Bernartz. *Marinemaler*. Herford, 1977.
J Bracker, M North and P Tamm. *Maler der See*. Herford, 1980.
M V and D Brewington. *Marine Paintings & Drawings in the Peabody Museum*. Salem, 1968.
D E R Brewington. *Marine Paintings & Drawings in the Mystic Seaport Museum*. Mystic, 1982.
P-C Caussé. *Album du Marin*. Paris, 1836 (Reprint 1971).
E W Cooke. 65 Plates of Shipping & Craft. London, 1829 (Reprint, 1970).
V Coronelli. *Ships & other sorts of Craft*. Venice, 1690 (Reprint London, 1970).
I DeGroot and R Vorstman. *Sailing Ships*. Maarsen, 1980.
G Groenewegen. *Verzameling van 48 Stuks hollandsche Schepen*. Rotterdam, 1789 (Reprint)
G Kaufmann, H Lungagnini and J Meyer. *Kapitänsbilder*, Catalogue of the Altonaer Museum.
J Meyer. *Segelschiffe auf alten Postkarten*. Norderstedt, 1975.
A L Morel-Fatio. *Marines*. (Reprint Grenoble, 1980).
A L Morel-Fatio. *Etudes de Marine Positive*. Paris, 1865 (Reprint Douarnenez, 1982).
N Ozanne. *Marine Militaire*. (Reprint Grenoble, 1969).
R Nooms. *Verscheÿde Schepen en Gesichten van Amstelredam*. Amsterdam *c*1660 (Reprint Amsterdam, 1970).
M S Robinson. *Van de Velde Drawings in the National Maritime Museum*. Volume I, Cambridge, 1973.
A Roux. *Carnet d'Etude de Marine*. (Reprint Salem, 1960).
D and J T Serres. *Liber Nauticus*. London, 1805 (Reprint 1979).
P F C Smith. *More Paintings & Drawings in the Peabody Museum*. Salem, 1979.
J Vichot. *L'Album de l'Amiral Willaumez*. (Reprinted by le Musée de la Marine, Paris).
J Vichot. *L'Album de Marine du Duc d'Orléans*.
J Vichot. *L'Oeuvre des Ozanne*.
Zeichner der Admiralität. Herford, 1981. (van de Velde drawings).

INDEX

A la cape 213
Aanhalen 74
Aanwenken 186
Aap 14, 217
Abaft 11
Able-bodied seaman, definition 17
Abreast 11
Absacken 201
Accidents 294-312
Achtergasten 91
Achtermast 54
Active, HMS *156*, 170
Admiralty anchor 231
Afhouder 2
Afterguard 91, 92
Aftermast 54
Aftersail 29, 50-51
Agincourt, HMS 238
Aiglet on reefline 139
Ajurie 300
Alas 163
Albero di mezzana 14
A-lee 11, 217
All in the wind 11, *11*, 62
Alliance, USS *136*
A-loof 10, 11
Alphen, Dutch warship *312*
Alternating sides 25-26
Amaranth 173
Ammarage à grelin 210
Ammarage à la serre 210
Ammarage en vache 210
Amazon, HMS *222*, *310*
America, ship 245
America, yacht 60
Amidships 11
Amure 74
Anchor 201, 210-211, 231-279; backing 244; casting 242-244, 277; laying at 277-279; shoeing 244; size and weight 232; tripping 270
Anchor bearings 255
Anchor buoy 241
Anchor cable 232-233, 235-237; cleaning 270; ranging 243-244; shipping 276-277
Anchor clinch 237
Anchor lining, billboard 268
Anchor tackle 264
Anchora spei 235
Anchoring 244-246
Anchors, line of 254
Ancre à jet 277
Ancres 235
Anker lichten 13
Ape 17
Apparent wind *58*, 58-59, 63
Arcboutant 23; *ferré* 161
Arciform frames 44
Ardency 56, 58, 176
Ascending 43
Asia, HMS 171, *229*, 244, *245*
L'Astrolabe 306
Aufbrechen 67
Aufholer 78
Avaler 199
Avast 14
A-weather 10
Axes, rolling, pitching and yawing 41, 42-43
Axiometer 174, *175*

Babord 176
Back cloths 108
Backboard 176
Backbrassen 225
Backing 199-201; an anchor 244; around 248; out 273; sails 184, 225, 226-227
Backing, of the wind 12, *12*
Backsgasten 91
Back-spier 161, *163*
Backstays 22-23, *22*, *23*
Bagien-ra 17
Bagpiping the mizzen 248

Bag-reef 132
Bakboord 176
Bakker 203
Balance reef 138, 152
Balanced rudder 71
Bald-header 38
Ballast, storage of *48*, 49
Ballooning *130*
en Bardouliere 277
en Bannière 130
Barbotin 266
Bareka 18
Barge 282
Barham, HMS 58
Barkas 282
Barn door rudder *71*
Barque rig 53
Barrico 18
Basta! 14
Bauch 212
Beam ends, on the 214
Bearing abaft of the breast backstays 23;
Bearing away 221-222
Bearing out of the breast backstays 23
Bear's hole *17*
Beating 12
Beaufort Scale 51-53, 60
Beckets 25, 33, 74, 185
Before the wind 11, *11*; backstays 23
Begijn-ra 17
Beibrassen 130
Belay 13, 14
Belfast rig 38
Belly-guy 56
Belvidera, HMS *278*
Ben Avon, merchant vessel 118
Bending, courses 98-100, *99*; cringle 97; headsails 102; jackstay 141; royals 98; spanker *103*; square sail 96-101; strop 97-98; topgallants 98; topsail *99*, 100-101, *106*
Bengal lights 291
Bernouilli's principle 60
Besaansmast 14, 54
Beschlagen 124
de Bezaan bollen 217
Bezaans-schoot aan 297
Bi-de-vind-stik 186
Bijdraaien 225
Bijlander 78
Bijleggen 213, 225
Bilander 78
Billboard 268
Binnacle 174, *175*, 215
Binnenlander 78
Bisection theorem 64-65
Bittacle 174
Bitter 243
Bittmen 93
Bitt-pin, Norman 238
Bitt stopper 239
Bitts 238
Blacking the rigging 23
Blake slip stopper 237, 238, 240
Blanketting 55, 56, 64, *64*
Bleorie Castle, ship *224*
Blindmen 174, 215
Blind-zeil 86
Blocks *34*
Blown into her courses 36
Blue lights 291
Board and half-board 12
Boat leadline 278
Boat rope 285-286
Boat tackles 283
Boats 259, 282-288, 291; on davits 284
Boatswain 18, 94
Bobstay carried away 298
Bobstays 23-24, *23*
Boeg ankers 235
Bojar 189
Bolster 238
Boltrope 14, 30
Bombay, HMS *311*
Bonadventure mizzen 36, 54-55, 80-81
Une bonne cape 217
Bonnets 72, 75, 137
Bonnette d'artimon 163
Bonnettes en etui 163; *maillees* 163
Boom brace (studdingsail) 166; flying forward 169; guy 29; tricers 92-93

Border 74
Boreing 182
Boss buntline 34, 144
Bosses à fouet 239
Bo'sun 18
Bouguer's theorem 61-62
Bouquet 34
Bourrasque 221
Boven blindzeil 87
Bovenbram 15
Boven branzeil 14
Bow rudder 71
Bow anchors 232, 235, 237-238, *250*
Bowline 13, 30, *31*, 45, *72*, 103-104, 132; parting of 298; steadying out 13, 132;
Bowsprit 19-20, *20*, 21, *21*, 81, 212; cap 20; Gammoning carried away 298; shrouds 23, *23*; sprung 299; steeve of 81;
Box the compass 189
Boxar, 189
Boxhauling 189-191, 219
Brace block *34*
Brace in and brace up 18, 63
Brace winch, Jarvis 69
Braces 26, 26-28, *72*, 212
Bracing 93; aft, by 130, 148, 225; counter 14, 51 *see also* Counter braces; sails 65-66; to 183; yards 14, *14*, 25, 26-27, *63*, 63-69
Brack gardiner 67
Bräckbom 264
Braguet 116, 120
Brails 31, 32, *33*, 78, 84
Brase bak 14, 225
Brase op and *brase ind* 18
Brasse 231
Brassen springen lassen 186
Breaker 18
Breaking off 11; sheer 247, 252-253; the trumpet 148
Breast backstays 23, 24, 185;
Breast gaskets 32
Bredindin 280
Breeches mat 259
Breech-rope 116
Breeze 51
Brig *57*, 78
Bring to 14
Broaching to 214
Broad reach 12
Brok 78, 116, 120
Brokupphalare 80
Broodwinner 76
Brooking, Charles *69*
Brought by the lee 214
Brown stopper 241, 243
Brunton's anchor trigger 243
Buckler 238
Bug anker 235
Buikreijers 108
Buiten lijzeilen 163
Buitengewoon stand 51
Bull earing 98, 144, *145*
Bull rope 75, 112
Bullentau 75
Bull-whanger 144
Bumpkin 73, *74*, 217
Bunt 22, 29, 84, 107, 212; gaskets *33*, 97, 107; jigger *33*, 33-34; whip *33*, 33-34
Buntline block *34*
Buntlines 17, 31, *32*, 66, *66*, *72*, 103
Buoy rope 280, *281*
Buoyancy 41
Buoys 241
Butluf 74
Butts 49
By and large 11
By the wind hitches 185-186

C.B. Pedersen, barque 155
Cabestan sans choquer 262
Cable 14; bends 237; laid 86, 232, 258, stopper 14
Cablet 262, 265
Caboteur 201
Cachemire, French steamer 303
Caesar, HMS *52*
Calcutta, HMS *308*
Calf in the reef 148
Caliorne 280, 307
Calm 51

Camels 203-204, *206*
Canot de parade 283
Un canot de porte-haubans 284
Canting a yard 14
Cantonniere 268
Canvas set 126
Cap 26
Une cape ardente 217
Une cape molle 217
Capon 267, 268
Capshore *120*, 121
Capstan 14, 260-263, 265, 266, 270, *275*
Captain of the crosstrees 93; of the mast 93; of the top 93, 114
Carbonero 14, 217
Carpenter 92, 211-212, 259
Carrick bitts 263
Carry lee helm 56
Carry weather helm 56
Casting anchor 242-244, 277; sail 271-272
Cat hole 17
Catback 267
Catenary 234
Cat-harpings 24-25
Cathead *74*; anchors 235
Cat-tackle 267
Catting the anchor 267, 268-269, *275*
Caulking 211
Centipedes 110, 169
Centre of buoyancy (CB) 41-42, 43, 44; of cavity 41; of effort (CE) *40*, 41-42, 43, 44, *54*, 56; of gravity (CG) 41-42, 43, 44, 70; of lateral resistance (CLR) 41-42, *41*, 43, 44, 56, 70
Chafe 212
Chafing gear 259
Chain cable 233-235, 270
Chain messenger 265
Chain sling 21, 26, *27*
Chain stoppers 239-240
Chaloupe 282
Chambrière 97
Chameau 203
Chapelet 203, 307
Chapman, Frederik af 47
Charles, French merchant barque *146*
Chas 74
Chatte 279
Check (in) 14
Check stoppers 239, 243
Checking around, of wind 12
Checking line 112
Cheerly 13
Chesstree 73, 74
Cheveaux-de-Frise 73
Chine and bulge 49
Chock 13
Choquer 13
Clamp 210
Clapper 135
Clean full 11
Clear anchor 247
Clear hawse 255-256, 257-258, *274*; breeches 267, *270*, 271
Clew 29, 127-129; hanger *34*, 97; jigger *34*, *34*, 214; outhaul 76
Clewgarnet 30, 34, 105; blocks 108
Clewing up sail 105
Clewline block *34*, 108
Clewlines 17, 30, *31*, *72*
Clewrope 31, 34, 78-80
Cliffords lowering gear 285
Climax, ship 137
Clinch 236; service 233
Clin-foc 14
Clipper 46
Close-hauled 11, *13*, 14, 25, *63*, 216
Clubbing 201
Clubhauling 195-198
Coaming stopper 239, 240
Coaxing 186
Cockbilled 201
Cockbilling, the anchor 243; the yards 123
Cod's head and mackerel tail 45
Coins 210
Collier 17, 263
Collier's purchase 264
Comb 73, *74*
Coming home, of anchor 244
Coming to 12, 13, 246

Coming up 11, 12, 13
Commands 182-185, 220, 224, 272, 284, 286, 292-293
Commodore Morris, whaler *227*
Communications 228-230
Compass *10*, 174, 175, 215
Compressor 240-241
Conding 177
Conning 177-180
Conqueror, HMS *178*
Constance, barque *213*
Constitution, USS 210, *278*
Contra-mezzana 15
Contrary wind 11
Controller 240-241
Corps-mort 203
Cottellazzi 163
Coude 268
Couillard 108
Couillons 107, *109*
Counter-braces 28, *72*
Counterbracing 51, 130, 184, 225
Course 14, *15*, 36, 37, 72-90, 214, 216, 222; ballooning *130*; bending 98-100, *99*; furling 98, 104-105, *107*; handling 131-132; reefing 140, 149-150; setting *132*; shifting 111; stowing 98, *99*; taking in *129*, *132*
Coutre 283
Crabs 260
Crankness 43, 44
en Cravatte 277
Creeping for an anchor 279
Crew 91-95, 193-195, 220; disposition of 135, 154, 172, 195, 258, 272, 283-284; numbering of 91; silence 93-94
Cringles 30
Croix de Saint-André 212
Crone chain 233
Cross in the cables 256
Crossjack yard 17, 21, 78, 212, 219
Cross-sail 81
Crowding 58
Cruiser, HMS, frigate *128*, 181
Crutching the backstays 23
Cuckold's neck 238
Cumberland, ship *275*
Cunning 177
Curved sail 60, *61*
Cutter 41, 282
Cutty Sark, ship 71, 161
Cutwater 73, *74*

Dävert 268
Davits 23, 211, 268; boats on 284
Dead block 73, *74*
Dead muzzler *see* Muzzler
Dead upon the wind 11
Deaden way 225-226
Deadman 18
Deadrise *45*
Deck stoppers 238-239
Deck tackle 244-265
Defiance, HMS 262
Dek-swabber 217
Depressing sails 59, *59*, 158
Desaix 227
Devil's claw 237, 238, 240
Dipped abaft all 167
Dipping sails 166-167, 168
Discourse 174
Disengaging gear 285
Displacement hull 46
Dog stopper 239
Dog-and-bitch thimbles 83
Dog's lug 148
Dog-vane 175
Dolphin striker 22, 23-24, 38, 73, *89*, 89-90, 203
Doove jut 23, 284
Dos d'âne 173
Double bitting 238, 243
Double breeching 210
Double capstan 261-262
Double purchases 25
Double target rule *62*
Douse 17, 124
Down by the head or stern 43
Downhaul 143-144; of the upper studding-sails 168-169
Drabbler 75, 137

Drake, Sir Francis 10, 36
Dräng 78, 134
Drawing splice 232
Dredging 201
Drehreep 25
Drift lead 255
Drifting 199
Drijven 199
Drijver 160
Drisse 25
Driver 76, *76*, 89, 163
Driving 199
Droits de l'homme, French two-decker *52*
Dronningens Qvarteer 91
Drop pawls 276
Dry provisions 49
Duc d'Alben 203
Le Duc de Chartres 302
Dukdalf 203
Duke of Wellington, HMS *107*, *275*
Dull in stays 182
Dusseuil's jury rudder 303
Dyce 180
Dynaschiff of Prölss 65, *65*

Earing *31*, 144-145, 163; jackstay 144
Easing the helm 176-177
East Indiaman 35
East Indian yaws 214
L'Eclair, French brig *305*
Edgar, HMS *95*
Effacer 228
El 231
Elbow in the cables 256, *274*
Elliott's eye 232, 236
English splice 232
Enkhuizer 263
Essex, East Indiaman 163, *164*
Estouin 163
Eugenie Swedish corvette *288*
Explosion 312
Eye of the wind 11, *11*
Ezels-hoofd 26

Fair loom gale 51
Fair wind 11, *12*
Faire servir 225
Fakes 18, 236
Fall 13
Fall (German) 25
Fall off 13, 43
Falling off 181
Falls 286
Fallwind 221
False tack 75, 155
Fancy lines 80
Fanga uggla 214
Fanning of the masts 56
Farranes, Swedish training ship *107*, *136*, *153*
Farthell, furl 124
Fast beting-stoppare 240
Fats 75
Fatz 75
Fausse amure 75
Fausses fenêtres 214
Faux-sabords 210
Favourable wind 11
Ferler 124
Fiche 300
Fiddle *17*
Fids 114-115
Fighting stoppers 299
Filer 74
Filling 199-201
Fire 310-312
Firing on the roll 48
First reef 146-147
Fish davit 258, 268; tackle 267-268
Fishtackle 280
Fishes 300
Fishguard, HMS *311*
Fixed points, reefing 140
Flag signals 123
Flakes 18, 236
Flaking the cable 237, 243
Flamming 182
Flare 45
Flatting in 67, 74
Flaw of wind 51

Fledermäuse 163
Fleeting 13; the turns 262
Flemish horse 25
Flensing 227
Floor, rise of 44-45
Flotation lines 45, *45*
Fly block 25
Flyer 22, 85
Flying backstays 212
Flying jib 14, *15*, 36, 38, 82, 89, 222; handling 133-134; stays 22
Flying jibboom *21*, 22, 90, 118
Flying moor 246, 255
Foc 14
Fock mast 54
Fock-segel 18
Foke sails 18
Following wind 11, *12*
Footropes 25, 104
Forbes, Robert B 137
Fore and aft sail 21, 29; casting *271*; reefing 138-139, 151-152
Fore mast 56;
Fore sail 18, 50-51, 72, *73*, 212, 213, 214
Fore sheet 74, 186
Fore tack 74
Fore topmast staysail 82; handling 134
Fore topmast studdingsail, setting 164-165
Fore topsail, backing *226*
Forecastle, heaving on 271
Forecastle boom 161, *163*
Foreganger 236
Forereaching 12
Forestay carried away 298-299
Foretopmen 91, 92
Forfait, Minister of Marine 262
Förlorad-stoppare 240
Forward jackline 140
Fots 75
Foul anchor 247, *270*, 271
Foul berth 256
Foul wind 11, *12*
Fouling hawse *255*, 256
Fox-hauling 189
France, barque 188
Francesca Themis, frigate *208*
Franklin lifebuoy 289-290
Franzoslches-takel 280
Frapping the hull 301
Freeboard 45
Freischläfer 91
French anchor *231*
French bunt 107, 108
French reef 34, 140-142
French flaking the cable 237, 243
Fresh gale 51
Freshening the nip 233, 294
Friesche Ruiter 73
Frihales 81
Frithjof, auxiliary barque 103
Frolic, HMS *171*
Froude, William 46
Full and by 11, 175
Funnel *19*, 20
Furlers 92
Furling, a course 98, 104-105, *107*, 108, 124; in a body 108; lines 32, *33*, 97; mizzen sails 110; royals 109-110; sails 17, 104-111, *134*; square sails 104-110; staysails 110; topgallants 109-110; topsail 98, *107*, 107-108; topsail and topgallant sail fashion 107, 108

Gabbia 14
Gabier 14
Gaff sails 103, 212, 217
Gaff topsail 29
Gaff trysails, reefing 138, 152
Gaffel-lee-segel 163
En Galère 201
Galhaubans volents 212
Galley 282
Ganger 236, 243
Garnets 87; tackle 280
Gaskets 32-33, *33*, 97
Op zign Gat draaien 185
Gata 15
Gate at crosstrees 114
Geared capstans 262
Geboied 306
Getting down the track 13, 74;

Getting under way 271-277
Ghosting 46, 155
Giek 282, 283
Gig 282
Giga och broka 78
Gigtag 78
Gigue 283
Girdling 48; the hull 301
Girt 131, 256
Glut 33, 144
Gob-rope *80*, 81, 134
Goeben, SMS 238
Going aloft 93
The Golden Fleece 128
Good full 11
Gooseneck 209
Goosewinging a sail 77, 82, 219
Gorch fock 46, 69
Gorgon, HMS 307
Gower, Richard Hall 61, *62*
Grab line 143
Grab rope 112
Grain sec 221
Granaat 280
Grande ancre 235
Granizda 221
Grapnels 235
Gretchen vom Deich 15, *17*
Grethe, brigantine 35, *106*
Grietje van dijk 15, *17*
Gripes 176, 286
Griping 56
Grommet 96, 98
Grossmast 56
Grua 267
Gun deck 260
Gun platform, ship as a 48-49
Gunners 91, 92, 259-260
Gunner's wedges 210
Gunroom 209, 260
Guns 209
Gust 51
Guys 23, *23*, 29, 89 *see also* Vangs
Gybe 29

Habitaculum 174
Hägg, Admiral J 174
Haha 90
Hailing 228-230
Hak-stoppare 240
Half-board 12, *13*
Half-booms, spreaders 90
Half-legged reef points 142
Half-man 173
Half-ports 210
Halliards 13, 20, 25, 26
Hals 77, 163
Hammerlock moor 256
Handing 17, *109*, *126*; square sails *109*, *126*
Handling, sails 131-135; square sail 126-127
Hands 93
Handsomely 13
Hanging mat 212, 259; nippers 267; pawls 260, 261
Harbour drills 94; furl 105-107, 108; gaskets 32-33, *33*; stow 31, 34
Harvey's Desire, West Indiaman 229
Hastings, HMS *207*
Hatch stopper 239
Hatches 211-212
Haul of headyards 185
Haul her wind 12
Hauling 12, *12*; aft the sheets 74; all yards, tacking 187; out to windward *147*, 148; wind 182
Hauptmast 54
Hawse 255-256, 257-258
Hawsehole 233, 235-236, 238
Hawser 120; laid 232
Hayes, Captain "Magnificent" 196-198
Head earings 30, 97
Headholes 96
Headreaching 12, 216, 227
Headsails 29, *80*, *82*, 84, 186; bonding 102; casting 272; reefing 138, 152; shifting 102-103; taking in *134*; unbending 102-103
Headway 12
Headyards, haul of 185
Heave 43

Heaving, athwart 225; in anchor 269-271; through all 271; to 216, 225-230
Heavy heave 270
Heel 42, 43; lashing 162; rope 116, 117
Heeling moment 43
Helm 56, 173, 175-176, 185, 209, 217; orders 56-57; weather and lee 56-57
Helms-a-lee 183, 186, 187
Helmsman 174-175, *176*, 214-215; orders 177-180
Hemp cable 234-235
Herzogin Cecilie, barque 46
High bunts 107, 108
Hinged rudder 71
Hitching the messenger 270
Hogging 48
Hogsheads 49
Hoisting a boat 283, *284*, 286, *287*
Holding a good wind 58
Holmes storm and danger signal lights 290
Hondefok 280
Horses 25, 86
Housing 13, 210; masts 117
Hove to 225
Howes, Frederick 137
Hull form 44, *57*
Hulling 125
Hullock 217
Hunier 14, 15

Idlers 91
In irons 181
Indefatigable, HMS *52*
Industrie, brig *206*
Irons *13*
Itague 25

Jaag-pad 204
Jaagstut 204
Jaag-tross 204
Jackass 92, 210, 238
Jackblocks 112
Jack-crosstrees *19*, 20, 22
Jack-line reef 10, 140-142
Jäckstag 30
Jackstay 30, *31*, 69, 85, 104, 141
Jackyard 160
Jacob's ladder 115, 286
Jagen 204
Jager 14
James Allen, whaler *227*
Jamming 11
Jarramas 79
Jarvis brace winch 69
Jeer block *34*
Jeer capstan 262, 263, 266, 269, *274*
Jeers 26, 121
Jemmy Green *89*, 90
Jewel block 163
Jew's harp shackle 231, 234
Jib 14, 29, 36, *80*, 81-82; brails 81; downhaul parting 294; halliard parts 294; handing 134; reefing 138, 151, *152*; sheets 81-82; shifting 111; stays 22, 82; stowing 82; tack & jib sheet parting 294-295
Jibboom 20, *20*, *21*, 22, 67, 81, 89, 118, 212; broken 299-300
Jib-headed mizzen 77
Jibstay, parting of 294
Jigger 264
Jiggermast 54
John Kay, ship 311
Jol 283
Jollyboat 282
Juanatero 17
Juanete 17
Jumelle 300
Jumper on yardarm 220
Jumper strut 22
Jury rig 300-301
Jury rudders 302, 303
Jylland, frigate 142

Kabelaring 265
Kalv i Revet 18, 148
Kapiteins-Sloep 283
Karnaat 280
Kastvind 221
Katt-am-Lande 203
Katten 244, 267
Kattenkopf 263, 267

Keckling 233
Kedge anchor 235, 256, 276, 277, 278
Kedging 278
Keelhauling 196
Keeping the wind 11
Kentledge 49
Kielzog 46
King George V, HMS 238
Kippen 268
Kites 89, 155
Klein-Fok 14
Kluiver 14
Knipare 267
Knop Stoppare 240
Kolder-luke 173
Kolder-stok 173-174
Kondwachter 86
Kongens qvarteer 91
Kopfschlag 186
Kotter 283
Kovending 193
Krahn 267
Kreuzmast 54
Kruis-marszeil 14
Kruis zeil 14, 36
Kuhlgasten 91
Kuntor 265
Kvaerk 84
Kwartier 91

Lacing a bonnet 72, 137
Lady Kennaway 206
Laeiszmast 54
Langard 78
Larboard 16, 176
Larbolins 91
Large wind 12, *16*
Lashing fore and aft 210
Lasket 137
Latchet line 137
Latching a bonnet 72
Lateen mizzen topsail 81
Lateen sail 21
Launch 13, 278, 282
Lavering 11
Lawhill, merchant vessel 118
Laying out anchor 277-279
Laying out marks 93, 123
Laying out on the yard 93, *94*
Laying the yard 147
Lazy tack 75
Lead line 211
Lead of the tacks 73-74
Leading wind 12, 276
Leaks 303-305
Lee brails 80
Lee clew 127-129
Lee helm 56-57, 176, 217
Lee helmsmen 174
Lee topsail sheet and clewline 297
Leechline block *34*
Leechlines 17, 31, *32*, *72*, 104, 105
Leegrossbrass-aufholer 185
Leeward service 233
Leewardly 58
Leeway 12, 58
Leg of mutton mizzen 77
Legger 77
in de lens liggen 249
Lenzen 213
Let fall 17, 124
Let fly 13
Leve-Nez 160
Levende 14, 18
Lever 74
Lie by 225
Lifebuoys 211, 289
Lifelines 93, 211, 285
Lift block *34*
Lift jiggers 127, 149, 162
Lifting sails 18, 59
Lifts *28*, 29
Ligga Uppbrassad 225
Light sails 29
Light yards 102
Lightening the ship 306
Lighting over 13
Lightning, ship 46
Lightning conductors 212
Lij-zeilen 163
Lijk 14

Lines 45
Link worming 233
Lizard 31, 66, 116, 121
Lloyd 218
Locking of yardarms 55
Lof 74
Long flaking the cable 244
Long tackle 119
Longboat 277, 282
Longitudinal stability 44
Loof 73
Loof hook 75
Lookouts 211, 291
Loom gale 10
Loose points, reefing 139-140
Loosers 92
Loosing sail 17, 103-104, *106*, 110
Loosing to a bowline 103-104
Loosing to a buntline 103-104
Losa Beting-Stoppare 240
Losing way 12
Louvoyer 11
Low bunts 107
Lower boom 161, 163
Lower brace, parting 296
Lower foreyard carried away 300
Lower lifts 29
Lower mast 20, *27*; sprung 300
Lower sails, unbending *100*
Lower studdingsail 158-160; setting 169; taking in 169
Lower studdingsail boom *162*
Lower tack or sheet parting *297*
Lower yards 26, 122, *123*, 212
Lowering boats 286, *287*
Lowering gear 284
Lubber's hole *17*, 113, 117
Lubber's line 174
Luff 29, 74; and lie 13; and touch her 13; tackle 73, 74
Luffing 12, 13, 17, 43, 181, 221-222
Luny, Thomas *16*
Luvseite 10
Luvwarts 10
Lying a hull 125
Lying heavy on the helm 71
Lying to 125, 213, 215, 225

Maas Estuary 237
Macedonian, frigate *301*
Mackerel tail 45
Mägerman 30
Magnificent, HMS 196-198, 276
Main brace, parting 296-297
Main sheets 74
Main topsail, backing *226*
Main yard, backing *226*
Mainmast 19, 54
Mainsail 72-73, *73*, 213, 216, 222, 223; aback 72; haul 184, 185
Maintopmen 91, 92
Maitresse brass 235
Making sail 17, 124-136
Malta, ship 139
Man-of-war fashion, anchoring 244, *245*
Man overboard 289-293
Manger 238
Manning the ropes 13
Manning the yards 93, *94*, *95*, 123
Mantel-takel 280
Mantelets brises 210
Mantelets volants 214
Mare's tails 36
Marguerite 264
Mariner's compass *10*
Marines 92
Marrying the falls 286
Mars zeil 14
Martin, HM Brig *106*, *170*, 197
Martinet 304
Martingale 23, 166; stay 22, 23-24, 89
Martnets 31, *32*, 78, 104, 105
Mast party 93
Mast rope *115*, 116
Mast tackles 280
Masts 14, 19-20, 29; accidents 299-301; number of 53-55; positions 55; rake 55-56; size 55
Mat de fortune 300
Mat de mizaine 14, 56

Mathematical principles 40
Meander 221
Measurement, units of 231-232
Medina 88
Mending sail 109
Merchant ship crews 195
Merchant ship fashion, anchoring 244, *245*
Mercury, training ship *274*
Messenger 260, 262, 265, 266, 270
Metacentric height 43, *44*
Middle staysail 22, 85, 151
Midship reefing buntling *143*, 144
Midshipman of the top 93
Misaine 14
Misère 76, 77
Missing stays 181, 189, 190-191
Mittelmast 54
Mizzen, bowlines 80; brails 78; course 36, 75-76, 134-135; lift 77; mast 19, 54, 56; reefbands *139*
Mizzen sails *15*, 37, 38, 75-81, 213, 216, 217; altering the area 80; backing 184; bagpiping 77, 80; changing the 77; furling 110-111; goosewinging 77; loosing 110; reefing 139; smiting 77; taking in *134*; turning effect 77-78
Mizzen stay 299
Mizzen studdingsails 155
Mizzen topmen 91, 92
Mizzen topsail 36; backing 184, 225
Mizzen vangs 80
Mizzen yard 21, 226
Mockage 177
Moltke, corvette *95*
Moment 40, 47
Moment altering trim 44
Moonlight Battle, 1780 48
Mooring 254-258; anchors 235; swivel 256-257
Mouiller en Creance 278
Mousings 265
Moustaches 29, 86
Muzzler 12

Najaden 206
Nantucket, training ship *136*, *146*
Nassau, SMS 238
Naufrage 310
Naval line 141
Nedhaler 159
Neptune 208
Neptunes 206
Nipper 237, 258, 262, 266-267, 269
Nock 29
Nock-Paard 25
Nock-Takel 283
Nonsuch, ketch 27, *79*, *178*
Nood-Anker 235
Noodmast 300
Nooms Reiner 38
Norma, Brig 302
Norman 263
Norrkoping 39
Nosebag *17*
Nun-buoy 241

Off the wind 11, *16*
Old sea 48
Omtrijsen 29
On the wind 11, 16
De Onderzoeker, brig *288*
Opbreker 262
Open house 255-256
Opsteken 74
Orange Pip Principle 41, 60
Oreilje-Blok 163
Orse 74
Outlicker 55, 73, *74*, 81
Outrigger 23
Overblowing 51
Overhauling 13

Paardelijn 204
Pacific Iron 161
Pakenham's jury rudder 303
Pallas, ship 302-303
Pamir 39
Panne ardente 225
Panne courante 225
Panne molle 225
Pappafico 17

Parallelogram of forces 40, 60
Parcelling 233
Parden 25
Parliament heel 45
Parrels *28, 29,* 69
Parrochetto 17
Passarado 75, 155, 169
Passaree 75, 155
Passing the nippers 269
Patent reefing 138
Paunch mat 212, 259
Pawl rests 261
Pawls 276
Pay off 13, 181
Pay out 13
Paying 181
 apeak 276
 en penau 201
Pendant d'Oreille 163
Penter-balk 268
Period of roll 47
Perroquet 15, 17, 108
Perruche 17
Phare 155
à Pic 276
Pilot 230
Pilot, HMS Brig 106
Pilot's luff 12, *13*
Pinching 175
Pinnace 282
Pipe, giving the 94
Pique, HMS 153
Pisbak 238
Pitching 43, 182
Plain sail 29, 124
Planing hull 46
Platting 233
Plegt-anker 235
Plug stock rudder 71
Plyades 223
Pocock, Nicholas *39, 218*
Point Velique *59,* 60
Points of the compass 10, 11
Points of sailing 11
Polar diagram *46, 64*
Pommern, barque 69
Pommes 265
Pompe royal 304
Pond 231
Pooped 214
Port 176
Port luff 74
Porte-lof 74
En Porte-Manteau 284
A-portice 74, 122
Portlast 21, 72, 74, 122
Portoise 72
Portsmouth, USS *16, 122*
Potosi, barque 188, 189
Pouillouse 14
Preventer braces *28,* 149, 212, 220
Preventer gasket 212
Preventer jackstay 141
Preventer sheets 75
Preventer stays 22, 212
Preventer tacks 75
Preventer top tackle 116, 120
Prins Willem 173
Pumps 211, 304
Purchases 25

Quart 91
Quarter 22
Quarter boats *285, 287*
Quarter gasket 32
Quarterdeckmen 91, 92
Quartering wind 11
Queen Mary 189
Quicksaver 212, 214
Quoins 210
Qvaerk 84

Ra 30, 96
Rabeca 14, 217
Racking turns 267
Rafale 221
Raising the ship 307-310
Rake of masts 55-56
Rake of rudder 71
Rake of stern 45

Rake of sternpost 71
Ram's head 26
Ranger, USS *136*
Ranging the cable 243-244
Rap full 11
Razeed frigates 48
Reaching 12
Reef bands *137,* 138, *139*
Reef buntlines 142
Reef lines 139, 140, 143
Reef pendants *143,* 144
Reef points 137, 139-140, 142-143, *148*
Reef rope 137
Reef tackles 143, 147, 222
Reefing 137-154, 159-160, 214, 216, 217,
 219; becket 140, 141; before the
 wind 148-149; buntlines 142, 144; by the
 foot 101; by the wind 145-146, *147;*
 commands 154; jackstay 141; sequence
 of 145
Reefs, taking and shaking out 17
Reeving line 116, 141
Reijer 204, 205
Relieving tackles 209, 215
Retribution 207
Revenge, HMS *16*
Rhadamanthus 207
Riding a portice 122
Riding a-portlast 21, 122
Riding bitts 238
Riding to windward and leeward 249-252
Riding trade 249
Riding turn 238
Rigging 22-29, 117; stoppers 299
Righting arm 43
Righting moment 43
Rijder 205
Ring stoppare 240, 269
Ring stopper 239, 240
Ring tail 55, *76,* 77, 85, 163
Ringing up 268
Ripon, steamer *308*
Ris de Chasse 146
Rise of floor 44-45
Risee 221
River mooring 258
Roband 30, *31,* 96-97
Robinson's disengaging gear 285, *286*
Rodney, George B 48
Roll, period of 43, 47
Roller reefing 138
Rolling 47-48, 213, 214; bunt 107;
 reef 160; tackle 29, *143,* 144
Rot-Tag 259
Rotten stops 164, 242, 272
Rounding in 13
Rounding up 13
Roundly 13
Royal George, HMS 45
Royal halliards 26
Royal Louis 156
Royal mast *19,* 20, 114
Royal rigging 22
Royal studdingsails 171; booms 162
Royal yard 111-114
Royals 14, 15, 29, 36, *83,* 84, 212, 222;
 bending 98; furling 109-110;
 taking in 130-131, *133*
Rudder 56, 69-71, 175-176, 214, 215, 216,
 217; accidents 301-303; angle 70-71;
 carried away 302; chains 302; chocks 209;
 forms of 71; raking of 71; stock 71;
 tackles 209
Rudderhead 209
Rudderhead fractures 302
Rug paard 25
Rule joint rudder 71
Run away 13
Rund-Stoppare 239, 240
Running aground 305-310
Running lifts 29
Running moor 255
Running rigging 25-29; accidents 294-298
Russell, John Scott 46
Rust-Ankers 235

Sail, plain 29
Sail drill 93-95
Sail plan 36-39
Sail point *59,* 60
Sailing large *16,* 65-66

Sails 14-18, 29-35, 49-61, 72-90;
 backing 184, 226-227; bending *31,*
 96-103; bracing 65-66; clewing up 105;
 furling 104-111; lifting and depressing 59;
 making and shortening 124-126;
 setting 131, *133,* 135-136, 163-171,
 271-272; shortening 136, 228;
 trimming 61-66
St George, HMS *52*
St Jean d'Acre 290
Salamanders 85, 102
Santa Ana 208
Savatte 268
Scandalising mizzen topsail and fore
 topsail 126, 158
Scant wind 11, 12
'scending 43
Schanzgasten 91
Schiff Bruch 310
Schooverzeil 72
Schuif-Blindzeil 87
Schwer anchor 235
Scopamare 163
Scotchmen 259
Scudding 11, 213-215, 216
Scuppers 210-211
Sea-anchor 211
Sea Fox, whaler *227*
Sea gaskets 33, 97
Sea Mew 215
Sea painter 285-286
Sea-turn 51
Sealark, HM Brig *16*
Seconde ancre 235
Secret blocks 83
Seljsingar 267
Selvage strops 267, 271
Semelle 268
Serrebaugiere 210
Serrer en chapeau 108
Serrer en chemise 108
Services of cable 248
Serving 233
Setting sails 131, *133,* 163-171, 271-272
Setting strop 167, 168
Settling halliards 13
Shackle, length of 232
Shaking down casks 49
Shaking out reefs 150-151
Shank-painter of 243, 269
Shannon, HMS *278*
Sheep's feet 117
Sheer, breaking 252-253
Sheering *200,* 248-249, *273;* to windward
 and leeward 247
Sheet anchor 232, 235, 237, 243
Sheet block *34*
Sheet cable 236, *250*
Sheet of a course, parting of 298
Sheeting home 13
Sheets 13, 30, *31,* *72,* 74-75, 76
Shift of wind 251
Shifting flying jibboom 118
Shifting masts 117, 119-122
Shifting sails 101-102, 102-103, *106,* 111
Shifting yards *113,* 118-119
Shingle ballast 49
Shiphandling 40-71
Shipwreck 310
Shoeing an anchor 244
Shoring up 306
Shortening sail 17, 104, 124-136, 228
Shot of cable 232
Show pole 116
Shrouding the foresail 74
Shrouds 22-23, 24-25, 212; parting of 299
Shuifpallen 260
Side tackles 280
Sighting the anchor 248, 253
Silence of crew 93-94
Simple rudder 71
Single anchor 247-254
Single purchases 25
Single sail amidships 49-50
Sinking 305
Sjomanskuntor 265
Skage, of wind 12
Skaka 13
Skiatic 283
Skjuta bjorn 214
Skotmatta 259

Skracka 13
Slab lines 31-32
Slab points 140, 142
Slab reef points 143
Slab reef lines 142
Slack mooring 256
Slacken off 13
Slackness 56, 58
Slaeber-Bom 163
Sliding pawls 260
Slings 22
Slip rope 277
Slipping the cable 276-277
Smart in stays 182
Smijt 77
Smiting line 77, 110
Smiting the mizzen 77
Smoke sail 17
Smyt 77
Smyth, Admiral William 10, 11, 14
Snaking stays 22
Snorter, snotter 112, 119
Snow 78
Snowmast 78
Snub 13
Soldier's hole 17
Soldier's wind 12
Southwell, frigate *39*
Sovereign of the Seas 36, 37
Spaansche Ruiter 73
Spaansche Waker 175
Span shackles 268
Spanisches Takel 280
Spanish catting 269
Spanish lifts 29, 86
Spanker *33,* 76, 222; bending *103;*
 gaff and boom *28;* reefing 138, 152;
 setting 131
Spare anchor 235
 pars, accidents 299-301
Speed 45-47
Spike bowsprit 38
Spilling line 31-32, 143
Spindle 260
Spiral bracing 63-64
Spirit room 49
Splashboard *260*
Splice the main brace 296-297
Split topsails 137-138
Splitsa storebrassen 297
Spooning 213
Spreaders 23, 89, 90; of chain cable 233
Spring 276; aloof 12; the braces 186
Spritsail *15, 17, 21, 27,* 85-87; lifts *28,* 29;
 reefbands *139;* reefing 152-153;
 tacking 187; topgallant sail 90;
 topmast 20; topsail *15, 21, 22, 27, 36, 67,*
 87-90, 187; topsail yard 21, 67, 90, 114;
 tricing lines 28-29; yard 21, 212
Spunyarn stops 272
Squalls 221-224
Square mizzen topsail 81
Square rigger 62-63
Square sails 29, 50; bending 96-101;
 casting 271; furling 104-110; handing *109,*
 126; handling 126-127; setting 131;
 unbending 101-102
Square yardmen 94
Squaring yards 122-123
Squilgee strap 167
Squilgees 164
Stability 41, 43-44
Stag-Gravaat 280
Stagvending 193
Standing lifts 29, 86, *127*
Standing rigging 22-25; accidents 298-299
Staples 32
Starboard 176
Starboard beam *16*
Starboard lift 11
Starbolins 91
Stark calm 51
Start 13
Start buntlines 67
Stay 29
Stay tackles 280, 283
Staying 12, 181
Stays 22; of chain cable 233;
 reefing in 153-154
Staysails 14, *15,* 17, 22, 29, 36, 37, 38, 84-85,
 151, 213, 214, 216, 217, 219-220;

furling 110, *134*; halliards 26; handling 134; loosing 110
Steadying out the bowline 30, 132
Steam tugs 205-207
Steamer, tacking 188
Steering 173-180, 302; by compass 175; by wind 175; gear *173*; wheel 173, 174
Steeve of the bowsprit 81
Stern boats *285, 286, 287*
Stern davits 285
Sternboard 12, *13*, 71; making a 185, 189, 199
Sternline 45
Sternpost, raking of 71
Sternway 12
Steun paarden 25
Stick-Stoppare 240
Stiff gale 51
Stiffness 43-44
Stjert-Stoppare 240
Stock lashing 269
Stock tackle 269
Stokers 92
Stootmatte 259
Stop-anker 199, 235
Stoppen 225
Stopper knots 239
Stoppermen 93
Stoppers 237, 238-240, *299*
Stopping a tide 244
Storm bonnet 75
Storm sails 212-213, 216
Storm staysails 22, 85
Storms 209-210
Stossmatte 259
Stotynge 162
Stowing anchor 235, 269
Stowing boats 284
Stowing cable 236-237
Stowing courses 98, *99*
Stowing topsails 108
Stream anchor 235
Streaming the buoy 241
Streep 232
Streichreep 116
Stretching the weather wheel rope 117
Striking masts 117, 119-122
Striking yards 122, *123*
Studdingsail 18, 77, 90, 155-172, 212, 222, 223; boombrace 162; boom irons 161-162; boom jigger 162; booms *21*, 22; commands 171, 172; Lower 158-160; reefing 151, *152*; setting 163-171; topgallant *160*, 161; topmast 160-161; wind and weather 156-157
Studs of chain cable 233
Styfhetspunkt 44
Styrman 174
Success, frigate 157
Surge 43
Surging 121; the messenger 262
Sway 43
Sway up 13
Sweeping for an anchor 278-279
Swifter 24-25, 26
Swinging all yards 187, 188
Swinging boom 161
Swivel 234
Sword mat 212, 259

Table Bay 221
Tack 29, *31, 72*, 73-75; and sheet 74-75; bumpkin 73, 74; of a course 298; studdingsail 166; tricing line 80
Tacke about 181
Tacking 12, 13, 14, 181-189, 217; in line 189
Tacks to weather 135
Taglich-Anker 235
Tail rope 75, 241
Takel 280
Taking in sails 130-131, *133, 134*, 166, 168, 169
Talje 280
Tallowing 244
Taloner 305
Tangon 161, *163*
Tau-Anker 235
Taut mooring 256
Teeth of the gale 12
Tend 12
Tenderness 43, 44
Tending to leeward and windward 247,

249-251
Texel Island 237
Thetis, HMS 271
Throat brail tackle 78, 134
Thrum mat 212
Thrumming 259, 304
Tidal estuary *200*, 201, *202*
Tide rode 247, 249, 276
Tideway 199-202, 253-254
Tiding it over 199
Tie 20, 25
Tie block *34*
Tierers 236-237
Tiller 56, 71, 173, *178*, 209, 214, 217; fractures 302; rope 209
Timenoguys 18, 74
Timmynocky 18, 74
Timonier 174
Toezetten 74
Toggles 164
Toggling the halliards 26
Topgallant halliards 26
Topgallant mast 19, 20, 114-118, 119, 121-122, 212, 213
Topgallant parrel carried away 295-296
Topgallant sails 14, 15, 17, 18, 29, 36, 38; bending 98; furling 109-110, *136*; handling 132-133, 151; reefing 151; taking in 130-131, *133*
Topgallant studdingsail *160*, 161; booms 162; dipping *167*, 168; setting 167-168; taking in 168
Topgallant yard 111-114, 212
Topmast 19, 20, 119-122, 212; sprung 300
Topmast staysails 212, 214, 217, 222; reefing 138
Topmast studdingsail 21, 160-161; boom 161; dipping 166-167; setting 164-165; taking in 166
Topmen 113-114, 127
Top rope 120, 122
Topping lift 161, *162*
Topsail yard 21, 118-119, 120, 212; parrel carried away 296
Topsails 14, 15, 17, 29, 36, 37, 38, 82-83, 83-84, 209, 212, 214, 216, 219-220, 221, 223; backing *226*; bending 99, 100-101, *106*; clewlines 83; furling 98, 107-108, *136*; halliards 185; handling 132; harbour furl 108; hoisting 25; leechlines 144; parrel 296; reef bands *137*; reefing 25, 138, 139, 140, 145-146, 149, 151, *152, 153*; setting *133*, 149; sheetmen 93; sheets 72-73; shifting *102, 106*, 111; split 137, *138*; stowing 108; taking in 130, *133*
Top-tackle 116, 120
Torque 40
Tournevire 265
Towing 203-208
Trafalgar 207
Transom-stern 277
Transverse metacentre 44
Travelling backstays 23, 144
Traverse wind 12
Traversière 268, 271
Triatic stay 280, 283
Tricing around spritsail yard 23-24, 89
Tricing lines 28-29, 74, 185
Tricing up 29, 93
Triesge 87
Trijsen 29, 87
Trim 41, 44, 57-58; of sails *62*; of yards 14, 63-64, 65, 222; out of 43, 44, 176
Trimmer 44
Trimming the sails 61-66
Trinchetta 14
Trinquete 14, 217
Trinquetilla 14
Trip shores 243
Trip strop 243
Tripping line 81, 84, 112, 119, 160
Trissen 87
Trompete 265
Trotman's Anchor 231
True wind 58-59, 63
Trunks 277
Truss parrel 29
Truss tackle 26, *27, 28*, 29
Truss yoke 69
Trysails 223
Tub parrels 69

Tugs 272
Tumblehome 44-45, *52*
Tumblers 135, 243
Turnado 51
Turning ability 40
Turning on her heel 185
Twiddling lines 71
Two blocks 127
Tye 20, 25

Uberstag gehen 193
Uitlegger 73, 81
Uitschieter 217
Unbending headsails 102-103
Unbending lower sails *100*
Unbending square sail 101-102
Underway 12
Unmooring 258, 274
Upper bracemen 93
Upper lifts 29
Upper studdingsails, downhaul 168-169
Upper topsails, reefing 151

Vackstag 30
Vadem 231
Vailing 199
Vaka 241
Vanda 193
Vangs 29 *see also* Guys
Vasa 56, 173, *179, 250*, 260, 263, *274*, 309
Vater-Bom 163
Veering 12, 191-193; ropes 13; sheets 74, *127*; wind 182
Veiller 241
Vela de gabia 15
Vela del humo 14
Velacho 17
Velical point *59*, 60
Vergue seche 17
Verjelijking 309
Verlikker 175
Vernon, HMS 58
Very large crude carriers, VLCC 53
Victory, HMS 25, 53, 57, 71, 90, 161, *208*, 209, 232, 240, 260, 261, 262, 263, 267, 284, 304
Vieren 74
Vinnen schooners 53
Viol 263, 265-266
Virer 193
Vlieger 22, 85
Volage, HMS 156
Volger 236
Vollbrassen 225
Voor den wind zeilers 23
Voorlooper 236
Vormann 193
Voyal 260, 263, 264, 265-266, 269-270

Wachen 241
Waist anchor 235
Waisters 91
Wake 46
Walk away 13
Walking back the capstan 14
Wall sided 44
Wardroom 209
Warley, East Indiaman *175*
Warp 277
Warping 203-208, 235, 278
Warrior, HMS *153*
Watch 91; bill 94; disposition of 195; mustering 91-92; officer of 223-224; working with 135
Watching a buoy 241
Water casks 49
Water sail 89, 163
Water whip 150, 280, *281*
Water zeil 163
Waterline plane 45
Waterspouts 224
Wave Line Theory *45*, 46
Wearing 12, *13*, 191-193, 217-219, 219-220; on her heel 191; short round 191; steamer 70
Weather anchor 272-273
Weather beam *16*
Weather bitting 238, 263
Weather braces 11, 13, 60-61, 222, 295, 296, 297
Weather clew 29, 72, 127-129

Weather cloths 211
Weather coil 219
Weather gauge 48
Weather halliards 25
Weather helm 56-57, 70, 176, 217
Weather leech 18, 29, 30, 61
Weather reef tackle 298
Weather topgallant sheet parting 297
Weather topsail sheet parting 297
Weather wheel rope 177
Weatherly 58
Weighing anchor 12, 258, 260-267, 270, *275*, 278
Wenden 193
Wending 193
Werfen 277
Werksloep 282
Werpanker 277
Wet provisions 49
Whalers heaving to 227-228
Wheel 215; accidents 301-303; rope parts 301-302
Whelps 260, 261
Whipstaff 173, *179*, 215
Whole topsail breeze 10, 48
Wien-takel 280
William Lee, whaler *227*
Wind 11-12, 193; across the tide 201, 276; ahead, leeward tide 273-276; arrows 248; fairer aloft *58*, 59, 63, 157; on sails 49-61; rode 247; shadow 64, 66; shift of 251; speed *58*, strength 60; true and apparent 58-59; veering 59, 182
Winding tackle 280, *281*
Windjammer 46
Windlass 263-264
Windward service 233
Wing stopper 239
Wingers 49
Winging out weights 47
Winter pole 116, 212
Wipe off the wind 131
Woid 264
Wolf's throat *17*
Wood's detaching apparatus 285
Worcester, HMS *156*
Working anchor 235
Working to windward 12, 13
Worming 233
Wuit 264

Yardarm horse 25
Yardarms 21-22
Yardmen 25
Yards 20-22, 26; blocks *34*; bracing 14, 25, 26-27, 63-69; clew down 30; cockbilling 123; crossing *111*; hoisting 20-21; manning 123; naming 21; parallelism 56, 57, rope 111; sending up and down 111-114; squaring 122-123; striking 20-21; tackles 280, 283; trim 63-64, 65
Yawing 43, 214
Yawl 282
Yole 283
Youyou 283

Zog 46
Zuigen 46
Zwakken-hals 239, 240